Eugene Jolas:
Critical Writings, 1924–1951

André Masson, *Portrait d' Eugene Jolas,* 1942. Courtesy of Mme. Diego Masson.
Copyright © 2009 Artists Rights Society (ARS), New York/ADAGP, Paris.

Eugene Jolas

Critical Writings, 1924–1951

EDITED AND WITH AN INTRODUCTION
BY KLAUS H. KIEFER AND
RAINER RUMOLD

Northwestern

University Press

Evanston

Illinois

Northwestern University Press
www.nupress.northwestern.edu

Copyright © 2009 by Northwestern University Press.
Published 2009. All rights reserved.

Printed in the United States of America

10 9 8 7 6 5 4 3 2 1

Library of Congress Cataloging-in-Publication Data
Jolas, Eugene, 1894–1952.
    Eugene Jolas : critical writings, 1924–1951 / edited and with an
introduction by Klaus H. Kiefer and Rainer Rumold.
      p. cm. — (Avant-garde and modernism collection)
    Includes bibliographical references and index.
    ISBN 978-0-8101-2581-0 (pbk. : alk. paper)
    1. Jolas, Eugene, 1894–1952. 2. Avant-garde (Aesthetics)—
History—20th century. 3. Modernism (Literature)—History and
criticism. 4. Literature, Modern—20th century—History and
criticism. I. Kiefer, Klaus H., 1947– II. Rumold, Rainer.
III. Title. IV. Series: AGM collection.
    PN56.M54J65 2009
    809.9112—dc22

                           2009016917

♾ The paper used in this publication meets the minimum
requirements of the American National Standard for Information
Sciences—Permanence of Paper for Printed Library Materials,
ANSI Z39.48-1992.

Contents

Editors' Introduction, xi

Remarks on the Edition, xxi

Part One: Rambles Through Literary Paris

Introduction, 5

Number 17 (June 8, 1924), 7

Number 18 (June 15, 1924), 14

Number 19 (June 22, 1924), 20

Number 20 (June 29, 1924), 26

Number 22 (July 13, 1924), 32

Number 28 (August 24, 1924), 40

Number 30 (September 7, 1924), 46

Number 36 (October 19, 1924), 52

Number 40 (November 16, 1924), 58

Number 2686 (November 23, 1924), 65

Number 2714 (December 21, 1924), 71

Number 2735 (January 11, 1925), 77

Number 2763 (February 8, 1925), 82

Number 2805 (March 22, 1925), 88

Number 2875 (May 31, 1925), 95

Number 2889 (June 14, 1925), 99

Number 2910 (July 5, 1925), 102

Part Two: Revolution of the Word: *Transition* Manifestoes and History

Introduction, 109

Proclamation ("Revolution of the Word," June 1929), 111

The Novel Is Dead—Long Live the Novel (November 1929), 113

Preface to the New *Transition* (March 1932), 115

What Is the Revolution of Language? (February 1933), 116

Frontierless Decade (April–May 1938), 118

Transition: An Occidental Workshop, 1927–1938 (1949), 121

Part Three: The Language of Night

Introduction, 129

The Revolution of Language in Elizabethan Theater (June–July 1933), 131

The King's English Is Dying: Long Live the Great American Language (June 1930), 134

The Language of Night (1932), 140

Wanted: A New Symbolical Language! (March 1932), 162

Wanted: A New Communicative Language! (March 1932), 163

Confession About Grammar (February 1933), 164

Introduction to *The Negro Who Sings* (1928), 165

Race and Language (June 1936), 173

Inquiry into the Spirit and Language of Night (April–May 1938), 175

Preface to *Words from the Deluge* (1940), 178

Logos (June 1929), 179

From Jabberwocky to "Lettrism" (January 1948), 184

Part Four: From Romanticism to the Avant-Garde

Introduction, 203

Romanticism and the Dream (June 1936), 205

Romanticism Is Not Dead (1941), 207

Pan-Romanticism in the Atomic Age (1949), 211

Romanticism and Metapolitics (after 1949), 214

Stars and Angels: Homage to G. Th. Fechner, Romantic Savant and
    Visionary (1941), 219

Prolegomenon, or White Romanticism and the Mythos of Ascension
    (undated), 222

Surrealism and Romanticism (undated), 227

Surrealism: Ave atque Vale (1941), 228

Part Five: Crisis of Man and Language: Verticalist/Vertigralist Manifestoes

Introduction, 241

On the Quest (December 1927), 243

Notes on Reality (November 1929), 248

Preface to *Transition Stories* (1929), 254

Literature and the New Man (June 1930), 257

Night-Mind and Day-Mind (March 1932), 264

Poetry Is Vertical (March 1932), 266

The Primal Personality (February 1933), 268

Twilight of the Horizontal Age (February 1933), 274

Vertigralist Transmutation (July 1935), 275

Paramyths (July 1935), 277

Workshop (July 1935), 278

Vertigral (June 1936), 288

Vertigralist Pamphlet (1938), 289

The Quest and the Myth (1941), 294

Poetry of Ascent (1941), 296

Threefold Ascent: Verticalist Manifesto (August 1941), 298

Part Six: Literary Encounters

Introduction, 303

Novalis

Homage to Novalis (November 1929), 307

Novalis, the Mystic Visionary (undated), 309

Novalis, or the White Romanticism (January 15, 1951), 315

Goethe

The Case of Goethe: Was He a Heroic Figure or Merely a Philistine?
    (March 1932), 329

Gide

André Gide, Mystic and Dionysian (July 13, 1924), 333

Kafka

Franz Kafka's Stories and Ascending Romanticism (1941), 343

Trakl

Georg Trakl, *Poetry* (June 15, 1951), 349

Benn

Gottfried Benn (August 1927), 355

Jünger

Ernst Jünger and the Twilight of Nihilism (November 1951), 361

Breton

André Breton's Surrealism in 1950 (June 1950), 371

Joyce

The Revolution of Language and James Joyce (February 1928), 377

Marginalia to James Joyce's *Work in Progress* (February 1933), 383

Homage to the Mythmaker (April–May 1938), 388

My Friend James Joyce (March–April 1941), 393

Elucidation of James Joyce's Monomyth: Explication of *Finnegans Wake*
     (July 1948), 405

Part Seven: Literature, Culture, and Politics

Introduction, 423

Super-Occident (February 1929), 425

Goodbye to Yesterday (October 1940), 431

Toward a Metaphysical Renascence? (October 1940–March 1941), 437

Super-Occident and the Atlantic Language (June 1941), 440

Arts and Letters in Latin America (July 1941), 442

German Letters in Ruins: A Report from Frankfurt (July 4, 1948), 451

The Migrator and His Language (1948), 456

Part Eight: Across Frontiers

Introduction, 465

Some Notes on Existentialism, Martin Heidegger, and Poetry Sales
     (November 1, 1949), 467

Reemergence of Heidegger (November 1949), 471

Heidegger in the Atomic Age (November 1949), 473

Irrealism, Immoralism, Naturalism, Concretism (November 8, 1949), 475

Origin and Aim of History (November 15, 1949), 480

A German Nationalist (December 6, 1949), 485

The Absent Avant-Garde (February 7, 1950), 489

German Letters Today (February 21, 1950), 493

Negro Culture (March 14, 1950), 497

Franco-German Cultural Exchanges (March 21, 1950), 502

German Literary Trends (May 23, 1950), 507

Biography of Eugene Jolas, 511

Notes, 515

Selected Bibliography, 555

Index, 583

Editors' Introduction

The little magazines—numerous publications based in Paris, Berlin, London, New York, and Chicago between 1910 and the late 1930s—constitute a vast field of research. Their study is of primary importance for grasping a dialogical relation between twentieth-century European avant-garde movements and Anglo-American literary modernism. Yet, despite their considerable historical and critical significance, these periodicals are only now being subjected to a wider academic inquiry, which may be accounted for by their geographical dispersion and their relative rarity, as well as their interdisciplinary aspects, the latter being of central interest to culture studies, a discipline that has replaced a traditional focus on national literatures.

Conversely, *transition* (Paris and New York, 1927–38), perhaps the most influential review of the lot, has been an object of long-standing interest to Joyce scholars, if only because it published *Finnegans Wake* seriatim as *Work in Progress*. Yet the journal was much more than a medium for Joyce's avant-garde summa. The sheer diversity of the journal's features—from German Expressionism to Zurich Dada, French Surrealism, and the first translations of Kafka—made it synonymous with all that was innovative in contemporary writing, since it brought these works together with equally significant productions of Anglophone modernism. The spirited ambition and ultimate reach of the magazine give us a notion of the driven editorial talent of the man behind it; moreover, we sense an uncanny intuition for which works of "the new" would persist. James Joyce would capture the essence of his faithful friend and editor, Eugene Jolas (1894–1952), in a limerick entitled "Versailles 1933":

> There's a genial young poetriarch Euge
> Who hollers with heartiness huge:
> Let sick souls sob for solace
> So the jeunes joy with Jolas
> Book your berths: Après mot, le déluge![1]

Joyce's praise for Jolas as both a poet and a patron of the arts who would steer a course through the imminent flood—unleashed by the revolution of the word—is an intimate response to a long and richly varied career. After all, "poetriarch" is a fitting neologism for the polyglot poet, critic, editor, and dynamic spokesman of a transatlantic modernism. In turn,

with Joyce in mind, Jolas envisioned an intercontinental, multilingual literature within a larger anthropological context. Yet his decidedly universalist stance was not just one of philosophical idealism. Rather, Jolas's positions stemmed more concretely from his unique experience of growing up
in the region of Alsace-Lorraine, as an American citizen by birth, speaking
French, German, and only later English. All of which would quite under-
standably animate his perpetual physical and spiritual motion from the
borderland to the metropolis, back and forth between Europe and America
throughout a lifetime.

Eugene Jolas was born in Union City, New Jersey, in 1894, yet his
Franco-German parents returned to the "old country" with him still a small
child. He was educated in Lorraine—after grammar school in a Catholic
seminary—where French, German, and a regional patois of both vied for
cultural domination. Amid rising political tensions, Jolas decided to return
to America in the paradoxical role of a native-born immigrant in 1909. His
"Wanderjahre" would lead him through the world of delivery boys, night
schools, New York City tabloids, German-language pressrooms, and even
to the U.S. Army Medical Corps. All along he was deeply immersed in
acquiring the American language in its entire wealth, vernacular and literary. However, it was his editorial work at the *Chicago Tribune* which would
send him back to Paris, where he took up the "culture beat" previously
in charge of Ford Madox Ford. In 1924 he began writing his "Rambles
Through Literary Paris," a mixture of refined analysis, intimate portraits of
writers and artists, and lapidary reviews of new publications in French and
German. One could easily reconcile Jolas's poetic and journalistic activities as an illustration of Pound's famous definition of literature as the "news
that STAYS news."[2]

The personal and professional connections that Jolas made writing
the "Rambles" helped him start his own literary review, *transition,* which
sought to bridge the gap between the iconoclastic artist and the common
reader, bringing the former to exposure and shaking the latter from com-
placence. With the benefit of hindsight, *transition* appears as an august
meeting ground for the international avant-garde, but at the time it was the
result of Jolas's personal curiosity and professional commitment to making the best art and literature available to the English-language public on
an ad hoc basis. Rather than listing a roster of its participants (from Joyce
to the Expressionists, from Dada to the Surrealists), we might measure
transition's pioneering role by pointing out that, for example, the very first
English translations of Franz Kafka's stories appeared therein as early as

1928. *Transition* was also the site of multiple manifestoes, the most famous of which remains the 1929 "Proclamation" ("Revolution of the Word"). We can judge the impact and the cogency of this key text for avant-garde poetics by the fact that Joyce himself, when writing notes for *Finnegans Wake,* would refer back to the manifesto in shorthand: "X revolution of the word / Manage—/ Burial of old sense."[3]

Jolas's life and career from his early peregrinations as a "neo-American" to his role in reconstructing the postwar German press are vividly described in his autobiography, *Man from Babel.* Jolas's memoir provides compelling anecdotal and sometimes idiosyncratic details about his dealings with the main actors of modernism and their political, aesthetic, and social concerns. Judging from the wide reception our edition of the autobiography received, it clearly helped to render Jolas's prolific creative persona accessible to a wider audience.[4] The present volume takes the relay in raising Jolas's profile while contributing to a much more detailed understanding of literary modernism in its aesthetic and increasingly political contexts as captured by a rarified sensibility.

This edition gathers Jolas's literary criticism and manifestoes from 1924 to 1951. It includes a representative sample of his writings as editor of *transition,* but goes far beyond this by gathering his manifold essays from the feuilleton of the European edition of the *Chicago Tribune* (1924–25), as well as his commentaries on the culture and politics of a divided Germany and Europe after 1945. Presently there is only a slim anthology of selected texts by Jolas available in English.[5] Another selection of his essays translated from English into French is exclusively devoted to James Joyce.[6] The materials collected in this edition are dispersed over literary archives, contemporaneous journals, and newspapers. The publication of his critical writings in a readily available format is intended to highlight Jolas's pertinence for modernist and avant-garde studies.

Our edition addresses and reveals the underlying unity of the major phases of Jolas's writings and activities. All of Jolas's thought, both in prose and poetry, is informed by his inimitable understanding of, and indeed, faith in literary language. His "religion of language," as one might call it, is unparalleled by any other contemporaneous modernist writer and critic, since it comes to him straight from early German Romanticism. It is this spirit that he wants to see resurface in recent modernity in the forms of the literary creativity of the avant-garde, which he actively propagates as poet, editor, and critic. His different activities thus signal his overwhelming concern for the freedom of creative language. He articulated these concerns in a central body of essays arguing for transnational communication on the highest level of poetry as *Weltsprache* (world language), tantamount to a revolution of the word in an age of transition. It is not simply hyperbole to argue that the ambition of *transition* has to do with revelation and renovation out of decadence, a meaning that lies implicit in the apocalyptic tones of its title.[7]

Spanning outward from Jolas's understanding and advocacy of the "Revolution of the Word," our edition reflects three major phases of his development, which are summarized below.[8] In choosing a thematic division rather than a chronological one, we are aiming to re-create Jolas's holistic vision, thereby allowing the reader to better understand his global project. The goal is not merely to gather what has been dispersed so far, but to use the texts as a prism of intellectual history, providing new perspectives not only for students of literary modernism, but also for historians, biographers, and sociologists of culture who may be interested to examine how literary coteries and movements come into place and fall apart.

Part I: The Avant-Garde Between Region and Metropolis

The "Rambles" included in part 1 document, for instance, the astounding productivity of poets and artists from the bicultural, multilingual region of Alsace, with Strasbourg at the center, which was transplanted to Berlin and Paris from 1910 to the early '20s. Regional writers' and artists' associations appear to have prepared the most characteristic developments for the self-understanding of the French Surrealist and the German Expressionist avant-garde. Jolas's articles explain the avant-garde's transnational cultural claims as evolving not necessarily in the metropolis, as previously assumed, but between region and metropolis. The "primitivism" and linguistic innovations of the regional writers, experienced in "crossing borders," proved to be a special source for the metropolis in search of new forms and energies—for a modernist culture that could appeal to, if not unify, the emerging multiethnic urban public.[9] In suggesting that proto-forms of Surrealism and Dada arise from the margins rather than in the metropolis, Jolas is turning a pervasive cliché on its head. This appears to hold major implications for comparative studies not as the study of "other" national literary traditions and cultures, but rather as the study of a "borderland" phenomenon that escapes historical and national grids.

Parts 2–6: The Critic in Progress Toward the "Revolution of the Word": From "Rambles Through Literary Paris" to *Transition*

The double focus in these parts is on both the function of the feuilleton, that is, Jolas's weekly column, "Rambles Through Literary Paris," and on the power of a "little magazine" such as *transition* in shaping our image and understanding of the avant-garde. Such understanding differs from the later projections of academic criticism confined to the disciplines of literature and the other arts. A major issue here is Jolas's interest in the interdisciplinary convergence of poetics, psychoanalytical and anthropological theories of language, images of the unconscious, and theories of myth and "primitivism" for the understanding of avant-garde aesthetic productions. Jolas's essays on these questions were initially inspired by Gottfried Benn (who would thoroughly disillusion him by, however briefly, turning toward Nazism years later). But it was Joyce whose *Finnegans Wake* challenged him to develop his literary criticism in the very forum where it first appeared. In Joyce's rejection and reworking of most of the key Romantic aesthetic categories, Jolas would also find somewhat of a counterbalance to his obsession with German Romanticism—above all the Schlegel brothers, Schelling, and Novalis—and the "language of night" as a form of expressing the unconscious. To be sure, *Finnegans Wake* legitimates Jolas's insight into the function of literature as a universal language capable of reconnecting with the "night-mind" on a new level.

While Joyce may have been "apolitical" in a normative sense, his inimitable originality only reinforced Jolas's long-standing conviction that the existence and survival of humanity rests on the cornerstone of individual creativity. Where Jolas's essays on language and literature, by extension, turn into essays on culture and politics, he is a stalwart defender of democracy and a relentless critic of totalitarianism, be it Nazism, Fascism, or Communism in any of their historical forms.[10] While Jolas's forthright suggestion that there is a connection between the avant-garde aesthetic and democracy may appear dubious at first, his essentially probing attitude toward tradition gives us a clue to what he meant. Observing the uses and misuses of literary history, Jolas was keenly aware that literature may not necessarily lead to savvy politics. Hence his view of the great European canon was inherently a destabilizing one. In his introduction to Carl Einstein's ambitious polemical centenary essay on the "Goethe legend," for example, Jolas questions the legitimacy of Goethe's monumentalized stature in modern poetry, while reminding the reader in a quiet aside that 1932 also marked the four-hundredth anniversary of the publication of Rabelais' *Pantagruel,* the hundredth anniversary of the birth of Lewis Carroll, and Joyce's fiftieth birthday. This alternative pantheon of writers, who each in his own way revolutionized language, culminates once more in Joyce, and "serves to emphasize once more the fundamental scissions . . . in the entire history of literature."[11] Such a shift seems emblematic of Jolas's critical idiom, which seeks at once to unsettle tradition from within, while programmatically valorizing the new writing as anticipating the future.

Parts 7–8: The Avant-Gardist and the War of Words

Jolas's wartime and post-World War II activities bore the traces of the avant-garde's project transferred into a sociopolitical sphere. His charge as a press officer of the U.S. Department of the Army's Information Services consisted in no less than the reconstruction of the German press as a democratic institution and the founding of a German news agency that eventually became the Deutsche Presse-Agentur (presently the *dpa*) at Bad Nauheim. This immense task, successfully carried out, along with reporting from the Nuremberg Trials, brought his preoccupation with language to a concrete level of political awareness. Jolas turned to the attempt to denazify the German intelligentsia and, last but not least, the German language. This orientation was accompanied by a number of essays, including a painful review of the legacy of his beloved German Romanticism which had first inspired him to write poems in his youth, as being partially responsible for the rise of German Nazism.[12]

With the existentialist philosopher Karl Jaspers as a member of the editorial board, Jolas set up the journal *Die Wandlung* (*Metamorphosis,* a title straight from the terminology of German Expressionism) for the reintroduction of democratic thought and reacquaintance with international modernist literature. Together with Dolf Sternberger, the editor of the journal, he developed the idea of prohibiting certain terms of National Socialist origin from use in all publications, which led to the later edition of Sternberger's *Das Wörterbuch des Unmenschen* (*Dictionary of the Monster,* Hamburg, 1957). The idea was to expose words that had been forced into the labor of giving false significance to nationalism and racism, to liberate an abused language, and to realign it with language as a universal phenomenon. After all, a language liberated from external constraints had been the very concern of Jolas's work as an avant-garde editor, poet, and critic. During the postwar years, he wrote a political and literary column for the *New York Herald* which reflected his views on the status of the language of irrationalism and nationalism in postwar German thought, literature, and politics—focusing especially on Martin Heidegger and Ernst Jünger.[13]

The critical landscape has changed significantly since Dougald McMillan laid the groundwork for recognizing the importance of the "little magazine" in the first significant assessment of Jolas and *transition*.[14] More recently, Anglo-American scholars may have been alienated by the magazine's Romantic predisposition, which was more in tune with the "geistesgeschichtlichen" temperament of Renato Poggioli's *Theory of the Avant-Garde* (1962) than with Peter Bürger's *Theory of the Avant-Garde* (1974), which was steeped in critical theory. Nonetheless, Jolas's programmatic stance for multilingual poetics and for an interdisciplinary understanding of literature and the arts invites a major review. Jolas's advocacy of a multilingual merger in the realm of poetry as well as in the social space makes him one of the most important members and critics of the avant-garde, with special relevance to current debates on multilingual creativity.[15] The institutional aspects of modernism have also been receiving increased attention since Lawrence Rainey's groundbreaking study of the sociology of modernist literature in England between 1912 and 1922.[16] By placing modernism in its institutional and economic contexts, Rainey draws attention to the crucial role played by little magazines as patrons. The burgeoning interest in little magazines can also be measured by a forthcoming three-volume history of little magazines commissioned by the Oxford University Press and edited by Peter Brooker and Andrew Thacker, or the Modernist Journals Project, an ongoing joint effort of Brown University and the University of Tulsa.[17]

In the current configuration, Jolas's critical essays should play a key role in launching a new vector of research in literary scholarship and culture studies. After all, his work not only situates Joyce's ideas and literary practice in a larger context, it also speaks to a series of interrelated issues which define modernist and avant-garde dimensions and moments. Jolas's critical essays unveil new aspects or refine our present understanding of then nascent movements: Yvan Goll's Alsatian-Lorrainean regional form of Surrealism as distinct from Breton's Parisian program; the dynamics of the concept of a transnational "avant-garde" literature, with its origins in the multilingual borderland as well as in the multiethnic metropolis; and the reception of Expressionism and Dada outside Germany. Moreover, his writings explore centrally, albeit essayistically, the relation of the linguistic sign to image and sound, or the complex of language, myth, and psychoanalysis. Finally, they are part of the post-World War II critical revision of the legacy of German Romanticism for the rise of Nazism, and the reconstruction of a democratic intellectual culture in postwar Germany. While some of the later writings may appear to be dated as historical commentary, the edition as such puts them into the context of Jolas's overall poetological concerns, which pioneered an exploration into modernist discourses as part of an epochal linguistic and visual turn which is at the core of our concerns today.

Notes

1. James Joyce, "Versailles 1933," cited in Eugene Jolas, *Man from Babel,* ed. Andreas Kramer and Rainer Rumold (New Haven: Yale University Press, 1998), 112.

2. Ezra Pound, *The ABC of Reading* (London: W.W. Norton, 1960), 29.

3. James Joyce, *Buffalo Notebooks,* 32, 210, cited in Jean-Michel Rabaté, *James Joyce and the Politics of Egoism* (Cambridge, Eng.: Cambridge University Press, 2001), 208.

4. A review of *Man from Babel* in the the *London Review of Books,* for example, found Jolas's memoirs to "stand alongside Wyndham Lewis's *Blasting and Bombardiering* and Gertrude Stein's *Autobiography of Alice B. Toklas* as a critical document in the history of Modernist fashioning and self-fashioning" (London Review of Books, July 29, 1999, 18).

5. Noel Riley Fitch, ed., *In Transition: A Paris Anthology: Writing and Art from "Transition" Magazine 1927–1930* (New York: Doubleday, 1990).

6. *Sur James Joyce/Eugène Jolas,* trans. Marc Dachy (Paris: Plon, 1990).

7. See part 3, "The Language of Night," or part 5, "Crisis of Man and Language: Verticalist/Vertigralist Manifestoes."

8. There are, necessarily, a number of subdivisions within the three parts whose purpose is not to "divide" but to emphasize certain historical and poetological issues and phases of Jolas's essays, and there are sub-introductions as well, for example, for Jolas's reviews of the work of individual authors from Novalis to Breton, or from Gottfried Benn to Joyce; see part 6, "Literary Encounters."

9. See part 1, "Rambles Through Literary Paris" (1924–25), which contains major reminiscences, reviews, and the fervent advocacy of the literary legacy of poets and artists like Yvan Goll and Hans (Jean) Arp (from Lorraine and Strasbourg, respectively) for the international avant-garde.

10. See part 7, "Literature, Culture, and Politics."

11. Eugene Jolas, "The Case of Goethe: Was He a Heroic Figure or Merely a Philistine?" *transition*, no. 21 (March 1932): 206.

12. See part 4, "From Romanticism to the Avant-Garde."

13. See part 8, "Across Frontiers."

14. Dougald McMillan, *"Transition": The History of a Literary Era, 1927–1938* (New York: George Braziller, 1975).

15. See, for example, Marjorie Perloff, *Logocinema of the Frontiersman: Jolas's Multilingual Poetics and Its Legacies* (Kunapipi: Wollongon, 1999), 145–63; or Klaus H. Kiefer, "Eugene Jolas' Multilinguale Poetik," in *Multilinguale Literatur im 20. Jahrhundert,* ed. Manfred Schmeling and Monika Schmitz-Emans, Saarbrücker Beiträge zur Vergleichenden Literatur- und Kulturwissenschaft 18 (Würzburg: Königshausen & Neumann, 2002), 121–35.

16. Lawrence Rainey, *Institutions of Modernism: Literary Elites and Public Culture* (New Haven: Yale University Press, 1998).

17. For *transition* and its contexts in the arena of modernist Anglo-American journals, see Céline Mansanti, "Bibliographie," in *Revues modernistes anglo-américaines: Lieux d'échanges, lieux d'exil,* ed. Benoît Tadié (Paris: Ent'revues, 2006), 287–304.

Remarks on the Edition

This volume is the culmination of a project whose initial supporters included the Deutscher Akademischer Austauschdienst and the American Council of Learned Societies from 1993 to 1994 and, subsequently, the Fritz Thyssen Foundation. The project was conducted by Klaus H. Kiefer (of the University of Bayreuth at the outset and of the Ludwig-Maximilians-Universität Munich since the winter semester of 1996–97), Andreas Kramer (Goldsmith College, London), and Rainer Rumold (Northwestern University, Evanston, Illinois) under the heading "*transition*—The Transatlantic Effect of the European Avant-Garde" or "Eugene Jolas (1894–1952)—Edition and Interpretation." The collaboration between Andreas Kramer and Rainer Rumold resulted in the publication of Eugene Jolas's autobiography, *Man from Babel* (New Haven: Yale University Press, 1998).

The editors here would like to express once more their gratitude to Betsy Jolas, daughter of Eugene Jolas, and one of France's leading avant-garde composers, not only for giving us permission to publish the texts contained in this edition, procured with the assistance of the Beinecke Rare Book and Manuscript Library at Yale University, but also for being so responsive to important details involved with our work. The completion of this second volume, presented here, was delayed by the customary vicissitudes of academic life. There was frequently a shortage of the necessary manpower and financial resources.

The work was nevertheless undertaken with considerable optimism. Klaus H. Kiefer's research sabbaticals at Northwestern and Yale, and Rumold's work as a visiting research fellow in September 1999 at the latter's Beinecke Rare Book and Manuscript Library, which constituted the source and scope of our edition, yielded an extensive collection of relevant and edition-worthy texts written by Jolas.[1] These were later entered electronically at the University of Bayreuth with the help of assistants Sioban Groitl and Hildegard Rupprecht. The texts were checked in Munich by Holger Zimmermann and Gabriele Holst, which led to the selection of writings that were reviewed and organized by the editors with the expert assistance of Ela Kotkowska (EK) at Northwestern University as well as by Tanja Trumm (TT) in Munich. Trumm also prepared the index, and a bibliography of the most pertinent critical literature on Eugene Jolas and *transition*.

In the context of an undergraduate research seminar, generously funded by the Weinberg College of Arts and Sciences of Northwestern University, the translation of the non-English texts (which were either in German or French) and the writing of some of the sub-introductions were directed, supervised, and finalized by our graduate assistant Ela Kotkowska. The translators are named by their abbreviations in the listing of the collaborators. The various introductions to the edition's parts were written in co-operation with Dirk Deissler (D.D.), Ayse Draz (A.D.), Zakir Paul (Z.P.), Christopher Reid (C.R.), Diana Rumrich (D.R.), and Laura Storz (L.S.). Storz also initiated the chronology ("Biography of Eugene Jolas"). Zakir Paul composed selected annotations and wrote commentary notes to the texts selected. The editors also acknowledge Paul's familiarity with intimate details of James Joyce's life and work in the Parisian contexts.

Jolas's writings presented numerous editorial problems due to the trilingual world in which he thought and worked. Most notably, Jolas's mother's German speech, as well as the language of his schooling in Forbach, often permeates his word formation and syntax. His "father tongue," French, is primarily evident in his false orthographic renderings in English of Romantic loanwords. Europe's Greek and Latin linguistic heritage is manifested in abundant neologisms and, most of all, compounds. Moreover, interferences resulted not only from the polyglot author himself, but also from the editors and the presses. French printers were responsible for putting out the English-language *transition,* English and American publishers had difficulties with foreign names and quotations, and British and American English would occasionally compete with each other.[2] Given all this, there was a balance to be struck between preserving Jolas's originality and the need to correct obvious errors.

Given Jolas's frenzied style of reporting, annotative comprehensiveness proved to be an irresolvable dilemma. Jolas seemed to know everyone. His address book—assuming he had one—likely bore a resemblance to the white pages of a medium-size city. Many of the names of the period have fallen into obscurity and are no longer verifiable. There are also obvious differences in the educational backgrounds of American, British, German, and French readers. An autodidact and a journalist, Jolas himself lacked academic training but possessed a unique erudition, and it is precisely for this reason that his writing is so rich with allusions. Certainly, there was much that needed to be put in order, and because of the sheer volume of the material, it was a challenge to do the bare minimum of what was absolutely necessary. In the case of "Rambles Through Literary Paris," publications have been referenced by name, publisher, and year placed in parentheses so that the footnotes would not snowball into a bibliography. Otherwise, text and commentary are strictly divided. Enumerated footnotes are from Jolas himself, and they have only been revised when it was required. The editors have chosen to abbreviate some of the "Rambles," using ellipses when the selections trailed off or veered into literary gossip.

Jolas's citations from literary works, even when he does not translate them directly into English (for there are always differences to be found with modern translations), do not always appear reliable. One example is when he quotes Joyce's *Work in Progress,* a text that would go through many transformations by Joyce after it had been in Jolas's hands. Because Jolas rarely gives information pertaining to a source, much less a page number, the original text or quote can often not be substantiated. Even in this instance, however, Jolas's manner of citation has been retained as much as possible, along with those obvious errors which may have escaped his, or the printer's, notice. As a basic rule of thumb, the orthographic peculiarities of the quoted foreign language (such as the German umlaut), which typically were not correctly rendered because foreign type machines or letter cases would not accommodate them, have been respected and incorporated.

The text selection excludes "poetical" works in the narrow sense, yet the literary quality of Jolas's essays, reportage, manifestoes, reflections, and so on can hardly be missed. It would be a commendable further task to anthologize the author's numerous poems and works of prose. Jolas created in part his own genres, particularly with respect to his multilingual works. The term "critical writings" should be broadly understood as a critical response to language, literature, and culture, concepts that always existed for him as a plurality. Jolas's societal critique also contains an unambiguous endorsement of the mediation of borders—between nations, cultures, races, as well as the human "physis" and "metaphysics" (verticalism/vertigralism).

Conceived as whole, the volume proceeds chronologically. It begins with "Rambles Through Literary Paris" (part 1), which strongly influenced Jolas as a journalist and writer, and continues through his monumental work on *transition* (part 2), his "verticalist/vertigralist" phase (part 5), and his last reports following World War II (part 8). Of course, continuities and intersections may be found. There are also elaborations and variations in emphasis, as found for instance with Jolas's thematization of the "Language of Night" (part 3) and the reception of German Romanticism (part 4), where he simultaneously finds himself and attempts to mediate past (Romanticism) and present (Surrealism). Part 6, "Literary

Encounters," presents a selection of essays assembled according to pertinent criteria.

The question of relevance guided this volume, which aims to put forward a representative selection of Jolas's works without, however, also offering justifications for the choices that have been made. There are indeed repetitions and redundancies in Jolas's works, which are the product of an obsessive commitment to *Wort* and *Sprache* (word and language). The editors, in immersing themselves in Eugene Jolas's writings, the modern literature of the period, and, in particular, that of the avant-garde, have silently excluded some of Jolas's less important works. By doing this, however, they do not intend to suggest that serious consideration of his still-unpublished writings would not also be a rewarding venture.

Notes

1. See Timothy G. Young, "Yale University: Beinecke Rare Book and Manuscript Library: General Collection of Rare Books and Manuscripts: Eugene and Maria Jolas Papers, Gen Mss 108" (1993), http://webtext.library.yale.edu/xml2html/ beinecke.jolas.con.html; see also Addition, Gen Mss 411 (1998), http://webtext .library.yale.edu/xml2html/beinecke.JOLASADD.con.html.

2. Beginning in 1932, the original, ambitiously avant-garde form of the title *transition* (in lowercase) was replaced by *TRANSITION* (in uppercase letters); yet for whatever reason one can later on sporadically still encounter the former.

Eugene Jolas:
Critical Writings, 1924–1951

Part One : **Rambles Through Literary Paris**

Introduction

In spring 1924, already a city editor with the Paris office of the *Chicago Tribune*, Eugene Jolas started his weekly column "Rambles Through Literary Paris." As an American journalist, Jolas had advocated using facts over opinions, and he developed his "Rambles" to be a form of hands-on cultural reportage. Just the same, his personal opinions colored and ultimately determined all of his statements. Following in the footsteps of Ford Madox Ford, a dean of Anglo-American modernist literature and criticism, Jolas's new position allowed him to come in close contact with the Parisian literary and avant-garde community. His vibrant potpourri reviews seized on everything new from Dada to Surrealist automatic writing, Freud's impact in France, current literary magazines, Sylvia Beach's and Adrienne Monnier's bookshops with a mission, and individuals such as the American avant-garde composer George Antheil, the poet Ezra Pound, or internationally less well-remembered writers like Valéry Larbaud, a friend of James Joyce. Jolas's observations and analyses reflect an exceptional achievement for a man of largely self-taught background.

Recognizing Paris as a melting pot of languages, second only to that of New York City, Jolas found his column for the newspaper to be the perfect starting point for his evolving ideas about bridging multiple languages and cultures. The particular significance of "Rambles Through Literary Paris" lay in its ability to transcend national and linguistic borders and to introduce up-and-coming European artists and intellectuals as well as American modernists to a global network of readers.

Echoes of Jolas's borderland mentality, his bilingual Alsace-Lorrainean heritage with a strong rooting in Romanticism, his horizon for understanding divergent phenomena as part a universal avant-garde movement, resonated in all of the reports. A crucial relationship between the provinces and the metropolis was reflected in Jolas's ongoing interest in two poets representative of the period's complexity, Yvan Goll and André Breton. Both were promoting Surrealism, but Goll, Jolas's countryman, tended toward a more Romantic, less programmatic Surrealism, as such favored by Jolas, while Breton established and masterminded the urban movement paradoxically as an institution which also took a political turn to Communism.

"Rambles Through Literary Paris" formed the foundation for Jolas's later literary project, *transition* (Paris and New York, 1927–38), in which he would fully explore his ideas of internationalism and universal bridging, and proclaim the achievements and productions of the Western avant-garde. His weekly column "Across Frontiers" (1949–50) would later take up the "Rambles" thread once again, albeit on a decidedly political note, since it emphasized the spirit of international democracy as of vital importance in the aftermath of the catastrophic Second World War.

"Rambles" appeared weekly in a section of the *Chicago Tribune Sunday Magazine* (European edition): no. 17 (June 8, 1924) through no. 40 (November 16, 1924). Afterward, the numbering of the newspaper changed: no. 2686 (November 23, 1924) through no. 3436 (December 13, 1925). The texts reprinted here only represent a modest selection, specifically only seventeen of the fifty-eight "Rambles," with the exception of two forerunner texts entitled "Through Paris Bookland" (May 25 and June 1, 1924) and two belated texts under the name "Chronicle of Reviews" (December 12 and 26, 1926). A reportage outside of "Rambles" concerning André Gide (no. 22, July 13, 1924) is printed under the heading "Literary Encounters" (see part 6). The criterion for selection relates to the literary and cultural historical importance of Jolas's articles.

The articles in this section of the book are reprinted with permission of the *Chicago Tribune;* copyright *Chicago Tribune,* all rights reserved.

—A.D.

Number 17 (June 8, 1924)

In wandering through Paris, the shimmering city, one's visual and auditory nerves are constantly ravished, and one has a veritable *embarras du choix* in trying to absorb the thousand and one things that the kaleidoscope of this city presents. Paris today is doubtless the cerebral crucible of the world. Nowhere does the visitor from America face such a plethora of ideas, revolutionary concepts, boldly destructive philosophies, ferociously new esthetic principles. . . . And the role of the spectator is the more interesting as the flux of ideas and the interchange of ideologies produce a constant war of the spirit which finds its expression in literary and artistic brawls of the most violent kind. Thus we take great pleasure in announcing a new fight which promises to surpass all of the preceding struggles in intensity and interest. This time the protagonists are M. André Gide and M. Henri Béraud. And the war is being fought in the *Mercure de France,* where M. Gide has massed his heavy battery, and in the *Paris-Journal,* where M. Béraud has dug his trenches. This little war has its genesis in the now well-known controversy between M. Jacques Rivière of the *Nouvelle Revue française* and M. Béraud, which, as our readers may remember, ended almost in a delightful little duel. We are watching developments with intense interest.

We have been much amused at M. George Migot's essay on "Henry Cowell and Musical Typography" in the *Gazette musicale et théâtrale,* in which M. Migot—of whom our readers have doubtless heard, thanks to M. Irving Schwerke's valuation of his work—examines Mr. Cowell's ideas.

Mr. Cowell, it will be remembered, is the heretic who some time ago shocked musical Paris by insisting on banging the piano with his elbows, thus producing somewhat crashing effects on tender nerves. "Without wishing to be Chinese, may we not hope for a part of that plastic and altogether spiritual joy which the design of a word gives the intelligentsia of China, in order to feel intensely the plastic, sonorous, and intellectual joy of a word which moves us, which one reads and understands," M. Migot asks. Evidently the frontiers of the arts are getting more and more vague, and soon we will have to redefine our concepts, if the E. E. Cummings and Henry Cowells continue.

That fantastic modern conception—*la réclame*—is giving Montparnasse enough vociferous tom-tom to prove that it is really the home of the Muses, in spite of it all. Here we have M. Michel-Georges Michel who just published *Les Montparnos* [Paris: Fayard, 1924], wherein the frequenters of the Rotonde, the Dôme, and other literary cafés are being sketched in audacious silhouettes. Aside from the fact that even the cinema has recently invaded the tranquil atmosphere of the cafés and forced the eloquent habitués to a reluctant appearance before the film, the fame of Montparnasse has been spread by other writers such as André Billy in *Scènes de la vie littéraire* [Paris: La Renaissance du livre, 1918], Mme. Marcelle Vioux, in *Les Amants tourmentés* [Paris: Charpentier & Fasquelle, 1923], M. F. J. Desthieux, in *Un Homme parmi les femmes* [Paris: Albin Michel, 1922], and other writers.

How James Joyce spends his hours in Paris is being revealed by Valéry Larbaud, brilliant French poet and *romancier,* and "European." Frédéric Lefèvre gives a scintillating causerie with Larbaud in *Les Nouvelles littéraires,* in which the latter, who is the discoverer and friend of many leaders of thought in Europe, chats about the great Irishman with remarkable frankness. "The last time I met Larbaud," says Lefèvre, "was in that American bar in the Latin Quarter, whither his friend James Joyce calls him, whenever he wants to read a new work to him." "We come here," states Larbaud, smilingly, "because we are very quiet from nine o'clock in the evening until one o'clock in the morning. The little dancers arise late." Valéry Larbaud, according to the writer, is at present supervising the translation of Joyce's *Ulysses,* although the work is to be given to the French public only in fragments, as it would take a lifetime to translate it.

"I met James Joyce towards the end of 1919 in the studio of a friend in the rue Dupuytren," Valéry Larbaud related. "Miss Sylvia Beach introduced us. Joyce is a man who does not speak; he is a man—*tout à fait en bois.* When I went away, Miss Sylvia Beach gave me the numbers of the *Little Review* in which fragments of *Ulysses* had appeared. On my arrival at home, I began to read them, thinking it would be an excellent preparation for sleep. I had a happy surprise; when I finished the last number, it was early morning. *A Portrait of the Artist as a Young Man*—is one of the greatest books I have ever read, and Joyce at this moment represents the entire English literature. Dedalus is in line with *L'Education sentimentale* and the *Trilogy* of Vallès. My admiration for Joyce is such that I am sure he is, of all contemporaries, the only one who will pass into posterity." Valéry Larbaud himself is one of the outstanding figures of French literature. Beside writing *A. O. Barnabooth* [Paris: Nouvelle Revue française, 1913], a tremendous hymn to modern life, and several novels, such as *Amants, heureux amants* [Paris: Nouvelle Revue française, 1923], he has been the chief link between French and foreign literature. It is interesting to note that he is the literary correspondent of *La Nación* at Buenos Aires, for which he writes his articles directly in Spanish, and that he has also written articles for English magazines directly in English. A universal genius!

We have found the most dangerous book written in many a year. During an interminable railway voyage recently, we read *Baal* [Abbéville: Paillart, 1924] by Renée Dunan, and we frankly felt a series of revulsions and attractions that made the trip comparatively short. Plunging into the Fourth Dimension, into weird occult madness, into grotesque distortions of the mind, we had the feeling, after finishing it, that we had just awakened from a nightmare. It is the story of a Paris *voyante,* or better, *magicienne,* whose esoteric powers are unlimited. Being in league with the forces beyond life, she knows the mysteries of the black art of the Middle Ages, and abuses her knowledge by atrocious murders and other criminal ventures. Her secretary Renée being sceptical of her art, the *magicienne* demonstrates her power by causing a fearful accident, by bringing about the appearance of a being from the fourth dimension—Baal—the fantastic reconciliation of a husband and wife, the transmutation of metals into gold through human blood, and finally a trip into the other side of life. Then comes disaster. The book is written with a dynamic force, although the very subject limits its esthetic appeal. An exceedingly dangerous book!

While the Dadaists continue to stammer their stylistic distortions, the conservators of French grammar persist in upholding the traditions of verbal sequence and logic. MM. Jacques Boulenger and André Thérive have just edited a remarkable book, *Les Soirées du grammaire club* [Paris: Plon, 1924], which gives a series of dissections of the language that anyone interested in linguistic purity should read. M. Abel Hermant, the novelist, some time ago published *Xavier: Ou les entretiens sur la grammaire française* [Paris: Le Livre, 1923], which gives a cross-cut of many subtleties of the French language.

Several of our private detectives are busy hunting up the identity of a chap who hides himself under the name of "Un Provincial," and who has made a stir in Paris recently by his biographical snapshots called "Franchises" which have appeared in *Comoedia* and other journals. These witty sketches of artists and writers—amazing drypoints of portraiture—have a certain malicious, albeit kind, spirit of understanding, their very briefness bringing out a whole human cosmos and giving a real insight into the essential character of the "victim."

We learn that M. Philippe Barrès, son of Maurice Barrès, is slated to receive the Grand Prix de Roman de l'Académie for his book *La Guerre de vingt ans* [Paris: Plon, 1924]. The literary path of M. Philippe Barrès has been made smooth throughout his career, which fact, of course, has been received with ill will by some of his less fortunate brothers-in-arms. The necessity of being eclectic in selecting a father seems again to be the moral of this little story.

We have great admiration for M. Poincaré, who appeals to us as the most intellectual of all political men in the limelight. To turn from reparations and internal politics to such an abstruse theme as a critical essay on Victorien Sardou, as he has recently done in speaking at the unveiling of a monument to the playwright, is a remarkable bit of versatility. Did he not make an address on Renan last summer that for sheer stylistic charm and penetrating analysis equals the best of any master of prose? M. Poincaré's style has all the lucidity and grace which is the sine qua non of French prose.

We select as the most beautiful title of any book published this year M. Paul Bourget's *Coeur pensif ne sait où il va* [Paris: Plon, 1924]. This profound study of a social phenomenon which would necessarily appeal to the famous *psychographe du coeur* rotates around a mixed marriage between a girl of the middle classes and a workingman. The purpose of the book is somewhat obvious, and we are not at all sure whether the famous *roman-cier* succeeded in convincing us that such marriages should not occur. The grace of style which all of Paul Bourget's works show is, of course, apparent in this novel.

We have just made a pilgrimage through Alsace and Lorraine, and had an opportunity of watching the fermentations of an artistic movement which may be called a modern Humanism. Strasbourg, we believe, bids fair to become the literary Athens of eastern France. There are powerful forces at work in the ancient Gothic city, and since its return to the motherland, it has forged ahead in an astonishing degree. It will be remembered that it was at the University of Strasbourg that Maurice Barrès gave his famous lectures on *The Genius of the Rhine* [Paris: Plon, 1921], which marks a milestone in the interpretation of French history. Le Groupe de Mai, which was founded in May 1920 by a number of enthusiastic young artists, furthers the artistic activities of the city, and is in close touch with the progressive minds of the interior. They have built the nucleus of a native art.

Another important, though vitally different, movement has grouped itself around *Les Nouveaux Cahiers alsaciens,* under the name of l'Arc. While intensely national in spirit, the young men of this organization have set before themselves the goal of building an intellectual bridge between France and the other nations. Under the leadership of M. Henri Solveen, brilliant artist and poet, the Arc movement proposes the shibboleths of a new Humanism in the arts. George Bernard Shaw, Romain Rolland, René Schickele, Ivan Goll, Maurice Betz, George Epstein, Jean Sebas, Raymond Buchert, and a host of nationally and internationally known writers will appear in the new magazine of the arts, *Rouge et blanc,* to be issued as the medium of the group. We spoke to M. Solveen, who told us that the writers of Alsace and Lorraine feel that Strasbourg, being at the *carrefour du monde,* is the ideal place for the execution of the program. One of the interesting features of this plan is the idea of issuing an all-American number this summer, in which some of the best-known writers and artists of America will make their appearance. We liked the atmosphere of the old Rhine city, and if Paris were not such an alluring sorceress, we might have stayed in Strasbourg, for all we know.

Young France celebrates the renascence of Pierre de Ronsard's Humanism. This Prince of Poets in the sixteenth century who was the leader of the Pléiade, and is doubtless one of the greatest lyric poets of all times, is being remembered now in connection with the four-hundredth anniversary of his birth. The publishers vie with each other in bringing out new editions of his work and dissertations about his life. We have been especially struck with M. Gustave Cohen's *Ronsard: Sa vie et son oeuvre,* which, although written by a professor of the Sorbonne, has the distinction of being a charming series of essays evocative of all the magic that Ronsard's poems contain. At a little gathering of enthusiasts, we heard a number of Ronsard's poems recited recently, and we felt that this ancient French has an indescribable beauty and music to modern ears. We did not care for his odes, which appeared to us as artificial, but his short poems have a beauty due to their very simplicity.

Ronsard lives in the pages of M. Cohen. With a graceful style, he paints the precursor of all French poetry. For Ronsard, the "galant" of Marie, the lover of Cassandre, the admirer of Helen, the disciple of Plato, Lucretius, Epicurus, and intense hedonist, has the very quality which we demand of the modern poet: that his work be the direct result of his experiences. *La Revue musicale* devotes an entire number to Ronsard and his relation to music, and comes to the conclusion that he has acted as a tremendous incentive to the development of French music. It may be noted in this connection that Ronsard wrote most of his shorter poems for the purpose of having them recited to the accompaniment of the lute. *La Revue de Paris* publishes the text of a lecture given by M. François Jammes, mystic poet, on Ronsard, the poet of nature. He emphasizes the fact that Ronsard drew his inspirations directly from the phenomena around him.

Was Victor Hugo the originator of the *romain urbain*—the novel which dramatizes the chaos of a city? M. Albert Thibaudet states this hypothesis in *La Nouvelle Revue française,* where he studies the origin of this type of modern novel. "Between the complexity, and the rumbling of a big novel and those of a big city, it seems that there is a real affinity, and that the idea of uniting them into the form and material of the same work should come natural to the mind of a fiction writer. Still, one does not find anything of the kind before the nineteenth century. And it seems to me that the author of this fruitful novelty, the creator of the urban novel, is Victor Hugo, with *Notre-Dame de Paris.*"

We are advised by *Les Amitiés françaises* that *La Marche au soleil,* a book of poems by M. Pascal-Bonetti, is being translated into English and will appear simultaneously in New York and London, as well as fragments from another work by this poet-Orgueils. The translation is being made by Prof. J. G. Walleser, a Rhodes scholar, who is now teaching at an American university. It seems that poetry does sell occasionally, notwithstanding the wails emitted by a thousand and one evokers of verbal rhythms!

The publication of Edgar Allan Poe's *Love-Letters to Helen* in a French translation by Emile Paul has created a considerable flutter among the numerous admirers of the great poet in France. The critics express a certain astonishment at the quality of these missives to Mrs. Whitman, but point out that they give a real index to the work of the writer. The psychology of the poet of the grotesque is still a mystery surrounded by a thousand legends and calumniations, and these letters open up many new vistas of his spirit.

We are awaiting with intense interest the appearance of *Kyra Kyralina,* by Panair Istrati, which Rieder is to bring out within a few days. The author, who is the son of a Greek smuggler, and of a Rumanian peasant, has lived an amazing life of adventure, traveling through the Orient for twenty years and supporting himself in the most fantastic ways. It is an autobiographical novel of the most colorful kind, and the fragments we have seen printed in reviews here and there have whetted our appetite.

Number 18 (June 15, 1924)

There is, after all, another side to contemporary French literature. Beside the blatant modernism and shrill Cubism of the cliques and *chapelles,* there is a movement that upholds the traditions of the eighteenth century. We had the pleasure recently of visiting the editorial offices of *La Revue hebdomadaire,* that typically Gallic magazine directed by M. François Le Grix and edited by M. Jean d'Elbée. In the high, cool rooms of the editorial sanctum, behind the church of St. Sulpice (known to lovers of strange books through Huysman's magic evocation of the "plaintchant" in *En route*), we spent some spirited moments with M. d'Elbée, who happens to be a marquis and a connoisseur of books. M. Le Grix, we learned, was on his way to see M. Paul Bourget, and we felt strangely envious of him.

"We are a rampart against the revolutionary tendencies of our age," M. d'Elbée told us. "We frankly and consciously believe in order and traditions. There is too much insincerity in the productions of the young men of this age, and we feel that a dam must be built by conservative hands. Somehow we believe that conservatism is more necessary today, with the war's effects producing many distortions of the spirit, than ever before. And we direct our magazine with that end in view. Thus, for instance, we have just devoted special numbers to Pascal and Paul Bourget, and are now preparing a special number on Ronsard and Maurice Barrès." The group of the *Revue hebdomadaire,* he told us, includes such names as MM. Henry Bordeaux, Charles Maurras, Tristan Derème, Marcel Bouteron, Edmond Jaloux, Henri Duvernois, Robert de Flers, Albert Thibaudet, Franc Nohain, Jean-Louis Vaudoyer, Marcel Boulenger, Francis Carco, Eugène Marsan, Pierre de Nolhac, Emile Henriot, François Mauriac, Paul Valéry, Julien Benda, Jean Balde, Henri Bremond, Lucien Fabre, and many others well-known in contemporary literature. The most recent number of the magazine brought the concluding chapters of Ferdinand Ossendowski's *Bêtes, hommes et dieux* [Paris: Plon, 1924] (which, when first published in New York [Dutton, 1922] created a furor), Princess Bibesco's *Le Perroquet vert* [Paris: Grasset, 1924], and some impressionistic poems by Louis Roché which we liked very much for their atmospheric charm.

For those of our readers who are interested in statistics, we have just dug up some figures that throw considerable light on France's literary activities. France is swept by an avalanche of books of the imagination, and the critics—overburdened as they are with tomes—are crying "halt" to the fertility of creative brains. According to a compilation just completed, one thousand five hundred and seventy-nine books coming within the category of belles lettres were published during the past year. They were: one thousand and nine novels, two hundred and eighty-four plays, and two hundred and eighty-six books of poetry. This is a steady increase as far as novels are concerned over the productions of previous years, the record for 1922 being: nine hundred and seventy-six novels, three hundred and sixty-six plays, and three hundred and ninety-five books of poetry.

If anybody would ask us who the most interesting poet of France is today, we would unhesitatingly cast our ballot for M. Jean Cocteau. A decidedly revolutionary, sincere, and original writer, M. Cocteau today seems to us to represent the absolute quintessence of modern French art. Not only does he write plays, books of poetry, and novels that are stamped with magic, but his interests also include such subjects as music and painting. He is a friend of Erik Satie, Poulenc, and the other members of the Six, whose herald he has been these many years. Just recently he appeared as an actor in his own version of *Romeo and Juliette* (wherein he dared to translate or adapt Shakespeare's lines through the medium of modern French argot). Some months ago, we remember, he published some sketches of his own in an "advanced" magazine, and we recall especially a bit called *Les Origines de la tragédie,* a primitive, hallucinated design of a Hellenic character, showing a man and a woman dancing upon the Parthenon. He has the amazing faculty of giving archaic and antique subjects a modern touch. His *Antigone* (first night: Paris: l'Atélier, December 20, 1922)—set to music by Arthur Honegger—gave a new interpretation of this Greek symbol of womanhood.

Mr. George O'Neill, author of *The Cobbler in Willow Street* [New York: Boni & Liveright, 1919], a book of poems that we have admired for many years, was captured by us the other day, just after he had landed in Paris from the Hudson city. He brought to us the impression that New York is today the literary center of the world. . . . As one of the editors of *The Measure,* one of the most energetic and ambitious of the art magazines in America, he would, of course, have more than an ordinary survey over the work of the young American writers. And he told us that America was on the threshold of a great era of artistic flowering. He chatted about the work of Eleanor Wylie, and grew enthusiastic about her novel *Jennifer Lorn* [New York: Garden City, 1923], a story of eighteenth-century England, which he regarded as a tour de force. He told us of the theatrical season in New York—of the production of Toller's *Masse Mensch* (which was a complete failure, because the revolutionary basis of the play had no reference to the American consciousness, it being purely German in background and conception), of the *Icarus Flight* of Norman Bel-Geddes, one of the most amazing of the modern American stage designers (he showed us his illustrations to Dante's *Divina Commedia* which we frankly regard as astounding creations), of an obscure Hungarian's play, called *Fata Morgana,* of Shaw's *Joan of Arc,* of Eugene O'Neill's failure in dramatizing *The Ancient Mariner,* although his *All Gawd's Chillun Got Wings,* he says, was a great success, and of a hundred things that made us proud of the old town, where we used to earn our daily bread.

We have just read *Oxford et Margaret* [Paris: Fayard, 1924] by M. Jean Fayard and were impressed by it. It seems to us a capital tale of an Anglo-Saxon civilization seen through French eyes. While the Oxford "esthetes" and "athletes" are busy with their sundry ideals, the Frenchman—and we are proud of him—interests himself in the only woman in the place: Margaret. What he thinks about her, about Oxford and Anglo-Saxon ideas, is tremendously interesting, showing how difficult it is for the various nations to understand each other. . . . If you have read *Ariel* [Paris: Grasset, 1923] by André Maurois you will understand what we mean. For only a Frenchman could have written this vibrant, and perhaps a little distorted, story of Shelley. . . .

We have perused with great amusement the reports of the now famous Grammaire club by M. André Thérive, laureate of the Prix Balzac, and by M. Jacques Boulenger. Both, it seems, are the archivists of this strange club, which has set as its goal the preservation of French grammar amid the facile introduction of many vulgarisms, argot, and other distortions into the language of Molière. The last number of *La Revue hebdomadaire* contains a delightful account of a session of the club. A chap named Anselme relates his adventures of a mission to the Sorbonne, his encounters with an automobilist, M. Xavier de Marais, who insists on using good old argot to express his annoyance, and a final violent discussion about a grammatical subtlety.

M. Pierre Reverdy, who, it will be remembered, won the *New World* prize, has a collection of poems in the June number of *La Nouvelle Revue française,* and in view of the fact that his selection for the honor has created a violent controversy, we decided to examine his verses most critically. These four poems in free verse seem to us a little bit academic, although we liked "Visage" best as a real lyrical evocation, as it has a strange beauty and seems to have been a direct result of an experience.

Swiss writers using French as their medium of expression are increasingly coming into their own in France. We have just read *Le Parricide* [Paris: Rieder, 1923] by M. Fred Berence, and it suggested nothing to us so much as a novel by Dostoevsky. It is the story of a youth, who after twenty years of suffering from his alcoholic father's brutality, kills him in final desperation. Werfel in Germany tried the same theme in *The Son.* We feel somewhat afraid of these pathological sketches, which all seem to proceed from the principle that "every son is an Oedipus, and every father a Lajos." Sigmund Freud! What sins have been committed in Thy name!

Every once in a while the newspapers report the distribution of prizes at the Flower Games in the cities of Arras, Rouen, Amiens, Valenciennes, and Toulouse. M. Joseph Bédier talks entertainingly about the history of the Jeux floraux in the last number of *La Revue de France.* It seems that this custom had its origin in the north of France, whence it spread to other cities, in the thirteenth century. "Without doubt our forefathers tried to show that the poets must not shut themselves up in cenacles, as in little chapels, to hear themselves sing, but that they should sing before the entire city. Such a thought was salutary, and although poetic contests have often been criticized, we have a right to say that French literature owes a great debt to this practice." The Nouvelle Librairie nationale has also just published *Anthologie des jeux floraux* by MM. A. Praviel and J. R. de Brousse, which traces the poems in the *langue d'oc* and *langue d'ail* from the first *leys d'amors* of Armand Vidal to our days.

Rudolph Valentino, the Sheik of the cinema, as our friends the newspapermen are wont to say in their inimitable style, is back in America, but there seems to be a little epilogue to his visit in France that has gotten into the papers. Apparently some garrulous gentleman has stated somewhere that Rudolph was displeased with France, that he expressed himself as antagonistic to French habits, and that he would not return here. Now, we learn through a letter published in the *Paris-Journal* by M. Jacques Hebertot that the movie star was really in love with France. "Having lived near him almost daily," says M. Hebertot, "I can only tell you that his dearest desire is to return to France to remain here always, that it is here that he buys his automobiles, his neckties, and his dogs, that he adores our country for its landscapes, its customs and the charm of its manner." . . . Thus a great international problem is automatically solved!

We were hugely disappointed in reading M. André Baillon's *Par fil spécial,* published by Rieder. This book of sketches by a journalist, or editor, when first announced aroused our curiosity, and we felt that we would get a great thrill out of it. Is it because we have no understanding for Continental methods of journalism, having been a cub reporter, reporter, and whatnot on American newspapers in our younger days—about thirty years ago? . . . Somehow we felt that this sort of journalistic revelation was absolutely uninteresting, and we felt a strange pride in the fact that, mechanically, our methods were different.

This *carnet* of a "secrétaire de rédaction" is very malicious in many ways, but somehow seems to us to lack the dynamics which an American newspaperman, with similar ideas, would have injected into his sketches. We have reported murders, and fires, and presidential trips, and political conventions and a hundred queer things that fall to the lot of a reporter, and we always felt that if any of our more literary colleagues would ever write that life of adventure and bitter disappointments and tragedies, we certainly had some very definite ideas about it. Now, we do not feel that M. Baillon's volume gives us any thrill, because somehow the direct contact with life which the American newspaperman gets was entirely missing from these pages.

Number 19 (June 22, 1924)

What does modern France think of American letters? We gained the impression during an afternoon with Paris writers that France is watching the work of our young men with intense interest. . . . This surprised us the more, as we have felt for some time that the Anglo-Saxon student of litera-ture on the whole is little interested in the tendencies of French letters after the war. A new Classicism, we believe, is in the offing here. Dadaism—a negation of art born out of the war—has died, not, however, without leav-ing its traces on the works of the younger men. We believe that the time is not very far off—say, perhaps, fifty years—when French artists will seek their inspiration in America, just as they go to the colonies today in order to refresh their creative imaginations which have become dulled by tradi-tion. We do not want to give the impression, however, that the novel of analysis and the exotic novel, as they appear in France at present, lack inter-est—never has there been such a feverish intensity in the creative arts as in France today. Bold experimenters are forging new methods of expression. France is still the apparently inexhaustible source to which the students of the world flock in increasing numbers. But there is a keen curiosity here about the creative forces across the Atlantic, and anyone who follows the currents here will notice the almost fetishistic hold America is gaining on Young France.

We recently had the pleasure of meeting a number of contemporary French writers. Thanks to the kindness of M. Jacques Rivière, critic, novelist, and editor, we were able to talk with them in the charming atmosphere of a literary home. M. André Gide, whose *Les Nourritures terrestres* [Paris: Mercure de France, 1897], *L'Immoraliste* [Paris: Mercure de France, 1902], *La Symphonie pastorale* [Paris: Nouvelle Revue française, 1919], and other books present a high-water mark in contemporary French letters, was there and enchanted us with his magical words. We met there M. Charles Du Bos, brilliant critic and author of *Approximations* [Paris: Plon, 1922], M. Jean-Louis Vaudoyer, critic, poet, and novelist, M. Simon Levy, painter and art critic, M. Ramon Fernandez, critic, M. Boris de Schloezer, of *La Revue musicale,* M. Henri Deberly, novelist, M. Jean Prevost, novelist, M. Jean Paulhan, editor, M. Gachot, poet, Mme. Van Rysselberghe, wife of the painter, and Mme. Jacques Rivière.

All of these writers have grouped themselves around *La Nouvelle Revue française,* which we daresay has no analogy in any other country. We were surprised at the knowledge of American writers shown by them; several of them, notably M. Gide, expressed the opinion that America will eventually produce the literature for which the present stage of transition is only a preparation. It seems that the work of Waldo Frank has made the deepest impression on French writers. They felt that his is the authentic voice of America, expressive of the rumbling chaos and electric fermentation of our country. Apparently the production of Eugene O'Neill's *Emperor Jones* in a French version here last winter did not leave any marked impression, the prevalent opinion being that it was monotonous. We pointed out that it was probably the fault of the translator, and we felt that it would be exceedingly difficult to transpose the essentially American psychology of the Pullman porter. M. Charles Du Bos, who has a vast knowledge of American and English literature, expatiated on the influence of Marcel Proust on contemporary literature and asserted that only by forgetting Proust could the young men of today assert themselves. M. Ramon Fernandez, who was born in Mexico, who lived in New York, and apparently knows a great deal about the psychology of languages, entertained us with his ideas about America, and astonished us by the revelation that he is one of the contributors to English as well as French magazines. We gained the impression that all of these writers are in close touch with American letters and are watching the work of the young men very closely. We heard some flattering comments on Gorham Munson, T. S. Eliot, and Carl Sandburg, and on the work of the Russians in Paris, who in many cases have conquered the difficulties of a new language by using it as a literary medium.

We asked Mr. Harold Vinal, editor of *Voices,* and one of the best known of American poets, the other day, whether it was not true that American poetry was on the decline today. Recent readings of books and magazines from New York and Chicago had given us the impression of a curious monotony and a certain artificial repetitiveness which seemed somehow to be entirely at variance with the idea one gains from this side that the crystallization of a native feeling in America would produce big things. Mr. Vinal did not agree with us. He admitted that there was a tendency nowadays to "intellectualize" too much, but he was decidedly of the opinion that a native school of poets is emerging. Sitting in a delightful Neapolitan restaurant and sipping Chianti with Mr. Vinal, Mr. Paul Tanaquil, well-known poet and short story writer, and Mr. Dwight Fiske, whose work created a sensation here recently, we looked over some of the recent books of poetry which Mr. Vinal has just brought from New York, *After Disillusions* by Robert R. Wolf and *Sunrise Trumpets* [New York: Harper, 1924] by Joseph Auslander, as well as the last few issues of *Voices.* While we did not feel that we could sympathize with these two poets very much—we had the impression that they are definitely out of tune with their age— we were constrained to pay high tribute to the artistic charm of their works. There was nothing American about them. They might have been written in Czechoslovakia.

Mr. Vinal, who is on a brief tour of Europe, told us some interesting details of his work as editor of *Voices.* This magazine which, like *The Measure,* projects some of the best lyric work of the American poets, had its beginning in staid old Boston three years ago. Unlike most ventures of this kind, it flourished, and Mr. Vinal has now been able to open a larger office in New York. Mr. Tanaquil, who has a remarkable short story in the last number of the *American Mercury,* told us that his novel *The Frontiers of the Flesh* would be published in New York this fall. Mr. Fiske's settings of Stevenson's poems as well as his *Milltown Lyrics,* we learned, will be given in New York this fall.

We have recently trumpeted our enthusiasm for the poetry of M. André Spire, and felt that we were somewhat solitary in this discovery. That enterprising weekly, *Le Paris-Journal,* devotes an entire page to "Three Poets Who Should Become Popular"—Spire, Fagus, and Vildrac—by M. Ernest Tisserand. We confess we never heard of M. Fagus, and were astonished to be introduced to a poet of such magic. Vildrac, better known as a dramatist (his *Le Paquebot tenacité* was given with great success in New York last year), is familiar to us chiefly for his *Chants du désespéré* [Paris: Nouvelle Revue française, 1920] that have tremendous power and beauty.

Modern music is still a bugaboo to many well-meaning people whose intellectual roots unfortunately are in the decades before the war. They forget that the nervous vibrations of the man of today—nourished, as he is, on Proust and Freud and the fanatic agony of machines—are totally different from that of his blithe and passive ancestor. But though they fight with all of the tenacity of the conservative, the new rhythms will doubtless become banal in another decade. We thought of this the other day, while listening to Mr. George Antheil, the American composer, as he unfolded to us the percussive power of his new string quartet *Hungariana,* which is to be given in Paris next month at the Conservatoire, where he and Mr. Ezra Pound will appear in a joint recital of their own compositions. Both recently returned from London, where their works acted on the British public like an electric shock. *Hungariana* is a composition that, we believe, has no analogy in musical history. It is a vast rhythmic sneer at melodic banalities. It is a philosophical negation. . . .

"Yesterday I became impolite to a certain superior person," Mr. Antheil told us, "because he insisted that a well-known ultra-Russian composer had written a certain Negro music from the Congo, simply because that Russian composer always wrote extremely rhythmic music, and that particular music happened to be very rhythmic. . . . The human mind is amazingly stupid and stereotyped with regard to the musical situation today. It is this stereotype which I think has influenced my quartet. It has come out meagre, stiff, conventional. It seems quite out of style . . . it is more on the side of musical photography than art. I do not like style . . . it has always seemed to me the point at which the intelligence becomes tired, and drifts down the stream two or three years late. The last work of this Russian composer is in style, even as his Spanish counterpart in painting is in the latest style . . . the smartest style." Mr. Antheil, incidentally, is now putting the finishing touches to his *Ballet mécanique* which is to be given, together with designs by M. Fernand Léger, at the Théâtre des Champs Elysées next season.

Will we face another Zola controversy? The erection of a monument to the father of the Naturalist novel at the intersection of avenue Emile Zola and rue Viollet recently has been the signal for numerous attempts to fix his position from the perspective of the distance which his contemporaries were unable to possess. MM. Léon Deffoux and Pierre Dufay contribute a joint article to the *Paris-Journal* on Emile Zola and his influence, in which they trace the tremendous impulse his work has given the younger generation. Among the men they regard as having been under his influence are Henri Barbusse, Georges Duhamel, Henri Béraud, Roland Dorgelès, Francis Carco, Emile Zavie, and others. *Les Nouvelles littéraires* recalls the manifesto of the famous Five issued by five contemporaries against Zola, after the publication of his *La Terre*. Zola treated this attack on his work with the utmost contempt.

Nothing has shaken us as much as *La Steppe rouge* by J. Kessel (Nouvelle Revue française), which fell into our hands recently. These amazing sketches in grey portray Russian life during the revolutionary period. These short stories evocative of terror and madness might have been translated from a new Chekhov. *Les Deux Fous*—a fragment during the Red occupation of Odessa—has a macabre note that stays with one long after one has put the book away. We would also put M. Kessel in the categories of the writers who were influenced by Zola.

M. Abel Doysie devotes an article to contemporary English poetry in *Les Nouvelles littéraires* and gives excellent translations of some of the poems of Masefield, Yeats, Kipling, Bridges, Sir Henry Newbolt, Rupert Brooke, and others. "Out of this brief essay," he concludes, "there emerges the conviction that English poetry, in every field, is vigorous, and that it does not tend to bend itself into official systems or hermetic forms that can only interest a restricted cenacle. It reaches power through simple processes, natural force, and is always near to life."

That bright and vivacious new magazine of the arts, *Cap,* edited by M. Marcel Hiver, has just appeared for the second time since its start. We liked especially an essay entitled "Reflections About Michel-Georges Michel, That Is, About Nothing." This is a savage attack on the author of

Les Montparnos. There is also an attack on M. André Salmon which we deem absolutely unjust and out of taste.

If the signs do not deceive us, France is on the threshold of a puritan wave. Witness the strange case of M. l'abbé Violet who, like a reincarnated Savonarola, got himself into trouble with the police by publicly destroying the *affiche* of a nude woman on one of the boulevards. Now, it seems that the police commissioner told M. Violet that his zeal would be better employed if he would go to the trouble of providing the young ladies in our music halls with camisoles and other necessary things. Soon we will have an anti-vice crusade here, if this continues!

Somebody called our attention to a book just issued here under the title of *Le Lid yidish en amérique* by Anna Margolin. This anthology of the Yiddish poets of America culled from their productions during 1923 gives a marvelous insight into the esthetic charm of this new literary phenomenon. It gives poetry by Keurtz, Kissin, Segal, Glatstein, Eizenstat, Halpern, Drapkin, and others. Most of these poems have a revolutionary nostalgia . . . and are typical of the Jewish immigrant in New York's East Side.

We have been greatly interested in a little brochure published by Les Editions G. Crés & Co., called *Literature,* which attempts to give a silhouette of the life and works of the various writers this famous publishing house has brought out. We confine ourselves to giving the names of the writers: Barbey d'Aurévilly, A. Gilbert de Voisins, J. K. Huysmans, René Lalou, Pierre MacOrlan, Jules Renard, Maurice Renard, André Rouweyre, Marcel Schwob, Victor Segalen, and A. de Villiers de l'Isle-Adam.

Number 20 (June 29, 1924)

Half the charm of the book lover's life lies in the spontaneous discovery of the little hidden corners of belles lettres that do not hear the echo of the tom-tom of the highway. There is no doubt that the last year has seen a certain, albeit quiet, swing toward literary statism, toward the resuscitation of the traditions. Cubism in letters, which really dates from Guillaume Apollinaire and found its strident climax in the negativism of the Dadaists, has fulfilled its functions, and there is a tendency toward a new Classicism. The experimenters are failing precisely because their art is deliquescing into rigid formalism and a fever artificially whipped to a crisis. It did our heart good, therefore, to stumble into the atmosphere of *Le Divan* recently, where we discovered a bit of contemporary French literature that for sheer poetic magic has no equal, it seemed to us.

We had a long chat with M. Henri Martineau, director of *Le Divan,* poet, editor, publisher, bookseller, and—physician. There is a certain colorful lure about the bookstore at 37 rue Bonaparte, where M. Martineau watches over the destiny of his books, where he receives his friends of *Le Divan,* and where he edits the various numbers of the magazine. He has a certain southern, exotic personality, and is one of the few poets who seem to us somehow to be the incarnate phenomenon of their fantastic preoccupations. "I founded the *Divan* fifteen years ago," he told us, "because I was very much alone. Living in the provinces as a physician, I occupied myself with literature, and in order to get in contact with kindred spirits in France, I founded the magazine which for a time was published in the provinces, and later was transferred to Paris. I soon had as collaborators most of the poets who are now members of the *Divan* group." The magazine had at first the usual fate of ventures of this kind—it had to fight every inch of the way, but gradually asserted itself. M. Martineau himself is the author of *Les Vignes mortes* [Niort: Clouzot, 1905] and *Acceptation* [Niort: Clouzot, 1907], two volumes of verse of beautiful sincerity and artistry. He has also written numerous critical books, such as *La Science de Zola* [Paris: Baillière, 1907], a volume on *Stendhal* [Paris: Société des trente, 1912], and estimates of the work of MM. Lièvre, Carco, Porché, Benoît, Jaloux, Montford, and Paul-Jean Toulet.

In looking through the anthology of the poets of *Le Divan* [Paris: Le Divan, 1923] published some months ago, one encounters many names that are famous today. There are poets like P.-J. Toulet, Francis Carco, Pierre Lièvre, Nicolas Beauduin, Lucien Fabre, Jean-Louis Vaudoyer, Francis Eon, Guy Lavaud, and others. Reading this *recueil,* one has the impression of entering a Gothic cathedral at twilight. There is no tropical luxuriance, rather a strange, introspective atmosphere of meditation. Having been gorged with the a-rhythmical cacophony of the poets of the day, we felt a curious sensation of relief in reading them. It is strange to find in this collection poems by such a radical as M. Nicolas Beauduin, whose *L'Homme cosmogonique* [Paris: Povolozky, 1922] made a sensation a year ago; Francis Carco; and Tristan Derème. We advise all bibliophiles to pay a visit to the *Divan* Temple in the rue Bonaparte.

Mr. John Dos Passos, the author of *Three Soldiers* [New York: Doran, 1921], has just dashed into the Seine city on one of his annual pilgrimages to strange lands, and we cornered him in a little out-of-the-way café, where one can talk uninterruptedly, and where the atmosphere is still somewhat pristine. He related to us the queer adventures of his latest book, *The Streets of Night* [New York: Doran, 1923], which raised a tremendous scandal in prim old Boston, where the publishers, indignant at the alleged libel of their beloved town, virtually boycotted the book. Mr. Dos Passos, who has a charmingly dynamic personality, told us many little bits of literary New York, where, he insists, modernism is in its last stages.

Just why did Freud's psychoanalytical theories never take root in France? This interesting question is answered by M. Edmond Jaloux in *Le Disque vert,* which has devoted the entire last number to the Viennese magician of the soul. When we think of the times our long- and short-haired Greenwich Village friends shrieked into our ears the parrot-formulas of complexes and libidos, we have a strange inclination to avoid every line ever penned about Freud and Jung. M. Jaloux explains the strange fact that Freud became a fetish in puritan countries, or countries with rigid ethical standards, while France remained free from the hysteria.

"If French doctors have so long refused to heed the ideas of Freud," he says, "it was simply because they have not been able to verify them. There are few cases of 'suppressions' in France, where a general tolerance gives human beings a relative liberty of action and seldom creates around sexual manifestations that atmosphere of anguish and suppressions which is obvious in the cases studied by Freud or Havelock Ellis. And as we live on the puerile idea of the classical man, who is always true to himself, we think that the phenomena so frequent in Vienna, Zurich, or London are rare in Paris, although they surely exist . . . For this reason Freud's pan-sexualism must appear exaggerated to most Frenchmen, doubtless because they have always loved pleasure too much to experience that profound abnormality of the individual under the influence of generic instincts which characterizes the patients studied by foreign neurologists." M. Jacques Rivière, the critic, has a very interesting study on "The Possible Generalization of Freud's Theories," while M. Ramon Fernandez studies the ethical aspects of psychoanalysis.

We met Mr. Gilbert Seldes on the eve of his wedding, in the company of his brother, Mr. Georges Seldes, Berlin correspondent of the *Chicago Tribune*. The young New York critic, and former editor of the *Dial*—who at one time in his career, we understand, was boosted as the greatest living expert on Henry James—recently made a decided success with his book *The Seven Lively Arts* [New York: Harpers, 1924], which attempts a new and esthetic valuation of the "arts" hitherto despised and neglected by the intelligentsia. His editorship of the *Dial* was coeval with a tremendous literary and artistic renaissance in the United States, for which much of the credit must go to the magazine.

The Daddy of Dada is tired of his age. M. Tristan Tzara, who founded the great postwar movement in Switzerland, confided to M. Pierre de Massot in the *Paris-Journal* recently that he was extremely bored, and he used a trip-hammer to put his literary adversaries out of commission. "I find that the present literary situation is extremely rotten," he said. "It is an uninteresting morass. There is a marked decadence, since everything is being vulgarized by so many newspapers. There is absolutely nothing that interests me. I withdraw more and more from literature and would like to do something else. If I write sometimes, it is because of habit, weakness, or illness. I find that one can no longer discern definite currents, as we did several years ago. And it is going from bad to worse.

"With regard to M. Reverdy, who won the *New World* prize, I could tell you a lot about him," he continued. "He is a poet whom I valued highly in 1916–17 for certain poetic qualities which since that time have remained static to such an extent that I cannot sympathize with them. His poetry is based on a certain stability that lies in a perfection of images or the style, which, because of this desire, loses its splendor, outside of its formal beauty. His poetry is purely literary, and if there is a spirit in it, it is that of Maeterlinck's melancholy and Viélé-Griffin's lyricism. I don't give a hang for the purity of the poet and his 'noble' heart; what makes the charm of life for me, and the thing he ignores are the impurities and the maladies of which I live and of which I die. I detest his 'ivory tower' Romanticism and the fanatic admiration shown by certain disciples. At present I am sleeping a great deal. Like the poet of *Mouchoir de nuages* [Paris: Editions de la galerie Simon, 1925], I die every day a little."

We looked through M. Reverdy's *Epaves du ciel* [Paris: Nouvelle Revue française, 1924] recently, and are sorry to say that we agree in part with M. Tzara. They are decidedly academic. We could enumerate any number of contemporary American poets who have done better work than any of the poems that won him the prize. In view of the fact that these poems are to be translated into English and presented to America as the quintessence of contemporary French poetry, we feel decidedly that it was a mistake. In fact, we think there is too much condescension toward American poetry on this side, anyway. Why not translate Frost or Sandburg or the *Spoon River Anthology*?

Ever since M. Michel-Georges Michel published his *Les Montparnos* with a plethora of fireworks—movies were taken at the Rotonde and the Dôme of the more prominent habitués of Bohemia—this book has been the center of a bitter wrangle. The author is accused of having distorted the picture of some of the well-known inhabitants of that charming province of Paris in an atrocious manner, of having made ataxic caricatures of his characters, and finally of having written a mediocre book. Some of the portraits are apparently so thinly disguised that they are easily recognizable, and there is considerable agitation among those sketched by the writer. Our boy-reporter is watching the situation at the Dôme, and will keep us informed about the bouts.

And since these are the days of political excitations, we propose to toss a little information your way that may help you throw some light on an important question. Mr. Prew Savoy just presented us with his thesis, *La Question japonaise aux Etats-Unis,* with which he captured his *doctorat en droit.* It seems that Mr. Savoy is entirely in favor of Japanese exclusion, but he advocates a different strategy from that which was used by Congress. He favors proposing restrictive legislation by Washington in order to force Japan into a treaty. But it's too late now. . . .

The Blumenthal Prize was distributed a few days ago among MM. Robert Coiplet, Marcel Sauvage, and Pierre Guegen. Each of the three writers gets the nice little amount of twelve thousand Gallic berries. The jury was composed of Mme. de Noailles and MM. Bergson, Jaloux, Paul Valéry, Gaston Rion, Albert Thibaudet, Henry de Regnier, and René Basave.

We just read M. Paul Géraldy's *Le Prélude,* a novel by the author of *Aimer,* which seems to us to give the exact limits of this very pleasant talent. It is a little bit too tenuous for our taste. We did like *Aimer* immensely, and felt that here was a sincere attempt to solve a triangle with a profound delicacy and lyric charm. M. Géraldy, it seems to us, is a real *intimiste* who always succeeds in showing these hidden, subtle evanescent *états d'âme* that more vigorous writers somehow neglect. It is an excellent "livre de chevet."

It is tremendously interesting to compare *Le Prélude* with the rhythmic prose of M. Valéry Larbaud. We have just read his *Amants, heureux amants,* which is dedicated to Mr. James Joyce, "my friend and the only begetter of the form I have adopted in this piece of writing." The story is entirely based on the inner monologue, with a story of imperceptible outlines. But there is a glorious atmosphere about the reflections, and we confess we even liked it better than some of his other short stories. We understand that *Amants, heureux amants* will be brought out in New York next fall.

Great interest is being shown in the Rémy de Gourmont exposition now being held at the Sirène, rue la Boétie. Friends of the famous writer appear every Friday and hold brief addresses on various aspects of his life and work. The "Amazone" and MM. Jean de Gourmont and A. Ferdinand Hérold were the first to mount the rostrum. Portraits, sketches, family portraits of Gourmont, his death mask, manuscripts, articles he gave the "Amazone," and other mementos are shown there.

For those who are interested in dynamically exotic poetry, we recommend *Kodak* by Blaise Cendrars. We will have occasion to speak of this poet's work some time in the future, as he seems to us one of the most interesting figures in contemporary French literature. He is one of the few poets who translate their lyrical nostalgias into action. *Kodak* is a transcription of his travels in America and other parts of the globe. He is at present in the wildest part of South America. . . . These poems have power and beauty and are shot through with passion and sincerity.

Number 22 (July 13, 1924)

We have just had a discussion with a group of young French poets—
very dogmatic young men—whose heretic notion it is that lyric poetry
in France was approaching intellectual bankruptcy. They feel that their
generation has burned itself out, and that the creators of today are merely
the last epigones of a dying age. Without drawing, however, the consequence of their heresies, they announce that the poetic instinct will cease
to function in another decade. It so happened that three very important
essays dealing with the modern poetry movement in France had come
under our observation, in which one writer agreed with this pessimistic
viewpoint, while the two others are of the opinion that France is on the
threshold of a great poetic renaissance. Tristan Tzara recently hammered
the mythos of this conception into chaos. But then he is a Dadaist and
he has a theory to defend. Now comes M. André Salmon, who in an illuminating essay in the *Transatlantic Review* asserts that "in 1924 French
poetry, the expression of a convalescent motherland . . . when all the currents of the world are running to a still unequal rhythm, is a very healthy
person." M. Bernard Fay analyzing the "recent state of poetry in France
1918–1924" comes to the conclusion that "not since the seventeenth century have we created a poetry as personal, strong, masculine as ours."
M. Ivan Goll, on the other hand, states in the *Paris-Journal* that "poetry,
being disquieting, foggy, mysterious, is being represented by Dadaists,
who want to be nihilists, and who are at bottom only Symbolists of the
worst kind, who walk about with a false boredom, and the withered car-
nation of Wilde's."

Vertical Rhythms Predominate

All of them somehow agree on the idea that Dada played an important part in the evolution of contemporary art; it filled a real function, for as M. André Breton, himself a Dadaist, pointed out in *Les Pas perdus* [Paris: Gallimard, 1924], these artists sought "a particular solution of the problem of our life." It was therefore essentially an ethical movement—Prometheus storming Heaven. With it goes hand in hand literary Cubism, of which M. Max Jacob is doubtless the greatest exponent. M. Pierre Reverdy's "plastic poetry" derives from the sculptor's studio. Paul Valéry, Valéry Larbaud, and others have been revolutionary in their work. Paul Claudel, Francis Jammes, and the other Catholic poets have been silent for some years. All of the work of the moderns is decidedly vertical and tends toward a new metaphysics. There is a new sense of beauty in their poems that is bewildering and full of the restlessness of the age.

A Bombshell from the *Little Review*

We recently said a kind word for the *Dial* and evidently have stirred up a hornet's nest. Miss Margaret Anderson, brilliant editor of the *Little Review*—ultramodern exponent of American art—has taken us to task, although we are second to none—as the phrase goes—in our admiration for the great services the *Little Review* has done for American art and letters. For that magazine's history is essentially the history of the emancipation from the incubus of insipid esthetics. "I am so tired," she says, "of hearing the *Dial* spoken of as the beacon light of modernism in America (the *Dial* which I always speak of as the 'de-alcoholized version of the *Little Review*')—that I am sending you the enclosed for Sunday's edition of your interesting book page."

Ulysses and the Critics

I am a bit fed up, as we say in America, with the literary critics who are now taking credit to themselves for having discovered James Joyce's *Ulysses*. Especially as I happen to possess all the inside information as to their refusal for three years to recognize Joyce as anything but an excrescence upon the literary horizon. As editor, publisher, and founder of the *Little Review* I may be said to be more or less au courant with the fact that it was I who published Joyce's *Ulysses* serially in the *Little Review* some five years ago. This was in the days before the professional critics knew that Joyce existed—in spite of the opportunities he had given them with his *Exiles, Portrait of the Artist as a Young Man,* and so on. No, I am unjust: several of them had already denounced him thoroughly on the grounds that in the *Portrait* he wrote of natural functions . . . naturally. When we urged the *New York Times* to help us in spreading a little publicity about this great book, our requests were ignored completely, except for sneers at "a decadent art magazine that delights in publishing the filth of diseased contemporary writers," etc. We ran *Ulysses* serially for almost three years, and from the first were attacked by the combined forces of literary, social, and civic America. The Post Office Department suppressed five different issues of the *Little Review*—not only suppressed them but burned them up— each issue of some four thousand copies, so that we were almost unable to carry on our business. (Fortunately the *Little Review* has never been a business: it is simply the most interesting review of art and letters ever launched in America and for that reason always without a cent of capital; so that to be burned up was only another of the perfectly normal disasters for which we were always prepared. In fact, we got so used to being burned that we didn't feel normal except under fire.) Finally the climax of our persecution arrived with our arrest by the Society for the Suppression of Vice, and we were brought to trial on the specific issue of a certain episode in *Ulysses*— (the chapter where "Gerty" raises her skirt a bit indiscreetly and Mr. Bloom is moved thereby to erotic meditation).

A Historic Trial

Mr. John Quinn, one of New York's ablest and busiest lawyers (who bears also the distinction of owning one of the best collections of modern art in America and of being a friend of Joyce) defended us. But in spite of his prestige, his brilliance, and his effective irony at the *défaillance* of Vice Societies who couldn't recognize literature because of a short skirt, he lost the case; and Jane Heap and I, the publishers, were forced to pay a $100 fine and have our fingerprints taken. We are now on record in the United States courts along with the fingerprints of thieves, murderers, the insane, and other criminals!

There were (among others) two beautifully ironic aspects to the trial: as we hadn't a cent, our fine was paid by a friend (an Irishwoman) who privately detested *Ulysses* and the *Little Review* as immoral and very shocking, but who had, in spite of her opinion that we were all mad or abnormal, a sincere personal respect for Joyce and for us. Second, at the end of the trial (at which there were three presiding judges, two of whom were white-haired and went to sleep during most of the proceedings), the prosecuting attorney announced his intention of reading aloud the alleged "obscene" passages in question. But the oldest of the two white-haired sleepers suddenly woke up and, regarding me with that protective paternity which is the outstanding characteristic of all American males, refused that such obscenity be read in my hearing! "But she is the publisher," said Mr. Quinn, smiling. "Yes, but undoubtedly she didn't know the horrible significance of what she was publishing," responded the judge, regarding me with tenderness and suffering.

A Cautious Silence

During the trial and afterward not a single New York newspaper came to our rescue: not a word was printed in defense of Joyce and his art; not a word about our courage in publishing what we considered the literary masterpiece of our generation; not an opportunity given our rather special ability to defend our point of view. We didn't have even any helpful publicity out of the trial, as every editor in the country was afraid to be identified with the "*Ulysses* scandal."

The *New York Times* was particularly silent. . . .

In our defense we had as witnesses Mr. Scofield Thayer, editor of the *Dial*, Mr. Philip Moeller, the dramatist, and Mr. John Cowper Powys, a literary critic too interesting and unorthodox to be recognized by the *Times*. Mr. Moeller analyzed *Ulysses* for the court by trying to give them a simple explanation of the Freudian manner of unveiling the subconscious mind, but one of the judges asked him "please to talk in words that we can understand." Mr. Thayer was forced to admit that if he had had the opportunity of publishing *Ulysses* in the *Dial* he would have consulted a lawyer first—and not published it.

Mr. Powys explained why he considered it a very beautiful piece of work and in no way capable of corrupting the minds of possible young girl readers. Jane Heap tried to explain that she saw no reason why the minds of young girls should be so carefully protected—if there was anything she really feared, it was the mind of the young girl. I expressed freely my rage against judges being allowed to express their opinion on literature; against the criminology of the American censorship; against the general and total senility of the whole situation. None of these things helped us any.

Where Credit Belongs?

It is true that if we had not published *Ulysses* it would never have been shown to the literary elite until Sylvia Beach brought it out in book form in Paris. As it was, by the time the book was ready, the elite were talking of *Ulysses* and gradually it was borne in upon the *New York Times* that it would be a disgrace to its future literary reputation to continue its silence. From this moment full pages of enconiums on Joyce and his masterpiece began to edify the astonished readers of the *Times*!

I shall never forget the day we received the first two chapters of *Ulysses*, sent to us by Joyce through Ezra Pound, foreign editor of the *Little Review*. I still remember my emotion as I read them: "This is the most beautiful thing that has ever come our way." I wrote Joyce that its publication would begin immediately, and I continued to be so exalted with the creative miracle of Joyce's work that the danger of publishing it never quite became a reality to me, even when we were burned at the stake! But it is probably the simplicity of this attitude that has allowed all the professional critics to ignore the fact that we were the only magazine in the world willing to publish *Ulysses*. If we had done it as arrivistes, to make a sensation for ourselves or for Joyce or the *Little Review*, we would have had columns of publicity. Even Mr. Gorman might have mentioned the fact in his new book: *James Joyce: His First Forty Years* [New York: Huebsch, 1924]. As it is, in the floods of *Ulysses* reviews that have appeared in the last year I have not seen one that felt it would be charming to state: "Published originally in the *Little Review*."

Music Lures Poets

Mr. Ezra Pound is not the only poet who has become unfaithful to the Muses and who seeks his esthetic expression in music. Mr. Louis Untermeyer, famous American poet and critic, writes us from Switzerland that Mrs. Jean Starr-Untermeyer will give two song-recitals in Vienna this autumn. Mrs. Untermeyer, who will be known on the concert stage as Jean Starr, is the author of two books of poetry which we always admired very much for their delicate beauty. The two poets have been on the Continent for more than a year, traveling through England, France, Germany, Austria, Italy, and Switzerland.

Witches Sabbath of Letters

Is modern literature seeking an escape from life in the fantastic quest after horror and the evocations of black magic and occultism? Mme. Renée Dunan, whose *Baal* we recently discussed here, devotes in *Vita* an interesting article to "the present tendency towards the love of miracles in literature." She is inclined to believe that this tendency is about to conquer the minds and imaginations of many writers, especially since the present spiritualistic and occultist mania has spread through many countries. She enumerates Huysman's *Là-Bas,* H. H. Ewers's *The Magician* (*Der Zauberlehrling*), whose *Mandragore,* a weird story of the mechanical production of a strange human being, was translated into French a year ago and was a considerable book success. The preoccupation with the diabolical has always held a place in literature, although we don't think it will ever overshadow the fundamental values of the normal spirit.

Algebra and the Poet

We learn that M. Paul Valéry, the poet, has been triumphantly received at Madrid, where he lectured on "Baudelaire et sa postérité," and on Ronsard before literary societies of the Spanish capital. M. Valéry is doubtless one of the most gifted poets of this generation. M. André Gide in his *Incidences* gives an affectionate appreciation of his friend who, after a brilliant debut as poet, laid aside his pen for more than twenty years to occupy himself with strange studies of algebra and geometry. "I am not a poet," he insisted at that time. "I am he who is bored. All moral, cubic, and affirmative beauty takes me away from poetry."

A Book of Genius

The July number of *La Nouvelle Revue française* brings the final installment of Raymond Radiguet's *Le bal du comte d'Orgel,* which is soon to appear in book form. This precocious novel of the young poet, finished shortly before his death last year, is a definite contrast to the diabolical fever that surged through his first book, *Le Diable au corps.* It gives an extraordinary story of love and renunciation with the background the emotionally chaotic days before the armistice. This number of the *NRF* also contains the final chapter of M. Léon Bopp's *Jean Darien*, which we have already had an opportunity to praise. M. Paul Morand is represented with a short story, "Les Amis nouveaux." M. Paul Fierens devotes an analytical essay to "Les Epaves du ciel" by M. Paul Reverdy, which was crowned with the prize of the *New World* some months ago.

A Rebel of Letters

Paris recently saw the unique case of a former German Uhlan officer who was well received by the lovers of new accents in literature here. Fritz von Unruh, a German novelist and playwright of the modern school, has been showered with homage in newspapers and magazines ever since the French translation of his *Opfergang—La Marche au sacrifice* by M. Benoist-Méchin was published here. These vividly realistic sketches of the German defeat of Verdun are second only to his dramatic works which captured the German stage during the past few years. He is a dramatic genius whose roots lie in tradition, although he is a revolutionary noble-man. His style has more Latin charm than the tortured "telegram style" of his contemporary, Georg Kaiser, one of whose expressionistic plays was given at l'Oeuvre last winter, proving a fiasco.

Paris Hails Alsatian Poet

The first work of an Alsatian novelist and poet to be presented to the French public has made a profound impression here. M. René Schick-ele's *Le Consolateur des femmes* [Paris: Rieder, 1924] was written before the war and aside from its artistic power has the distinction of having given a remarkable horoscope of the war. Although M. Schickele has spent most of his youth in Paris—his mother being French and his father Alsatian—he wrote the book in German and it had to be translated into French. His racial background causes him to synthesize in his intellectual life the French analytical power and formal sense and the German love of spec-ulation. When we met M. Schickele at Strasbourg for the first time, we heard from him one of the most amazing stories produced by the war. After telling the German government which had prepared to draft him that he was "unable to participate in its undertaking," M. Schickele fled to Switzerland, where he became editor of *Die weissen Blätter*, the refuge of the young German poets who in their works fought for the overthrow of the kaiser and his clique. German Expressionism found its cradle in that group, which included men like Werfel, Becher, and others. M. Schickele is the author of numerous books of poetry, plays, and novels and frequently appears in Paris, where he has many friends. We have the most delightful memory of an evening spent in a famous Strasbourg inn, together with a group of Alsatian poets and artists, listening to the amazing conversation of M. Schickele.

An American Boswell

We cannot imagine anything more delightful than listening to Mr. B. J. Kospoth, whose interviews with Rachilde and other celebrities have recently appeared in this magazine. Mr. Kospoth, who at one time was a correspondent attached to Wrangel's army and at that time was made a Cossack of the Kuban, probably knows more men and women who have made history during the past twenty years in Europe than any other American.

Number 28 (August 24, 1924)

When visiting American literary critics, who omnivorously absorb the entire modern literature of France, Italy, Germany, and Czechoslovakia in a wild dash of three months or less, get the brilliant idea of interviewing James Joyce—which is à la mode—they usually beseech Miss Sylvia Beach to pave the way to the orphic Tusculum of the Gaelic Master. But they never succeed. For James Joyce has a panicky fear of newspapermen. They disturb him, misquote him, and with the usual journalistic imbecility distort the ideas he expresses. That is why the legends around Joyce grow by leaps and bounds. The literary gossips construct fantastic fables around the mysterious figure of the writer. It seems to have become one of the "idées fixes" of every American or British journalist that he must see James Joyce. Hundreds have been here in the last few months and tried their luck. This phobia of Joyce's may be another legend—but we have it directly from Miss Beach.

The Romance of a Bookshop

Miss Beach is probably the best-known American woman in Paris. Ever since she launched her ambitious scheme of running a bookshop exclusively devoted to American and British books of the day, her name became known throughout Paris. And when she became the publisher of *Ulysses,* her fame spread through the world. One does not overstate the case in asserting that Miss Beach, who is the friend and adviser of many French and Anglo-

Saxon writers, is one of the important figures in contemporary letters. She told us that the idea of opening a bookshop came to her shortly after the war, and encouraged by French friends, notably Mlle. Adrienne Monnier, she opened the Shakespeare Bookshop at 8 rue Dupuytren. One of her ideas was to provide a meeting place for French and American writers and artists. The store flourished, and after a little while she was able to move into larger quarters, the present premises in the rue de l'Odéon. In the meantime she met James Joyce at a party; and because the latter has a great love for bookshops, he visited her place the following day. It was here that she introduced him to Valéry Larbaud shortly afterward—a meeting which was to be a red-letter day for European literature. Valéry Larbaud had already taken a great interest in her undertaking. In a picaresque mood he had given her a miniature replica of Shakespeare's house, which can be seen near the entrance of the store. He was the first to introduce Joyce to France.

Job and the New Style

When the plan for publishing *Ulysses* was first broached, James Joyce thought the book "too dry" to become a success. Miss Beach, however, with characteristic American optimism, had a different idea about it and events have proven her right. When the first installments of *Ulysses* came out in the *Little Review,* she gave the various copies to Valéry Larbaud, and he later told her that he sat up all night, so interested had he become in the work. *Ulysses,* Miss Beach told us, has now gone into its fourth edition. James Joyce does not regard the introduction of the "interior monologue" in the story as specially original, for, he wrote to her in a recent letter, Job used it successfully many centuries ago.

The Book-Friends' House

Opposite the Shakespeare Bookshop there is its French pendant—La Maison des amis des livres—which is run by Mlle. Adrienne Monnier, friend of poets and *romanciers.* It was here that Valéry Larbaud gave his famous lecture on Joyce in December 1921, when the first translated fragments of *Ulysses* were presented to a sceptical audience, which gave the Irish writer a tremendous ovation. When Valéry Larbaud had finished, Joyce, who had hidden behind a screen, was dragged to the stage and embraced by the enthusiastic Larbaud, while the room rocked with applause.

A Translator's Whim

The first French translation of fragments from *Ulysses* to be published will be brought out by a new magazine, *Commerce*, of which Mlle. Monnier is to be the publisher. Paul Valéry, Léon-Paul Fargue, and Valéry Larbaud are the editors. The translation is by Auguste Morel, who, we understand, has retired to Belle Ile, Sarah Bernhardt's former home, to complete the translation, a task which will take at least two years. The first issue of this magazine, which is to come out shortly, will contain, in addition to the *Ulysses* fragment, contributions by Paul Valéry, Léon-Paul Fargue, Valéry Larbaud, St. J. Perse.

A Strange Poet Laureate

And since we are talking about Valéry Larbaud, whose *Barnabooth* incidentally is in the hands of every young French poet today, we might mention the fact that he has blossomed forth as the poet laureate of the miniature Republic of San Marino. He writes to his friends on the official paper of the republic and takes huge delight in this poetic caprice. He has prepared an essay to be published in the *Nouvelle Revue française* soon in which he will make short shift with the Gaelic-American writers, who have had a grudge against him ever since he announced that "with *Ulysses* the young Irish literature has made a triumphal entry into high European literature." Mr. Ernest Boyd, who evidently has been grieved by this—as it left out Yeats, and so on—and who has been sending steel-barbed shafts in the direction of M. Larbaud, had better watch for the article.

A Jewish Poet in Paris

The arrival here of M. A. Leyeles, a Yiddish poet who has been hailed by his compatriots in America as the lyric apostle of the new consciousness, has caused considerable interest in Paris. M. Leyeles is the protagonist of the so-called Introspectivist movement in New York's East Side, and in that capacity has influenced the younger generation in Yiddish literature to a large extent. This poet, who hails from Poland, has been a resident of New York for more than twenty years and edits there the review *In Sich* as well as *Der Tag*, a literary daily. His latest collection *Rondoes and Sonnets* will be published in Warsaw shortly.

King Ramon de la Serna

One of the greatest services Valéry Larbaud has done French letters was to introduce the work of that quixotic Spanish writer, Ramon Gomez de la Serna. The life of this Hispanic Balzac, whose productivity is enormous, is as bizarre and astounding as are his novels. M. Jean Cassou in the last issue of the *Nouvelle Revue française* gives some details of his life at Madrid, where Ramon holds "court" in a fantastic café—Pombo—and where his friends gather once a week to witness the extravaganzas of their "King." "In a corner of the café of Pombo," says M. Cassou, "under the triple protection of a painting by Solana, a street lamp, and ventilator, Ramon officiates every Saturday night. Here he collects strange characters, fools, bums, maniacs, versifiers, and all kinds of original types—a menagerie, a burlesque court, and stages his galas of the world. The shrieks and laughter of triumph, which Ramon shows amid this nocturnal fair, may give the key to his books, to their hilarity and diversity. I must add, to explain this phenomenon better, that the face of Ramon, in addition to his 1830 disguise and certain imitations of the crooks of Madrid, offers an evident resemblance to one of the most alluring and joyous artists of our times— the smile of Ramon resembles that of Douglas Fairbanks. . . . Throughout this immense and miserable Madrid, Ramon chases curious beasts, runs through the streets, gardens, and cafés, and every object elicits a strange story, an absurd imagination, a puerile and fantastic hypothesis. It is not a process of metaphysics, a system of deformations and associations which the author applies to every spectacle. The reactions of Ramon before the world are always unexpected, because a drama is played between himself and the world, and because he does not bring to this play the frigidity of a brain organized in such and such a manner, but the ardent soul of a man of genius."

A Weird Ego

The egoism of this writer is apparent in a little brochure he wrote about himself under the title of *Ramon,* according to M. Raymond Cogniat in *Comoedia.* Here he describes his inner life, speaks complaisantly of his own person or his collections, which are the strangest things one could imagine. This illustrated brochure contains a large quantity of reproductions of sketches and photographs of Ramon in every pose, at every age, and in every costume. One of them shows him under five different aspects. He wanted to commemorate a year when he published five new books. His fetishes are numberless and have all a story: in a corner of his study there is a street lamp, on which Ramon wrote his name; next to it you will find a big waxen doll, his Muse, as he calls it, which he dresses and undresses, according to circumstances, and which plays the role of Molière's servant girl—for he reads his manuscripts to her before publishing them.

The End of the Cenacle?

Ever since Dada and Expressionism have gone to pieces, students of literature have noticed a rebound toward individualism. Schools and cenacles are probably things of the past, simply because of the intensified ego of the young writers, who, having matured at a vertiginous speed, refuse to acknowledge a Master, as did, for instance, the Symbolists, who gathered in the rue de Rome every week to listen to the conversations of Stephane Mallarmé. Examining "the crisis of the artistic conscience" in *Les Cahiers du mois*, M. Maurice Betz comes to the conclusion that the "ismes" are dead, and the rare prophets, who still continue their preaching, are not heard. "Individualism is à la mode," M. Betz says. "Everybody is busy following his own faith. He finds his dignity in the fact that he adheres strictly to this attitude. At least he believes that he safeguards it in this way. While yesterday twenty individualists, burning with the desire to each affirm his own particular faith, grouped themselves together accidentally under the banner of a school, it happens that today twenty writers who follow perhaps the same thought, have no other wish but to run away because of love of individualism."

The Hebrew in France

Has there been a Hebraic influence in French literature? M. André Spire, categorically affirming this question, explains his viewpoint in an article he recently contributed to the Jewish review *Menorah* published in New York. According to *Paris-Soir*, he mentions Mikael, at the end of the Parnassian movement, Marcel Schwob, during the movement of the "Romantic purification," and Catulle Mendès. He asserts that Durkheim was the father of Unanimism. "Beside Bergson," he continues, "there is also another writer, who is a traditionalist, syndicalist, and utilitarist at the same time—George Sorel, one of the most enlightened minds of the age. Pupil of Bergson and

Kant and perhaps of the Spinozaist Brunschvicg, the poet Henri Franck, who shortly before his death wrote *La Danse devant l'arche,* remains one of the finest minds of Jewish French literature. Edmond Fleg, pupil of Bergson, wrote *Ecoute, Israel."* M. Spire also mentions MM. Claude Anet, Jean-Richard Bloch, Bernard Lazare, André Maurois, Fernand Vanderem, Léon Werth, and others.

The Pathos of Music

Gopher Prairie leaves its traces even in the modern art movements. As proof we receive the latest *Quarterly Bulletin* of the Franco-American Musical Society, published in New York. "The most interesting thing about the brochure," someone says, "is the quotation from Jean Cocteau—'Le tact dans l'audace c'est de savoir jusqu'ou on peut aller trop loin.'" The bulletin reads mostly like a weekly pamphlet issued by the Ladies Sewing Circle, as it gives copious notes about the activities of various chapters, where each member is allowed to toot his own horn and to talk about his latest creative smear. No wonder there ain't no American music!

Number 30 (September 7, 1924)

There are few bookshops with personality. Most of them are just bibliographical warehouses. You feel somewhat constrained, as you wander in front of the shelves, an atmosphere of frigid business hovers over the place, and you feel the categorical imperative of the impersonal *magasin*. You get, however, a glimpse of magic sometimes, when you discover a store that has the imprint of the owner's psyche. That is the case with the Maison des amis des livres, where Mlle. Adrienne Monnier holds open house. Situated near the venerable Odéon, in the heart of one of the most charming quartiers of Paris, you find here all the modern French books and magazines, and you also have an opportunity of becoming a member of La Société de lecture, which gives you the right to borrow books and reviews or to spend leisurely moments in the quiescent milieu of the store. And here you will always find Mlle. Monnier ready to give you information.

The Poets' Friend

For Mlle. Monnier is a friend of all the important and struggling poets and *romanciers* of France today. She is their adviser on the hard road to recognition. They write her about their troubles and she gives them the horoscope of her ideas. But she herself is—what very few booksellers are—a writer and poet of fine sensibilities. Did she not publish her charming *recueil de vers La Figure* [Paris: La Maison des amis des livres, 1923] last year in which she celebrated her friends Jules Romains, Léon-Paul Fargue, Paul Claudel, Paul Valéry, André Gide, Valéry Larbaud, James Joyce, Luc Durtain,

Jacques Benoist-Méchin, Sylvia Beach, and her sister Mlle. Marie Monnier, in musical and sincere accents?

To Paul Claudel she says:

Ta puissante prière vient troubler mon sommeil
Elle assiège ma nuit par la peur et le feu.
J'implore malgré moi la force de ton Dieu.
Je sais qu'il peut chasser la troupe qui tourmente
En moi la fille née de ceux qui le servaient.

Of Fargue she writes:

Comme un astre fidèle,
Il paraît tous les soirs,
Son heure est incertaine,
Asservie aux nuages.
Et docile aux regards.

James Joyce she calls "Homme de Péché, Homme de Colère, Homme de Patience," while Valéry Larbaud is "le voyageur dont la course relie comme un sang généreux les membres de l'Europe." She told us that, in order to give young poets eager to have their works published a wholesome example, she purposely printed on the title page: Imprimé aux dépens de l'auteur.

The Magic of Books

She began running the store "with very little money and a great deal of faith" about eight years ago. In a delightful brochure she published some time ago, she told about the initial phases of the venture, and tinctures it with her brave philosophy. For she had very little help when she began realizing her vision. "At that time," she says, "I had no business experience, I did not even know bookkeeping, and I was so afraid of appearing businesslike that I always tried to give the impression of neglecting my interest, which, of course, was childish. People like to believe that life extinguishes enthusiasm, that it deceives our dreams, and that it deforms the first conceptions, realizing somewhat accidentally our projects. Still, I might say that in the beginning of my enterprise, my enthusiasm and faith were a little less big than they are today. Our first idea was a modest one: we only tried to start a bookstore and reading room devoted to modern works. We had little money, and that little detail caused us to specialize in modern literature. . . . A man like Gide was given recognition only late in life. It is almost unbelievable that it took eighteen years to exhaust the first edition of *Les Nourritures terrestres* [Paris: Mercure de France, 1897]. It seems to us that Jules Romains does not occupy the place he really should have: for the last few years we have given young men, who come to us, books to read which seemed reserved for the elite; they always grow enthusiastic over the poems of Paul Valéry and Léon-Paul Fargue, *Barnabooth* [Paris: Nouvelle Revue française, 1913] by Valéry Larbaud, *Livre d'amour* [Paris: Nouvelle Revue française, 1914] by Charles Vildrac, *L'Etape nécessaire* [Paris: Sansot, 1913], by Luc Durtain, for instance, although most of them never heard of these authors."

A Recalcitrant Poet!

Her interest in these poets is not merely cursory. She also publishes their books, as well as magazines. We had occasion recently to refer to a new magazine, *Commerce,* published by the Maison des amis des livres—and we were the first to mention it—which contains, beside the fragments of *Ulysses,* and other contributions, "Epaisseurs," an exquisite ideological fantasia by Léon-Paul Fargue. Mlle. Monnier told us that she had to force the poet to write this sketch. He finally dictated it to her, after he had wasted precious days in "talking his poems." Valéry Larbaud, who had one of Fargue's books, *Tancrède* [Paris: Raymond, 1911], published at his own expense, had to lock up the divinely lazy poet at Vichy to get him down to work.

A Literary Phenomenon

There are few bilingual poets in the history of literature, but there is always the danger that this manifestation may become mere verbal acrobatics. The artistic conscience in this type of mind has to be extraordinarily acute. Some years ago we remember reading an article by Prof. Brander Matthews in the *Boston Transcript,* in which he attempted to prove that no foreigner can completely absorb the spirit of a language which he did not learn at his mother's knees. He will stumble over the nuances which are of the mechanics of the language, he thought. We have just spent an afternoon with Ivan Goll, who is both a French and a German poet, and one of the leaders in both countries. If we are not mistaken, he has completely demolished Prof. Matthew's thesis. (So has Joseph Conrad, for that matter.) M. Goll, who hails from Metz, creates lyrics and dramas in both languages, and it is impossible to discover any verbal lesion in either language he uses. We have read his *Le Nouvel Orphée* in both versions [Berlin: Die Aktion, 1918; Paris: La Sirène, 1923], his *Eiffel Tower* [Berlin: Die Schmiede, 1924] poems, his *Memories from the Underworld* [Berlin: Fischer, 1919], his *Chaplinade* [Dresden: Kaemmerer, 1920], and others. He is the poetic Stravinsky. Modern life hammers through his rhythms. His *World Anthology of Contemporary Poetry* [Paris: Renaissance du livre, 1922] gives a bird's-eye view of the lyrical work of almost every country on the globe. Among the Americans represented in this book are Carl Sandburg, Edgar Lee Masters, Amy Lowell, Ezra Pound, Sherwood Anderson, and Orrick Johns.

A New Theory

[Goll] told us that art in France was ripe for a synthesis of the various movements born in the past decade. Thus he is of the opinion that *Surréalisme* will be the new orientation. "Let us be alogical," he said once. "It is the best weapon against the platitudes that strangle life." He is still of that opinion, he said. Two groups in Paris are, therefore, today struggling for leadership in this movement, each of them claiming intellectual priority. One section is headed by Ivan Goll and Paul Dermée, and the other by André Breton, who has now forsaken Dadaism.

A Poet of the "Movies"

Mme. Claire Goll is also a poet of great gifts. She became known in America through her German translation of contemporary American poets, which was a remarkable example of empathy of one who has never seen America. Her *Lyrical Films* [Basel: Rhein, 1922], a collection of her own poems, has a modern note and an intensely dynamic force.

American and European Writers

It is strange what a romantic lure the immensity of America has for the Continental mind. From this perspective, of course, he sees the outlines of America more sharply than a native could, and his traditions and temperament give him a different viewpoint. Thus the European artist hungers for a chance to see America, because he projects an a priori conception of intensity and dynamism that really is a subconscious desire, we think, to get away from the static mood of the European landscape. Ivan and Claire Goll told us of their great desire to wander through America, to see the inchoate outlines of New York. Chicago, which they know through Sandburg's poem, which both translated, lures them, and the Great West has appeared in their poems in a strange nostalgia of anticipation. Although there is in America, in our opinion, no literary art as yet, but a higher journalistic art, an adaptation of Continental emotions and attitudes—witness, for instance, the grotesque spectacle of Dadaism in a country where a positivist philosophy is the very antithesis of this negative attitude—the two poets believe that America will be the country in which literary art will ultimately reach its twentieth-century apogee.

A Document of Pathology

Suzanne Kra contributes an article to the *Journal littéraire* on Sacher-Masoch in which she quotes the amazing contract that the writer had entered with his first wife, Wanda: "Blind obedience. The slave will execute every order of the sovereign," the agreement reads. "Every disobedience will be vigorously punished. The slave shall follow every order carefully and shall serve with absolute attention, while she dresses, undresses, and bathes, and shall submit to ill labor with conscience and scrupulousness. The sovereign does not need to do any domestic work. The slave must serve breakfast to his sovereign every morning on bended knees. The humblest adoration, the most devoted solicitude, a continuous gratitude shall be the first law of the slave. He shall, in speaking to the sovereign, use only the terms fixed by her. He shall formulate every request on his knees. Without the permission of the sovereign the slave can only kiss the hem of her robe. The sovereign has the right to put the slave temporarily at the disposition of her women friends. She has the right to see in the slave only a plaything, without will, an instrument of her humors, a serf without any rights. Every consideration, compassion, and pity shall be excluded. Without any motive, the sovereign has the right to cruelly torment her slave, to martyrise him, to force him to the lowest and most vulgar labors. The slave has only two days of liberty every week."

"Bluff" and the Dictionary

The controversy over the refusal of the American word "bluff" by the French Academy is merrily going on. M. W. Mayr in *Le Journal littéraire* takes issue with the academicians for closing the dictionary in the face of this "picturesque word." "We understand very well," he says, "that the honorable Company of Forty (reduced to three or four that day!) admits the strangers who crowd before the columns of the dictionary only with the greatest circumspection. But it seemed to us that 'bluff' had already made sufficient headway, and that nothing can replace that picturesque word, whose meaning evokes a ball that bursts." (M. Mayr, who has been in the literary struggles in Paris for many years, has given us an interview on his adventures throughout this feverish epoch, and we will give our readers an exposé of his reminiscences shortly. It will give them a look behind the curtains of the cliques and cenacles!)

The Year's Crop

M. Benjamin Crémieux devotes an instructive article to a recapitulation of the literary year in the last issue of *Les Nouvelles littéraires*. He points out that as one of the arbiters chosen by the Commission of Intellectual Cooperation of the League of Nations, he has selected *L'Enquête au pays du levant* [Paris: Plon, 1923] by Maurice Barrès and *Eupalinos* [Paris: Gallimard, 1924] by Paul Valéry; *Amants, heureux amants* [Paris: Nouvelle Revue française, 1923] by Valéry Larbaud and *La Brière* [Paris: Grasset, 1923] by Chateaubriand appealed to him as being next in line. He also mentions Morand, Max Jacob, and Rabevel.

Number 36 (October 19, 1924)

The one thing almost every European writer expresses about American art and letters is scepticism. Condescendingly they refer to the artistic endeavors of our traditionless youth. They know little save Poe and Whitman, who undoubtedly wielded an immense influence on Continental evolution. Waldo Frank and possibly Theodore Dreiser among the moderns represent the extent of their horizon. But they always insist that America will eventually produce the art for which this age of epigones is waiting. It is so much more facile for them to write about America, the cubes of its visionary skyscrapers, the roar of the Chicago pit, the singsong of jazz, which Milhaud discovered for them. The real America they do not know. They are ignorant of the groping psyche of the nation as manifested throughout its limitless spaces. Ivan Goll publishes a *World Anthology* [Paris: Renaissance du livre, 1922] and gives a cross-cut of the Poetic Renaissance, featuring Sandburg, Edgar Lee Masters, Amy Lowell, Sherwood Anderson (the poet), Orrick Johns, Ezra Pound, James Oppenheim, and Vachel Lindsay. Novels, probably because of the technical difficulty of translation, are practically unknown. The work of Eugene O'Neill is not understood, simply because the premises are unknown. To be sure, the realistic—or regionalistic—movement, as exemplified by the writers of the Middle West, has no real analogy in France. Rather, it is a movement which owes its impulse to the central European *Heimatkunst* of 1908–13. It is, therefore, comprehensible that its period of greatest production fell in the years during and after the war. Sinclair Lewis, Sherwood Anderson (who is, however, also a mystic), and also Homer Croy! (Dreiser, being a naturalist, does not belong in this group). . . . As Homer Croy is now in France and has just finished his latest book—*R.F.D. no. 3* (New York: Harper, 1924)—we were happy to chat with him the other day.

The American Farm

The author of *West of the Water Tower* [New York: Harper, 1923] and *R.F.D. no. 3* represents the American consciousness in its very essence. He has become the voice of the inarticulate moods of the neglected towns and farms. . . . When you meet him, he impresses you with a certain dynamic intensity. He looks at life with a kindly smile, and his humor is contagious. On the day we met him with Mr. and Mrs. John A. Chapman he had just sent off the contract for his new book—*R.F.D. no. 3*—which is now on the bookstalls in America. It will be remembered that he was the subject of a great literary mystery when Harper's published his *West of the Water Tower*. Rescued out of a prize competition, it was published anonymously, and the secret was kept for almost three months. "Because I had previously confined my literary activities to writing humorous and lighter yarns, Harper's, when they decided to publish *West of the Water Tower*, did not want to bill me as a 'serious thinker,'" he said to us whimsically. "Everybody engaged in the guessing contest, and the only critic who guessed right was Miss Fanny Butcher of the *Chicago Tribune* Literary Section. A few of my friends, of course, knew that I had been responsible, but they kept it under cover—until Percy Hammond of the *New York Herald Tribune* got hold of the fact one day, while we were having a party at the home of Burns Mantle, dramatic critic of the *Daily News* and *Chicago Tribune*. Somebody evidently put him wise, and when he asked me some questions about it point-blank, I did not realize that he was not aware of it. I gave it away. Then he wrote a long, laudatory article revealing my name. The next morning Harper's called me up, and there was a great deal of excitement. I had to dictate a flat-footed denial of the authorship, but it was considered too strong, and I finally decided on a humorous, evasive answer. The reply was published, but it was too late. I had become a 'serious thinker.'" He told us incidentally about the curious way publishers have of selecting a title for a book. As a rule, the author's title is submitted to the scrutiny of the office force and salesmen; and if it does not meet with their approval, a list is circulated, and the highest number of votes wins.

France and American Writers

Mr. Croy told us his reasons for coming to France to write about the Middle West. "I did not come to France for the reason you imagine," he said, "because I had all I wanted back home. . . . There was merely a change in price. The reason is that the farther you get away from the scenes you are writing about, the better you are apt to do them. I live in a place, absorb all I can, and then go off and incubate. I would never write stories of the Latin Quarter while living there. I'd probably write 'em in the Middle West, and then living in the Latin Quarter, I'd write about the corn rows. I go on the theory that if you can't remember a thing, it isn't worth writing about. The novel I wrote here in France is *R.F.D. no. 3* and it has just been published. I wrote some of it in Paris, some of it in Nice, and finished it in Sainte Maxime (Var). . . . I have my family with me and every now and then we get the itch to move, and then we fasten a Michelin guide on the windshield, hang out the baby carriage on the front bumper, and ride into the unknown. Just at this minute I am living in one of the suburbs of Paris, banging away on a new novel."

A New Realism

"*R.F.D. no. 3* is laid on the farm in the Middle West where I was born and lived until I was twenty-two. Then I went away to the city and into the newspaper business to lead a fast life. I found that about the only thing fast about the newspaper business is the way you have to work. And the way your pay goes. . . . One thing that made me particularly anxious to do a farm novel is that one-third of the people in the United States live on the farms and yet nobody is writing about them realistically. Gene Stratton Porter has done a few farm stories, but her heroes are handsome, broad-shouldered sons of toil whistling as they go jauntily down the corn rows. I don't see farm life that way. I tried to put, as I know it, into *R.F.D. no. 3*. . . . I don't know whether I have hit it with *R.F.D. no. 3* or not, but I know that I put all I had into it. When I was through, I was a squeezed lemon. It seemed to me that I should never be able to get up steam again, but at last the drivers began to turn. . . . France is a good place to work."

The Age and Genius

Genius is notably absent in our days. There is no supreme intelligence or leadership, only a mixture of contradictory individualities. This is the view of our age which M. Paul Morand expressed to us recently. The Freudian psychology and the urge of exoticism are the two main impulses behind the modern ideation. He told us that he was planning to visit America some time this winter—which will give him his first glimpse of America. He has a great affinity with the Anglo-Saxon spirit and has always been an assiduous reader and admirer of its literature, especially the Elizabethans.

A Literary Event

The long-awaited first novel by André Gide to be called *Les Faux Monnayeurs* [Paris: Gallimard, 1925] will at last be published. We learn that the next few numbers of *La Nouvelle Revue française* will contain the incipient installments of the novel. The entire literary world is looking forward to the publication of the book with the keenest interest, since M. Gide has been silent for a long time. He writes with infinite care and devotes usually many years to a single volume.

A Pathetic Gesture

Has anybody noticed the following queer and pathetic item in the newspaper? "Tired of life, M. Alphonse Raus, a citizen of Czechoslovakia, committed suicide on the grave of Heinrich Heine in the Montmartre Cemetery by sending a bullet through his head." Are we to witness another current of Werther depression? This is a symbolic gesture of Romanticism which has the substance for a curious study in pathology! Heinrich Heine, the Rhenish Aristophanes, lived in Paris for many years and from his "mattress-grave" sent out the *Lieder* that still live. We cannot help thinking in this connection of that beautiful poem by Louis Untermeyer—"Monologue from a Mattress-Grave"—which seemed to us at the time one of the finest expressions of the Romanticist's tragedy ever written.

The Battle's On

In a recent talk with Ivan Goll, author of *Le Nouvel Orphée* [Paris: La Sirène, 1923], we were told that he was girding his loins for a literary battle that would echo and re-echo throughout Paris. He said that he loved the dynamic struggle in modern letters. He was being violently attacked at that time together with his friends by another group that insisted on having priority rights to the designation of "sur-realists." The battle has now reached a decisive stage. In *Les Nouvelles littéraires* Maurice Martin Du Gard explains the sur-realist theories of André Breton, leader of the left-wing party of the new school. Paul Dermée edits *Les Interventions surréalistes,* while Ivan Goll publishes the first number of *Surréalisme.*

Automatic Writing

There is no doubt that *Surréalisme* is the most important literary movement in French literature since the Symbolists. It is a final adieu to Dadaism. It is the one vital expression of the age and seeks to lead literature from the psychiatric ward, in which it has been drooling in the years after the war, to sanity. The idea goes back to Guillaume Apollinaire, who in 1916 developed the new concept as an antithesis to Realism, Naturalism, and other genres that were flourishing at that time. While André Breton insists on—let us say—automatic writing, on the complete destruction of the critical function in the creator, Ivan Goll and his group, although agreeing with the importance of the unconscious function of creation, would not eliminate the analytical element. The theories of Paul Dermée are still unknown.

Down with Decadence!

In his manifesto, Ivan Goll says: "Art is an emanation of life and its functions. *Surréalisme,* the expression of our age, takes into account the symptoms that characterize it: it is direct, intensive, and rejects all arts that are based on abstract and secondhand notions: logic, esthetics, grammatical effects and plays with words. . . . *Surréalisme* is a vast international movement. It signifies sanity and rejects the tendencies of decomposition and morbidity that emerge everywhere where something is constructed. . . . The art of divertissement, the art of ballets and the music hall, the curious, picturesque art, the art based on exoticism and eroticism, the strange, restless, frivolous, and decadent art, will soon have ceased to amuse a generation that after the war was in need of forgetfulness. . . . And that counterfeit of *Surréalisme,* which a few ex-Dadaists invented, in order to continue shocking the burghers, will soon be destroyed. . . . They affirm the omnipotence of the dream and make of Freud a new Muse. If Dr. Freud uses dreams to heal too-terrestrial troubles, well and good! But to apply this doctrine to the world of poetry—is that not confounding art with psychiatry? Our *Surréalisme* rediscovers nature, the primary emotions of man, and goes with a completely new artistic material straight to a construction, to a new will." The first number of *Surréalisme* contains a poem by Pierre Reverdy, an article by Joseph Delteil on "Esthetes et anges"; "La Route obscure" by Marcel Arland; "Je ne vendrai pas la commode de mon grand-père" by René Crevel; an esoteric, semi-scientific prose poem by Jean Painlevé, son of the president of the Chamber of Deputies, which he calls *drame néo-zoologique;* and sketches by Delaunay, whose work we have admired for a long time.

The Freudian Influence

André Breton, according to Maurice Martin Du Gard, derives directly from Freud. He was for a long time one of the most ardent adherents of Dadaism. In 1919 he published with Philippe Soupault *Les Champs magnétiques* [Paris: Au sans pareil, 1920], which is now being hailed as a forerunner of the new method. "My attention was then fixed," he says, "on more or less fragmentary phrases, which were perceptible to the spirit in solitude at the approach of sleep, although it is impossible to discover an a priori determination." This, of course, goes straight to Freud, and it will be interesting to watch the application of the method, devoid, as it will be, of all critical corrections.

Number 40 (November 16, 1924)

German civilization is looking to the East. It has become caught up in the cult of Dostoevsky, according to Mr. Louis Untermeyer, American poet, critic, and anthologist, who has just returned to Paris after a year spent in Vienna, the literary Capua of the Germanic South. A brooding, nebular mysticism apparently has gotten hold of the younger minds of Germany and Austria. The war had created the field for an ethical conception of the arts. A new, ecstatic Humanism swept over these countries, which was apparent in the works of the Expressionists. The latter had revolted not only artistically against the impressionist banalities of the years immediately before the war, but had imbued their productions with the spirit of a frequently distorted sentimental Humanism. The movement finally deliquesced into a macabre dance of the senses. . . . Dadaism, coming via Switzerland, was à la mode for a time, but never really created the impression it did in France. It remained an isolated, fragmentary attempt to negate the arts, without any profound influence on the big line of development. . . . Suddenly they discovered Dostoevsky. . . . Steiner and Count von Keyserling, with his *Schule der Weisheit* (*School of Wisdom*), and Oswald Spengler, with his *Untergang des Abendlandes* (*Decay of the Occident*), led the spirits of the younger men to the Eastern orientation. The arts became vertical . . . a mystic Romanticism is the only refuge the new creators have found for their efforts. . . . This mysticism, Mr. Untermeyer explained to us, gives the present works of the Germano-Austrian writers their distinct note. . . .

The Lure of Vienna

Mr. and Mrs. Untermeyer have just come to Paris, on their way to London where Mrs. Untermeyer is to make her debut on the British concert stage, following her two successful appearances in Vienna. They were enthusiastic about Vienna, which apparently has what most North German cities lack, a certain Gallic charm and vivacity that lures many American artists and writers there. We had a rude shock in learning that Vienna today is not the intellectual laboratory it always seemed to us from this distance. Vienna, the American poet explained to us, is essentially a city of tremendous traditions. The resignation of Dr. Richard Strauss from the State Opera and the struggle it reveals between the forces of the modern and traditional viewpoints in music, for instance, is symptomatic of this orientation. . . . Mr. Untermeyer intimated that he felt a need for American air to continue his creative work . . . or at least get the revivification of the electric impetus America seems to give the creative artist. . . . Two of his chief friends in Vienna were Arthur Schnitzler and Beer-Hoffmann, two of Austria's most representative writers. . . . During his travels on the Continent, Mr. Untermeyer met Ernst Toller, the German poet and playwright, whose fantastic *Mass Man,* translated by Mr. Untermeyer, was produced in New York and London last winter. Toller, who had just been released from his Munich prison where he had served a five-year sentence for participating in the Munich Red Rising in 1919, told him that he had lost hope in mass action. . . . Mr. Untermeyer is translating just now Toller's new play *Hinckemann* which, in spite of its macabre theme, he hopes to see produced in New York next winter. Mr. Untermeyer has written a considerable number of poems during his stay in Vienna—which are being published by the *New Republic*—and has also completed an adaptation from Gottfried Keller's stories for children.

Open Letter to Ernest Hemingway

Dear Hemingway. We discussed you the other day with some American writers and we expressed to them our conviction that you have one of the most genuinely epic talents of any youngster writing in English today. In fact, we said that, in our opinion, you were destined to create a new literature on the American continent. We have never hesitated in expressing this view, in spite of some contradictions from men who disagreed with us. When we met you for the first time at Dave O'Neil's hospitable home here, we felt an aura of masculine strength about you that we like to connect with our dreams of America. . . . You have the root of the matter in you. . . . You have created in stark, acid accents the medium which is symptomatic of a great deal of modern hopelessness. . . . To be brief, we like most of your stories . . . they have power and often a beauty that leaves one with a sense of the terror of life. . . . Now, we just picked up *Der Querschnitt* and noticed your two poems in them. . . . We ain't able to follow you there. . . . We simply give up. . . . We believe you're on the wrong tack. . . . If you don't watch out, Dr. Sumner will give you a raft of free publicity and then what's going to happen to you. . . . Please give us another "My Old Man" and let it go at that. . . .

The Modern Chaos

If you want to get a concept of the hopelessness of our age, as far as the arts are concerned, get a copy of the autumn number of the *Querschnitt* (*Cross-Section*). Technically following American ideas of periodical journalism, the *Querschnitt* is a sardonic reflex of the artistic thought of the world. It is catholic in taste, *tendenzlos,* and presents the work of American, French, German, English, and Italian painters, poets, and composers, in epitome. It is interesting to detect, for instance, poems by Raymond Buchert, an Alsatian, Ernest Hemingway, a Canadian; Pierre Reverdy, a Frenchman, William Carlos Williams, an American, Joachim Ringelnatz, a German, scattered through the magazine in the various languages they use. Paul Morand is represented with a short story, "Fleur Double." Ezra Pound gives a new and heretic interpretation of the *Merchant of Venice.* Carl Sternheim contributes an article on Oscar Wilde, from which we quote:

> History? Who believes in its truth or probability? Have the last generations, in addition to all the fearful things they experienced, not also found that the best conceptual images of the twentieth century have been tortured to death and that dull imitators were set up in its stead? Did not their unworthy countrymen demolish Heinrich Heine, Van Gogh, and finally Oscar Wilde? And still does not nearly the entire conceptual contents from 1825 to 1925, as far as it is still useful for better Europeans, come from these three exiles?

B. Marcus has an article on George Antheil which was originally published in *L'Arlequin.*

The Significance of Jacques Rivière

If the history of modern French literature is written, the name of Jacques Rivière will appear in a prominent place. This brilliant *romancier,* critic, and editor has forged into the front rank of the constructive minds of his age. As editor of *La Nouvelle Revue française,* M. Rivière has made that review the intellectual center of the young men whose creative genius blossomed forth following the storms of the war. He has created a medium for the literary artists who, walking more or less in the footsteps of André Gide and Marcel Proust, are seeking the expression of the "I" as the chief function of the newer ideology. It is through the study of the soul and all its queer ramifications that the men of the *NRF* group sought to solve the riddle of the universe. . . . We had a chat with him recently following his return from a lengthy vacation. . . . He was just getting ready to reissue his war book *L'Allemand,* and complained that his editorial work interfered seriously with his creative plans. . . . The novel on which he has been working for some time is approaching completion, he said, although his work as an editor takes a great deal of his time. . . .

The Neo-Proustians and Massis

There are several distinct currents in present-day French literature, or rather the literary attitude of its leading writers. In a recent number of *La Nouvelle Revue française,* Jacques Rivière outlined his thesis in a debate with Henri Massis, and these two writers may be said to represent two of the sharply developed tendencies of modern groups. While Rivière takes up the cudgels for an almost pathological subjectivism in the arts, for the most ceaseless analysis of the "moi," Massis seeks the salvation of the artist in tradition, in transcendentalism, in the return to a medieval scholasticism. Thomas Aquinas vs. Marcel Proust! Massis believes that by basing art on dogmatism, he can avoid the pitfalls of intellectual anarchy and restlessness. He is essentially the Catholic philosopher. In his works, especially *Jugements* [Paris: Plon, 1924], he hammers this idea, and never lets an opportunity go by without accentuating the gulf that he sees between himself and some of his contemporaries. Rivière, on the other hand, is all for intuitional examinations of life. . . . That is probably one of the reasons why the group he headed—*La Nouvelle Revue française*—was believed for a time to be the torch-bearers of Unanimism. Jacques Rivière has never denied his indebtedness to André Gide, the classicist of the modern "I."

Received Blumenthal Prize

"My life has been very uneventful," Mr. Rivière told us. He hails from Bordeaux. After completing his studies at the lycée there and other schools, he came to Paris and attended the Sorbonne, where he received a degree in philosophy. Early in his career he devoted himself to his philosophical studies, which were mellowed by a temperament of poetic intuitions. The turning point in his career occurred when he met André Gide and his group, and became a contributor to the *Nouvelle Revue française.* In 1919 he became the secretary of this magazine and after the war assumed editorial leadership. During the war he fought in the infantry and was made prisoner. In 1920 he received the Blumenthal Prize.

Modern Study of Love

In his novel *Aimée* [Paris: Nouvelle Revue française, 1922], Jacques Rivière gives the story of an amatory development of infinite delicacy, power, and psychological verism. It is the story of a young man, his nascent love for the wife of one of his friends who had forsaken her. Listen to this strangely sincere monologue of the protagonist:

> I was unusually sophisticated in those days. . . . And still how strong was my desire, my waiting for something distant! I did not belong to those whom intellectual work consoles. I felt to the very point of exasperation all the numberless seductions into which I had been plunged. The magic of Parisian love never touched me without my becoming faint. I remember my walks on the boulevards, the wish, the cry that was in me and that something which was stronger than everything else, that insurmountable sense of reticence which caused me to be silent. If only every woman I saw could have known the storm that was in her wake! It was not alone with kisses that I silently persecuted her, it was not only that exquisite place on her shoulders I wanted to touch: all my heart followed her every movement; I was ready for every sacrifice: already I was offering her all my devotions.

The psychological struggle between those passion-whipped beings is sketched with infinite nuances. This love develops before us in all its magical and cruel character, and reaches a tremendous climax, as the hero finally tears the chains which tied him to the woman he adored. There is no plot in the usual sense. It is a plot of a cerebral distress that grips and moves one profoundly.

Portraits of the Soul

The critic set himself a monument in *Etudes* [Paris: Nouvelle Revue française, 1924]. They represent studies of Baudelaire, Paul Claudel, André Gide, Rameau, Bach, Franck, Wagner, Mussorgsky, Débussy, Ingres, Cézanne, and Gauguin. His critical viewpoint is intensely subjective, and has none of the pedantic schoolmaster-attitude one notices so often among modern writers. They seem to be tremendous prose poems of appreciation, of rejection, of a certain voluptuous adoration of words for their own sake. . . . "A critic has accused me of having a bookish soul," says M. Rivière. "He claims that I never had any 'adventure save in the domain of literature and esthetics.' He is mistaken. He knows me very little. But still, in the degree in which he used my *Etudes* to study me, his reproach is justified: it is evident that they betray an exaltation, a somewhat abnormal fervor and transfer to the artists and their works of sentiments that I might have expended somewhere else." This is the very personal note in his critical ventures. . . .

A Critical Horoscope

Whither are the moderns drifting? In the November issue of *La Nouvelle Revue française,* M. Benjamin Crémieux (whose book *XXe Siècle* has just been published) presents an essay on "Sincerity and Imagination," in which he analyzes recent tendencies in letters and prognosticates the constructive art of the future. He gives a careful outline of the Proustian psychologism and the Surrealist attempt to present the subconscious fragmentariness of life, and takes up the cudgels for an expansion of the artist's interests. He is afraid of the pitfalls into which a too frenetic analysis of the "I" may lead the artist. "Can one not conceive a constructive art, a creative art," he asks, "where the personal ideas of the artist, based on whatever originality his experience and imagination give him, replace the universal ideology of Classicism, the modern and local ideology of the Romantics, a creative art which would be above all else solidly cohesive correspondences, forming an intelligible sequence, and which in the case of genius and success (as with Ariost, Balzac, Dostoevsky, and possibly Proust) would produce an art that would be an affirmation, that would present human values, instead of pursuing the intangible reality of a mythical 'I'?"

Number 2686 (November 23, 1924)

In talking about Jacques Rivière last week, we mentioned the fact that the neo-Proustians were attempting to interpret life in terms of the more or less mythical "I." There are certain writers in France today who regard the external struggle between the "I" and the external world as the most important problem with which the artist of letters has to deal. The complexities of modern life, the age of steel and stone, of terrific electric energies, clash with the psychological phenomena and create attitudes of an amazing interest. Thus Valéry Larbaud, author of *The Journal of A. O. Barnabooth* [Paris: Nouvelle Revue française, 1922], *Les Poésies de A. O. Barnabooth* [Paris: Nouvelle Revue française, 1923], of *Enfantines* [Paris: Nouvelle Revue française, 1918], *Beauté, Mon beau souci* [Paris: Nouvelle Revue française, 1920], *Fermina Marquez* [Paris: Bibliothèque Charpentier, 1911], and other books, has set himself the task of interpreting the intense reactions of his psychophysical mechanism to the world around him. He is the poet of the wagon-lit, the cosmopolite par excellence, the "good European" in the best sense of the word. We never had the chance to meet M. Larbaud, although he is the one contemporary writer we always had a nostalgia to see in the flesh . . . And we are therefore compelled to be content with the indirect interview we managed to get via his Paris friends. For M. Larbaud is seldom in Paris. Phantasmally he wanders through the four corners of the world. . . . From exotic and strange places he sends delightfully hedonistic souvenirs of his travels. . . . He stands above the ruck and routine and the imbecility of human bickering like a Superman who observes every wrinkle in the cosmic comedy, but unlike Nietzsche's hero, looks on with a great deal of pity. . . . It is through Mlle. Adrienne Monnier, of the Maison des amis des livres, and Miss Sylvia Beach, of the Shakespeare Bookshop, that we managed to get real glimpses into the personality of the evanescent Globetrotter of the Spirit.

A Modern Croesus

This ecstatic singer of the modern world's electric energy has just made his debut to the Anglo-Saxon world. His *Journal of A.O. Barnabooth* [New York: Doran, 1924] has been translated into English by Gilbert Cannan, and we understand that London and New York literary circles have reacted to the work with great interest. . . . For *Barnabooth* is the quintessence of the modern spirit. It is the Song of Songs of motion, of immensities, of the destruction of space and time. . . . More precisely, it is the diary of a young South American Croesus who seeks to conquer his ennui by traveling. . . . Whipped by an eternal hunger to escape from the loneliness into which his isolation of luxury has thrown him, he travels in special trains through the spaces of Europe. . . . He has adventures galore. . . . But all he really seeks is the happiness which he finds is denied him somehow . . . the happiness which even the most ragged denizen of Whitechapel seems to have. . . . The book is an evocation of Florence, San Marino, Venice, Trieste, Moscow, Sarajevo, St. Petersburg (it is, of course, prewar atmosphere), Copenhagen, and London. . . . "When I examine my existence during these last few months I am astonished," he says. "Nothing has happened to me. . . . And yet I asked only to meet adventures: I invited them. Henceforth delivered, without ties, absolutely free, to do everything and go everywhere—what? . . . My wealth and independence seemed to promise a hundred romances of high adventures, and this is my diary: hours spent in hotels, visits from friends, letters, and at last, at great expense, a miserable intrigue with one of those women that come to you at a nod."

His Cosmopolite Influences

Valéry Larbaud was born at Vichy and is today about forty-two years old. It might be interesting to note that the name on the more or less well-known and popular bottles of healing water is his name, as his father is the discoverer of the famous source Larbaud. . . . He attended the Collège St. Augustin, which became decisive for his intellectual development and literary orientation in many ways. . . . For this college was attended by a cosmopolite congregation of students, among whom there were many students from South American republics. . . . The Hispanic influence is noticeable in all his works. . . . In *Fermina Marquez,* Valéry Larbaud set a monument to his old alma mater, weaving about it a story of great charm and psychological penetration of the international mind. . . . He began to travel at an early age, saw Italy, Spain, Great Britain, Germany, and many other countries. . . . All of his impressions are transmuted in his *Barnabooth.* . . . His cerebral cosmopolitanism is not the usual pretension of a sit-by-the-stove, the bookish fellow, the chap who hangs around bookstores and wanders over continents via the atlas. . . . He knows and loves the people with whom he has come in contact. He knows their languages intimately. They accept him as a compatriot. . . . Does he not write his weekly literary articles on French letters for the *Nación* of Buenos Aires directly in Spanish? And at one time in his life he wrote weekly articles for a London literary weekly directly in English. . . . In spite of his almost frenetic, his futuristic modernism, Valéry Larbaud is all for tradition. . . . He loves the old French writers, and in his bibliographic explorations has discovered many forgotten writers of unusual gifts and charm, as, for instance, Raoul de Nervaise. . . . He has a hobby for tin soldiers . . . and for the Jardin des Plantes, where he has chosen the hippopotamus as his "patron animal." . . . Beside being a creative artist, Valéry Larbaud has also a potent influence on contemporary letters as the interpreter of many of the most unique minds of the age and anterior decades. . . . He is the translator of Butler's *Erehwon,* and is the man who introduced James Joyce to the French public at a memorable occasion at the Maison des amis des livres, when he whipped his audience of sceptical French men of letters to such a pitch of enthusiasm about *Ulysses* that he had to drag the timid James Joyce from behind the curtain where the latter was hiding, and force him onto the stage to receive the plaudits of the public. . . .

Dithyrambics of Our Age

We have always liked his *Poésies de A.O. Barnabooth* best of all his works. . . . These huge Stravinskian rhythms of trains and hotels and the thousand-and-one things of modern cities have elemental power. . . . Borborygmes . . . savage word!

Give me your giant noise, your gentle singsong charm.
Nocturnal roaring through the continent's lighted

O train de luxe! and the aching rhythms of your music
That sounds along your corridors of golden leather,
While back of lacquered doors, that have heavy copper latches,
The millionaires are slumbering . . .
I wander through your corridors while whistling little songs,
And I follow your tremendous sweep to Vienna, Budapest,
Mixing my voice with your ten-thousand voices,
O Harmonica Zug!

This inadequate translation may give a faint idea of the powerful beauty of
these poems. . . . They represent fundamentally the lyric expressions of this
young South American multimillionaire as he races across the Continent
in search of mythic adventures. . . .

Apropos of the *Querschnitt*

"Thanks for your open letter of last Sunday. The two poems in the
Querschnitt are not intended to be serious and were written three years ago
and a year and a half ago, respectively. So if my writing is going bad it must
have been going bad for some time.

Unfortunately for passport purposes, working for a Canadian newspaper does not make me a Canadian. I have always been told that I was
born in or near Chicago. I have a son who was born in Canada. Perhaps
he is the Hemingway you were thinking of when you referred to talented
youngsters.

If you would like to read some new stories in manuscript to ease your
mind as to my present mental and spiritual state, come around some
Sunday afternoon soon. There is a long bullfight story you might like.

With best regard to your column and yourself."
Ernest Hemingway

Women and Cities

Valéry Larbaud knows women as he knows cities. "J'ai des souvenirs
de villes comme on a des souvenirs d'amours," he sings. . . . He has penetrated into the soul of the adolescent boy and girl and, in *Les Enfantines,*
he gives unforgettable portraits of the little perturbed souls of the young
. . . Rose Lourdin and Eliane belong to the world's literature because they
are real. . . . As in *Barnabooth,* he has created living characters . . . he has

given us vistas into the landscapes of nostalgia. . . . That only one of his books—the *Journal of A.O. Barnabooth*—has been translated into English is regrettable. . . . (Incidentally, it can be obtained at the Shakespeare Bookshop.) But to make the Anglo-Saxon world acquainted with *Fermina Marquez* and *Enfantines* is one of the most delightful tasks still awaiting a pioneer's audacity. . . . And that would be only fair exchange, for Valéry Larbaud has done more for spreading the knowledge of English writers in France than any other modern man of letters, next to M. Du Bos and M. Victor Llona.

"The Interior Monologue"

The great esteem in which his contemporaries hold Valéry Larbaud was emphasized when the revue *Intentions* brought out a special number devoted to appreciation of the poet by his friends and admirers. Among those who contributed to this remarkable symposium were René Chalupt, Marcel Chaminade, Benjamin Crémieux, Charles Du Bos, Léon-Paul Fargue, Jean Giraudoux, Ramon Gomez de la Serna, Edmond Jaloux, Pierre de Lanux, Adrienne Monnier, Paul Morand, Jules Romains, and others. Benjamin Crémieux points out that Larbaud's works partially foreshadow the "interior monologue" which later was to become the quintessence of *Ulysses*. In *Amants, heureux amants* [Paris: Nouvelle Revue française, 1923], Larbaud pays a tribute to James Joyce, to whom he gives credit for having discovered the form he (Larbaud) is using in this short story. This edition, published by the Maison des amis des livres, is a rich mine for those who wish to learn more about this literary phenomenon. . . .

E. E. Cummings and France

We are not violating any confidence in quoting Mr. Louis Untermeyer as saying recently that he regarded E. E. Cummings as one of the most original of the young poets of America today. Now we read in *Le Journal littéraire* in an article signed by Bernard Fay: "Mr. Cummings has just published a book of poetry, *Tulips and Chimneys* [New York: Seltzer, 1923], which is one of the finest we have ever seen. I believe that Cummings has genius, and those who have read his book are also of this opinion, but this book was not written for large circulation—it has guarded its dignity. He was doubtless right. It does not help a poet to be too well known: a sure means of being little known, and then misunderstood. Still, Cummings emerges more and more from the group of young American writers and is marching at the head of his generation."

The Gumps Enter Literature

Andy, Min, and Chester Gump have admirers even in France. M. Bernard Fay, in discussing contemporary developments in American literature, says: "America: read the articles of Brisbane in the New York *American,* and follow Chester Gump traveling in Australia (*Chicago Tribune*). You will find there a wisdom which is not ours—a pleasure denied to us." M. Fay believes that the chief preoccupation of contemporary American literature is "documentary." "The novel and the theater are entirely dominated by this ideal," he continues. "America has so well succeeded in creating a gigantic world, hard and beautiful, that it likes to touch it, palp it, and perceive it with every sense. . . . There is therefore at the present time not much room for the individual talent in the United States, and the foreigner can be interested in any gifted writer only in the degree in which he (the foreigner) interests himself in that life . . . which is so feverish, colorful, and constantly creative—the life that flows each day in the thirty pages of every newspaper of Boston, Chicago, San Francisco, and New York, in the thousands of periodicals that flood bookstores, stations, and shops. Here there is excitement and audacity, invention, joy, and success. The newspaper cries to the world night and day what America is doing and dreaming: white editions at seven o'clock, pink editions at nine o'clock, green editions at midnight, and all the pallid editions that follow each other from four o'clock in the morning until the end of day. The newspaper is not literature nor ideas, but paper and news; flesh and frissons. . . ." and so on.

Number 2714 (December 21, 1924)

We stand before a new epoch in literature. The miasma of the postwar period is almost exterminated. New legends arrive. A new mythos is on the horizon. The Impressionistic, Cubistic, Dadaistic consciousness is already archaic. We are on the threshold of the great affirmation. The year 1924, we believe, is the prelude to an age that corresponds chronologically to the Romantic interlude. . . . Léger and Delaunay and Stravinsky and Antheil are here . . . they give us the accents of the age in painting and in music . . . the rhythms of the things that move. . . . Only literature still lags somewhat behind. A few men, however, have caught the vision of reconstruction. . . . Ivan Goll, it seems to us, is the quintessential force of our decade's creative literary forces. He concentrates in himself the international psyche . . . the nostalgia for a great dynamic synthesis . . . the power of evoking the metaphysics of the piston rod. We do not believe in schools. We are against the pedagogy of the elders . . . the tyranny of a theory. . . . Even when Max Jacob and Guillaume Apollinaire were known as the group of the rue Ravignan, it did not destroy the idea that they were individual artists of a sharply silhouetted originality. . . . Literary Cubism! It was merely a term to denote an esoteric quantity. . . . But it is necessary sometimes to find a generic term for historic purposes. In other words, it is convenient to invent a more or less artificial nomenclature to find a common denominator for a series of variegated ideas. . . . Thus Ivan Goll believes that Super-Realism is the generic word to describe the ideology of the constructive age in the arts. . . . He believes that the time is ripe for the welding together of the creative forces in the various countries, especially America. . . .

Speed, Speed, Speed!

We discussed three questions with Ivan and Claire Goll in their charming home in Autueil recently. . . . "We need a new mythology," he said. "The imagery of 1913 is no longer satisfactory to an age with stronger nerves. . . . Super-Realism is not a new invention or technique . . . it is simply a general term for the entire modern literature and art. We are retaining the roots of such movements as Futurism, Cubism, Expressionism, Dadaism . . . but each of these is essentially the modern orientation of one people. . . . We need a synthesis that will include all. Super-Realism, by retaining the basis of the phenomenal world, attempts to build upon it a psychological superstructure. . . . Super-Realism will probably be the leading idea for the next ten or twenty years. . . . It is a constructive movement . . . it is an international movement. . . . The age of technical explorations is more or less over. We can now stand back and estimate the accomplishments. . . . We are creating the mythology of the aeroplane, the dynamo, and all sorts of machines for a new lyrical world—we are using these things to help us express the evolutions of the unconscious world."

X-Raying Love

Both Ivan Goll and his wife are poets and playwrights. . . . One interesting result of their poetic collaboration will be the publication soon of a book of verse to be called *Poèmes d'amour*. This title, we suspect, is voluntarily banal . . . for the poems translate the erotic emotions in terms of a modern consciousness. . . . Chemistry and physics rub elbows with psychiatry and general medicine. . . . We were privileged to get a glimpse of some of the manuscripts and confess to a violent shock . . . the "new mythology," of which Ivan Goll had been speaking to us, is used here to the last analysis. . . . The book will contain about twenty poems each. We are quoting two of these poems:

Radiographie
J'ai vu tes chairs diluées comme l'eau
Monde inconnu: chairs que j'appelais miennes!
J'ai vu les aigues ultra-violettes
Où traînait mon amour.
Ton cœur pontu, wrack d'un bateau sombre.

Gisait au fond des rêves
Parmi les coraux oxydes
Un rocher bleu
Plein d'un silence impénétrable
Sur quels secrets?
Alors, moi, lourd scaphandrier,
J'ai voulu y descendre, y chercher l'or perdu
Et l'on ne m'a jamais vu revenir.
    —Ivan Goll

A Ivan
Où que tu sois
Des roses explosent
Toutes les hirondelles du monde
Se réfugient dans mon cœur
Qui est grand ouvert et rouge
Comme le portail de Notre-Dame
Je ne sais plus
Sur quel continent nous vivons
Pourtant je vois flamber
Le rouge international du géranium
Et les tramways transportent le temps
Ici comme ailleurs.
Je voudrais me jeter sous un autobus
Tant je suis heureuse
Si je savais lequel va au paradis.
    —Claire Goll

Charlie Chaplin as Poet

Ivan Goll is a figure of towering stature in contemporary literature. . . .
We have before us his collected works: *Le Nouvel Orphée* (Aux Editions de
la Sirène—29 Boulevard Malesherbes). In 1923 he won a prize given by
L'Intransigeant for his groups of poems included in this book under the
title of "Editions du matin." *La Chaplinade* (or *Charlot Poète: Poème ciné-
matographique* [Dresden: Kaemmerer, 1920]) is a metaphysical evocation
of the Immortal Genius of the Screens. It depicts Charlot emerging from a
poster and his erratic wanderings through the world. . . .

Mais qui comprend ma souffrance bouddhique
Je rends aux hommes ce qu'ils ont perdu depuis des siècles
Le joyeau de leur âme, Le Rire!

Babbitt in the Pillory

In *Mathusalem ou l'eternel bourgeois* (*drame comique*), Ivan Goll lashes the burgher in the person of a gouty shoe manufacturer; his son Felix, the modern businessman, who "carries on his head a telephone, a little lamp, and an intermittent bell"; his sentimental daughter Ida and her student lover and a host of caricatural personages. . . . It is a cosmic burlesque . . . a huge sneer at the imbecility of the parvenu and his circle of war profiteers. . . . Technically, it is extremely novel—the subconscious of these ataxic pretenders is portrayed in a masterly manner. . . . Mathusalem is shot dead by the student-lover of his daughter's, after a mob had threatened to lynch him. . . . His wife and son decide on a third-class funeral, and Mme. Mathusalem is upset because the invitation of her fellow profiteer's has to be canceled. . . . The whole play is like a nightmare with its automaton and its symbolical beasts. . . . Grosz has illustrated the drama with weirdly distorted drawings. . . . When the play was given in Berlin two months ago, the nationalist press raised a hubbub, going even so far as to petition the government to stop this outrage on patriotic citizens. . . .

A Burlesque on Idealism

In *Assurance contre le suicide* (*drame rapide en deux actes*), Goll presents a *danse macabre* of the humanistic intellect. . . . It is a grotesque drama of a lecturer on the "Superman of Tomorrow." He promises "sensational revelations on Universal Peace." . . . A journalist, who attends the lecture, convinces him that only his death can bring him immortality, and when the professor consents, the journalist runs off with the lecturer's wife. The morning papers report the death . . . sensation . . . but the lecturer had a second thought and reappears very much alive . . . a collection is taken up for his "widow" and they find that "speeches for the salvation of humanity are good business."

Orpheus's New Music

In his poems "Paris brûle," "Astral," "Editions du matin," and others, Ivan Goll gives the measures of his Super-Realist conception of lyric poetry. . . .

"Paris brûle" is an attempt to portray the city . . . an immense speedy drama. . . . "Le Nouvel Orphée" is a delirious description of the poet of the new age. "Astral" is another evocation of modern illusions. . . . In "Editions du matin" one finds short, dynamic, telegrammatic poems of exquisite beauty.

A Woman Poet's Magic

Mme. Claire Goll has given numerous proofs of her high creative gifts. Her poems have an almost nervous sensibility and freshness and are shot through with imagery of an apocalyptic splendor. . . . Although born in Munich, she always felt at heart a Parisian . . . for the last five years she has been living here. . . . She made her debut in 1916 with a little volume of poems, and a year later created a stir in central Europe by publishing a pacifist book of short stories entitled *The Women Wake Up*, which was prohibited by the censor. . . . She has appeared in numerous magazines and anthologies. . . . In 1922 she published *The New York*, an anthology of modern American poetry, in which she presented Young America to Germany for the first time. She has given excellent translations of Vachel Lindsay, Edgar Lee Masters, Carl Sandburg, Louis Untermeyer, Orrick Johns, Amy Lowell, and many others. Her own *Lyrical Films* appeared in 1922. In this she caught the spirit of Paris with the most remarkable intuition . . . she does not present the tourists' bagatelles, but a frenetic reaction to the colorful drama of the Seine city. . . . In *Movie of the World* she gives a gorgeous, rapidly moving evocation of her age with "Pathé Review," "Paris Round Trip," "To Autobus No 12." . . . Soon there will appear, besides her book *Poèmes d'amour*, which she wrote jointly with Ivan Goll, her first French book in prose: *Le Journal d'un cheval*, which will be illustrated by Chagall (whose interesting exhibition began here last Wednesday). . . .

An Intercontinental Mind

Ivan Goll was born in Alsace in 1891—"in that corridor," as he said somewhere, "where one became used to the currents between the soul of France and the German spirit which they taught us at school in those days. . . . Everybody catches bronchitis there." After studying law at Strasbourg University and other colleges, he published in 1912 *The Panama Canal*, which was a hymn for the fraternity of the races. . . . Then he lived in Switzerland, where he wrote a great poem, "Requiem for the Fallen in Europe," and then followed *The Netherworld,* poems which described the misery of the world and the great pity. . . . Then came the long poem "Astral," "The New Orpheus," "Dithyrambs," which have just been gathered into a collective volume under the title of *Eiffel Tower.* After coming to Paris he soon forged to the front, especially when in 1921 he received one of the coveted prizes of the *Seize* of the *Intransigeant* for his poems "Editions du matin." One of his remarkable contributions to literature was the world anthology *The Five Continents,* which contains excerpts from modern poetry of every nation. Many of them have been translated by himself. . . . The American poets represented with translations are Sandburg, Amy Lowell, Vachel Lindsay, Sherwood Anderson, Edgar Lee Masters, Robert Frost, and others.

Number 2735 (January 11, 1925)

The antithesis between the dogma and the instinct has always been a tragic problem. On one hand, there is the theological maxim, intransigent and immutable. . . . On the other hand, the eternal impulse toward the destruction of the law. . . . Without entering into any scholastic problems, one might say that the Catholic faces this dilemma more intensely than anyone else. . . . This fearful conflict is mirrored in the works of many writers today who have accepted many of the cerebral emancipations of their age . . . but feel themselves eternally at war with the philosophic posture of tradition. . . . How can it be solved? Not that a writer who is consciously moralistic or reformatory could interest us for a second. . . . Art has nothing to do with convictions per se. . . . Art is interested primarily in presenting the reflexes of a sensitive psychic mechanism. . . . Therefore the work of François Mauriac has always interested us ever since we read *Le Fleuve de feu* [Paris: Grasset, 1923] and *Génitrix* [Paris: Grasset, 1923]. . . . Here was a writer who, like M. Henry de Montherlant, is rooted in a Christianity of almost the profundity and primitiveness of the catacombs. But, unlike many Catholic writers, he did not run away from those terrifying conflicts the modern man faces today, in an age where all values have been transvalued. . . . He recognizes the fact which Thomas à Kempis has established—that life is essentially a tragedy, a jest, a symbol of a symbol. . . . Christianity is a pessimistic religion. . . . We were therefore eager to get his views recently, when we saw him in his Passy studio.

The Destruction of Nietzscheanism

M. François Mauriac is primarily interested in reestablishing the subtle relation between good and evil. "In this I am, of course, at variance with many of the tendencies of my age," he told us. "In the novels of today you will find that there is no conflict anymore, properly speaking. . . . The question of the flesh has become all-important. . . . If I have read the signs aright, the great writers of the past were always religious—religious, I mean, in the mystic sense. . . . No one was more so than Dostoevsky. . . . The problem of the flesh is essentially tragic. . . . And when the Catholic Church insists on opposing it, we must admit that reality justified it. . . . Now a modern writer cannot escape the problem. . . . It stares him in the face in an age where sex is neurotic. . . . I am not, however, a Catholic writer in the sense of dogmatic presentation of a mystic ideology. . . . My work attaches itself to the work of such men as Morand and others, precisely in the fact that I introduce the problem of sexuality under a new consideration . . . for this sexual knowledge is a key that opens the doors to an understanding of others. . . . Freud's idea has been in the air for some time . . . it was inescapable. . . . We moderns have learned to know the complexity of human beings. . . . While formerly the writers chiseled their personages out of one block, we dissect and analyze . . . hence the *roman d'analyse* . . . hence the great cult of Dostoevsky.

Barrès Launched the Poet

M. Mauriac told us he owed much to Maurice Barrès, both intellectually and materially. . . . For it was Barrès who launched the young poet when he published his first book of poetry, called *Les Mains jointes* [Paris: Bibliothèque du temps présent, 1910], shortly before the war. . . . Barrès was so impressed with the mystic charm of the verses that he devoted a long article to it in *L'Echo de Paris*. . . . M. Mauriac later came under the influence of André Gide (the Gide of *L'Immoraliste* [Paris: Mercure de France, 1902], *La Porte étroite* [Paris: Mercure de France, 1909], that is, the Gide of the period of inquietude, metaphysical searching, delving after an esoteric solution of soul problems). . . . He feels, however, that he cannot follow the Gide of *Corydon* [Paris: Gallimard, 1925]. . . . M. Mauriac was born in Bordeaux in 1885. After graduating from the Catholic College of his hometown he came to Paris, where he wrote a great deal without, however, achieving any success until his *Le Baiser au lépreux* [Paris: Grasset, 1922] and later *Génitrix* were published. . . . In *Le Baiser au lépreux* he presents a terrific conflict between two human beings in the lonely landscape of the Landes. (The Landes as a background of his stories repeats itself in his works, because, he told us, he spent a great deal of his youth with relatives in that forsaken, solitary country.) . . . A new book of his, called *Le Désert de l'amour* [Paris: Grasset, 1925], will be published in the collection *Cahiers verts* (Grasset) shortly. . . . It is the story of human solitude, he indicated to us, with a father and a son as protagonists.

A Strange Conflict

In *Le Fleuve de feu*, M. Mauriac presents a poignant metaphysical drama. . . . In a little lonely summer resort in the Pyrenees, Daniel Trasis meets a young girl, Mlle. Gisèle de Plailly . . . the arrival of the latter's friend, Lucile de Villeron, unleashes a conflict . . . it is a triangle of an almost mystical quality . . . for Mme. de Villeron is the symbolical conscience of the young girl . . . the epitome of asceticism of Christian renunciation . . . in spite of all their struggles, however, the young man and young girl are unable to resist the lure of their magnetism on the eve of her departure for Paris . . . only by fleeing the temptation did Gisèle think of solving her problem. . . . Centuries of tradition weigh upon her . . . for this is the second time that she has torn down the wall that held her desires caged . . . the struggle becomes intense as she reaches Paris. . . . Daniel follows her . . . but in the end Mme. de Villeron, subtle evangelist, is triumphant . . . in a final scene, typical of Catholic psychology, the young man seeing the girl in church renounces his desire for her and goes away. . . . In *Génitrix*, M. Mauriac told the story of a mother and her son . . . against the bleak landscape of the Landes. Mme. Cazenave and her son Fernand are depicted in a masterly manner. . . . Her mother love has broken all resistance in the son in spite of the fact that he is already fifty years old. . . . When he marries, after all, she retains her supremacy, and the wife loses in the struggle. . . . Even after the mother's death, her influence hovers over the house, and the tyranny of her will continues to assert itself. . . .

MM. Larbaud, Boyd, and *Ulysses*

The controversy about *Ulysses*, which has been somewhat muted for some time, is again flaring up. . . . Thus M. Valéry Larbaud, the creator of *Barnabooth*, in a leading article in the last issue of *La Nouvelle Revue française*, entitled "A Propos de James Joyce et de Ulysses . . . Réponse à M. Ernest Boyd," takes issue with the Irish-American critic on the question of valuating Joyce. . . . The contest began in 1922, when, in a lecture held before a group of writers at the Maison des amis des livres, M. Larbaud took up the cudgels for the Irish heretic. Mr. Boyd, in his *Ireland's Literary Renaissance*, attacks M. Larbaud for maintaining that Joyce does not come within the general current of the Irish Renaissance. . . . The position of Mr. Boyd is precisely that James Joyce is merely the continuator of the great Irish literature. . . . M. Larbaud maintains, on the other hand, "that with James Joyce, Young Ireland has made a sensational entry into European literature." . . . For this, says M. Larbaud, Mr. Boyd accuses him of a "colossal ignorance of Anglo-Irish literature." . . . M. Larbaud answers his critics in a decisive fashion. "My ignorance is apparent," says M. Larbaud,

> when I said that with James Joyce "Ireland made a sensational entry into European literature." And this phrase really implies a complete ignorance of the great Anglo-Irish writers who preceded the most recent Irish War of Independence: Synge, Moore, Yeats. But I wrote: "Ireland, or rather Young Ireland." . . . That is, the Ireland of the time after 1914; the one whose definite triumph all the newspapers of the world were then announcing (1921); the one that had just taken its place of independence among the nations of Europe. . . . And for my French audience this expression "Young Ireland" meant that Ireland, without any equivocation. Then, Mr. Boyd remarks (apropos of the same phrase which he mutilated with so much *sans-gêne*) that it is "supremely naïve" and even "touching" to believe in the existence of a European literature. . . . And still he himself seems to admit that there have been and still are in several countries in Europe a small number of writers who are read by the connoisseurs of literature of all the countries and whose influence has been felt (or is making itself felt) in the literature of all the countries. Well, it is the small number of writers, who are read, studied, and imitated beyond the frontiers of their home country, which I call "European literature."

M. Larbaud concludes: "Surely I never dreamed that some day the Irish nation would give me a vote of thanks—a vote of thanks which is due above all to Miss Margaret Anderson, editor of the *Little Review*—but it is a disagreeable surprise for me to see that an Irish critic, who says he is an admirer of *Ulysses,* seeks to reduce to nothing the effort I made to bring *Ulysses* to the attention of the Continent."

A Critic on Literary Schools

In talking to M. Mauriac about contemporary literature, we happened to ask his views about the movement called *Surréalisme* which is at present raising so much dust here. He called our attention to an article "Propos sur le Surréalisme" in the last number of the *Nouvelle Revue française* which, he said, expressed his views. The article in question by M. Jean Cassou makes short shrift with the tendency of creating schools and forcing ideas into the straitjacket of definite theories sharply circumscribed. "The success of literary magazines," says M. Cassou, "teaches us that the men of letters are more interested in literary life than in literature. And those who came last feel the necessity to push to an extreme attitude the doctrine of which future historians will not retain anything except what pleases their fancy. . . . Every doctrine, with its pretension to place itself in an age registered by the historians and with its preoccupation with the 'public' factor, is impure. This chronological vanity corrupts a work of the spirit as much as the most unimportant moral, political, or anti-alcoholic intention. I think I see in the noise that M. Breton and the friends make—whom he cultivates and whom he praises—nothing but a strange prolongation of a crisis in adolescence. That does not militate against my opinion of the lyrical power of M. Breton nor my admiration for M. Louis Aragon, for instance, who is really the greatest living French prose writer. But the adolescents find themselves in that divine state of innocence which makes them discover America already traced on the map and which makes them give their first cigarettes and their first cocktails an undeserved importance."

Number 2763 (February 8, 1925)

It is platitudinous to say that here is always an intellectual wall between the various nations. . . . That wall is rarely scaled. . . . The difficulties of this enterprise are accentuated by the fact that a host of leprous intellects is trying to do it. . . . People with a superficial knowledge of art, letters, and psychology, as far as the alien nation is concerned, insist on setting up shop as teachers, interpreters, and prophets. . . . In looking through American and English magazines recently, we were struck with this fact . . . imbecile wordmongering to hide ignorance . . . apish repetition of glittering phrases filched from the leaders of the alien race . . . philosophic dullness drooling across the verbose pages of ataxic essays. . . . We always wondered at the credulity of editors who allow this grotesque prolixity, written to bamboozle their public, to be published as authoritative interpretations of another race. . . . The impulse to understand the mentality of other races has been given a tremendous impetus in France during the past few years. . . . Here we find an honest and sincere attempt to penetrate the psyche of other languages, other people, other artistic impulsions. . . . We discussed these matters recently with M. Robert Aron, of the *Nouvelle Revue française,* who pointed out to us the fact that modern France has a real hunger for an understanding of what M. Joseph Delteil recently termed "mondialisme." . . . In other words, young France is interested primarily in gaining an informative conception of the minds of other nationalities. . . . We emphasize *informative* because it is the very essence of the French genius to first seek the "phenomenal" aspect of an idea and then to dissect it. . . .

The Interpreters of the Alien Spirit

For this reason, M. Aron told us, the *Nouvelle Revue française* is attempting a novel scheme of circulating international knowledge. . . . It consists of a program comprising lectures, cinematographic performances, and vocal and instrumental hearings anent the accomplishments and the quintessential quality of other nations. . . . Beginning April 23, these conferences will be held partly at the Collège de France, and partly at the Vieux Colombier. . . . M. André Maurois, author of *Ariel* [Paris: Grasset, 1923], *Les Discours du Colonel Bramble* [Paris: Grasset, 1918], and other charming subjects with an Anglo-Saxon background, will lecture on Great Britain. . . . M. Bernard Fay, one of the best-known younger French critics, and whose literary erudition has been commented upon in the columns several times, will entertain his audience with instructive information about the United States. . . . He will give an exhaustive tableau of our literary evolution, of our artistic and musical evolution, and will attempt to valuate the potentialities of our country. . . . Germany is next on the list with M. Philippe Soupault as interpreter. . . . M. Soupault belongs to that group of brilliant young men who have been associated with the revolutionary history of the *feuilles libres* for the past few years. . . . His recently published novel, *Les Frères Durandeau* [Paris: Grasset, 1924], has just come off the press, and we are to have the pleasure of meeting him just in time to report our reactions in a subsequent issue of this causerie. . . . M. Soupault is thoroughly familiar with the German language and has been a thorough and critical student of the modern currents in Germany. . . . M. Benjamin Crémieux will attempt to interpret the Italian genius . . . its cultural and philosophic significance. . . . Spain will find its interpreter in M. Jean Cassou, whose critical estimates of several modern Castilian writers we have had occasion to mention here several times. . . . Russia, the enigmatic, with its half-European, half-Asiatic civilization, will be presented by M. Kessel who, although born in Russia (Odessa, we believe), has made the French language his medium of expression and, with several books published in recent years, has forged ahead in modern French literature. . . . The intellectual cicerone for French civilization will be M. Aron himself.

A Cultural Cross-Cut of the World

"I believe this will be the first time that cinema will be used as a consciously intellectual weapon in modern life," M. Aron told us. . . . "Our cinema will represent primarily geographical ideas. . . . We will try to show the general landscape of the countries under discussion, as well as the psychological geography, that is, the manner in which the people of the various countries live, and the manner in which they are typically different from other racial entities. . . . We will present not primarily the literature of the people under discussion. . . . Our lectures will be about their entire civilization. . . . And all the men who have been chosen for the task are thoroughly familiar with their subjects. . . . The music we will present of the various nations will be absolutely the most direct native expression of their tonal or polytonal capacities. We expect to rouse great interest in this movement, not only here, but also in other countries. For the age demands a more thorough understanding of the soul of other peoples."

The Duse in Retrospect

We have always been a great admirer of the genius of Eléanore Duse. . . . And few books have gripped us during the past few weeks as did M. Edouard Schneider's anecdotal and deeply felt sketch of the great actress. . . . This book, with the simple title of *Eléanore Duse* (B. Grasset), had its genesis during days when the author stayed at the great artist's summer home in Merano during the last few years of her life. . . . He had conceived the ambitious project of writing a play with the fantastic idea that she might interpret the chief character. . . . "It is too late to speak of love at my age: what blasphemy," she told him wistfully when she refused his request. . . . What golden words are there scattered through this book about a woman who was what so very few of our creative artists are today, a human being first and then an artist. . . . For her life was netted into every fiber of her art. . . .

French Letters and Burton Rascoe

The last number of *Le Journal littéraire* publishes, among other things, an article by our friend Victor Llona on Mr. Burton Rascoe, the American writer. The heading of the article is "La Littérature française jugée par les grands ecrivains étrangers." The interview quotes a plethora of platitudes emitted by the American writer, their quality being such as probably capable of even shocking the dullard sensibilities of a college youth. Now, let's see—what did Burton Rascoe do to contribute to the American literature?—Oh, yes, he published a literary potpourri under the heading *A Bookman's Daybook*!

Devastating Anatole France

Just what Anatole France has meant to at least one writer is poignantly told in a letter to *Clarté* by M. Panait Istrati, the amazing Rumanian whose *Kyra Kyralina* has recently roused such a plethora of enthusiasm. "I was one of those," he says, "who demanded from Anatole France something with which to quench my thirst, a little warmth for my cold, a reason to sustain me in my quotidian manual labor, a stilling for my love hunger, a direction for my restlessness, an encouragement for my despair, and a clear road for my revolt. And Anatole France was a traitor to my sincerity. Having bought his book with money which allowed the author to sneer at life from the depths of his upholstered fauteuil, I carried the work shivering to my room, and it did nothing else but poison my soul, throw me still more into despair, confuse my reasoning, and make me oscillate for weeks between my hunger for life and my desire to die. For here lies the danger of his criminal act: he enters the organism like an opium. He is superior in action and ignoble in the results. Under the whip of his sarcasm a thousand despairing verities emerge before the eyes of the poor reader, but all these truths are without heart and are pure lies."

Words, Words, Words!

Surréalisme has captured as its chief citadel *Commerce,* the magazine of the avant-garde published under the guide of Mlle. Adrienne Monnier at the Maison des amis des livres. M. Louis Aragon (whom M. François Mauriac in a recent conversation with us designated as one of the greatest among the young French talents) gives a strange explanation of *Surréalisme* in the last number of *Commerce,* under the title of "Une Vague de rêve." Among other things he says: "I lived in the shadow of a great white building decorated with flags and echoing with cries. I was not allowed to leave this chateau, nor its society, and those who stepped up the staircase produced an atrocious cloud of dust on the doormat. . . . But slowly I unraveled their most definite beliefs. They can be reduced to very little. 'The tendency of every being must be to persevere in its being' is one of their favorite formulas . . . the ignoble expression 'enchanted with *finalisme*' suffices for them to condemn everything. Then they inaugurate paragraphs of their intellectual lives by this phrase which they like: 'Let us take the veil from words.' They never suspect that such methods drag them to the realization of hypotheses and hypotheses a posteriori. Their spirits are hybrid monsters, etc." In reading the article one comes dangerously near the feeling that, after all, the philosophic background of the new consciousness is not new. For we have heard those accents before. . . .

René Crevel Scores

Amid the many good things one finds in the last number of *La Nouvelle Revue française,* the contribution that struck us most was René Crevel's *Minutes au ralenti,* a bit of great power and beauty. . . . François-Paul Alibert contributes a poem, "Stances à l'automne," which failed to move us. . . . The number also contains the final installment of Joseph Conrad's *Coeur de tenèbres.* M. Albert Thibaudet contributes a remarkably lucid analysis of the Thomist philosophy as developed by M. Maritain in a recent brochure called *Descartes ou l'incarnation de l'ange.* . . . M. Thibaudet makes short shrift with the anti-Cartesianism of the orthodox thinker. . . . This is another side to the controversy which has been raging here for some time and which formerly had as its chief antagonists MM. Jacques Rivière and Massis.

Melisande Learns Philosophy

Judging from the excerpts we have read of *Les Lettres à Melisande pour son éducation philosophique,* this book by M. Julien Benda just published by Nicole ought to become very popular. There are some very charming epistles dealing with such varied matters as "Divisions of Philosophy," "Philosophy and English Politics," "A Method Dear to Melisande or Intuition," "Pragmatism and Several Other Schools of Morals," and so on. Their style is of a great charm with a profundity that makes them stimulating.

Africa and Literature

Literature has done much in recent years to vivify the longing of travelers for North Africa, according to M. Jules Bertaud in the *Gaulois.* "Literature has an important part in diverting the stream of travelers to the sunny climes of Algiers and Tunis and the far-off oasis of Gabes and Tozeur. Literature followed almost immediately the Moroccan conquest and created its legend in this beautiful country. A writer like les Tharaud has done more for making known the beauties of Fez and Marrakech than all the stories or conversations of thousands of tourists." This writer enumerates among those who have written about Africa: les Tharaud, M. Louis Bertrand, M. Jean Vigneaud, Mrs. Myriam Harry, and M. Léandre Vaillat.

Number 2805 (March 22, 1925)

What is wrong with the Middle Western school of writers? Simply this: they substitute the banalities of a police reporter's imagination for the creative process of art. They lack a sense of sublimation. They have no vision. It is time that they be catalogued and eliminated. . . . The currents of thought today are in the direction of a new Romanticism . . . not the French or German Romanticism of 1830, but toward a sense of the dynamism of dreams, of the magic of psychic mysteries. We cannot escape the power of the occult. . . . There is no categorical law for emotions. In looking though the last number of *Commerce* (*Cahiers trimestriers publiés par les soins de Paul Valéry, Léon-Paul Fargue, Valéry Larbaud*), we were conscious of the gulf between the Zolaistic Naturalists of the American landscape and the violently accentuated beauty of the spirit which the writers appearing in this medium reveal to us.

Léon-Paul Fargue Dissects His Conscience

In *Suite Familière*, Léon-Paul Fargue presents his lyric vision broken into shimmering fragments of thought:

I call bourgeois everybody who renounces the struggle and love—for the sake of his security. I call bourgeois everybody who puts anything above sentiment. . . . He does not go near a language or an idea without believing it dead and without seeing it mummified in a show-window, and without realizing that it can no longer bite, and he goes near it on cat's feet. He has a sense of caste as an animal has the sense of danger. He is a sentimental madman. When Rimbaud wrote the "Bateau Ivre," he had never seen the sea. . . . Descartes arranged marriages of reason. Rimbaud made marriages of love.

Somebody translated some poems of Rainer Maria Rilke, the Czechoslovakian mystic. (And it so happens that M. Maurice Martin Du Gard gives us an excellent sketch of the poet in the last number of *Les Nouvelles littéraires*.) The same issue contains translations of Robert Herrick in old French that retain the tang of the original to a nicety. . . . Valéry Larbaud writes a "Lettre à deux amis" which is an intellectual causerie on Spanish things. . . . Louis Aragon gives us "Une Vague de rêve," which we mentioned here before.

"Qui Est La? Ah, Tres Bien! Faites Entrer L'Infini!"

Thus Louis Aragon in the amazing essay or prose poem which *Commerce* publishes under the title "Une Vague de rêve." From this, one elicits the facts that catalepsy was one of the manifestations of the new consciousness and that a new liberty has been born "where the marvelous begins." He explains the miracle of Cana and the victory of Valmy. . . . "An idea which has been formed does not limit itself to the fact of being; it reflects: it exists. Thus the concept of super-reality for the last two years came back to itself, bringing in its wake a universe of determinations. In the light of Surrealism, the dream begins to clarify itself, and takes its significance. For this reason André Breton's notations of his dreams—for the first time since the world was young—retain the character of dreams in the telling. Because the man who recounts them has accustomed his memory to correspondences other than the poor realities of the people who are awake. Thus Robert Desnos learns to dream without sleeping. He succeeds in expressing his dreams verbally, at will. Dreams, dreams, dreams, the field of dreams becomes larger every stop we take. Dreams, dreams, dreams, the blue sun of dreams causes the steel-eyed birds to scurry to their dens. Dreams, dreams, dreams, on the lips of love, on the figures of happiness, on the sobs of the attentive faculty, on the signals of hope, in the timberyards, where people rest on their axes. Dreams, dreams, dreams, everything is a dream, where the wind wanders, and the barking dogs run on the roads. O great dream, in the pale morning of buildings, don't abandon anymore, attracted by the first sophisms of the morning sun, those calk cornices where you lean and where you mingle your pure and fragile traits with the miraculous immobility of statues!"

The Cinema of Hallucinated Faces

"There is a *surréaliste* light in the eyes of every woman. They are tearing down a great bit of Realism on the boulevard de la Madeleine, and through this breach you can perceive a little landscape which is also in the work of the Moulin Rouge, cité Vernon, in the demolitions of the Parisian fortifications, in the fields of the Tuileries statues, the Gobelins flaming the word *Pardon* in phosphorous letters against the night, in the vaults of the metro where the golden horses of the Poulain *chocolat* jump, in the diamond mines where the smugglers expose themselves to greedy surgical cavities, in the sulphurous regions where the little dogs die away. . . . Paul Eluard, I have seen kicked by the policemen and the machinists on the piano and in the shattered phials—they were thirty against this shimmer of stars. Delteil, he is the young man whom Francis Jammes entreated in the name of his white hair, this young carnivorous animal who spends his days in the forest of Meudon with bleeding images. Man Ray who tamed the greatest eyes of the world, dreams in his fashion with knives and saltcellars: he gives light a meaning and now he can talk. Suzanne, are you brown or blond? She changes with the wind and you may believe it: water is just like man. Who is this man strangely entrapped? The signs of Antonin Artaud from afar cause a curious echo in my heart. Mathias Lubeck, surely you are not serious about it, you are not going back into a colonial atmosphere? He says he is ashamed not to have been tattooed. Jacques Baron, on his boat, has just met beautiful white women: do you remember, my dear friend, an evening I left you near Barbès, there were so many night-prowlers that you did not think of Eastern seas anymore—you had suddenly hurled yourself into the summer. André Breton, here is one of whom I can say nothing. If I close my eyes I find him again at Moret-sur-le-Loing, in all the dustiness of the towing-path. At his curly hair one has long recognized Philippe Soupault, who talked with chair repairers, who laughed outrageously towards noon."

The Movies and Dream-Psychology

The Surrealists are bringing up their heavy guns to invade the territory of the cinema. . . . In an article published in *Comoedia,* M. Jean Goudal takes up the cudgels for the application of the new theories to the production of the modern film: "It is about time that the *cinéastes* begin to realize the great advantage of opening up the unexplored regions of the dream to their art. This has up to now been done merely fragmentarily and, as it were, accidentally. They ought not to hesitate to mark their productions with the three essentials of the dream which are: *visual, illogical,* and *penetrating.*"

Group Movement a Modern Tendency

This seems to be an age of artistic collectivism. . . . Schools and groups emerge everywhere with astounding rapidity. Thoughts whirr like a horde of airplanes marshaled in battle-formation. . . . The individual genius is finding it harder and harder to penetrate through the forces of mutually helpful squadrons. . . . It may be necessary for men of an analogous tendency to group themselves together, when one considers the fact that the general chaos of the intellectual forces today makes it difficult to silhouette the contours of various mental mechanisms. . . . But we still think that the original, independent mind will penetrate, no matter what the difficulty. . . . With the publication in Strasbourg recently of *L'Arc: Anthologie* [Strasbourg: Editions de l'arc, 1924], Alsace seems to enter into the domain of the modern consciousness. . . . Here we have a group of writers who, proceeding from a common nostalgia for an international Humanism, have presented their creative efforts in a medium of virile charm and alluring bibliography. . . . It is an attempt primarily on the part of the creative men of the province to escape the bilingual problem they have been facing and to orientate themselves toward a unified attitude in the arts. . . .

Toward a Literary Renaissance?

"From the days of Otfried and the epic of *Garin le Loherain* up to our own days, Alsace and Lorraine have provided a valuable contingent for the intellectual history of France and Germany," the manifesto written by Henri Solveen states. The writer insists on a reevaluation of the mission of the province, and demands an objective judgment and understanding in order to prepare the way for a literary renaissance which would provide a means of expression for the bilingual tendencies there.

Poems, essays, extracts from novels, and plays, together with reproductions of paintings, and vignettes, comprise the contributions of the various writers. . . . Among those represented are Maurice Betz, René Schickele,

Jean-Richard Boch, Henri Herrmann, Raymond Buchert, Th. Maurer, O. Mannon, Claire and Ivan Goll, Georges Schaffner, Charles Wolff, Claus Reinolt, Henri Solveen, Sulvain Cahn, C. A. Frantz, Jean Sebas, Nathan Katz, and others. . . .

Poetic Fragments from Boston

In the *Stratford Monthly*, the Boston international review, which has just reached us, we discover among other contributions a poem by Pierre Loving, entitled "A Mountain Child's Morning," which impressed us with its strength and beauty. Mr. Loving has in the same number an excellent English translation of two poems by the German pre-Romantic poet Friedrich Hölderlin. Paul Eldrige is represented with three pseudo-Chinese poems. Louis Ginsberg, whose work we remember having seen before, gives us a fine conception in "The Spirit of Beauty." There are articles by Ethel Marjorie Knapp, Edward Sapir, and others.

A Literary Portrait of the Amazone

The portrait of Miss Natalie Clifford Barney, "L'Amazone," is sketched by Mme. Aurel in the last number of *Le Monde nouveau*. This American woman, whose mind has totally absorbed the French genius, is represented with a touch of almost rhapsodic understanding. . . . "When the demon of letters breathed to me: 'Considering that this foreign woman has the strongest and most biting trait of the great moralists and immoralists of France—that she has done you the honor of writing in your language, the homage to her country alone would demand that you define her,' I awkwardly replied to myself and today am still replying to myself: 'It must be done.'" Mme. Aurel says later: "Natalie Clifford Barney has invented grace without love. You live in that half of ardor where nothing rests heavily on us, but we must consent to the burdens in order to live. Your art, therefore, is too fine, too pretty, too artistic for me, but it has a consummate intelligence. . . . What a miracle of balance you are, you who fled your roots! . . . But where have you learned, dear anarchist, that rectitude of countenance, that discipline of the word, and above all else that divine negligence which makes you so easy to read, when you write words like these: 'La dame, une femme expurgée.'" Mme. Aurel quotes a word of Miss Barney's on men: "All those penguins who do not know how to wear their clothes. Dispatch them, if not into the flames, at least into the cold."

Jean Cocteau Makes His Bow to America

America will at last be able to take the measure of Jean Cocteau, following the tremendous mythos created around him several years ago. . . . Lewis Galantière has translated *Thomas l'imposteur,* and the book has just been issued by D. Appleton & Company [New York, 1925]. . . . It is a good, linguistically accurate bit of work, though we feel that the aura of Cocteau's style has not been entirely caught. . . . Cocteau's very personal style is impossible to reproduce in a foreign version. . . . Mr. Galantière gives us the rhythm, however, and the story reads smoothly and retains often the tang of the original. The introduction is well worth reading.

Thomas the Impostor Analyzed

In his introduction to *Thomas the Impostor,* Lewis Galantière says: "Thomas is a fairytale. It happens to be a 'war book.' Believe me, it is no less beautiful for that. Indeed, the war of itself is no more an integral part of the story than Guillaume Thomas's heart, which had to beat until the tale ended. I mean that no element of fiction is important except in relation to the other elements. It was inevitable that our hero be identified with the war, just as it was inevitable that Pinchwife bring his rustic young woman to London. . . . Had there been no war, Guillaume Thomas would have lived and died without the magnificence in which his memory is now clothed; no London, and Mrs. Pinchwife would have continued in innocent imbecility with her husband. . . ." Of Cocteau he says: "Cocteau stands apart from his contemporaries. They are jealous and afraid of him; he is decently courteous to them. . . . He is a magnet, but he is also a leader, though no despot. Many young men have revolted against his leadership, prompted by personal exacerbation. . . . Cocteau continues (the tradition) of *La Princesse de clèves, Adolphe, La Chartreuse de Parme.*"

French Authors Introduced to American Public

American translations of French writers are reported from New York in ever-increasing numbers. We learn that aside from Lewis Galantière's translation of *Thomas the Impostor,* Ernest Boyd is bringing out the complete works of de Maupassant, which the critics regard as the best of its kind. *L'Homme traqué* [Paris: Michel, 1922], under the title of *The Hounded Man* [New York, 1924], by Francis Carco, has also recently been brought out by Seltzer.

American Writers, Artists, Musicians, Attention!

The American Chamber of Commerce in France is preparing to issue a directory of Americans in France. Particular efforts will be made to give a complete list of the names and addresses of writers, artists, and musicians who hail from the United States, and are making their headquarters here. Those who wish to be included in this directory are requested to communicate at once with Mr. Brace or Mr. Leeds of the American Chamber of Commerce at 32, rue Taitbout.

Love Poems in the Newer Vein

The first volume of the *Collection surréaliste* has just been published by Jean Budry & Co. The book is *Poèmes d'amour* by Claire and Ivan Goll, with four sketches by Marc Chagall.

Number 2875 (May 31, 1925)

Super-Realism as an epochal force in contemporary thought continues to assert itself. Two events of the past week have quickened the movement apparently from the empirical phase into the period of creative accomplishments. . . . The premiere of Louis Aragon's *Pied du mur* at the Vieux-Colombier represents the first dramatic attempt to envisage the revolt against pure intelligence. . . . Then there occurred last week the publication of "Le Bar de l'amour" by Philippe Soupault in the *Cahiers du mois,* apparently the first *surréaliste* story. Any critical orientation toward these events must of necessity be premature now.

The Modern Adolphe Appears

"Le Bar de l'amour" is a story that postures the problem of the modern youth and his emotional instability. . . . In rapid staccato sentences, Soupault draws his character and his pathological inquietude. . . . For Julien, as he himself says, "looks often into himself as into a mirror. When he lifts his eyes (the world turns), he continues to see his own face and his familiar gestures in the eyes of his equals. . . . Sometimes unconscious, sometimes conscious of his dizzy rotation of mirrors, he does not wish to fight against himself, he analyzes himself and seeks disconsolately points of support. . . . Is it for this reason that he prefers the bars? . . . When the phantom of love passes before him, he stretches his hand, touches it, drinks. Then he realizes that he was not thirsty at all. 'Love,' he says to himself, 'I know that.' And he is not lying. He knows everything and nothing." Thus the love story of Julien with Mme. Leroy-Beaumont is negation . . . neurotic futility . . . ephemeral madness. . . .

Enter: "*Le Nouveau Mal du Siècle!*"

André Berge contributes an interesting study of Soupault's orientation to this issue of *Les Cahiers du mois.* He believes that "after the wars of the Empire there was the '*mal du siècle*,'" and that the late war's heritage is '*le nouveau mal du siècle*'. . . . "Doubtless, there is today, as then, a profound trouble in the souls of men: the same need for revising all values that proved unable to assure happiness and the equilibrium of the preceding society. But the values at stake are not the same anymore, and our eyes are not directed to the same side. . . . The Romantics believed in words and the Absolute: today, no! There is a great empty space, and that is one of the reasons for the present crisis: those who accept this new condition take refuge in a painful inertia of which the heroes of Drieu La Rochelle are a pathological example. Others—the heroes of Soupault, Crevel, Arland—are suffering because they are in quest of some thing. Their malady (if malady it be) tends toward an equilibrium: let us rather call it 'inquietude' and recognize that it reveals a profitable effervescence of the soul."

Stating the Cerebral Conflict

"What does it consist of? There is the individual problem: Aragon, the problem Delteil, etc. . . . Each one explains according to his manner of seeing the problem: a disproportion between the grandeur of the human being emerged from the war and the smallness of civilized life? Absence of God? Excess of the intelligence? Perhaps all three . . . and why should that be everything??? But remark well: whatever the cause, there is always the question of 'suppressed' (in the Freudian sense) ardor; the trouble has a more or less intellectual origin in proportion to temperamental qualities, from which proceeds a difference in theories; in general, a too lucid scepticism keeps back the great élan, the desire for which is inherent in youth and all life. From this comes the interior conflict, malaise. How can one calm this eternal thirst which only a little bit of the absolute succeeds in quenching? . . . Because we do not give any credit to facile generalizations of language anymore, we attempt the conquest of the universe, sensation after sensation. A superhuman task which in most cases results in an insatiable febrility. One demands that everything have an intense savor. Contempt for the sensation that weakens and therefore most often: contempt for sentimental prisons. The hero of *Détours* (René Crevel) [Paris: Nouvelle Revue française, 1924] renounces tenderness to safeguard 'his liberty, his beautiful new liberty.' Julien in the 'Le Bar de l'amour' is also incapable of enduring a stable happiness. Gide has put into modern hearts a love for 'Possibilities' which are incompatible with the lazy satisfaction of the definitive."

Important Document for Surrealists

Super-Realism is still holding its own. . . . It is wielding a profound influence on the minds of the creative workers of the world. . . . Therefore the man from whom the group has taken the name is more than ever being read. . . . Under the strange title of *Il y a* there will soon appear a book containing the writings of Guillaume Apollinaire which he penned during twenty-four years of his life. It will comprise forty-one poems, some of them printed for the first time, as well as his articles on the new painting and his monographs on Henri Matisse, Le Douanier, Picasso, Van Dongen, and others.

Jean Cocteau and "Pure Poetry"

An illuminating reaction to the work of Jean Cocteau is published in the last number of *Les Feuilles libres* by M. Jacques Maritain. He says, among other things: "Among contrasting fashions there appears thus the profound unity of the work of Cocteau: a constant seeking after pure poetry. From this result those eternal renewals, that will to free oneself constantly from the acquired and accustomed ideas, a dangerous game, where it seems sometimes that the human substance vanishes, but which is at bottom nothing but a faith in the 'Angel,' in the exigencies of secret virtues which engirdle the poet and lead him where he would not go."

Helping the Young

M. François le Grix, editor in chief of *La Revue hébdomadaire,* will edit, together with MM. Gaston Chérau and Henri Massis, a new collection of modern writers which will be called *L'Aubier.* According to an article in *Les Nouvelles littéraires,* M. le Grix states: "We wish to reclassify certain values, to put a little order into literary production. . . . We do not believe in the improvisations of genius, we do not expect to find prodigies, but we wish to find young writers who give distinct promise and whom we may aid in their progress. We have no idea of publishing masterpieces, but works where trained eyes will recognize certain promises. We shall seek authors capable of giving us in ten or fifteen years perfect fruits of their labors and books that are not ephemeral, and which one may read again later on: many artists today have no longer a sense of duration but are too much taken up with their sense of relativity: 'I am writing for three I's,' said Paul Morand to me one day."

Number 2889 (June 14, 1925)

Do you know Paris? Or are you merely one of those pitiful fellows whose horizon is dominated by the background of a *terrasse* swirling with bibulous humanity? We know of many an otherwise amiable chap who spends years in the cerebral and artistic capital of the world and knows nothing of its moods save obvious phenomena or the topography of a limited section. . . . A real Parisian has a plethora of contempt for him. . . . There are three kinds of Parisians . . . those who are born in Lutetia (lucky devils!); those who came from the provinces in various stages of their adolescence; and the rest are the foreigners . . . to which most of us belong. . . . It reminds us of the amused sneer a certain friend of ours used to have for amateurs, dilettantes, immature rhapsodists who crashed into New York after the war, when there seemed to be a general uprooting in the United States. . . . He would become somewhat bitter whenever he heard those pseudo-New Yorkers grow ecstatic, write ponderous dramas and poems about Manhattan, and generally assume the air of being privy to Father Knickerbocker's intimate thoughts. . . . For he knew what he used to call "the real New York . . . the New York of Hungarian cafés, charming bookshops, continental effervescence." After the armistice, he used to say, New York became a grotesque box containing sterile automata. . . . All these, somewhat confused, remarks are anent a beautiful essay with which M. Valéry Larbaud opens the initial number of *Le Navire d'argent,* the new magazine of the arts and letters published by the Maison des amis des livres. . . .

Wandering Through Paris with a Poet

In "Paris de France" M. Larbaud gives us a masterpiece in the understanding of Parisiana . . . or, as he calls it, *Parisianité*. . . . He looks at his amazing world-city from the cabin window of *The Silver Vessel*, muses over the psychology of the real Parisian consciousness, smiles discreetly at the provincial pretenders who would bluff themselves into the belief of having lived here all their lives, reminisces charmingly over his own experiences here and then presents a delightfully bizarre argument. . . . He takes up the cudgels for the establishment of a chair of *Parisianité* at the Sorbonne "for the use of foreigners, provincials, and even the inhabitants of Paris who think they know their city." He then proceeds to give an examination paper to win the "brevet élémentaire de Parisianité."

YOU ARE A PARISIAN IF—
Here it is: Examination in writing.

1. Prepare a list of the streets and passages of Paris that are still illuminated by oil-lamps. Indicate the arrondissements where they are. Describe two at random. . . .

2. Which are the hotels, châteaux, farms, and inns of the eighteenth century that are still in the twentieth arrondissement?

3. Enumerate and describe the impasses that are on the Ile Saint-Louis.

Oral Examination:

1. In which churches do you find the tombstones of Descartes, Racine, and Mlle. de Scudéry?

2. Trace on the blackboard, indicating and naming the gates, the appearance of the enclosures of the Fermiers généraux, from the right bank of the Seine west as far as the Boulevard de Belleville. . . .

3. In what arrondissement is the rue de la Py? Is there a street in Paris that has a still shorter name?

4. Where can one see the statue of Goldoni?

5. Which, besides the British Embassy, is the house in Paris that is juridically situated in British territory? What street, what number, what other details do you know about it?

6. Which is the shortest route from the Rat Mort to the Musée Carnavalet? If you find the Carnavalet closed, and if you desire to see, while waiting for its opening, a beautiful fig-tree, where do you go? . . .

In reading this picturesque and charming essay one grows veritably hostile to the journalists who dash to Paris every year, send their imbecile droolings to the *Saturday Evening Post,* and bamboozle the American hinterlander into the belief that he gets an earful of the Seine-City. . . . M. Larbaud's essay is, in our humble belief, one of the best he has ever produced. . . .

Miss Beach and Mlle. Monnier Translate American Poet

Some historian will some day write the story of the Shakespeare Book-shop and the Maison des amis des livres. Mlle. Adrienne Monnier—who is the director of the *Navire d'argent*—and Miss Sylvia Beach, proprietor of the Shakespeare Bookshop, will doubtless go down into history as brilliant animators of French and Anglo-Saxon literature. . . . The current number of *Le Navire d'argent*—the appearance of which was incidentally mentioned in these columns first of any newspaper in Paris—contains the French version of T. S. Eliot's "The Love Song of J. Alfred Prufrock," well known to American readers when it first appeared in the *Imagist Anthology* in 1916. . . . Both Miss Beach and Mlle. Monnier collaborated on the translation, which may be said to retain the spirit of the original to a nicety. . . . Read, for instance, the opening stanzas:

Allons alors, vous et moi,
Quand le soir est étendu contre le ciel
Comme un patient anesthésié sur une table;
Allons à travers certaines rues mi-désertes,
Murmurants retraits
Des nuits agitées dans les hôtels de passe
Et des restaurants à la sciure et aux coquilles d'huîtres;
Ces rues qui ont l'air de suivre une discussion interminable
Avec l'intention sournoise
De vous conduire à une question bouleversante.
Oh! ne demandez pas "Qu'y a-t-il"
Allons faire notre visite . . .

The same number contains a poem, "Le Portrait," by Jules Supervielle; an analysis of Paul Valéry's thought as revealed in Le Cahier B 1910 by M. Jean Prévost, who is the editor of the review; "L'Abbaye de bonheur" and "Homme buvant du vin" by J. M. Sollier—the latter an example of interior monologue. It also comprises a bibliography of English literature translated into French, and some excellent critical études.

Number 2910 (July 5, 1925)

The Super-Realists have entered the militant phase of their stormy evolution. . . . As the revolutionary hiatus between the postwar ideology and
the new art we all await, they hammer their steel-hard concepts into the
brains of the journalists. . . . This department has been the first among
the American reviews to mention the work and the projects of this group
more than a year ago. . . . Since that time we have followed their development through their career, and the little *bagarre* at the Closerie des Lilas
the other night was amusing in the revelation of the fact that the Super-
Realists had really become "news." . . . Mme. Rachilde was the object of
attacks during a dinner tendered by the Super-Realists to the poet Saint-
Pol-Roux le Magnifique—chairs and shattered crockery flew through the
air—fists hammered on skulls and backs. "The Open Letter to M. Paul
Claudel," in which the group hurls its anathema against the author of
L'Annonce faite à Marie [Paris: Gallimard, 1912] for attacking its members,
was only published a few hours before the row on Montparnasse got under
way, and it came somewhat like a fearful explosion into the summer quiet
of Paris. . . . The new issue of *La Révolution surréaliste,* the proofs of which
we saw the other day, will be published within a few days, and will doubtless create a still more troubled state of mind among the traditionalists . . .
and although we understand from M. André Breton that most of the bookstores and kiosks refuse to carry the magazine, it seems somehow to find
enough purchasers to flourish. . . . It so happened that we had a talk with
M. André Breton, intellectual leader of the movement, shortly before the
Montparnasse episode, and we also met M. Paul Eluard, poet of *Mourir de*

ne pas mourir [Paris: Nouvelle Revue française, 1924], and M. Louis Aragon, the author of *Anicet* [Paris: Nouvelle Revue française, 1921] and *Le Libertinage* [Paris: Nouvelle Revue française, 1924]. . . .

M. André Breton Explains Basic Ideas of Surrealism

Situated at the edge of the Place Pigalle in the rue Fontaine in an old Montmartre retreat, the home of the leader of *Surréalisme,* and therefore the meeting-place of the poets, is evocative of the violent explosiveness of their electric chants. . . . In the large study clustered with pictorial and bibliographical mementoes of other incarnations—notably that of Dadaism—M. Breton spoke at random about some of the basic ideas that horrify the modern bourgeois. . . . For they want to re-create a world. . . . Never in French literature has there been such a violence of spirit, such a destructive chaos of concepts. . . . Youth is tired of academic rattle-brains, stinking imbeciles of dogmas, sadistic writers, sterile critics, and evokers of roaring banalities. . . . That is the feeling back of the movement. For they are hysterically explosive against their age. . . . We must ask for the indulgence of our readers if our report of the conversation we had with M. Breton may seem inadequate. . . . For it went with the speed of a Twentieth-Century Limited. . . . Therefore we will only attempt what some of our French colleagues have called "an interview express." . . . "The idea for the *dictée automatique* came to me while I was engaged in studying the cases of maniacs during the war," M. Breton said.

"I noticed that the flight of ideas in insane persons made a definite appeal to certain instinctive postulates in me. . . . Poetry is alone capable of codifying the compromise between dream and reality. . . . The phenomenon of the *dictée automatique,* I felt, may produce astonishing results. . . . I believe that it is difficult to create any kind of difference between the image and the idea as such . . . for poetry proceeds by the image. . . . Certain poets succeed in approaching those two terms in a most remarkable manner. . . . The reason Cocteau is not a poet is exactly because his images are literary and artificial. . . . Compare with him Apollinaire. . . . We consider poetry not as an end, but as a means. . . . What is our end? We accept absolutely nothing. . . . We believe that we are capable of reducing reason and *le faux bon sens.* . . . We believe in an Oriental contemplation of some sort. . . . We are convinced that our age is built on a compromise. . . . This latter is such as to justify the most daring acts on our part. . . . For this reason we feel a certain sympathy with all revolutionary parties, even the class struggle. . . . We do not believe in human progress nor in anything. . . . We want to support all movements of the opposition from whatever side they come. . . . We want to support them violently at the peril of our lives, if necessary. . . . Philosophically, our ideas go back to the German philosopher Hegel. . . . *Surréalisme* has discovered that time does not exist. . . . I would rather destroy than construct. . . . We insist on a complete revision of all modern artistic values. . . . We insist on the denunciation pure and simple of all people who have presented a certain spiritual guarantee— a guarantee sheltered by their utilitarian success—and later renounced it. . . . That is why we are attacking Paul Valéry now, in spite of our admiration for him. . . . We exclude all literary talent and literary quality we consider of secondary importance. . . . Joseph Delteil's expurgation of his version of Jeanne d'Arc is a '*vaste saloperie.*' A man who could write *Sur le fleuve d'amour* [Paris: La Renaissance du livre, 1925] and then do this upon the demand of the Catholics has passed a judgment upon himself. . . . We have a kind of explosion of wrath against the present reality."

Clinic of Ideas Closed to the Public

M. Breton told us about the Bureau de recherches surréalistes, which was a kind of clinic on the rue de Grenelle where experiments in the new orientation were examined. . . . The clinic had finally to be shut down, simply because "there were too many duchesses and other boresome people" who insisted on participating in the work. . . . "We lost too much time." Nevertheless this unique feature continues behind closed doors, and the next number of the *Révolution surréaliste* will contain many results of the work. . . . "Who talks about disposing of us, of making us contribute to the abominable terrestrial comfort?" M. Breton continues. "We desire and we shall have the 'beyond' of our days. It suffices for this that we only listen to our impatience and that we remain, without reticence, ready for the marvelous. Whatever the means which we deem well to use, it is impossible, because of our faith in its vertiginous and endless aptitude, that we should ever forfeit the spirit. Let it, however, be well understood that we do not wish to take any active part in the murder which man commits against man. That we have no civic prejudice. That in the present state of European society we remain faithful to the principle of all revolutionary action, even if it should take as point of departure the class struggle, and provided only that it may lead rather far." M. Breton told us that the painter from whom all the modern painters derive is Picasso. . . . "La musique m'ennuie," he continued. "It gives me no pleasure . . . it is noise . . . whether that is due to any physiological condition, I have no means of knowing."

Pope and Dalai Lama or Spook and Idol

The previous number of *La Révolution surréaliste* has a very significant series of contributions that would illuminate somewhat the philosophical position developed by M. Breton. One is an "Adresse au Pape," in which he is told that "the confessional is not you but we," and in which the Catholic idea is berated in bitter accents. . . . The other is a proud "Adresse au Dalai-Lama" in which the latter is told that the *Surréalistes* are his "faithful servants." Among the *textes surréalistes,* it may be interesting for the understanding of their viewpoints to quote a piece, "La Révolution," by Robert Desnos:

It is the instauration of the Revolution and the Terror that interests me, and its arrival alone can today still give me the hope for the disappearance of the canailles that encumber life. The present hellish atmosphere will triumph over the noblest impulses. Only the guillotine can, with its somber blows, enlighten this crowd of opponents against whom we stumble. Oh! May it at last be erected on a public place—this sympathetic machine of delivery.

Ho hum! as Andy says. . . .

Part Two : **Revolution of the Word: *Transition* Manifestoes and History**

Introduction

While Jolas was a successful journalist throughout a long career, he also became critical of his own trade. Hence he always sought in the medium of poetry a radical alternative to the age's sociological prose of public manipulation. For the poet-critic in tune with and partaking in the discourse of the early twentieth-century avant-garde, poetic creativity comprised an aversion to the narrow social and aesthetic rules of realistic and naturalistic writing, and the epistemological problem of representation in general. Poetry required the will to confront modernity's "malady of language" by exploring the realm of "neologistic possibilities." Where language is lowered to a form of shorthand in the service of consumerism, where economic and technological interests are dominant factors in an ideology of "progress," the writer should altogether reconsider language as the means of transition, transformation, and metamorphosis.

Jolas's own abundant experiments in language poetry (a sample of which is reprinted and introduced in Jerome Rothenberg's 1974 anthology *The Revolution of the Word: A New Gathering of American Avant-Garde Poetry 1914–1945* [New York: Seabury]) emphasize a striving for "kinetic" speech, where movement is "vertical" and spiritual (thus differing considerably from the Futurists' idolatry of the machine and technological speed). In his prototypical "To the Tremendum" we accordingly read: "You are silverglast in starspace/Slowly lood the millarales of our hungers/Filla oo bilda alastara tinka/Es ist warm im eiswirbel deiner nacht." Neologisms are derived from a fusion of several languages offering evocative associations and sonorous, rhythmic effects; traditional syntax is overturned, if not canceled, while English transforms into German and vice versa. The eccentricity of Jolas's own poetic production is in unison with *transition*'s programmatic 1929 manifesto, "Proclamation" ("Revolution of the Word"). The journal's manifesto constitutes a first synthesis and poetic platform from which one could begin to understand the rich linguistic creativity of the international, "frontierless," avant-garde movements from Zurich Dada to Expressionism and Surrealism (contrary to Jolas's somewhat idiosyncratic denial of Breton's movement as merely a syntactical revolution). One center remains, of course, the genius author James Joyce with his magnum opus, *Finnegans Wake,* which was published seriatim in *transition.* Hence the provocative statement that "narrative is [. . .] the projection of a metamorphosis of reality" (point 4), or that "the writer expresses, he does not communicate" (point 11), and of course the conclusion: "The plain reader be damned."

Yet, in spite of appearances, there is something uniquely conservative in Jolas's transatlantic, "Eur-American" mediation of then still relatively little-known avant-garde productions in (often first) translations. After all, his provocative stance, motivated by the desire to stretch and break linguistic as well as national boundaries, maintains a link to tradition. Jolas himself recalls Friedrich Schlegel's Romantic notion of *Universalpoesie* and *Sympoesie,* where a "plain reader" becomes the receptacle of what he calls a "paramyth" (or, *avant la lettre,* a form of "magic realism"). The fusion of genres as the erasure of the distinctions between prose and poetry is to result in a transformation of the normative modern state of mind. In its conscious recourse to the "marvelous" of Romanticism, Jolas's and *transition*'s program must thus be addressed as a widened idealist Humanist view of the international avant-garde. Thus it has ultimately no place for the warlike and chauvinist Italian Futurists, and perhaps too little genuine sympathy for Gertrude Stein's linguistic exercises and meditations within the medium of her "little household words," and Jolas has the greatest difficulties to evenly accommodate André Breton's mainstream French Surrealism, not only politically, but also in its ambiguous relations toward Freudian psychoanalysis and its later embrace of Communist politics.

—C.R.

Proclamation ("Revolution of the Word," June 1929)

Tired of the spectacle of short stories, novels, poems, and plays still under the hegemony of the banal word, monotonous syntax, static psychology, descriptive Naturalism, and desirous of crystallizing a viewpoint . . .

We hereby declare that:

1. The revolution in the English language is an accomplished fact.
2. The imagination in search of a fabulous world is autonomous and unconfined.
   (*Prudence is a rich, ugly old maid courted by incapacity.* . . . Blake)
3. Pure poetry is a lyrical absolute that seeks an a priori reality within ourselves alone.
   (*Bring out number, weight and measure in a year of dearth.* . . . Blake)
4. Narrative is not mere anecdote, but the projection of a metamorphosis of reality.
   (*Enough! Or too much!* . . . Blake)
5. The expression of these concepts can be achieved only through the rhythmic "hallucination of the word." (Rimbaud)
6. The literary creator has the right to disintegrate the primal matter of words imposed on him by textbooks and dictionaries.
   (*The road to excess leads to the palace of wisdom.* . . . Blake)

7. He has the right to use words of his own fashioning and to disregard existing grammatical and syntactical laws.
   (*The tigers of wrath are wiser than the horses of instruction. . . .* Blake)
8. The "litany of words" is admitted as an independent unit.
9. We are not concerned with the propagation of sociological ideas, except to emancipate the creative elements from the present ideology.
10. Time is a tyranny to be abolished.
11. The writer expresses. He does not communicate.
12. The plain reader be damned.
    (*Damn braces! Bless relaxes!* . . . Blake)

Kay Boyle
Whit Burnett
Hart Crane
Caresse Crosby
Harry Crosby
Martha Foley
Stuart Gilbert
A. L. Gillespie
Leigh Hoffman
Eugene Jolas
Elliot Paul
Douglas Rigby
Theo Rutra
Robert Sage
Harold J. Salemson
Laurence Vail

The Novel Is Dead—Long Live the Novel
(November 1929)

The novel as practiced today is an archaic form that no longer answers the needs of the modern psyche.

It presents a rigid, exhausted formula, and has grown unwieldy as an instrument of expression.

It lacks the possibility of further evolution, because it clings to the descriptive requisites of a banal universe.

It has grown artificial, and, like the rhyme, represents a straitjacket to the creative visionary of our age.

The novel of the future will take no cognizance of the laws imposed by professors of literature and critics.

The novel of the future will be a compendium of all the manifestations of life in a timeless and spaceless projection.

The novel of the future will use telegrams, letters, decrees, fairy tales, legends, and dreams as documents for the new mythos.

The novel of the future will be a plastic encyclopedia of the fusion of subjective and objective reality.

The novel of the future will synthesize all the styles of the epoch in an effort toward unity.

The novel of the future will plunge into the underworld of our being and create fables in consciousness.

The novel of the future will produce the new myths of the dynamic movement of the century.

The novel of the future will express the magic reality in a language that is non-imitative and evolutionary.

Harry Crosby
Stuart Gilbert
Eugene Jolas
Theo Rutra
Robert Sage

Preface to the New *Transition* (March 1932)

We are still living in an epoch of transition, the chief characteristic of which is the crisis of man.

In the face of a materialistic despotism which places the "concept" before the living imagination, and the force of the will before that of life, in the face of a naive optimism of progress, in the face of machine-mammonism, we feel the necessity of a revolution of the soul.

While the general crisis is being liquidated, the new *Transition* proposes the revision of all values that no longer answer our deepest needs.

The new *Transition* proposes to defend the hallucinative forces now trodden underfoot, and to maintain their primacy under any social system that may come.

The new *Transition*, having little faith in Reason or Science as ultimate methods, proposes to establish a mantic laboratory that will examine the new personality, particularly with relation to the irrational forces dominating it.

The new *Transition*, in a spirit of integral pessimism, proposes to combat all rationalist dogmas that stand in the way of a metaphysical universe.

The new *Transition* proposes to encourage all attempts toward a subliminal ethos through mediumistic experiments in life and language.

What Is the Revolution of Language? (February 1933)

When I wrote the manifesto "Revolution of the Word" which was published in *transition* 16–17 (June 1929), I was aware that the opposition to this action would be considerable. I was not prepared for the formidable abuse which was heaped on this document, both in Europe and in the United States.

The term has now become part of the literary baggage of our day. There are signs that the idea is beginning to be discussed with more objectivity than at the time it was first launched. There are also signs that it is being received with more sympathy than in the days of *transition*'s pioneering.

The impulse for the revolution of the word owes its genesis to such precursors as Arthur Rimbaud, James Joyce, the Futurists, the early Zurich Dadaists, certain experiments of Gertrude Stein's, and Léon-Paul Fargue. It owes nothing to Surrealism.

I claim for *transition* priority in formulating the problem on an international scope, in developing it independently, and in giving it a systematic dialectical substructure. I based myself primarily on a study of the Freud-Jung-Lévy-Bruhl explorations into the unconscious in order to discover the laws dominating the mutation of language.* In all the numbers of *transi-*

---

* It always seemed to me strange that none of the psychologists themselves tried to tackle the problem. It is, therefore, with great interest that I notice in the last number of the *Psychoanalytische Bewegung* (Vienna) an article by A. J. Storfer, "Chancen einer psychoanalytischen Wortforschung," in which the question is studied for the first time, to my knowledge.

tion I proposed and encouraged a radical criticism of language, both from the communicative and the symbolical viewpoint, and tried to prepare the ground for a general reconstruction.

Today I feel that the battle has been partly won. Although the work of many writers is still in the narrow circle of traditional language matter, there is a small group in Europe and in the United States who are beginning to break away from academic prejudices, and who are engaged in building a new and more pliable form of expression.

It may be opportune, therefore, to redefine the problem of the Revolution of the Word, or, better still, of the Revolution of Language:

Revolution of Language:

(1) An attitude which regards modern language as inadequate for the expression of the changing background of the world, and which posits the necessity of a radical revision of its communicative and symbolical functions.

(2) It regards both the individual creator and the collective folk speech as mediumistic instruments for bringing about the change.

(3) It envisages creative language as a pre-rational process.

Frontierless Decade (April–May 1938)

With this number *Transition* completes the tenth year of its existence.

It was founded, in 1927, as a more or less eclectic organ, with the basic aim of opposing to the then prevailing photographic Naturalism a more imaginative concept of prose and poetry. It encouraged a new style by postulating the metamorphosis of reality.

As a documentary organ, *Transition* began by bringing to the attention of Anglo-Saxon readers translated stories and poems from various camps, including Expressionism, Post-Expressionism, Dadaism, Surrealism. It also introduced original work by most of the unorthodox writers of the British Isles and America, as well as countless Continental independents who had heretofore been ignored by both the conservative and the radical magazines.

Beginning with the first issue, it published seriatim eighteen fragments from James Joyce's *Work in Progress*. A number of *Transition* writers also served as interpreters of this new and difficult work. (See *Our Exagmination Round His Factification for Incamination of Work in Progress*, Shakespeare & Co., 1929, in which are published nine articles that had originally appeared in *Transition*.)

Among the translations published, it introduced the texts of the then emergent school of Surrealism, a full decade before London and New York became aware of it, and this despite the fact that the Surrealist ideology was not identical with that of *Transition*.

Almost all the new painters, photographers, and sculptors were reproduced, beginning in 1927, when many of them were little known outside of a small circle on the Continent.

Transition was not satisfied, however, to merely be the mirror of Continental advance-guard movements, although it always considered the construction of a bridge between creative Europe and America an important task.

It created a new narrative in a magic realism (paramyth) and a new form of dream-poetry (hypnologue).

After the first year of research, it became an independent workshop for the development of a new style and a new language through a continuous effort to expand the frontiers of expression. It was the first modern review published in Europe or America to recognize the "malady of language." It sought the de-banalization of creative language by encouraging the phantasmatic metaphor and the exploration of neologistic possibilities.

This linguistic revolution was already in the air when *Transition* began. But *Transition* organized for the first time, in Europe and America, and brought into focus, the efforts being made in that direction by writers in English, French, and German: James Joyce, Léon-Paul Fargue, certain left-wing representatives of German Expressionism (Sturm), Zurich Dada, the editor's own interlinguistic experiments, and so on.

The manifesto "Revolution of the Word" was the outcome of this attempt at synthesis. It did not imply that every writer should invent a language of his own, but simply that the writer should have more liberty than he had possessed heretofore in subjugating syntax and vocabulary to his individual ends.

Transition progressed from an experimental into a constructive phase by associating the mutation of language with the new discoveries related to the expansion of consciousness (night-mind) and the intercontinental, social amalgations occurring today. It was the first to relate this problem to the reconstruction of the myth. It asked for a linguistic reformation, not out of esthetic caprice, but because such a reformation was actually taking place in real life, especially in America. Here it was not H. L. Mencken's *American Language* that was at stake, although Mr. Mencken undoubtedly was a pioneer in the recognition and elaboration of the new Elizabethan tendency toward word-making, existent in modern America. *Transition* sought a welding-together of all the linguistic elements that are about to make the new English language, of all the contributions to Anglo-American speech to be found in the interracial crucible which the North American continent represents. The results of the great Western migrations of the past hundred years are only today being coordinated. *Transition* is in search of the Euramerican language of the future.

Throughout its ten years of existence, *Transition* has faithfully adhered to a belief in the primacy of the creative spirit. Nor did it climb on the bandwagon, when a split occurred in the ranks of writers everywhere simultaneously with the world depression in 1930, but took its stand on the side of a metaphysical, as opposed to a materialist-economic, interpretation of life. In 1932 it announced: "Poetry is vertical." The bankruptcy of sociological literature and art should now be fairly obvious even to the most zealous activist of the arts.

Transition will continue to seek a pan-symbolic, pan-linguistic synthesis in the conception of a four-dimensional universe.

Paris, France
Nov. 1937

Transition: An Occidental Workshop, 1927–1938 (1949)

The aim of *Transition* between the wars was to forge a chain that would link together America and Europe. To me it was the realization of a youthful dream that had brightened my immigrant years before World War I: the vision of a linguistic and creative bridge between the countries of the Western world. I had spent most of those years in the crucible of New York, absorbing its universe of races and languages, and it had been my hope that my experience might one day help to span the Atlantic with a two-way flow of ideas between men of different races and tongues.

I started *Transition* in Paris in April 1927 with my friend, the American novelist Elliot Paul, who remained associated with the review for two years, after which he returned to the United States. We agreed that the magazine should present an amalgam of Eur-American writing, and in the very first issue set the standard with the following table of contents: a sample from James Joyce's *Work in Progress* (later to be titled *Finnegans Wake*), an "elucidation" by Gertrude Stein; a translation of a story by the German Expressionist Carl Sternheim; a translation of work by the French novelist Marcel Jouhandeau; narratives by three American writers, Kay Boyle, Robert Coates, and Ludwig Lewisohn; a translation of a story by the Swedish writer Hjalmar Söderberg; and translations of poems by André Gide, by the Surrealists Robert Desnos and Philippe Soupault, as also by the German Expressionist poets Else Lasker-Schüler and Georg Trakl. Early poems by such young American poets as Hart Crane, Braving Imbs, R. Ellsworth Larsson, Archibald MacLeish, and Evan Shipman completed this list.

Almost immediately, *Transition* assumed the role of what it was to become later on; that is, a workshop of the intercontinental spirit, a proving ground of the new literature, a laboratory for poetic experiment. I had at the time, and I have still, an almost mystic concept of an ideal America, and I wanted to make of *Transition* a continuous manifestation of this concept. In a later essay (1929), entitled "Super-Occident," I wrote: "I should like to imagine a Super-America which might be the idealistic intensification and sublimation of the Occident."

Our chief agent was Miss Sylvia Beach, owner of the famous Shakespeare & Company bookshop on the rue de l'Odéon in Paris, publisher of *Ulysses,* and our good friend, who helped us through many difficulties. It was she who intervened with James Joyce in our favor when, as yet unknown to him, we envisaged the bold plan of printing serially the already famous Irish poet's new work. It was also in her hospitable little shop on the Left Bank of the Seine that we met many of the writers who later became contributors to *Transition.* Indeed, at the very outset, we were fortunate in obtaining the collaboration of writers who were representative of both continents, and their courtesy is still remembered with gratitude.

The reception by critics and readers was fervid, often violent, and the controversies raised continued for a full decade. The first of these controversies was due to the fact that the title was printed with a lowercase "t," for no other reason, really, than because Paul and I thought it might be fun to bait the critics with this innocent enough innovation; and we were right. Later, as we grew in stature, we reverted to the capital letter, but the change back was considered almost as irritating as had been the original little "t." There was no pleasing certain of the more captious of our critics.

The first issue appeared just two years before Wall Street "laid an egg," as *Variety* announced in its famous banner-line. Materially, therefore, the moment was not a propitious one. We managed to continue, however, with varying fortunes, and faced with occasionally serious financial problems, were twice rescued by the generosity of friends and well-wishers. The last issue appeared in May 1938. The by-then inevitable approach of World War II made it no longer possible to concentrate on abstract laboratory problems, or to daydream about new forms in art and language. The totalitarian menace was looming on the international horizon, and I came more and more to feel that the writer could defend the spirit only by participating actively in the battle against the enemy. During its slightly more than ten years of existence, *Transition* had passed from an eclectic period through a thoroughly exploratory one into a final constructive period. The following writers, named in the chronological order of their association with the magazine, acted at one time as associate or advisory editors: Elliot Paul, Robert Sage, Matthew Josephson, Harry Crosby, Stuart Gilbert, Carl Einstein, James Johnson Sweeney. I should like to take this opportunity to express publicly my warm appreciation of their contribution toward making *Transition* possible.

Paris in the 1920s was a center of intellectual ferment, the undisputed capital of creation and experiment. *Transition* entered this moiling world with the avowed purpose of combining the various tendencies in art and literature into a single channel, which I once called "magic realism." All the narratives and poems we published bore this mark, and by retaining an anti-realistic, anti-photographic bias in favor of the metamorphosis of reality we went on exciting voyages of discovery. We stressed work with a fantastic, dreamlike, apocalyptic trend and sought to give to expression a sense of the "marvelous." In fact, as *Transition* continued, we abolished the term "short story" in favor of the term "paramyth," because we considered that the narrative should be given a mythological prolongation. We also felt strongly that the notion of delimiting prose and poetry should be combated, for we regarded poetry as an existential entity.

In the beginning, Paul and I wrote resounding and, I fear, somewhat prolix editorials: "*transition* will attempt to present the quintessence of the modern spirit in evolution," we announced in an early number. "We do not hold with the dogma that contemporary works of art cannot be evaluated. It is easier to judge a contemporary work because it arises from sources more readily and directly understandable. . . . We believe that although art and literature are, in many quarters, growing more definitely national in coloring and texture, their appeal is becoming distinctly international. . . . The reader is coming into his own." And again: "We need new words, new abstractions, new hieroglyphics, new symbols, new myths."

In looking back, however, it is probably no exaggeration to say that a new literary style resulted from this heightened esthetic awareness, a style that broke with the imagistic-objectivistic tradition in order to seek a symbolical form. This style, which derived from Expressionist, Dada, and Surrealist experiments, flowed finally into the cosmological imagination of Verticalism. Among its more daring American exponents should be mentioned Wayne Andrews, Hamilton Basso, Erskine Caldwell, Hart Crane,

Kay Boyle, Morley Callaghan, Ernest Hemingway, Anaïs Nin, Katherine Anne Porter, Gertrude Stein, and William Carlos Williams. Among the Europeans, it gives me pleasure to recall that we translated the work of Franz Kafka well before the appearance of the Kafka "cult,"* that we were the first to translate Léon-Paul Fargue and St. John Perse,[†] and that the work of the Surrealist group appeared in *Transition* when Surrealism was as yet known only to a handful of *lettrés* in Paris.[‡] Let us add that another of our most cherished aims—to bring about a sort of poetic "Internationale"— was realized, and that we actually did publish the work of writers from some twenty countries.

Parallel with its efforts to extend the notion of reality was *Transition's* interest in language experimentation and, in this connection, we published the work of a number of British, French, Irish, and American writers who were conscious of the increasingly serious malady of language today. James Joyce and Gertrude Stein, of course, dominated the Anglo-Saxon experimenters, to whom were added such Europeans as Hans Arp, Robert Desnos, Léon-Paul Fargue, Kurt Schwitters, and many others. The sonorist Iconoclasts appeared side by side with the pure Neologists, and the attempts of yet a third group to find a "language of night" through dream writing were also numerous. In 1929, exasperated by the critical scorn and ridicule that greeted these innovations, *Transition* initiated a declaration of linguistic independence by publishing a manifesto entitled "Revolution of the Word," which started a storm in the paper forests of two continents. Although this was undoubtedly the most controversial of the *Transition* manifestoes, there was another, written by the editor and signed by the following: Hans Arp, Samuel Beckett, Carl Einstein, Thomas McGreevey, and James Johnson Sweeney, which, under the title "Poetry Is Vertical," sought freedom from the purely materialistic conceptions then in vogue (1932) in order to find a nexus with cosmic and mystic forces. Numerous subsequently published documents—stories and dream-texts—implemented this tendency, and certain attempts to find a language adequate for its expression were made, not without success.

Needless to say, however, our bellwether in the neologistic pilgrimage was James Joyce, substantial portions of whose new *Work in Progress* were

---

* The first time, in 1928.

† 1927.

‡ 1927. At this date, Surrealism was still in what might be termed its heroic period. It had not yet discovered the Marxist ideology, nor had it shown esoteric or gnostic-mystic tendencies.

published in *Transition* before it appeared in London and New York under its ultimate title of *Finnegans Wake.* For the sake of history, I should like to recall here that seventeen installments of the *Wake* were published in *Transition* between 1927 and 1938. The preparation of these installments was always exciting, for it entailed close cooperation with the author, who had to consult numerous notebooks, accumulated over the years, before he considered that any portion of the work was ready for publication. In addition to this already difficult task, he nearly always made last-minute neologistic additions which caused the French printers to tear their hair in desperation. Simultaneously with the work itself, *Transition* published the first exegetical essays on *Work in Progress,* which were later collected in book form by Sylvia Beach under the title of *Our Exagmination Round His Factification for Incamination of Work in Progress.**

It was from Paris, then, that *Transition* was edited during those confused years between the two great wars. A number of British, Irish, and American writers were living there as "exiles"—an appellation I always thought ludicrous—because they felt that the Seine capital offered the essential background for creative work. In reply to one of the several *enquêtes* organized by *Transition,* "Why do Americans live in France?" Gertrude Stein who, at that time (1928), was "dean" of exiles, wrote as follows: "The United States is just now the oldest country in the world, there always is an oldest country and she is it, it is she who is the mother of the twentieth-century civilization. . . . America is now early Victorian, very early Victorian, she is a rich and well-nourished home, but not a place to work. Your parents' home is never a place to work, it is a nice place to be brought up in. Later on there will be place enough to get away from home in the United States, it is beginning, then there will be creators who live at home."

This paradoxical answer was only one of numerous extracts from the work of Gertrude Stein published by *Transition.* Among the more important of these were *Tender Buttons* (which had long been out of print) and the first version† of *Four Saints in Three Acts* (later made into an opera by Virgil Thomson).

Although for technical reasons‡ it is impossible to give pictorial representation in this anthology to the very valuable contribution to *Transition*

---

* Later republished by Faber & Faber (London) and New Directions (Norfolk, Connecticut).

† 1929.

‡ Most of the copper plates were seized by the Germans during their occupation of France, and the photographs used were swallowed up in the disaster along with the other papers that composed the *Transition* archives.

made by the painters, sculptors, and photographers of the epoch, it should be recalled that certain of its covers were signed Picasso, Léger, Miró, Kandinsky, Arp, Duchamp, Man Ray; that reproductions of the work of these men appeared frequently in its pages, as did also the work of such painters as Braque, de Chirico, Ernst, Gris, Grosz, Klee, Hélion, Masson, Mondrian, Picabia, Tanguy, Rouault; of such sculptors as Brancusi, Calder, Giacometti, Gabo, Moore, Nicholson; of such photographers as Abbott, Brugière, Powell, Man Ray, Sheeler; of such architects as Moholy-Nagy, Le Corbusier, Nelson, S. Giedion.

The task of making this selection of representative material from such a wide spate of contributions has been a particularly delicate one. There were many others to be found in the twenty-seven numbers of *Transition* which I should have liked to see included in such a miscellany, and only my agreement with the publisher to remain within definite space limitations is responsible for their omission. It is my sincere hope that this choice will, nevertheless, give a fair idea of what *Transition* tried to accomplish and—however short of the mark—what it did accomplish. The great period of transition through which humanity seems destined to pass so painfully into the as-yet-unforeseeable new era is surely not ended. I believe it is not impossible, however, that the review *Transition* may, for future generations, constitute an important record of certain of its earlier manifestations.

Part Three : **The Language of Night**

Introduction

In attempting to articulate for modernity a space of the imagination, Jolas turns fundamentally against the conceptual model of Freudian psychoanalysis as symptomatic of the age's misled, sterile rationalism. In a sequence of perhaps some of his very best as well of some of his altogether over-the-top idealist essays, he develops a vision of "the language of night" as an extended part of the "Revolution of the Word," the antidote to the age's perceived crisis of language. A self-avowed spokesman for and participant in the avant-garde, he takes recourse to a tradition from Schelling's to Jung's visions of the relation between the unconscious and conscious dimensions in the creative process. Simultaneously, he is always in awe of James Joyce's evocation of a universal linguistic unconscious from the major languages of the ancient and modern world, the "big language," for our comprehensive awareness. By contrast, the rationalist ideology of "progress" is without memory, its hierarchies based on material criteria only, resulting in a process of spiritual disintegration in which the aura of poetry no longer exists. Calling on the history of the human imagination, Jolas uncovers and translates for the reader a multitude of linguistically innovative poets from past eras and writers of his own time, most notably François Rabelais and William Shakespeare, Arthur Rimbaud and Stéphane Mallarmé. His genealogy continues to the pioneers of the early twentieth century, the prophets of Zurich Dada (Hugo Ball, Hans Arp), Expressionism (August Stramm, Gottfried Benn, Carl Einstein), and Surrealism (not Breton's but that of Robert Desnos and Michel Leiris); also invoked are American writers like E. E. Cummings, T. S. Eliot, and Ezra Pound, all as poised against the "utilitarian word." On a transatlantic scale, it is the sheer inexhaustible vitality of the American language, nourished by so many contemporary languages from within, including the sounds and forms of slang, that is most promising as a crucible of an evolving "Eur-American" mind in transition. Aware of the era's obsession with the Primitive, Jolas objects to the excesses of the contemporary entertainment industry which threatens to also corrupt African American music, from spirituals to jazz. Nevertheless, he clings to a nostalgic belief in the primal rhythm, unique magic, and aura of black culture (of the deep South) as strong enough to retain a mediating influence in American literature and even European modern music.

Recalling the "nocturnal empire of the pre-logical," Jolas cites several states beyond waking (neither of which actually had escaped Freud), that is, "dream, daydream, and pathological hallucinations," which form a dimension of language as an autonomous process. The modernist poem is to unlock, reveal, and illuminate a repressed pre-logical unity of word and image, in unison with Rimbaud's "hallucination of the word." We intuit that Jolas's "vertical" idealism is nourished by these arcane sources, but he leaves it to the reader to associate the sociocultural implications of the secretive and seductive nature of the night as a phase of the day of human existence. In fact, Jolas, the critic, editor, and poet of the avant-garde, turns out to be nostalgic for an Adamic language and the fulfilled experience of communication before the hubris of the tower of Babel: "And the poet, in giving back to language its pre-logical function, makes a spiritual revolution—the only revolution worth making today." Yet in spite of the manifest idealism of such proclamations poised against the "malady" of modernity, in particular the German reader of Jolas's texts will here become aware, and perhaps wary, of a certain "sound" that in the 1930s, with, for example, Gottfried Benn's short-lived embrace of Nazism, turned out to be a seductive siren's song of a new irrationalism. At any rate, the critical reader here will want to be aware of the limits as well as the potential of any "White Romanticism" that entrusts itself optimistically to an encounter with the "language of night."

—D.R.

The Revolution of Language in Elizabethan Theater (June–July 1933)

As the Middle Ages came to an end, and the period freed itself from the influence of the spiritual community, England began to turn its interests toward man. Individualism, resulting from the impulse of the Renaissance, stretched itself into all intellectual domains. An age overflowing with strength and the vigor of genius blossomed. This burgeoning of creativity found its outlet in literature, above all in poetry, which became the expression of the age par excellence.

In the general effervescence of ideas, the instrument of language was radically reshaped and sharpened. Because the imagination was not searching for a fixed model, but was flowering with a freedom never reached since, the means of expression became plastic and malleable. During this time, the vocabulary and the syntax shattered all traditions.

It was a time of luminous chaos. Dr. Johnson had not yet begun his famous dictionary, whose etymology, full of errors, unfortunately stopped the vertiginous evolution of language. The establishment of the Tudor dynasty announced itself with an anarchy of syntax that was supposed to feed the most fiery of spirits. The transition of the English language from its birth during the Conquest (Middle English) to that of Modern English had begun.

Each poet assumed all possible rights to change the sense of words, to invent new ones, to deform the orthodox vocables, and to play with the laws of syntax. Shakespeare, Marlowe, and their contemporaries filled their works with daring neologisms and verbal allusions. Nouns, verbs, and adverbs were employed in a highly idiosyncratic manner.

Language, under French and Italian influences, became cosmopolitan. Neoplatonism, as well as Montaigne, Rabelais, and Calvin, influenced the intellect, and Latin words slid little by little into the English vocabulary, naturally undergoing a phonetic change in the process. The word *malgré*, for example, became *maugre* in Shakespeare's *Twelfth Night*.

During this period of adolescent creativity, "the first quality of Elizabethan English," according to M. George Gordon,* "was its power of hospitality, its passion for free experiment, its willingness to use every form of verbal wealth, to try anything. They delighted in novelties, and so exultingly that prudent word-fearing men became alarmed. The amusing thing was that even the alarmists were unable to deny themselves the very contraband they denounced; in this matter of language they were all smugglers. Thanks to this generous and unlicensed traffic we discover a quite astonishing number of words, introduced, apparently, by the Elizabethans, which today we could not do without."

According to the same author, there were three prominent contemporaries who violently opposed this poetic debauchery: Richard Puttenham, Thomas Nash, and Ben Jonson. But, curiously enough, almost all of the censored words persisted in the language, and a good number of them have entered into the modern vocabulary. Among these words, we might include *scientific, idiom, method, function, refine, compendious, prolix, figurative, impression, numerous, grammatical, penetrate, savage, obscure,* and so on.

This game of etymological invention manifested itself in the Elizabethan theater. Shakespeare, in particular, led the way. In the edition of his work, revised by Craig,† we find a glossary containing a multitude of neologisms. There are some that were abandoned by the later generations, but many have also remained in usage.

We might cite, among others, *lumpish, mash, mate, merchant, mess,* and so on. According to M. Gordon, there was also *aerial, auspicious, bump, castigate, clangor, conflux, control, countless, critic* and *critical, crop-ear, disgraceful, gloomy, gnarl, heartsore, herblet, hurry, home-keeping, hunch-backed, lackluster, lapse, laughable, pedant, perusal, savagery, sprightful.*

It is above all in Shakespeare's last plays that we find the poet devoting

* At the Clarendon Press, Oxford.

† Oxford University Press.

himself to the "alchemy of the word." In a single play, *Cymbeline*, we find such audacious words as *after-eye* (v.), *chaffless, under-peep, straight-pight, imperceiverant, wrying, cravens,* and so on.

It seems that anything was possible in the grammar of the time. The poets used verbs as adjectives. For example, the adjective "happy" was used as a verb. One "happied a woman." The same transformation appears in the use of the adverb "askance" as a verb. Shakespeare also said: "Be guilty of my death, since of my crime." The adjective "malice" was used as a verb as well. On the other hand, there were also adverbs that were used as nouns.

Already we can see that the dynamism of the thought of the time was rather irrational. Words were overturned without any pedantic order.

There is an analogy between this marvelous age and our own that relates particularly to the problem of language. As in the sixteenth century, the English language today is undergoing an immense crisis that is far from having reached its climax. We are witnessing a slow disintegration of traditional grammar at a time when words have lost their original sense, and we fail to recognize the distinction between *communication* and *expression.* This linguistic crisis is also a human crisis. The values of mythology have been broken down, and we are beginning to move away from the determinist doctrine. In addition, the English of the British Isles is suffering the assault of the American idiom that seems to possess all the possibilities of renewal.

In James Joyce's work (above all in *Work in Progress*), we can trace an evolution toward a synthetic language. The great Irish poet finds the existing linguistic means insufficient for expressing the experiences of the unconscious. He therefore invents a language of his own and shakes up traditional philological conceptions. It could be that through him we are entering a new Elizabethan age.

The King's English Is Dying: Long Live the
Great American Language
(June 1930)

The Modern Quarterly, *of Baltimore, Md., devoted its last number to a debate with* transition *as to the advisability of continuing the "Revolution of the Word" inaugurated by me a year ago. Messrs. V. F. Calverton, Herbert Gorman, S. D. Schmalhausen, Pierre Loving, and others explained their viewpoints, challenging my friends Stuart Gilbert, Robert Sage, and myself on the question. In order to simplify the discussion, we thought it advisable to deal with Mr. Calverton's essay exclusively, since it seemed to concentrate the arguments of all our opponents.*

The mechanical acceptance of language which pedantic philology and utilitarian literature continue to force upon the writer is drawing to its close. The struggle to give the poet unlimited liberty to re-create each word in his own image is still going on, but a new sense of the word which professors, newspapers, and novelists have abused to the point of sterility is now developing, and a modern mythos of language is being established.

In a world which is in a state of flux, the assumption that language for purposes of creative expression has been fixed once and for all is no longer tenable. We know now that language has a definite relation to anthropology, and we can see its historic evolutions in connection with the evolution of man himself. There is an incessant growth and mutation in it.

In order to trace this kinetic development of language, a brief consideration of its origin may not be amiss. Its genesis and growth is identical with all races. The desire for communication undoubtedly played a major role in the creation of words. Then, as man became more cultivated, the need for facilitating thought expression was added to the need for communication.

Speech, or oral expression, developed relatively late. The explorations of the French Jesuit Father Jousse have illuminated this problem. He found that the gesture was the first sign of communication. Later on sound enchainments followed. He found that in the ancient history of mankind the grammatical arrangement of spoken words is entirely different from those of the written scheme of phrases. *On ne parle pas comme on écrit.* The rhythmic *recitatifs* of the Koran, the biblical verses, and so on thus find a new explanation. The gesture of the primitive man, in other words, was replaced later on by sound expression in the form of a rhythmic repetition of words and phrases.

The primitive sign was the first expression. The attempt of the prehistoric man to reproduce naturalistically an aurochs or a tree can still be traced in the caves of southern France. But there were also signs that did not *reproduce* the phenomenal outline of a subject. Hieroglyphs and other abstract designs were used from time immemorial. These instrumentalities are the very essence of the human desire to *express,* and the more cultivated the human mind became, the more abstract became its form or composition.

"Words are social in origin," says Mr. Calverton. I admit that for the purposes of plain everyday speech, language has always had but one function—that of transmitting information. But when Mr. Calverton insists that "words are the irreducible data of communication," I am puzzled. To be sure, language used for purposes of documentation and exposition, as in scientific literature, newspaper information, critical elucidation, can only use the signs transmitted to the mass, that is, the condensation of words that have a common denominator in every mind accepting them.

There is, however, a state of mind that worries little or not at all if the masses understand its implications. It is in no way concerned with the problem of considering an audience. It is primarily interested in stating in its own terms an irresistible aggregate of experiences that come from mysterious sources. This state of mind is a gratuitous one. Words are treated instinctively as a fluid medium of a vision.

The creative writer does not convey information for just *any* audience. His aim is to express himself regardless of the consequences. He delineates his theme with the material he possesses, and creates an absolute. The audience is his objective self, the prolongation of his critical consciousness. The spectator, as Jean Paulhan calls him.

Mr. Calverton worries considerably about his age. "And finally we must see that the whole direction of our age is social and that any attempt to revolutionize the word which tends to isolate the individual from the group is moving, not with the age, but against it."

The tendency toward a mass psychology has been nurtured by the tremendous economic groupings of today. Capitalist America and Communist Russia are both mass phenomena. But do not let us mix our categories.

The creator is always and fanatically an individualist. This does not prevent him from seeing his work in relation to the general mythology of his group. But he always sees himself as an autonomist of the spirit, a nonconformist, a rebel, a subversive element in any group as far as his inner life is concerned. If that were not the case, and he were merely running along the line of social movement, he would doubtless be obliged to lower his intellectual values in order to reach the masses. He would have to give the mere replica of a mass hierarchy in his creative expression. He would have to play the role of the polite journalist who is the echo of the powers that be.

The creator, no matter what specific social structure surrounds him, is contemporaneous only by chance. He cares little whether he is for the age or against it. As a matter of fact, he is as often as not either indifferent, or against the main current.

Social communication, then, is in no way connected with creative expression. The nature of the work of art and its manifestations prove sufficiently that this conception plays no role whatever in the esthetic structure. If communication exists, it is indirect and by chance.

Mr. Calverton points to my statement that "it is the fact of becoming *conscious* that makes the creator," and tells me I failed to understand "that Freud has endeavoured to make the chaos of the subconscious mind intelligible by the device of analysis and classification."

Here I must point out to Mr. Calverton that I have always defended my conviction that the creator organizes his material in highest consciousness. But the idea of "intelligibility" does not enter in. The poet condenses the symbols of his subconscious mind into form. The multiplicity of these symbols, sometimes of a mythical primitive nature, sometimes of a purely personal reminiscence, necessitates, doubtless, the intervention of reason for their organization.

According to Schelling, there occurs in art a reconciliation of the conscious and the unconscious. It is the creative imagination that has the function of synthesis, as has Freud's psychoanalytical process in the case of the individual pathological condition. Mr. Calverton, however, seems to me to wander wide of the mark when he tries to draw an analogy between the therapeutic process of the Freudian system and the creative process of becoming conscious. I agree with Dr. Jung in rejecting the theory that the artist is per se a neurotic one.

This seems to me also the error of the *Surréalistes,* which I have pointed out several times. The Surrealist tries to evoke the subconscious in its raw and absolute state "without the intervention of reason." He does not try to organize the symbolic mechanics. He fails to see that here is a difference between the symbols of the dream and those of art. The dream is a biological function of the instinctive. Art demands, however, that the entire personality be in play and that a conscious action follows the movement of the symbolic images.

"If an artist writes merely to express and is unconcerned with the element of communication, to be consistent with himself he should never print what he writes," according to Mr. Calverton. The function of the work of art is not action. At the bottom of all artistic movement there is the dream and play. They are self-sufficient functions. But the artist prints his creation, because printing itself is a heightened form of expression, a graphic expression.

Mr. Calverton asserts: "To be revolutionary in this age one must experiment with better means of communication rather than with more muddled methods of expression, for the aim of the age, with its new science and new logic, is to clarify rather than to confuse."

"Better means of communication" for whom? If Mr. Calverton—or *This Quarter,* which took up the same argument against us—is eager to have an international method of communication, they have merely the embarrassment of choice. Esperanto, Volapük, and now even Dr. Jesperson's Novial—all tend to simplify social communication for scientists, preachers, grocers, drugstore clerks, and even writers. It is a commendable effort, and I, for one, see no objection to it.

Neither Esperanto nor Novial will ever bring about the dream of international brotherhood. The international languages will, I believe, remain forever mere technical, auxiliary equipments for specialists. They will never influence the organic development of a linguistic unit. For at the bottom of all human differentiation—the sole condition to be desired, in spite of economic collectivism—there is the native language, the dialect, slang.

Economic interpenetration is doubtless influencing the various languages. As a result they are enriched. But the creative writer really has nothing to do with this, although he takes advantage, of course, of this enrichment. His own contribution must remain an intensely personal one, a word metamorphosed by the force of his own vision.

"Any revolution of the word, therefore, if it is to mark an advance, has but one function to perform, and that is to make the word a finer, because a more precise and clarifying form of social communication," says Mr. Calverton. I repeat: precision and clarity are absolute necessities in those forms of writing that are primarily informational. These virtues are not necessary in the process of creating. In attempting to convey a metaphysical state of mind, the poet does not ask himself if such and such an expression is precise and clear to the reader. It is enough that it is to him.

Mr. Calverton is at one with me in his desire "for revolutionary change in the arts and letters." But he believes "this change must occur in literary form and technique and not in the word-substance."

Transition has never been afraid of presenting new forms and techniques. But that is not enough. The instrumentalities of expression have been so abused by repetition that they will have to be overhauled, repaired, renovated. I do not demand that every writer henceforth invent his own vocabulary. I merely believe—and that was the impulse of my *proclamation*—that he has the right to make lexicographical changes if there is an organic necessity for it in the substance of his work itself, to tear syntactical and grammatical arrangements to pieces if they seem to approach the monotony of a *New York Times* editorial, and if the subject he is treating seems to require it, to use the language of the street, of erotic-physiological processes, of the prison, of the tenement house, of the baseball grounds, of slang, to give voice to the irrational both of his own and of the collective mind of a people, to organize all this into an art of the word deeply rooted in the living movement of things.

The mysticism surrounding the "purity of the English language" has, I believe, lost its force. In the crucible of the immense racial fusion of indigenous and immigrant America there is occurring today an astounding creation that ultimately will make the American language,* because of its greater richness and pliancy and nearness to life, the successor of British English. This is already happening in speech, and as soon as the age-old delusion that there must be a difference between written and spoken words has had its day we will probably see the American language colonize England and all English-speaking countries.

Our writers of the Middle Western school (with the exception of Sherwood Anderson) and those of the New York school (with the exception of Murray Godwin, Ernest Hemingway, Robert E. Coates, John Dos Passos) still continue unfortunately to use a medium that derives from the reporter's notebook.

It is in the immigrant development of the new America that the possibilities for a fundamental revolution of the word are inherent. Here the foreign background, the world mythos lying dormant and being blended with the reality of the new continent, will eventually sweep the word-lore of the mother country away—although retaining the latter's primal elements—and thus will bring to fruition the language of the century to come.

* See H. L. Mencken's *The American Language.*

For Stuart Gilbert

The Language of Night (1932)

The Crisis of Language

The crisis through which we are passing is not only politico-economic in character, but encompasses all the manifestations of the spirit. We are emerging from the intellectual hypnosis of the postwar period. A new attitude toward life is gradually silhouetting itself.

The dogmas of materialism which the pessimism produced by the war brought to a brief supremacy are being thrown into the discard. The Eur-American mind, inebriated by the technological intelligence, sought in mere "concepts" a substitute for the living organism of the imagination. It sneered at metaphysical values. It overrated the potentialities of the machine. It uprooted the "I" and replaced it with an illusory "mass mind." But signs are not lacking that we stand at the threshold of an epoch that will reestablish the personality as the primary element of modern life.

The problem of man is becoming again a fundamental one. Max Scheler has pointed out that there never was an age in which the beliefs concerning man's essence and origins have been so confused as in our own. We observe the liquidation of a world form that was given a mortal blow by the war. We stand before the necessity of redefining the individual in relation to a world that we no longer consider bound by the laws of causality. We are going toward a view of the universe that will deny the intellectualism of the last decades, that will tend to rebuild an idealism as precise as physics itself, and envisage a new epoch of the soul.

The process of decay which, as a corollary, we notice in literature, is connected with the disintegration of language. As in every historic cycle that has run its course, expression has become a paralyzing factor in the development toward the new worldview. Since we live in a period of latent revolution, a radical metamorphosis of language is a prerequisite condition of its realization.

The crisis of the communicative functions of language acts as an impediment in the creation of a new universe. Although the intellectual content of words has undergone profound changes during the last few decades, we still use a vocabulary that retains obsolete meanings and is unaware of the enormous changes in meaning brought about by the flux of events. Because words evoke played-out concepts, confusion sets in. We find it necessary again and again to redefine each term as we go along. The ideological transformations in recent history have shifted the significations of many terms to such an extent that the original ideas are obscured, necessitating wearisome redefinitions in order to avoid the misunderstandings produced by the difference between the primary image and the superimposed one. I do not deplore the decay of these words—decay being a law of life—but I do deplore the lack of invention and the resistance of an orthodox majority that oppose their renewal. It is time to make tabula rasa.

Two or three persons, as a rule, are unable to agree on any set of words we might bring up for discussion. If they be terms like "Metaphysics," "Romanticism," "Classicism," "Humanism," the chaos is complete in every case. The subterfuge of affixing the adjective "new" or "neo" to any of these terms, with the hope of avoiding a misunderstanding, or of clarifying an intellectual complex, only increases the disorder. Let us take "Romanticism" as an example. The expression "New Romanticism" has invaded literary history again and again since the great Romantic epochs in France, Germany, and England. Each time the new label distorted the original idea. We find it necessary to seek other reference points. In the field of international politics, the fact that the various nations still use the terminology of prewar days veils the issues. The original differences between "conservative" and "radical," "republican" and "democratic," and so on, no longer exist. The positions of the various ideas have been shifted by events. I would suggest the elimination of all words that tend to confuse us. They have reached the age of retirement. Let us pension them off so that they may end their lives in the studies of pedants and in obsolete dictionaries!

It might be worthwhile, in this connection, for the writer bent on "clarity" to ponder the lesson given him by the man in the street. For while educators, radio announcers, editorial and scenario writers adhere to Ruskin's gentleman's tradition, new and more vigorous means of verbal communication are constantly being created in colloquial speech.

Slang, in every language, develops with increasing speed. The American language, for instance, boldly disregards inherited diction. Its speech is far removed from polite literary expression. This astonishingly vital organism may well become the basis for the sociological evolution of the English language.

The instrumentalities of poetry are particularly involved in the general chaos. The line of demarcation between communicative and symbolical expression has almost disappeared. We face the crisis of the orphic language.

The fictions evolved by the mechanical mind of the age have prostituted the language of poetry and smothered its sacred character. Poetry still lives in an era of rationalism.

Dialectic materialism insists that the poet is primarily conditioned by his environment, and as such has no right to follow any individual caprice of expression. He functions only in the degree in which he is an active member of society in the construction of a better world. It is treason for him to give voice to the eternal elements of his being, to the great human fissions which have pre-conscious relationships.

This grave error is caused by the inability to separate the idea of expression from that of communication. For the conflict between the poet and his audience has always been an acute one. To be sure, language used for purposes of documentation and exposition should use the signs that have a common denominator in the intelligence of the readers. There is, however, a state of mind that worries little or not at all if the masses understand its implications. It is in no way concerned with the problem of considering an audience. It is primarily interested in stating an aggregate of experiences that come from mysterious sources. It is a gratuitous state of mind. Words are treated instinctively as a fluid medium of a vision.

The language of poetry is passing through a tremendous crisis today. It no longer mirrors the primal emotion. It does not express the many-colored entities which we know now to be in the creative consciousness.

Poetry needs a new instrument.

Revolution of the Word

Language, like man, is in constant mutation. The poet, being the possessor of a heightened visionary faculty, duplicates the morphological process of mankind. His right to bend language to his sublime needs has its causes in the organic movement of words.

Folk-speech, with its primordial sense of mythos, shows no timidity about creating words. Sir James Frazer* tells us of "tabooed words" among certain primitive tribes today with whom the invention of new words becomes a religious rite.

Those literary ages that coincide with important political transformations are more fertile in language changes than others. The Renaissance, with its emphasis of individual liberty, gave language, in almost all European countries, a powerful impetus. "The first quality of Elizabethan, and, therefore, Shakespearean English," says Mr. George Gorden,†

is its power of hospitality, its passion for free expression, its willingness to use every form of verbal wealth, to try anything. . . . They delighted in novelties and so exultingly that we discover a quite astonishing number of words, introduced, apparently, by the Elizabethans, which today we could not do without. . . . Shakespeare was, by every sign, in the first rank of the advance, and of all its members the most exuberant; an experimenter always, though in the diction of his time; making his language as he went along. . . . Only the Americans today profess to do this.

In Spain Gongora y Argote hammered out his Baroque syntax in prodigious fantasies. In France, next to Rabelais, whose invention of words was based on Latin, Greek, and sometimes Hebrew, it was the theories of the Pléiade that infused the language with new vigor. Ronsard, in his preface to the *Franciade* (1572), says: "Je te veux bien encourager de prendre la sage hardiesse d'inventer des vocables nouveaux, pourvu qu'ils soient moulés et façonnés sur un patron déjà reçu du peuple." The revolt of Ronsard's friends against medieval forms and rigid Latinisms began a fruitful epoch in French letters. Their insistence on using not only the French of Paris, but also the *picard,* the *gascon,* the *poitevin,* the *normand,* even the *wallon,* gave their vocabulary freshness and earthiness.

* *The Golden Bough,* abridged edition (London: Macmillan), 254.
† S.P.E. Tract XXIX, *Shakespeare's English,* at the Clarendon Press.

Although the organism of language in France continued to undergo changes during the Moyen-Age by means of deformation, phonetic alterations, combinations, duplication of meanings, the period following the Renaissance was hardly favorable to any important development along this line, and it was not until the Romantic movement that a new interest in language asserted itself. Victor Hugo, who wanted to put a "bonnet rouge" on the dictionary, gave the signal for the insurrection.

Baudelaire, whom Rimbaud called "le premier voyant," discovered the elements of the new poetry. But his own use of language, in spite of certain apparent audacities and foreign terms, remained within the circle of tradition.

Comte de Lautréamont (Isidore Ducasse) in his *Chants de Maldoror* was the first to wrench the ancient poetic realities apart. He was the first to show enough audacity to present the unconscious relationships, instinctive phantasms, violent hatreds and sadisms, in his poems. His language, however, remained within tradition, although its content was revolutionary.

With Arthur Rimbaud we enter upon the epoch when language became properly subordinated to the movements of the unconscious. He envisaged "the hallucination of words." In his *Alchimie du Verbe* he said: "Je réglai la forme et le mouvement de chaque consonne, et, avec des rhythmes instinctifs, je me flattai d'inventer un verbe poétique accessible, un jour ou l'autre, à tous les sens." Rimbaud, however, failed to take the step further toward *minting* new words.

The Symbolists, under Stéphane Mallarmé, gave language new "correspondances," but also refrained from attacking the organism of the word itself. Mallarmé, according to Bernard Faÿ*

resorted to the use of rare, technical, or ancient terms, or else employed the usual vocables in their etymological sense, or with oblique meanings. . . . He did not use punctuation to mark the stops fixed by grammar and logic, but rather the pauses which his thought and sentiment had chosen. He did not group words according to grammar and logic, but suppressing personal pronouns, verbs, prepositions, and adverbs, transforming epithets so as to set them in relief, he sought unity not in the phrase, but in the verse.

In *La Pénultième,* this tendency is shown at its best:

* *Since Victor Hugo,* trans. P. R. Doolin (Boston: Little, Brown).

Je sortis de mon appartement avec la sensation propre d'une aile glissant sur les cordes d'un instrument, trainante et légère, que remplaça une voix prononçant les mots sur un ton descendant: "La Pénultième est morte," de façon que

La Pénultième

finit le vers et

Est morte

se détacha de la suspension fatidique plus inutilement en le vide de signification. Je fis des pas dans la rue et reconnus en le son *nul* la corde tendue de l'instrument de musique, qui était oublié et que le glorieux Souvenir certainement venait de visiter de son aile ou d'une palme et, le doigt sur l'artifice du mystère, je souris et implorai de vœux intellectuels une spéculation différente.

Stefan George, whom we may consider the German representative of Symbolism, also attempted to create poetry that had the immanence of a religious emotion and rhythm. His preference went to the Romance languages. He tried to wrest the word out of its quotidian ambience and give it the quality of magic. Such was his desire for verbal purity that he invented a language of his own. "Many linguistic experiments," says his friend and biographer Carl August Klein, "which went back to his early youth, preceded that period when he created a strange, secret language entirely incomprehensible to the uninitiated, in accordance with a highly symbolic system. He collected the bricks with which to build it from elements of the Romance languages, especially the Italian and the Spanish. In this language which he baptized 'lingua romana,' he created his *Zeichnungen in Grau* and the *Legenden*."

The following is an example of a poem in "lingua romana."

Rosa Gelba
En la atmosfera calida tremulante de odores
En la luz argentea de un diffallaz
Ella respira circunfundida de un gelbo fulgor
Envelata toto en una seta galba
Multo vagamente conaria extranea
No lassando deomar distinctas formas
Que si sua buca se contracta en moriento scibudor
E suas spatulas o suo seno en un leve altiar
Dea misteriosa de Brahuraputra e Gange

Pareceste creato de cera inanumota
Sin tuos oelos dusamente ad umbratos
Quando lassos del reposo subito se levaron.

The irrationalist movement which developed in France and Germany during the war was a modern Romantic explosion. Its chief feature was a violent onslaught on academic language. Expressionism and the original Zurich matrix of Dadaism were mostly instrumental in leading this movement after Marinetti, with his "words in liberty," had given the initial start. Surrealism ignored the problem, retaining, in spite of the primacy of irrationalism it demanded, a more or less traditional language-matter.*

In Germany it was August Stramm who, in the magazine *Sturm,* edited by Herwarth Walden, disintegrated the lyrical language of the Liliencrons and Dehmels: *Lichte dirnen aus den Fenstern* (Lights streetwalk out of windows) is the beginning of a famous poem that had the influence of a declaration of independence.

Gottfried Benn demanded the "southern word," and Kurt Schwitters in his *The Rights of the Artist for Self-Determination* initiated his Merz poetry ("Anna Blume") with primitive stammerings. Carl Einstein in *Bebuquin* created language as neurosis.

It was the Zurich movement of Dadaism, however, that originated the most radical conceptions of language. In his *Flucht aus der Zeit,* Hugo Ball, the inventor of the word *Dada,* and the *animateur* of the early movement, says: "We sought to give the separated word the fullness of a spell, the flame of a star. And strange to say, the magically filled vocable charmed and bore a new phrase which was not conditioned by any conventional sense. Touching upon a hundred thoughts, without naming them, this phrase evoked the sunken, irrational being of the hearer; it awakened and strengthened the lowest strata of memory."

He invented a new genre of verses, sound poems, in which the "balancing of the vowels was measured and distributed only according to the value of the initial line":

gadji beri bimba
glandridi lauli lonni cadori

* Only Roger Vitrac, Michel Leiris, Benjamin Péret, and Robert Desnos in this group gave the problem their attention.

gadjama bim beri glassala
glandradi glassala tuffm i zimbrabim
blassa galassasa tuffm i zimbrabim

Hans Arp, Tristan Tzara, and Richard Huelsenbeck entered this Dionysian dance of words with poems in which an attempt was made to discover once more an absolute quality in poetry.

Arp, whose sculptures are better known than his writings, is undoubtedly one of the great German poets today. In his experimental work, *das lichtscheue paradies, weisst du schwarzt du,* and so on, he creates neologisms that are born out of strange, abstract imagery:

Arabische Sanduhr
so wie der panikvogel
sich brüstet mit den brüsten
im chor vokalkabalen
aus portraitierten büsten

und wie wie sie sie laden
blitz ab der leiter frieden
entwed und od und ader
als doppeltes hinieden

rundräder um die reiche
reißein reißaus verdücken
flieht als verkappte hüte
auf euern fleischperücken

dort mäht ihr schlagerblumen
im wetter so wie alle
dort backt ihr schnee im maule
mit wasser in der falle

Tristan Tzara, a Rumanian by birth, chose French as his medium. He left Zurich, where he had collaborated with Ball, and unleashed the Dada spirit in Paris after the war.

"Pour faire un poème dadaïste," he says, in *Sept manifestes Dada,**

---

* Jean Budry, Paris.

Prenez un journal. Prenez des ciseaux. Choisissez dans ce journal un article ayant la longueur que vous comptez donner à votre poème. Découpez l'article. Découpez ensuite avec soin chacun des mots qui forment cet article et mettez-les dans un sac. Agitez doucement chaque coupure l'une après l'autre dans l'ordre où elles ont quitté le sac. Copiez consciencieusement. Le poème vous ressemblera.

French Dadaism attacked the problem of language less vigorously than its Swiss initiator despite the fact that the ground had already been well prepared through the work of Guillaume Apollinaire and Alfred Jarry, its immediate predecessors.

The poet of *Alcools, Calligrammes,* and so on reintroduced the magic of the eye into poetry. Jarry, in *Ubu Roi,* gave his work many neologisms (*merdre, phynances, oneilles, decervelage,* and so on) that have passed into the language. Roger Vitrac, in *Le Langage à Part,** presents an excellent study of Jarry's importance as an innovator. Jean Cocteau, in his magazine *Le Mot,* attacked the dictionary of the academicians with brilliant effect.

After Marcel Duchamps, writing under the name of Rrose Sélavy, had published his *jeux de mots,* paradoxical and picaresque word derangements, André Breton and Philippe Soupault, in their *Champs magnétiques,* inaugurated the autonomism of composition by giving the unconscious thought its first systematic expression in literature. Breton's *Manifeste du Surréalisme* unleashed the movement which, taking Freud's theories as a basis, tore the orthodox style asunder. It was a syntactical revolution, however, rather than a word revolution. Breton, inventing the *texte surréaliste* (*Poisson soluble*), pushed the free association to amazingly daring regions. It is to be regretted that this enormous discovery was not developed further. It was subsequently abused by writers without organic creative equipment who used the method as an easy way out of esthetic difficulties.

The darkling, a-syntactical rhythms of Paul Eluard come from a spring of pure poetry. Benjamin Péret, Roger Vitrac, and Robert Desnos made audacious attacks on the language, the latter inventing a species of poems in *langage cuit* that deftly play with both grammar and words. Michel Leiris contributed his *Glossaires.*

Henry Michaux, a Belgian poet, invented his own language in *Mes propriétés* (ed. J. O. Fourcade).

The most important innovator of language in France today is Léon-Paul

* *Transition* 18.

Fargue. He dissociates, in his *Poems in Prose,* the classical word, and by charging it with rhythms and phonetic "caricatures" taken from the speech of the people, gives it power and magic.

Jean Paulhan, in his *Jacob Cow, le Pirate: Ou si les mots sont des signes,*[*] studies words in relation to a Freudian conception. "We do not directly speak our thought," he says. "We speak our words. . . . The words engage us. . . . It is enough to turn the order of words around for the sense to become turned around. . . . We no longer need to think, the phrases are enough."

Modern English and American poetry has occupied itself little with the problem of language. Lewis Carroll, with his "portmanteau words," made the first successful frontal attack on the dictionary. In magnificent verbal fantasies, he coined alogical expressions that have already entered English speech. He remained, however, the only writer in the last century to make this insurrection in English.

The Imagists, during the war, mistook the replacing of the classical phrase by "democratic speech" for a revolutionary gesture. While this did not prevent the emergence of real poets, the disregard for the unconscious life of the creator in relation to expression made the movement abortive from the beginning. They failed to recognize the automatic character of the "image."

Gerard Manley Hopkins organized a verbal world of his own, a world of a-grammatical movement, mystic and beautiful.

But the great composer of the word arrived with James Joyce. In him we see the decay of a sterile language and the prophecy of the future creative language.

Already in *Ulysses,* he is engaged in disintegrating words. In the Proteus scene, Stephen monologues: "Listen: a four worded wavespeech: seesoo, hrss, rsseeiss, ooos." "She trudges, schlepps, trains, drags, trascines her load." In the Siren scene there is a witches' sabbath of new word arrangements that foreshadow his subsequent development.

With his still unnamed *Work in Progress,* Mr. Joyce goes beyond *Ulysses* and invents a language of his own. It is a language that, in line with Vico's theory of repetitive cycles, combines in a vast saga the elements of the language of the gods, the heroic language, and popular speech. Numerous modern and ancient tongues have been welded together by him.

"The technique of much of Mr. Joyce's verbal creation," says Mr.

---

[*] Au sans pareil.

C. K. Ogden,* "may be illustrated by the principle of the infix. English works almost entirely through suffixes and affixes. . . . If we separate the functions of language into four main divisions—Sense, Feeling, Tone and Intention— it is clear that Mr. Joyce's neologisms chiefly provide blends of the three last. He is not concerned, as is the scientist, with the creation of new names, so much as with the development of fresh emotive and invective gestures."

Proceeding from a planetary concept of time and space, Mr. Joyce presents a fantasy of prehistoric, historic, and modern man across the vista of legends and fairy tales. It is a lyrical story of mankind related during the period from dusk to dawn. "Mr. Joyce," says Samuel Beckett, "has desophisticated language. And it is worth while remarking that no language is so sophisticated as English. It is abstracted to death."

The opening passage of "The Ondt and the Gracehoper"† reads:

> The Gracehoper was always jigging a jog, hoppy, on akkant of his joyicity (he had a partner pair of findlestilts to supplant him), or, if not, he was always making ungraceful overtures to Floh and Luse and Bienie and Vespatilla to play pupa-pupa and pulicy-pulicy and lantennas and push-pygygyddyum and to commence insects with him, there mouthparts to his orefice and his gambills to there airy processes, even if only in chaste, ameng the everlastings behold a waspering pot. He would of curse melissciously, by his fore feelhers, flexors, contractors, depressors and extensors, lamely, harry me, marry me, bury me, bind me, till she was puce for shame and allso fournish her in Spinner's housery at the earthbest schoppinhour so summery as his cottage, which was cald fourmillerly Tingsomingenting, groped up.

No systematic effort for renovating the creative capacities of language had been made in modern English literature until I founded *transition* in 1927. By publishing James Joyce's *Work in Progress,* most of the foreign writers mentioned above, and new-sounders like Gertrude Stein, Theo Rutra, Murray Godwin, A. Lincoln Gillespie Jr., Robert M. Coates, Laura Riding, Walter Lowenfels, Charles Duff, Elsa van Freitag-Loringhoven, and so on, *transition* laid the groundwork for my "Revolution of the Word," which I published in June 1929.

* Preface to *Tales of Shem and Shaun* (Paris: Black Sun).

† See *Three Fragments from Work in Progress,* Black Sun Press; amplifications from *transition.*

This manifesto tried to crystallize the mood against the utilitarian word and was a declaration of independence in which I was joined by the following writers: Kay Boyle, Whit Burnett, Hart Crane, Caresse Crosby, Harry Crosby, Martha Foley, Stuart Gilbert, A. L. Gillespie Jr., Leigh Hoffmann, Elliot Paul, Douglas Rigby, Theo Rutra, Robert Sage, Harold J. Salemson, Laurence Vail.

The Proclamation was as follows:

Tired of the spectacle of short stories, novels, poems, and plays still under the hegemony of the banal word, monotonous syntax, static psychology, descriptive Naturalism, and desirous of crystallizing a viewpoint . . .

We hereby declare that:

1. The Revolution in the English Language is an accomplished fact.
2. The imagination in search of a fabulous world is autonomous and unconfined.
3. Pure poetry is a lyrical absolute that seeks an a priori reality within ourselves alone.
4. Narrative is not mere anecdote, but the projection of a metamorphosis of reality.
5. The expression of these concepts can be achieved only through the rhythmic "hallucination of words."
6. The literary creator has the right to disintegrate the primal matter of words imposed on him by textbooks and dictionaries.
7. He has the right to use words of his own fashioning and to disregard existing grammatical and syntactical laws.
8. The "litany of words" is admitted as an independent unit.
9. We are not concerned with the propagation of sociological ideas, except to emancipate the creative elements from the present ideology.
10. Time is a tyranny to be abolished.
11. The writer expresses. He does not communicate.
12. The plain reader be damned.

Among American poets, E. E. Cummings, T. S. Eliot, and Ezra Pound attacked the problem of language by introducing into their work the colloquial element of the living speech.

Says E. E. Cummings:*

i do however protest anent the un
spontaneous and otherwise scented merde which
greets one (Everywhere Why) as divine poesy per
that and this radically defunct periodical. I would
suggest that certain ideagestures
rhymes, like Gillette Razor Blades
having been used and reused
to the mystical point of dullness emphatically are
Not To Be Resharpened

Ezra Pound, in his *Cantos,*† writes as follows:

So I said to the old quaker Hamish,
I said: "I am interested." And he went putty colour
And said: "He don't advertise. No. I don't think
You will learn much." That was when I asked
About Metevsky Melchisadek.
He, Hamish, took the tractors up to
King Menelik, 3 rivers, and 140 ravines.
"Qu'est ce qu'on pense. . . ?" I said: "On don't pense.
"They're solid bone. You can amputate from just above
The medulla, and it won't alter the life in that island."
But he continued. "Mais que'EST-ce qu'ON pense,
"De la métallurgie, en Angleterre, qu'est-ce qu'on
"Pense de Metevsky?"
And I said: "They ain't heard this name yet.
"Go ask at MacGorvish's bank."

Gertrude Stein presents mathematical abstractions in her work; her rhyth-
mograms proceed by repetition, thus producing a kind of hypnosis. In the
a-syntactical movement of her work she tries to find a solution to the problem of the sentence and the paragraph. Her method derives from painting.
   She uses words as gestures in the primitive sense of the idea. The delib-
erateness she shows in limiting her vocabulary to the most quotidian, the
most colorless words, has puzzled many of her readers. She has no interest
in giving the emotive element of the mind. Her economic language con-

* Is 3 (New York: Liveright).
† *This Quarter*, no. 2, edited by Ernest Walsh and Ethel Moorhead.

denses the creative process. And yet, in *The Making of the Americans,* the very paucity of words succeeds in presenting a narrative of engrossing qualities. Her most recent work, *How To Write,** gives the quintessence of her esthetic credo.

I quote one of her portraits:

Guillaume Apollinaire
Give known or pin ware.
Fance teeth, gas strips.
Elbow elect, sour stout pore, pore caesar, pour state at.
Leave eye lessons I. Leave I. Lessons. I. Leave I lessons, I.

Depth and the Chthonian Image

What is creative expression today other than cowardly genuflection before positivist dogmas and social idols? Progress and evolution as watchwords. Machine-mysticism as an illusion of progress. The hegemony of intellectualism, the dance around money, the principle of causality—all enemies of the absolute. Biedermeier orderliness. Depersonalization. Mass man. Sport as a substitute for deep emotions. Fear of the symbol. Language as Fordian standardization. Literature in terms of honoraria. The urban feeling as anti-nature primitivism. Sobriety of photographic realism. Sexus instead of Eros. Anonymity. Fear driving the I to mass-opium. Melioristic world ideals. Aversion to facing the individual conflicts inherent in our irrational being. Utilitarian metaphors. Metaphors as substitutes for primal images. Onslaught against the subjective. Sachlichkeit (Why *Neue* Sachlichkeit?). Pseudo-tranquillity because of a uniform rhythm. Conversation as neurosis. Pornography. Snobish "isms." American detective stories. *La mystique américaine.* Geographical escape as a means for finding literary themata. Normalization. False Humanism.

Instead of encouraging the revolt of the sunken "I," Eur-America continues to raise her indigenous pragmatism and objectivism to a canonical mode of thinking. She emphasizes will and behaviorist consciousness as a priori requisites for idealistic action. She worships an ephemeral reality.

We need a revolution of our notion of man, whose body and soul are identities. Even in a collectivized social organization, it is inconceivable

* Plain Edition, 27 rue de Fleurus Paris.

that the personality, in its multiple stratifications, should be submerged by a mass imperative.

The creative man today should guard the magical forces of life from deterioration. If he accepts a new social system—and in the face of mankind's economic misery he must hope for the replacement of the present plutocratic oligarchy—it will be on condition that this act be not accompanied by the sacrifice of his inner vision. He reserves the right of secession.

Our age has lost the sense of transcendental introspection. It shuns the visionary and the irrational. It avoids the meta-real possibilities which are properly creative. The mechanistic-physical explanation of processes, the remnant of a blind belief in natural science, is still the predominating *Weltanschauung*.

There is, however, a view of the world that has been in man from the beginning of time, and which is the antithesis of the rationalistic one. It is the magic view: the world seen from within, from out of the living unconscious movements of life in a spaceless and timeless projection. It is the hallucinatory view, properly speaking, and proceeds from the depths of the personality.

A vast cosmos lies slumbering in us. Personal and ancestral memories are hidden in our being awaiting the spell of the conjuror. In order to understand this condition, we must need dissolve the personality first before constructing the new ethos. Only by recognizing the fact that the primordial background of life is characterized by enormous scissions can we recapture the lost qualities of our psyche.

All cognition is anthropocentric. We think subjectively. For the romantic, or magical, motif of thinking has been in man from time immemorial. It still exists.

The Eleusinian mysteries epitomized a state of mind that was the antithesis of the "serenity" and formality of classical Hellas. Here we have the mystic act, dancing as a means of cognition, a ritualistic search for the underworld. Thus Hellas consisted of both the Ionic and Doric principles, the Apollonian and the Dionysian, as Nietzsche showed in his magnificent essay *The Birth of Tragedy from the Spirit of Music*. We find the same mystic interrelationships in all primitive races, past and present.

The history of gnosis gives us remarkable examples of this attitude of mind, which aimed at metaphysical knowledge in a direct manner. Christian, Judeo-Christian, Persian, and Egyptian gnosis agreed in the attempt to discover an immediate knowledge of divinity in a variety of ecstatic methods. This gnostic mythology has never changed and still dominates our beings in one way or another.

Plotinus, in talking about the "world-soul," claimed that it existed, undivided, in each individual soul, and that the cognition of pure ideas was made possible through illumination and trance.

The unconscious side of life—particularly as revealed in the dream—has been the subject of speculation and exploration throughout history. Heraclitus and Aristoteles devoted much thought to the problem. Christian theology did not hesitate to approach the subject, and Albertus Magnus, as well as his disciple Thomas Aquinas, paid considerable attention to the dream.

The exploration of the irrational celebrated its greatest triumph, however, with the Romantic movement. This immense revolution of the spirit which once revealed itself in German, French, and English manifestations continues to be an important part of the human psyche. A hundred years ago it saw in the fusion of spirit and nature the real problem of mankind. Its persistent attempt to enlarge the knowledge of consciousness opened a gap for the exploration of neglected regions of the mind. It strove for a revolutionary sense of life, and sought in fanatic opposition to the rationalism of the *Aufklärung* a development toward an emotional orientation of the European spirit. It penetrated into the instinct and saw its principal aim in a mystic interpenetration of the world. It did not hesitate to occupy itself with the Ahriman forces of the telluric.

But it is wrong to assume that it was an anarchic movement. Its avowed aim was to assure the triumph of consciousness over chaos, although it insisted on going through the netherworld first. To its representatives, art was primarily unity and synthesis. It was the conscious construction and organization of all the discoveries which had been made in the nocturnal empire of the pre-logical. Thus, in contradistinction to the Classical idea, which demanded rigorous canonical standards and adhesion to preconceived ethical and ideological principles, the Romantics used consciousness as a fluid thing and created the basis for a cosmos in movement.

We children of the twentieth century are unable to return to their background. It is impossible for us to revive Gothicism, moonstruck ruins, and evocation of knights and tournaments. It is the Romantics' fundamental belief that the forces of life are irrational ones before they become creative entities which establishes our method of thinking in a link with theirs. Our point of contact with them is precisely the reawakened interest in the pre-conscious and daemonic qualities of life. But our age demands a different realization. Against the background of a dynamic world we hope to create a sense of the miraculous that is not a looking-backward into the Middle Ages, but a use of more modern elements of development.

Novalis believed that the dream gives us glimpses into the supernatural, that it brings us nearer the world spirit. Nature is incomprehensible in itself, he says, and we are able to understand it only as a symbolic picture of the spirit. Franz von Baader said: "In the language of dreams, inherent in every man, we find revealed a peculiar capacity of our nature to become one with something other than ourselves, with something higher or lower, i.e., to come into contact with the more essential regions of the divine or the diabolical." The pneumatologists (Kerner, *The Seeress of Prevorst*) also considered the dream as a gate to the supernatural.

Modern psychology, beginning with Janet and finding its climax in Freud, has discovered that the subconscious is the basin into which flow all the inhibited components of our being. According to Freud, they are mostly sexual in character. Dr. Jung, a dissident of the Freudian school, found, however, that into the subconscious flow not only the unfulfilled elements of our personal lives, but that it contains also the continuation of a collective mythos. He finds in it a connection with the social organism and even with cosmic, mythological forces. We stand in contact with the entire evolution of mankind, with all the demonish and benevolent powers, and from this inner world emerge both the religious and the bestial phenomena of life.

Other psychic states are revealed to us by the so-called hypnogogic hallucinations. These occur at the moment between waking and sleeping, and are usually automatic images reflecting certain thoughts we had before falling asleep. The image continues the thread of conscious thinking. Daydreaming, too, has a connection with this. What Léon Daudet calls "le rêve éveillé" has an important relation to the workings of the mind.

A new element has come in with recent findings by brain specialists and paleontologists. The capacity for "mystic participation" which, according to Lévy-Bruhl, exists in the primitive mentality, survives in civilized man, albeit in an atrophied form. The pineal body—a fragment of the exclusive cerebral organ of our ancestors—is still part of the brain structure. The growth of the big brain has smothered this unit which the ancients called "the seat of the soul," "le troisième oeil," "das Scheitelauge."

We have lost relation with nature. Modern paleontology has discovered that man is not, as Darwin's theory insisted, a recent evolutionary product. His existence goes back to forgotten epochs. He existed many billion years ago in a form that has undergone psychic modifications in the same way in which the earth has passed through geological epochs.

The primal man, who is still in us, was a visionary of nature. He had a somnambulistic mind. Modern life has succeeded in relegating his ancient capacity for vision to a condition of passivity.

What methods should be used to rediscover the lost vision?

We need to seek the hidden depths of the "I." The absolute is not a mere static product of the past. It has to be conquered again and again through an activistic idealism.

The experience of reality is a hermeneutic task. We can find, in a preliminary disorganization of the senses, the point of departure for the capture of the chthonian universe. The poet is a mediumistic element. In order to create the state of mind adequate for orphic emotions, he develops in himself once more the practice of divination. Like Plotinus, he shuns discursive thinking in an attempt to find the great identity.

His mind is related to the minds that practiced alchemy, the Kabbala, Neoplatonism, and other mantic states. Master Eckhart, Jan van Ruysbroeck, St. John of the Cross, Eastern mysticisms, and the gnostic systems are identical with it. The messages of telluric images emerging from the primordial background are transmitted through ecstasis, the dream-state, and psychiatric conditions. In the quietistic state, the poet becomes aware of the eternal relationships. He automatically creates a cosmos of phantasms and proceeds from the irrational of his collective and personal life to the *ratio* of the creative. He comes to us from the empire of the mothers.

Why should the poet be afraid to face the telluric aspect of the world? All organic life is composed of antinomies, and the classical idea of "harmony" is not the final aim. Through a knowledge of the chthonian, the poet is able to conceive a new beauty that synthesizes the world spirit in all its ramifications.

The poetic "method," then, aims at the creation of myths. It is, in Nietzsche's phrase, "a lying in the extra-moral sense." The inner world is brought to the surface with blinding suddenness. The highly sensitized individual sinks into himself, he tries to penetrate to the unutterable, he lives for a flight "of the alone to the alone," as Plotinus says.

He then seeks a sublime individuation which encompasses all the world. When this goal has been reached, he feels the irruption of a higher power. Mystic cognition sets in. The frontiers between man and man fall. Ancient mythologies emerge. He comprehends the contents of humanity's consciousness. Not only the living races, but the dead races appear to him. His psychical and mental faculties are enormously heightened.

The period of cynicism and disillusion is over. We are entering upon an era which should adopt again a vertical attitude toward life.

The mechanistic period dispensed with gods and myths. It placed its faith in technology, economy, and science. We need faith again, faith in something beyond us, a Heraclitean god, a kinetic idea of cognition.

Only with this as a basis can we find a new style of creative expression. Here may lie the basis for a great twentieth-century collective art, when the unconscious of the masses will have been stirred again into an act of faith.

Art will be vertical instead of merely horizontal. The inner life will be again the center from which everything proceeds. A perpendicular movement from the nocturnal to stellar constellations will create a new emotion of wonder. Ecstatic immediacy!

In this mystic manticism of the inner life, the unconscious expression has the characteristic of the dramatic dialogue.

Already Friedrich Schlegel, the Romantic critic, asserted more than a hundred years ago that "there is an inner dualism that exists not only in our dreams, but also in our waking state, so that we really think in twos."

M. Jean Paulhan, in his series "Carnets du spectateur,"* came to the same conclusion.

This interior dialogue has not only a dual character, but is also multiple in movement. There is a simultaneity of stratified dialogues. In the dream and the daydream the dramatic character of our thinking can easily be proven.

Despite all that has been written on the subject, I do not believe that there is such a thing as interior monologue.† The real background of the interior thinking is a primitive one. As yet conscious reason has not blown over it. It is raw material, concrete, like the thinking of primitive races, a linguistic chaos. It is connected with all the pre-conscious processes and these are very fragmentary. Its primordial stratum is composed of images

* See *Nouvelle Revue française,* no. 15. November 1928: "Le portrait de Briand, l'assassin naïf, et les gens qui sont toujours en retard."

† I disagree with my friend Stuart Gilbert when he interprets the Proteus scene in *Ulysses* (see James Joyce's *Ulysses,* London: Faber and Faber) as a monologue: "I am getting on nicely in the dark," muses Stephen. "My ash sword hangs at my side. Tap with it: they do. . . . Am I walking into eternity along Sandymount strand? Open your eyes now. I will. One moment. Has all vanished since? If I open and am forever in the black adiahphone. *Basta.* I will see if I can see." The process here is one of question and answer. In *Work in Progress,* Mr. Joyce is using almost exclusively the interior dialogue.

the multiplicity of which is in exact ratio to the psychic potentiality of the possessor. Here an emotional conjuration occurs. The image seeks a new connection with another image. We observe the birth of the word as the symbol of the image. There is a reaching between an "I" and a "you," between an individual world and a group world, between a night and a day mind.

Gradually the conscious will intervenes. Words seek enchainments. The metaphor (alas—conscious comparison!) emerges. Grammar is born.

The Vertical Language

But once the nexus with a new universe has been established, how can the poet express his vision adequately with words that are bound by utilitarian necessities? Is it possible for him to give voice to the *unio mystica* which he experiences?

Language must be given a mediumistic function. It must be charged with the mood of liturgy.

Since the poet, in an age of positivism, has the task of rediscovering the sacred character of the religious emotion, of the shudder before the mysterious night, he must become a maker of language in his own right. He is no longer interested in the language of the nerves celebrated by the postwar epoch. The physical world collapses around him. He faces eternity. From the underworld, the tenebrous depths of his soul, he tries to emerge toward a Paradise of his own fashioning.

He is not interested in changing the world. He only wants to change himself. His form is in movement. He struggles against nothingness. He composes the vision he suffers.

The disintegration of consciousness which he understands better today requires a more comprehensive attitude toward the expression of his hallucinatory world. Since we witness in our night-mind the movement of our pre-conscious and unconscious layers, the inherited symbols of billions of years, the poet has the task of organizing the matriarchal images transmitted to him.

In his night-world he feels a new sense of time. For he knows today that the idea of "time" has a cosmic character. His mind carries in it the concentric point of all prehistoric and historic time. Everything is eternal, but he also knows that nothing is ever the same.

The vertical sense of language can be recaptured only by a revolutionary attitude toward its function of creative action. The character of conjuration implied in the sacred faculty of the word is reestablished by the poet who attempts to express the unconscious in magic potency.*

In the dream, the daydream, hypnogogic and pathological hallucinations, we frequently observe the fragmentary or decomposed character of words. They develop organically into neologisms. They become deformed. They assume superimposed meanings. They are phonetically changed. They are changed optically. They become polysyllabic, where once they struggled with one syllable.

The poet whose psychic life is identical with that of the mystic and other mantically gifted persons creates his own language of night. In the cosmogony which he builds for his own compensation, he transmits the symbolic and dramatic character of his vision by means of an autonomous language. His vocabulary runs the gamut from the lowest depths of the acherontic to the planetary reality of a sublimation.

He struggles, therefore, for the metaphysical words, considering this his most essential task. He undermines reason in language. He unmasks the pragmatic spring. The vertical language is the true international language.

Since the heart of all of mystic mankind beats with him in an immense rhythm, the poet does not hesitate to invent his own expression. The mythological images are identical. They are fixed stars in the psychic constellation. Every man gifted with vision can look at them and interpret them.

The new language has no terror for him. The new nouns made by verbs, the new verbs made by nouns, words made by juxtaposing adjectives and nouns, words made by wedding dream-signs, words made by the lopping off of inorganic syllabic structures—they all create the true universal language.

But because the primordial images find a nexus in an alogical way, any attempt to present the juxtaposition of contrary realities in a revolutionary manner is justified. It is permissible, therefore, for the poet to disregard the laws of grammar and syntax. The conventional rules of word enchainment have been responsible for the elimination of a metaphysical emotion in this age.

Thus if the so-called logic of syntax interferes with the pure development of a vision, the poet bends syntax to his own uses. He employs inversions where the internal rhythm demands it. He leaves out prepositions,

---

* Mystics, according to Görres, often invented their own secret language. Psychiatrists found the growth of an inner language, where analogy with ancient language-systems was discovered and new assonances and agglutinations were predominant. The stammer of the child and its word inventions are also part of this phenomenon.

adverbs, pronouns. He gives the phrase a changed substructure. By the dislocation of old sentence-schemes he achieves a delusional logic that is identical with that of the nocturnal. The sentence, being chthonian in origin, has a mediumistic rhythm. The new grammar forges an elemental and a fabulous world.

Thus language will become once more a primal and a sacred sign. It will be gravid with the deepest wonders of living. It will be the mother of a sacramental attitude toward eternal things.

And the poet in giving back to language its pre-logical function makes a spiritual revolution—the only revolution worth making today.

Wanted: A New Symbolical Language!
(March 1932)

The instrumentalities of poetic expression are particularly involved in the present chaos of the spirit.

The line of demarcation between sociological and symbolical media has almost disappeared. We face the crisis of the orphic language. The inroads made by the pragmatic forces have prostituted the language of poetry and deprived it of its autonomous, primal character.

The poet struggles for the metaphysical word, considering this his most essential task. He unmasks the mechanical grimace and undermines the rationalist elements of expression. He seeks in the visionary word the means for voicing the dissolution of the unconscious personality.

Since he combines in himself a mythos of his own with the mythos relating him to all of humanity, he has the right to invent his own language.

The poet who gives back to language its pre-logical functions, who re-creates it as an orphic sign, makes a spiritual revolt, which is the only revolt worth making today.

Wanted: A New Communicative Language!
(March 1932)

The process of decay, which as a corollary to the general crisis, we observe in literature, is primarily connected with the disintegration of language. As in every historic cycle that has run its course, a reactionary use of sociological terms paralyzes the evolution toward a new picture of the world.

The crisis in the communicative functions of language creates the intellectual chaos which characterizes all human relations today. Although the contents of words have undergone profound modifications during the last few decades, we still struggle with a vocabulary that statically retains now-obsolete words and is unaware of the enormous changes in meaning that have occurred. The vast political, philosophical, and psychological revolutions in recent history have shifted the signification of many terms to such an extent that the original ideas have become obscured, necessitating wearisome redefinitions to avoid the misunderstandings produced by the indifference between the primary image and the superimposed one.

It is high time to make tabula rasa. The old words have reached the age of retirement. Let us pension them off!

We need a twentieth-century dictionary!

Confession About Grammar (February 1933)

Language is passing through a crisis today. Words and syntactical rules have become inadequate to express a world in violent flux. The necessity of revising language should once and for all be admitted.

Grammar, as the basis of language, is no longer capable of serving its creative functions. It is tainted with the brush of the mechanistic categories, and is decaying with the logic of a bourgeois philistinism that is the last remnant of a rationalist epoch.

The principles of grammar today represent merely a common denominator of pragmatic experiences. But the grammar of the creator needs fresh air, liberty, a radical impulse.

I do not believe in the grammar of my age.

I feel in using it—as I do now—that it has become a chain and a nuisance.

Phonology, accidence, syntax, as taught by the philological old maids, have grown impatient under the domination of academism.

Grammar is not a static thing.

I believe in the right of the creator to ignore the law of subject, predicate, copula, and so on, to make any irrational alliance he damn pleases, to follow the law of his vision.

Since we must go back to the prehistoric and unconscious strata of our beings, it is necessary that grammar become alogical again.

I believe in the dynamics of an inner grammar.

Introduction to *The Negro Who Sings* (1928)

Although several modern writers insist on the absolute hegemony of the white civilization, we can easily trace the influence of certain foreign or savage races on our psychology. The Asian spirit and the African spirit both strive for supremacy in our time. As a matter of fact, savage art is redefining the traditional concept of art or, more precisely, it is becoming a driving force of a broad artistic revival.

Since Satie employed ragtime polyrhythm in his *Parade,* and many American and European composers introduced jazz rhythms into their works, a new spirit revealed itself to the old civilization: that of the American Negro soul. We heard the "spirituals" sung by blacks such as Roland Hayes, Paul Robeson, the Fisk Singers; we heard the modern songs of Irving Berlin; we watched, perplexed, Josephine Baker's erotic dance at *La Revue nègre;* we bathed in the delirious rhythms of cabarets where charleston reached a convulsive climax.

However, we should make a clear distinction between authentic and imposturous Negro expressions in the United States. First there is the pure primitivism of blacks who live beneath the Mason-Dixon Line that is in the South. To a large degree, they have kept all the naive and infantile charm of their ancestors who toiled in cotton and tobacco fields under the yoke of slavery. There are also blacks who mimic the whites, who willingly assume odd mannerisms in order to exploit the white nostalgia for the exoticism of color, and who become corrupt by renouncing their own race. This group of blacks lives mostly in the big cities of the North.

The interest for the particularly primitive Negro spirit intensified in

America after World War I. A great "black wave" descended upon New York, where journalists and intellectuals "discovered" the beauty of Negro songs. We could then see the revolting spectacle of commercial exploitation that threatened the purity of the African American phenomenon. Journalists, who never had any predilection for American folklore, and who were mostly interested in poker or baseball, were spilling lots of ink to depict their discovery of a new exoticism. Educated people had known the Negro song for a long time. They worked modestly, and without any public support, to preserve the primitive song—the only folklorist expression in the United States with the exception of Native American songs. There were, particularly in the South, many men and women who loved these direct manifestations of the poetic soul of a people enough to devote themselves to the task of recording them.

The visitor from the North of the United States arriving in any Southern town immediately notices a radical change in the relations between the races. While the Negro in the North is, to a certain degree, equal to the white, Southern Negroes definitely find themselves in an inferior position. They have to use designated compartments on the trains and they are assigned separate seats in the streetcars. The Southern white has a lot of affection for the Negro and understands his peculiarities; however, he watches over him with an almost beastly ferocity in order to maintain his own social and political superiority. As a result, the Negro withdraws into his traditions if he stays home and, if he has the energy to fight against the moral restrictions imposed on his race, he migrates north. The aged white civilization of the South, which suffered defeat in the Civil War, is on the verge of vanishing. It is being slowly suffocated by the power of the machine, standardization, and the madness of materialism. Yet a sense of the marvelous persists, recalling the old days when the Negro, an enslaved uncultured child, lived under his master's feudal system.

Despite the industrialist onslaught, the Southern Negro continues to create a magic aura that he instinctively needs. Living in a wooden hut he often shares with domestic animals, he dreams, meditates, and works as little as possible. He plays dice, makes love, and enriches his life with spontaneous or traditional songs. He solves the problem of life by simplifying his desires, by loving the sun, and by singing.

The Negro has an innate sense of rhythm. While in the African kraals, his ancestor was interested in pure rhythm only for the sake of expressing his pleasures and his physical ecstasies; the African transplanted to America in the seventeenth century adds other elements to the rhythm: melody and harmony. A return to African folk art thus resulted in a thriving American music of a prominently indigenous character. The slave, in listening to Protestant hymns, likely absorbed and distorted them.

The first time I heard Negro voices in unison, I had the impression of a mystical frenzy. The Negro's whole being is imbued with a very strong religious instinct. I recall the South Carolina and Virginia Negroes whom I encountered during a visit to these states. I always found in them a strong intuition of God's presence. Their stories struck me with their mediumistic quality. They heard God speak to them; they conducted long conversations with Christ; and many of them had visual hallucinations of God and angels.

To understand their need for metaphysical liberation, we should remember that the Negro in times of slavery could find only one way of overcoming his physical and moral misery and that was by means of the Christian faith. He created the possibility of a future emancipation through biblical images. Most blacks did not know how to read or write. They placed all of their trust in the preachers of their own race who, equally ignorant as they, evoked a future life and particular relations between the divinity and men.

This spirit persists even today in Southern towns and villages. I witnessed strange scenes in Savannah, Georgia, while I was strolling in the Negro district at sunset. There was an old grey-haired man who, sitting at a street corner, was preaching to people of his race. What a confusion of images! King David spoke to Abraham and the mountain of Sinai was located in Mexico. The old man yelled at the sinners, beat his chest, and wept with true mystical abandon. Most of his audience listened to him fervently, although a few more emancipated young people teased and mocked him. Suddenly, he started to play his banjo and to sing in a sweet melancholic voice.

This affinity for the beyond is reaffirmed in the church reunions. In Savannah, I often attended Baptist religious services. In this pretty town on the Atlantic coast, the Negro has preserved to a large extent the sense of his race with all of its nuances. Imagine a very simple wooden church where the congregation meets at night. A withered old lady is conducting the song. In a high-pitched voice, she starts singing hymns, and then the congregation accompanies her in a chorus of moving orchestral beauty. A woman collapses in delirium and is carried outside. When he sings alone, the voice of the Negro rarely attains its full beauty. But in chorus, the effect is astonishing. The rich and profound timbre of these voices possesses an exhilarating emotional appeal. The singers completely give themselves over to the inspiration. Swaying their heads and their bodies, they express their need to physically experience a rhythmic manifestation, even in the devotional songs. It is an impressive spectacle: the whole assembly, engrossed by a collective emotion, while singing in a wood church on a summer night.

In some regions of the South, we still observe the survival of religious songs that resemble primitive African dances. These shout songs derive from hymns, but also spring from a pagan impulse. After the service, the Negroes gather in a circle outside the church and start moving to the sounds of savage music, slow at first, until their steps then escalate to a terrifying rapture. They sing with a strange monotony, whirling all the while. The pervading Christian spirit and the stupidity of the authorities, who strive to eliminate all that is indigenous, have nearly succeeded in destroying this expression of the magical.

There is another kind of song that developed from the creative instinct of the American Negro and which resonates in the profane song, the work song, "the blues," and "the mellows." In these songs, the Negro devotes himself to the matters of life with a mixture of sorrow and humor that is the essence of his character. Most of the mellows (a Negro deformation of the word "melody") were born in Louisiana. Replete with imagery, they combine indigenous inspiration with soulful traditions.

To taste the charm of this culture, we have only to visit New Orleans. A strange and enchanting town, pulsating with color and memories, we can discover here a complete synthesis of French, Spanish, Indian, Negro, and American traditions. I experienced the extraordinary beauty of this town on the Mississippi River when I lived in the Vieux Carré. I arrived on the eve of the Mardi Gras Carnival, which is the only surviving manifestation of this sort in the United States. On the day of the carnival, the town was dark with crowds. The inhabitants from all parts of Louisiana, above all the descendants of the Cajun French, who were driven out of Canada by the English more than a century ago, had gathered to attend the colorful spectacle that was about to unfold before their eyes. The Negroes danced in the streets the night of the carnival, and I could hear their songs all night long.

In this quarter, a number of Negroes speak the Creole language, which is a mixture of old French and their own brand of English. The spirit of singing in New Orleans is also expressed in the cries on the streets where Creole continues to reign. Cotton and cane fields resound with loud and high-pitched Negro voices. The Negroes improvise their songs and, on the roads where they break rocks, they accompany their movements with songs that are full of joy and sorrow.

The African origin of the Negro songs is no longer disputed. Research on the rhythmics in African folklore has made considerable progress in recent years, allowing us to trace the development of the Negro song in America. According to the findings of the American critic H. E. Krehbiel, it is clear that the two musical genres—the song of the American Negro and the African folk song—share a rhythmical basis. However, as I have previously mentioned, the American Negro brought a new nuance into the African music: his sense of melody and harmony.

The Negro language took shape slowly after the arrival of the first slaves to America in 1619. In the beginning, they used their own dialects, but it was difficult for the Negroes from all parts of Africa to understand each other. Naturally, they searched for ways to communicate and eventually adopted English or French words that they mixed in with their own idioms. This interaction gave rise to a peculiarly Negro dialect that, however, tended more and more toward pure English.

The Bible has always been a major source of inspiration for the Negroes. They developed scriptural themes, often distorting images in such a way that they created a magic spell of words through truly unprecedented transformations. The language was simplified in such way that all sharp sounds in English were eliminated. The dialect thus obtained, by virtue of its naiveté, a very special charm for the white ear. But these dialects differ vastly depending on the region in the South from which they come. They possess a softness as elisions have replaced modalities.

The poetry of the spirituals, as well as of the traditional songs, is nearly untranslatable because it has resulted mainly from image deformation and from spontaneous transposition. We find in the poetry a great tenderness and sadness expressed through nostalgia. Some critics have emphasized the relation between the Negro's and the Hebrew's inspiration in their lyrical expressions. Not incorrectly. In both manifestations we can discover a need for liberation and the melancholy of a persecuted race. This is the subject of all the spirituals. Just listen to one of these religious songs, whose lyrical innovations are of great simplicity and beauty. It suggests a child speaking to God, deploring his lot, intoxicated by the idea of finding peace in the other world.

The spirit of this pariah race is also found in its work songs, and in all of its other traditional songs. The Negro is a storyteller at heart. That is why his songs begin with an anecdote as a basis for evocation, which the "music physicianer" or "musicianer" improvises. In the old days, these creative men traveled from town to town with their guitars or violins and many of the songs became widely known as a result.

The Negro's self-representation as an exile within the American culture is the source of many of his songs' themes. The black is a perfect ethical dualist, an unconscious gnostic. If he experiences a mystical ecstasy, it is quite certain that the animal spirit of his nature will prevail soon after. His conversions are just as violent as his convulsing in the sacred mud of life. Before the conversion, he remains overcome with sorrow for several days. He avoids his friends. *He is seekin'!* Then comes the revival, the religious awakening during which he is publicly converted in an unbounded frenzy. But this does not last long. One converts, after all, so easily.

While I was working as a police reporter in a number of Southern towns, I had many opportunities to observe the Negro grappling with the authorities. He is a natural anarchist. He has no sense of the law, which he knows benefits the white and the rich. To be arrested is, for him, an everyday affair. Like a *bad man,* he likes the role of the *rowdy.* That's why the Negroes' songs are often an apology for all sorts of crime. That's why they celebrate the power of alcohol, murders, and forbidden love.

Love above all. American puritanism violently rebels against the publication of these so-called obscene songs. Nevertheless, sexual relations are depicted in thousands of unpublished songs, where imagery exaggerates erotic emotions even further. The Negro has an absolute sense of life. In moral matters, he is untouched by middle-class hypocrisy, and he pokes fun at a more idealized notion of love.

Since the Negro is essentially a nomad, he also has no sense of belonging. His philosophy requires absolute freedom; and although he often sings of homesickness, he seldom establishes a home for himself except when he becomes attached to a plot of land. The Negro travels across the South, from Atlanta to New Orleans, working little, but loving his independence, while, at the same time, occasionally complaining of his loneliness.

The Negro conveys a sense of eternity in his work songs. Time and space do not exist for him anymore. He intertwines historical periods arbitrarily, but it is mostly the present that he evades. His imagery allows us to appreciate his ramblings, which approximate modern literature. Many contemporary works seem to proceed from this same primitive concept.

Another type of the Negro song is known as the blues. We often say,

"I've got the blues," to express a latent melancholy. Blues stanzas generally have only three lines. The last one is a shock, a kind of emotional explosion. The blues, although historically less primitive, is an integral part of the African American psychology.

The influence of Negro psychology is observable in the new American music, as well as in the works of George Antheil, Aaron Copland, and some French and German composers. It must also be noted that the sense of rhythm that is the very basis of the Ethiopian spirit has penetrated American life. The Americans have learned to seize these difficult rhythms, whereas the Europeans have seldom understood them. All the European jazz bands I have heard lack authentic spirit. The white singers who try to fiddle with the spirituals always turn out to be ignorant of the genius of the race whose music they are trying to perform. Such false exoticism is revealed when a white female singer tries to sing religious hymns by herself, without having studied them among the blacks. The simplicity of the hymns usually disappears when they are performed in public, even if by the blacks themselves.

Jazz, which is the application of the Negro rhythm to music, presents enormous difficulties for the whites. The Negro plays with tempo with an expertise that no white could ever attain. When you hear the Negroes sing, you can get an idea of the capricious rhythms that baffle the white. They sing traditional songs, and accompany their movements with the clapping of hands and the stamping of feet. The movement of only one foot indicates the base rhythm, while the singers simultaneously clap their hands. The last motion is very difficult because it expresses rhythms that seem to be quite different from the base rhythm. Thus, the syncopation is kept with the rhythm of the foot having a free and sure accent. We could easily find an illustration of this idea in the charleston. For the Negroes, dances have never been more than an accompaniment to their songs. The same attitude can be found in their apparently conflicting rhythms, which, in reality, are the condition for the magic of this dance that conquered Europe as well as America.

The Negro is the pure poet of the American continent, and he shares this title with the Native American, whose primitive art is hardly known in Europe. The Negro is a child who is unfamiliar with mechanized civilization, the disciplining of muscles and nerves, and the conventionalizing of emotions. He discloses his dreams in direct and tangible phrases, but he also always manages to imbue his expressions with sensual fervor. Modern American literature has been inspired by the African American psychology, and it is for this reason that American poets and novelists present such vigorous diction and imagery.

The dream principle accords well with the Negro spirit. Human anguish is revealed in impulsions toward anarchy and transcendental nothingness. Negroes find refuge in the pathos of forgetting through the exhilaration of their songs, the intoxication of their rhythm, and the magic of their fetishes. In their collective imagination, life and dream are inseparable. Representations of their taste for the infinite are their only means of revolt against white domination. Negroes invent scenery that exists beyond time and space, and take vengeance with an absolute that is the abstraction of their power. They are immersed in the mystical. The black man's laugh is softer than the howling of the machines across the immense American continent, more powerful than the sobs of his brothers who are suffering from the whites' injustices. Oh, memories of the blue sunset along the Mississippi River when I heard the songs of Negroes at work, unloading the cotton bales! Oh, the liberating laughter of young black girls wearing white dresses, who sang in the obscurity of narrow half-illuminated streets, where life revealed its strangest mysteries! Far from you, I feel the nostalgia for a sunlit land where the fever of your voices brings the somnambulism of the agonizing myths!

Race and Language (June 1936)

If the liberation of man is the chief aim of action, the function of the creator is as essential as that of the politician or the economist. The creator liberates with the instrument of the word, the plastic organization, the rhythmic composition. His revolution aims at a complete metamorphosis of the world.

The function of the poet is that of conjuration, invention, illumination. Standing on the threshold of a new age, he tends to become less and less subjectivistic, and to seek for an expression of the totality of human experience. He builds a bridge between the personal and the collective unconscious in a superconscious creative act.

A new race is slowly emerging from the crucible of the intercontinental mutations. Due to the vast migrations of the past decades, and the unprecedented biological interminglings now going on, the new race, the emergent characteristics of which can be noticed chiefly on the soil of the American continent, is groping toward a new vision of man that will be as different from that of the past centuries as was the Renaissance man from the Gothic man.

The poet visions this new conception of man by reconstructing the link with the pre-logical or mythological age—still dominant in mankind in the form of the ancestral memory—and by anticipating, in an expanded consciousness, the supra-rational faculties which partake of, and even surpass, the mystic mode of thinking. The new poet, following the law of motion, seeks a form of expression that will attack principally the problem of language. He is aware of the inadequacy of the traditional means of expression. He watches the malady of language and attempts to find a remedy in analogy with its historic mutation. He builds the creative language of the future by consciously welding together the elements of all the languages in flux due to the interracial synthesis now going on. He seeks a new syntax and vocabulary in order to give voice to the enormously complicated world of psychic changes that are the result of the biological and politico-economic metamorphoses today. The linguistic mutation which is developing now on the American continent justifies the poet in the exploration of new possibilities for creative expression. He may fuse the major languages of Europe as well as the linguistic remnants of ancestral forms of speech with a superlanguage the basis of which, on the North American continent, for instance, may be considered a definitely Eur-American language. The latter is already being spoken in all the big cities of America, where immigrant and Anglo-Saxon words have a growing tendency to intermingle.

We are perhaps on the threshold of a new art of the word.

Inquiry into the Spirit and Language of Night
(April–May 1938)

I have asked a number of writers to answer the following questions:

1. What was your most recent characteristic dream (or daydream, waking-sleeping hallucination, phantasma)?
2. Have you observed any ancestral myths or symbols in your collective unconscious?
3. Have you ever felt the need for a new language to express the experiences of your night-mind?

The replies to the inquiry I addressed to British and American writers about the night-mind in relation to creative expression speak for themselves. Perhaps I may be permitted to once more summarize briefly my viewpoint about this problem.

All my life I have been haunted by the idea of Night. All my life I have dreamed and daydreamed. In the little border town of Lorraine, where French and German civilizations sought and fled each other in a ceaseless tension, I spent my childhood before the World War dreaming escape from the millenary struggle of languages and races. There I dreamed my boyhood away in the phantasma of a utopian America, where I was born and which my immigrant parents had abandoned for the ancestral loam when I was two years old. I dreamed my days away, when I worked as an immigrant in my native land—paradoxically my native land—and wrestled with the Columbian reality, with the English language, with the ambience of a continent passing through an industrial revolution. I dreamed my days away as a vagabond newspaperman, gypsying through the North American cities, seeking to solve my intercontinental problem as a human being, as a linguist, as a poet.

Ever the question followed me: Is it I who am dreaming or am I being dreamed? Am I the stage on which some mystic or cosmic forces are playing their apparently irrational dramas? Were the Romantics right in assuming that in the dream we see a game of polarity between the powers of the earth, the daemonic powers, and those of an invisible, celestial, world? Did my dreams reveal the angelic and Luciferian perspectives which my indigenous Catholicism had instilled in me? How can this be expressed?

From a study of my dreams over a period of many years, I am inclined to believe that this vertical principle is definitely at work in my unconscious.

Modern psychology and the discoveries of J. W. Dunne (*An Experiment with Time*) opened new vistas in this exploratory process. The Romantic conception of the night-mind found its prolongation and elaboration in Freud and Jung. Jung's idea of the "collective unconscious"—the demonstration that we continue to carry in our night-mind the ancestral mass inheritance—has been definitely established in my own experience. What Jung calls the "archaic man" is still part of our psyche. Dunne, the engineer, studied his own dreams for many years and established to his satisfaction the existence of a multidimensional world which, he claims, our three-dimensional being is as yet unable to grasp—and I might add, to express.

In my most personal dreams I have often seen an analogy with the secular myths of mankind. The mythological world was revealed in definite reconstructions of the following images: *Death and Resurrection, the Cosmic Fear* (Kierkegaard's *Begriff der Angst; la grande peur de l'an mil;* Heidegger's hypothesis of apprehension before nihility as the basis of metaphysics; Lévy-Bruhl's demonstration of the primitive's fear of thunder, and his discovery of the consequent birth of the supernatural myths, and so on); *the biblical motif of the Conflict Between Satan and Michael; the Nostalgia for a Paradise; the Tower of Babel; the Birth of the Planets; the Legend of Flying, or Conquest of Gravity,* and so on.

Objectively, I have always used the concept of "Night" in a Romantic-mystic sense. It approximated the representation that seems to have been that of Novalis in his *Hymns to the Night,* or that of St. John of the Cross in his vision of the nocturnal universe. The inner dynamis of cosmic time.

Night as the ensemble of unconscious thinking—an emanation of the race and personal memory, as well as of transcendental revelation.

In attempting to express this world of the "night-mind," I instinctively used my native German language at first, since it continued to be the language of my unconscious. I discovered a de-rationalized grammar in which the word and syntax followed the organic laws of metamorphoses contained in the psyche. Gradually I came to try this new grammar in English and French as well, and sometimes attempted an interlinguistic alloyage which seemed to be the exact replica of my trilingual conscious experiences. The images translated themselves into German sounds first and then into new amalgamations which led me to a dream-language of irrationalist nuances. I am still engaged in a search for this *language of night*.

Preface to *Words from the Deluge* (1940)

A new language is developing in the United States. It has no name as yet. It is never used by writers of prose and verse, yet its existence is very real, especially in the urban centers of the country. Nor is it H. L. Mencken's *American Language,* but rather an intensification and expansion of it. It is a super-Occidental form of expression. It has polyglot dimensions. Millions speak it throughout America. It is the embryonic language of the future.

I call it the *Atlantic,* or *Crucible, Language.* It is the result of the inter-racial synthesis that is going on in the United States. It is American English, with an Anglo-Saxon basis, plus many grammatical and lexical additions from more than a hundred tongues. All these languages are being spoken in America today. They form an intercontinental idiom used by millions of Neo-Americans, an idiom that is the result of the ceaseless migrations of peoples of all races and tongues going forever westward during the past hundred years. It is an attempt by the autonomous tongues to retain certain sound-values from the past, and to incorporate these, together with archetypical myths and images, *naturally* into the scheme of the existing American language.

I have lived this language for many years. As a young immigrant I welded the languages of my parents—French and German—with the newly acquired English words, out of sheer necessity for communication. I have observed it in use again and again, in all parts of the United States, wherever I was working as a roving newspaperman. I invented my own *Atlantic* language. I made the discovery of a multilingual form of poetry which corresponded to an inner need in me to express the linguistic monism which was my organic mode of thinking. Part of this poem is written in *Atlantic Language.*

Logos (June 1929)

Poetry is at the crossroads today. The confusion about its essence and power seems to be universal. On the one hand, there are those who, basing themselves on sterile theories consecrated by tradition, seek a retention of values in their formal precision and give us simply a monotonous description of their mediocre universe. Their belief in a new art for art's sake conception through the insistence on false classical analogies tends to celebrate a hyper-individualistic *morale* that makes for the error of positivism. On the other hand, there is a handful of visionaries who, proceeding from a natural disquietude, seek in an inner vision possibilities of hallucinations. They are trying to revise certain values which the past has transmitted to them. They are in open revolt against all naturalistic concepts.

A dilemma faces the modern poet at the threshold of his development. He either will have to abandon completely the attempt to express his universe with the decadent instrument of unpliable and exhausted language matter, or else he will have to try to resuscitate the comatose word. The first alternative is a renunciation of despair. I know of some who have had the courage to do it, who have preferred the immediacy of living and experiencing the primary elements of life to the necessity of handling rusty tools. This attitude proceeds from a profound incompatibility with the efforts of a century that, in its mania for collectivistic leveling, gives the commonplace an opportunity to approach the orphic mysteries without feeling or understanding them. The superficiality of universal education drives the apperceptive mind into a *moral* region of its own, where it hopes the intruder may not penetrate, unless ready for the experiment. The creator

179

who would go on, in spite of the knowledge of a hopeless struggle, has a real love for the great creations of the past, and it is for this reason that he withdraws from the spectacle of the vulgarization of their media.

Not only does the orphic poet try to find the territories of the unknown, to penetrate still deeper into the most abstract limits of his conscious and subconscious personalities; he is also eager to explore new ways of transmitting his discoveries. The problem of language and of the processes of intellection have as great an importance to him as life itself. But it is necessary here to make certain distinctions. The imitators, the sterile parasites, who have misused words to the point of exhausting them, and who, therefore, attempt to give themselves a new lease on life by verbal freaks and literary acrobatics, should be ignored and tracked down. The poet has in himself a vision that is direct and pure. He is interested, first of all, in living life, in experiencing its multiple mysteries. Then he struggles to give adequate expression to his impulse for the essential. It is the conflict between the intensity of his vision and the inadequacy of the existing instrumentalities that force him to seek other methods.

The pure expression of a poetic concept outside of all documentary adhesions may be seen in the experiments made by one or two modern film creators. Through mechanical means they flash before our eyes a series of rhythmitized images which produce illuminations without slavish reference points in our sensual lives. The poet is interested primarily in giving us his world stripped of all superfluous elements. Poetry, using the word as mechanics, may, like the film, produce a metaphoric universe which is a sublimation of the physical world.

The frontiers of the poetic universe have still not found exact delimitations. If we examine the history of humanity, we find certain absolute and immutable values. The psychic personality in its state of spontaneous manifestations is still very much of a mystery to us. But we know that forces are at work below the surface that deform and demolish the conscious recognitions we have of reality. Here life is fundamentally automatic. The rational impulse is without power. The conscious state with its projection of the will through reason tends to lead us away from the enormous forces which create spontaneous movement. We have, however, not yet been able to learn if this conflict between the rational and irrational can be solved. We know that life in its psycho-physiological aspect is a syncretism of two hostile conditions, and it is impossible for us to determine precisely where the scission begins and where it ends.

Poetry seems to develop through the conflict between those two forces.

The tension toward the spontaneous and the organic is the tension toward a state of mind that is functionally an other-world reality. We are near the borderland of the visible and the invisible. The poet passes from the natural order of things into the supernatural. At the extreme limits of his consciousness there is a reality that presents immediately a transfiguration of the concrete. Through his lyrical confessions transmitted in prismatic movement, we get the creative action toward a beyond. He strives for the immediacy of a metaphoric mental perception.

This magic idealism which is a means for destroying the mediocrity of the universe is translated into metaphysical terms. The poet acts in terms of the universal. He feels it to be his function to create the unity of an organism which is composed of elements by nature hostile to each other. Through the autonomy of his visionary operations, he proceeds to the synthesis which alone can satisfy him. He brings together realities far removed from each other, that seem without any organic relationships, that are even tending to mutual destruction. But his imagination demolishes the tyranny of the world by eliminating its customary analogies and substituting new ones.

In order to give spontaneous and radical expression to this impulse, the poet becomes a composer of the word. His artistry lies precisely in the degree in which he succeeds in producing adequately and violently a chemistry of words.

In doing this, he is merely using certain automatic laws that have governed the development of language from time immemorial.* The "genius of language" is simply the insistence of a collectivity on perpetuating a world conception. It is the incessant desire of humanity to find the common denominator. The idea that a loosening of the linguistic material is either a divine prerogative or happens as a sudden phenomenon of common impulses has, of course, been exploded long ago. Changes in the organism of language are made as a result of instinctive individual activity, and the history of philology shows conclusively, through a vast deduction process, that the linguistic evolution from early days was one of constant metamorphosis, synthetism, deformation, adjustments. The unity of human

---

* Universal parallelism in linguistic psychology has recently been demonstrated by the Rev. Marcel Jousse, a French Jesuit. The "rhythmic gesture" which he found to be common to all primitive expression led him to the discovery that the propositional gesture is the universal basis of oral expression. Within those balancings occur the rhythmic particularities. He has found that parallelism, which is "psychological automatism," is the fundamental impulse of poetic art. After studying numerous primitive languages, he applies this to certain modern poets like Mallarmé and Péguy, and demonstrates this general law to his satisfaction.

life shows us that expression had a parallel characteristic in the beginning. The history of Indo-European speech gives us an illustration of the fact that there was a constant growth and mutation through phonetic changes, combinations, duplication of meanings, changes in grammatical canons, sound transmutations, assimilations, abbreviations. Phonetic experimentation played an important role in this. The sound evocations often had the result of changing completely the meaning of the mutilated word. In this historic development we find sometimes that one language borrows from another language and assimilates the foreign word completely. In modern history we have the example of deformations which English, French, and Spanish words underwent in America, as in the case of Creole French on Mauritius, Guyana, Martinique, Haiti, Louisiana, and Colonial Spanish.

The poet should not be dominated by the ideas of pedantic semasiologists. In seeking the flexibility of his language, he is at liberty to create his own laws. He finds that by watching his inner life he is thinking in broken images. The arrangement of these images is a more or less conscious process. But in order to transmit the integral movement of the development, he should have the power to break up the structure which a rigid kind of syntax has imposed on him. Grammar should lose its didactical inevitability when the poet tries to escape the degradation of artificial conformity.

The sharpness and power of the metaphorical vision gives him a superiority in understanding the primordial creation of life. The expression of this should be made through a technique of the word that is parallel with the incentive guiding the evolution of the images in his mind, because we are beginning to realize that, by putting words together in identical and repetitive relationships, we arrive ultimately at creative abortions, and are not faithful to ourselves.

The juxtaposition of contrary realities demands an analogous effort in expression itself. The autonomous vocable can, in a changed interdependence, assume a splendor it never had before. The conventional sense of it is transmuted into something that has suddenly become hallucinatory. It is possible for this word to give us unheard-of allusions and illusions. It is possible for us to arouse the hidden sources of the wonderful in the listener.

By using words that have no longer their traditional meaning, we may thus achieve sensations never felt before. The fusion of components that ordinarily have no relation with each other is a process that has as a premise the unconscious movements within us. For in the dream and the half-dream we find enormous and fantastic affinities which to the rational analysis seem absurd. But they have the magic of transmuting the mediocre values of the real world and of opening up territories which are revelations to the voyager.

The eternal elements in our lives rescued from the treadmill of daily existence through the magic word—that is the aim of the new mythos. The natural passion for synthesis, Unanimism, unity, which the true poet has, becomes the dominating one, when he attempts to develop the interchangeable correlations of the real and the unreal.

The sound of the word which we elicit following an instinctive law becomes new to us, even with old words. If we repeat, for instance, a familiar word long enough we gradually discover that the rhythmic quality dominates us. If we keep on repeating it we find that it will lose its primal etymological meaning. There occurs a subtle metamorphosis. The transmuted meaning approaches an almost abstract concept.

The powerful tendency of children to create words of their own is an embryonic impulse which the poet duplicates. It is also a scientific fact which our observations may bear out that we form strange and exotic words in the state of sleep—words that often are without the slightest reference to those we have known in our waking condition. We cannot doubt that there is a deep-rooted instinct in humanity to make changes in speech. The poet by deforming traditional words or by creating word combinations is only following an organic law of linguistic psychology.

The photographic conception of the word can no longer interest us. We desire a nomenclature that evokes an immediacy and the essence of an abstraction. The *état-limite* of the spirit cannot be expressed through the words which, by dint of having been used and abused, no longer evoke in us the primary image. Words have a reality which the dictionary does not know. Etymology is for the archeologists of letters. We demand the etymology of approximation and apperception.

From Jabberwocky to "Lettrism"
(January 1948)

Aeae Iuo Iao Oia Psinoter Ternops

Nopsiter Zagura Pagura Netmomaoth

Nepsiomaoth Marachachta

Tobarabrau Tarnachachau

Zorokotora Ieou Sabaoth

— Gnostic ritual, 300 B.C., quoted by Hugo Ball in

Das Byzantinische Christentum

The language of poetry has undergone more radical changes in the past fifty years than were recorded during the previous three hundred years. During the seventeenth, eighteeenth, and nineteenth centuries language remained generally static, with the exception, perhaps, of the addition of certain technological terms. Esthetic language, however, hardly varied at all from Racine to Valéry, from Marlowe to Eliot. And this despite the fact that all-important scientific discoveries were being made, that human consciousness was continually expanding, that new dimensions of thought cried out for new expression. Even today, it cannot be truthfully said that academic language has greatly altered during the last four or five decades, and the tragic misunderstandings resulting from persistent use of exhausted terms are only too numerous. What has characterized this period, however, is the continuous metamorphosis which has been taking place on the periphery of academic language, where individuals with sensitive antennae, sensing linguistic decomposition and conscious of the growing trend to abolish the frontier posts of words, have understood that one of the solutions to the problems of verbal Symbolism is to be found in *phonetic* transformation.

When the English mathematician Charles Lutwidge Dodgson took the pen name Lewis Carroll to write "'twas brillig, and the slithy toves," the Victorian public smiled indulgently and placed *Through the Looking-Glass* on the lists of children's books, where it remained until only recently. Today the children have grown up and throughout the world, in many languages, are making their own inventions, some in fun, some in deadly seriousness.

In the latter category belongs the most recent searcher in the jungle of words, a young Sorbonne student of Rumanian origin, Isidore Isou. Two years ago, in a one-number review entitled *La Dictature lettriste,* he proclaimed himself the initiator of a new school of poetry: "Lettrism." Isou is surrounded by an active group of disciples, and their public demonstrations are among the attractions of the Latin Quarter. He has now published a four hundred-page Lettrist manifesto: *Introduction à une nouvelle poésie et à une nouvelle musique,** summarizing his views and claims and giving examples of Lettrist writing. It is a highly charged volume with explosive and frequently megalomaniacal titles such as "From Charles Baudelaire to Isidore Isou," "Outline of Musical Evolution from Claude Debussy to Isidore Isou," and so on and so on. Although the style is frequently obscurantist and the author occasionally indulges in the pseudo-philosophical verbiage that is the plague of modern critical writing, it cannot be said that his ideas lack interest. Nor is it diminishing Isou's merit to say that the Lettrism he defends is primarily a general, didactic theory descriptive of a current that has been noticeable in European letters, as well as in certain parts of the Americas, for almost half a century. In fact, he acknowledges this in his preface when he says: "If this material existed before, it had no name that might make it known."

In France, scepticism concerning the notion that the language of poetry should be limited to traditional, stereotyped phonetics began with Stéphane Mallarmé at the turn of the century. He it was who, under Baudelaire's dictum of Symbolism, translated the sensation of esthetic rapture into a mysticism of language. No one was more keenly aware of the pathology of words than the author of *Hérodiade.* The experience he sought to project belonged to a category for which the old Classical and Romantic vocables were insufficient. He did away with explanations, anecdotal associations, and similes and made things identifiable by means of metaphors. He searched for an almost mystic experience of words, for the triumph of the isolated word as emblem of the Absolute. Mallarmé did not find the language he was looking for, and died still on the quest.

In the line of Symbolist progression, the greatest linguistic virtuoso of modern times was undoubtedly James Joyce. With *Ulysses* he began his self-imposed task of forging "within the smithy of his soul the uncreated conscience of his race," and faced resolutely the problem of the disintegration

* Paris: Gallimard, 1947.

of language. Joyce used onomatopoeia as a major function of his medium and even lifted the despised pun into the realm of poetry and music. He brought into the flux of his narrative of a day in the lives of certain Dubliners the sonorities of the unconscious: hallucinations, dreams, daydreams, human and bestial cries. Here compound words mingle with meaningful sound-words in a bewildering foliation, and not even the cadences of the lowest animal forces are neglected. See, for instance, how humorously he describes such a physiological process as the *borborygme:*

Prrprr.
Must be the bur.
Eff. Oo. Rrpr.
Nations of the earth. . . . Then and not till then. Tram. Kran, kran,
     kran. Good oppor. Coming Krandlkrankran.
I'm sure its the burgund. Yes. One, two. Let my epitaph be.
Written. I have.

Pprrpffrrppf ff.
Done.

This tonal pattern is even more accentuated in *Finnegans Wake.* Here we witness a titanic effort to orchestrate the language or languages of night, through physiological as well as psychic changes, mythological deformations, pluralities of sound rotating around birth, war, death, resurrection. On the first page we find the following *sonorist* evocation:

The fall (bababadalgnaraghtakamminarronnkonnbronntonnerronntun
onnthunnthrovarrhouanwskawntoohoohoordenenthurnuk!)

and a few paragraphs later:

What clashes here of will gents wonts, oystrygods gaggin fishgods! Brekkek Kekkek Kekkek Kekkek! Koax Koax koax! Uala Uala Uala! Quaouauh! Where the Baddelaries partisans are still out to mathmaster Malachus Micgranes and the Verdons catapelting the camibalistics out of the Mhoyteboyce of Hoodie Head. Assiegates and boomerinstroms. Sod's brood, be me fear! Sanglorians, save! Arms apeal with larms, appalling. Killykillkilly; a tol, a toll. What chance cuddleys, what cashels aired and ventilised!

As every student of Joyce knows, these are not nonsense words. On the contrary, they all have meaning. The first quotation contains a multilingual word for thunder, being the celestial cry during the fall of HCE (HERE COMES EVERYBODY; the protean hero of the story); and the second describes the tumult of primitive and historic battles fought around the hero.

Joyce himself, a music lover and singer of great talent and who, as a result of increasingly poor vision, came to possess a correspondingly sensitive ear, was always conscious of the relations of music to language. The theme of the singing, prattling River Liffey is a constant transcription of sounds in *Finnegans Wake*. The ever-changing Heraclitean flow denotes in musical melodies and atonalities a hundred world rivers: the Mississippi, the Nile, the Ganges, the Rhine, the Irrawaddy . . . and being in Vico's sense the cyclical symbol of time-space (riverrun) it characterizes the fluidity of the art of music. The motif of erotic music is also indicated in an early passage beginning: "Sir Tristam violer d'amores, fr'over the short sea, had passencore rearrived from North Amorica," while the motif of discord and conflict is constantly translated in sound-words through the description of the antithesis between Mutt and Jute, Shem and Shaun, and especially between those two characters Joyce himself used to chuckle over while writing the book: Buckley and the Russian General. But throughout, there are constant musical projections, as in the section he once called "Mime of Mick, Nick and the Maggies,"* where we read:

> . . . for Wold Forrester Farley who was found of the round of the sound of the lound of the Lukkedoerendunandurraskewdylooshoofermoyportertooyzooyspnalnalnabortansakroidverjkapakkapuk
>
> Byfall
> Upploud!
> . . .
> Ha he hi ho hu.
> Mummum.

This is a repetition of Vico's thunder motif. HCE slams the door, and the singing children of the household suddenly grow silent. The sonorities of numerous world languages can be traced throughout *Finnegans Wake*.

Contemporary with and in some instances preceding Joyce's musical

---

* Cf. *Transition*, no. 22, 1933.

word researches, was the trend noticeable in European literature before, during, and immediately following the First World War, toward a sonorist hypnosis in poetry. Certain poets began to sense that traditional language was breaking up and that the language of poetry, which still depended on the classical vocabulary for its expression, needed new blood. The structure of creative language seemed to be suffering from a malady which posed a definite problem. With stupefaction these poets realized that they were unable to use the language of their predecessors. In 1912 Hugo von Hofmannsthal published his "Letter of Young Chandos to Lord Bacon," in which he said: "I can no longer write, because the language in which it would perhaps be possible for me to write or to think is neither English, nor French nor Italian nor Spanish, but a language not a single word of which is known to me, a language in which mute things will speak to me, and in which some day I shall be called to account by an unknown judge." Marinetti and the Futurists had just announced their "words in liberty," and in France, Germany, Czechoslovakia, and Switzerland an identical direction was to be noted. These Continental poets sought new sonorities, and some even tried to abolish words entirely. They began to write incantations. Like primitive peoples, they sought a liturgical spell by emphasizing the phonetic value of words, eliminating entirely any preoccupation with mere semantics. Here it is only fair to recall that already in 1897, the poet and novelist Paul Scheerbart* had written sonorist verses. It can truly be said that sonorism (or Lettrism) was fathered by Scheerbart when he wrote:

Kikakoku!
Ekoralaps!
Wiso kollipanda opolosa.
Ipasatta ih fuo.
etc.

Still before 1914, we find Stefan George creating poems in a strange secret language of his own, composed of elements of Romance languages mingled with German sounds. He baptized this language "lingua romana," and it was his chosen vehicle for a series of legends of which the following lines are a sample:

* Born in Danzig, 1863; died in Berlin, 1915. Quotation from Carola Giedion-Welcker's anthology *Poètes à l'écart* (Berne: Ed. Benteli, 1946).

Rosa Gelba
En la atmosfera calida tremulante de odores
En la luz argentea de un diffalaz
Ella respira circundundida de un gelbo fulgor
Envelata tot en una seta gelba
etc.

The Expressionist movement which flourished during and after the first war was particularly active in the liberation of language. The review *Sturm,* edited in Berlin by Herwarth Walden, encouraged primitive stammerings, and published the first purely sonorist verses by Rudolf Bluemner and Kurt Schwitters, as well as the word deformations of August Stramm. Dada, which began in Zurich in 1915, with Hugo Ball, Richard Huelsenbeck, Tristan Tzara, and Hans Arp as cofounders, continued this trend.

Hugo Ball, who planned the programs of the Zurich Café Voltaire, scene of the first Dada manifestations, kept an interesting diary of that period.*

I have invented a new series of verses, verses without words, or sound poems, in which the balancing of the vowels is gauged and distributed according to the value of the initial line. Tonight I recited examples of these poems for the first time.

I wore a specially designed costume. My legs were encased in cothurns made of luminous blue cardboard reaching up to my hips, so that I looked like an obelisk. Above this I wore a huge cardboard collar, scarlet inside and gold outside. This was fastened at the throat in such a manner that I was able to move it like wings by raising and dropping my elbows. In addition, I wore a tall blue and white striped hat. I recited the following verses:

gadji beri bimba
glanridi lauli lonni cadori
gadjama bim beri glassala
glandridi glassala tuffm i zimbrabim
blassa galassasa tuffm i zimbrabim
etc.

Before reciting my verses I read a few program notes: with these sound

* Cf. *Transition,* no. 25, for more complete extracts from Ball's diary.

poems we should renounce language, devastated and made impossible by journalism. We should withdraw into the innermost alchemy of the word, and even surrender the word, thus conserving for poetry its most sacred domain. We should refuse to make poems secondhand; we should stop taking over words (not to mention sentences) which we did not invent entirely anew for our own use. We should no longer be content to achieve poetic effects which, in the final analysis, are but echoes of inspiration.

Tristan Tzara, who left Zurich in 1917 to organize Dada in Paris, manifested his suspicion of words in a different way. His was an exotic drunkenness, and his verbal cascades often produced an exhilarating resonance. In his *Sept manifestes Dada** he gave the following advice to budding poets:

To make a poem take a newspaper. Then take a pair of scissors. Choose from the newspaper an article having the length you wish to give the poem. Cut out the article. Then cut out carefully each of the words that comprise the article and put them into a bag. Shake the bag gently and put the cuttings side by side in the order they come out of the bag. Copy conscientiously. The poem will resemble you.

While still in Zurich, Tzara once copied some African sound poems from an ethnographic volume and, in a spirit of Dada fun, passed them off to his friends as original creations. It is historically true that they appeared under his name in the *Dada Almanach* of that period. This one was called "Toto Vaca":

ka tangi ta kivi
kivi
ka tangi te moho
moho
ka tangi te tike
tike.

But the tendency to orchestrate sound verses was generally much in favor at the Café Voltaire, and Tzara organized combined *Simultanéist* and Dada recitals composed of violently grotesque sonorities that are said to have shocked the staid Swiss habitués of the café.

* Paris: Jean Budry et Cie, 1924.

Another Dada poet and painter, Kurt Schwitters, founded a German variety of Dada in Hannover, in 1920, under the name of Merz. Schwitters's hatred of words became a veritable dogma, and in his desire to rid humanity of words, he wrote what he called his "Ursonata," in 1922:

. . .

lanke tr gl
ziiuu lentrl
lumpf tumpf trl
lanke tr gl
pe pe pe pe pe
ooka ooka ooka ooka ooka
lanke tr gl
pii pii pii pii pii
zuuka zuuka zuuka zuuka zuuka
lanke tr gl
rmp
rnf
lanke tr gl?

But Dada was not alone. Other poets, in different parts of Europe, were also showing marked sonorist tendencies. Among these, one of the first to be cited must be Léon-Paul Fargue who, in addition to a number of prose poems in this vein, also invented beautiful sound poems in which a spirit of Paris folklore is wedded to his linguistic innovations. Listen to his "Air du rat blanc":

Abi, Abirounere
Qui que tu n'étais don?
Une blanche monere
Un jo
Un joli goulifon
Un oeil
Un oeil à son pépère
Un jo
Un joli goulifon
    (Appel)
Tillibeet, mon tí fi fi!

The bilingual Franco-Chilean poet Vincent Huidobro wrote "Altazor" in 1919, in Madrid. Following is a fragment from this sound poem:

. . .
Déjà s'approche oche oche l'hironbelle
Déjà s'approche l'hironselle
Déjà s'approche l'hironfrele
L'hirongrele
L'hironduelle
Avec les yeux ouverts l'hirongele
Avec ses ciseaux coupant la brume l'hironaile
L'hironciel
L'hironmiel
La belle hironréelle
Et la nuit rentre ses ongles comme le léopard
etc. . . .

The Russian poet Iliazd, who settled in Paris immediately after World War I, invented a language he called Zaoum. Iliazd stems from Russian Futurism before 1914, and as early as 1912 he had organized a Zaoum manifestation in Paris. In 1923, still in Paris, he published *Ledentu le Phare,* written partly in Russian and partly in Zaoum, for which the French poet Ribemont-Dessaignes wrote the following introduction: "Zaoum has necessarily a Russian appearance. But there may also be a French, German, English, and international *zaoum.*" Iliazd himself claims that *zaoum* is the "natural language of children and lovers."

After Dada, Surrealism. At the beginning, this group showed a strong respect for linguistic tradition, and it was one of their tenets that all so-called *textes surréalistes,* or dream transcriptions, should be written "in good French." It is interesting to note of late, however, the beginnings of an awakened interest in the problem of phonetics. But Surrealism burst asunder traditional word realities, in itself of immense importance. André Breton brought into modern letters a subversive vision and a scientist's passion for exploration. In the early twenties and later, he systematically sought an explosion of the world of the unconscious, and his *Poisson soluble* marked a date by introducing automatic writing. From this stemmed the *textes surréalistes* which influenced poetry diversely. *Les Champs magnétiques,* written in collaboration with Philippe Soupault, contains known and quotidian words used in astonishing juxtapositions based on the movement of the unconscious. Reading Breton's early texts, one is catapulted into an extraordinary world of sensations by the fact that the habitual situation of the vocable is thrown overboard and new associations formed.

Robert Desnos, one of the early Surrealist poets, who died in a Nazi concentration camp in 1944, wrote poems in what he called *langage cuit*, of which the following fragment is an example:

Mon mal meurt mais mes mains miment
noeuds, nerfs non anneaux. Nul nord
même amout mol? mames, mord
nus nénés, nonne ni Nine.
etc. . . .

Benjamin Péret, in his novel *Mort aux vaches et au champ d'honneur*, has a chapter entitled "Les Paradis voyagent" containing strange phonetic innovations:

un bavard se posa sur mon occ, roula sur mon
cornu, de là sur ma valise, descendit sur mon
percot et me brula une tige. . . .

André Breton wrote recently in *Le Surréalisme en 1947:*[*]

There will be long debates as to the more or less figurative sense which Rimbaud (we can never insist too much on the fact that he was nourished on occultistic reading) intended should be attributed to the words "Alchemy of the Verb"; we shall continue to wonder if the secret of the passionate interest periodically aroused within Surrealism itself by the wordplays of Marcel Duchamp, or Robert Desnos, the discovery of the entire work of Jean-Paul Brisset and the last work of Raymond Roussel, "How I wrote certain of my books," is not due to the extraordinary advance which, through them, the activity of the so-called phonetic cabala has made in our time. Ambelain recalls that it is traditionally cabalistic to maintain that in the "world of sounds" two words or two sounds whose resonances are contiguous (and not merely their assonances) have an undeniable contiguity in the "world of images."

[*] Paris: Editions Maeght.

Breton himself, in a recently published poem, shows a definite interest in sonorist conceptions and even approaches the Joycean neologism:

La Porte Bat
à Matta

La por por porte por
La fe nê tre
Sur l'odeur amère du limurerre
Qui me rappelle Milady de Winter
Hissant son cheautru derrière les losanges et la pluie
Brifouse-bifrousses le plancher est si vieux
Qu'à travers on voit le feu de la terre
Toutes les belles à leur coumicouroir
Comme les hirondelles
Sur les fils où je joue dans les gouttes
D'un instrument inconnu
Oumyoblisoettiste
Au coeur de ce noeud de serpents
Qu'est la croix ses quatre gueules fuyantes suspendues
aux pis cardinaux
   (janvier 1943*)

Although apparently far removed from examples noted thus far, it is not wholly irrelevant to recall here that the primitive peoples of Africa, Asia, and Polynesia are known to use simple sonorities even today as ritual incantations. Certain tribes have a secret, jealously guarded holy language that consists entirely of meaningless sounds. Jules Monnerot, author of *La Poésie moderne et le sacré*,† recently called attention to the existence of an African dialect—Banda—studied by the late Félix Éboué, governor-general of French West Africa, in which the meaning of the language is given through the differences in length and intensity of sounds. Monnerot states that, as a result, every text edited in Banda can be transcribed by musical notation, and he adds that this, in fact, is the easiest method of transcription.

But contemporary folklore has many examples of sound communication, or sound ritualism. The entire world, through the cinema, is famil-

---

* *Les Quatre Vents,* no. 8, Paris 1947.

† Paris: Gallimard, 1945.

iar with the purely phonetic vociferations of Donald Duck, and children's nursery rhymes—*amm stramm gramm* or *eenie meeney miney mo*—belong in this category. Certain popular American songs show increasingly sonorist tendencies—*Mairzie Doats, Hutsutt Rawson on the Rillera, Hey Ba-ba-re-bop*—which approach pure non-word fantasy.

In North and South America there exists a rich sonorist lore among the Indians and Negroes. In Iowa, the Fox tribe has composed dance songs, entirely without meaningful words, to accompany the ritual eating of the narcotic cactus-fruit, or "peyote."* The following is sung as an accompaniment to the swan dance:

ye he wi ya
ye—e he wi ya
yo yo he
yo wi yo wi ya he yo
yo he ya—e
yo he yo
yo he ya—e

The Mexican poet Alfonso Reyes has named the Negro sonorisms of Central and South America *jitanjaforas,* from a poem by the Cuban poet Mariano Brull, "without sense or sentiment," in which that word occurred. Brull's poem, entitled "Leyenda," follows:

Filiflama alave cundre
ala olalunea alifera
alveolea jitanjafora
sula salumba salifera

Olivea oleo olorife
alalai canfora sandra
milingitara girofora
ula ulalundre calandra

Writing of the *jitanjaforas* in his country, the Cuban poet Fernando Ortiz[†] points out that they are "the poetic form of the magical language, a literary

* Noted by Martha Champion Huot (cf. *Transition,* no. 25, 1936).
† Cf. *Transition,* no. 25.

survivor of the mysteriously liturgic black art of conjuration which is still alive and cherished by many who listen to it because of the irresistibly hypnotic, emotive force of its rhythm." In the opinion of Ortiz, it is African rhythm, through its onomatopoeia, that has produced new syllables in the languages with which it has come into contact. Among a number of examples, he gives the following:

tam-bor (drum)
timbal
bombo ba-to
en-co
cum-bo
tum-ba
tam-tam
chan-gi
tun-tun
rum-ba
bon-go.

It is of course not possible within the framework of this article to do justice to all the experimenters in this field.* It has been our desire to name the pioneers and chart the main currents, in so far as they have been represented in Occidental literature during the period under discussion. But however cursory, it is nevertheless evident from this short account that Isidore Isou has done little else than to gather these currents together and organize them into a personal theory. Curiously enough too, although claiming direct descendence from a most distinguished line of French poets—Baudelaire, Verlaine, G. Kahn, Apollinaire—he neglects to mention any non-French precursors (all the more to be wondered at in view of his own non-French background), with the result that when the "Lettrists" organized their first public manifestation in Paris (January 8, 1946), there were a number of claims to priority. For the sake of history, it should be recorded that M. Iliazd, the father of Zaoum, organized a counter-demonstration during which he proved to the satisfaction of his audience that others had had a major share in the "Lettrist" revolution. The title of his lecture was: "Après nous le lettrisme."

Monsieur Isou's book is a vigorous *apologia pro verbo suo*, an ardent justi-

* Cf. *Transition*, nos. 1–27 (1927–1938) for numerous other examples of linguistic experimentation.

fication of his "Lettrist" ideas. Like Schwitters and a number of others, he wants to abolish words entirely, only he is in favor of a fusion of poetry and music. "With this synthesis," he says, "we shall constitute a single art, a stream which will flow on, without bearing within itself traces of any original differences. The old forms are already transformed into a single formulation, and the two rivers have now joined together in a single idea." He sees concert halls being used by poets and musicians, without distinction.

Developing his theory further, Isou draws a sharp line between the two artistic categories he calls *ciselant* and *amplique:* the "cerebral chemistry of bookish art," the personal, *nuancé* art, on the one hand, and an amplifying, epic-lyric, impersonal art with communal trends, on the other. He created these two categories, he says, because existing categories no longer correspond to the modern temper: neither the antithesis of Apollonian and Dionysian, nor that of Classical and Romantic, nor that of Symbolist and Realist, have any meaning today, because one personality may possess several of these simultaneously. For Isou the *amplique* hypostasis is the full moment of any art; it appears with the first artistic tendencies. The work is massive, and because it is creation on a grand scale, it is rudimentary. All this would appear to bear close resemblance to post-Wagnerian *Expressionism.* In any case, "Lettrism," we are told, announces an "amplic" period.

Isou wants to create word symphonies, and he considers that the new art of the word "should produce a new series of creators, the first of whom will be Isidore Isou." In a footnote, he adds that he wants to play the same role in poetry as that "played by Jesus in Judaism, that is, it is Isou's intention to break a branch and make a tree of it. . . . Isouism: a Christian form of poetic Judaism." Isou is too young to have heard the great Polish pianist de Pachman who, when he had played a particularly brilliant passage before an adoring public, would turn and say for all to hear: "Bravo, Pachman!"

In his concluding chapter, entitled "La Lettrie," after repeating his imperative for a synthesis of poetry and music, Isou gives full rein to grandiose visions of the future:

Lettrist poetry, which was a sect of poetry in its beginning, will become a new separate and true poetry. . . . We know there will be frightened persons who will utter cries of warning because they will only see the past in this present and a mixture in this new form. For all these traditionalists we shall show ourselves to be as usual even more *passéistes* than they are. We shall hark back to more ancient times than they are accustomed to recall. We shall bring to the bar witnesses of *the prehistory of their wanted knowledge.* Because at the beginning of *their* beginning (in the true beginning, *which was before all differentiation between music and poetry*) there had been the years of primitive growth. At that time, there was *an identical flow,* the result of *an identical source.* There was no question then of musicians and poets, but of *storytellers who sang and spoke at the same time.*

With unwonted modesty, Isou adds:

> As for the author, Isidore Isou, and the role he wants to attribute to himself at the beginning, it must be said that he does not know just how the new scales, bars, and letters will eventually be transcribed. Nor does he know who will make this discovery. . . . But in the end certain composers will turn to him. As in every art, they will converge toward their origins and their beginnings.

Rejecting, finally, his immediate elders, he affirms that "Surrealism is dead and quote, dead," and that he and his friends mark the end and the beginning of an era. But let him speak for himself:

CALVAIRE
Iouda ! Iouda !
cloacalacloun, foulcalacloun
SALE JUIF, saljuif, saljuif !
   CROOUDA ! CROOUDA !
M* ouaste—waste—wist A† B‡
Jésuischrist
JESUS CHRIST !
CHRIST !

JE TE SUIS DANS TES ILES, GAUGUIN
Hioké ! Kioké ! rkioké
Koklikokette !
Haîhaîîarara

* M, m = gémissement.
† A, a = aspiration.
‡ B, b = expiration.

Gui ! Tahitiha tapapaoula !
Tapapaoula ! tahitipé !

It is of course inconceivable that the poetry of the future will be based exclusively on Isou's "Lettrism," and his fate will in all probability resemble that of his precursors, for it only represents one facet of the complex linguistic situation we face today. Yet, with this reservation, the writer does not hesitate to say that "Lettrism" is a valuable movement. Isou's own poems are often filled with a mysterious, fluid, and dynamic "amplic" force. They remind us of cries and exclamations which are vital elements in carrying the emotional flux of a collective fraternity. My own research, while including a quest for sonorist rhythms, follows a more ecumenical direction.

Part Four : **From Romanticism to the Avant-Garde**

Introduction

Perhaps the most common indictment leveled against German Romanticism points to its potential for a nationalist, *völkische,* if not totalitarian ideology, exemplified by some of Johann Gottlieb Fichte's writings, which Jolas singled out in his broad post-1945 review of the era. Jolas now had doubts about the legacy of the movement, as suggested by his distinction between "White" and "Black" Romantics, and his hitherto unthinkable inclusion of the idol of his own poetics, "gentle Novalis" (whose work he still continued to translate after 1945), in such revision. How then are we to understand Jolas's persistent vision of a "new Romanticism" during the troubled interwar period, and even as the Second World War raged on in apocalyptic force, when the atrocities of National Socialism were no longer a secret? All along Jolas stubbornly maintained that "Romanticism is not dead."

Obviously, Romanticism did not simply connote a historical time period or particular movement for Jolas, but rather the creative process as a spiritual phenomenon. He was always clear in his belief that art needed to be transnational and transcultural, in short, "universal," and as such "timeless," to challenge stale traditions. These qualities are seen at the center of Romanticism's exploration of the unconscious as manifested in the dream, in folklore, myths, and legends. We must not forget that in spite of his essential belief in the primacy of the spiritual in art, Jolas stayed a Catholic at core. As such he was also attracted to Romanticism in terms of an aesthetics still rooted in religion and containing a narrative of the "struggle between Lucifer and the angelic forces."

The representatives of his "Pan-Romanticism," whom Jolas wanted to recognize in the twentieth century, were a varied array of modernist and avant-garde writers (as documented by us in part 6, "Literary Encounters"). None of these authors would have even understood such an idiosyncratic label for their work, just as it is difficult today to take seriously Jolas's grouping of Kafka with Benn, Carl Einstein, or Joyce. Nor can we readily follow his Romantic genealogy which valorizes Dada (his Alsatian preference for Arp, or the mystic Hugo Ball) over Breton's Surrealism. Yet, despite its obvious differences, the best of modernist and avant-garde writing for the editor of *transition* constituted not a "break" (Peter Bürger's theory of the avant-garde) but rather a continuity with idealism (Renato Poggioli's view). Characteristic, indeed, is the century's experimentation toward an alternative literary language, while we simply can no longer connect a Jolasian "vertical," "spiritual," dimension with the understanding of an epochal "linguistic turn" since Nietzsche.

—C.R.

Romanticism and the Dream (June 1936)

Modern interest in the dream began with the Romantics.

Yet the dream has been a subject of preoccupation from time imme-morial. Primitive man translated his dream into sagas and myths. The Greeks examined the problem of the dream particularly from the view-point of its mantic interpretations. Penelope's dream of the eagle swooping down among the geese in the *Odyssey* is well known. Plutarch talks about dream-books of a crude kind that flourished in his time. Aristotle wrote about dreams, in which the Freudian wish-idea was anticipated. Heraclitus studied the image-associations in the dream.

But it was the great, the unique experience of the Romantic move-ment that brought the dream-problem to the attention of the recent era. Hamann's statement that "passion alone gives hands, feet, and wings to abstractions and hypotheses" showed a deep insight into the workings of psychic phenomena. The powers of the unconscious, alogical, daemonic, instinctive were suddenly recognized as having a preponderant influence in life.

The Dionysian principle was discovered. Men like Hamann, Herder, Novalis, Jean Paul, Schlegel, Tieck, Schelling, Brentano, Achim von Arnim, Franz von Baader, and later Fechner, E. T. A. Hoffmann, Justinus Kerner, G. H. Schubert, and so on opened a gap.

To Herder "the dream was the paragon of all poetry." To Novalis it became a religious and metaphysical experience and was incorporated in his esthetic. He said: "The dream is prophetic—the caricature of a mar-velous future." In *Ofterdingen* he said: "It seems to me that the dream is a rampart against the regularity and commonness of life, a free diversion of the chained imagination, where it mixes up all the images of life and interrupts the constant seriousness of the adult with a merry children's game." Tieck's William Lovell believes that "a deep meaning can be found in apparently confused dreams, if only man would observe well enough and be less held down by terrestrial things." Jean Paul states that "the dream is involuntary poetry." Fr. Schlegel finds "an inner duplicity in waking-thinking as though we were thinking in twos." Franz von Baader asserts that there is "an inner seeing which is not communicated by the external senses." Schelling states that during the moment of falling asleep and in the dream there is a state "which surpasses the liveliest representations in the waking state."

The dream with the Romantic poets became the real basis for all creative action. It is for this reason that I have always insisted in *Transition* and other places that this was the modern creator's link with Romanticism. Much in that movement seems to us today obsolete, dusty, ready to be thrown overboard. But the great irrationalist researches of the Romantic poets continue to fructify our conceptions.

Romanticism Is Not Dead (1941)

When the great revolution of the spirit which history called Romanticism was paralyzed by the advent of the positivist-mechanistic age a hundred years ago, it seemed to have run its course. To be sure, dialectically inclined minds who remembered that Romanticism was precisely the heterodox antithesis of a previously existing state of mind—illumination, *Aufklärung,* enlightenment—could easily have deduced that a similar development of polar counteraction would follow the apparent demise of historic Romanticism. As a matter of fact, this is exactly what has happened. Mechanistic rationalism seemed to be in the saddle for a long time to come, although Romanticism as a state of mind continued to live a catacomb-like existence throughout the last century—the stupid century, as Léon Daudet unjustly called it—and toward the end of that century it began to flourish once more, slowly, at first, in fragmentary elements of the Symbolist movement, then in Expressionism and Dada, and finally in Surrealism. It was in Surrealism that it found its most recent apogee.

Now we are again in the midst of a Romantic revolution in the arts—and in life—which is sweeping across continents with the force of a tidal wave. It is part of the apocalyptic sensation which we all experience in the present social convulsions accompanying the war, and it is also the expression of vast creative forces that are preparing the way for a spiritual resurrection.

The electric conflagration which passed through Europe between the period of the French Revolution and about 1835 did not really leave a unifying doctrine behind. It was constantly fighting for its own definition.

207

There was rarely an agreement between all the adherents of the movement. It never arrived at a final conclusion, and contradictions of temperaments and philosophies were frequent. Yet its adherents did agree on one important issue: they were all anti-rationalists. They were all explorers in the vast empire of the psyche. They were voyagers on incessant columbiads for the understanding of the night-side of life. They wanted to pierce the mystery of the great currents in the unknown territories of the human soul. The search for unity in life was their principal objective.

The cult of the unconscious which the Romantics had as their common aim was prepared by certain precursors who had fought against the "enlightenment" of the preceding centuries and had tried to reinstitute an interest in the freely growing organism. Rousseau undoubtedly was the great dynamic force that loosened this direction. Herder's discovery of the folk-soul of the races, Hamann's researches into the inner world of man, the Storm and Stress epoch, the mood of the English Gothicists, the cult of genius, and many other similar tendencies of the day all gravitated around the preoccupations with this psychic liberation. The French Revolution gave the entire movement a decisive impetus. The Romantic war began in the mood of social decay and death, and continued for several generations in a march toward a rebirth.

The Romantics worshipped everything that bloomed organically and died; that which existed through the power of its inner life, not through will; that which was calculated to unite, rather than divide. This, they maintained, could be found in art, religion, nature, history. Philosophically it was "the possession of the transcendental self." They were attracted by the magic and beauty of medieval Europe, Gothic Europe, and many of their rank thought they could rediscover that period in the Catholic Church. A number of them, therefore, became converted to Catholicism, and their Catholic Romanticism went like a golden thread throughout the entire movement. The Orient lured them, magically, with the evocation of far-off wonders, and philologically, for it was the source of Indo-European discoveries concerning the genesis of language. Never before had the human spirit seemed so bent on voyages of discovery. Philology, mythology, psychology, folklore, religion, history were reexamined from the angle of this fluid mentality. They discovered the creative force inherent in all the sagas and legends of the peoples. They discovered the proverbial wisdom of vanished times. They wanted to arrive at a great synthesis, to portray the wholeness of existence, the unity of life. The dream and daydream were studied by Novalis, Jean Paul, Schlegel, Tieck, Lichtenberg,

Troxler, Carus, Schubert. The poets and storytellers saw in the dream the exact analogy of their creative work.

The Romantic surge became a great reservoir of new ideas in France, Germany, England, and America. Although the creations rarely achieved the last polish, rarely achieved total greatness—the *fragment* was a characteristic of the Romantic mentality—it left an enormous heritage in belles lettres and critical analyses that have fructified our modern thinking. There is a direct line from Nerval, Novalis, Coleridge to Nietzsche and Freud, and it is difficult to imagine the modern evolution of our understanding of irrationalism in psychoanalysis without the spadework done by the Romantic precursors.

The proliferation spent itself on the rocks of the mechanistic rationalism which appeared toward the middle of the last century. G. T. Fechner, the physicist and dreamer, remained one of the last links with the Romantic past. For five decades or more the Romantics were neglected, or denigrated, or simply rejected. The Victor Hugo of the latter period, Baudelaire, Rimbaud, Saint-Pol-Roux, Lautréamont, Wedekind, Hofmannsthal, Maeterlinck, Rilke were the prophets of the Romantic reconstruction. The World War unleashed again the long-hidden world of the night, and the explosion of Dada became the very symbol of the new Romanticism in Europe. Surrealism systematized the revolt, under André Breton.

There had been numerous signs in the beginning of this century that Romanticism was about to awaken. Already in 1906 the late Jacques Rivière published an essay in the *Nouvelle Revue française* entitled "Introduction to a Metaphysics of the Dream" which marked an important date in literary history. It was the first time that a modern writer had proposed the investigation of the unconscious as a source of literary creation. "The vertiginous reality of the first sagas," he said, "is to be found in the silent whirring of the dream, and the writer must look for it in the somber and magical upsurge in which things become as beings." The interest in primitive culture—folklore and plastic representations—which was developed by the early Fauves and Cubists before 1914 was already a sign of the times. Everywhere form began to loosen. A new sense of reality appeared in the lyrical and prose texts of the Continental writers.

The postwar crystallized the new Romanticism. But it became apparent, as the Second World War got under way, that it favored only the darker and more sinister side of Romanticism. Today, while the world is on fire, it is apparent that the Romantic spirit dominates once more the collective mood of the age. Although abhorred by Fascist corruptors, it colors the monumental struggle through which warring mankind is passing. It is a process of metamorphosis which still remains without conclusion in psychic, political, or artistic manifestations.

But the Occident is beginning to think in terms of metaphysical categories again. Certain of the basic ideas of the Romantics are to be found once more in the politico-social and cultural philosophies which are beginning to emerge today. We can only hope that the new Romanticism will be an ascending one. We can only hope that the creative spirit may follow the transcendental idealism of Novalis, Coleridge, Troxler, Baader, or even Brentano. We can only hope that the new orientation will be directed toward metaphysical ascensions and celestial perspectives. This direction, containing possibilities of universal and cosmic relations, may then expand our consciousness into a superconsciousness in search of an absolute reality.

Pan-Romanticism in the Atomic Age (1949)

If there exists a single unifying line traversing the entire activity of *Transition,* it might be called *Pan-Romanticism.* Many of the writers whose original or translated work appeared in the twenty-seven numbers of the review belonged to that heritage of visionaries which was epitomized by the continuous attempt to find a synthesis through philosophical and philological transformation. *Transition* contained elements of Gothic, Romantic, Baroque, mystic, Expressionist, Dada, Surrealist, and, finally, verticalist modes of thinking. In the last phase it tried to blend these traditions into a cosmic, four-dimensional consciousness.

Most of the writers were aware that the social convulsions of the epoch could be exorcised only through psychic freedom. In this striving toward a magic idealism, some of them sought the redefinition of old terms that had become exhausted and overladen with a contradictory aura. They invented new words for the expression of newly discovered areas of the psyche. In the war against all forms of totalitarian nihilism, they strove for complete liberation of the creative mind.

James Joyce pursued a Pan-Romantic objective by breaking through archaic literary forms. He explored the mythic unconscious of his heroes and invented a new language of many dimensions. Ernest Hemingway is a Pan-Romantic in that he searches for geographical and spiritual realities which will transfigure the nostalgia for love and death. André Breton is a Pan-Romantic in that he has continued Gérard de Nerval's and Achim von Arnim's descent into the abyss of chimeras and liberated the imagination by applying Freud's theory of free association and automatic writing. Franz

Kafka was a Pan-Romantic in that he recognized Kierkegaard's doctrine of existential fear as a basic emotion and presented man's tortured migration toward the light as the will to escape from the prison of existence. Dylan Thomas is a Pan-Romantic because of his metamorphosis of Welsh folklore, his use of the myth of man's renascence, and the wealth of his metaphor.

Romanticism was presented in *Transition* as early as 1928, by translations of Novalis, Jean Paul, Hölderlin, and others of this epoch. The *Hymns to the Night,* which I translated into English in 1929, do not sing of the bitter conflict between the finite and the infinite but grow out of a certainty of redemption, a spiritualization of the sensual, in which the real and the transcendental worlds interpenetrate. Preoccupation with the nocturnal was a characteristic of the early Romantics, for whom the dream and the daydream, the fairy tale and the fable constituted sources of a future literature. To them poetry and life were identical. This may have been mere *Schwärmerei,* as the philistines insist, but it was also an attempt to demolish the dualism of spirit and nature, of the I and the non-I.

After periods of *Realism* and *Naturalism,* the *Romantic* idea came to life again in the great *Symbolist* movement of Mallarmé. It ended in the dream-monologues of Maeterlinck's plays. (Maeterlinck, it should be recalled, was the first to translate Novalis's *The Disciples at Sais* into French.) There were *Neo-Romantic* movements in both France and Germany in the early years of the twentieth century, but not until the explosion of the First World War did a modern form of Romanticism, under the aegis of Freud and the psychoanalytical school of Zurich, foster the magical operation of the inner world again. Such *Expressionists* as Franz Werfel, Georg Trakl, Carl Einstein, and others presented a frontal attack against naturalistic materialism and made possible a revolution of the soul. They liberated both form and language and reintroduced the metaphysical and the numinous into life and art.

Dada was born in Zurich in 1915, when Hugo Ball, a German poet, Tristan Tzara, a Franco-Rumanian poet, Hans Arp, an Alsatian poet and sculptor, and Richard Huelsenbeck, a German poet, along with a few others, gathered at the Café Voltaire for readings and lectures. The wild irrationalism of their utterances expressed their insurgence against a war-mad world. Looking for a suitable appellation, Ball and Huelsenbeck chose the word *dada,* which they found quite by chance in a Franco-German dictionary. They invented sonorist verses and developed an anti-literary style in which the absurd was the quintessential element. The war ended, the movement soon reached Paris. By this time Hugo Ball had withdrawn, having returned to the quietism of his Catholic faith. With the early Dadaists, language was a method of conjuration, and their poems—especially in the case of Arp's verbal phantasmagoria—became fairy tales in sound.

Surrealism, under the leadership of André Breton, continued the irrationalism of Dada, but systematized its anti-doctrinary elements into a rigid dogmatism. It was based on certain Romantic and post-Romantic predecessors (Achim von Arnim, Lautréamont, Rimbaud) and drew heavily on Freud's discoveries. In 1924 Breton gave impetus to the movement with his *Manifeste du Surréalisme.* He surrounded himself with a brilliant group of young poets and painters, among whom were Benjamin Péret, Robert Desnos, André Masson, René Crevel, Antonin Artaud, Paul Eluard, Philippe Soupault. The exploration of the dream and other tenebrous aspects of Romanticism found expression in automatic writing and the famous *textes surréalistes* which Breton and Soupault inaugurated with *Champs magnétiques.*

Harking back to Novalis and Jean Paul's symbolism of the flying dream, *verticalism* revolted against the nightmare quality of its predecessors and inaugurated an attempt to liberate the human personality from the possession of nihilism. It stressed the creative urge toward a liturgical renascence by reconstructing the myth of voyage, migration, flight, and particularly ascent, in all its Romantic-mystic manifestations. It sought the "marvelous of the skies" in the poetry of aeronautical flight, in the conquest of the law of gravitation, and in an aspiration toward aerial perspectives. It also developed the poetry of cosmic or sidereal flight, tried to sing of the stellar spaces, and accentuated the vision of the "third eye." In the poetry of mystic flight it sought a transcendental reality. This new poetry of ascent wanted to express its vision in a language that would make possible a hymnic vocabulary.

Romanticism and Metapolitics (after 1949)

When, at the close of World War II, members of the allied Psychological Warfare Division undertook to denazify and democratize German intellectual life, they were obliged to face the fact that certain elements of Nazi "ideology" had undoubtedly been rooted in Romanticist currents of over 150 years before. Many of the Nazi documents found revealed a parallelism between the murderous tenets of the Hitlerian usurpers and those professed by the poets and philosophers of what had been one of the richest periods in any modern literature. Liberation of the concentration camps was to uncover further horrible evidence of what long fermentation of the seemingly innocuous utterances of that time had done to the German spirit. The fates of millions of human beings tortured and massacred in the name of Teutonic supremacy were shown to have been linked to that older epoch when, traditionally, an elegiac idealism was supposed to have prevailed.

In the face of the collective sadism which the descendants of the Romantics had demonstrated with such unbelievable violence, those Allied representatives who loved poetry and the manifestations of star-hungry Humanism that had marked the activities of the earlier group could not help but feel a sense of betrayal. Indeed, they asked themselves if it was still possible to speak of the German Romantics in terms of pure idealism and absolute poetry. Was it still possible to evoke the example of the incomparably sublime writings of those night-drunken creators without recalling that their work had foreshadowed to a certain extent the systematized terrorism of the Nazis, that it had contained the germs of the most vicious anti-Humanism? In the light of recent events, biological racism, anti-Semitism, aggressive nationalism were all detectable to a greater or lesser degree in the works of such writers as von Kleist, von Arnim, Hölderlin, Görres, and others, all of whose writings bore the mark of the Promethean, even Luciferian, elements apparently inherent in the Teutonic soul.

It is well known that many Romantics were attracted by chaos, dementia, the "abyss"; also, that some of them were authoritarian and anti-democratic in spirit. Johann Gottfried Herder, pioneer of the Sturm und Drang movement, and friend of the Romantics, sought to develop a concept of Nordic superiority over Latin civilization by advising his countrymen to "spew out the ugly slime of the Seine." He also insisted on the *Volk-Nation*, asserting that "the light of the so-called 'Enlightenment' was eating round about itself like a cancer." And this at a time when France was about to launch the "Declaration of the Rights of Man" with the immortal slogan of "Liberty, Equality, Fraternity!"

Even that most Dionysian of poets, Hölderlin, stated in his novel *Hyperion*:

A people in which spirit and greatness have ceased to beget spirit and greatness has no longer anything in common with those who are still men. Such a people has no more rights, and it is but an empty farce, a superstition, to insist on honoring those corpses that have no will of their own. . . . Away with them! They steal light and air from young life ripening toward a new world. . . . This will be the burden of my song . . . there is no need to say more. . . . Oh, light me a torch that I may burn these weeds from the heath, give me dynamite that I may blast these inert clods from out the earth!

There was also that other enthusiastic Hellenist, the Hanoverian philosopher Friedrich Schlegel, who, discussing the "tribal" aspects of the nation which should be "unconditionally its own master," wrote: "The older, purer, and less mixed the stock, so also are its customs: and the more this is true as regards customs and a really persistent attachment to them, the more this stock will constitute a nation."

It is not, however, until Fichte and, after him, Hegel, have made their contributions to philosophical thought that we find an absolutely clear statement of the aims which Germans were to follow doggedly from then on until their recent *Götterdämmerung*. Fichte was the first to urge a "new order which alone is the true order," and it is interesting to note that he also argued in favor not only of total national autarky, planned economy, quota systems, concealed inflation, a blocked currency, and state barter agreements, but also of artificial production of substitute materials, intensive armaments, *Lebensraum* for German nationals, forcible occupation of neighboring territories, complete economic coordination of such territories, transfer of populations, and an aggressive, consciously cultivated nationalism and anti-Europeanism. This was embryonic, essentially German Socialism—and National Socialism, in other words—and it must not be forgotten that its genesis dates from 1800, when the Romantic movement dominated the entire mode of thinking in Germany.

After Prussia's defeat at Jena, Fichte delivered his *Reden an die deutsche Nation*—a series of lectures; given in Berlin, in which he made an impassioned appeal to his compatriots to recognize their "national greatness" which, he claimed, could not be denied them in view of their all-pervading originality and superiority. This was particularly exemplified, he claimed, by their language, "which has been alive ever since it first issued from the forces of nature, whereas other Teutonic races speak a language that has movement but is dead at the root." According to Fichte's theory, it was obvious that "only the Germans . . . are really a 'folk,' and entitled to count as such; that they alone are capable of real and rational love for their nation." These are but a few samples of the theories which encouraged Germans to adopt any means that might make it possible for them to emerge from their, at that time, prevalent sense of inferiority. On the political side, the fact that the new German cult of nationalism was to a considerable degree imitative, looking as it did to the already flourishing national life of France and of England, tended to make it all the more emphatic and megalomaniacal in proclaiming its originality.

There were other Romantics, poets this time, who fell in line with these notions: Heinrich von Kleist, for instance, declared that "things would have gone better for Europe if Voltaire had been forgotten in the Bastille and Rousseau placed in a lunatic asylum." Achim von Arnim distinguished himself by founding a "Christian Germanic Society" from which "Jews, Frenchmen, and philistines were to be especially excluded." There was also that mediocre poet Ernst Moritz Arndt, who declared: "We are Germans. . . . We are the navel of the European earth. . . . We know that the Greeks set their Delphi in the center. . . . Where are our oracles and prophecies? . . . The fighters and avengers will come: Let this be the latest oracle." Arndt also wrote: "Must this be only a dream? I trust not. . . . The

German eagle will fly higher and higher with new spirit and energy, and the sound of its wings will attract the white Nordic falcon, whose feathers droop in lonely sorrow upon rock and cliff now that the Gods and Heroes are gone to their graves, and history is silent." In a lesser degree, the gentle Novalis too showed traces of these innate Germanic tendencies, and the dialectical principle, which was to be adopted by Hegel, was one of the philosophic concepts noted by him in his *Fragments:* "Thesis and antithesis are the terminal points of a line, and the line is synthesis." The French philosopher and poet Jean Wahl has written the following comment on this note:

> In the Novalisian sense, there is no animation of thought except when extremes communicate. . . . The man Novalis dreamed of is in constant contradiction with himself. He unites extreme sensibility and extreme energy, surplus and dearth, seriousness and gaiety, melancholy and enjoyment, childhood and wisdom.

In 1814 Fichte died and his chair at the University of Berlin—he was its first rector—was occupied by the philosopher Georg Friedrich Hegel. There is little need here to go into Hegel's philosophy, except to recall his notion of the State as a superior entity. The modern concept of the autocratic State is, however, directly traceable to Hegel, and both Hitler and Stalin based their ideas of an anti-Occidental oligarchy on his teachings. For Hegel, too, the Germanic spirit was "the spirit of the new world, the aim of which is realization of absolute truth as endless self-determination."

Despite this rather damning evidence, we may entertain legitimate doubts as to whether the Romantic poets, whose vision was a cosmic one and whose dream was of liberty and universal love, would ever have accepted the abject, anti-Humanist regime of vicious illiterates and criminals known as National Socialism. In his preface to the postwar edition of *Le Romantisme allemand* (first published in 1937),* Albert Beguin writes:

> Never did the Romantics push the experiment of chaos so far, with such blind constancy and such internal logic, as did the contemporary Germans. . . . The spiritual adventure of the German Romantics never sinks to the depths in which the larval "myth" of Hitler and Rosenberg came

* *Cahiers du sud,* Marseille, 1949.

to flower. . . . But to ignore their inner correlations would be to under-estimate both the exceptional grandeur of Romanticism and the true nature of Hitlerian frenzy; as also the particular misfortune of a nation destined to manifest with such precision, and at the cost of so spectacu-lar a downfall, the present state of all humanity.

Stars and Angels: Homage to G. Th. Fechner, Romantic Savant and Visionary (1941)

One of my favorite intellectual companions in my migrations has been Gustav Theodor Fechner, the poet-scientist who lived from 1801 to 1887. His monumental book *Zend-Avesta,* not yet translated into English, to my knowledge, has always stirred me in moments when I felt the hideous universe of larvae too much with me, when the hypocritical dogma of mechanism and materialism seemed to be triumphant. He was a discoverer of genius in the physical sciences, but more than that: he was an explorer in the domain of the psychic and poetic, and his transcendentalism had a cosmic dimension.

I think it was James Joyce who first mentioned his name to me. Since that time I have seen references to his work again and again in scattered places: Algernon Blackwood, in his fantastic novel *The Centaur,* speaks of him with elegiac enthusiasm. William James in his *Pluralistic Universe* pays homage to Fechner in the following words: "I doubt whether we shall ever understand certain abnormal or supernormal facts without using the very letter of Fechner's conception of a great reservoir in which the memories of earth's inhabitants are pooled and preserved, and from which, when the threshold lowers, information ordinarily shut out leaks into the mind of exceptional individuals among us."

Fechner dreamed the "world-soul." Human consciousness was to him a universal consciousness. The world, he thought, is not at all the antithesis between the natural and supernatural, it is simply the natural and the spiritual combined. The whole universe has a soul: stars and planets, birds and plants, every organism has a soul. (He also wrote a book called *Nanna,* in which he attempted to prove that plants had souls.) The universe is a living organism and each part of it is articulate. Everything, whether it be stone, plant, a piece of loam, a star, has a definite consciousness, and man thus has an organic connection with the entire world. To Fechner the world was monistic. We live in each other and are part of each other. There is a deep spiritual meaning in everything of the natural order. He called his main work *Zend-Avesta,* because this sacred book of the Zoroastrian system stirred him deeply, when he found that good and evil had been personalized and made into living things. The world has a plurality of souls, and is thus a plurality of sentient beings.

Fechner applied this idea to the whole of the universe. He believed that stars and planets were higher beings, living, articulate organisms, and that they represented angels. I have selected for English translation a brief chapter from *Zend-Avesta* where this idea is expressed.

Every element has as inhabitants its special organisms which are adapted to it in their structure and mode of living. The solid earth beneath us has its moles and worms within, and human beings and animals on it; the water has fishes and the air has birds and butterflies. The heavenly ether, the element that fills the entire worldspace, has as its inhabitants the world-bodies, sun, moon, stars, and planets, and they are adapted to their element like the fish to water, like the birds to the air.

The cosmic bodies are higher beings adapted in the higher element to a higher way, to a higher life which, of course, cannot be immediately comprehensible to us in our lower mode of thinking. They swim in the ether without fins, they fly in it without wings, they wander about in it, hugely and quietly, the way everything that is sublime wanders about; they do not race anxiously around; nor do they look for food; they are satisfied with the light they send to each other. They do not shove each other about, but wander in a clear and harmonious direction, each following the slightest urge of the other. And in thus submitting externally to an eternal order, they develop internally the greatest liberty, an inexhaustible wealth in intellectual and bodily creations, formations, and aspirations.

All the religions of antiquity, especially the oriental ones, prove the fervent correspondences between star-service and angel-belief. We want merely to reduce the old faith to its true origin. The viewpoints of the Old and New Testaments, which lift God out of the world, and take Him into a void, as it were, had, when meditated upon with consequential logic, naturally to take the angels, who are God's subjects, also away from the cosmic bodies and direct them into the void. And the same anthropomorphism, which forms God according to our image, had also to make beings resembling men out of angels. But if we let God again fill the body of the cosmos with His omnipresence, then the angels, too, will take up their old places as stars among stars.

Prolegomenon, or White Romanticism and the Mythos of Ascension (undated)

In my European childhood an emotion I shared with most of my young friends was that of a vague nostalgia or *Sehnsucht* for Sirius-far phenomena that we grouped under the name *das Wunderbare*. The *Märchen,* poems and folk tales we read or listened to during long, snow-whirling winter evenings, evoked the "marvelous" of Grimm's and Andersen's magic tales, as well as that handed down by word of mouth through local legends in which the irruption of the supernatural was like a lyrical explosion. We experienced the wonderland of night, with its sidereal splendors, as seen from the tops of old, medieval castles and expressed for us in Ludwig Tieck's enchanting, albeit facile verses:

> Wunderbare Mondennacht,
> Steig' empor mit alter Pracht.

We were indeed youthful visionaries playing in old gardens and mysterious forests, or in meadows redolent with *primula veris* and fragrant herbs. We lived on intimate terms with the neighboring forests and rivers, and we worshipped birds because we felt they were messengers of freedom. Once we had consciously situated this fairy-tale world, we began to talk pretentiously of our "romantic souls." The words *Nacht* and *Sehnsucht* became almost sacred, and when our teacher read us the dream of the blue flower as told by Novalis, we set forth on pilgrimages to that occult symbol, which became a veritable obsession. Our idealistic professor had a private library in which the classics predominated: Goethe and Schiller, naturally, but especially the Romantic works of Novalis, Tieck, Heine, Hoffmann, and Jean Paul; and we were allowed to borrow them for reading at home, whenever we wished to do so. We hated the modern Germany we saw about us, the Germany of grotesque militarists of world expansion, and we lived mentally in the pious legendary country of 150 years before, when the great Romanticist Jean Paul Richter could proudly say: "To England belongs the empire of the sea, to France that of the land, and to Germany that of the sky."

Our imagination was both intuitive and utopian, and we dreamed of landing on far-off shores in some yet-to-be-discovered America of the mind. I personally developed this fantasy to the point of frenzy. I wandered across vast prairies in an invented Western land, I lived in Rousseau-like simplicity in surroundings of unspoiled nature. Some years later, after my actual emigration to America, which was my native soil, I was still under the spell of these childhood dreams, longing for lands of saffron sunsets, for a repetition of the Columbian voyage. Already I aspired toward Eur-American unity, an Occidental monos, interracial synthesis, a universal language. I envisaged a frontierless cosmos, a future world in which the genius of poetry would reign. I dreamed of a world from which nationalistic feeling was absent, and where love was the only law.

While working as a reporter in numerous American cities, I envisaged a metropolis of crystal skyscrapers that would compensate for the wretchedness of the existence I observed about me. My first poems, written in German during my early American reintegration, mirrored this metallic Romanticism.

The wander-urge drove me east again, and for years I roamed across Occidental Europe and then back to America. But the Romantic quest has taken me even deeper into the inner universe. Immediately after the First World War, I settled as a newsman in Paris, where I became acquainted with Maeterlinck's studies of the Romantic epoch and his translation of Novalis's *The Disciples at Sais*. I picked up André Lichtenberger's *Novalis* (1912) on a stall along the Paris quays, and this, too, opened up new perspectives. The French Symbolists seemed to me to have points in common with the Romantic writers.

In the 1920s I detected with excitement certain Neo-Romantic currents that were beginning to be visible, and this excitement increased when I met a number of French poets whose outlook seemed to be dominated by tendencies analogous to those found in the works of the early Romantics.

Dada irrationalism had its source in the oneiromantic idealism of Novalis and Lichtenberg, and Surrealism, as defined by André Breton, was but a modern prolongation of many Romantic doctrines. In Germany, too, the explosion of the Expressionists quite evidently constituted a modern manifestation of notions that stemmed from their Romantic predecessors. In each case, of course, a profound extension of the original ideas had taken place. Thus, under the influence of Freud's and Jung's teachings, a distinctly contemporary efflorescence of unconscious manifestations was accompanied by attempts to discover new words for their expression. The poems of Rimbaud, Mallarmé, Hugo, Baudelaire, Lautréamont, and de Nerval kindled our imagination.

From its very inception, in 1927, I conceived the review *transition* as a Neo-Romantic organism. Under an approximately collective ideology, I tried to gather into it the leading Pan-Romantic writers—Surrealist, Dadaist, Expressionist—who were striving to expand human consciousness. James Joyce, leaving behind him his naturalistic-Expressionist period, which stretched from the *Portrait of the Artist* to *Ulysses,* was entering upon a Pan-Romantic period with his *Work in Progress,* in which the night-world was to be explored once more by a poet of genius who, in addition, was able to invent the linguistic instrument that would permit him to give expression to these irrational concepts.

In the late 1920s, in the pages of *transition,* I sought to revive interest in the work of Novalis by translating and publishing certain of his poems and fragments. However, "Homage to Novalis," which appeared in 1929, attracted little notice, the critics of that period being interested primarily in what they termed "Proletarian Realism." They were inclined to look with disdain, in fact, on all metaphysical or metapsychic manifestations. So the gesture was classified as untimely, and it was not until several years later that the ever-receptive Mary Colum picked up the idea in her excellent *From the Roots.* In *Axel's Castle* Edmund Wilson sought to situate Villiers de l'Isle-Adam's drama *Axel* as the fountainhead of a Neo-Romantic outlook. Early in 1931, I myself composed a modest *plaquette* entitled *The Language of Night,* in which the Novalisian genesis was strongly emphasized. In 1937, M. Albert Béguin brought out his *L'Ame romantique et le rêve,* and there appeared as well a remarkable issue of the *Cahiers du sud* devoted to a collective study of German Romanticism. These two books marked a date, and interest in Romanticism began to grow apace in France. Béguin's contributions, particularly, had a profound influence on French writing before the Second World War, and continue to have it today.

Rereading carefully the writings of Novalis, one is struck by a leitmotif which is apparent in his philosophy of "magic idealism," that is, a grandiose attempt to merge life's contradictions into a higher unity, into a superior amalgam of nature and spirit, world and God, reality and idea. To this poet, life was ascent and descent in continuous alteration, and his final solution was an upward metamorphosis in which man was envisioned as a star, or sidereal being, tending toward realization of the ascensionist affirmation of a new "golden age." Certain features of later thinking have revealed a similar direction. The philosopher and psychoanalyst G. T. Fechner believed in animate star-dwellers, thus anticipating certain modern hypotheses concerning a possible challenge to the law of gravitation. In 1943 the French philosopher Gaston Bachelard published a work entitled *L'Air et les songes,* in which he studied the theory of psychic ascensionism in the writings of Blake, Novalis, Shelley, Rimbaud, and others. The Swiss psychologist R. Desoille, in his *Le Rêve éveillé en la psychothérapie* (1949), used the dialectics of rise and fall in the waking dream as an active form of therapy in the treatment of neuropathic patients. Finally, Gustave L. S. Mercier, in his philosophical work *Le Dynamisme ascentionnel,* synthesized the methods of philosophers and scientists, from Bergson to Einstein and Bohr, in an attempt to create a new ontology to be based on the most recent discoveries.

For over fifteen years the present writer—under the banner of "verticalism"—has been pursuing parallel investigations in the creative domain, in an attempt to find a four-dimensional consciousness having cosmological perspectives. *Verticalism* or *vertigralism,* which I launched first in *transition* and later independently, represented a modern application of extreme Romanticist notions. It was a "white" Romanticism, however, in contradistinction to such "black" Romantic manifestations as nihilism, Dadaism, Surrealism, existentialism. It sought to discover the transcendental principle dormant in the daemonic chaos of the age, and hailed the astronomic and mystic imagination. It proceeded from Kierkegaard's concept of primordial anguish toward the primacy of poetry's spiritual transmutation. As the years passed and humanity progressed into the apocalyptic age (which may be said to have begun in the early twenties), my own development followed more and more a verticalist direction. I wrote an astronomic fantasia, *Session in Astropolis,* which had certain elements of the paramyth or what was later to degenerate into "science fiction," based, for the most part, on the American dream of the nuclear fantastic. My poems "Planets and Angels," "Vertical," "I Have Seen Monsters and Angels," "Mots-Déluge," and so on were all strongly influenced by the philosophy of Novalis's *magic idealism.*

It is quite possible to distinguish between *Black* and *White Romanticism.* If, for instance, we call Achim von Arnim, with his cruel fantastic stories, a *Black Romantic,* we may also assume that Novalis, who saw mystic or transcendental night as the Romantic ambience par excellence, professed a *White Romanticism;* and Jean Paul, who wrote dream-sagas of space travel, was the antipode of E. T. A. Hoffmann who, with his evocations of grotesque and hallucinatory events, symbolized the Luciferian side of Romanticism. For Romanticism constantly sought its own definition, but without ever finding an ultimate formulation. Novalis alone, who in his brief life attained to the role of both poet and seer, attempted to discover a new territory through an ascensionist, seraphic vision.

This is still the quintessence of the philosophical quest of today; the struggle between Lucifer and the angelic forces is still in progress. And poetry is more than ever the logomantic art of the word which tries to incite the human being to take wing to spiritual summits. It also seeks to exorcise the lower, or daemonic, powers.

For us, Novalis remains the poet and seer who sought the reality of the invisible world: "The heart seems to be the religious organ," he wrote, "and the highest product of the creative heart is perhaps nothing other than the sky." His mystique was that of the ascensionist mythos.

Surrealism and Romanticism (undated)

The analogy between German Romanticism and French Surrealism has been pointed out many times, especially by Albert Béguin in his great work *The Dream and the Romantic Soul*. Now comes the Mauritian poet Malcolm de Chazal, and in a letter to André Breton—which the latter reprints in the "Surrealist Almanac of the Half Century" in the current issue of *La Nef*—he states the following: "France saddens my heart. She is lost to true spirituality. You are not a Frenchman. You are a German—of the race of Novalis and Rilke—whose mind is turned arrow-like to the Orient—the ever-lighted lamp in the belfry of Divine Wisdom." This is the most direct statement about a phenomenon in France that always seemed to me more Celtic than Latin that had to go beyond its frontiers to become a living reality.

Is it not a significant fact, however, that Surrealism has conquered certain circles in North and Central America, in England and Ireland, but has never taken root in Germany, which gave the Surrealists of the early period their direction? Achim von Arnim, Novalis, Jean Paul, and so on, over a hundred years ago. The two books I mentioned above have had hardly any repercussion so far, as one might have expected, and during my long stay in the ruined cities of the Rhine I have encountered little interest in unconscious expression.

But the high objectives he set himself in the early years—the metamorphosis of man—have certainly not been realized. I believe in an ascending Romanticism as the only answer to the problems we face today, a spiritual verticalism which leads to a subliminal consciousness.

Surrealism: Ave atque Vale (1941)

Mr. Jolas, after being in the vanguard of various literary movements for many years, has settled down temporarily to write of his part in them. It gives us great pleasure to publish a first section from his autobiography now in progress, an autobiography which is to be not a mere anecdotal narrative, but a panorama of an often amazing period in its intellectual and spiritual quests. For evidence that Mr. Jolas has not deserted his position of prominence in the new literature, we suggest that you consult Truncations *for notice of "Vertical."*

The age-old city of Marseille presents a curious spectacle today. A year ago it was still France's busiest, most colorful port. Today its population is swollen by the presence of thousands of strangers, the majority of whom are marking time while waiting; some for visas that will permit them to envisage an escape to a happier life, others simply for the end of the war which, they hope, will restore to them their liberty of thought and movement. Among those who have been drawn by the tempered climate of this Mediterranean city are to be found the names of some of France's most distinguished intellectuals. And so it happens that in a little inn, famous for its port wine, in the old harbor, where one can see the Chateau d'If, not far from the cosmopolitan brothel district, there meet today the last remnants of the French Surrealists. Their leader, André Breton, still presides over his faithful adherents, as he did at the Café Cyrano and the Café des Deux Magots in Paris, before the cataclysm began. In the apocalyptic twilight of Europe, this insurrection against modern civilization continues its explorations into the sub-rational powers of the unconscious. From a friend who recently left Marseille, I learn that the game of the *cadavre exquis*—an automatic collective experiment that flourished among the Surrealists in Paris in the twenties and thirties—is the pastime of these exacerbated rebels today. Despite a belated attempt at transplanting the complex of this irrationalist nihilism to the American continent, I, nevertheless, predict that, in the Phoenician city, we are witnessing the death-throes of this movement. There is every indication that this revolutionary Romanticism is nearing its end, for the horror of the present reality has surpassed the wildest attempts of its members to create a universe of monsters.

Yet when it began, in the early twenties, the hopes for a total revolution in the arts and letters seemed to be justified. It was in 1923, in Strasbourg, that I first heard of Surrealism through the medium of my friend Marcel Noll, then one of its earliest militants. At that time I spent many of my leisure hours in the Alsatian capital, and Noll talked to Henri Solveen, another poet-friend, and myself about his Paris friends. He insisted that I should meet André Breton and Paul Eluard, with whom he was then intimately associated. The Surrealists themselves frequently visited Strasbourg during that period, because the city seemed to them a symbol of the Romantic outlook they were seeking. This was also doubtless what had always attracted me to the frontier city from early childhood. Curiously enough, however, we never met in Strasbourg, and it was only some six months later that Noll introduced me to Eluard in Paris. Noll, Solveen, and I would wander through the cathedral city on the Rhine, and, thanks to the cheering flow of Traminer wine, our conversations often lasted until the early morning hours. René Schickelé, the Expressionist leader, the border-man, the dreamer of the Alsatian bridge-idea, occasionally joined us. In the old-fashioned inns near the cathedral, we experimented in the writing of collective poems. One of us would start a line, another followed, a third added to this, and the results were read with great hilarity. Sometimes we managed to produce a kind of verbal dementia, a wild *coulée de mots* that excited our lyrical imagination. We usually wrote these *poèmes en commun* in German, but on several occasions Noll added French lines, and I added English lines, thus creating what we felt to be a new multilingual genre.

Back in Paris, Noll presented me to Eluard, and we became friends. Eluard and his Russian wife, Gala (now Mme. Dalí), lived then in the suburban town of Eaubonne, where I visited him with Noll and my brother Jacques, the pianist. He had a remarkable collection of paintings, principally Picassos of the so-called blue period, and primitive objects from the

South Seas and pre-Columbian America. He had recently returned from a long voyage that had carried him as far as Easter Island, and he narrated his adventures with gusto. Eluard was then, and has remained, the most gifted of all the Surrealist poets. But I always felt he was a pure poet, in spite of Surrealism. Sometimes in a café he would suddenly begin to write a poem on the shabby notepaper supplied by the proprietor, and I was always astonished at the rapidity with which he penned his incantatory meditations. My brother shared our apartment then, and he played for us—Chopin and Schumann and Scriabin—whenever the Eluards came to see us, although Eluard confessed to an intellectual suspicion of music. I would argue that it was certainly the most Romantic of the arts, but he said he felt an inability to *feel* music. This attitude was part of the early Surrealist creed. A year before the war Eluard told me he had changed his mind, that singing especially delighted him, and that he had allowed his poems to be set to music. There were days when Eluard, Noll, and I would wander all over Paris in search of primitive objects for Eluard's collection. We would visit the flea market where he was usually lucky, and where he showed a fine instinct in distinguishing the shoddy from the unusual or decoratively facile.

Benjamin Péret, Robert Desnos, Max Morise joined us during the following months. I was then working as a journalist on the Paris edition of the *Chicago Tribune,* and Noll often brought his Surrealist friends to the office at night. The real exodus of Americans to Paris had not yet started. Elliot Paul, with whom I was to launch *transition* some years later, had not yet joined the newspaper staff, and our American organization was composed of old-fashioned newsmen from every part of the United States. My colleagues would goggle at these weird Surrealist bohemians who brandished their anarchic gestures with gay nonchalance.

Péret, a tall, powerfully built man, possessed, undoubtedly, the most subversive mind I have ever encountered. He wrote luridly vehement poems against the Church, the State, the Family, the Fatherland, the Army. They were redolent of coprolalia, but often had a lyrical tang which redeemed them creatively. He had a remarkable genius for language, and his essays in a phantasmal Paris argot, invented by himself, always amused me. I think his writings, in general, were the most irrational of any of this group. He was fond of public scandal, and his private manifestations in the streets of Paris showed a certain courage, if not callousness. The sight of a priest's cassock aroused his anger, and he never failed to hurl the most scatological insults at an ecclesiastic, whenever he passed one. One day I was sitting on the *terrasse* of a café with him when he saw a little nun walking by. The sight of the poor woman seemed to lash him into an insane rage. He left his seat and shouted: "Ah, vieille vache!" His face was livid, and he shook his fists at her. Other customers took the nun's part, and there arose a bitter brawl that ended only when a policeman intervened. The humble little sister did not file a complaint, and the matter was dropped.

Robert Desnos, on the other hand, was more urbane. He was a pure lyric poet, and had also strong mediumistic gifts. I think his *La Liberté et l'amour,* a fantastic and illogical parody of the detective story, which we later published in *transition,* influenced many American writers. André Breton would organize seances at which Desnos' occultistic *talents* diverted his friends. He seemed to be really living in a universe of the unconscious, and his automatic writings had an air of the genuine. In those years he wrote certain of his poems in what he called *langage cuit* (cooked language), that often resulted in striking word fantasies. His inventive virtuosity derived from his Dada experiences and added new color to Surrealism. Max Morise wrote comparatively little. He seemed more interested in the anti-literary negativism of the movement.

I think of others who emerged in that crucible of the phantasmatic and Romantic during that period. Michel Leiris, neurotic and unpredictable, who decomposed the words of the dictionary in order to reconstitute it with poetic *calembours.* He is now a prominent member of the Musée de l'Homme at the Trocadero in Paris. Philippe Soupault, who seemed to synthesize in himself that new *mal de siècle,* whose poems were tinged with a far-ache for visionary Americas, who smashed everything in front of him. His latest letters to friends in this country are filled with a nostalgia for America. I think of Joseph Delteil, already ill, yet feverishly working in Montmartre. I interviewed him in his little room on the top floor of a dilapidated building. A *foire* was in progress in front of the house. He was reading proof on his *Jeanne d'Arc,* and spoke of Surrealism as the beginning of a new age. Unfortunately a vehement quarrel broke out between him and Breton, who declared that *Jeanne d'Arc* was a "saloperie," and booted him out of the group with an acid letter, at the very beginning of the movement. I think of Roger Vitrac, who wanted to reintroduce the drinking of absinthe, and who was primarily interested in a Surrealist theater based on Jarry and his grotesque humor. He did not stay long in the group, being quickly at loggerheads with the dictatorial policies of Breton, and left, "slamming the door." There was Antonin Artaud, poet, playwright, cinema actor, who took drugs, and had apocalyptic visions. I remember Georges Ribemont-Dessaignes, who had written Dada plays and poems, and, after a while in the Surrealist fold, left the "shame of literary Paris" to become a humble innkeeper in an Alpine village. There were Maxime Alexandre, Jacques Baron, and others. Georges Hugnet, then the darling of Gertrude Stein, complained to me that he would like to be a member, but that his advances had been repulsed by Breton. He finally entered the sect in the lean years of the thirties. Louis Aragon, who shared leadership with Breton, participated in the paroxysm with brilliant manifestoes, especially with *A Wave of Dreams,* which crystallized certain directions.

Painters and sculptors flocked to the Breton standard in the spirit of the irrationalist dementia. There was Max Ernst, who had come to Paris from his native Cologne, after having been a German Dada revolutionary. He was a great friend of Eluard's, and we met in Eaubonne. He spoke very little, but sat quietly, absorbed in the visions of his "haunted brain." There was Giorgio di Chirico, and his brother, who would sit in cafés for hours, occasionally exchanging a word or two, then falling into silence once more. There was André Masson, with his submarine magic and Dionysian madness. There was Hans Arp, one of the founders of Dada in Zurich, who hailed from Strasbourg. Arp is a sculptor as well as a poet. He read me his strangely constructed quatrains, written in a deformed German language, which always struck me as picaresque word fairy tales. He told me stories of the Zurich Dada revolt: of Hugo Ball, its real founder, who after a year of the Dada tumult, retired to a Swiss mountain in 1918 and became a mystic, writing his *Byzantine Christianity* with a hagiographic pen. He spoke of Tristan Tzara, the *anti-philosophe,* who had come to Paris a few years before from Zurich and created a lunatic Dada mood in the French capital; who wrote prose poems of great beauty and verbal felicity; who presided at public manifestations in which everything was intermingled: futurist *Bruitism, Simultanéism,* poetic license, sneers at bourgeois prejudices—a maniacal tom-tom. Arp lived in Meudon, near Paris, with his wife, the sculptor Sophie Taueber-Arp, and I often visited them in that mood of an unreal dream which characterized their atelier. The newly founded school of Surrealism had not accepted Tzara into the fold, after Breton and his friends had decreed the death of Dada, because of a personal quarrel between Tzara and Breton, which was not patched up until some years later. When I first met Tzara he seemed at loose ends.

A group publication, *La Révolution surréaliste,* appeared, after *Champs magnétiques* by Breton and Soupault had crystallized the new orientation. This book of automatic writing marks a literary date. The two poets had begun these *poèmes en commun* with an explosive richness of imagery, and it proved to be a discovery, Freudian in its genesis, that was to create a new style of writing in France. Whether or not this was a fruitful insurrection, it is still too early to say, but it was the first conscious effort ever made at collective automatic expression. The book crackles with a disarming illogic and contains grammatical innovations that impinge on the reader like sputtering machine-guns. Breton, a short time later, issued his *Manifeste surréaliste,* which became the Bible of the group. In it he continued, alone, the experiment of the *Champs magnétiques,* and his *Poisson soluble* was a success in subjective-idealistic writing. The first issue of the *Révolution surréaliste* was a disappointment to some. It contained manifestoes, essays, and poems by diverse persons more or less loosely connected with the new group. But somehow it did not seem to hold together. With the third issue Breton himself took over the direction, and from then on, it was truly "the world's most scandalous review." It became a laboratory for the exploration of sub-rational forces, publishing automatic dialogues, dreams, hypnological experiences, erotic investigation with the emphasis on Freudian pan-sexualism, poems, and reproductions of photos, paintings, sculpture, and objects. All the artists and writers mentioned above participated in it, and each number seemed to whip the delirium more savagely than the preceding one. During this period Breton organized a dream-laboratory in the rue de Grenelle, but this did not last very long because of the intrusion of the bourgeois element, not to mention the numerous aristocratic hangers-on.

I met André Breton at his home in the rue Fontaine, Montmartre, early in 1925, when I called on him in connection with the literary column I was then contributing to the Paris edition of the *Chicago Tribune.* A heavyset young man, who at first sight seemed phlegmatic, but who soon revealed a tendency to acrid utterances, received me. A wild shock of hair encompassed a magnificent head of leonine dimensions. He had a courteous manner, but his inner tension betrayed itself by a nervous walking up and down, and a staccato manner of speaking. His study was filled with Picassos, Massons, Tanguys, di Chiricos. Through a window could be seen nocturnal Paris, could be heard the vague rumble of the megapolis.

He explained his philosophy with an emphatic delivery. "The Surrealists," he said, "were trying to apply the revolutionary principle to everything. We are interested in a total metamorphosis of life and man," he insisted. "*Il faut changer le monde*," said Rimbaud,

> and we intend to do it with every means in our possession. . . . We are for the subversion of the bourgeois ideology in all its forms of life and art. . . . Our philosophical idealism is dynamic. . . . It includes an integral nominalism. . . . We want to fight the Church and the State, the entire odious morality of the middle classes. . . . When I hear the word God, I feel like vomiting. . . . We have found a subversive instrument in the dream, for it helps us transform the reality we loathe. . . . Our Freudian conception of love is another instrument for battering down the bourgeois mentality. . . . When someone cries *Vive la France,* we cry Vive l'Allemagne. . . . We want to uproot our civilization through black humor.

But at that time Breton was already moving toward a Marxian reorientation. He showed me a batch of documents, mostly letters exchanged between himself and members of another group in Paris, that of Esprit (which had nothing to do with the present review *Esprit*). The attempt was made to find a common ground for Communist revolutionary action. They even discussed the founding of a collective review to be called *Clarté,* but it was impossible to make the synthesis, and the collaboration ceased. Politzer, Morhange, Gutermann, of Esprit, withdrew, and the Surrealists continued alone. Breton did not see any conflict between his nascent Communism and his earlier proclaimed idealism. He vehemently defended this evolution, and quoted Hegel and Berkeley, Marx and Engels, Freud and Lautréamont. "We really have no literary ambitions," he continued to me. "We do not want to take part in their filthy games of prizes and judgments uttered by cretins of the blackest kind. . . . *Nous sommes en quête du merveilleux.*" His insistence on the word "marvelous" stirred my curiosity, for I had been a reader of the German Romantics since early boyhood, and was aware of the identity of viewpoint between the Romantics and the Dada and Surrealist tendencies. The word "wunderbar," "merveilleux," was the objective of creative work posited by the Romantics a hundred years before, and was part of their vocabulary. The dream, too, had been decidedly a Romantic preoccupation. Breton spoke of this parallelism, and even repeated the dictum of Novalis that "the novel must end in a modern fairy tale." He spoke of the English Gothicists, notably Monk Lewis, and of Hölderlin. He said he had read Novalis in the translation by Maeterlinck. His knowledge of psychoanalytical literature was extensive—he knew German rather well—and he related Freud to the Romantic movement. He also claimed that certain late Symbolists were Surrealist before the letter: among them St. John Perse, Léon-Paul Fargue, Saint-Pol-Roux-le-Magnifique. He spoke with admiration of Achim von Arnim and the imagination of the monstrous. He rejected all the other Romantics.

I was a friend of some of the Surrealist poets and artists, but I never was an official adherent of their principles. I approved of their general direction, which, then, still seemed to be aimed toward a metaphysical end. Sometimes I participated in their morning and evening sessions at the Café Cyrano, where Breton discussed the new problems with his friends, and where plans were made for their subversive forays into the bourgeois world of Paris. Numberless were their public demonstrations in the galleries, in cinemas, in theaters. They kept the spirit of heresy alive with the sniping and shooting of their destructive actions.

I remember accompanying them one evening to the Closerie des Lilas, the well-known café in Montparnasse, for a banquet given by the Surrealists in honor of the aged poet Saint-Pol-Roux. They had invited the Symbolist recluse to come to Paris from his hermitage on the Brittany coast and receive the homage of the young poets. They had also invited a number of other members of the Symbolist school, notably Rachilde, the aged novelist, to be their guests. Soupault, Desnos, Aragon, Eluard, Baron, Vitrac, Leiris, and all the others were present. Desnos spoke excitedly about an interview that had appeared that afternoon in the *Intransigeant*, in which Mme. Rachilde had stated she would never receive a German into her home, no matter what the pretext. This was about 1925. Desnos considered this an affront to the human spirit. The banquet began. Saint-Pol-Roux, a white-haired patriarch, had the seat of honor. One felt electricity in the air. Suddenly Desnos rose and shouted: "I refuse to stay in the same room with a woman who this very day expressed such sordid sentiments." Someone cried: "Vive l'Allemagne!" and others followed it with: "A bas la France!" A bottle flew across the table, and soon a general melee ensued. Mme. Rachilde fled into an adjoining room. Saint-Pol-Roux ducked under a table. The police were called, and the battle continued with clubs and fists, Leiris being particularly bent on assaulting the *flics*. At the police station they were booked under the general heading of: Brawl Between Intellectuals, and released a few hours later. Breton, the next day, officially withdrew the homage to the Symbolist poet.

On another occasion they decided to avenge some derogatory remarks that had appeared about them in the *Nouvelles littéraires*. They went to the offices of the journal, barged into the editorial rooms, threw all the typewriters into the street, and created a wild disorder on the premises. They were arrested again and released. At a *matinée poétique* given by a traditionalist group of poets in the Vieux Colombier, Breton interrupted a reader of poetry with the remark: "We refuse to listen any longer to this exhibition of cretinism. *A bas la poésie française!*" Scattered in the audience, the Surrealists then began to scream and catcall, and they were arrested again. Their manifestions also took the form of pamphlets written with extreme fury. Now it was against Paul Claudel, whom they attacked for his Catholicism and patriotism during the war, now against di Chirico, who, they considered, had betrayed his early creed. Or again they wrote in favor of Rimbaud, quoting his strongest anti-French statements during the Franco-Prussian War, and they rode to the poet's hometown in Charleville, to placard the walls with posters against the reerection of his statue, destroyed by the Germans during the war. The bourgeois of Charleville, they said, had never appreciated Rimbaud during his lifetime. Meanwhile the internecine war inside their group went also apace. Early in 1927, Soupault was ejected by Breton. That same evening I had invited the Eluards and the Soupaults to be our guests, without being aware of the expulsion that had taken place a few hours earlier. Eluard refused to speak to Soupault, and the latter left in great emotion.

In this Pan-Romantic tumult, I started *transition*, with Elliot Paul as my associate. It seemed to me that we were on the threshold of an Elizabethan flowering in Eur-American letters. A visionary and magical renaissance was dawning in Paris, and I wanted *transition* to be a part of this élan. I wanted to present English translations of Surrealist texts, and thus help free the imagination which I thought was shackled by the Midwestern desiccation. At that time the Surrealists were loath to collaborate with any review other than their own *Révolution surréaliste,* or at best, *Commerce.* It took time therefore to obtain permission to make the transliterations. It was finally given, and I was able to present dreams, poems, *textes surréalistes,* and so on in Englished forms, by Eluard, Péret, Noll, Desnos, Leiris, Soupault, Breton, as well as reproductions of all the painters. That was in 1927, and after a year of this, *transition* became mistakenly known as the American Surrealist review. Under the impression that we had sold out to the Surrealists, Communists, and other Bolshevik *fauves,* Wyndham Lewis, in his *Enemy,* and later in his *Diabolical Principle,* made a frontal attack on *transition.* Other critics pounced on the novelty, and their heavy artillery kept up the barrage from America, England, Australia, and even India. Some six years later Surrealism was acclaimed by the snobs, literati, dealers of London, and thanks to Dalì, a latecomer to the fold, it also finally became the fashion in the United States. But *transition* undoubtedly had borne the brunt of the attacks during the pioneering days. I accepted all this cheerfully, because I felt in sympathy with the Neo-Romantic outlook and anti-bourgeois passion of the Surrealists, and because Breton—whose spirit I admired always—had succeeded in gathering around him the most provocative and the purest poets and artists of modern times. I wanted to make *transition* an organ for a modern Pan-Romantic revolution. The *early* Surrealists and ourselves were undoubtedly fellow travelers.

But was it possible to go on piling metaphor on metaphor without a mythic or religious basis of any kind? Could one, in the thirties, when the shadow of the new world-cataclysm began to fall on us in the strange, alien mood of Paris, go on celebrating the exclusively monstrous, the grotesque, nihilistic, chthonic, as the sole points of departure of a new vision? Could man, with an increasing spiritual nostalgia, find his roots in the gallimaufry of phantoms and fetishes, of cheaply hermetic texts that finally ended in the *poncif* and the pseudo-Romantic cliché? Maggots began to crawl through the living corpse. It had become a hybrid made up of Marxism and idealism, of Trotskyism and Freud, of Sade and Jean Paul Richter, of schizophrenia and the *Foire de Paris*. The movement, with all its deadly contradictions, has spread to England, to North and South America. But in France it was already dying, some time back, in spite of the drugs administered by its leaders. It became a mysticism without a mystique, as someone said of it. It avoided the ontological problem, and turned with revulsion from all transcendentalist preoccupations. The principle of *chance* ended in a hysterical subjectivism. The postulates of the unconscious and the erotic instincts led to the stupefaction of chaos.

I lost interest in this movement in the early thirties. Certain of its adherents have split with Breton and joined the Social Realism of Moscow. Others have grown silent, or have launched independent activities. The war in France has undoubtedly given the *Surrealist Revolution* its death-blow, and the *cadavre exquis,* despite its migration to the Mediterranean port, remains an escapade into a vacuum.

Part Five : **Crisis of Man and Language: Verticalist/Vertigralist Manifestoes**

Introduction

Staying in a New York "sky scraper hotel" in 1933, riding up and down precipitous elevators, Jolas could, as it were, tangibly experience the Western spirit of "verticalism" of which he stubbornly wrote, much more abstractly, before and after the rise of Nazism and its myths of "blood and soil." Yet Jolas rejects much of the contemporary experience, for instance, the "photographic or acoustic realism" of "mechanical inventions" such as radio, cinema, or television, at least in their contemporary and merely functional state, for his review of the significance of modern culture. Written and spoken language, after all, was the richest medium for the communication of transcending ideals. "Interlingual" New York was foremost a bubbling crucible of nationalities, where differences were overcome in improbable harmonies by means of the lingua franca, an American English enriched by the experience of multiple immigrant cultures. If Jolas "fell in love with Manhattan all over again," it was because New York, the "Weltstadt," spoke to his transatlantic heart and his desire for a universal society.

Jolas thus was led to view even the Depression as foremost a *spiritual* and *aesthetic* crisis. Politics, especially radical political visions, were bound to remain mere symptoms of the era's crisis of the imagination, perceived as such by the best European and American writers, he felt. His concept of community, as at stake in modernity, was also informed by his experiences in Paris as a member of a wider international circle of creative minds, the center of which for him was staid James Joyce. Yet in his insistence on a "vertical," or spiritually "ascendant," *Weltanschauung,* Jolas was often further apart from the writers whose work he translated into English than he wanted to realize. For him art had a cultural mission to fulfill: to generate a "collective spirituality" based on individual creativity. Jolas's vision of the "primal personality" was clearly influenced by Gottfried Benn's essays on the subject, which he had translated for *transition*. The German poet's turn against the Cartesian subject was marked by a return to preconceptual man as an aggregate of ultimately unintelligible biological forces. Nevertheless, Jolas took a fundamentally idealist stance against any form of regressive "dark" Romanticism as the harbinger of the excesses of racism, nationalism, totalizing authoritarianism, or worse. His idea of a global community of the "new man"—here he borrows a key notion of German Expressionism—was essentially based on forms of expression experimenting with the linguistic medium in its aesthetic *and* ethically communicative dimensions.

A creative approach to language would bring about forms of *myths* adequate to the crisis of meaning in the modern age. A constructive balance needed to be found between the irrationalism of the past and the rationalism of the present; the primal emotion had to be given concrete form anew. In Jolas's new mythology such is the task of the "logomantic" poet, whose "paramyths" are to dissolve the boundaries between the physical and the metaphysical, the word as concept and the image as experience.

—C.R.

On the Quest (December 1927)

The misconception with which the experiments of *transition* are being received in many quarters necessitates once more a clarification of the general ideas underlying our venture. We have no intention of indulging in dogmatic pronunciamentos, for we are interested primarily in research. We should like to feel that each being reinvents the world for himself.

The philosophic problem of the twentieth-century spirit seems to us to lie especially in the attempt to discover a new notion of man. The relationship between the I and the dynamic totality needs to be definitely analyzed, in order to elucidate the process of evasion from the disquietude in which we live.

We are struggling for a new faith which may help us create the mythos for which every true artist is waiting today. We hope for an esthetic synthetism in which not only Europe and Asia will coalesce into a new flowering, but to which also the two Americas will bring their vision.

This conception of universalism, however, opposes all attempts to neutralize or destroy individualism. We think of the new spirit as a vast orchestra in which each instrument brings its share of the rhythmic and harmonic creation. We are against the abdication of the indigenous forces. Art and literature do not represent a geographic condition, but as in the most fruitful historic events, when each nation contributed its share to the whole, they can conquer again the universal supremacy of the spirit.

The vertiginous pseudo-progress of industrialism has blinded us to the immense psychological importance of the machine. The latter, which surely is the greatest single esthetic contribution of our age, has enslaved the human spirit, instead of liberating it. It is chiefly responsible for the fact that our civilization is a decadent one.

But America, where the technical-mechanical development of our age reached its zenith, shows conclusively to what destructive ends the instrument of the machine can lead. For the blind belief in the omnipotence of the mechanistic psychology produces a disintegration of the free spirit and an automatic mentality, a glorification of intellectual laziness that seems to us to be the gravest danger modern civilization faces.

America, swollen with mercantilism, content with its mediocrity, is influencing the world more and more. It creates a caricature of optimism and persecutes every genuine attempt to give voice to the deeper beauty of life, to discover the eternal and changeless magic of things. She develops in her colossal organism a hierarchy of the materialistic preoccupations that crashes brutally into the silences of the spirit.

The arts suffer as a result of this hysteria. Noise has become the surrogate of beauty. The faculty to vocalize the platitudes of newspapers and pulpit and the plethora of perfumed magazines is the new criterion for excellence.

The machine has the capacity—as with Gothic art—to create a new sense of the vertical. The plastic arts, which are perhaps the most representative of the arts, show this impulse at its best. It is up to the young and growing generation to take this fact into consideration and we feel distinctly that America may eventually find the solution, once the slags have been cleared away.

Human history is a collection of coarse solutions, according to Paul Valéry. The solution of a neurotic kind of activism rooted in a stupid nativistic determinism and sentimentality is the last one we can admit. The arts, in order to grow in such a soil, need a maximum of evasions. The old frames must be ruthlessly destroyed, and new ones substituted. The human being cannot breathe freely in this civilization.

For the immediate result of this state of things is the critical danger to intellectual liberty which is the consequence of the increasing industrialization we face today. The terrifying conception that the minority has no place in the general scheme of things and must be destroyed with all the weapons at the disposal of the mob is asserting itself more and more. This sinister prejudice finds its greatest aid in the marshaling of political ideas that are out to crush whatever poetry has created.

A certain kind of barbarism which to some seems for the moment the only solution is motivated by the profound disquietude in which the sensitive man of our age lives. He has trusted to pure reason too long. He lives in the obsession of despair. Call it a new *mal du siècle,* if you wish, it is none the less a real thing that goes deep into the consciousness of our epoch. The intellectualism vaunted so long leaves him cold.

Our nerves live in a vertigo. The will to dream, to meditate is slowly being undermined. It is for this reason that the Oriental sense of the contemplative may be called upon to counteract the increasing sterility of the modern vision. It is conceivable that a synthesis of the primitive, the technical, and the contemplative may resurrect the faculty of creating beauty.

We are dissatisfied and propose to let this feeling come to expression. We have no sense of equilibrium anymore. Our center is gone. We are waiting in fear, in insolence, in boredom for the light beyond the horizon.

We are through with the mendacious brutality of literature. We stand in admiration before the classical achievements, but we are through with the epigones of Classicism or any other source of the past. We revolt against the idea that by grafting on our consciousness an antique ideal fresh sources of inspiration may come. The hunger for evasion which is the symbol of our generation can find expression in certain definite ways.

Realism, as it is still preached in America, is a movement with which we have no sympathy. We believe that the police reporter's mentality has nothing whatever to do with poetry. We are against all methods that believe that the photographic representation of life is the aim of true art.

What really is needed is a new feeling. We need a greater naiveté, a greater simplicity, a greater sense of adventure. The dual realism we think of has the two planes of the subconscious and the instinctive and the physical consciousness.

The movements of the dream have a value that surpasses all deliberate attempts to emerge into a state of serenity. Out of them may come new landscapes, new ecstasies, which open the way to the Arabian Nights. Whether this process is essentially a mystic one or leads to a complete denial of transcendental forces is unimportant. It is important, however, that passion and dream be expressed.

The movements of life in its physical sense added to the hermetism of the instinctive can conceivably create a beauty never dreamed of before. The dynamism of the newer manifestations such as electricity, cinema, auto, telephone, aeroplane, radio, may give a new artistic basis leading to fantastic functions of the poetic mind.

This duality could give the American poet an opportunity to disport himself to his heart's content, absorb the rhythms of the indigenous

Afro-American and Indian traditions, if he be so inclined, and find the sky-scrapers of the fourth dimension he dreams of. Thus he may find a partial escape in the sense of the vertiginous movement of his country, by using its rhythms to express his visions in an accelerated way. If dynamism is intrinsically a new atmospheric means, it cannot alone produce the magic we demand. It must be wedded to the sense of the unreal, the imaginary, the fantastic.

We are not hostile to the whirling symptoms of the modern world of machines. But they must be subordinated to the expression of the imaginative aims which are the very essence of poetry. The cinema, in spite of the imbecility surrounding its present evolution, can give us possibilities for hallucinations that check successfully the pedantry of the puritan. The telephone, that marvelous instrument for disaster, for saturnine proceedings, for strange visions, can conceivably become a real basis for esthetic communication. The radio, in spite of its urge to parallelism, lets us participate in the spontaneous rhythms of continents. But it must not be forgotten that these things are methodological, not creative per se—a mistake that has frequently been made.

The intercontinental tendency for simultaneity today does not, we emphasize again, exclude the expression of the indigenous. The American poet, for instance, to whom his age is a torture, may very well follow the advice of William Carlos Williams and return to the origins of the American mythology. Here is a species of American Romanticism that evades the dynamism of the present age. He might go back to his earth, that rich, fruitful loam which is now being violated by the sadistic hand of industry.

By going back to his primitive forces, Dr. Williams hopes to find again that impetus to the imaginative life now being choked in sentimentality and ignorance. The Mound-builders, the Indians, the Incas, the Aztecs, the Mayas, Negro art offers a liberation of the spirit that may help the new artistic forces of our generation. People like De Soto, Daniel Boone belong to that race of truly great pioneers who had their roots in the soil. They were the great internationalists.

We are not interested in the limitations imposed on the mind by political considerations. It is true that we owe an incalculable amount of things to the influence of the Russian Revolution, but we cannot allow this conception to dominate us. The stimulus of the emancipation which we gain from the Cyclopean effort of the October rebels has been our constant encouragement, but not in its political, nor in its dialectic aspect.

But let there be no misunderstanding. We reject the insinuation that any political affiliation whatever can master us. The question at stake in this respect is bigger than all the ephemeral solutions of history. We are for the reestablishment of liberty in its deepest sense.

We have no patience with the idea that the spirit of revolt can be expressed through political means. Poetry in itself is a revolt. The mistake some of our contemporaries made is precisely that they failed to recognize that the poetic instinct has nothing whatever to do with the programmatic principles of politics.

Poetry can be renewed through the re-creation of the word, if the dynamic scheme of our age gives us really new artistic methods to express our vision. That vision, however, can be found only in silence. The roar of steel does not give the new mythos we crave. We must dream again.

To capture the eternal values in the flux of the modern world, to create a cosmos, each in his own way, to find a new Humanism in a marriage of reason and instinct—this, it seems, should be our universal goal.

By contrasting the two realities—the beyond and the living—we can create a verbal organism that may increase esthetic enjoyment. Let the word in prose and poetry find its different planes and its new associations in order to make it impossible that art be again and again the sycophant of reality.

Notes on Reality (November 1929)

The creative effort of this age goes toward totality. To achieve the new image of the world which we dimly perceive on the horizon, we disintegrate the universe with all the means at our disposal and transform chaos into cosmos.

We live in disquiet and disorientation. "Isms" come and go; the crisis of the imagination continues. What characterizes most this age is its lack of revolutionary faith. This age proceeds through a dialectic of acceptance and seeks transcendental surrogates in intellectualist knowledge. The New Impressionism which we observe blossoming out is an attempt to resuscitate the Naturalism of a purely mechanical epoch, when evolutionary materialism dominated the world. The immediate senses are celebrated as the prime factors in the esthetic organization. In this positivist metaphysics, however, the enigmatic or the pre-logical is ignored. Neo-Classicism fights for the reestablishment of traditional rationalism. Going beyond mere analogy, it seeks the return to a historic, long-exhausted conception of life with which it identifies itself in a final gesture of despair. It is eager to graft upon our consciousness an ideology which is the modernistic interpretation of dogmas and seeks its esthetics in Racinian order and Cartesian rigidity. The Neo-Romantic attitude toward life and art is doomed from the outset, because its aim is irrationalism. It is unable to escape from the chaos which it worships for its own sake, although it is well to state in its favor that its preoccupation with the primal being gives its movement an experimental force. The proletarian primitives, and their brothers, the skyscraper-futurists, approach the creative spirit inadequately, because their empirical vision leads to pure pragmatism.

The majority of philosophic systems up to recent times attempted to explain nature rationally. Hegel's identity of opposites still presented reason as the only important agent in the formation of reality. The unknown element which is a priori to knowledge was recognized and separated by Schopenhauer. It is to his eternal credit that he proved the relativity of reason and the importance of the sense of "will." He revolutionized the epistemological conception of idealism. He found that knowledge is simply the substitute for will which is the unity of organic and inorganic reality. He concluded that reason can attain its perfection only through the process of development beyond the primal limitations. By bringing the empirical-psychological element of the will into the front rank, the new idealism found an escape from the dilemma into which it had fallen.

The explorations into the pre-logical regions were given a strong impetus during the Romantic period. This movement developed from pure irrationalism into the classical synthesis of rationalism and irrationalism and reached its zenith in absolute irrationalism. Never were the powers of the nocturnal, the alogical, the instinctive, the earth-magical explored with more passion than by the representatives of this conception of life. All the branches of philology, philosophy, esthetics, and even jurisprudence were influenced by the current. Herder, under the aegis of Hamann, had already given, in his *History of Mankind,* a powerful impetus to the movement, and in his *Adrastea* epitomized his ideas. While most of the Romantics opened up new vistas into an understanding of the instincts, they failed to solve the main problem of knowledge, and with one or two exceptions, notably that of Novalis, sank deeper and deeper into chaos. It is a curious fact that their modern successors and imitators have not recognized this fundamental error.

There are certain eternal organic impulses which pragmatic dynamism has been unable to eliminate. The primitive mythos is a subterranean stream (held up by "civilized" consciousness) which we observe again and again in such manifestations as the dream, neuropathic conditions, and the poetic inspiration as such. Explorations into the irrational continued even during the reign of pure materialism. In the beginning of this century they recaptured their position, and became in certain cases the all-absorbing, almost exclusive preoccupation. When Freud, in his *Totem and Taboo,* showed us the astonishing relationship between neurosis and primitive humanity, an immense step forward was made in the understanding of life. In his struggle to cure psychic disturbances by transforming the subconscious into the conscious, he developed the technique of psychoanalysis. The discoveries of the French psychologist Janet at the same time opened a gap along almost identical lines. This new psychology quickly burst its medical frontiers and is slowly assuming the picture of an interpretation of the universe. The subconscious is the immense basin into which flow all the inhibited components of our being. This is the primal psychic principle. But it was found by Dr. Jung, a dissident of the Freudian school, that into the subconscious flow not only the unfulfilled elements of our lives, but that it contains also the collective mythos, thus establishing connection with the social organism and even the cosmic forces.

Although it is only since very recent times that the dream has been scientifically disintegrated into its component parts, the problem has occupied thinkers and poets for many centuries. Beginning with Heraclitus and Aristotle, the Greeks already made attempts to penetrate into the mysteries of sleep. Heraclitus asked himself the question why it was that in the dream every man has his own world, while in the waking state we all have a world in common. The wish-dreams were known to the ancient Greeks, for they discovered that, in his dream, the hungry man eats and the thirsty man drinks. Aristotle sketched the first psychological explanation of the dream, the genesis of which he did not seek outside man, but in his interior life. This revolutionary conception definitely broke with the idea of the dream as a supernatural revelation. Hippocrates recognized also the psycho-gnostic possibilities of the dream. Later we find that Christian Aristotelianism examined the question, especially as exemplified by Thomas Aquinas and Albertus Magnus. The latter compares the dream-picture with the sensual illusions which we have in a state of being awake.

To understand the exact nature of the dream and its relation to creative life, certain states of mind may be studied which precede or follow the dream, or more properly the sleep. There are certain hallucinations which we experience before falling asleep or immediately upon waking. These so-called hypnogogic hallucinations represent mostly imagistic reflexes of a thought we were engaged in before half-sleep overtook us. The image experienced is the surrogate for the logical development of the preceding thought. A reality of associations appears. The return to the objective world makes us aware of the exact contour of this image. The transition of these half-sleep hallucinations to the actual sleep is connected with the most amazing images which, as the French psychologist Maury has established, often are prolonged into the dream itself.

In examining this region, the psychology of depth has facilitated the comprehension for the processes of creation. The old dogmas of critical dictators are automatically thrown overboard. We now have come near knowing the sources of inspiration, and the secret of genius is out. Visionaries create instinctively their substantialities out of their demonish or religious constellations. The projection of the will in Schopenhauer's sense—through sublimation—is the creator's solution of his problem. The revolutionary agent is that which becomes conscious and proceeds from the instinctive to a fusion with the objective reality. The individual and collective forces seek a union. It was the failure to recognize this principle that led the Neo-Romantics to the error of applying too literally the new psychological discoveries, with the result that their work was incoherent and without completion.

The creator presents and sometimes interprets his instinctive symbols. Since the esthetic state is a transition between the active tendencies and those of the interior impulses, it is necessary, in order that the expression may truly achieve that hard, athletic beauty which is its sublimation, to descend into the night-side of life, before we can attain perfection. To this end we need not necessarily accept Fechner's idea of the "day-view" and the "night-view" in all of its implications, but we are aware that the modern mind tries to approximate the distinction. The symbols of the subconscious contain many dimensions in their mythological-individual developments. The condensation of these symbols, showing us, as they do, the strata of a variegated, affective organism in the dream, is reproduced in the creative reaction.

Enough has been written about the various theories of dream interpretation for me to forgo delving into the problem at this stage. But the absolute importance of the dream for the creative artist must now be assumed.* The dream is the reflex of the eternal struggle between our instinctive, unhampered life and our civilized being. For this reason, as Stekel has

---

* It is understood that I do not consider the childish applications of Freudian theories which certain English and American writers have indulged in as of the slightest importance. They failed to understand the elementary magic of the pre-logical. With typical pragmatic insensitiveness they have "psychologized," celebrating a narrow pan-sexualism as a new "philosophy of life," and using the textbook information they had gained to engage in their little literary game. The most obvious case is that of Eugene O'Neill, who, in his *Strange Interlude,* and his other Biedermeier dramas has not recognized the subconscious as a new well of inspiration, but has worked rather from the exterior, never going beyond the all too simple task of artificially constructing his protagonists around the more familiar "complexes."

pointed out, Freud's definition of the dream as pure wish-fulfillment is not entirely correct, since there enter also other elements, such as fear, warning, and so on. But the study of the dream mechanism opens the door to the recognition of a world which was dim and obscure before. The dream is pure imagination. Here we are verily beyond good and evil. In that world happen the most wonderful, pathological, criminal, demoniacal, beautiful things. The imagination takes revenge on reality. All objects in their pragmatic virtue fade. They carry only the poetic emotion.

At the limit of the creator's spirit there is always the pre-logical. Its expression is the prime factor in poetic operations. The creator is the carrier of all these images and associations, and the difference between him and the neuropath lies precisely in his capacity to get rid of his burden by means of his expressive power. The creator and the dreamer have identical roots. They both try to return to the primitive condition of humanity, and create a condition where the frontiers of the real and the unreal vanish. We have now controlled reality to some extent. In physics, chemistry, and mathematics we have witnessed the prolongations of its frontiers. The atom, once the last reality, has given way to new disintegrations which open up possibilities for tremendous evolutions.

The repercussion of this on creative expression is very important. We are near the very limits of the infinite. The Heraclitean picture of modern life confronts us at the same time. The subconscious is not enough. We must organize. The flight from the excessively rational must go on. It is blind fanaticism to deny the conscious will as a creative agent. I am not one of those who now turn suddenly against Surrealism. In spite of all the snobs who, following in the wake of our pioneering work for that movement, today discuss it glibly and pretentiously, I persist in regarding the Surrealist effort as having crystallized a viewpoint in the modern spirit. The importance of the *Surréalistes* which I tried to emphasize, when I first introduced them in this review, lay in their recognition of the primal being as a basic element in creative activity. Theirs was a revolt against the hegemony of reason which historically goes back to Romanticism and more recently to Freud. Their mistake lay in the fact that, after applying Freudian and Dadaist discoveries, they did not transcend them. For the transition from life as a biological existence into the formed existence of creation brings with it a concentrated change. The spontaneous emergence of the disintegrated symbols is the a priori condition of the creative activity. And it is here where synthetist reality begins.

The new composition must thus become mythological action. The primitive mythos and the modern mythos are fused, and the union of the collective and individual at the point of the immediate conscience produces the universal condition. The timeless and spaceless forces lie hidden in the instinctive. Consciousness is merely the result of an effort toward a state of mind that is control. In what degree we also control the daydream and all the emotional currents that lie in consciousness itself is a moot question.

The new creator is out to make the alliance between the Dionysian-dynamic and the nocturnal realities. He is out to discover the unity of life. Conquering the dualism between the "it" and the "I," he produces new myths, myths of himself in a dynamic environment, myths of new machines and inventions, fairy tales and fables, legends and sagas expressing a hunger for beauty that is not passive and gentle like that of former ages, but hard and metallic like the age toward which we are going. He brings the fabulous again within our reach. Cause and effect are transposed. The distances of the earth are vanquished, past, present, and future disappear in a unity, there remains a time-space stream which is homogeneous. The new composition is polyphonic and on many planes. It is as exact as possible and tries to produce harmonic unity by balancing the negative and positive. It is the static point produced by the balancing of the dynamic representations of the world with the spontaneous movement of the dream.

The persistent cry for the expression of life in all of its crudity based on social and moral imperatives does not answer our needs. Zola's method is not for us. He expressed a milieu and described a segment of his time and world by copying it, although, it should not be forgotten, his passion and bitterness transcended his means. Artistic creation is not the mirror of reality. It is reality itself. The writer of tomorrow using a Romantic-realistic orientation will give us the tempo and the development of the gigantic forces which he finds in a fusion of metaphysical space with nature. His subject is life, enigmatic and utopian.

This new sense of life, this world sense, which goes toward a totality, will probably characterize the next generations. But before that is possible, we must disintegrate and help batter down the present structure of a pathological civilization. By going toward this pure idea, we are individualists and universalists; subversive agents also whose vision is the synthesis of *all* the forces of life.

Preface to *Transition Stories* (1929)

The problem which every writer faces as he struggles with the expression of his vision is that of reality. In what degree are we to retain the integrity of the sensual phenomena outside ourselves? Is the inner vision, in the idealistic sense, the final criterion for the artistic manifestation? Thus the eternal search for the absolute has been going on, while the economic and political confusion of our age is juggling the significant values we need. The attempt to arrive at a complete denial of reality by way of a consistent and dogmatic exploration of the subconscious remains one of the important actions of our creative life. Our contemporaries have been unaware that miracles and adventures were still possible. It became necessary to legalize the mystic researches in order to create a rampart against a conception of life that is non-conscious and non-creative. It is obvious that such a decision celebrating the instinctive and the psychically automatic has opened up many new relations and associations for the mind that had previously found itself hampered by the exigencies of natural science. The domination of pure reason was abolished in the twinkling of an eye. But what of the dynamic totality, the new rhythm of twentieth-century reality? The revolt against the descriptive idea of literature has become imperative. For the creator, having discovered the dream and the daydream as functions of his subjective existence, should try to bring them into a more definite relation with the phenomenal world which his conscious mind perceives. This dual reality of dream and life can alone bring us liberation.

The tendency of modern life is toward universalism or collectivism. Mechanical science is producing a condition which is the triumph of rationalistic categories through the destruction of time and space. But is it not true that we should proceed from the individual to the collective, from the regional to the universal? A good deal of the present chaos is due to the inversion of this order. We are not against the machine, which is, after all, the most important single esthetic contribution of our age. We are against its blind glorification, against the resultant planning of the spirit and the general destruction of the magical detail which this produces. We may use the mystery of the new instruments as a base from which to proceed into the world of adventures. Sociologically speaking, it is conceivable that the machine will make it possible for humanity in the future to devote more time to pure laziness, to the beauty of the dream, when once the capitalistic hierarchy has been vanquished by the masses themselves. For this is the chief fault of the rule of the machine as obtaining now in capitalistic countries: it is exploited for the benefit of the few, while the majority employing its appendages for economic facilities become interested primarily in the superficial aspect of bourgeois comfort. In this, as well as in the political domain, it seems important that a process of decentralization should set in. The creative activity of our age should also be made aware of the need of disintegration. It is therefore important for the writer not to reflect his time in a photographic sense, but to help first in the struggle for the eternal autonomy of the spirit, and then to work for a mass-spirit that will continue to have its roots in variation.

We are no longer interested in the bourgeois forms of literature. We are against the esthetic chaos which, using decadent dogmas, continues to weigh upon our minds. We demand a sense of adventure that leads the individual toward a collective beauty, that is for every movement tending to demolish the current ideology, that seeks again the root of life in an impulse toward simplicity. For this reason we encourage the tendency to find new associations in theme as well as word. Life, in the new spirit, becomes transmuted, and the mind, wedding the magnificence of the inner world with that of a plane from which emanate different visions and rhythms, creates a mythology that is real-unreal. To express this straining toward a new magic, language, which heretofore has been chained in traditional regimentation, must be dissolved and re-created with new elements. It is impossible to use the mechanism of the old word for the delineation of such conditions as are between waking and sleeping (for a more detailed exposition of this I refer the reader to Edgar Allan Poe's *Marginalia*), or for abstract correlations, or for the marriage of the physical and the miraculous. It is necessary to break up the word, to construct an organic world of the imagination, and to give life a changed and spontaneous reality.

Transition, which I began with Elliot Paul in the spring of 1927, and which I have continued with him and Robert Sage, in the face of criticism and costly censorship, has attempted to encourage the liberation of the imagination in all its forms. We have tried to bring together the significant international forces in the creative field, although always remaining fundamentally American in spirit. Contemporary America, suffering from a democratic illusion, is still groping, but signs of an intellectual fermentation may be noted that, we hope, will lead to a Periclean age. May the American writer go to the roots of his indigenous consciousness and thus create through a mythology of his own the expression of a vision that differs from that of Europe and the Orient as much as those two differ from each other!

Literature and the New Man (June 1930)

Review of an Evolution—The Night-Mind and Day-Mind—Lévy-Bruhl, Freud, and Jung—The New Anthropology vs. the Error of the New Humanism—Objectivism, or Vagaries of the New York School—Poetry and Anti-Poetry—The Beautiful and the Ugly—Toward Synthetism

I confess to a feeling for life that postulates the pre-logical and tries to bring it into relation with conscious man as well as with reality in movement. The individual and not the group creates a vision.

Poetry—I use the term in its generic semantics as indicating the primal impulse to create—is enmeshed today in a materialistic consciousness of a contemporaneous process. It seeks to compete with machines and newspapers. It has become political. It seeks its subjects in the mass-man, and insists on presenting life as a reportorial document.

For three years *transition,* almost alone of all movements today, set its face against the pragmatism of the age. Almost alone it fought for the vision of a new humanity. Its arrival coincided with a crisis of the imagination. In the chaos of the postwar period a confusion of values had set in. In an epoch that was interested primarily in reducing all creative expression to a mere auxiliary and conductor of a collectivistic program of living, *transition* sought to present an ideology that would combine the primitive, instinctive mythology with a modern consciousness. We therefore fought the realistic idea of poetic values. We encouraged the imagination in all its intuitive associations by positing a conception of reality that refused to entangle itself any longer in an archaic dualism.

By publishing and defending *Work in Progress,* the new creation of James Joyce, *transition* established a basis for literary insurrection that included a radically new conception of the processes of consciousness and the development of language. Like the second *Faust, Work in Progress* will, I am very sure, continue to baffle the non-visionary minds, although the immensity of its plan and execution as well as the magnificence of its humor and cosmic imagination cannot fail to interest those who do not see in creative expression merely a means for communication.

To show to what extent the disintegration of conventional methods of literary communication was progressing among foreign writers as well, I published the work of Hans Arp, Léon-Paul Fargue, Henri Michaux, Eric de Haulleville, and many others. By revealing the work of the Surrealists in translation, *transition* introduced a spirit which, nurtured on Rimbaud, Freud, and Lautréamont, sought in the discovery of another reality the exclusive aim of expression. Although my own definition of reality differs from theirs in the implication of methodology, I have no hesitancy in saying that the Surrealists, following in the wake of Dada, were the only ones to recognize the importance of the explorations into the subconscious world. But the movement remained incomplete, in my opinion, because it refused to consider the problem of the word in the struggle for a new reality. Its revolutionary activity did not transcend the traditional style.

Transition published the work of Gertrude Stein, whose psychological experiments with language have made a profound inroad into the conventional ideas of philology. She has made possible word correspondences and rhythmic enchainments that will forever make it impossible to consider literary composition as the mere evocation of documentary phenomena.

In order to demonstrate the parallel development in other arts, *transition* published the work of the new painters, and was the first of the Anglo-Saxon reviews to introduce the art of creative photography. It is regrettable that this should now be taken up by snobs and epigones.

The influence of the experiments of *transition* is making itself felt in the work of the young writers in both England and America. Instead of the purely reportorial-objective realism of the "Middle Westerners," who have been cluttering up the pages of the magazines with their sordid boredom, we reestablished the reign of the imagination.

Parallel with this more or less "evangelical" effort went the attempt to find an ideology based on the new psychological and philosophical viewpoints as well as on the fact that America and Russia are creating a reality with which the artist of the future cannot fail to reckon. I found that it was impossible to retrace our steps, as many of our contemporaries are doing, and seek in a resurrection of past ideals the basis for our outlook. But it was obvious that as a result of recent explorations into the unconscious and the discovery of its relation to the eternal mythos, the Freudian symbol of the personal did not suffice to explain the complexity of the human spirit.

Thus the ideas that *transition* has stood for may be briefly summarized as follows: the mythos and the dream, that is, the evocation of the instinctive personal and collective universe; the attempt to define the new man in relation to his primal consciousness; the revolution of the word. All of these are interdependent functions of the modern spirit.

Transition attempted a discipline. The absolute denial of reality, we found, is often beyond human capacity. Only a mystic, living with his hallucinatory world, can properly achieve this. It is difficult for us who are rooted in the earth. But there *are* things beyond reality. It is the duty, then, of the creator to find the bridge between the primal and the objective worlds and to consciously fuse his discoveries into an organic whole.

Throughout history men have struggled with the daemon. The nineteenth century, being mostly preoccupied with rationalistic ideas, ignored it, but philosophers and psychologists have since given the study of the inner world a new impulse.

In France, it is Professor Lévy-Bruhl who has penetrated the primitive processes of thinking. His discoveries are only now beginning to react upon the younger generation. In Vienna, Dr. Freud continues his correctives. Although we stand in reverence before the genius of the scientist who in *The I and the It* and more recently in *The Malaise in Civilization* has gone beyond his initial point of departure, we feel nevertheless that he does not entirely meet our conceptions of the creative spirit. By reducing everything to the dogma of a neurosis, he eliminates layers of the poetic genesis that are essential for esthetic understanding.

The enigmatic in the human soul is approached from another angle by Dr. C. G. Jung. In the essay which *transition* is publishing in this issue, an epochal step forward has been made. Not only does the unconscious contain the repressed elements of the personal life of the creator, says Dr. Jung, but it is also the vessel containing ingredients that relate him to the collective life of humanity. The latter force may be menacing in the suprapersonal dementia, or else beneficent in the poet's vision, or the religious sentiment. But the poet gathers these forces in him and presents them through his conscious act as a revivified condition of the personal-collective unconscious. Past generations emerge and manifest themselves. In dream and fantasies there are symbols that are identical with those of the sagas and the fairy tales of humanity.

It is in the recognition that in the human being there is a good deal of nocturnal chaos dating back from his primitive ancestors that the discoveries of the new psychology interest us. The night-mind of man crops out in a thousand ways, and although the intellect is the final arbiter and corrective, poetry draws its strength from the sources of the hidden forces of nature. All poetic experience is a struggle toward the light, or as Bachofen put it a hundred years ago, from the "mother empire to the paternal reign."

The creative imagination is not a priori a rational one. It proceeds from the primal, almost somnambulistic phase to that of intuition. Then the intelligence sets in, when, as Novalis said, "everything involuntary becomes voluntary."

A scission has occurred between our conception of the traditional man and the modern man.

Of all the attempts to find a basic philosophic concept to guide us out of the postwar confusion, it seems to me the most muddled one so far has been the New Humanism. It is interesting to watch from this vantage point the gyrations of the littérateurs who, having floundered around in the collectivistic mire for so long, suddenly find it expedient to climb on the reactionary bandwagon.

With Allan Tate, I regard the theories of the New Humanists as dangerous to art. The ethos which these pragmatic mystics wish to filter into literary expression is somewhat reminiscent of that wave of holier-than-thou sentimentalism that destroyed a good deal of expressionistic literature a decade ago. Literature has nothing to do with this ethos. It is itself ethos.

The criticism of the utilitarianism and pagan expansiveness of the age, which Irving Babbitt and his disciples are engaged in, is nothing new. *Transition* has been fighting the naturalistic spirit for three years. But it is also true that there have been a good many minds in America—Sherwood Anderson, Waldo Frank, Van Wyck Brooks, and others—who have long ago recognized this fact and have opposed the sordidness of the mechanistic impulse.

The values which the New Humanists wish to set up, because man has lost his humility before a whole transcending him, are traditional, ethical, and humanistic principles. The problem of a moral consciousness is more than ever with us. But it is not by turning back that we can find the solution. What Mr. Babbitt and his friends propose is a pseudo-philosophy rooted in theology and a distorted metaphysical literature. The application of moral dogmas of this kind to literary expression is unacceptable.

What is really needed is a study of man in relation to his modern world. The individual, in an age of flux, wavers between many clashing currents, and finds it difficult to find a unity to direct him. The integrity of the individual is being attacked from many sides. American civilization deludes him into facile beliefs in progress, although the mechanical conformity to which he finds himself subjected confuses him at every step.

The new man should combine in himself the possibilities for universality. He will not be the *homo faber*, the *homo sapiens*, the metaphysical man, the Dionysian man, the automatic man, the economic man. He will be all of them in one. He will become conscious to a very high degree, because he will finally, through analysis, come to know himself. The industrial revolution needs an individual who will blend the intellectual and emotional side of his nature, who will harness science to eternal humanity, who will nullify the antinomy of nature and man. He will proceed from the premise that the eternal mythos remains unchanged, that only the conditions of living have changed, and that our biological changes occur only in the degree of the intensity of our nervous reaction to reality.

The new man, represented by the creative spirit, will build his work on the consciousness of a purified individualism. It will be an individualism that is sufficiently deep to produce a compensation with groups, races, civilizations, economic systems, and even linguistic aggregations. He will be able to bend with pity over humanity's stumbling attempts to see the light. He needs must be against the excessive, decadent individualism which produced the art of the neurons. The individualism of a *mal du siècle*, with its puerile narcissism, is not for him.

In the domain of epic literary expression we observe the phenomenon of a current toward a New Naturalism. In France the emergence of the populist school of Lemonnier and Thérive has been hailed in some quarters as the forerunner of Neo-Realism, an attitude which seeks in a documentary description of the people the aim of the epic manifestation. In Russia we have an identical attitude, although still more emphasized on the sociological side. The writer is called upon to dispense with "invention," since the proletarian reality, it is held, surpasses the poetic imagination. The direction is toward a reportorial literature. The writer's mission in Soviet Russia henceforth is to write for the primitive reader. In Germany we have the concentration of the "New Objectivism" and the demand that the writer concentrate on a *Niveau-Senkung,* that is, leveling down of his values in order to reach the masses.

We have here a curious phenomenon. The enormous influence of Sinclair Lewis, Upton Sinclair, John Dos Passos, and so on is not foreign to its development. An American Romanticism has caught the imagination of many European writers. It is not to be denied that the forceful and colorful quality of modern America reacts upon the outsider like an almost occult fact. But the shallowness of the literary photographers of the New York school, their pretentiousness in demanding the prerogative to give voice to the impulses of the people, their misunderstanding of the relationship between expression and communication—all these factors help in the general confusion. Many a talented young American who came to Paris during the past three years with a manuscript in his pocket thought it essential to reveal his optic dexterity by presenting a story of his life or that of his neighbors. Let us forget for a moment that, as a rule, the story was atrociously written. It usually claimed as its chief merit absolute verity to life. This naive attitude forgot that even the police reporter—consciously or unconsciously—deforms the facts he has gathered. The passion for the "document" is now at its height. How long it will last I cannot say. It all depends upon the organizations which have succeeded in constructing Babylonian literary factories on Manhattan Island, and which will go on doing this as long as literary guilds and other book clubs continue to bamboozle the reader of the provinces.*

The period immediately following the war was one of disquiet and despair. But let us not forget that the war did not particularly influence the arts. It interrupted temporarily an anti-positivist movement, and I am inclined to believe that we are only now returning to the point where we left off.

The revolt against poetry is a very real one. We are facing a movement of anti-poetry. The vegetative-materialistic-concrete-optimistic is celebrating its cheap little triumph. A melioristic dementia has seized the world. But,

---

* Joseph Roth, a young Austrian novelist, recently stated in an essay: "The works of the new Americans satisfy the curiosity of the simpleminded reader for the private life of his fellow men, just as the works of pseudo-evolutionary objectivity in Russia satisfy his interest in the extraordinary, the world-historic, and the erotic."

as Gottfried Benn declares in a recent essay, poetry will survive only if we return to the "self-conscious I, this late mood of nature." The mind of man will continue to look into its own mysterious forests where the unicorns wander and where demonic beings dance before the miraculous fires. Nothing can ever destroy in him the immense night of the prehistoric.

Poetry has suffered too long, however, from the imperative of a frail, androgynous kind of beauty. It is high time that we revise our notions of the beautiful and its supposed antithesis. I feel we should no longer accept the classical definitions without revising them. Against mere glacial and static beauty there should be placed the monstrous, the grotesque, the tenebrous, the diabolical, the things the night has hidden. The will to illusion, in Nietzsche's sense, includes the will to penetrate into the darkest recesses of the human spirit. It is here where American poetry, with the exception of Jeffers, has not yet stepped out of the Calvinistic atmosphere.

Pure objectivism fails, because it is the antithesis of subjectivism. It follows the extreme swing of the pendulum toward a craze for actuality and factual experience which can only end in artistic sterility and a return to the literature of the commonplace. If we wish to find a standard for life and literature, we cannot, of course, escape the results of the personal and collective experiences. But creative expression envisages the combined forces of the human spirit. The writer proceeds from his own individuality to a connection with the humanity around him. He does not shirk the dark and sinister aspects of life. He presents life in its universal relationships and is not afraid to destroy in order to create his vision.

The epic writer of the future will not copy reality. He will create, with the material he possesses, another world in which he will make his own laws. This other world is not above his own world, but identical with it. Like James Joyce in *Ulysses,* he will seek the fantastic of the real world.

"The highest indication of will is the belief in the illusion," said Nietzsche. The phantasms of the new man are not very different from those of his ancestor. They are only differently expressed. For this he needs an attitude of the mind that presents the unifying process of thought by the organizing intellect via pre-logical passivity, intuition, conscious hallucination. Thus he can create, through synthetism, the unity of science and life, mythos and consciousness. He will be able to *invent* a new world in which appearance blends with reality, and in which the delusional mechanism is a voluntary act.

Let us have myths and more myths!

Night-Mind and Day-Mind (March 1932)

Metaphysics is an attempt to find the unity of man and nature. The ultimate reality back of the phenomenal world, the transcendental universe, is the aim of this research. The process eventuates by means of a mediumistic act, the release of reason "from the pressure of an objective world."

Mystic action proceeds from the lower strata toward a higher region. It is vertical motion and seeks a final synthesis in a world beyond a world. Any metaphysical experimentation that does not first investigate the night-side of life deprives itself of the necessary precondition of success.

Gnosis accepted the principle that the universe partakes of a dual nature. Matter, it claimed, is an active principle. Therefore the tenebrous regions, it believed, are identical with the evil principle and exist as autonomies. Derived from the ancient star-religions of Hebraic, Egyptian, and Asiatic origin, gnosis grafted the Christian purity of the catacombs onto the basic structure and developed a cult the aim of which was the conquest of the dark regions by an audacious penetration into them, with the idea of using the acquired knowledge for reaching a primal God by a process of redemption.

Gnosis is still with us. In order to understand the very springs of the human psyche it is imperative to study the nocturnal manifestations of the spirit. They reveal themselves in all collective desires for sadistic hate as in war, in sexual aberrations, in "the malaise of civilization," in scatology, in psychiatric regressions, in our dream-life, in primitive tribal lore, in religious-erotic manticism, in the revival of witchcraft and black masses. They are found in such states as somnambulism, hypnotic sleep, stigmatization, telepathy, telekinesis, possession, and the numerous occult accidents of consciousness discovered by Dr. Freud and his disciples.

Weary of the struggle with gnostic duality imposed on him, modern man relegated the principles of both darkness and light to a neurosis, or to a fairy tale suitable for children. This latter conception has worn itself out, quite as definitely as the dual conception it has attempted to combat was abused by autocratic dogmatists.

We have today means for investigating the night-mind and day-mind that have never existed before. We must use them and probe as far as human possibilities will permit. Modern science is no longer afraid of mysticism. Theoretical physics gives us daring speculations in a new idealistic way of thinking. The imagination becomes exact. The modern physical reality is a cosmos in which there exists a transcendental entity. Psychology has opened the gates to the chthonian world. It is a world within our reach.

Poetry Is Vertical (March 1932)

On a été trop horizontal,
j'ai envie d'être vertical.
—Léon-Paul Fargue

In a world ruled by the hypnosis of positivism, we proclaim the autonomy of the poetic vision, the hegemony of the inner life over the outer life.

We reject the postulate that the creative personality is a mere factor in the pragmatic conception of progress, and that its function is the delineation of a vitalistic world.

We are against the renewal of the classical ideal, because it inevitably leads to a decorative reactionary conformity, to a factitious sense of harmony, to the sterilization of the living imagination.

We believe that the orphic forces should be guarded from deterioration, no matter what social system ultimately is triumphant.

Esthetic will is not the first law. It is in the immediacy of the ecstatic revelation, in the alogical movement of the psyche, in the organic rhythm of the vision that the creative act occurs.

The reality of depth can be conquered by a voluntary mediumistic conjuration, by a stupor which proceeds from the irrational to a world beyond a world.

The transcendental "I" with its multiple stratifications reaching back millions of years is related to the entire history of mankind, past and present, and is brought to the surface with the hallucinatory irruption of images in the dream, the daydream, the mystic-gnostic trance, and even the psychiatric condition.

The final disintegration of the "I" in the creative act is made possible by the use of a language which is a mantic instrument, and which does not hesitate to adopt a revolutionary attitude toward word and syntax, going even so far as to invent a hermetic language, if necessary.

Poetry builds a nexus between the "I" and the "you" by leading the emotions of the sunken, telluric depths upward toward the illumination of a collective reality and a totalistic universe.

The synthesis of a true collectivism is made possible by a community of spirits who aim at the construction of a new mythological reality.

Hans Arp
Samuel Beckett
Carl Einstein
Eugene Jolas
Thomas McGreevy
Georges Pelorson
Theo Rutra
James J. Sweeney
Ronald Symond

The Primal Personality (February 1933)

The City of Chicago is preparing a world exposition under the grandiloquent slogan of "A Century of Progress."

Progress in what? In capitalism? Technology? Machine supremacy? Materialism? Wars? Exploitations? The mechanistic philosophy? Standardization? Pragmatism? Behaviorism?

It might not be amiss to ask: What has happened during this century to the eternal elements in man? Have they not been overwhelmed, choked, hidden under the slag of an artificial automatism? Has not science deformed the irrational forces into empirical, statistical facts? Have we not witnessed in the last few decades the triumph of cerebralization, the destruction of metaphysical autonomy, the idolization of all intellective functions? Have not the primal processes of life become externalized? Have we not watched the dehumanization of mankind?

It is possible that the present worldwide crisis is a turning point. We are witnessing a crisis of man. We stand before the development of a new anthropology.

For we are living in an epoch of latent revolution. The change occurring in the present social and economic structure is slowly silhouetting itself. Only blind, fanatic reactionaries can still oppose the transformation of the dominant plutocratic regime of slave methods into a new, proletarian rule which will dispossess the exploiters and redistribute the wealth of the world.

But we also know that this new development is endangered by a tendency to simplify reality, to think in terms of a radical neo-rationalism, to standardize the personality. Although economic collectivism is desirable, the scissions in the human personality will never be eliminated by any governmental system, be it ever so melioristic, and this condition will always obtain.

The new feeling of life which is emerging today is based on a revolutionary view of the human personality. This revolution aims at the totality of man and nature. Philosophers and psychologists are exploring the inner mysteries of man, the attitude toward reality is changing, we are before the resurrection of a new ontological orientation. This metanthropology, as the late Max Scheler called it, no longer considers man an *animal rationale,* but a being, with a partly daemonic, partly transcendental inner universe.

Science is beginning again where the great Romantic movement left off, when the age of Naturalism overwhelmed it. It is symptomatic for this new phase that such long-neglected thinkers as Schelling, Carus, Novalis, Fechner are being studied again. Men like Kierkegaard, Nietzsche, Lévy-Bruhl, Bergson, Freud, Jung, Klages were the only ones during the naturalistic reign who continued the explorations of the irrational side of life. A new interpretation of history, like that of the Swiss scientist J. J. Bachofen, with its discovery of the matriarchal law, helped the evolution along.

The cosmic-organic view of the world, which, according to Leisegang, is one of the four methods of thinking (the others being the ethical-moral, the physical-mechanical, and the rational-mathematical), is coming into its own again. It is, in Comte's term, the "metaphysical" method of thinking.

Modern philosophy is turning to metaphysics again, after it had neglected it for many decades. The epistemological problem is giving place to the ontological one. Man's attitude to the *ens a se* is once more in the foreground.

The new irrationalism now silhouetting itself is as yet only demonstrated in a tendency to nihilism. But it is significant that an academic scientist like Martin Heidegger should attempt to approach the problem of being from the standpoint of metaphysics. In his remarkable essay *Was ist Metaphysik?** he says: "Every metaphysical question always comprises the whole problematical complex of metaphysics. It is always the WHOLE itself. Every metaphysical question can be asked only so that the questioner—as such—be included in the question, i.e., that he be placed within the question." What exists outside of being? he asks. We know there is nothingness. But how do we know it? How can we prove it? Through

* Bonn: Verlag Friedrich Cohen, 1931.

logic? "Can the reign of logic be attacked? Is reason not really master in this question concerning nothingness? With its help we can, as a matter of fact, determine only nothingness and posit it as a problem, even if it should devour itself. For nothingness is the negation of the totality of the existential, the properly non-existential." Every principle of logic thus combats the possibility of determining nothingness. Then why not examine the rights of logic itself in this matter? Logic, he says, is incapable of grasping nothingness except through its "no." But supposing nothingness really existed before the negation? The impotence of logic would then be clear. Heidegger asks: "Does there occur in the existence of man a being-in-the-mood in which he is placed before nothingness itself? This event—albeit rare enough and happening for moments only—is possible in the basic mood of *apprehension . . . apprehension reveals nihility.*" Heidegger's criticism of logic is a fact of historic importance. But as long as he has not given us a more precise definition of nihility or non-being, his research must necessarily remain incomplete.

The criticism of the intellect has found its most violent protagonist in Ludwig Klages. His philosophy of expression proceeds from the recognition that the nineteenth century mechanized the body and intellectualized the soul. He insists that the mistake of Naturalism lay precisely in the fact that it failed to examine psychic processes in direct relation with the physical side of the personality. Basing himself on Nietzsche, Bachofen, and Carus, he developed a new psychology which envisages the complete unity of body and soul. His characterology places the emphasis on the totalistic personality, thus making the break with the Platonic-Christian-Cartesian dualism. He calls for the "Dionysian" man, in contradistinction to the "Apollonian" man. His vitalistic conception believes in a "voluptuous ecstasis" as an escape to the irrational forces. It is from the latter alone, he says, that man can find true strength for living.

The Pan-Romanticism of Klages has some very important insights into life. That the daemonic forces have been driven back into themselves, and thus deprived man of a most essential source of life, can no longer be doubted.* But it seems to me that the irrationalism of the *telluric* alone is not sufficient. There is also a *transcendental* element of irrationalism which should be taken into account.

The researches of Heidegger and Klages have crystallized an important

---

* Count von Keyserling, in his latest book, *Süd-Amerikanische Meditationen,* gives us some astonishing observations of the Indian as the last remaining "earth-man," whose psychic makeup, he claims, contains "metallic properties."

psychological problem. They have dealt the death-blow to the naturalistic conception which saw in man primarily a being impelled by reason.

Meanwhile, experimental work along similar lines continued in France and Switzerland. Lucien Lévy-Bruhl's monumental *La Mentalité primitive** showed the thinking methods of the primitive to be pre-logical ones. This fact, he says, explains why in the few still existing tribes of savages we are face to face with the capacity for "mystic participation," a capacity which modern man has practically lost. Only the creative mind has here and there retained it. "Parmi les différences qui séparent la mentalité des sociétés inférieures de la nôtre," says M. Lévy-Bruhl,

> il en est une qui a arrêté l'attention d'un grand nombre de ceux qui les ont observées dans les conditions les plus favorables, c'est-à-dire, avant qu'elles eussent été modifiées par un contact prolongé avec les blancs. Ils ont constaté chez les primitifs une aversion décidée pour le raisonnement, pour ce que les logiciens appellent les opérations discursives de la pensée; ils ont remarqué en même temps que cette aversion ne provenait pas d'une incapacité radicale, ou d'une impuissance naturelle de leur entendement, mais qu'elle s'expliquait plutôt par l'ensemble de leurs habitudes d'esprit.

The primitive idea of causality is different from ours. In a recent book, M. Lévy-Bruhl examines the primitive mind in its relation to the idea of the meta-real. It is significant that, like Heidegger (and before the latter, like Kierkegaard), he should arrive at the conclusion that the primal force revealing trans-reality to the savage is fear, or rather, apprehension.

Edgar Dacqué, a German paleontologist, also finds that the primal man possessed an inherent visionary faculty which modern man has partially lost. He says: "The anatomical properties of that primal man consisted most probably in the possession of brain-organs which we still find as remnants in us, but which the intellective great brain has overgrown, so that they no longer stand in relation with the outer world through the cranium, as once they did."† Dacqué expresses the daring theory that the naturally visionary, prehistoric faculties may some day redevelop anatomically in man.

The Swiss psychologist Dr. C. G. Jung, whose revolt against Dr. Freud's pan-sexualism opened a new chapter in psychology, found, through a study

---

* Paris: Librairie Félix Alcan.

† *Natur und Seele* (Berlin: R. Oldenbourg).

of the dream, that there are not only personal memories in the unconscious, but also antique symbols and primitive images. The latter, he discovered, often come from ancient mythological "archetypes" which represent the "collective unconscious."

The question concerning man is posited against the background of a disintegrating worldview. Which will be the ultimate synthesis among the various conceptions? *Homo Faber? Animal Rationale? Ens Irrationale?*

The new man's chief characteristic will be a violent revolt against the intellect. The insurrection of the unconscious against the conscious, of the night-view against the day-view, of instinct against reason, is now in full swing.

Man is beginning to think about the structure of his being. Being as such is questioned. Metaphysics has become revolutionized.

What we see today is this: science, tending in a totalistic direction, tries to see man in relation, not to his historic evolution, but to the immense cycles through which he has passed, in relation to the billions of years of oor-world he has hidden his structure, in relation to the prehistoric background of life. Science is beginning to think again in universal terms, it is discovering once more correspondences with the cosmic.

This means primarily a new capacity for immediacy. An intuitive experience. A sinking into the stream of life. A hallucinated attitude before the object-world. The feeling of humility before the fundamentally irrational essence of being *Wesensschau.* The inner eye.* The third eye. The attempt to experience an absolute reality with alogical means. The elimination of discursive thinking as an a priori thing. Ecstasis. Meditation about the *ens a se.* The union between the I and the you, between the subject and the object. The new eros.

The creation of a new mythological mother-world is possible through the search for the inner meaning of life, through the search for the sign, the symbol, the primal image and sound. The search for God. We proceed from the daemonic to the supra-individual and supernatural forces. We go through all the scales of existence, and seek totality in a dialectics of spirit and instinct.

The new man will combat the nihilism of his age. He will go nearer the pre-logical forces, seek a synthesis, the great *unio mystica* of being which is

---

* "There is an inner seeing which is communicated by the external senses, and there is action corresponding to this inner seeing (*actio ad extra*) which is just as little transmitted by the external actions." Franz von Baader, "Über den innern Sinn im Gegensatze zu den äussern Sinnen," in *Schriften von Franz von Baader,* ed. Max Pulver (Insel Verlag).

triune in nature, man, and the absolute, he will vibrate between the polarities of the above and the below.

The new man will recapture the cosmological worldview and search for the primal logos.

Hugo Ball, in *Das Byzantinische Christentum,* describes the ecstatic and hymnic language of gnosis which was used during the mystic rites. He quotes the following magic invocation:

AEAE IUO IAO OIA PSINOTER TERNOPS NOPSITER ZAGURA
PAGURA NETMOMAOTH NEPSIOMAOTH MARACHACHTA
TOBARABRAU TARNACHACHAU
ZOROKOTORA IEOU SABAOTH.

Twilight of the Horizontal Age (February 1933)

Nihilism is fighting its last stand.

On the flat plane of consciousness, man tried, in the past few decades, to see life with dreamless eyes, the stars were hidden behind the smoke of his machine-mind, his senses moved in the dull rotation of blind forces.

But in the face of the collapse of mechanistic utopias, man is beginning to revolt against the dogma of evolution, and turns again to the eternal elements of his being.

Man is beginning to think in cosmic terms again.

The Vertigral Age brings with it a recognition of the ahistoric man, the religious man, the man who seeks a mystic union with the logos.

The Vertigral Age sees modern philosophy turning deliberately to metaphysics after a long interregnum.

The Vertigral Age hails the cognition of a nonmechanical reality on the part of astronomy and physics.

The Vertigral Age believes that we stand in direct line with the primeval strata of life.

The Vertigral Age is rediscovering the mantic forces of prehistoric man.

The Vertigral Age wants to discover the supernatural reality through the dreams that lead to the transfiguration of life.

The Vertigral Age wants to give voice to the ineffable silence of the heart.

The Vertigral Age wants to create a primitive grammar, the stammering that approaches the language of God.

Vertigralist Transmutation (July 1935)

The vertigral wants to abolish the era of nihilism and rationalism by postulating a metanthropological transmutation.

The vertigral spirit seeks a creative synthesis through Pan-Romantic irrationalism and through the dreams of the individual and the collective, in order to attain a total personality, the superconscious man, the interracial man, the man with a pineal eye.

It seeks cosmologic knowledge in the ecstasy and in the intoxication of myth and mythical images.

It seeks an interplanetary and transcendental dimension in the tension between the demoniacal and the metaphysical.

It seeks the supernatural.

The vertigral spirit seeks to discover new means of expression in order to express its inner dialectic.

It seeks the mantic metaphor that would be a kind of exorcism and incantation.

It raises the question of the transmutation of language and of the language of night.

It raises the question of the plastic subobject of night.

It raises the question of the music of night.

Traditional literary forms such as the poem, the short story, and the novel have become obsolete. We need new forms for new myths.

Paramyth: a prose form partaking of essay, legend, magical fairy tale, folk tale, prose poem, story, and which offers a psycho-synthetic diagram of experiences of dreams, daydreams, hypnogogic hallucinations, eidetic images, fantasies, visions, and of the individual and collective unconscious.

Hypnologue: a logomantic form that approaches a traditional poem because it equally expresses organic rhythm yet differs from it as a result of its emphasis on mediumistic and imaginative inspiration by means of the transmutation of words and of syntax. It wants to achieve a liturgical and incantatory spirit.

Polyvocables: a hypnologue spoken in several languages that seeks above all to express the dynamic of the interracial unconscious by means of an identical rhythm and the synthesis of mythical images.

Ontogram (Georges Pelorson): the loud, kinetic, and instantaneous voice of being. Thus it admits contradictions, provided that they partake of eternity. It may also be called the gesture of eternal being. Thus it admits all definitions.

Paramyths (July 1935)

(The literature of the future will have no interest in competing with the possibilities for photographic and acoustic realism offered by the cinema, the radio, television, and similar mechanical inventions.

I believe, therefore, that the literature of the future will tend toward the presentation of the spirit inherent in the magic tale and poetry, toward the poet's exploration of heretofore hidden strata of the human personality. It will probably express the irruption of the supernatural, the fantastic, the eternal into quotidian life.

This mantic night-world will need new forms for its expression. What is now known as the short story, the novel, the poem, and so on will give way to forms that are as yet unnamed.

I suggest the paramyth as the successor to the form known heretofore as the short story or *nouvelle.* I conceive it as a kind of epic wonder tale giving an organic synthesis of the individual and universal unconscious, the dream, the daydream, the mystic vision. In its final form it might be a phantasmagoric mixture of the poem in prose, the popular tale of folklore, the psychograph, the essay, the myth, the saga, the humoresque.

The language of the paramyth will be logomantic, a kind of music, a mirror of a four-dimensional universe.)

Workshop (July 1935)

Expression and Activism—The Intercontinental Man—Creation of the Mantic Compost—The Language of Night as a Postulate—Its Relation to the Collective Language—Toward a Metaphoric Syncretism—The Supernatural and the Subobject—Phantoms and Exorcism—Vertigral

The art of expression is suffering from a paralysis that is one of the symptoms of a civilization in collapse. It struggles for its autonomy against the sociological flood. On every side we are belabored with the question: how can the artist of the word continue his search, when the nursery of humanity is without parallel in history, when wars and catastrophes threaten everywhere, when the destruction of world capitalism is the only task that should occupy him? He is untrue to the mission of the spirit, say these arguments, his flight into the dream is treason to man. The moment has come for him to reject facile compromises and to join in the class struggle.

The fight to abolish the exploitation of man by man is undoubtedly entering a decisive phase today. World capitalism will not recover from the blows it has received during the past decade. We are entering a revolutionary epoch that will become progressively more intense until the solution has been found. The artist of expression, as a human being, as the intuitive type of mankind, can only respond sympathetically to this revolutionary wave which must end by giving justice to the victims of the profiteering system. He is in favor of every effort made to metamorphose the present economic reality, to create a new social order which will give the masses power and leisure, to eliminate racial and national discords caused primarily by the international plutocracy. Yet he cannot obey the instructions of militant ideologists who have proclaimed the dogma that the "poet" must henceforth place his art at the service of propaganda. He cannot be activistic in that special sense without abandoning the premises of the creative motor of life. His is not the task of the tract or the pamphlet. He is not a reformer. He does not preach ethics. He does not aid in a religious revival. The creative can never be bound by political frontiers. It is never concerned with being "left-wing" or "right-wing." It is by its very nature syncretistic. It takes life as a totality. It lives it and expresses it. It blends the unconscious and conscious, the mythic and historic, the individual and the collective, into a superconscious reality.

The new human type that is emerging as an elite is not dominated by environmental changes, social revolutions, or chiliastic conceits, but by the explosive force of an inner mutation that may very well run parallel with the social mutation, but is hardly caused by it. It seems to me that we are witnessing the slow emergence of a new creative personality. I see it not as a Fascist or Bolshevist or New Dealist type, but as an interracial and intercontinental synthesis, a type that has become conscious of the ancestral strata in man—the primitive and pre-logical heritage in our structure— and of a new collective human sensibility. It may become the blending of the Nordic and the Mediterranean type of man, a kind of super-Occidental man capable of transcending cycles and continents.

A new kind of creator is due who will liquidate the putrefaction of present-day bourgeois literature and art, who will sweep away the decaying expression used by the clowns of estheticism, who will unite the mantic and interracial forces in man. He will organize the vast material which biology, psychology, philology, anthropology, and other sciences have put at his disposal. The universal identity of the inner psyche which has now been proven and which transcends cultural, racial, or linguistic antinomies opens up new possibilities to him. He knows that there is an identity between the creative psyche and the spirit of illumination. He anticipates the fact that the horizontal consciousness which, through Naturalism, has dominated the past hundred years, will be followed by a psychic revolution, through which the creative man will look at his life in terms of high and low, in terms of antinomies in fluctuation, in terms of a systole and diastole between the irrational and the superconscious. He seeks the laws of totality. He seeks a *restitutio in pristinum*. He develops whatever embryonic mystical faculties he may have. He lets new perceptions inundate him. He watches in himself the efflorescence of extra-normal states of consciousness. Or better:

he redevelops in himself ancient and mutilated sensibilities that have an analogy with those used in the mythological-magical mode of thought in the primitive man, with prophetic revelations, with orphic mysteries, with mystic theology such as that of Dionysius Areopagita, with the Kabbala, Tao, Hindu philosophy, with Egyptian wisdom, with gnostic rapture, with mantic experiences like those of van Ruysbroeck, Böhme, Master Eckhardt, St. John of the Cross, with the attitude of the early Romantics, with the mental habits still extant in folklore and fairy tales, with clairvoyance, clairaudience, day and night dreaming, even with subhuman or psychotic thinking. This attitude to the creator is the antithesis of one that believes in the primarily conscious genesis of creation. The two attitudes are best represented in the antipodes: Mallarmé and Rimbaud, Hölderlin and Goethe. Yet we know that the identification of the "poet" with the *vates* or seer has always existed. Novalis and Rimbaud were at one in postulating this union. It is only in periods of "Enlightenment" and positivism that the tendency has been temporarily buried. (This is what was happening after the war.) Yet it emerged again and again explosively after each period had run its course. The new creator builds the bridge between the two attitudes of the unconscious inspiration and the superconscious creation: the line passes from irrationalism to a transcendental superlogic. I believe that we stand today at the threshold of a new flowering of this spirit: the resurrection of the vertical attitude toward life.

It is, of course, impossible to return to the historic past. We can no longer indulge in a nostalgia for the Middle Ages, in a search of Ofterdingen's *blue flower,* in a return to Gothicism. The return to a New Romanticism, as many continue to call this inner revolution, is an absurdity (just as is the return to a New Classicism, or a New Humanism). Let there be no mistake about it: Romanticism is dead, and it will never be resurrected. Yet we cannot but acknowledge that there is a link binding some of us with a certain aura that hovered around Romanticism. We feel that we are living in a mental climate that, in its collective alienation and apocalyptic mood, resembles the one in which Romanticism flowered in the beginning of the last century. We cannot forget that our interest in the night-side of life is identical with that manifested by the Romantic thinkers and seers. They were the first to emphasize the importance to the creator of irrationalism, of the dream and the daydream, of mysticism and mythos. The preoccupation with the dream, especially, haunted all Romantics from Coleridge to Nerval, to Petrus Borel, to Novalis, to Tieck, to Jean Paul. They considered it an integral element of the "novel" and of "poetry," after Goethe, strange to say, had led the way by being the first to use the dream as part of an anecdote in *Wilhelm Meister.* They regarded it as the principal esthetic organon. They identified it with the fairy story. They interpreted the symbols through metaphysical categories.

We feel a relationship with the aura of that age. But that is as far as we go. We are through with its forms of expression, with its language, with its style. The period of the "lyric" and "poem" is definitely over. The world of sonnets, ballads, octaves, elegies, odes, is over. The "poem" with its narcissism, descriptions of the milieu, paeans of land and loam, lovesick whines, melodramatic anecdotes of bloodlust and incest, Hellenic parallelisms, propaganda of "living issues," little individual aches and troubles, cynically objective naturalism, is liquidated. A new style is in the making that will present the dramatic unity of "body and soul," that will be *subobjective.* New forms to present the identity of the ancestral world and the present world will have to be found; epic word-symphonies will have to be discovered; an interracial language will have to be forged to express the collective inner vision of mankind. The "poem" must change into a *mantic compost* which organizes the expanding consciousness of "the expanding universe." It will go parallel with science which is no longer afraid of intuition, which is joining the ideations of mystics and seers, which has discovered the cosmic rays as the confirmation of the gnostic pneuma, which has annihilated three-dimensional space. The *mantic compost* will be the expression of the noumenal reality, the super and interplanetary cosmos, the dynamis of a new imagination.

The chief need for the expression of this inner mutation is a new art of the word. We need a new plastic word composition that has nothing to do with the pedantry of modern philology, or the sterile dogmas of "estheticism." It is related to the existential, to anthropology, to depth psychology, to metaphysics.

The artist of the word who participates in this process of inner metamorphosis attempts to forge language into a mantic instrument. In calling for the *language of night* some years ago, I had this in mind as an aim. I expressed a wish-image, a postulate, a nominalistic fiction. I knew this language did not exist today. It existed in the past, it was the Homeric language of the gods, the language of the heroic age of the races, the inner language of the mystics. Poets like Angelus Silesius, St. John of the Cross, Blake, Nerval, Novalis, Francis Thompson wrote in a manner approximating it. So did the anonymous poets who created their hymns in "mystic

Latin." Yet we can only use their expression as a base. They did not solve the question. They merely attempted with the means at their disposal to give voice to the inner vision they had. Theirs was the liturgical, hymnic attitude to the word, which is the attitude we should try to recapture today.

The extension of consciousness which modern science places within the zone of possibility today seems to require a new form of expression. I noticed in my own linguistic development that the words in my native and acquired tongues were beginning to wear out. Having used creatively the three principal European languages, I saw how in each one of them I was reaching a dead point beyond which there was no use going. In this trilingual difficulty I had no precedent to go by. Creative language, I feel, is sick. A curious muteness lies over it. The nihilistic collapse of a world is mirrored in it. It is inadequate to transmit even the simplest psychic phenomena. There no longer exists any language for our deepest emotions about love and death. The "lyrical" language today is filled with banausic clichés and metaphoric banalities. To the epigones the thematic material is everything. Their language is poisoned by the *déchets* of the utilitarian mind. It suffers from the vacuity of the "little housekeeping words," and from the logic of the conceptualist system. The use of words in what is known as "poetry" occurs through the reflective and conscious hammering of sense-impressions into the objective language. Language has lost the Heraclitean sense of movement.

A new "alchemy" is needed. This has been felt by a few isolated word-artists for the past hundred years, but the full clinical picture of the pathology has been recognized only in the last decade or so. The Romantic poets had a presentiment of it. Edgar Allan Poe, now passing through an unjustified eclipse, was struck with it. Lewis Carroll tried to find a solution of his own. Rimbaud had a grandiose vision of the need of "hallucinated words." Mallarmé fought heroically for his own inner language. Marinetti, albeit in a non-metaphysical sense, was the first in this century to open the offensive by making the word autonomous and dynamic. The Expressionists and early Dadaists, following in his footsteps, made the isolated word anarchic. James Joyce, the greatest word-artist of the age, mirrored his independent vision of the disintegration of language in *Ulysses*, and is now hammering out his own polysynthetic solution, which cannot be imitated.

We are beginning to sense the metaphysics of language again. I envisage the *language of night* as a mediumistic organ, the attempt to cognize the meta-real value of the word and syntax. Here we come face to face with those processes that cannot be sensed with the intellect. For it is the unconscious vision which created language, and we stand before the task of redis-covering the knowledge of the daemonic-magical things that lie hidden in words and have been lost to modern man. This is, I take it, the real sig-nificance of Emerson's dictum: "The corruption of man is followed by the corruption of language."

The word was song and liturgy in the beginning of man's verbal expres-sion. The epos existed before the novel. Sagas were recited as litanies. Today's "poetry" has lost this sense of the ancestral rhythm in which the word was considered a *formule magique,* in the literal sense. We have in us the heritage of billions of years of common mutation. The *language of night* does not want to break with the past. Numberless words in every language are eternal, because they carry the weight of mythical experiences with them. The ancient symbols still live, but we have to experience them again and again in order to open the way for other experiences by the liberated imagination. Once there was a language of parabols, runes, and fairy tales. We no longer understand the fervor with which past epochs employed the *Word.* It was sacred, it was the atman's echo, it was the Johannite logos. The ancients felt it contained the inner wonder of the Godhead. It was a means of conjuration and creation. When the Hindu spoke AUM, the interjec-tion became power through the forty different ways of its pronunciation. The poets of the Veda regarded the word with religious fanaticism, they examined each intonation, and meditated every grammatical and rhyth-mic relationship. The primitive man—the *homo divinans,* as he has been called—had the same attitude to the word. Among certain tribes in Africa, America, and Australia, it is still the custom, on special occasions, to sing in a sacred language handed down from primeval days. In the magical texts of the past there are to be found extraordinary sound formations that refer to the sacred elements of language. These forms of ancient wisdom were transmitted liturgically, they represented enigmatic sigils, they had exorcis-tic potency. In this alchemy of letters the mythological mind approached the hidden or supernatural powers.

We cannot break with the past, but we cannot return to it either. For language cannot stand still or go back. It is in constant movement and simply carries the symbolic remnants of the past in its stream. It carries with it the phylogenetic mass. The psychic liberation which new discover-ies have made possible (eidetic images, the collective unconscious, all the oneiromantic or hermeneutic operations) opens up new means of expres-sion. The artist of the word whom these psychic experiences have liber-ated finds the contact with the mystic seer's view of the world and uses language in its function of *suggestion,* as M. Paulhan has called it. He acquires changed faculties of expression. He is in search of new symbols and sigils, and weds them, in a voluntary arrangement, with ancient words inherited from an ancestral past. He seeks hieroglyphs to express what to many seems the inexpressible. In his process of the mystic metamorphosis of reality, he also metamorphoses the means of representation. The experiences of the *yore-world* vibrate in him, he senses abysmal life through the operation of dreams, diurnal fantasies, hypnogogic hallucinations, visions of rapture. His words themselves become mediumistic. They live a life of their own, like all living organisms. They have the power to create a universe that heretofore existed only as a fiction.

The *language of night* being the total expression of all the material that goes to make up the experiences of the daemonic-cosmic dynamis of the inner world in flux needs a liberty such as the recent literary epochs have denied the creator. The artist of the word having extended his consciousness and created in himself an intuitive apprehension of the invisible world must be free to de-rationalize the language of an intellectualist age. There are two ways of approaching this problem. His temperament may be such as to make him limit himself to a mere *phantasmatic* rearrangement of his material. In that case, I believe it essential that the irreality he presents should find voice in the mysticism of a *montage in words,* in a *semantic* revolution, in an attempt to dislocate mediumistically all those vocables that have become poisoned by the contact with the empirical reality. He is not bound by the syntactical laws of logic used in the language of communication, although he may use them if his inner vision makes it necessary to do so. He is out to create a new syntax: the sentence becomes conjuration. On the other hand, if his temperament be more impatient and if he finds many words definitely useless and pathological for the purpose of manifesting the mediumistic experience, he ought to have the right to invent new ones. In this *revolution of the word* he does not forget that he always builds on a language saturated with the ancient mythic symbols. He does not forget that the substratum of the unconscious psyche is identical in all races throughout the world. Age-old magic texts well up from the tertiary memory. Word-images emerge somnambulistically. He makes a "spiritual wedding" of the old and new sigils and thus gives language wings again. His primary aim is the creation of a new metaphoric language that might approach the mood of illumination.

In this revolutionary process he does not neglect the collective language as speech. The *language of night* absorbs the language of communication in a metaphorical syncretism. It passes through continents and centuries, through dead and living worlds. The mutation now going on, which is helped dynamically by the new technological means such as the cinema, the radio, and other mechanical forces, is about to create a linguistic inter-penetration that will doubtless have its effect on the final morphological process of modern languages. There will be modifications eventually that will kill certain weaker branches and develop new ones. The migrations of peoples since the war have also contributed to this process. I see today a vast intercontinental revolution of language.

The *language of night* I have in mind will make the intercontinental syn-thesis of the inner and outer language. It may thus become the truly uni-versal language. Not that of the "educated philistine" who demands signs to simplify his world of communication, not an auxiliary language that will never remind him of his solitude, not a quotidian language of gestures that flees from consecration. But a language that will dance and sing, that will be the vision of the "troisième oeil," that will bind the races in a fabu-lous unity.

One of the steps toward this language is the entrance into the pre-logical. We are still on the threshold to the discovery of an authentic language of the dream.

During a number of years when I attempted to transcribe my dreams verbally, I encountered considerable difficulties. Certain objects of the unconscious world often appeared to me to have no analogy whatever with the objects which they might have resembled in the waking state. They were definitely *new* objects created automatically in the state of sleep, or half-sleep, deformations of well-known objects, synthetizations of them. Since the objects were subjective creations, I felt that naming them objects was a misnomer. I invented the word "subobject" for these phenomena.

In naming them according to approximate correspondences with the objects known in the waking condition, I realized I was making a com-promise. For often they were, in fact, *other* objects. I therefore proceeded to invent certain vocables for them. It so happened also that in the dream itself words presented themselves spontaneously to me as pure neologisms. I noticed a selective relationship between the objects and the words. The semantic sense of the dream-word and their sound character determined their interpretation. I saw that the *jeux de mots* in the dream were full of meaning. Behind each new word stood another word, another reality.

I had suggested to myself during the dream, or else I name-invented such words as Grala, Ascaton, Alzneiwein, Spaenlein, Sickermore, Old Griper, Verstehung, Hiera Ut, Gillabet, Cosmosa, Zweegey-Weegey, Bourgeoisin, Géantade, Grandoloquet, Lussurus, Garillon, Mélodore, and numerous others.

During hypnogogic experiences I often caught isolated sounds that I have not been able to explain satisfactorily. Usually they are Franco-German sounds that have no relation to anything I have read or heard.

In this subobjective oneiromancy it is important to remember the experiences of the daydream. We are always dreaming, and it is only the irruption of the outer-world of civilization that puts brakes on this process. The night-world of the daydream has not been studied thoroughly up till now, although the [James] Cooks of psychology are preparing to do so. Here we enter the mutation of the metaphor.

One of the chief faults I have to find with the present art of the word is that it tends to ignore almost completely the daemonic content of language. By this I mean the word that is the reflex of the descent into the mythological world, into the ritual universe. Some years ago, during the infant stages of *transition,* I once spoke of the *diabolical principle* in connection with an analysis of Lautréamont's work. Wyndham Lewis pounced on the idea, and, misunderstanding completely my purpose, belligerently published a book using as its title my *transition* term. Since his premises were wrong, his arguments against the stand I then took fell flat.

I still feel today that, creatively speaking, the preoccupation with this principle cannot be overrated. I am inclined to substitute for the word "diabolical" (which now smacks too much of old-fashioned theology) the more precise term "daemonic," which was first used by Goethe, I believe, to describe that inner dynamics in man denoting the experience of the lower or subhuman forces. Life is a polarity between the subhuman, or daemonic, and the supra-human, or cosmic, an energetical process, in which both principles flee each other and sometimes join. This phenomenon can be traced in every mystic and gnostic philosophy, the Chinese knew it as Yang and Yin, the dualistic Manicheans built a marvelous cosmogony around the idea. Even the Catholic Paschal acolyte says triumphantly: "O certe necessarium Adam peccatum." It is what Bachofen called "*the road to the mothers.*"

In studying the unconscious—my own, of course, for, *n'en déplaise aux collectivistes,* it's the only one I really know well—I came upon certain phenomena that, by dint of repetition, attracted my attention. I found that the dream symbolism was subject to laws that apparently went beyond mere psychoanalytical interpretation. Urged on by the mystic and gnostic writers I was then studying, I understood that that material in my dreams was not only non-personal, but definitely related to certain myths or legends I had learned to know in my childhood. There seemed to be a polarity between the daemonic and celestial images. What struck me, as I went on, was that behind the objective images there stood other images. Hidden behind the foreground of the realistic symbols, there apparently was a universe inherited from the ancestors. It was the unconscious of mankind that was revealed.

These dream-beings were mostly phantoms, sometimes also light-beings. Grotesquely masked apparitions, cobold-like creatures, animal-men predominated in these phantasmata and chimerae. I had the impression that my night-world was the playground of the Luciferian and celestial powers, to use the terms of the biblical mythos. The depersonalization I sensed in the dream-state was a kind of schizophrenic phenomenon. I felt that we are split personalities in our dreams, that we are really *being* dreamed, that there are other "I's" in us, that we are like persons possessed.

We have to face these demons and phantoms. What is at stake here is this: the artist of the word who seeks transcendental perceptions cannot hesitate to confront chaos. He must accept it as a necessary step to a higher medial cognition. He must pass willingly through what St. John of the Cross called "the dark night of the soul." Ordinarily men try to ignore these maleficent forces. They live in the cynical belief that their little intellect suffices to approach the immense complexity of the unconscious. To go down into this troubling labyrinth, to descend into the abyss is a catharsis. As I have watched these phenomena, I have tried to transcribe the conflict in words. This presented itself to me as an exorcistic process, the redemption from the larval power of what the gnostics called *daimones*. The exorcism translated itself through a word-synthesis that seemed to solve the tension between the subhuman word of the "I" and the transcendental word of the "you." The inner duologue found its conclusion apparently in a language of mantic metaphors, in a superconscious synthesis.

Vertigral looks toward the future for an elite of interracial men and a new art of the word that will create the myths of a supernatural universe in logomantic terms.

Vertigral (June 1936)

Eur-American Anthropology
Expansion of Consciousness
Synthesis between Ur (*Scheitelauge,* Pineal Eye, *Troisième Oeil*) and New
    Vision
Phantasmata
Ontological Experience
Mystic Metamorphosis of the World
Ecstasis
Exploration of the Irrational
World Rhythm
The Spirit of Night
Incantation and Ritual
The Liberation of Man
From Tellurism to Uranism
The Language of Dream and Night
The Interplanetary Imagination

Vertigralist Pamphlet (1938)

> And the Lord scattered them from that place into all lands, and they ceased to build the city. And therefore the name thereof was called Babel, because there the language of the whole earth was confounded; and from thence the Lord scattered them abroad upon the face of all countries.
>
> —Genesis 2:8

> Let us assume that a person has often been flying in his dreams, and that, during a dream, he becomes conscious of the faculty and the art of flying, as well as of his privileged situation, and of an enviable happiness . . . why should not such a person find that, in his waking hours, the word "happiness" is tinged and determined quite differently for him?
>
> —Friedrich Nietzsche

> Time is a spiral.
>
> —P. D. Ouspensky

> Truly elevated, I flew vertically into the deep blue, starry sky, and besang the cosmic structure while flying.
>
> —Jean Paul

> Nous descendons spiralement, depuis quinze années, dans un vortex d'infamie et notre descente s'accélère jusqu'à perdre la respiration.
>
> —Léon Bloy

> Language is Delphi.
>
> —Novalis

One of my principal objectives in *Transition* (and outside of *Transition*) during the last seven years has been the search for a new art of the word based on a mystic renovation.

In giving the name of *vertical,* or *vertigral,* to this tendency it has been my intention to emphasize my opposition to the mechanistic mode of thinking, to the frenetic intellectualism accentuated by the world crisis, and, at the same time, to help build a bridge between creative expression and the eternal pan-symbolic (or mystic-Romantic) *experience* of life.

In stating that the crisis was a psychic one rather than a politico-economic one, I posited as a premise the malady of human consciousness and language. I postulated *"a subliminal ethos," "the being with the third eye," "cosmological cognition," "the language of night."*

The expression of this view seemed to me to be justified at a time when contemporary creators, in the first phases of the world depression, sought escape in the philosophy of materialism, and attempted to solve their esthetic problem in a militant *sociological activism.* A plea for a metaphysical reconstruction would appear to be more than ever justified today.

Creative manifestations today are in the shadow of a primeval *fear,* a rationalist *possession.* This is an epoch of ontological despair and nihilism.

We are afraid. A nameless apprehension lies over us like a stupor. We bend under the weight of a cosmic fear, an existential anguish, a *weltangst,* which is the mark of our collective emotion.

Through Kierkegaard, Heidegger, and Kafka we understand what a primordial role this sensation of *urangst* plays in the life of man. Like *la grande peur de l'an mil,* we experience it again today, with heightened force, as an apocalyptic apprehension that paralyzes us in an almost blinding terror.

We have lived too long in the telluric cavern. We have been preoccupied too long with the demoniacal universe, with the world of the larval, subhuman phenomena, with schizophrenic monsters. Ours has been a "descending mysticism."

True, it was a necessary experience, for we need to cognize the phenomenology of *le mal.* It is a cognition of the innate polarity of life that, for instance, the works of Bernanos, Mauriac, and other literary transcendentalists bring to our attention today. Not the "Satanism" of the last century, but the daemonism of the Anti-Christ in whose existence these writers really believe!

The poet *exorcises* this *possession* through the mantic word. From his visionary experience he expresses the metaphysical depths of modern *man in pain.*

We need the conscious will to batter down the gates of "the narrow prison of life" (Pascal) by a search for a mystic nexus, for a *total* reintegration of the eternal elements of life.

The will to *ascension* still slumbers in us.

It has astral and transcendental directions.

It is the hunger for the *tremendum.*

We find traces of this urge in many of the archaic myths of humanity as an *astronomic* desire, and even today, primitive Indian races, on both the American continents, preserve the ancient star-myths as a living heritage.

There are many legends, many sculptural and architectonic ritualistic sigils of ascension throughout prehistory and history. To mention only a few:

Daedalus and Icarus.

The Nordic saga of Wieland, the goldsmith.

The Hellenic Nike, the archetypal image of

The Angel, seraphic flyer through space, cherubic messenger of God.

Yggdrasil.

The pyramids of Egypt, Mexico, and Guatemala.

The menhirs of Brittany, Ireland, England.

The communal faith of the Middle Ages produced the ogival aspiration of Gothic cathedrals.

This intuitive reaching toward the *above,* toward the liberation of the human being from the chains of the law of gravitation, manifests itself technologically in the aeronautical triumph of modern times; the helicopter rises *vertically* into space.

Lindbergh is the perfect symbol of this *verticalism,* which, although it has a *mechanical* direction, is merely the twentieth-century solution of an age-old *psychic* problem.

Modern aeronautics is the physical manifestation of an "as if" that has haunted mankind from time immemorial; for the human mind has tried heroically, again and again, to make its wish of imitating the flight of the birds come true.

But there is a deeper psychic significance. The imprisonment of Daedalus reflects the human feeling of being "imprisoned" in the material world, it is the symbol of the desire to "ascend," to "rise," to "mount," to "fly"—to destroy the fetters of human limitations.

The Nordic races, in their unceasing migrations, carried with them the universal symbol of the world-ash, which mirrored existence as a dynamic ascensionist concept, binding together hell, earth, and heaven. This was the tree of life, the tree of time and space.

In the Middle Ages it changed optically into the Gothic cathedral, the architectural form of a collective faith in and aspiration toward God. The Romantic notion of the *cosmic night* (Novalis), the dissolution of consciousness in the objective universe by means of *ecstasis,* is related to the idea of this *unio mystica.*

The mystics used numerous geometrical or architectonic metaphors to express the will to "ascent," "elevation," "levitation," "angelic flight," and so on.

In this connection let us recall:

The desert saint Joannes Climacus (the name alone is a program!) and his book: *Scala Paradisi.*

The entire gnostic movement with its liturgy of the *celestial ladder.*

The Spanish mystics, especially St. John of the Cross, and his *Ascent of Mt. Carmel.*

Flemish and Rhenish mystics such as Ruysbroeck, Master Eckhart, Tauler, the *Strasbourg Friends of God,* and so on.

Böhme, Swedenborg, Blake.

Our racial memory is still preoccupied with the dream of flying. In our archaic unconscious we repeat the experiences of primitive man and the mystic alike.

These flying dreams evoke the erotic instinct and the mystic spirit, as well.

But they also mirror the *future* life.

In them we vision a new age of man.

One of the outstanding inadequacies of psychoanalysis, in my opinion, has been its failure to recognize the transcendental potentialities of the dream, by making the past the sole arbiter for the mythological understanding of the night-mind.

We know today that oneiric ascension is a kinesis announcing the new human being, the *cosmic being.*

It announces an epoch when anthropological development will have made such progress that the human being will be again *homo divinans,* with faculties that will permit him to reach, organically, the *fourth dimension.*

In this connection, it is interesting to note the recent experiments made by Professor Rhine of Duke University in an effort to determine the possibilities of "Extra-Sensory Perceptions" (E.S.P., as they are commonly referred to in accounts of the experiments).

We may be passing through an inner mutation which, eventually, will give us the capacity for a new vision, the *third eye,* the *zenith-vision,* the gift of peering into eternity, which will permit us to comprehend the idea of *Psychic Time,* the multidimensional stratification of Time, cosmic Time.

This will probably be the human being foreshadowed by the great scientist and visionary, C. G. Fechner, in his astonishing book *Zend-Avesta:* the man who will participate in the collective consciousness of the universe, who will find contact with the interplanetary consciousness, with the "world-soul."

This eternal principle can no longer be found in the creative arts today.

I am convinced, however, that the creative instinct should be identical with the instinct of ascension. The arts are analogous to existential mysticism and, as such, should once more become *conjuration,* a mantic means of liberation or *exorcism.*

Their role should be to emancipate the human being from the obsession of fear in the world of matter.

They should mirror the *expansion of consciousness* in a migration to higher space, to the supernatural, to "the divine dark."

For this a cosmic expression and form, a *planetary imagination,* are needed:

The cloudglass-city.

The skyscraper-cathedral of New York.

The interstellar tower.

Monumental sculptures as ritualistic symbols of a *communal* celestial aspiration.

Polyphonic music as *hymnic* expression, pan-rhythmic liberation, the *chorus mysticus.* Synthesis of the terrestrial and the celestial emotion. The human being participating in a seraphic chant. This music to be executed not only in concert halls, but diffused in the open, or in gigantic buildings that are adequate to its architectonic universalism.

Absolute painting giving the color-vision of the bridge between the *finite* and the *infinite.*

Poetry taken in the universal sense of *Dichtung,* or the sacred logos.

A new art of the word in a constant interweaving of lyric and epic expression.

Pan-logos.

Invention of new languages to voice the inter-linguistic sense of *unio mystica.*

The word as rune, as liturgy, as a hymnic eulogy, as incantation.

The phantasmatic metaphor.

All the arts interpenetrating in the mutation from the frontier-world of the three-dimensional consciousness to the experience of a multidimensional, frontierless cosmos.

All the arts, combining past, present, and future, building the new myth of the heightened creative life.

The Quest and the Myth (1941)

In an age of Fascist barbarism, it is high time to return to the myth as a creative source. The *mythical marvelous* reflects the millennial war between the spirit and chaos, between the satanic imperative and the redemptive principle.

The myth is still part of our psychic heritage. It exorcises fear, suffering, desire, and resolves them in a sequence of images that occur again and again in our cerebral structure, being primordial "archetypes" that hardly vary in the process of time. We poets should resuscitate the *mythical marvelous* during this period of convulsions and suffering by reviving narrative, epic poetry with heroic dimensions.

Myths—which are ancestral, collective dreams—besing the hero as well as the saint.

I am interested in the myth of migration—or the wander legend—which I have lived in my own life and which millions of beings are living today, when the dictatorial dominators bludgeon human beings from their homes and send them forth on vast, unwilling odysseys. I have myself been working on an epos of this kind with multilingual elements.

There are many others, the contemporary symbolism of which moves us all:

The voyage of the Argonauts under Jason, in quest of the Golden Fleece.

The Quest of the Holy Grail, still a dynamic myth that has not lost its immediate significance.

We think of the great Columbiads in the Middle Ages that are still going on today, less as geographical utopias, than as scientific explorations, or astronomic investigations.

We think of the mythical migration from the cavern to the mountain—as seen in Dante's *Divina Commedia*—which is still a living, fabulous symbol.

I am also interested in the myth of celestial ascent, or of the vertical journey. It is deeply rooted in our unconscious. The Icarian dream is now realized. But the cosmic-mystic journey still awaits its interpreter.

It is, of course, an ancient story: many primitive peoples had this mythology as a central motif. The Babylonians, the Polynesians, the Aztecs, the Mayas, the Hindus, many African tribes, as well as Indian tribes of North America, organized their world into vast patterns built horizontally one above the other until they felt they had reached the heavenly apex. The polarity was conceived with the areas of death in the lower regions, those of life in the earth's surface, and the supernatural ones located in the higher spaces of the cosmos. In psychological application, this would mean the unconscious, the waking conscious, and the superconscious.

The mythology of *elevation* has always been part of the sacred architecture of primitive peoples. It was the carrier of theogonic ideas in the pyramids and temples. Gnostic and alchemistic theories of *elevation*—the passage through planetary spheres—imply this ceaseless journey to a *unio mystica.*

Astronomic myths—which were also common with primitive peoples—are again being revived. And we know much more about the spiral universe today than our ancestors, although their collective myth-dreaming anticipated many of the notions now projected by the sidereal sciences.

There are many others: the Christian myth of death and resurrection; the myth of Apollo and Dionysos, as the antithesis between logos and ecstasy; the myth of the Labyrinth and Minotaur; Theseus and Ariadne; the birth of the planets; Babel; creation of the world; the flood; end of the world; to name only a few. These are some of the countless patterns used by humanity everywhere for the weaving of the tale of its mysterious existence.

The revival of mythical thinking may lead us back to that universalism which the nationalist corruptors have tried to demolish.

Poetry of Ascent (1941)

Poetry, in an age of apocalyptic struggles, should confront the daemonic existence of evil and fear, face resolutely the terror of suffering, and attempt to liberate the human personality from the possession of nihilism.

The direction of poetry in our age should go toward the zenith.

It should seek a revolution in lyric and epic expression by a revolt against mechanistic thinking, by leaving the catacombs of primal irrationalism, by beginning a journey toward eternal objectives.

Poetry must emphasize the creative urge toward a communal feeling of living, toward a collective spirituality, toward a liturgical-ritual renascence.

Poetry must become a medium for the emancipation of the human personality by accentuating its voyage to the invisible, its hunger for the transcendental reality, its nostalgia for God.

The new poetry, in its daemonic-celestial tension, reconstructs the myth of voyage, flight, ascent in all its Romantic-mystic dimensions, and seeks the *marvelous of the skies.*

I. *The poetry of aeronautical flight* expresses the myth of the physical magic of technology. It sings and praises the deliverance of man from the law of gravitation. It gives voice to his aspiration for aerial perspectives and freedom, in spite of the abuse of this conquest by the daemonic forces of Fascism.

II. *The poetry of cosmic or sidereal flight* opens up four-dimensional possibilities in Occidental thinking. It sings and praises the luminosity of the stellar spaces and makes the dream of an astronomic imagination a reality.

It eulogizes the vision of the third eye, once known to primitive man. It reestablishes the belief in the existence of angels as elements in a huge vertical stratification of the universe.

III. *The poetry of mystic flight* seeks the absolute and the transcendental reality, the apex of which is God.

The new poetry of ascent wants to express the verticalist vision in a revolutionary language, a new religious form of expression which will make possible a hymnic vocabulary and a sacred syntax.

Threefold Ascent: Verticalist Manifesto
(August 1941)

We are living under the sign of a great dying, and a world aeon is crumbling.

The stability of the inner life has been demolished, and there seem to be few sigils to which man can cling, from the irradiations of which he can extract new hope.

We are in an epoch of convulsions and blasphemies, for the reason that modern man has rejected the universal solidarity of original guilt and lost the sense of liturgy, myth, and dream.

The disquiet of the individual is growing in proportion to the increasing bankruptcy of all the cultural values in which he believed up till now, and modern man contemplates the disintegration around him, rootless and bewildered.

The dissolution of the social ties throws the individual back into a glacial solitude from which apparently there is no deliverance. The psychic malady approximates to the point of alienation.

The false peace between two great wars only created a sense of nihilism and brought about a dilettante preoccupation with the diabolical forces of life.

Biological materialism has tried to throttle all metaphysical nostalgias, and a sense of vertigo grips contemporary sensibility, which is in the stupor of heretical ideologies.

The crisis of modern Humanism literally haunts the individual, who has lost the unity of existence in a labyrinth of contradictions and nightmares.

The human personality feels paralyzed in what Pascal called "the narrow prison of life." Its vision has become a fragmentary one. Everywhere man confronts the sordid parody of the marvelous.

Hitlerism, with its pseudo-philosophy of racial intolerance, militaristic inhumanity and terror, and the megalomaniacal deformation of ancient myths, is the chief cause of our disquiet.

But the monstrous tyranny of its tribal regressions and the barbarism of its state despotism, engulfing all of Europe and threatening our own American hemisphere, must make the creative mind more than ever determined to defend the democratically conceived state as the only organic political community in which the existence of freedom constitutes an ever new and living vision.

Fear, existential apprehension, cosmic anguish—this emotion is sweeping over the masses of the continents. A terror that is innate in all of us now emerges again in this moment of human crisis, like a wave of collective emotion, bringing a sense of rupture.

It is the tragic symbol of evil personified by "that wicked man," as Winston Churchill has called Hitler; by the emergence of the myth of the Anti-Christ; by a mechanistic anthropology; by the sadistic abuse of technology; by the anti-spiritual rationalism which Nazism encourages.

Creative man today must *confront* both evil and fear, he must face the social and inner convulsions, he must enter the cavern of nightmares and larvae, he must encounter the grimaces of irrationalism, in order to find redemption from daemonic possession.

He must conquer the anemia of the intelligence and the heart which dominates the individual and the community in the presence of the social and political spasms of history. He must seek the rediscovery of psychic freedom through an effort of the will tending toward a group liturgy and collective exaltation.

In the struggle against the pseudo-religion of Caesarism, he must reconstitute the great myths which its abject lies and paroxysmal distortions are trying to crush. Especially must he reconstitute the myth of continuous ascent as being the myth underlying mankind's ceaseless aspiration toward the liberation of the soul.

The metaphysical evolution of man from time immemorial has expressed itself in the symbolism of myths which voice the *marvelous of flight and ascensions:* the astronomic-planetary myths of the primitives; those of

Icarus and Daedalus, Pegasus; Nike; Wellan; Christ; the winged horses of the Norse; the magic carpet of the Orient; the levitation of saints; the sacred elevation of menhirs, pyramids, temples, Gothic cathedrals.

Even the modern urge for aeronautical flying is the contemporary signature of a Neolithic dream, the physical and technological expression of a psychic urge to conquer the law of gravitation.

Man's hope to elude the three-dimensional prison and search for the four-dimensional universe through the conquest of Time emancipates the creative personality by making him look at the stars again and develops a living nexus with the cosmos.

Modern science is making miraculous strides toward the conquest of many problems in physics, chemistry, astronomy, medicine, that a short time ago seemed insolvable, and the alchemistic dreams of the transmutation of the elements and the realization of the great unity of life are being slowly realized today.

Creative art must seek a union with the new sciences.

It must go on a quest for a transcendental and supernatural reality by reviving the great eras when communal ecstasy was a natural phenomenon, when the instincts of a group were tightened in inspired gestures, when ceremonial rituals were the usual, rather than the exceptional, functions.

We stand on the threshold of a new cycle—perhaps the super-American cycle—with cosmological properties, and the higher revelations will be found in a spiritual liturgy of all the arts, all of which are exorcistic instruments for destroying the anguish and tension created by a Fascist barbarism.

A mystical will is needed to ruin the fraudulent Romanticism of totalitarian imperialism. It can establish an ascending direction in an integration of the telluric and the marvelous by means of a brotherhood of initiates of the numinous.

We stand before the Era of the Paraclete.

Part Six : **Literary Encounters**

Introduction

Jolas met and interviewed a countless number of authors, journalists, publishers, intellectuals, philosophers, and men of letters whom he depicted, interpreted, and criticized in his writings. Frequently Jolas gives only short commentaries, as with his "Rambles Through Literary Paris," but there are also longer pieces, such as his essay on André Gide. Jolas wrote for a variety of other literary organs, typically journals, about the representatives of literary and, less frequently, intellectual life whom he considered important. Although the preponderance of his articles are sympathetic, he reserves criticism for Goethe—appearing to adopt the thrust of Carl Einstein's polemical "obituary" in the same issue—and Ernst Jünger, whose fascistic aesthetic at once fascinated and appalled him. The subjects who met with Jolas's approval are his most significant touchstones, the majority of which are German authors. There are the Romantics (above all Novalis) and also the mystics, on the one hand, and the Expressionists, Trakl and Benn, on the other. Kafka, in addition, must be understood here as meeting Jolas's criterion of a priority of the imagination that shows itself in the medium of language, whereas André Breton, the leading spokesman of French Surrealism, was someone to whom Jolas devoted special attention, but always with considerable reservations as to a certain deficit of "spirituality." In Jolas's view, the Romantics and the artists of the avant-garde shared a particular brand of Romanticism. No doubt, he was indebted to Novalis for inspiration and, of course, to James Joyce, whom he considered to be the twentieth century's truest example of literary genius, but whose originality was also beyond reach. It is a testament to the strength, if not stubbornness, of Jolas's convictions that despite Joyce's hostility to any kind of Romanticism, Jolas nonetheless always tried to incorporate him into his own preferences.

The significance of James Joyce's oeuvre for Eugene Jolas, both as a critic and a poet, however, cannot be underestimated. In a period of enormous creative upsurge, when artistic movements were constantly being announced and groups were coming apart at the seams, Joyce represented the kind of singular genius that seemed almost anachronistic. Indeed, Jolas liked to invoke the fifteenth-century master painters Hieronymus Bosch and Matthias Grünewald when describing the color and vibrancy of Joyce's more grotesque evocations. Joyce, in turn, found in Jolas a kindred spirit, a sympathetic editor, and most plausibly, a pioneering polyglot reader for his final *Work in Progress.* Their relationship, formed over the seventeen years of gestation of *Finnegans Wake,* would make Jolas, according to the biographer Richard Ellmann, one of the central dramatis personae in Joyce's life. Jolas saw Joyce primarily as a poet and a mythmaker; the chapter on Joyce in his autobiography *Man from Babel* is called "Ananke Strikes the Poet." His desire for a "Revolution of the Word," for an invention of a potent new vocabulary that would unleash the repressed imagination of the night-mind in a "rhythmic hallucination of the word," found its realization in the drafts of *Finnegans Wake* that Joyce would allow him to publish. Jolas thus came to consider Joyce as the poet who would incarnate his radical manifestoes with enormous creativity.

—K.H.K, Z.P.

Novalis

Homage to Novalis (November 1929)

> Nothing is more poetic than transitions and heterogeneous mixtures.
> —Novalis

The hunger for the infinite and the absolute found in Novalis* a deep and complete expression.

This ecstatic of the night refused to recognize the bipolarity of individual and universe, subject and object, and in his "magic idealism" demanded the spiritualization of external reality as well as the concretization of the spirit. He insisted that the creative being, the poet, is the synthesis of the sensual and spiritual universe. The problem of knowledge was solved by him in the Hegelian sense: that all conscious apprehension is the union of opposites. The identity of being and non-being became in his mystic metaphysics the root of his ideology. He thought and felt "pan-psychically."

This conception developed in him a latent mysticism which, although strongly infused with his indigenous Herrnhuter Pietism, remained free and undogmatic, like Blake's. In his poetry and prose he expressed the miraculous, explored the mysteries of the night and the chthonian, and gave voice to his longing for death, which he felt would be a creative act and the objectivation of his desires.

It is not to be wondered at that the dream became a factor of the utmost importance in his life. According to him, we know only that which knows itself. Nature is incomprehensible in itself, and we are able to penetrate it only as a symbolic picture of the spirit. This anti-intellectualist attitude led him to the idea that man alone is the absolute point of contact for all opposites, and that the study of our subconscious is the first essential

* Pseudonym of Freiherr von Hardenburg (1772–1801).

in our development toward a liberation. In the dream he found the very roots of poetry. He worshipped all the manifestations of the pre-logical and the mythic. In his *Heinrich von Ofterdingen,* the dream of the blue flower became the symbol of his longings, and the quintessence of an entire state of mind. And since the fairy tale is the result of the dream and shares with it many characteristics, he demanded its literary canonization.

Novalis created unconsciously a magical reality. For he demanded that the poet create in a state of highest consciousness in order to proceed from disassociation and anarchy toward the liberty of the pure spirit.

Novalis, the Mystic Visionary (undated)

Novalis was endowed with prodigious psychic and creative antennae. He was also a contemplative man, one who projected a striking light on religion, sought to abolish the frontiers separating the arts, and viewed life from the "dialectical" kinesis of height and depth, always on the quest for a superior consciousness. "Each descent into ourselves," he wrote in his *Fragments,* "each glimpse into the inner world is ascension—assumption—a glimpse into the true reality." And in the same collection of aphoristic statements, he declared: "The sloughing off of self is the source of all *descent,* as well as the basis of all veritable *ascent,*" for "the mysterious path leads inward" (*nach innen geht der geheimnisvolle Weg*). He did not see life as a journey toward darkness, toward the "underground" described by Dostoevsky, but as a slow progression toward the luminous, the spiritual night, a night analogous to that described by St. John of the Cross. Nor did he seek the chthonian, demoniacal night; but a night of galaxies, of angels and the "Divine Spark." Like certain more recent poets—Victor Hugo, who believed in the physical existence of angels; Saint-Pol-Roux and his "vertical voyage"; O. V. Miłosz and his experience of levitation—Novalis strove for the "ascending mysticism," which J. J. Görres, another Romantic, opposed to "descending mysticism" (*aufsteigende und absteigende Mystik*). He belonged to that class of *verticalist* dreamers whose poetic vision remains turned toward the heights.

After the death of his fiancée, Novalis's desperate grief soon gave way to a decision "to regard Sophie's tomb as the magnet of his new life and the place of his own redemption." He even resolved to follow her in death, observing that this "would also be a troth, albeit of a superior order." Writing to his friend Just, he said: "If thus far I have lived in the present, I shall now have to live entirely in the future, with faith in God and in immortality. It will be very hard to separate myself from this world which I have studied with so much love; there will be backslidings which will cause me many moments of distress. But I know that there is a force in man which, if carefully nurtured, can develop into a curious sort of energy." As this experience ripened it was finally metamorphosed by him into a series of mythic *Hymnen an die Nacht* which are among the purest examples of religious-Romantic poetry.

In 1799 Novalis abandoned his philosophic and scientific researches to devote himself exclusively to poetry and religious speculation. This resolution found its highest expression in the three great poetic works, *Hymns to the Night, Spiritual Canticles,* and *Heinrich von Ofterdingen.* In the *Hymns* he amplified the themes of his personal experience in a nocturnal intuition that resumes the Böhmist mysticism of the night in the cognition of nature and the soul of God. Here we also find the great themes of his creation: the metamorphosis of man, death and resurrection, continual ascension. It was through love that he found God. "My intelligence," he wrote to his friend Just, "had developed gradually and impinged little by little on the domain of the heart. It was Sophie who restored its lost Throne to the Heart." In his immense sorrow he had wanted to join his beloved in the other world. But a moment of mystic ecstasis experienced beside Sophie's grave tore the veil from his eyes. This illumination delivered his soul from its prison of grief.

The *Geistliche Lieder* are expressions of Novalis's experience of death, sorrow, and faith. Contrary to the heterodox trend of the *Hymns,* they reveal a certain orthodoxy, an evangelical belief in Christ's sacrifice, and an almost Catholic devotion to the Virgin Mary. Indeed, they recall the Pietist convictions of the poet's youth. They also have an emotional ebullience approximating the Baroque sentimentality of the old Herrnhuter poets, and for that reason represent Novalis's antipathy toward the growing rationalism of the hymns he heard being sung around him. A number of them, set to music, were incorporated in the Pietist hymnals and are, today, still very popular.

The innate mystic optimism of Novalis is evidenced in these hymns by the fact that they reveal no sense of sin. The *felix culpa* of St. Augustine seems never to have influenced him, and contrition and repentance are completely absent from these poems. They convey, in fact, an impression of childlike innocence, not to say naiveté, which Novalis further stressed by referring to the "ancient, burdensome illusion of sin." He did not believe in evil, and thus was liberated from the fear of death.

But what Novalis sought above all else in his metaphysical voyage was a new religion, an ecumenical church within the Christian theology. In 1799 he published an essay entitled "Christianity or Europe," in which he championed the cause of medieval Catholic Christianity and declared himself openly against *Aufklärung* and progress. His friends, especially Goethe and the entire group surrounding the Schlegel brothers, did not fail to rebuke him for what they considered his "reactionary" attitude. In the *Hymns,* however, there is no question of orthodox religion, as there is in the *Canticles,* but interpretation of a religion of the heart and of love, stemming from his sorrow over the death of his beloved. The *Hymns* are addressed to the Night (the Unconscious); and they greet Death and the inner vision. In a letter to Friedrich Schlegel, dated June 20, 1798, he wrote: "In interpreting *Hemsterhuys,* I have come upon an idea for a moral astronomy, and I have made the interesting discovery of a religion of the visible universe. Don't you think that this is the proper way to treat physics *symbolically,* in the most general sense of the word?" This *astronomic* mysticism played a great role in his thinking.

With Novalis (and Jean Paul), literature began to be dominated by the irrationalism of the dream and the unconscious. The oneiric life was explored, and symbols never met with before emerged as a result of these explorations. Here, too, the cosmogonic dreams of both poets tended toward ascension. We know very little about the results of Novalis's own researches, however, since he did not reveal his personal dreams. For him the dream uncovered irrational images "in a strange fashion," and he noted "the facility with which our soul penetrates into every object, transforming itself instantly into that object." He also wrote: "Is not the dream, even the most disordered, a curious phenomenon which, without even invoking divine origin, discloses a rift of inestimable worth in the mysterious curtain that hangs in myriad folds before our soul?"

The key to the *Hymns* may be found in the third hymn, in which the poet evokes his experience of ecstasy: "Suddenly I felt the birth-cord, the chain of light, snap asunder. Terrestrial splendor fled and with it fled my mourning—My melancholy melted into a new, unfathomable world." And he continues: "The landscape seemed to *rise* gently while above it soared my delivered, newborn spirit. The grave became a dust-cloud—through which I saw the radiant features of my beloved." And the hymn ends with the following words: "It was the first, the one dream—and only since then have I felt an eternal and immovable faith in the heaven of night and in its light—the beloved." Here we have an aerial verticalism of night, a suave sensation of gliding, the destruction of gravitation and of chronological time. "Thousands of years rolled away like thunder," he noted in his ravishment, and everything assumed a mythical nature.

Here Novalis reveals himself as a seer, a visionary, not of the artificial paradise to be attained through the use of drugs (as some of his letters would seem to indicate), but of the mythical "lost paradise," the new "golden age." Mysticism and magic bring him closer to the secrets of nature. His poetry becomes extraliterary incantation, the aim of which is to attain to the supernatural. In his inner experience he envisions vast cosmogonies, and his words become liturgy. His attitude toward the sacred is related to a seraphic faith, as revealed in the ninth poem of the *Geistliche Lieder:*

> Once more an angel shields you
> And leads you to the strand,
> And joyfully you rest your gaze
> Upon the promised land.

The spirit of night in the works of Novalis is quite different from that manifested by most other Romantic and post-Romantic writers. There is in it the notion of light, as exemplified by the Böhmist Virgin of Light or the myth of the Great Mother. It also projects the existence of being, a naturalist and supernaturalist notion of magical revelation, an expression of hope and belief in a world without monsters. The Novalisian night symbolizes union and perfect love in its accomplishment, a return to the maternal womb. This is the night of the cosmos and of the mythological night itself; the night of nuptial joy, the symbolical night of prophecies and of the *Ungrund;* the clairvoyant, irrational night, the night experienced by the individual and by all humanity.

The *Hymns to the Night* do not symbolize angry flight from the world, nor the ascetic disembodiment of older mysticisms. These night-songs ignore the bitter conflict of the finite and the infinite. On the contrary, they stem from the certainty of salvation, the sensual-super-sensual healing nexus of religious mythology. For him who succeeds in sensualizing the spiritual and in spiritualizing the sensual, both worlds are at hand. He elevates the sensual to God, but he also sees God in that which is sensual.

The *Hymns to the Night* glorify especially the Great Night, which is both

Sophie and Jesus the Redeemer. Being considerably attracted by theosophical ideas, Novalis identified Sophie with the Universal Sophia and Christ, when he wrote in his diary, "Sophie and Christus." His night of death leads to life eternal, and the meditation on the subject of the "sweet fiancée" ends in an apogee of love. The poems—originally written in regular verse and then recomposed in the tradition of poems in prose—begin with a lamentation and end on a note of profound religious optimism. Little by little the terrors of death vanish, and the monologue finally becomes a grandiose incantation of hope that the path may lead to the "house of the Father." In these lines we find a synthesis of the Pietist faith of his ancestors and of Catholic belief in the intervention of the Virgin. Hymn V has a particular significance: "In the poetic hut of poverty—a Son of the first Virgin, the Great Mother . . . fruit of mysterious embracings," we find the revelation of Christ, the real myth of night, drawing closer to the mysteries of India, to the conversion of the Singer. This, according to Maurice Besset,* is "the supreme union with Christ and His Mother, the Queen of Night."

In this obsession with the nocturnal spirit, Novalis owed much to Oriental thought, which was one of the dominating interests of his friends Schlegel and Schelling. In fact, his poetry cannot be understood unless we take into account the spread of Vedic writings introduced in the West by the Englishman William Jones, and by such French scientists as Anquetil-Duperron, who published a translation of the *Zend-Avesta* in 1771, before Jones had founded the Asiatic Society. As a result of these Anglo-French contributions, Hinduism gained adepts among such early Romantic philosophers and poets as Schlegel, Schelling, Schopenhauer, and Tieck, and indeed the dream of a universal religion, having its cradle in India, seemed then on the point of being realized. In his desire to change man, to raise him to a higher estate, these Oriental ideas—particularly the notion of transition from one plane of human evolution to another—encouraged Novalis in his own speculations. Here we may recall that in the *Hymns,* Novalis gives the name "Hindustani" to his nocturnal Orient.[†]

M. Maurice Besset retraces the lines of the poet's evolution by following

---

* *Novalis et la pensée mystique* (Paris: Aubier, 1947).

† In his *Renaissance orientale,* Raymond Schwab sketches the Hindu filiation of Novalis's *Hymns:* "What we call magical idealism established relationships between a system of clairvoyance and a mysticism of history, poetry, and human love. The two *gitas* visit the Occident in order to sanction these. The themes of a Hindu fatherland of art and the soul, fountain of wisdom, ocean of metamorphoses, and always the universal soul, circulate back and forth between Herder, Maier, Schelling, Novalis, and F. Schlegel. Among others inspired by the Vedic hymnal, William Jones had written a *Hymn to the Night* some years before Novalis."

the phases of his religious destiny. According to Besset, Novalis's quest is based not only on his studies of Orientalism, but also on his knowledge of Böhme, and his poetry can only be understood against the background of mystological research. Böhme undoubtedly played a capital role in his evolution, and both his letters and "fragments" testify to his passionate interest in the works of the Görlitz visionary. The ideas which Novalis developed after the death of his fiancée do resemble a good deal Böhme's quest as presented in *Aurora*. Böhme conceived a schema in which the "centrum" would be simultaneously "the source of radiation" and the "point of crystallization," and his speculations were based on the necessity of reconciling the existence and power of evil with the existence of an all-powerful God. He faced this difficulty boldly, and the eternal conflict between the two principles furnished the theses of his faith. Divinity or the Godhead appeared to him as *abyss* and *quietude without essence,* and contained as well "eternal nature" or the *mysterium magnum,* which is the principle of contradiction illuminating the two facets of the antithesis. For Böhme, divine love delivers us in a "ravishment of lightning flashes."

If the Böhmist influence is evident in the poems of Novalis, there are, however, other influences which are no less powerful. He had boundless admiration for the philosopher Fichte, for the mystic philosopher von Baader, for Schelling, the creator of the philosophy of transcendental idealism—all men who marked his evolution toward the magic realism that was to become his true credo.

Novalis, or the White Romanticism
(January 15, 1951)

The plethora of translations of Novalis's works published in France over the past few years is a sign of a growing interest on the part of the anguished public for that spirit inebriated with the aspiration to transcendence. Defined by anxiety, our apocalyptic age desperately reaches out for a spiritual consolation. Novalis has touched upon many philosophical and even scientific problems unsolved to this day. From the perspective of 150 years (Novalis died in 1801, at the age of twenty-nine), his poetry and prose acquire a prophetic aura. Surrounded by pessimism and nihilism, we welcome in him a man of affirmation, a man for whom the return to the Golden Age was an article of faith. Curiously, it is after the capitulation of Germany that his writings have won a large readership abroad (especially in France, Great Britain, and the United States), while in Germany we notice that not only Novalis but Romantic ideas in general have suffered a decline.

Indeed, it is difficult to speak with objectivity of Novalis and of the German Romanticism after the Nazis' crimes, after having witnessed the systematic sadism of these dreamers' descendants. It is impossible to put aside the Romantic heritage of totalitarian horrors and to remain blind to the biological racism present in the works of certain Romantic thinkers. As we read Novalis, Kleist, von Arnim, Hölderlin, and other lesser poets of German Romanticism, we easily detect intellectual deviations and, to use the expression borrowed from the admirable work by Michel Carrouges,

Mystique du surhomme,* many "Promethean" or even Luciferian elements whose seeds lay dormant in the Teutonic soul only to germinate in our days as a megalomaniac pan-Germanism, a brutal anti-Semitism, and the "universe of concentration camps." As we recall, the Romantics felt an attraction for chaos, for the abyss, and nearly all of them were anti-democratic. Let us not forget Herder's disdain for "the age of reason" and democracy in favor of the nation (of the *Volk*), nor his counsel to the German people to "vomit the infected mud of the river Seine" at the moment France vibrated with the promise of the Declaration of the Rights of Man. Let us also not forget the words of Heinrich von Kleist, who said that "everything would have turned out much better if Voltaire had been forgotten in the Bastille and Rousseau locked up in an insane asylum." There was also the Christian Germanic Society, founded by Achim von Arnim, from which he wanted to exclude "all Jews, Frenchmen, and Philistines." Romantic philosophers and poets no doubt share the responsibility for the Holocaust of 1939–45; Arndt, Fichte, and even Hölderlin are all more or less guilty.

And yet, would these poets of cosmic vision, who dreamed of total liberty and universal love, have accepted an abject and anti-Humanist regime and the dictatorship of a vicious swine? We can agree with Albert Béguin, who declares in his "Foreword" to the new edition of *Romantisme allemand* that "the spiritual adventure of the German Romantics never touches the vile regions in which swarmed Hitler's and Rosenberg's larva myths." He adds: "Yet to ignore these internal correlations would be, in my opinion, to underestimate both the exceptional greatness of Romanticism and the true nature of Hitler's madness, as well as the particular misfortune of a nation destined to manifest with such clarity, at the cost of an immense downfall, the present state of humanity."

Armel Guerne, who has recently given us a new French translation of the *Hymnen an die Nacht,* supplements the edition with valuable exegetical notes. He has managed to revivify the somewhat musty language of the original and even to preserve the subtly nuanced rhythm of these poems with a touching fidelity. Henri Stierlin has chosen the first version of the fifth hymn (a version differing from the second, translated by Guerne, in that it is written in blank verse), to which he adds a beautiful translation of the "Bergmannslied" (the Underground Castle) taken from the first part of *Heinrich von Ofterdingen.* Gustave Roud, Geneviève Bianquis, and Marcel Camus have equally translated the same fragments a few years earlier. A

---

* Michel Carrouges, *Mystique du surhomme* (Paris: Nouvelle Revue française, 1948).

philologist will have the pleasure of comparing their works from linguistic and esthetical points of view.

As we reread Novalis in the original, in 1950, we are struck by his nervous and spirited style, as well as by tautologies and redundancies, and on occasion even by a lyrical banality which often prevents the reader from gaining insight into the author's intentions. Novalis uses sterile, worn-out words of the Gothic vocabulary that cannot but meet with a certain resistance on the part of a modern reader. Can we still accept today the repetition *ad absurdum* of adjectives such as *anmutig, freundlich, wunderlich, lieblich, seltsam,* and so on without a slight reflex of revulsion? Novalis's style is characterized by a somewhat puerile *Schwärmerei;* and we are tempted to rewrite the whole work by substituting new words, words that are more alive. Moreover, the poet has never found a four-dimensional language necessary to express the creations of his cosmological imagination. Having said that, we admit with astonishment that one can still read his poems and his prose with pleasure.

For they are suggestive of freedom, of an ascending movement that delivers us from the laws of gravity and to a new vision. Indeed, an ascensional vision is at the heart of the poet's work, and the appeal of his writing consists in the fact that it opens a vast horizon onto the future and outlines the configuration of the future man.

Endowed with an acute psychic and creative sense, Novalis is a contemplative who sheds a radiant light upon religion and abolishes boundaries separating the arts, forever in search of a higher consciousness. "All descent into oneself," he says in his *Fragments,* "all insight is at the same time an ascent—an assumption—a glimpse at the true inner reality." In the same work, he declares: "Self-renunciation is the source of all abasement, just as it is the ground of all true exaltation" . . . because "it is toward the interior that leads the mysterious path" (*Nach innen geht der geheimnisvolle Weg*). He does not perceive life as an advance toward darkness, toward Dostoevsky's "underground," but as a slow progress toward a luminous spiritual night, analogous to the one described by St. John of the Cross. He does not seek a chthonic and demoniacal night, but the night of galaxies, angels, and divinity. As did other younger poets—Victor Hugo who believed in the existence of angels, Saint-Pol-Roux and his "vertical voyage," O. V. de L. Miłosz and his experience of levitation—Novalis lives an intense and precocious life of "ascending mysticism" (*Aufsteigende Mystik*) which Johann-Joseph von Görres, another Romantic, contrasted with the "descending mysticism" (*Absteigende Mystik*). He belongs to the category of verticalist dreamers, his poetic vision always facing the heights. He beckons us to follow him on the road climbing toward the regions of a dreamlike *Märchenwelt*.

The deeper we penetrate Novalis's creation, the more we are struck by its modern qualities. He has anticipated the psychological and metaphysical currents of our times, and his speculations approximate recent eschatological research. All his writing—his letters, his journal, his *Fragments*—seem to announce ideas that fascinate us today. Novalis speaks of the stratification of the human soul, of the unconscious, and of individual and collective dreams. And his conception of an ideal man is a synthesis between man endowed with a third-eye vision (*homo divinans*), contemporary technological man, and cosmological man of the future. H. G. Wells, Jules Verne, and the dreamers of nuclear fantasy all come to mind, as do the current interstellar Romantics—flourishing in the United States—who have abolished space and time in their tales of astronomical marvel.

As we return today to the writings of this poet, we feel a pressing need to revise some of our notions of Romanticism. Albert Béguin has already invited us to do that in the work cited above. Gaston Bachelard's book *L'Air et les songes* is a historical and analytical contribution to the study of the poetry of the marvelous, based upon the notion of psychic verticalism in the works of Novalis, Shelley, Poe, Baudelaire, Rimbaud, and Nietzsche.* Robert Desoille, applying a verticalist theory to psychopathology, has introduced, as a psychotherapeutic method, the principle of a dialectic produced in a waking dream between the ascent and the fall. Finally, Gustave L. S. Mercier published in 1949 a book of philosophy entitled *Le Dynamisme ascensionnel* in which he expounds a new ontology based upon certain recent technical and philosophical discoveries, from Bergson to Niels Bohr. And hasn't Blaise Cendrars lately written an ascensional hagiography, that of saints and aviators? A neo-occultism strives today to answer certain questions put forth by Novalis and his friends of the first wave of Romanticism. Likewise, in the works of the Surrealists grouped around André Breton, in Georges Bataille, and in other contemporary authors we discern a nostalgia for rapture, transport, and ecstasy viewed as a possible means of tearing through the curtain of everyday reality. We see here the same desire to blur the boundary between interior and exterior, between subject and

* Paris: Corti, 1943.

object, between the reality of day and night, in order to attain a state of heightened consciousness that could be experienced by individuals as well as by a collective. Novalis's work thus continues to evoke fresh interest.

Armel Guerne remarks: "If everything he writes has that charm of purity, that breath of heights, and that mysterious spark of artless transparency, it is because he carries the unmitigated burden of pain." We are familiar with the stages of his life from his birth in Wiederstedt on May 2, 1772, to his death on May 25, 1801. During his short life, he experienced love and death, and aspired to a universal religion. His mysticological research tended toward a synthesis grounded in his study of Jakob Böhme, Fichte, Schelling, and von Baader. But above all, it was the Pietism of the Herrnhuters, his spiritual ancestors, that left a mark upon him from the very start. His ability to reconcile the opposing poles of light and darkness with such lucidity has its source in his spiritual quest. In his study on the modes of philosophical thought in Novalis, Jean Wahl* explains:

> Novalis's esthetics is dominated by a necessary and fertile contradiction. A thing can find its full expression only in its opposite. A poetic work remains infinitely poetical and yet simple. . . . There is a unity of repose and movement, of enthusiasm and reason, of truth that elevates and illusion that soothes, of strange and familiar, of clarity and mystery, of order and chaos.

In *Novalis et la pensée mystique*, Maurice Besset retraces the lines of the poet's thought following the stages of his religious itinerary. According to Besset, Novalis's quest relies mainly upon his study of Jakob Böhme and on the philosophical idealism of Kant, Fichte, and Schelling. His poetry can be understood only against the background of his mysticological research. The cobbler Böhme has played a capital role in his evolution; Novalis's letters and "fragments" speak of his passionate interest in the visionary from Görlitz, as well as for the theosophical tradition that originated at the beginning of the eighteenth century. Novalis makes a constant effort, following Böhme's principles, to unite the tangible world and the invisible world.

Böhme's idea presented in *Aurora* bears a striking resemblance to the one developed by Novalis after the death of his fiancée, Sophie von Kühn. Böhme conceived a structure whose "center" would be at once "the point

* *Romantisme allemand,* 161.

of radiation and of crystallization." His speculations are based upon the necessity to reconcile the existence and the power of evil with the existence of an omnipotent God without falling into Manicheism, on the one hand, and into a naturalist pantheism, on the other, which would negate the reality of distinction between good and evil. He defiantly stands up to the challenge, and the eternal conflict between the two principles provides him with the foundations of his own faith. He envisions divinity as *Ungrund* (the abyss), *Stille ohne Wesen* (stillness without essence), and that divinity is the locus of the "eternal nature," or of the *mysterium magnum,* which is the principle of contradiction illuminating both sides of the antithesis. According to Böhme, whose ideas were always expressed in an esoteric and often very imaginative language, it is the love of the divine that transports us into the "lightning flash of rapture."

Böhme's influence can be felt throughout Novalis's work, but there are others whose impact was no less potent. Novalis professed unbounded admiration for the philosopher Fichte, the mystical philosopher von Baader, as well as for Schelling, the founder of the philosophy of identity. These men directed Novalis toward a magic idealism that was to become his veritable credo. Fichte, who fundamentally modified Kant's critical idealism, transposes everything into the interior. Reality has its basis in an absolute I. Besset tells us that Fichte's doctrine of "non-I" as a resolution of the "I" in a dialectic movement recalls "Böhme's doctrine of manifestation." Little by little, however, Novalis turns away from Fichte and studies Schelling and Hemsterhuys, whose Platonic mysticism advocates man's perfectibility through a process of positive moral development. He becomes interested in Galvanism, as well as other aspects of *Naturphilosophie.* Orientalism equally comes to bear upon his creative development.

In 1799, Novalis abandons his philosophical and scientific studies in order to devote himself to poetry and religion. This sudden change finds its expression in two great poetical works: the *Hymns to the Night* and *Heinrich von Ofterdingen.* He writes other books and booklets as well, such as the *Devotional Songs, The Disciples at Sais,* and so on. The *Hymns* build upon the theme of the experience of nocturnal intuition that informs Böhme's mysticism of the night in the sphere of knowing Nature, the Soul, and God. Here we also encounter the grand theme of Novalis's creation: the theme of death and resurrection, of a continuous ascent, of man's metamorphosis. It is through love that we approach God. "My mind," Novalis wrote to his friend Just, "developed little by little and gradually started encroaching upon the realm of my heart. Sophie has reinstated the Heart on its lost throne." In his immense sorrow, he wishes to rejoin his beloved in her grave. A moment of mystical ecstasy before Sophie's tomb opens his eyes; this illumination liberates his soul, while a nostalgia for death becomes his dogma.

It is then the experience, described in the *Hymns to the Night* and in *Heinrich von Ofterdingen,* that elevates him to the next step in his evolution: "My whole being has acquired unity and consistence; I can feel the seeds of my future life sprout within me." Henri Lichtenberger* observed: "An incorrigible idealist, despite his life's disappointment, he dreams of severing the ties that bind him to the earth solely by the effort of his will." We observe clear parallels with Gérard de Nerval and his sanctification of Jenny Colon. Isis plays an almost identical role in *Aurélie* as in *The Disciples at Sais.*

Without abandoning Christianity as his larger framework, Novalis seeks above all in his metaphysical journeys a new religion and an ecumenical church. In 1799 he publishes an essay entitled "Christianity or Europe," in which he openly opposes the *Aufklärung* and progress by making an apology for medieval Catholicism, a reactionary attitude that met with an unwavering reproach on the part of his friends: Goethe and the clique gathered round the brothers Schlegel. In the *Hymns,* it is not a question of an orthodox religiosity, as it is in the *Devotional Songs,* but of an interpretation of religion of heart and love that issued from his desolation in the face of death. The *Hymns,* addressed to the Night and to the Unconscious, were for Novalis an acknowledgment of Death and of an inner vision. In a letter to Friedrich Schlegel, from June 20, 1798, he wrote:

> I have developed an idea of a moral astronomy (in Hemsterhuys's sense of the word), and have made an interesting discovery of a religion of the visible universe. Don't you find this an appropriate way of symbolically approaching physics, in the broader sense of the word?

With Novalis (and Jean Paul), literature enters the reign of a dreamlike irrationality and of the unconscious. The exploration of the oneiric life yields previously unknown symbolism. Here, once again, the cosmogonic dreams display an ascensional tendency. However, we only vaguely know the results of his quests, since he never transmitted any of his own dreams to us. Dreaming, with its irrational images, represents to him, "in a

---

* Henri Lichtenberger, *Novalis* (Paris: Bloud, 1912).

strange way, the facility with which our soul penetrates each object, instantaneously transforms itself into it" (*Fragments*). "Isn't even the most disorganized dream a singular phenomenon which, without even invoking a divine origin, reveals a precious opening in the mysterious curtain, with its thousand folds, in the hidden recesses of our soul?"

The key to the *Hymns* can be found in the third hymn, where the poet makes a eulogy of his experience of ecstasy: "From the heights, my ancient ecstasy: a twilit tremor awe—/And the bonds of birth were rent, the/Fetters of Light—Black fled the earthly masters and/my sorrow with them. Sadness flowed together into/an unfathomable world." And he continues: "The scene itself gently rose higher—my unbound, newborn/Soul soared over the scene. The hill became a dust cloud/and through the cloud I saw the clear features of my Beloved." The hymn culminates with these words: "That was the first dream in you./It lingered long, and its reflection/endured as the eternal, unshakable Trust/in the heaven of Night and its Sun, the Beloved." We have here once more the aerial verticalism of the night, the suave sensation of a gliding flight, the abolishment of gravity and of chronological time. "Millennia fled like storms," he said in rapture, and everything truly becomes mythical: the hill becomes Mount Tabor, as Besset points out in his interpretation of the hymn.

Nocturnal ecstasy of the *Hymns* brings us closer to the White Romantic poetry, to the Icarian poetry, to the poetry of magical transfigurations. Novalis appears here as a seer and a visionary, not of artificial paradises found through the use of drugs (as his letters might have indicated), but of a lost paradise and a new Golden Age. Mysticism and magic guide him through the secrets of nature. His poetry is an extraliterary incantation; its aim is to attain the supernatural. In an interior experience, he surveys vast cosmogonies and his words become a liturgy. The sacred is associated with a seraphic faith, for example in the tenth poem of his *Devotional Songs:*

An angel saves you and pulls you
Once more upon the beach,
And you gaze with joy
Upon the Promised Land.

The night spirit in Novalis is quite different from the one understood by most Romantics and post-Romantics. We find there the notion of light, of Böhme's *Luminous Virgin,* and the myth of the *Great Mother.* It is the sleep of death without awakening, but also the existence of being. It is the naturalist and supernatural notion of magical revelation and the expression of hope and of the absence of monsters. Novalis's nocturnal life symbolizes the accomplishment of the union and of a perfect life, a return to the maternal womb. His is the cosmic and mythological night, the night of nuptial voluptuousness; it is the symbolic night of prophecies and of the *Ungrund;* the clairvoyant and irrational night; the night of individual experience and of the experience of humanity as a whole.

The *Hymns to the Night* celebrate, above all, the Great Night—that is Sophie—and Jesus the Redeemer. Novalis is influenced by theosophy and identifies Sophie with *Universal Sophia* and with Christ. He writes in his *Journal,* after the death of his fiancée: "Sophie and Christus." The night of death opens onto an eternal life, and the meditation of his "sweet fiancée" has its apogee in love. His poems—written at first in regular verse and then composed in the tradition of prose poems—start out as lamentations and end as chants filled with religious optimism. The terrors of death gradually recede, and the monologue turns into a lofty incantation invoking a path that leads back to the "Father's house." These hymns represent a synthesis of Pietistic and Baroque faith of the Herrnhuters and of Catholic faith evoking the Virgin Mary. The fifth hymn, in Armel Guerne's and Henri Stierlin's rendering, contains a peculiar remark: "In poverty,/In a marvelous shed—/A Son of the First Mother,/Mysterious offspring/Of Infinite fruit." Here we find the revelation of Christ, the true myth of the night, the progression toward Hindu mysteries, and the conversion of the Singer. It is, according to Besset, "the supreme union with Christ and Mary, his mother, the Queen of the Night."

In his obsession with the nocturnal spirit, Novalis is profoundly indebted to the Orientalism that dominated the interests of his friends Schlegel and Schelling. Novalis's poetry will remain incomprehensible if we do not take into account the popularization of Vedic and Persian writings introduced by the Englishman William Jones and by French scientists of the time, such as Anquetil-Duperron, who published the *Zend-Avesta* in 1771, even before William Jones founded his Asiatic Society. In the wake of the British and French discoveries, Hinduism attracted young philosophers and poets of the first wave of Romanticism: the brothers Schlegel, Schelling, Schopenhauer, Tieck, and others. The dream of a universal religion with its cradle in India seemed almost realized. Novalis desired to change man, to lift him up to a higher stage. It was the ideas borrowed from the Orient that spurred him in that direction. The notion of transition from the sphere of human evolution to another belongs to that initiation. . . .

Thomas Carlyle said of Novalis: "With his calm, with his profound love of nature, with his soft, elevated, and spiritual contemplation, Novalis shows us his Asiatic side." Let us recall that in his *Hymns* Novalis calls his nocturnal Orient his "Hindustan." The Oriental imaginary was the fashion in England and in France, as well as in the United States; Emerson's transcendentalism also draws its inspiration from Oriental discoveries (*Zend-Avesta, Rig-Veda*). Raymond Schwab in his book *Renaissance orientale** outlines the Hindu sources of the *Hymns*: "What we call magic idealism forms ties with a system of seership and a mysticism of history, poetry, and human love sanctioned by both *Gitas*. Hindu home of art and of the soul, the fountain of wisdom, the ocean of metamorphoses, and the universal soul, these ideas pass from Herder, to Maier, Schelling, Schlegel, and to Novalis." William Jones had composed, before Novalis, his own *Hymn to the Night*.

Heinrich von Ofterdingen is Novalis's cosmological novel. It is in 1799, after Sophie's death, that he starts to realize his creative dream. He conceived it as a vast series in six volumes, of which only the first was completed under the title *Erwartung* (*Expectations*). The tale was designed as a Romantic counterpart to *The Years of Apprenticeship of Wilhelm Meister* and to the *Apologie for Poetry*. In his journeys through the labyrinth of the mind, Novalis seeks a "new man." Tieck, who had long conversations with his friend, tells us that Novalis also wanted to demonstrate, with the help of magic, the close relationship that binds the invisible world to the visible one. He cites a poem that Novalis wanted to include in the second volume and which he considers as the key to the whole work:

> When numbers and figures are no longer
> the key to all creatures;
> when those who sing and those who love gain
> a more profound knowledge than scholars;
> when the world turns again to a free life
> and reenters an inner universe;
> then, finally, light and shadows will be married
> in order to radiate once more the true light,

* Paris: Payot, 1950.

and when in poems and legendary tales
one will have recognized true cosmogonies
—then a single mysterious word will suffice
to chase away all unnatural creations.*

The protagonists of this poetic quest are barely sketched out: Henry, Mathilda, Klingsohr, and the Princess all lack definite contours. We could even say that they are personified symbols: the Stranger, the Singer, the Minstrel, the Old Man, and so on. . . . Everything is vague, even the landscapes; everything is dream and illusion. Novalis uses the literary techniques of fairy tales (*Märchen*), which he called "the cannon of poetry." The novel is a narrative forming a continuous current of metamorphoses. (In *Finnegans Wake,* James Joyce also employs a system of analogies and transformations: the interpenetration of the ages, the transmutations of characters.) *Ofterdingen* is at once an alchemical tale and a fantastic allegory; and we know that Novalis was familiar with Kabbala and occult authors. Novalis awaits a new era of humanity—an era when man will be transformed into a supra-terrestrial being. His ascensional psychism is expressed in a dialogue in which Ofterdingen tells Mathilda:

> Yes, Mathilda, the higher world is nearer to us than we commonly think. We are already living in it here, and we perceive it most intimately interwoven with earthly nature. . . .Who knows whether our love may not some day turn to wings of flame that will lift us up and carry us to our heavenly home before age and death overtake us.

For all its classical features, Novalis's language is nevertheless strongly marked by mythology. The mythical aspect is particularly salient in *Ofterdingen.* Novalis seeks to master the immanent dualism and to proclaim the unity of the world in a style where the blue flower symbolism plays a capital role, the blue flower being an embodiment of that unity. For Novalis, poetry assumes the task of fulfilling the Idea, and "everything is marvelously coherent, everything is vivified, all of nature intermingles with the spiritual world in a most curious manner."

It is in the unfinished second volume, for which, however, Novalis left ample notes, that the future man enters the scene. *The Fulfillment* (*Erfüllung*) begins with a poem bearing a theosophical title, "Astralis," "born of

* Translation by Marcel Camus (Aubier).

a sidereal man, the first fruit of Mathilda and Henry." After Mathilda's death, Henry continues on his journey in search for universal poetry revealed through love, and destroys the "empire of the sun." According to Novalis's notebooks, Henry "becomes flower, animal, stone, star," and in the end enters the City of God. The work terminates, according to Tieck, with a grand poem, "The Marriage of Seasons," a theophanic and planetary myth in the pure occult tradition. The different stages of metamorphoses conclude with Henry's resuming his human form and with a new cycle of history.

In both his life and creation, Novalis embodies a sensitive soul's drive toward the highest summits. He prefigures the man of our times, a holder of secrets of nature's marvels, yet still a slave to his original slime, to the *Urschleim,* from which he rose. Novalis, filled with an aerial optimism, believed in man's perfectibility. He believed the man of our times capable of developing new senses, of flying through galactic space and putting an end to the state of disharmony and chaos, of definitely affirming the return of the Golden Age that existed before Babel. Hasn't this poet, whom we count among prophets who wish to transform man and the world, foreseen certain discoveries and hypotheses of today's thinkers who, in turn, seek to decipher the universal enigmas and to fathom the evolution of our expanding cosmos?

Goethe

The Case of Goethe: Was He a Heroic Figure or Merely a Philistine? (March 1932)

The printing presses of almost every country today are turning out thousands of books to celebrate the hundredth anniversary of Wolfgang von Goethe's death. We may soon expect a vast orgy of eulogies, panegyrics, paeans, platitudes, hosannahs, *lieux communs, Binsenwahrheiten,* about the Olympian oracle. We may expect to be inundated by anthologies, breviaria, albums of quotations.

(Curiously enough, 1932 marks other anniversaries as well: the four-hundredth anniversary of the publication of Rabelais' *Pantagruel,* the hundredth anniversary of the birth of Lewis Carroll, the tenth anniversary of the publication of *Ulysses,* and the fiftieth birthday of its author. The incongruity here presented only serves to emphasize once more the fundamental scissions to be found in the entire history of literature.)

But what is Goethe's real stature in modern poetry?

Carl Sternheim, the famous playwright, silhouetted him in his *Tasso, or the Art of the Juste Milieu,* more than ten years ago. He found that Goethe was a philistine, a standpatter, a pseudo-Hellenic Babbitt, a reactionary who escaped every emotional responsibility. He accused Goethe of having preached "cadaver obedience and watch-parade before the inalterable, before the existing facts of life." He called him "immensely cowardly and limited" because he changed "humanity's first impulse of insurrection" into "the flat moderation of the *juste milieu.*"

Herwarth Walden, the editor of *Sturm,* disposed of the poet Goethe in the following words:

> He did not write, he described. He stated impressions, impressions of nature, of voyages, of human beings, of Greek and Oriental art. . . . In his dramas he interprets sagas, history, and Kant's thought in a human way. Dramas to him are illustrative examples of his *Weltanschauung,* which was that of a liberal, sybaritic burgher of the world. His poems are descriptions of personal and erotic experiences. They are never immediate.

Carl Einstein, who belongs to the extreme left wing of modern German literature, explains in this essay, especially written for *Transition,* the immense gulf that exists between Goethe's Classicism and the attitude toward life today. His penetrating analysis demolished the professorial "Goethe legend" and exposes what he believes to be profound lacunae in the creative writer.

Gide

André Gide, Mystic and Dionysian
(July 13, 1924)

In meeting M. André Gide in the flesh for the first time, one has a curious sense of his timidity, not to say humility, as he talks about himself with hesitating gestures through verbal mysteries. The luminousness of his eyes sinks into one's consciousness. His quivering, sensitive mouth becomes a symbol. In the book-haunted atmosphere of his friend, M. Jacques Rivière, critic and novelist, amid a group of dynamically brilliant conversationalists, we met him hiding himself in a corner, talking almost in a whisper, with a strangely emphasized *pudeur.*

A Faustian cosmos is graven on his face. Rude contact with the mysteries of life has drawn his lips into pity. Genius of letters, discoverer of unheard-of rhythms in his native language, metaphysical emancipator of his nation's spirit, he is the center of gravity around which pendulate the new forces. He has hurled a new ecstasy into the soul of France, drugging the despair of the spirits.

Success was slow in coming. He has dreamed his dreams for a few decades and has made music of unheard-of tonal combinations, but France would have none of him, except the few spirits that loved him. Foreign countries have taken him up in increasing numbers and have paid homage to his strange genius. Knopf in New York recently brought out his *La Porte étroite* [Paris: Mercure de France, 1909], but his most representative works, such as *Les Nourritures terrestres* [Paris: Mercure de France, 1897] and *L'Immoraliste* [Paris: Mercure de France, 1902], still await the audacity of progressive publishers in England and America. Whether it is the complex and intensely sensitized ideology that hides behind his accents or the Anglo-Saxon fear of facing the blinding magic of a rebel, nobody has as yet tackled the translation of his many books that will be classics in another decade.

If art, as Oscar Wilde said, is surface and symbol, M. Gide—who, incidentally, was a friend of the unfortunate Irish poet—has solved the quintessence of the esthetic consciousness. When Mallarmé dominated his age, M. Gide, still in his twenties, shocked his Symbolist friends by writing a book that was a liberation from the formulas of the rue de Rome, and by catching the voluptuousness of the nuance, created a new art, essentially human, direct, and devoid of the verbal acrobatics that led the *harmonistes* into murky spaces.

Novelist, dramatist, critic, and human being, M. Gide represents today the intellectual bridge between the old and the new school. He is the last of the Humanists and the quintessence of the French intelligence. He is an artist of the word, who creates the texture of his words with as much virtuosity as did Debussy in the field of impressionistic music. Not that he is a literary Impressionist. He penetrates into the very depths of the human soul. Not since Flaubert has there appeared in French literature such a master of prose, who was able to relieve the language of mechanical formulas and tear it away from the sterility of the academicians. His is a synthesis of the Celtic's visionary qualities with the racially Gallic intelligence.

In his four novels—which he insists on calling *récits*—and his so-called *soties*—the resuscitation of a form of art which flourished in the fourteenth century and accentuates the pathological elements in human society—he descends into the very depths of the human soul. When he wrote on the flyleaf of his *Morceaux choisis* [Paris: Nouvelle Revue française, 1921]: "Les Extrêmes se touchent," it was not merely a phraseological gesture, but a symbol. For M. Gide is a modern mystic who pendulates between the sultry exoticism of the Oriental's singsong laughter and the icy atmosphere of Calvinistic thought.

His background may explain the contradictory complexity of his mind and work. Born in Paris in 1869 "of a father who hailed from Uzes (Gard) and a mother who came from Normandy," he was reared in the Huguenot faith of his fathers. After studying at the Ecole Alsacienne a few years, his frail health necessitated an interruption, and he was taken on various journeys through Europe. A few years later he returned to school, where he became the intimate friend of Pierre Louys, later the author of

Astarté [Paris: Librairie de l'art indépendant, 1891], *Aphrodite* [Paris: Borel, 1896], and other books, and at the age of twenty-two he published his first book—*Les Cahiers d'André Walter* [Paris: Librairie de l'art indépendant, 1891], which, although showing already the silhouette of his genius, had a mediocre success. It earned him, however, the friendship of men like Maurice Barrès, Marcel Schwob, and Maeterlinck. A short time later his failing health compelled him to seek another climate, and with his friend Paul Albert-Laurens he proceeded to North Africa. In Tunis he became critically ill, but finally recovered and returned to Paris, where he stayed a few years. Then he took up his abode in the Jura for a few years. Since that time he has traveled through many climates and absorbed many land-scapes and souls.

"I am sure I would have continued living in solitude, like a savage, if it had not been for Pierre Louys," he said later in reminiscing about his Paris days. "Not that I lacked the desire to frequent literary circles and to search for friendship there; but an unconquerable timidity held me back and that fear, which often continues strangling me, of importuning or embarrassing those toward whom I feel the strongest inclined. Pierre, much more aggres-sive and bolder, certainly also much cleverer and whose talent had already become formed, had dedicated his first poems to those of his elders we admired together. Urged by him, I decided to take my book to Hérédia.

"But I was bewildered, when I saw that Hérédia did not come up to the idea I had created for myself in thinking of a poet. There was no silence in him; no mystery; no nuance in the shrillness of his voice. . . . He was inter-ested almost exclusively in the external world and in art; as a matter of fact, he remained exceedingly embarrassed in the field of speculation and knew nothing else but gestures. . . . Rather an artist than a poet and more still, an artisan. I was at first terribly deceived."

Throughout the work of M. Gide there runs the nostalgia for an escape from life. In his psychic topography, which comprises the entire range of human suffering and ecstasy, his people grope from chaos into light. He is avowedly in love with the literature of pathology and decadence, precisely because his interest in the aberrations of the soul is second only to his love of letters. Pity and tenderness—and cruelty—play a savage dance in his consciousness.

M. Gide has a style that echoes all the agony of his conception of the world. It has an almost Cartesian simplicity, carried, however, by a tem-perament of an intense sensitiveness. There is no bombast—he sparingly uses the epithet. All of his phrases project autobiographical sensations and are essentially kaleidoscopic and aphoristic. A psychoneurotic spirit hovers over them, and they mirror that *frémissement* which derives directly from life. His language is anything but *livresque*—it is marvelously attuned to the almost feminine passivity of his thoughts. It has a conversational intimacy that stimulates and rests. He is the most emphatic individualist writing in France today. His least ideas are tinctured with a subjective magic. He looks at the world in terms of the exceptional experience and never lets himself be blinded by a too-facile conception of illusions.

His world is so saturated with sun that one almost becomes blinded. This example from *Les Nourritures terrestres* indicated his manner:

> I have known the heavy wine of inns—a wine which drugs the senses with an evocation of violets and brings the long noonday slumber. I have known intoxications at dusk, when it seems that all the earth is shaking beneath the weight of your full-blown thought. . . . Nathanael, I will talk to you about drunkenness— . . .
>
> Drunkenness—from fasting, when one has walked at early dawn, and when hunger is no longer an appetite, but a sensation of dizziness; drunkenness of thirst, when one has walked till dusk.
>
> The most frugal meal thus became to me excessive, like a debauch, and later I tasted the intense sensation of my life with lyric ecstasy. . . . I have known the drunkenness which lightly deforms the thoughts. . . . I have known drunkenness which makes you believe that you are better, bigger, more respectable, more virtuous, richer, etc.—everything you are not.

Nowhere can his dithyrambic pathos, his infinite depth of feeling, and his gift of empathy be found in greater synthesis than in *Les Nourritures terrestres.* It is a mystic hymn, an ecstatic chant from the mountains of the world. Next to *Zarathustra,* there is no work of the imagination in any literature that is so completely an elementary, Dionysian chant and an affirmation of joy. Here is plastic music, the quivering magic of earthy things, a tremendous lyricism in elementary rhythms, sometimes whipped to a demoniacal intensity of rebellion. And over it all blazes the southern sun— Amalfi, Syracuse, Blidah, Rome, Fiesole, Biskra. Songs tender as Chinese silk! And crashing polyphonies! And orphic evocations!

While *Les Nourritures terrestres* did not have any success until recently— although the book was written more than twenty years ago—his *récit L'Immoraliste* has had a different fate. Like part of *Les Nourritures terrestres,* its action is laid in North Africa. The author was accused of accentuating the concept of "beyond good and evil" and has been attacked especially by the traditionalists for his audacious morality, or amorality. Michel, the protagonist, who tells the story to his friends, is stricken with consumption while on his honeymoon trip in North Africa. Under his wife's tender care he recovers, but is suddenly seized with such a hunger for life that his ethical sense is completely crushed. In his fever for a new lease on life, he becomes responsible for the death of his wife—although he loves her—after the latter had herself become ill, by frantically taking her to places where the climate would hasten her death.

In *La Porte étroite* M. Gide, the mystic, reveals himself in the astonishing role of telling the story of asceticism. It is a love story more northern than Latin in spirit, written with a tender pathos that lingers with one long after one has put the book aside. The young Protestant girl, Alissa, is in love with her cousin, Jérôme, who reciprocates her affection, but she feels the desire for a life of sacrifice, when she notices that her sister Juliette is also in love with him. Deliberately she renounces love. Although her family urges her to marry, Alissa shrinks from it, and when, after a separation, she sees Jérôme once more, he finds her weighted beneath the burden of her humility, doing menial work. Three years later he holds in his hands the last tender message written by her before her death:

> "I understand that my life is useless unless I find happiness," she writes. "Ah! And still you have promised it, Oh Lord, to the soul that sacrifices itself. . . . Must I wait until death? For now my faith is being shaken, O Lord! I cry to you with all of my strength. . . . I am wandering through darkness, waiting for the dawn. . . . Come, satisfy my heart! I am thirsting now for this happiness. . . .
>
> Oh, Lord—thus to advance toward you, Jérôme and I, together, going through life like two pilgrims, one of whom would say sometimes: 'Lean upon me, Brother, you are so weary,' while the other replies: 'It is enough that you are near me.' But no! the road you teach us, Lord, is a narrow road . . . so narrow that two cannot walk together."

This delicately wrought tale does not contrast two viewpoints with any shrill definiteness, but mirrors the immense irrationality of the real problems of life.

Isabelle [Paris: Gallimard, 1921], another *récit*, belongs to the strictly experimental phase of the writer's work. It has been called a satire on

Romanticism, although many do not agree with this concept. It is a kind of an ironic modern *Adolphe* [Paris: Treuttel et Würtz, 1816] in the sense that the hero, Gérard, persists in analyzing his fatuous sentiments about Isabelle de Saint-Auréal, his dream-love. He tortures himself in the anticipatory delineation of her charms, but when he sees her in reality, his vision of her proves to be distorted and ironic. M. Gide succeeds in giving a remarkably chiseled atmospheric picture of the background of his story, which does not lack in the sense of pity and tenderness he always shows.

Probably the most completely successful of his *récits* is *La Symphonie pastorale* [Paris: Nouvelle Revue française, 1919]. All of his genius is concentrated in this beautiful story of love and—renunciation. It is a novel of poignant appeal set against a background of Calvinistic austerity. His art of dramatic condensation is shown here at its best. A snowy landscape is sketched against the drama with extraordinary reserve and effectiveness.

It is the story of a Protestant pastor in the lonely village of the Jura who, upon being summoned to the deathbed of one of his parishioners, finds the latter's blind servant-girl, Gertrude, wandering desolately through the house. He takes her to his home, and although his wife, Amalie, receives the new guest with ill grace, the pastor applies Christ's principles, takes care of the forsaken girl, and gradually falls in love with her. Under his tender care, Gertrude develops mentally and spiritually and Jacques, the pastor's son, also falls in love with her. Here follows a conflict between father and son of a most fearful poignancy which ends in the pastor's eliciting Jacques' word of honor that he desist from his plan of marrying the girl. Soon after that Gertrude undergoes an operation and regains her sight. It is then that she notices the suffering the pastor's love for her has caused his wife, and she tries to drown herself. She is rescued, but a grave illness follows and she prepares for death. In her last talk with the pastor, she tells him that she had seen Jacques for the first time and realizes now that she loves his son and not him.

"After Jacques had gone," the story continues,

I knelt down beside Amalie, asking her to pray for me, for I needed help. She simply recited Our Father . . . but put between the words long silences which filled our pleas.

I would have liked to weep, but I felt my heart more arid than the desert.

Among the *soties,* the most important of M. Gide's works is *Les Caves du Vatican* [Paris: Nouvelle Revue française, 1914], which marks a new phase in his evolution. This is the essence of his preoccupation with psychic abnormalities. It is the story of Lafkadio Wluiki, the murderer—a story that is related to Dostoevsky's *Crime and Punishment.* The "plot"—for a real "plot" is here postured for the first time—is somewhat complicated and lacks M. Gide's customary simplicity. Lafkadio murders without any motive other than the irrational desire to kill. Like Raskolnikoff in the Russian story, Lafkadio finds the love of a young girl, Geneviève de Baraglial, who although aware of his crime, clings to him and gives him understanding. Around these characters rotates Julius de Baraglial, who visits Lafkadio upon the solicitation of his father, Count de Baraglial, Lafkadio being the latter's illegitimate son. On his way to Italy Lafkadio meets Fleurissoire— his victim, who is on his way to Rome on a fantastic mission to liberate the pope from the "Cellars of the Vatican," and he murders him in cold blood. *Les Caves du Vatican* is surely not M. Gide's best work—it belongs to a transitional stage, but the reader will find rich reward in plunging into this borderland of sanity and psychopathy, where M. Gide evokes the horrors of the soul.

Gide, the critic and translator, deserves a place by himself. Aside from *Prétextes* [Paris: Mercure de France, 1903] and *Nouveaux prétextes* [Paris: Mercure de France, 1911], his critical essays appear in *Morceaux choisis* (Paris: Nouvelle Revue française, 1921) and the recently published *Incidences* [Paris: Nouvelle Revue française, 1924]. The *Morceaux choisis* is largely a collection of previously published essays. Here he discusses his ideas about nationalism, Germany; in his delightful "Billets à Angèle" he expatiates on Classicism, Proust, *La Nouvelle Revue française*—which he helped to found— Maurice Barrès, Jacques Rivière, Jean Cocteau, Francis Jammes, Gautier, Baudelaire, Paul Valéry, and even Dada. Gide has taken a great interest in the Dadaistic movement, precisely because Dada is a primordial attempt to recapture the naiveté of the mystic, and he feels its significance as a liberating movement closely related to his own work. There is a strangely touching description of his meeting with Oscar Wilde, after the latter had come to Dieppe following his release from prison. Although M. Gide does not himself attribute much importance to his translations, we feel that he has succeeded in transmuting his foreign subjects into the French spirit with amazing success. We may mention his translations of Rabindranath

Tagore's *Lyric Offering*, Joseph Conrad's *Typhoon*, Shakespeare's *Antony and Cleopatra*—which was played in Paris—and William Blake's *Le Marriage du ciel et de l'enfer.*

As one analyzes his work in the light of tradition, the fact emerges that he is closely related to the classical spirit. He derives from Montaigne and Pascal—especially Montaigne, whose scepticism as shown in his *Essais* approaches his own spirit. The capriciousness and intense subjectivism of Montaigne can also be found in the minute observations of M. Gide's. He delights in digressions of a bizarre nature. He is what Montaigne says of himself: "Je suis moi-même la matière de mon livre." His style is as personal as the latter's.

"Classicism—and with this I understand French Classicism—is the art of expressing something by saying the least," M. Gide asserts. "It is an art of modesty. Everyone of our Classicists is more moved than he appears to be at first. The Romantic, by bringing into his expression a certain splendor, appears always much more moved than he really is."

Arsène Dumont, according to Mr. Havelock Ellis, points out that civilization holds within itself a "toxic principle." M. Gide has set himself the task of discovering this law and attempting an escape from it. That is why his work is so intensely an echo of life—not of the rude barbarities of the street nor the rumbling madness of cities shaking with steel, but of the cyclones of the soul, the intoxications of evanescent moments, the magic of finding a hidden God in the chaos. M. Gide is the destroyer of Plebeianism.

The architecture of his language is entirely new and frequently audacious. He has breathed a new sense of rhythm into the words of Racine. He has poured a new fuel into the motor of his verbalism. He has sensitized the language and has opened new vistas into heretofore unknown landscapes of the soul, and has liberated literature from academic pedantry. That is why one may look forward with keenest interest to the appearance of his—first—novel, *Les Faux Monnayeurs* [Paris: Gallimard, 1925], of which extracts have already been published.

He is the creator of new sagas. No one can understand the France of the last twenty years without knowing his work. For he has given us new gods, new rhythms, new attitudes.

Kafka

Franz Kafka's Stories and Ascending Romanticism (1941)

Franz Kafka belonged to that small group of writers whose basic force lies in a spiritual and Romantic consciousness. His work has become a touchstone for the evaluation of a new mythological attitude toward the narrative. In the cultural materialism of our age, Kafka remains the pioneer of tomorrow's story with the new dimension.

He has brought into existence a new genre of the narrative that approximates the fantasia, the magic tale, the nightmarish grotesque, the psychograph, the paramyth, in which certain elements of the archaic memory are resuscitated in a sober, concrete style. His storytelling has that timelessness of the dream which is the criterion of great literary creations.

He knew that the *inventive* faculty alone is creative. He knew that the newspaper, the photograph, the movies in his lifetime—not to mention the radio in our own—suffice to portray a realistic contemporary scene. He matured in the turbulence of the First World War, when the mechanical media for the transmission of reportorial facts sufficed and made unnecessary the writer's repetition of these facts. He formed in his stories a living myth.

With the men of the great Romantic and mystic movements he shared the nostalgia for the infinite; the sense of the dream as a dialectical source, of the daemonic-transcendental relationship; the mystic aspiration for the "kingdom of God;" the spiritual apprehension before the occult forces of the beyond.

Kafka was historically a Romantic Expressionist. What springs to mind at once in his writings is his undoubted kinship to certain of the leading Romantic storytellers, especially to Heinrich von Kleist. His biographer, Max Brod, has pointed out that Kafka was an admirer of Kleist and was apparently influenced by his crystal-clear style of narrating fantastic events. Kleist, in *Michael Kohlhaas* and *The Marquise of O.,* employs a somnambulistic way of telling a story that we find again in Kafka. In the *Marquise of O.,* in which a mythical pregnancy is the motif, we find the tendency to anonymity in the character designations which Kafka uses often with such telling effect.

Kafka's *paramyths* are also religious narratives. His mythic thinking was related to the transcendental categories. The symbolism of his style points toward mystic objectives. Although it was sober and precise, the reader is always aware of some signpost indicating a spiritual speculation. The universe of the metaphysical reality is never presented as distinct from finite existence, but seems somehow to absorb it. The finite and infinite melt into each other. One always expects a sudden irruption of otherworldliness.

In this connection Max Brod indicates that one of Kafka's intellectual ancestors was Sören Kierkegaard, whose *Fear and Trembling,* he says, he read and studied seven times. The basic emotion, the archaic mythos, of his narratives seems to me to be fear, anguish, apprehension. It is not an ordinary fear, but a cosmic anguish, an existential apprehension, suffered in the compulsive urges of his characters.

In *The Care of the Housefather* (*Transition,* 1937), the terror of daemonic possession is symbolized by a spool in the house. In *The Metamorphosis* (*Transition,* 1936–37), metaphysical anguish dominates the whole structure of the story. The transformation of Samsa is, I believe, the image of the degeneration of the European order during the First World War. Modern man has to face the metaphysical revolution that is beginning. And Samsa too has to transform his life and adjust himself to the conditions created by a new ethos. He is unable to do so, and annihilation follows. The short story "The Sentence" (*Transition,* 1928) symbolizes the son's search for his "heavenly father" in the mood of his organic fear of life. In the story *In the Penal Colony* (*Partisan Review,* 1941), we have the theme of guilt: original sin gives birth to terror—in Kierkegaard's interpretation of the "concept of anguish"—and redemption is far off, or can never be attained.

The metaphysical search for a higher religious order of life is obvious in Kafka's novels. Max Brod, his friend and biographer, points out that *The Trial, The Castle,* and *America* represent the fanatic quest for admission to the "Kingdom of God." They are desperate attempts to find divine grace. But the search seems in vain. In vain the protagonists stand at the "gate of the law." Only in *America* does Kafka appear to have depicted the geometrical point where all contradictions are dissolved in the redemptive vision of the "natural theater."

Kafka always leads us into an oneiromantic landscape. To be sure, we may feel that we are in a simple, petit-bourgeois world. The quotidian reality surrounds us. People move through painfully familiar scenes. But suddenly we become aware of an irruption, an irrational transformation. Time and space have lost their ineluctable power. The law of causality is abolished. We no longer have any sense of verisimilitude. We feel that the laws of possibility are violated, yet somehow we fail to be shocked. Everything becomes alien. We feel that events are taking place which are incomprehensible to our rational understanding. Everything changes into signs and symbols.

In a heretofore unpublished and untranslated fragment, Kafka wrote the following sentence: "I can understand the hesitation of my generation; but it is no longer hesitation; rather the forgetting of a dream dreamed a thousand nights before, and forgotten a thousand nights before." Kafka, the Talmudic scholar, was obsessed with what he called "the forgotten law" in one of his unpublished dialogues. He learned Hebrew in order to study Jewish theology, and he felt that the world had "stepped out of this law." For it was the law of the phenomenal fertility of the dream.

Kafka believed in this dream, in everything that was natural, simple, childlike.

Trakl

Georg Trakl, *Poetry* (June 15, 1951)

Among Austrian poets who emerged before, or during, the First World War, Georg Trakl is little known abroad. Besides a few poems translated and published by Ivan Goll in his remarkable anthology *Les Cinq Continents* (*The Five Continents,* 1922) and a small collection of poems translated by Henri Stierlin and included in one of the latest issues of the revue *Le Temps de la poésie* (*The Time of Poetry*), Trakl is hardly more than a name in modern literature. The recent publication of his complete poems, edited by the tireless Otto Müller, in Salzburg—where Trakl was born on February 1, 1887—offers us a new perspective on his works, scarce as they are, and allows us to estimate their importance today.

Trakl belongs to that desperate generation of German-speaking poets who took part in the ordeal of the war in 1914–18 or who were crushed by the cataclysm. Kurt Pinthus introduced them to us in his anthology entitled *Menschheitsdämmerung* (*The Dawn of Humanity*), which electrified poetry lovers in the 1920s. There figured, side by side, the entire constellation of young poets: van Hoddis, Klemm, Benn, Werfel, Goll, Stramm, Schickele, Stadler, Rubiner, Heym, and others. To some of these poets, among whom we must mention Werfel, whose novels and lyrical dramas are familiar to us, the anthology brought a worldwide renown.

Although Trakl started out as a pharmacology student, he devoted himself to poetry since his youth, which was spent in Tyrol. He published his first poems in *Der Brenner,* an Innsbruck review founded and still run today by his friend Ludwig Ficker. At first, it was neo-Baroque poetry, solemn eclogues in which one could already discern the signs of future catastrophes. Trakl rarely traveled abroad, but during a short visit in Berlin in 1912, he encountered a few poets rebelling against Impressionism, who had founded a new so-called Expressionist school. Shortly thereafter, Kurt Wolff, the group's first editor (and today the director of the Pantheon Press in New York), published a volume of Trakl's poetry. When the war broke out, Trakl served in the medical corps at the front. In a surge of depression, he committed suicide on November 3, 1914. This desperate gesture was ascribed to the fact that he was left alone in charge of a hundred wounded men, in a barn near Grodeck.

The Expressionist movement was in its essence anti-Naturalist; it drew its inspiration from an inner literary revolution and from the fine arts. Born from a union of Neo-Romanticism and inflamed apocalyptism, Expressionism formed a harmony of voices which predicted, in the midst of war, a future fraternity across borders. They believed in the natural goodness and innocence of Rousseau's man, as well as in universal and anti-militarist democracy. This was particularly true of the poets Schickele, Rubiner, Otten, Goll, and Werfel. Another wing of the group, while similarly in pursuit of the ideal of man's metamorphosis, gave voice to physical and psychic convulsions, wartime destruction, the universe intoxicated with chaos. "Weltunglück geistert," wrote van Hoddis before his death in 1912, evoking in his frenetic verses "the demons of great cities" and foreboding the catastrophe. At that time Trakl muttered psalms, in his solitary contemplation of autumnal nature, far from the megalopolis. Van Hoddis, Heym, and Trakl were all destined for a violent death.

Even before the war, the apprehension that weighed over all of Trakl's writing turned into the certitude of decline. He was haunted by the twilight and by the night, by human solitude and a sense of being overpowered, by violence and death. He accepted evil and the primordial guilt, in St. Augustine's sense of the word; he was conscious of a demoniacal possession of the world:

You, a face of fire inside green metal that wants to go and sing about the mound of bones, of dark ages, and the flaming fall of the angel.
(from "Transformations of Evil," translated by H. Stierlin)

Or:

O the madness of the great city, when at nightfall
Crippled trees petrify beside the black wall,

The spirit of evil gazes from a silver mask.
    (from "To the Silenced")

The titles alone of the different sections of this collection give us a sense of the evolution that took place in the poet's mind. Starting with an almost serene vision of the world, evident in his juvenile poems ("The Beautiful City," "Small Concert"), his work quickly reaches a climate of despair, fear, and the void. As the tragedy gets closer, other titles, even more somber, follow: "The Dream of Evil," "Autumn of the Lonely," "Sevenfold Song of Death," "Dream and Derangement," and so on. Now we sink into a gray fog, we shudder in the atmosphere of disasters. Significantly, the words that recur in his poetry with hallucinating insistance are *Verfall* (decline, decay), *Verwesung* (putrefaction), and *Einsamkeit* (solitude). The first poem in the collection is entitled "Verfall": "A breath of decay makes me shudder."

Children of the apocalypse had a predilection for the themes of massacre, death, and dissolution; an individual and collective neurosis captured their imagination. Trakl was not an exception. He lacked Benn's pathological scepticism—Benn who later found himself drawn toward Nazism—but he shared his, as well as Heym's and van Hoddis's, sentiment of physical decadence of life. He was haunted by a nostalgia for a lost paradise:

Men perform warlike dances . . .
O our lost paradise!
    (from "Psalm")

Tinged with dark pessimism, Trakl's imagery reflects future war cruelties, it seems to prefigure the laments of concentration camp victims. We can already feel the putrefaction of the sacrificed flesh and the human anguish. The poems emanate eschatological unease:

At nightfall, white birds flutter up
Over collapsing cities
Of steel.
    (from "Sleep")

Although he had no ties with any traditional faith, his last poem, written a few days before his death, strikes a prophetic cord:

O prouder grief! You, brass altars,
Today the hot flame of the spirit is fed by a more violent pain—
The grandsons still unborn.
   (from "Grodeck")

Here, life itself seems to come to a stop in face of the abyss.

Rereading these *Dichtungen* from the perspective of twenty years, we feel slightly deceived, especially from the esthetical point of view. The reader is struck by the structural asymmetry of the poems, as well as by their amateurish rhetoric; we sense that, at his death, Trakl has not yet achieved the full mastery of his art. The influence of Rilke and Hofmannsthal is easily discernible in the use of words, which, by force of repetition, become stale and monotone. And at times, his work seems to resemble that of an epigone. His verses do not soar; the wings of his creation remain glued to the ground. The express pathos of his style often rings false.

Today's reader will seek in vain to find out what exactly is meant by Trakl's "avant-gardism," so vaunted in his time. Not that Trakl was insensible to the crisis of language. He simply lacked the audacity of an inventor; with the exception of a few syntactical and metaphoric innovations, he preserved the heavy and drab style of the Naturalist period. However, certain adherents of the Expressionist group, later cited by the first Dadaists, were conscious of that "malady of language" that Nietzsche spoke of, and the Walden review *Der Sturm* was in large part devoted, from the very beginning, to the works of reformers such as Carl Einstein, Stramm, Schwitters, and Scheerbart. (We know, moreover, what happened to their efforts in Hitler's Boeotia.) But perhaps, instead of attacking the poet, we should ask ourselves whether it is not his instrument, the German poetic language itself, which is out of fashion. That question must remain open to further investigation.

Benn

Gottfried Benn (August 1927)

The tragic feeling of standing isolated in his cosmos is a fate the sensitive man of today cannot escape. In spite of the progress of machines, this ever-present antinomy between his wishes and his phenomenal world produces in him a negative attitude, a nihilism that is a paralysis. While the metaphysical preoccupation projects the longing for a transcendental solution of this dilemma, the man who has sensed violently the currents of his age frequently sees no such possibilities and postures grotesquely a kind of anarchy.

The registering of this internal scission is to me an ever-fascinating interest. The poet's awareness of the condition leads him to an explosion of dynamic and aphoristic self-expression. The conscious will to disintegrate the structures which the intellectual mechanization of our age has produced can alone liberate the imagination which has been held enchained by the dictatorship of the cliché, the newspaper, the Calvinistic surrogate of magic.

The scission between the I and you is more and more the predominating interest of the significant writers of our age. Fleeing into his own empire of the imagination becomes the only means of defense against the phalanx of mediocrity and swinishness which we see everywhere. Only a savage ideology and a deformation of the current architectonics can satisfy the poet who attempts to find fresher regions of expression. This tendency can be observed analogously in a few of the advanced spirits in almost every country today.

When Gottfried Benn in his *Gehirne* (*Brains*) began to smash the order of things dear to the critics, he embarked on an experiment against chaos which left the observer bewildered. There was no criterion by which his bold insurrection against the language and spirit of Goethe could have been evaluated. Instead of evoking romantically rhythmed phrases of a moonstruck sentimentalism, his vision deformed the objective and placed the lonely individual upon a new terrain.

He and his fellow Expressionists declared war on the materialistic-impression ideology of their time. Instead of attempting to imitate nature—considering man as a mechanical product of external circumstances—instead of projecting merely the consequence of a condition, these writers made a creative function out of their own chaos. Nothing was considered of objective importance save the manifestations of their visions and dreams.

Benn's cosmos was that of a man wounded by life. As a physician who for years had been active in hospitals, his consciousness of the pathology of existence did not produce in him any sense of metaphysical solutions, but, on the contrary, the feeling for a cerebral escape. Objects became spooks and distorted representations. In anarchic accents he began to dissect his own mind, as if it were an anatomical segment, and ended in a psychic nowhere. Life is an aimless idea to Dr. Werff Rönne, the hero of his book.

The immense loneliness of an individual thrown against the suffering of his world is the theme of the stories which inchoately relate his odyssey through time and space. It is excessively Nordic, this brooding introspection, this preoccupation with the I, this hunger for "Southerlinesses." This surgeon has only the desire to create a huge world of magic in his brain in order to find oblivion, if possible, from the horrors of life about him; nothing really interests him save the eschatological, the thirst for finding the ultimate things.

Benn brings new rhythms for his cosmos. In his poems and his prose, there is a dynamic staccato quality which is exactly the medium for the neuropathic evocations of his mind. His images are sharp and explosive. They startle the reader, because his imagination projects deformations and disassociations in a manner to which a life of superficial reading has not accustomed us. It is the instinct dictating rapidly and blindly. But the wonder is that in this new mythos we do not become chilled by the atmosphere of a laboratory, but are made to sense a contact with an individuality of marvelous directness.

In his language there may be noticed the influence of that great poet whose *Zarathustra* still remains the most important lyrical expression of the last epoch in Germany. There is also the stylistic influence of Arno Holz, whom the professional interpreters of literature have neglected for years. Both gave the German style a plasticity it had not had before. Benn has subdued these two influences in his own starkly accentuated personality, and the fact that his images frequently derive from his medical experience only adds to the forcefulness of his vocabulary.

In *The Voyage* he says:

> But Rönne thought, I know you, animals; more than three hundred nudes each morning! but how strongly you play with love! One woman I knew, on one day alone she was the drunkenness of twenty-five men, their trance and their summer about which they blossomed. She provided the shape, and the real occurred. I want to seek forms and go about them; realities, a chain of hills, a terrain of things!

Gottfried Benn is a courageous poet. He brutally and consciously works for the disintegration of the universe he knows, throws his reflections against the screen of his perceptions, strips off the hypocritical garments of concepts, and evokes smells and visions in cancer barracks into which most men rarely dare to go. The preciosity that still is the current medium of "beauty-haunted" minds is not for him. Life is a hospital. There only remains his dream.

Jünger

Ernst Jünger and the Twilight of Nihilism
(November 1951)

Nihilism, whose spiritual fathers, according to Jünger, are Nietzsche and Dostoevsky, is coming to an end. Jünger affirms this in his new book entitled *Über die Linie* (*Over the Line*), and he announced it already in his war journal, *Strahlungen* (*Irradiations*), published in Germany in 1949 and recently translated into French. It is thus interesting to examine the two latest works of the former apostle of the total war, who is known in France mainly for his two stories published during the war: *In Stahlgewittern* (*Storm of Steel*, 1920) and *Auf den Marmorklippen* (*On the Marble Cliffs*, 1939). *Gärten und Straßen* (*Gardens and Roads*, 1942) and *Der Friede* (*Peace*, 1948) complete the list of French translations. The first and last of these books reflect two, apparently antithetical, attitudes.

If there is a German writer open to psychoanalytic reading, it is Jünger. He embodies the dilemma presented by his ambivalent nation: the oscillation between an aggressive subjectivism and a theological Humanism and which has determined with its feverish and deformed dialectic Germany's entire history since Bismarck. As Nietzsche remarks, the German "philosophizes with a hammer." This tendency, reinforced by an innate opposition to dialogue, constitutes the main characteristic of Jünger's writings, before and after his "conversion." Does he not declare in *Strahlungen* that "few men are worth the trouble of being contradicted"?

A talented and skilled writer, Jünger, who is nearing sixty, has passed through all the stages of German thought since 1918: from militarist impe-rialism and pan-Germanism, through atheist nihilism, to anti-Hitlerian pacifism. He is a typical German, a historical Teuton, whose life and work reflect the deep currents of his nation: a synthesis of atavist irrationality and extroverted authoritarian dynamism, enamored at once of catastrophic visions and of spiritual revelations. We have no proof of his opposition to the war in September 1939; on the contrary, many notes in his journal indicate that he approved of it. Yet he advocated peace after the invasion of Russia and led a secret battle among the German soldiers stationed in Paris against Hitler's party and its barbarisms. He is already a legend in Germany, where he continues to exert a great influence on the defeated generation.

Jünger participated in the First World War and then, in 1920, in the ille-gal actions of nationalist commandos. He professed his reactionary beliefs by saying: "We are not guided by the goal of our combat but by the act of combat itself." He spoke Goebbels's gibberish even before Goebbels. Later on, Jünger published militarist and "nationalist-revolutionary" books and pamphlets. Alongside *In Stahlgewittern,* one can cite *Der Kampf als inneres Erlebnis* (*The Combat as an Interior Experience*), in which he expresses ideas that are marked by a great anti-Western cynicism. In 1932, in *Der Arbei-ter* (*The Worker*), he foresaw a political system of absolute technocracy with "total mobilization." He did have, however, more peaceful preoccupa-tions, publishing the results of his zoological, geological, and philological research in *Blätter und Steine* (*Leaves and Stones*), followed by the admirable *Lob den Vokalen* (*The Eulogy of Vowels*). After acknowledging the effects of Hitlerism upon the life of his country, he then undertook a revision of his own philosophy. He turned against Nazism without, however, abandon-ing his own conception of an authoritarian and aristocratic state. *Auf den Marmorklippen,* published just before the Second World War, is a story, or rather, a half-Dionysian and half-tragic fairy tale. In that book, Jünger symbolically depicts the regime of a political usurper and his destruction by the mind's magic powers. His first war journal, *Gärten und Straßen,* reports observations and meditations during the invasion of France by the German army in which he served. This journal of a helmeted tourist who quite clearly rejoices at the Nazi victory casts a fresh light upon the "resis-tance" of its author. In *Strahlungen,* written at the Hotel Majestic on the Russian front and in Germany between 1941 and 1944, Jünger never stops denouncing the evil acts of "Kniebolo" (a code name he invents to desig-nate the false prophet). After five years in the Wehrmacht, Jünger returned to Germany, where he has lived since in the town of Ravensburg, in the French zone.

Über die Linie is a philosophico-theological divagation, filled with tortuous and often self-contradictory meanderings. This short post-existential essay, written in a dry, didactic tone, forms part of a larger collection, entitled *Anteile* (*Participations*), in which a dozen German poets and thinkers pay homage to Martin Heidegger on the occasion of his sixtieth birthday. Here, Jünger picks up certain arguments already outlined in his treatise on peace dedicated to "the youth of Europe and to the youth of the world." (It would have been more appropriate to dedicate it to that German youth overcome by the fanaticism of a madman who set the world ablaze.) *Der Friede* was the first step in a fight "against nihilism," and its author offers the world ethical advice that is not free of self-satisfaction. Since the war was, in Jünger's opinion, a result of Nazi nihilism (to whose genesis and expansion he was no stranger), the former militarist turned toward what he calls a "new theology" that, under "new forms," is supposed to influence men.

In *Über die Linie* Jünger strives to extricate himself from nihilism after having diagnosed it. Moreover, he looks forward to a counter-movement that would augur its twilight. Departing from Nietzsche, who used to call himself "the first accomplished nihilist in Europe, the one who in himself has traversed nihilism until its own end," and from Dostoevsky, who believed in healing through pain, Jünger proposes his own definition of nihilism, which is somewhat vague and grandiloquent. To him, nihilism is the "destiny of the power of a natural force, a destiny which no one can escape." He insists upon the fact that it is neither chaos, nor evil, nor pathology, but a "process of reduction." We think here of Jünger's theory which states that one must deliberately face the demons in order to accomplish any real therapy. Man sees the marvelous disappear in facing the void, says Jünger, for whom contemporary history operates outside of the sphere of the mind. In the world of fire (*Feuerwelt*), the barbarian and the sadist continue to act instinctively, disregarding moral action. Authors such as Poe, Melville, Rimbaud, Hölderlin, Tocqueville, Nietzsche, Dostoevsky, Bloy, and Kierkegaard have sensed the coming convulsions of this satanic era, the era of concentration camps that Jünger also calls the "world of Lemurs."

How do we react? How do we escape the power of the void? Where do we find refuge in the face of totalitarian degeneration? For the sake of self-preservation, is a free man obliged to think? What position should he take in a world where not only does nihilism rule over everything, but where such a state of affairs has become normal? "Man," says Jünger, "should stand upright before the temples of Hobbesian Leviathan, of the organized world." As a solution, he suggests seeking refuge in the "desert," which we should recognize as "the home of death, of Eros, and of poetical creation." Philosophical reflection itself would lead us to this "non-separated" world. But we should look, after all, for refuge in the human heart. Even though the task is to pay homage to Heidegger in unfolding his theme, Jünger lets the equivocal filter through: "We reside in the realm of the immeasurable, where the diminished security is accompanied by an increased hope of realization. *Holzwege,* expressing this in a beautiful Socratic formula, pretends that we are already in the 'non-separated,' at the threshold of high roads and amidst treasures. Such hope also implies the possibility of a failure." And Jünger piously concludes:

> The accusation of nihilism is one of the most frequently pronounced today. Hence, we should take this reproach upon ourselves, rather than remain on the side of those who always search for the guilty. He who has not himself experienced the enormous power of the void, who has not succumbed to the temptation, knows nothing of our times. His own heart is, as it once was, in a solitary retreat, the center of the world, of the desert and of the ruin. It is a cave where demons converge. It is there that everyone engages in an unmediated and sovereign combat, and where the world can be transformed through his victory. He will abandon his riches upon the beach. These will be recompensed by sacrifices.

We have the sense of having heard this before, and even better expressed. The eschatological stupor of one Gabriel Marcel, for instance, unveils a divergent vision of our crumbling civilization. Jünger wanted to cross "the line," the point zero, in order to reach a "refuge." Immersed in the flux of history, Jünger appeals to the mysteries of transmutation and attempts to find a firm ground in the Heraclitean current of the present in order to touch transcendence. An optimist, he believes that we are at a "historical turning point." By means of a Lautréamontian expression, Jünger seeks to emerge from the domain of what he calls *das Fürchterliche.* Here, he claims, we find the grand literary theme of the past fifty years, the one that recurs in Proust, Rimbaud, Faulkner, Malraux, Saint-Exupéry, Graham Greene, Hemingway, Kafka, and so on. We find a theme, in other words, marked by a sense of the provisional and an awareness of the terrible threat that hangs over human individuality. We are surprised to notice that Jünger hardly pays any attention to the liberating role that has been played by James Joyce, whom he mentions only briefly and rather offhandedly in his *Strahlungen*. On the contrary, taking Eros as a symbol of liberation to a man caught in the trap of nihilism, he praises Henry Miller who, as Jünger states, desperately fights against the machine by advocating redemption through sexuality. When he refers to the "desert of freedom from which man will emerge one day as a lion," Jünger seems to believe he has made a discovery. Engaged in his anti-nihilist struggle, he is happy to remark that theological subjects predominate more and more in contemporary literature, even though he does not believe that theology is at present directed against nihilism. Certain branches of science, especially astronomy, physics, and biology, approach, he says, "images" that could invite theological exegesis. He points out that, in Anglo-Saxon countries, the theological novel is on the rise.

But the nihilism that Jünger deplores has not managed to discourage the German youth who, in his opinion, is possessed of an "enormous force of resistance." Resistance, however, to what? He does not specify. "A defeat is always deplorable," he observes,

> but it has its advantages. Among others, the most important might be in the order of morality: because a defeat precludes all action, it does away with any resulting guilt. . . . Thus it favors the development of a notion of legality superior to the legality of men of action. . . . The shadow of new conflicts already spreads over our country. The German becomes very desirable in the eyes of his enemies, not only due to the central position of his country, but also due to the elemental force that resides within him. . . . This improves his situation all the while creating new dangers. This will force him to delve deeper into problems that only vulgar minds would call political.

The estrangement of the Germans from the rest of humanity has rarely been expressed more clearly.

In *Strahlungen,* Jünger paints a picture of totalitarian nihilism in action. It is a book rich in philosophical reflection, from which the sense of catastrophe is never absent. But it is also a book that causes in us a great unease. An attentive reader is embarrassed at the thought that such a talented German writer, apparently an avid advocate of individual freedom, could have remained silent, while French poets and writers risked their lives expressing their love of liberty. And yet, we are swept away and stimulated by these *Strahlungen,* where esthetical, theological, and scientific aphorisms mingle with often picturesque and bizarre reports. Although our interest is not infrequently sparked by the resistance that the book provokes, it is awakened, above all, by what it reveals about the author himself.

As in Nietzsche, we find in Jünger a heightened sense of the pathology of language; and he does not hesitate to mock the Nazis' gross linguistic inflatedness. Already in *Auf den Marmorklippen* we can sense the author's preoccupation with the precision of expression. "Above all," he confesses, "our labor concerns language, since in the word we recognize the magic sword whose radiance dulls the tyrant's power. We believe in the Holy Trinity of word, liberty, and spirit." Keeping in mind what we've already said, it is interesting to examine Jünger's own vocabulary. What are the keywords, those that often give us a better idea of the author's unconscious than his whole phrases ever could? Words such as "chivalry," "aristocracy," the "plebs," the "elite," the "honor of arms," the "old German decency," and so on, and the manner in which they are employed allow us to detect a true antipathy for democracy.

Although in his preface to *Strahlungen* Jünger revindicated a violent anti-Romanticism through his predilection not only for the *Naturphilosophie* and utopias but also for dreams, nightmares, the apocalypse, and death, he seems to belong to the tradition of Black German Romanticism. He lacks, however, the true mystic hermeticism, the sine qua non of a real Romantic; his irrational life, such as recounted in his journals, has little to do with a cosmological world. Here is an oneiro-critical sample:

A dream in which we carry the corpse of an assassinated man, unable to find a hiding place, and the awful anguish that this causes must be quite common and of ancient origin; for Cain is one of our great ancestors. The time of Genesis is also reflected in these buried oneiric figures that enter the scene at night, and even every night. Here, it is also quite clear that they derive from sources and documents more ancient than human history. Thus, next to the dream of Cain's curse, we find Genesis figures such as the serpent and the naked man, or rather the unclothed man, exposed to our glances at a public place.

And another entry, dated Paris, July 13, 1943:

> I dreamed of serpents, of tenebrous black serpents devouring other serpents dappled with the colors of the sun. Most of the time, I felt no horror at the sight of these beasts that play such an important role in our dreams. It seems that they represent my existential side, the fluid, rapid, mobile character that my brother, Friedrich Georg, has expressed so well in one of his poems. The primitive force of these animals resides in the fact that they embody life and death, and good and evil; while acquiring the knowledge of good and evil thanks to the serpent, man also received mortality. To me, the vision of the serpent constitutes an inexpressible experience, more powerful than that of sex with which it is associated.

Commenting upon these dreams, the German critic Fritz Usinger writes: "Goethe's world is still Luciferian, Jünger's already Satanic." For Usinger, the structure of cosmos proposed by Jünger is close to that of gnosis, while the genesis of history and of the lie represented by the image of the serpent form an integral part of Jüngerian mythology.

The *apologia pro vita sua,* for his inner attitude, is quite sensitive in *Strahlungen,* which Jünger presents as his "contribution, from the literary point of view, to the Second World War" ("regardless of who the winner is," he adds in *Der Friede*). We cannot but ask ourselves if such passages would not have been expressed differently had the fortune of the Nazi armies changed. But from the psychological point of view, his aphorisms, precipitated by his Russian adventure, are doubtless a faithful echo of Hitler's failure. His travel journal equally stands out by its powerful style and its remarkable gift for observation. Through fleeting and often brilliant impressions, the author plunges us into the everyday events of occupied Paris, viewed through the occupants' eyes. We must insist on this point. For if we are convinced that Jünger counts as one of "Kniebolo's" adversaries, it is also true that the Frenchmen, whom he frequents and whom he quotes on his pages, do not belong to the Resistance and are resigned in advance to the idea of France under the German rule. Moreover, when he does speak of the Resistance movement, he uses the term "shoeshine boys." His incessant proclamations of love for Paris, "his second fatherland," strike a sentimental note, but he seems to forget that he is in Paris thanks to Hitler's battalions.

Jünger speaks of his own mission in Paris, where he lived in the German district. As any tourist, he takes walks and visits bookshops. He rummages through antique stores in search of art objects and old books. He spends hours in the company of his French friends discussing literature, art, and philosophy. He participates in *agapes* organized chez Maxim's and at other similar places where Teutonic gourmands can enjoy the French cuisine. From time to time, sadness and a sense of solitude cloud the horizon, but his taste for the refined luxury of choice venues in the capital is more remarkable. And each day, he reads the Bible.

Jünger's life and work, replete with contradictions, provoke a certain mistrust toward his later books. What is the relation between the one who writes: "In my mind, the only durable world is the one in which we (i.e., the Germans) occupy the first place," and the self-proclaimed partisan of a spiritual revival through prayer? In fact, the latter has never denounced his opposite. "I do not contradict myself," he says. . . . "Rather, I move through different layers of truth."

Nevertheless, the fact remains that this highly talented writer around 1925 praised the aristocratic hierarchy of the German community, which would be governed by "a group of young and pitiless führers," by "heroes led to commit the worst acts, without fear of spilt blood." Today he should be pounding his chest in repentance of the horrors he helped unleash rather than seeking refuge in exhortations. He had good reasons in predicting the "Lemurs" of Hitlerian nihilism.

Breton

André Breton's Surrealism in 1950 (June 1950)

The world movement called Surrealism, founded by André Breton in Paris just after World War I, is still a tidal force. For nearly thirty years, this irrationalist explosion, which is a modern manifestation of the pre-logical mentality (it is no accident that it followed closely upon the discoveries of Sigmund Freud), has swept over the continents. Nor is it an exaggeration to say that it has liberated the imagination as no other doctrine of modern time has succeeded in doing.

When I first met Breton, in the early twenties, he was already living in the little rue Fontaine, in Montmartre, where he still lives today, in an apartment filled with modern paintings, especially those of Picasso, de Chirico, Masson, Tanguy, Ernst. It was here that he organized the now historic and frequently stormy meetings, devoted to automatic writing, mediumistic experiment, the penning of so-called *textes surréalistes,* and so on, as a result of which the main tenets of the movement were formulated. At the aperitif tour, the group would usually gather at a café on the nearby Place Blanche, where Breton quite naturally assumed the role of leader in the discussions. His talk was brilliant, at times even violent, and his iconoclasms recognized no idols of exception.

After a period during which these meetings took place on the Left Bank, Breton returned to Montmartre of the "heroic" earlier time, and today he may be seen there, as before, expounding his theories to an attentive group of followers. He still talks and writes with the same coruscating profundity about the things he believes in—which may range from the science of numbers or defense of an esthetic principle to the abolition of political parties and to world citizenship—and it is evident that, despite many premature announcements on the part of impatient would-be successors to the effect that "Surrealism is dead" (only recently another very young aspirant referred to "that poor wreck of Breton"), his influence is still very far-reaching.

An Inventor of Genius

The year 1950 has, so to speak, marked the apogee of Breton's career as a writer and inventor of genius. In addition to his own contribution, to which each year new titles were added, a number of books have been published about him and his ideas: the most important are those by Julien Gracq, Claude Mauriac, Michel Carrouges, Victor Crastre, a group testimonial edited in Switzerland by Marc Eigeldinger, and Jean-Louis Bédouin's presentation of a "little anthology" in the series "Poètes d'aujourd'hui" (Seghers).

There emerges from these monographs the picture of a rare nonconformist creator, as well as a unique personality. One has the impression, too, that the opulence of his discoveries is untarnished; he has not only gone more deeply into his original themes, but has also branched out into new fields of investigation. There is, however, a direct thread that runs from his first *Manifeste du Surréalisme* (1924) to his latest manifestations, and his theory of the interrelationship between dream and action, between the unconscious and the conscious, has never ceased to be an essential feature of his entire thinking.

Interest in Occultism

But the outstanding phase of his recent evolution is, in reality, a systematic continuation of certain earlier phases, such as were outlined in the "Lettre aux voyantes" (1925) and which may be termed mystagogical. Although he has always been interested in occultism, this branch of his explorations now seems to have become of prime importance to him, and it was, in fact, stressed at the last international Surrealist exhibition (Paris, 1947).

In my opinion, Breton's attempt to achieve hermetic understanding is rich in promise. It has nothing to do, however, with the religious concept (as some have claimed) for, unless I am mistaken, he has never budged from his position of agnosticism or atheism. It is, in fact, more akin to the "illuminationism" of the age of "Enlightenment." But the recital of his esoteric experiments is impressive, and I for one will continue to follow them with interest.

Stems from Romanticism

Although Surrealism undoubtedly stems from German Romanticism, it is curious to note that the land which was the cradle of the European Romantic movement shows little interest today in unconscious phenomena, and has even taken unkindly to the irruption of Surrealist irrationalism. (Many probable explanations of this fact come readily to mind.)

In Western Germany, where until recently, due to the obscurantism of the Nazi "estheticians," Surrealism was known only vaguely as one of the forms of modern art, two books have recently appeared on the subject: a translation of Alain Bosquet's *Surrealism,* and another, identically titled, by a German writer, Dieter Wyss. Although they constitute excellent introductions for the layman, they appear to have found little echo beyond the Rhine.

Most Recent Summary

The last issue of the Paris review *La Nef* is entirely devoted to Surrealism and constitutes the most recent attempt on the part of the group to establish a "bilan" of its accomplishments and potentialities. In it, I was much interested to read the following lines, in a letter addressed to Breton by the Mauritian poet Malcolm de Chazal: "France makes me heartsick," writes the author of *Sens Plastique.* "For she is lost to true spirituality. You are not Frenchmen, but Germans, of the race of Novalis and Rilke, whose minds point arrow-like toward the Orient, with its perpetual lamp burning in the belfry of Divine Wisdom."

This affirmation constitutes an unusually direct interpretation of a development in France that turns its back on the traditional Cartesian mode of thinking, and would appear, in essence, to be more Celtic than Latin.

For myself, I have, and have always had, great admiration for André Breton's pioneering genius. Today, as I read his "bilan" in *La Nef,* I ask myself if the high objective he set himself in those early years—the nominalist metamorphosis of man and the world—is any nearer realization as a result of Surrealist efforts. I shall even go further and recall that, already in 1928, when Surrealism abandoned the effort toward the spiritualization of

Novalis to pursue a daemonic myth, I felt they were on the wrong path. In 1950, I still feel this. The artist's solution, it seems to be, lies elsewhere: in an ascending, White Romanticism, a spiritual verticalism which may lead to a sublime superconsciousness.

Melos

A four-page manifesto—what would we do without them—has been launched by a group of young Paris musicians calling themselves "Melos," against what they term "scholarly," as opposed to inspired, music. André Breton, Claude Debussy, Erik Satie, Mussorgsky, even Beethoven and Mozart are quoted to prove their point.

Among many other things they have had enough of are intellectualist estheticism in music; algebraical formulas, empty of all substance, which are being proposed as the only music of our time; inflation of technique; scholastic pedantry; compositional problems devoid of all human interest. Their first concert will be held this evening. Let Rene Leibowitz and his little group of dodecaphonists look to their laurels. This is a timely, almost overdue revolt, unless I am mistaken.

Marginalia

Erika Mann, daughter of Thomas Mann, is preparing a book in memory of her brother, the late Klaus Mann, which will contain contributions by thirty international writers. . . . St. Germain-des-Prés is having its own fortnight during which twenty art galleries are showing new exhibits and authors will sign their books in nineteen bookshops. The recent vernissage of a deluxe edition of Jean Cassou's book of sonnets, with illustrations by Jean Piaubert, was one of the first events of the "fortnight." . . . The critic Jacques Lassaigne, writing in *Arts,* speaks of Tal Coat's current show as representing "one of the most original experiments of our day." The youth of Western Germany is getting a great "kick" out of Duke Ellington's concerts, which come to them as a complete novelty.

Joyce

The Revolution of Language and James Joyce (February 1928)

The word presents the metaphysical problem today. When the beginnings of the twentieth century are seen in perspective, it will be found that the disintegration of words and their subsequent reconstruction on other planes constitute some of the most important phenomena of our age. The traditional meaning of words is being subverted, and a panic seizes the upholders of the norm as they contemplate the process of destruction that opens up heretofore undreamed-of possibilities of expression.

In considering the vast panorama of the written word today, one is struck with the sensation of its endless and monotonous repetitiousness. Words in modern literature are being set side by side in the same banal fashion as in preceding decades, and the inadequacy of worn-out verbal patterns for our more sensitized nervous system seems to have struck only a small minority. The discoveries of the subconscious by medical pioneers as a new field for magical explorations and comprehensions should have made it apparent that the instrument of language in its archaic condition could no longer be used. Modern life with its changed mythos and transmuted concepts of beauty makes it imperative that words be given a new composition and relationship.

It is in the new work of James Joyce, the first book of which has been published serially in *transition,* that this revolutionary tendency is developed to its ultimate degree, thus confounding those timid minds who regard the English language as a static thing, sacrosanct in its position, and dogmatically defended by a crumbling hierarchy of philologists and ped-agogues. Words have undergone organic changes throughout the centuries. It was usually the people who, impelled by their economic or political lives, created the new vocabularies. The *vates,* or poetic seer, frequently minted current expressions into a linguistic whole. James Joyce, whose love of words and whose mastery of them has been demonstrated in huge creations, should not be denied the same privilege as the people themselves hold. He has used this privilege, and an avalanche of jeers and indifference has greeted him.

While Mr. Joyce, beginning with *Ulysses,* and in his still unnamed novel, was occupied in exploding the antique logic of words, analogous experiments were being made in other countries. In order to give language a more modern elasticity, to give words a more compressed meaning through disassociation from their accustomed connections, and to liberate the imagination with primitivistic conceptions of verbs and nouns, a few scattered poets deliberately worked in the laboratories of their various languages along new lines.

Léon-Paul Fargue in his prose poems creates astonishing neologisms, although retaining in a large measure the classical purity of French. He slashes syllables, transposes them from one word to the subsequent word, builds new words from root vocables, and introduces thus an element entirely unknown before in French literature. The large place he leaves to the dream as a means for verbal decomposition makes his work unique among contemporary French writers.

The revolution of the Surrealists who destroyed completely the old relationship between words and thought remains of immense significance. A different association of words on planes of the spirit makes it possible for these poets to create a universe of a beauty the existence of which was never suspected before. Michel Leiris, in his experimental glossaries, departs radically from academic ideas and presents us with a vocabulary of iconoclastic proportions. André Breton, demoralizing the old psychic processes by the destruction of logic, discovered a world of magic in the study of the dream via the Freudian explorations into the subconscious strata and the automatic expression of interior currents.

Miss Gertrude Stein attempts to find a mysticism of the word by the process of thought thinking itself. In structurally spontaneous compositions in which words are grouped rhythmically she succeeds in giving us her mathematics of the word, clear, primitive, and beautiful. In her latest work this compression is of the utmost power.

Verbal deformations have been attempted by German poets, notably August Stramm and Hans Arp. Stramm limited himself to the problem of taking nouns and re-creating them as verbs and adjectives. Arp, more ironic, played havoc with the lyric mind by inventing word combinations set against a fantastic ideology. Certain others went so far as to reproduce merely gestures by word symbols, which, however, often remained sound paroxysms.

Very little can be said for the futuristic theory of "words in liberty." It did not solve the problem of words, since it ignored the psychic contents of poetry. Because a work of art is a vision expressed through rhythm, Marinetti's idea, insisting on movement as the sole basis of expression, remains abortive.

James Joyce has independently found his solution. The texture of his neologies is based on a huge synthesis, and there is an artistic logic back of every verbal innovation. The English language, because of its universality, seems particularly fitted for a rebirth along the lines Mr. Joyce has envisaged. Those who have heard Mr. Joyce read aloud sections from *Work in Progress* now being published in *transition* know the immense rhythmic beauty of this word technique. It has a musical flow that flatters the ear, that has the organic structure of works of nature that opens up the Hegelian world of the "higher synthesis." The rhythmic association of his words is beautiful, because every vowel and every consonant formed by his ear is painstakingly transmitted.

Audibility as a factor in prose has always been of secondary importance in the history of literature. In the new work of Mr. Joyce, this element should be considered as of primary importance. Reading aloud the following excerpt from the installment in *transition* no. 6 will give an excellent idea of this.

If you met on the binge a poor acheseyeld from Ailing, when the tune of this tremble shook shimmy on shin, while his countrary raged in the weak of his wailing, like a rugilaut pugilant Lyon O'Lynn; if he maundered in misliness, plaining his plight or, played fox and lice, pricking and dropping hips teeth, or wringing his handcuffs for peace, the blind blighter, praying Dieuf and Dumb Nostrums foh thomethinks to eath; if he weapt, while he leapt and guffalled quith a quhimper, made cold blood a blue mundy and no bones without flech, taking kiss, kake or kick with a suck, sigh or simper, a diffle to larn and a dibble to lech; if the fain shinner pegged you to shave his immartial, wee skillmustered

shoul with his ooh, hoodoodoo! brooking win that to wiles, woemaid
sin he was partial, we don't think, Jones, we'd care to this evening,
would you?

The root of this evolution can be traced to *Ulysses*. There Mr. Joyce con-
templated already the disintegration of words. There he developed a very
sensitive medium for the expression of his vision. In the interior monologue words became disjointed from their traditional arrangements, and
throughout the book the attempt to give them new timbres is apparent.

James Joyce gives his words odors and sounds that the conventional
standard does not know. In his supertemporal and multispatial composition, language is born anew before our eyes. Each chapter has an internal
rhythm differentiated in proportion to the contents. The words are compressed into stark, blasting accents. They have the tempo of immense rivers flowing to the sea. Nothing that the world of appearance shows seems
to interest him, except in relation to the huge philosophic and linguistic
pattern he has undertaken to create. A modern mythology is being evolved
against the curtain of the past, and a plane of infinity emerges. The human
being across his words becomes the passive agent of some strange and inescapable destiny.

His word formations and deformations spring from more than a dozen
foreign languages. Taking as his physical background the languages spoken in the British Empire, past and present (Afrikaans—Dutch in South
Africa; French in Canada, etc.), Mr. Joyce has created a language of a new
richness and power to express the new sense of time and space he wishes
to give. Everything that the student of languages could learn is being used
to create this amazing flexibility of expression. Even modern American, so
fertile in anarchic properties, has been used by him. The spontaneous flux
of his style is aided by his idea to disregard the norms of orthodox syntax.
His construction of sentences follows a psychological logic rather than a
mathematical one, but this destruction of the usual sequences occurs only
where the particular substance requires it.

Take, for instance, the sentence: "This is the wixy old Willingdone picket
up the half of the three-foiled hat of lipoleum fromoud of the bluddlefilth."
The evocative quality of the neologism "bluddlefilth" cannot be missed.
We have here the word "blood," the effect of blood on the ground and
the entire word "battlefield." In the dialogue between Jute and Mutt, we
have such words as "meldundleize," a German association of two adjectives

taken over into English sounds from the opening of Isolde's "Liebestod." The expression "thonthorstrok" takes up the root idea of Thor. He takes a French word, "constater," and transmutes it into an English word. The deformations "shoutmost shoviality" and "woebecanned and packt away" are of a humor that only a confirmed misanthrope could withstand. Sometimes the humor is enhanced by a curious syntactical innovation: "and, er, constated that one had on him the melton disturbed, and wider he might that zurichschicken other he would one monkey's damages become."

Vico's *New Science* gave Mr. Joyce the philosophic impetus for his work. Vico, a seventeenth-century Italian philosopher, was resuscitated in modern times by Michelet, Auerbach, and Croce. A man of colossal knowledge, he approached the analysis of history from a universalist standpoint, fought the rationalistic ideas of Descartes, and concluded that there is an eternal recurrence of civilizations which he divides into three phases: the age of the gods, the age of the heroes, and the age of man.

It is in Vico's concept that the divine and heroic ages were poetic ages that the root of his linguistic analysis lies. Before the prosaic language there was the rhythmic one, before the rational or epistolary language there were gestures and metaphors. A modern scientist, the French Jesuit Marcel Jousse, has recently published a book in which he traces a similar pan-ethnic origin of language. He finds it in rhythm and gesture with all the nations of the earth.

In his epic work, Mr. Joyce takes into consideration this common nature of linguistic origins. It is not to be wondered at, therefore, that he should try to organize this idea by the creation of a polyglot form of expression. Whirling together the various languages, Mr. Joyce, whose universal knowledge includes that of many foreign tongues, creates a verbal dreamland of abstraction that may well be the language of the future. In this evolution, Mr. Joyce continues to be the master of form he has revealed himself to be from the very beginning, and although the problem of expressing his vision holds an important position in his present orientation, his work is organized on a scale that seems to have few analogies in literature.

In reading *Work in Progress,* let us not forget that it is a joyous creation. The universe, through these newly minted words, these grotesque and striking dissociations, these rhythms and timbres, appears flooded with laughter. The eternal flux of time through space is exteriorized with the humor of an insurgent mind. He moves by a sequence that inheres in the form itself. He has his focus on a scheme of sounds that deviates from the norm merely because we have not yet had the courage to get out of the beaten track. It would be worthwhile for some of the critics who persist in belittling this work to clear their minds of the prejudices they have, and follow with greater willingness the story of H. C. Earwicker across the acrid, lyric, jubilant words that express James Joyce's idea of life and its complexities.

Marginalia to James Joyce's *Work in Progress* (February 1933)

I

No collectivist system, whatever its ultimate economic and political aspect, will be able to destroy two essential entities of man: the saint and the genius. The dogma of sociological interpretation in the creative sphere—based on the belief that the creator is essentially an instrument for bringing about melioristic utopias—is inadmissible, for the scissions in man go beyond all attempts at uniformization. It is in the two forces of the genius and the saint that all the extreme possibilities of the human personality are incorporated. They represent the synthetic functions of life.

II

The principal criterion of genius is the capacity to construct a mythological world. In creating the saga of Anna Livia Plurabelle, James Joyce has given us the modern idea of Magna Mater, the super-Occidental vision of the Anatolian Cybele, of the Egyptian Rhea. In the fragment being published in this number of *Transition*, he presents the modern saga of the infancy of mankind.

III

Every effort to force the work of James Joyce into a literary-historic mold has heretofore been a failure. By the time the critics had caught up with *Ulysses*, identified it, and neatly pigeonholed it into the category of

Naturalism, his new work had already progressed beyond all academic signposts, having no reference point other than a *visionary* quality of invention. *Work in Progress* is, if we must indulge in identification, anti-Naturalist, and, on the positive side, mythological. For it is primarily the story of mankind and the universe. The first mantic myth written in our age. A cosmography in hierophantic terms.

IV

The Anamyth of Childhood begins with the presentation of the various characters, or rather, of the amalgam of characters with which the book deals. There is Hump, the protagonist, the symbol of the male principle, the Besterfather, the Titan of the Scandinavian sagas, known previously under other names, such as Here Comes Everybody, H. C. Earwigger, Lipoleums, or plain He. In the present installment we also trace him again as Meisther Wikingson and Heer Assassor Neelson. Then there is Ann, better known as Anna Livia Plurabelle, *das Ewig' Weibliche,* the Great Mother. Alongside of the minor characters, the Customers of the inn whose conversation, hacked into fragmentary dialogues, we listened to in the beginning of the book, are reintroduced. Glugg and Chuff, the sons of the house, also known under the names of Shem and Shaun, confront the seven girls, the Floras, with whose doings at "lighting up o'clock sharp" we are specially concerned.

V

An "argument" representing once more symbolically the Mookse and the Gripes—this time in the antithesis of Chuffy and Glugger—begins the description of the story. Its basis is the Manichean principle of light and darkness. Quickly the scene shifts to the sketch of the Floras. We watch the kinematics of the seven colors of the rainbow, a theme which reoccurs, under numerous guises and hieroglyphs, throughout this fragment. Taking as his starting point the Irish children's game "The Angels and the Devils," the author builds a richly textured word-pageant, in which we see pass the legend of all the children of the world, past, present, and future, during which we hear Joycean versions of children's songs from many languages, such as "Sur le Pont d'Avignon," "Little Bo-Peep," "Mary Had a Little Lamb," and so on.

VI

The dramatic background of the events is an inn near Dublin. It is dusk and the children are playing in front of the house. The angels and the devils of their game become huge mythic figures passing down prehistory and history. The children have tried to remember their lessons. Glugg's scholastic achievements are rather meager. Then it is time to go to bed, they rush into the house, the door crashes to. *Beifall.* They say their prayers to the "Loud"; in the zoo nearby in Phoenix Park the animals move with nocturnal sounds; the customers in the inn continue swapping stories.

VII

Thomistic and gnostic elements are dovetailed into the text. The paradisaical fall and the birth of sin give the keynote to the story, the struggle between Ahriman and Ozmud resounds, "for felix is as culpas does." The spirit of evil, the archfiend, the apostate angel, is presented with a plethora of names taken from the folklore of the ages. He is Aguliarept, the Joycean nomenclature for the more classical Aghatharept. When "they fleurelly to Nebnos," we watch the change of the noun Fleuretty into a verb. Rofocale is changed into Rosocale. We see the four elements: air, earth, sun, and water, fit into the evocation of the four evangelists: "He askit of the hoothed fireshield, but it was untergone into the matthued heaven. He soughed it from the luft, but that bore ne mark ne message. He luked upon the bloomingrund where barely his corns were growning. At last he listed back to beckline how she pranked alone so johntily." The seven sacraments, baptism, confirmation, eucharist, confession, priests' consecration, extreme unction, and marriage, are humorously described:

> He dove his head into Wat Murrey, gave Stewart Ryall a puck on the plexus, wrestled a hurry-come-union with the Gille Beg, wiped all his sinses, martial and menial, out of Shrove Sunday ManFearsome, excremuncted as freely as any froth-blower into MacIsaac, had a belting bout, chaste to chaste, with McAdoo about nothing, and childhood's age being aye the shamleast, inbraced himself for any time untellable with what hunger over from the MacSiccaries of the Breeks.

In the passage beginning "Ukalepe. Loathers' Leave etc.," we have the author's version of the *Theodicee ex consensu gentium* synthesized with the Odyssean pilgrimage.

VIII

A new development of Mr. Joyce's linguistic experiments can be noted in this fragment. His attempt to reproduce the language of children is particularly felicitous. In the girls' address to Shaun, we notice grammatical deformations that approach infantile stammering. He attempts a primitive syntax: "He possible he sooth to say notwithstanding he gaining fish considerable to look most prophitable out of smily skibluh eye"; "Is you zealous of mes?"; "He relation belong this remarkable moliman." That he is following the most modern philological researches can be deduced from the passage: "But up tighty in the front, down again the loose, drim and drumming on her back, and a pop from her whistle what is that, o holytroopers?" This is a picaresque illustration of the theory expressed by Sir Richard Paget in his *The Nature of Human Speech* (at the Clarendon Press, S.P.E. Tract no. XXII), in which the acoustic of speech is studied from a new angle. We have here again a reference to the rainbow motif, it being in this particular passage an attempt to sound-describe the word "heliotropes" from the viewpoint of Sir Richard Paget's idea of gesture.

IX

Nota bene: we might observe here the reoccurrence of Mr. Joyce's preoccupation with the irrationalism of numbers. Seven, being the symbolism of space-time, emerges here—as it does throughout the book—in the seven colors of the rainbow (the seven names of the Floras), while four, the number of mystic space, can be found in numerous allusions, such as the passage: "No more turdenskaulds" (No more thunder), "Free leaves for ebribadies" (Free love for everybody), "all tinsammon in the yord" (all canned goods in the earth), "with harm and aches till Farther alters" (with ham and eggs till the end of the world).

X

Into the mythological texture the author sometimes weaves bits of autobiographical material, making particular allusion to the tragedy of exile. "Allwhile preying in his mind he swure etc." is a restatement of the famous maxim of Dedalus, in the *Portrait of the Artist as a Young Man:* silence, exile, and cunning. Bruce here is a reference to the story of Scotland's Robert Bruce and the spider, silence being in this case identified with patience. Coriolanus refers to the tale of the exiled Roman, and Machiavelli is the illustration of cunning. Paname-Turricum indicates the author's stay in Paris and Zurich. Laurentius O'Toole is the native saint of Dublin who died at Eure (France). This is the hint in *Euro pra nobis.*

XI

The mythological symbolisms used include numerous past and living references. From the Egyptian *Book of the Dead* has come: "Your head has been touched by the god Enel-Rah and your face has been brightened by the goddess Aruc-Ituc." The deformations of the original terms are once more in line with the color motif. An American Negro song occurs in the passage of Meisther Wikingson, still the gigantic, pneumatic figure he always is in the book: "It's his last lap, Gigantic, fare him weal!" This is from the Louisville (Ky.) Negro song composed by some vagabond singer after the sinking of the *Titanic:* "It's yer las' trip, Titanc, fare thee well." In giving a picture of the night, the author says: "Was even ere awhile. Now conticinium. The time of lying together will come and the wildering of the nicht till cockee doodle aubens Aurore." This is a flection of the five Roman watches of the night: *vespers, conticinium, concubium, intempestas noctis, gallicinium,* and *aura ante lucano.*

XII

In this passage of *Work in Progress,* the author returns once more to Vico's cyclical conception of history. "The same renew." The triune evolution: theocratic, heroic, and human, is the basis of the work. The fear felt by primitive man is still in us. The thunder motif in the invocation to the "Loud" is based on Vico. It is, however, obvious that Mr. Joyce is not in the least interested in demonstrating any theory. He is merely following a vision of his own: the sense of the prehistoric and the historic as one great stream. It is interesting, in this connection, to observe that M. Lévy-Bruhl, the French sociologist, has come to some definite confirmations in his own researches. The primitive mentality, according to him, is characterized chiefly by the pre-logical function of the mind. He finds—as did Vico—that the basic emotion which impelled man to create his gods and myths is fear, or rather, apprehension. In his recent book *Le Surnaturel et la nature dans la mentalité primitive,* M. Lévy-Bruhl develops the idea still further. The German metaphysician Martin Heidegger has also found apprehension to be man's principal impulse.

XIII

An inkling of the author's most definite belief can be found in the final prayer. He looks at the universe with cosmic humor, creating a world of symbols, building a "witchman's funnominal world."

Homage to the Mythmaker (April–May 1938)

James Joyce is completing the last pages of his protean book of the night. *Work in Progress,* eighteen fragments of which have been published by *Transition* during the last ten years, will appear in book form in 1938, and will doubtless attract the attention of the intercontinental world with the electric shock of the thunder-word that epitomizes polysyllabically one of its leitmotifs.

Fifteen years of word-ecstatic labors are about to close.

To the very end, like one of the Celtic ornament-makers, the Irish writer has worked, in painstaking solitude, at the gigantic vision which has possessed him ever since he sent *Ulysses* on its world migration. As his Nocturne reaches the ultimate note of a word mutilated in the night-mind, as a final challenge to the spirit and grammar of the sun, he accelerates the rhythm, suffers the ensemble of his highly charged pan-logos once more, organizes into one synoptical prose poem the most tenuous threads of the three parts and postlude that compose his tale of humanity's progress through the abyss of the ages.

Soon our curiosity as to the mysterious and jealously guarded title of the book—a title that was first conceived fifteen years ago—will be satisfied.

What will the finished book be like?

This complex, this enigmatic work has challenged contemporary speculation as no other book has done for a long time. Its fragmentary appearance will probably have militated against an immediate acceptance, but the reader has doubtless now been prepared through *Transition* and the exegetical efforts of *Transition* writers. There have been a few indications in the past fifteen years sketching the ultimate silhouette.

We know that Mr. Joyce's ambition has been to write a book dealing with the night-mind of man. We have already followed most of the purgatorial, multiple characters, blundering through their larval and anthropological transmigrations. We have had glimpses of that titanic city-mountain synthesis: Humphrey Chimpden Earwigger, and have watched his countless human metamorphoses. We have followed the pan-symbolic pattern in the creation of Anna Livia Plurabelle, the river-woman, *magna mater.* Shem and Shaun, the adopted daughter, the household slut, the topers and gossips of prehistory and history, have passed by, in their primordial drama; the contour of the conflict that dominates the conception on the nocturnal stage plays in a continuous mutation of locality, objects, happenings, language, characters. Examining with new eyes Mr. Joyce's revolutionary conception of the paragraph, we have tried to keep in mind that the dramatic dynamis is based on the Bruno theory of knowledge through opposites, and on Vico's philosophy of cyclic recurrence.

We are once more in the ambience of Dublin, "The Black Pool," yet there is a new topographical background, the action of the "story" being played in a suburb: Chapelizod. We are in the Valley of the Liffey. Phoenix Park, the Wellington Monument, the Magazine, and so on . . . are constantly before us. Chapelizod is said to have taken its name from Iseult, made famous in our day by Tennyson and Wagner. All these elements are constantly used in the structure of *Work in Progress.*

The "story" deals with the outer and inner world of a lower-middle-class family living in a hotel beside the prattling Liffey, in the vicinity of Phoenix Park. It is a sultry summer night. Lightning rolling over the Dublin mountains strikes primal fear in the hearts of the inhabitants. A thunderclap roars through the phantasmal dusk. The customers in the pub forget their gargantuan tales. Rain clears the atmosphere. The children play on the square. Then the house goes to sleep. We are in the abyss of time and space, in the world of phantoms, in the night-memory of the family—and of the human race.

Mr. Joyce is now finishing the last pages. We may expect technical innovations that go beyond Marion Bloom's monologue in audacity. For now the author deals with the dream-fantasies, with the hypnogogic hallucinations, the inner scissions of an entire household, of mankind in general.

Nietzsche says somewhere: "In sleep and dream we pass once more through the early phases of mankind." Modern psychology has made enormous progress in delineating the *mythological* remnants of the unconscious. Man, in his night-life, relives the fantasies that were those of the Magdalenian man, the dream-phantoms which produced the great myths of all the races.

In *Work in Progress,* the pre-logical or pre-conscious mind of the ancestors is continuously at work. Mr. Joyce presents his phantasmagoric figures as passing back and forth from a mentality saturated with archetypal images to a contemporary kinesis, from the past of childhood memories to a vision of future construction.

History being, in his earlier words, "a nightmare," Mr. Joyce gives us the multidimensional idea of Time in sleep. His conception of Time is born out of his deep sense of race-parallelism. It has relations with the newest discoveries of physical science as well as with oneiromantic experiments. The Joycean idea is cosmic Time, a colossal vision that negatives Bergson's theory of *durée.*

Legend tells us that prehistoric man possessed a third eye, which was the "seat of the soul" in the Cartesian philosophy. The pineal eye was said to have given ancestral man the natural intuitive faculties which modern man has apparently lost. The man with the third eye may come back again, according to certain modern paleontologists, who foresee the eventual redevelopment of that anatomical organ.

Perse O'Reilly, hotelier at Chapelizod, Vico Road, is a man with the third eye.

One of the chief myths which *Work in Progress* treats exhaustively and with glacial objectivity is that of original sin. The myth of the fall of the angels; the idea of the "diabolical principle"; the gnostic-mystic idea of the demiurge; the antithetical dynamism of good and evil.

It has always been diverting to me to see my Catholic co-religionnaires assail Mr. Joyce's work because of its apparently heretic content. Is it necessary to point out to them the enormous role the concept of evil plays in Catholic theology? The Paschal acolyte does not hesitate to eulogize "the sin of Adam" in a famous liturgical passage. St. Augustine himself declared "Felix culpa! O fortunatissimum Adae peccatum!" The obscene distortions of gargoyles on Gothic cathedrals show the very luxuriant imagination of the conformist architects. The satanic chimeras of the paintings of such believers as Matthias Grunewald and Hieronymus Bosch lead us into the abyss of the grotesque. And what of the Book of Kells? Mr. Joyce, who knows his fathers of the church, assumes the right which the Catholic

Church has always given to the artist, to present the carnal side of man's consciousness with all the mastery of his verbal art.

The opposition of Catholic puritans is not shared by the highest ecclesiastical authorities, and it might be of interest to hear what the *Osservatore Romano,* world-organ of the Vatican, has to say about James Joyce. In a recent issue of that famous newspaper (Oct. 22, 1937), we find the following reference to him in an essay on modern Irish literature:

> . . . e infine James Joyce, di fama europea, iconoclasta e rebelle, che dopo aver cercato di ringiovanire il vecchio naturalismo, tenta nell' *Ulyxes* di tradurre plasticamente la realtà interiore, e nell' *Opera in Corso* attraverse una esperienza onirica et insieme linguistica si sforza di aprire altre vie all' espressione del sentimento umane.*

The Catholic Church is apparently far removed from the philistinism and hypocrisy of some of the orthodox literary critics of Dublin, London, and New York.

It is now more than ten years since I read the first version of *Work in Progress,* then a comparatively small manuscript. I had the privilege of seeing it grow bit by bit, of watching its expansion at close range. In Mr. Joyce's word-alchemical laboratory I have had the pleasure of glimpsing the amalgamations he made of his journeys into the unconscious of mankind.

The publishing of any one of the seventeen fragments in *Transition* has always been an event in the editorial life of the review. It was not the simple process of taking over from the author a completed manuscript, but required the active collaboration of members of the *Transition* staff, of friends and sympathizers. It was necessary to go through a number of notebooks, each of which had esoteric symbols indicating the reference to a given character, locality, event, or mood. Then the words accumulated over the years had to be placed in the segment for which they were intended.

It has been interesting to see Mr. Joyce's very special method of working. His interest in the little events of every day, during a period filled with political upheavals, is a constant source of wonder. Rivers, and mountains, and children, and apparently insignificant occurrences in the streets,

---

* "And finally James Joyce, of European fame, iconoclast and rebel, who after having sought to renovate the old Naturalism, attempted in *Ulysses* to translate plastically the inner reality, and, who, in *Work in Progress,* in an experiment, both oneiric and linguistic, is seeking to open up new paths for the expression of human sentiments."

preoccupy him. He incorporates continually into his work the living folk-lore and mythology gathered in his travels through Europe and the British Isles. His verbs transmute the quotidian gesture, which Jousse and Paget tell us was man's primal language.

"This book," he sometimes says, "is being written by the people I have met or known." Sometimes he hardly seems to be listening to the conversation around him. Yet nothing escapes his prodigious memory, whether the dialogues be in English, French, German, or Italian. It may be a slip of the tongue, a phantasmatic verbal deformation, or just a tic of speech, but it usually turns up later in its proper place.

Only absolute indifference to the sociological habit of thought could make possible such a devotion to the purely creative élan. Joyce does not take sides. He tells the pessimistic story of mankind's internecine war with a smile of irony and sometimes pity. He presses seconds into interplanetary aeons by looking at everything from a "funnominal" perspective. He has no "ethical" axe to grind. Yet is it not a fact that all his characters—beginning with those in *Dubliners* and continuing through *Work in Progress*—are people of the lower social strata, the so-called proletarized lower middle class, the poor white whose struggles in the never-changing world of Cain and Abel, or Shem and Shaun, he presents with the detachment of a whimsical understanding? The martial antinomies of life are the elements with which he deals. In lowly puns, irrational junctions, cross-currents from more than forty languages, we see the child-play of "The Mime of Mick, Nick and the Maggies," the legend of the "Mookse and the Gripes," the myth of "Anna Livia Plurabelle," the fantasia of "Shem and Shaun," the grotesque of "Haveth Childers Everywhere," the fable of "The Ondt and the Gracehoper"—all of them folk of the common, human run, yet made sublime by the creative imagination of a poet.

Work in Progress is "a compendium, an encyclopedia of the entire mental life of a man of genius," a definition which Wilhelm Schlegel posited, more than a hundred years ago, for the novel of the future.

Soon the Book of Proteus will appear in its entirety. We who have watched it grow hope that there will be ears to hear and rejoice at the fabulous new harmonies of this All-World Symphony!

My Friend James Joyce (March–April 1941)

To those who knew him intimately, James Joyce was a human being of great warmth and charm, although, at first approach, his personality could seem almost forbidding. In fact, it took him some time to accept an easy comradeship in social intercourse. He often appeared to be on his guard, an attitude that was particularly noticeable during the period of excessive curiosity concerning him that followed the publication of *Ulysses*. But once he had given his friendship, nothing could swerve him from his granitic loyalty. He was never an ebullient man. His moments of silence and introspection frequently weighed, even, on his immediate surroundings. Then a profound pessimism, that seemed to hold him prisoner within himself, made him quite inaccessible to outsiders. Usually, however, among his intimates, there finally came a festive pause, when he would begin to dance and sing, or engage in barbed thrusts of wit; when he would show flashes of gaiety and humor that could, on occasion, approach a kind of delirium.

He was never an easy conversationalist, and had a tendency to monosyllabic utterances. He did not relish being questioned directly on any subject. He never gave any interviews, and I was always careful not to quote him for publication. When he was in the mood, his talk, given in his mellifluous Dublin speech, was a ripple of illuminating ideas and words. Once he had left his anarchic and misanthropic taciturnity, he could enjoy the companionship of his friends, on whom, in some ways, he was very dependent, with a demonstration of good fellowship that brought out another facet of his nature. He eschewed all esotericism in his talk. Nor was he interested in high-flown abstractions, but engrossed rather by the drama of human relations, human behavior, human thought and customs. The range of subjects he enjoyed discussing was a wide one: poetry prodigiously remembered and faultlessly recited; music and musicians, especially singing, of which his technical knowledge was astonishing; the theater, where his preferences went to Ibsen, Hauptmann, Scribe; the various liturgies; education; anthropology; philology; and certain sciences, particularly physics, geometry, and mathematics. He was little interested in pure politics and economics, although he followed events faithfully.

I am conscious of difficulty in writing about him, for he was often amused by the article that concerned his private life. He seemed to resent the constant macabre preoccupations with the condition of his eyes. Once, when I read a particularly inept piece about his personal habits, written in German, he said: "What are they writing about? *Es ist eben nichts zu malen.*" (There really is nothing to paint, anyway.) During the fourteen years of our association—which coincided with the writing of *Work in Progress,* or *Finnegans Wake*—I had many opportunities to observe his kindliness, his humor, his pathos. I saw his stoicism before fate. I saw him in moments of insouciance and in moments of distress. In spite of the frailty of his physique, there was a certain toughness in him which saw him through the ups and downs of his destiny. This tenacity was part of his honesty of conviction, his horror of cheap compromise, his fanatic belief in his own intellectual powers. His being was compact and fashioned by a will of steel. He was a man of deep tolerance, and objected to all denigrations of friends, or enemies, in his presence.

I met James Joyce for the first time in 1924, three years before I launched *transition.* It was at a rather dull banquet given at the Restaurant Marguéry in honor of Valéry Larbaud, his first French friend and translator. (By a curious turn of fate, Larbaud was the last French writer Joyce saw anything of. While in Vichy, during the war, he went frequently to visit the now incurably ill author of *Barnabooth.*) Joyce was beaming in the aureole of *Ulysses,* and in a happy mood, when I was introduced to him. He thanked me courteously for something I had written about the book in a literary column I was then conducting for the Paris edition of the *Chicago Tribune.* We did not meet again until early in 1927, when I was preparing *transition* with Elliot Paul. We had approached Miss Sylvia Beach, his publisher, to ask her for a manuscript from Joyce, but with very little hope that anything would be forthcoming. Miss Beach consulted him, and within a few days we had the manuscript in our hands.

On a Sunday afternoon, in the winter of 1927, Joyce invited Mlle. Adrienne Monnier, Miss Sylvia Beach, my wife, Elliot Paul, and myself to his home in the Square Robiac to listen to his reading of the manuscript in question. We listened to the Waterloo scene, which subsequently appeared in the first issue of the review. His voice was resonantly musical, and at times a smile went over his face, as he read a particularly exhilarating passage. After he had finished, he said: "What do you think of it? Did you like it?" We were all stirred by his verbal fantasy, excited, even, but puzzled. It was not easy to reply with conventional phrases. There was no precedent in literature for judging his fragment, with its structure of multiple planes and its novelty of a polysynthetic language. Some weeks later, he let me read the entire manuscript. It was not more than 120 pages long, and had been written, he said, within a few weeks during a stay on the Riviera in 1922. Yet it was already complete in itself, organically compressed, containing the outline of the entire saga. Even the title had been chosen, he indicated, but only he and Mrs. Joyce knew it. It was still a primitive version, to which he had already begun to add numberless paragraphs, phrases, words. In a moment of confidence he told me something about the genesis of the idea. His admirer, Miss Harriet Weaver—who, some years before, like a Maecenas of other days, made it possible for the struggling writer to be freed of financial worry—had asked him what book he was planning to write after *Ulysses*. He replied that now that *Ulysses* was done he considered himself as a man without a job. "I am like a tailor who would like to try his hand at making a new-style suit," he continued. "Will you order one?" Miss Weaver handed him a pamphlet written by a village priest in England and giving a description of a giant's grave found in the parish lot. "Why not try the story of this giant?" she asked jokingly. The giant's narrative became the story of Finn MacCool, or *Finnegans Wake*.

The first issues of *transition* containing installments from what was then known as *Work in Progress*—Joyce told me that this provisional title was the invention of Ford Madox Ford, who had previously published a fragment in his *Transatlantic Review*—brought forth a fanfare of sensational outbursts. The confused critics in France, England, and America snorted, for the most part, their violent disapproval. Miss Weaver herself regretfully wrote Miss Beach she feared Joyce was wasting his genius; an opinion which disturbed Joyce profoundly, for, after all, it was for her that the "tailor" was working. His friend Larbaud said he regarded the work as a *divertissement philologique* and of no great importance in Joyce's creative evolution. H. G. Wells wrote him that he still had a number of books to write and could not give the time to attempt to decipher Joyce's experiment. Ezra

Pound attacked it in a letter and urged him to put it in the "family album," together with his poems. Only Edmund Wilson was intelligently sympathetic. After a while the reactions became more and more vehement, even personal, and on the whole journalistically stereotyped. Joyce continued working at his vision.

We saw a good deal of him during those years. Our office was not very far from his home, near the Eiffel Tower, and his urbane presence amid the disorder of our primitive hotel room was always a welcome one. All his friends collaborated then in the preparations of the fragments destined for *transition:* Stuart Gilbert, Padraic Colum, Elliot Paul, Robert Sage, Helen and Giorgio Joyce, and others. He worked with painstaking care, almost with pedantry. He had invented an intricate system of symbols permitting him to pick out the new words and paragraphs he had been writing down for years, and which referred to the multiple characters in his creation. He would work for weeks, often late at night, with the help of one or the other of his friends. It seemed almost a collective composition in the end, for he let his friends participate in his inventive zeal, as they searched through numberless notebooks with mysterious reference points to be inserted in the text. When finished, the proof looked as if a coal-heaver's sooty hands had touched it. Once the work was done, we would dine with him at his favorite restaurant, the Trianons, where he liked the atmosphere and cuisine, and where he was sure to find his dry, golden Chablis, or, if the evening grew more hilarious than usual, an excellent Pommery champagne. His nearly whispered conversations never had any nuance of scatology, and whenever one of the more Rabelaisian of his companions would indulge in some too robust *gauloiserie,* he would deftly, almost impatiently, lead the dialogue into other channels. Sometimes he would bring with him a page he had written and hand it around the table with a gesture of polite modesty. He never explained his work, save through indirection.

At that time Joyce's family life was closely knit and happy, and his humor was a natural manifestation of this ambience. It did not yet have that mordant quality which it acquired in later years, after great sorrow had entered his home circle. And yet, even then, it was rather what André Breton has called somewhere *un humour noir.* Later, he grew more asocial. But his friends succeeded in cheering him up. Once he celebrated, on the same day, his fiftieth birthday and the tenth anniversary of the publication of *Ulysses.* The events were hardly noticed by the literary world, which was then discovering Social Realism and considered Joyce outmoded. On that occasion, we gave a small dinner at our home in Paris attended by

Mrs. Joyce, Thomas McGreavy, Samuel Beckett, Lucy and Paul Léon, Helen and Giorgio Joyce, and others. The birthday cake was decorated with an ingenious candy replica of a copy of *Ulysses,* in its blue jacket. Called on to cut the cake, Joyce looked at it a moment and said: "Accipite et manducate ex hoc omnes: Hoc est enim corpus meum." The talk at the table turned on the subject of popular sayings. Someone expressed a suspicion of all of them and gave voice to his dislike for the adage: *In vino veritas,* which he held to be untrue and bromidic. Joyce agreed warmly and added: "It should really be: *In riso veritas;* for nothing so reveals us as our laughter." He was always astonished that so few people had commented on the comic spirit in his writings.

I was preparing a short homage to him in *transition* and had, among other features, ordered a sketch of Joyce by the Spanish artist César Abin. The result was an impressive study of a distinguished *homme de lettres,* with pen in hand, his own volumes reverentially piled beside him. But Joyce would have none of it, and insisted on giving the cartoonist precise instructions for the design and execution of the job. He wanted it, first of all, to look like a question mark, because friends had told him once that his figure resembled a question mark, when seen standing meditatively on a street corner. For more than two weeks he kept adding new suggestions, until he was finally satisfied with it. He asked to be drawn with a battered old derby hung with spiderwebs and bearing a ticket on which was inscribed the fatal number 13. He asked that a star be put on the tip of his nose, in memory of a criticaster's description of him as a "blue-nosed comedian"; that his feet be suspended perilously over a globe called Ireland, on which only Dublin was visible; that he have patches on the knees of his trousers; that out of his pockets there should emerge the manuscript of a song entitled *Let me like a soldier fall.* For his "luck," his "fate," had already started down the somber path it never left again. It was as though he had a premonition of the immense trials that lay before him. It was during this period that he suggested that we plan a *bal de la purée*—which is French slang for general insolvency—since the depression was beginning to be felt in Paris more and more. The gayest of the guests was Joyce himself, who finally inveigled all the ladies present to give him the first prize for his costume: that of an old Irish stage character famous once as *Handy Andy.*

At that time, the sudden death of his father came to him as a profound shock. He had never made any bones about his great affection for his father, and the autobiographical elements of his work reveal this in numberless symbolical and mythological allusions. *Ulysses* was man in search of his father, and *Finnegans Wake* is once again the expression of that filial quest. In those days, he dreamed much about him, and one evening he said suddenly: "I hear my father talking to me. I wonder where he is." Sometimes he would tell picaresque tales of his father's wit, and the last one I remember was one that concerned his father's reaction in Dublin to a minuscule sketch of him made by Brancusi. It was merely a geometrical spiral study symbolizing the ear. "Well, Jim hasn't changed much," said his father on seeing the portrait.

During the summer and fall of 1931 his daughter Lucia suffered a nervous collapse, and we spent several months with the Joyce family in a little frontier town in the mountains of Austria. Joyce had not been writing for some time, due, partly, to the intense worry he felt over his daughter's condition, partly to the general mood of inertia caused by the depression. So we took long walks together along the swirling mountain river Ill nearby, or we climbed the wooded hills. He had a deep love for mountains and rivers because, he said, "they are the phenomena that will remain when all the peoples and their governments will have vanished." Yet he was not at all a nature Romantic. He was rather a man of the megapolis. Toward dusk, after a siesta, he would go walking again. Eight o'clock was the hour he had set for himself many decades before as the time for his first glass of wine of the day. That summer he evolved a sort of ritual which, to me, had an almost grotesque fascination. At half past seven, he would race suddenly for the railroad station, where the Paris-Vienna Express was due to stop for ten minutes each day. He would quietly walk up and down the platform. "Over on those tracks there," he said one evening, "the fate of *Ulysses* was decided in 1915." He referred to the fact that in this Austrian town of the border he had almost been prevented by some jinx from crossing into Switzerland during the First World War. When the train finally came in, he rushed to the nearest car in order to examine the French, German, and Yugoslav inscriptions, palped the letters with the sensitive fingers of defective vision. Then he would ask me questions about the persons getting on or off the train. He would try to listen to their conversations. His fine ear for dialectal nuances in German often astonished me. When the train continued on its way into the usually foggy night, he stood on the platform waving his hat, as if he had just bid godspeed to a dear friend. With eight o'clock approaching, he almost skipped back to the hotel for his first draught of *Tischwein*—or, as Mrs. Joyce, who thought the drink of rather inferior quality, used to say, *dishwine*.

After a while I started making preparations for a new issue of *transition,* and this stimulated him to work. He attacked the problem with savage energy. "How difficult it is to put pen to paper again," he said one evening. "Those first sentences have cost me a great deal of pain." But gradually the task was in hand. It was to be known later as "The Mime of Mick, Nick and the Maggies." He wrote steadily on this fragment during those frenetic months, constantly interrupted by moments of anxiety about the health of his daughter, and by his own resultant nervousness. At his hotel, where we would work in the afternoon, he gave me a densely written foolscap sheet beginning with the words: "Every evening at lighting up o'clock sharp and until further notice. . . ." which I typed for him. After a few pages had thus been transcribed, we began to look through the notebooks—which he lugged around on all his travels—and the additions, set down years before for a still-unwritten text he had merely outlined in his mind, became more and more numerous. The manuscript grew into thirty pages and was not yet finished. He never changed a single word. There was always a certain inevitability, an almost volcanic affirmativeness, about his primal choice of words. To me, his deformations seemed to grow more daring. He added ceaselessly, like a worker in mosaic, enriching his original pattern with ever-new inventions.

"There really is no coincidence in this book," he said during one of our walks.

I might easily have written this story in the traditional manner. . . . Every novelist knows the recipe. . . . It is not very difficult to follow a simple, chronological scheme which the critics will understand. . . . But I, after all, am trying to tell the story of this Chapelizod family in a new way. . . . Time and the river and the mountain are the real heroes of my book. . . . Yet the elements are exactly what every novelist might use: man and woman, birth, childhood, night, sleep, marriage, prayer, death. . . . There is nothing paradoxical about this. . . . Only I am trying to build many planes of narrative with a single esthetic purpose. . . . Did you ever read Laurence Sterne . . . ?

We read Goethe's *Farbenlehre*, but he finally said he could use nothing from it. He was interested in a comic version of the theodicy, and he asked me to get one of the Jesuits nearby to give me an Augustinian text. There was a famous Jesuit school in the town, and he occasionally reminisced about his Dublin days with the fathers. But his anti-religious convictions were unshakable. I had come back from a talk with his daughter, who seemed to be interested in knowing something about Catholic dogma. Joyce, on hearing this, grew suddenly quite violent and said: "Why should a young woman bother her head about such things? Buddha and Confucius and all the others were not able to understand anything about it. We know nothing, and never shall know anything." He discussed Vico's theory of the origin of language. The conception of the cyclical evolution of civilizations born from each other like the phoenix from the ashes haunted him. He began to speculate on the new physics, and the theory of the expanding universe. And, while walking with him, I always had the impression that he was not really in an Austrian frontier town, but in Dublin, and that everything he thought and wrote was about his native land.

He completed the "Mime" in Zurich, after our return there. We used to take a motorboat in the late afternoon and go out on the lake. Or else we would go walking uphill to the zoo, where one evening he suddenly quoted to me the magnificent nocturne of Phoenix Park, with the verbal magic of animal sounds dying off in the gathering night. Or else we would walk up and down the Bahnhofstrasse, and I would think of his poem about this street. He would talk about his World War experiences in the Swiss town and chat about old friends, especially his English friend Frank Budgen, who was his companion in those days. Then we would dine at the Kronenhalle, which he now preferred to the more colorful Zum Pfauen that had been his *Stammlokal* in the old days. His guests were the few friends he had in Zurich: Dr. Bernard Fehr, of the university; Dr. Borach, and Mr. Edouard Brauchbar, English pupils during the First World War; Dr. and Mrs. S. Giedion. He was very fond of the Swiss *fondant* wine from the Valais, and we often left the restaurant in a grape-happy mood.

A British clipping came saying that Joyce was trying to revive Swift's *little language* to Stella. "Not at all," said Joyce to me. "I am using a *Big Language.*" He said one evening: "I have discovered that I can do anything with language I want." His linguistic memory was extraordinary. He seemed constantly *à l'affût*, always to be listening rather than talking. "Really, it is not I who am writing this crazy book," he said in his whimsical way one evening. "It is you, and you, and you, and that man over there, and that girl at the next table." One day I found him in a Zurich tea shop laughing quietly to himself. "Did you win *le gros lot*?" I asked. He said he had asked the waitress for a glass of lemon squash. The somewhat obtuse Swiss girl looked puzzled. Then she had an inspiration: "Oh, you mean *Lebensquatsch*?" she stammered. (Her German neologism might be translated by "life's piffle"!) Joyce retained all such scraps of conversation, lopped-off syllables said in moments of inertia or fatigue, *jeux de mots,* alcoholically deformed words, slips of the tongue—all the verbal grotesques and fantasies which he heard issuing in unconscious moments. His knowledge of French, German, modern Greek, and especially Italian stood him in good stead, and he added constantly to that stock of information by studying Hebrew, Russian, Japanese, Chinese, Finnish, and other tongues. At the bottom of his vocabulary was also an immense command of Anglo-Irish words that only seem like neologisms to us today, because they have, for the most part, become obsolete. His revival of these will some day interest the philologists. Language to him was a social as well as a subjective process. He was deeply interested in the experiments of the French Jesuit, Jousse, and the English philologist, Paget, and *Finnegans Wake* is full of strange applications of their gesture theory. He often talked with a derisive smile of the auxiliary languages, among them Esperanto and Ido.

Back in Paris he became more and more absorbed by meditations on the imaginative creation. He read Coleridge and was interested in the distinction he made between imagination and fancy. He wondered if he himself had imagination. As the political horizon in Europe grew more threatening, his high Olympian neutrality asserted itself more and more. In those days I remember reading to him a German translation from a speech by Radek in which the Russian attacked *Ulysses,* at the Congress of Kharkov, as being without a social conscience. "Well," said Joyce, "all the characters in my books belong to the lower middle classes, and even the working class; and they are all quite poor." He began to read *Wuthering Heights.* "This woman had pure imagination," he said. "Kipling had it, too, and certainly Yeats." His admiration for the Irish poet was very great. A recent commentator, asserting that Joyce lacked reverence for the logos in poetry, inferred that he had little regard for Yeats. I can assure the gentleman that this was not true. Joyce often recited Yeats's poems to us from memory. "No Surrealist poet can equal this for imagination," he said. Once, when Yeats spoke over the radio, he invited us to listen in with him. I read *A Vision* to him, and he was deeply absorbed by the colossal conception, only regretting that "Yeats did not put all this into a creative work." At Yeats's death he sent a wreath to his grave at Antibes, and his emotion on hearing of the poet's passing was moving to witness. He always denied, too, that he had said to Yeats that he was too old to be influenced by him.

Joyce had a passion for the irrational manifestations of life. Yet there was nothing in common between his attitude and that of the Surrealists and psychoanalysts. Nor did his experiments have anything to do with those of the German Romantics who explored the mysticism of the individual world. Joyce was an intensely conscious observer of the unconscious drama. During walks in Paris, we often talked about dreams. Sometimes I related to him my own dreams, which, during the prewar years, began to take on a strangely fantastic, almost apocalyptic silhouette. He was always eager to discuss them, because they interested him as images of the nocturnal universe. He himself, he said, dreamed relatively little, but, when he did, his dreams were usually related to ideas, personal and mythic, with which he was occupied in his waking hours. He was very much attracted by Dunne's theory of *serialism,* and I read to him that author's brilliant *An Experiment with Time,* which Joyce regarded highly. He told me one of his dreams, and subsequent events seemed to confirm Dunne's multidimensional conceptions. He was walking through a big city and met three men who called themselves Minos, Eaque, and Rhadamante. They suddenly broke off their conversation with him and became threatening. He had to run to escape from their screams of obloquy. Three weeks later I noticed a feature story in the *Paris-Soir* to the effect that the police were looking for a crank who was sending explosives through the mails. This fanatic signed himself: Minos, Eaque, Rhadamante, the judges of Hell. One of Joyce's less complicated dreams, however, caused considerable chuckling, each time he thought of it. This was a dream the climax of which was the titanic figure of Molly Bloom, seated on the side of a high hill. "As for you, James Joyce, I've had enough of you," she shouted. His reply he never remembered.

Some six months before *Work in Progress* was scheduled to appear, there was an amusing incident in connection with its title, then still known only to Mr. and Mrs. Joyce. Often he had challenged his friends to guess it. He even made a permanent offer to pay a thousand francs in cash to the person who would guess it. We all tried: Stuart Gilbert, Herbert Gorman, Samuel Beckett, Paul Léon, and I, but we failed miserably. One summer night, while dining on the terrace of Fouquet's, Joyce repeated his offer. The Riesling was especially good that night, and we were in high spirits. Mrs. Joyce began an Irish song about Mr. Flannigan and Mrs. Shannigan. Joyce looked startled and urged her to stop. This she did, but when he saw no harm had been done, he very distinctly, as a singer does it, made the lip motions which seemed to indicate F and W. My wife's guess was *Fairy's Wake.* Joyce looked astonished and said "Brava! But something is missing."

For a few days we mulled over it. One morning I knew it was *Finnegans Wake,* although it was only an intuition. That evening I suddenly threw the words into the air. Joyce blanched. Slowly he set down the wine-glass he held. "Ah, Jolas, you've taken something out of me," he said, almost sadly. When we parted that night, he embraced me, danced a few of his intricate steps, and asked: "How would you like to have the money?" I replied: "In sous." The following morning, during my absence from home, he arrived with a bag filled with ten-franc pieces. He gave them to my daughters with instructions to serve them to me at lunch. So it was *Finnegans Wake.* All those present were sternly enjoined by Joyce not to reveal it, and we kept it a secret until he made the official announcement at his birthday dinner on the following February 2.

The reception given this labor of seventeen years was to be a disappointing one. Among the few whose analysis struck him as being comprehensive and conscientious were, in rough order of his appreciation, William Troy's essay in *Partisan Review,* Harry Levin's article in *New Directions,* Edmund Wilson's essays in the *New Republic,* Alfred Kazin's review in the *New York Herald Tribune,* and Padraic Colum's piece in the *New York Times,* as well as one or two from England and Scotland. From Ireland there was little reaction, and the reception in France, on which he had counted so much, was lamentable. This state of affairs was a source of deep depression during the last year of his life, and was responsible, more than anything else, for the fact that he was completely indifferent to any suggestion for a future work.

For Joyce himself, *Finnegans Wake* had prophetic significance. Finn MacCool, the Finnish-Norwegian-Irish hero of the tale, seemed to him to be coming alive again after the publication of the book, and, in a letter from France I received from him last spring, he said: "It is strange, however, that after publication of my book, Finland came into the foreground suddenly. First by the awarding of the Nobel Prize to a Finnish writer, and then by the political door. The most curious comment I have received on the book is a symbolical one from Helsinki, where, as foretold by the prophet, the Finn again wakes, and volunteer Buckleys are hurrying from all sides to shoot that Russian general." "Prophetic too were the last pages of my book," he added in this same letter. The last pages, that had cost him such profound anguish at the time of their writing. "I felt so completely exhausted," he told me when it was done, "as if all the blood had run out of my brain. I sat for a long while on a street bench, unable to move."

"And it's old and old it's sad and old it's sad and weary I go back to you, my cold father, my cold, mad father, my cold mad feary father, till the near sight of the mere size of him, the moyles and moyles of it, moananoaning, makes me seasilt saltsick and I rush, my only, into your arms."

There was no turning back after these lines, my friend. You knew it well. Adew!

Elucidation of James Joyce's Monomyth:
Explication of *Finnegans Wake*
(July 1948)

Finally, we have the long-awaited exegesis of *Finnegans Wake*, the last book by James Joyce. A perceptive and bold undertaking by two California professors, Joseph Campbell and Henry Morton Robinson, this elucidation of the "monomyth" (a word coined by Joyce himself) was published in the United States during the war, and it constitutes an almost indispensable reading guide. This master or "skeleton" key opens doors that unimaginative and hasty critics would have passed without notice. Light has been shed upon the labyrinth.

As the book was ready to print after sixteen years of work, the Hitlerite war was imminent and Joyce was rushing to complete his task. During the final months of 1938, he worked night and day with the assistance of some friends who corrected the proofs and took care of his remaining research in his numerous notebooks. These notebooks, containing preparatory remarks made over the course of sixteen years, were filled with sibylline signs underlined in different colors and symbolizing the main characters of the saga. One of the first copies of the book arrived in London on February 2, 1939—Joyce's birthday. In keeping with his customary ritual, this was an occasion for a party that reunited his French, American, English, and Irish friends who came not only to congratulate him on his birthday, but also, and above all, on the completion of his oeuvre. Although fatigued and already affected by the illness that would lead to his death two years later, Joyce appeared to be in high spirits. He spoke of his work with an ironic tenderness, recalling how he got the original idea during his stay in Nice in 1922 and later developed and expanded it during his long sojourn in Paris.*

It was in Paris, moreover, that the first fragments of the *Work in Progress* were published (the definitive title was revealed only with the complete edition). At first, excerpts from the book appeared in journals, such as *Le Navire d'argent, Contact,* and *This Quarter.* The work was then published in installments over a period of ten years in the journal *transition,* alongside explicatory essays, often written after a conversation with Joyce, by Samuel Beckett, Marcel Brion, Thomas McGravey, Frank Budgeon, William Carlos Williams, Victor Llona, Elliot Paul, Robert Sage, Robert McAlmon, Stuart Gilbert, the author of these lines, and an anonymous reviewer. Miss Sylvia Beach later collected these articles into a single volume, which Joyce furnished with a mocking and symbolic title: *Our Exagmination Round His Factification for Incamination of Work in Progress.* Meanwhile, *la grande critique* in English-speaking countries confined itself in general to a prudent silence broken only by virulent or simply disdainful attacks.

Three months after the war broke out, Joyce left Paris to join his friends in a village in the Allier. It was there that he was surprised, with his wife and son, by the exodus of June 1940, and forever separated from his daughter, who remained ill in the occupied zone. The arrival of his friend and long-time collaborator, Paul Léon, prompted him to take up *Finnegans Wake.* During the emotional summer months of the defeat, they reread the entire book together, correcting the misprints that had slipped into the first edition, adding a word here and there, and clarifying punctuation. Paul Léon, who returned to Paris in September 1940, would die during deportation in 1942. After many ordeals, Joyce and his family managed to gain entry to Switzerland in December 1940. Joyce died on January 13, 1941, after a difficult surgery, in the city of Zurich, where he had already spent the First World War.

No one who became close to Joyce while he was writing *Finnegans Wake* has any doubt that his death deprived us not only of any other works he might have written (although he had not started anything), but also innumerable pleasures that would be derived from reading his last work under his guidance. Campbell and Robinson, for instance, wishing to elucidate a

---

* In Paris, Joyce stayed at rue Jacob, avenue Charles Floquet, square Robiac, rue du Cardinal-Lemoine, rue Galilée, rue Edmond-Valentin, rue des Vignes, et à l'Hôtel Lutétia.

passage, explain that the inhabitants of Laurens County, Georgia, are called *gorgios*.* (They add in a footnote that "gorgio" is also a Gypsy word to designate a "non-Gypsy" and that, besides, it means a "teenager.") Doubtless the clarification is well-informed, but Joyce's intimates also know that his only son, George Joyce, was called in the family by his Italian name Gorgio, which brings affectionate paternal harmonies to the entire passage, devoted to young boys.

This is but a minor criticism and, in bringing it up, by no means do I intend to depreciate the value of a work so remarkably executed by the authors of the *Skeleton Key*. Their diligence is all the more commendable considering that they were unable to consult either Joyce or his intimates. It is also true, however, that the book cannot supplement the reading of *Finnegans Wake* in the same way as, for instance, Stuart Gilbert's book,[†] for instance, supplemented *Ulysses*, which was written in close collaboration with Joyce himself. For the same reason, any attempt to translate *Finnegans Wake* must seem doomed to a less than rough inaccuracy, mostly because of the linguistic deformations which pose the greatest, almost insoluble, problems to the translator, the intentions behind each word being usually multiple and the sources reaching into the author's most intimate experiences.[‡] We can nevertheless rejoice, thanks to the *Skeleton Key*, at seeing the gates open: with this topographic map in hand, we are no longer at risk of losing ourselves completely.

Finnegans Wake was published simultaneously in London and in New York at the beginning of 1939. The few critics who approached it seriously limited themselves to expressing their astonishment at, and more rarely their admiration of, the density and the complexity of the work, but they surrendered without a fight before its hermetic, if not daunting, aspect. Most of them quickly put it back on the shelf, among other inaccessible works, which, they claimed, were only able to spark the interest of specialized scholars and esoterics. A "literary curiosity," such was their verdict. The critics cowered behind circumspect phrases and perplexed reservations, in the realm of ignorance and ill will. The overtly malicious critics, moreover, did not refrain from evoking "psychopathology" or ascribing the work to

* *Skeleton Key*, 28.

† *James Joyce's Ulysses* (New York: Knopf, 1934).

‡ See *Memories of James Joyce* (Paris: Fontaine, 1943) by Philippe Soupault, who describes the manner in which the translation of a short passage of *Finnegans Wake* was accomplished under the direction of the author.

"a sick mind," or using even more pejorative expressions. Nevertheless, a few rare minds understood the capital importance of the book. A young Harvard professor named Harry Levin published a study in 1940 that was widely noted in literary and university milieus and devoted to the totality of Joyce's writing from the *Dubliners* to *Finnegans Wake.** That study was forwarded to Joyce, who declared it the best to date. Writing for the *New Republic,*[†] the renowned American critic and novelist Edmund Wilson devoted two articles to *Finnegans Wake:* "H. C. Earwicker and His Family" and "The Dream of H. C. Earwicker," both of which were later incorporated in his book *The Wound and the Bow.*[‡] Finally, in 1944, Campbell and Robinson published their *Skeleton Key,* which intends to outline the narrative structure of *Finnegans Wake* rather than "to elaborate fully any passage or group of images." After devoting several years to their study, a work resulted that will henceforth remain the starting point of any attempt at solving Joyce's tremendous riddle. For they have succeeded in retracing the mythological elements, the conflicts, the innovations in characterization, the collective and individual dramas, the multiform and multilingual characters that compose this disconcerting book. Campbell and Robinson have demonstrated that this story—this Joycean mythology—does not represent either "the perverse triumph of the unintelligible" or a mere "philological entertainment" as certain critics would have it, but that the saga contains a logic, a humor, and a profound analysis of modern civilization. For those who find Joyce's English too difficult, the two erudite guides translate the book into a clear language without, however, absolving us of a diligent reading of the text itself.

Finnegans Wake is a novel whose content and language are both equally inaccessible. It is a novel that marks the end of all novels, a roman à clef without precedence, a narrative circular in form. It is a novel of a single family and the whole of humanity—a global novel. The customary chronology of events is not respected here, time is abolished, and the characters move in nocturnal and dreamlike penumbrae. One searches in vain in the novel for temporal markers, since all the incidents are telescoped, superimposed, or metamorphosed. We encounter fairy tales, dreams, nightmares, poems, slogans, myths, folklores, monologues, dialogues, sermons, prehistoric evocations, popular songs, jokes, radio plays, blasphemies, scientific

* *James Joyce* [reissue, Penguin 1982].

† New York, 1940.

‡ Boston: Houghton, Mifflin, 1941.

theories, manifestoes, proverbs, and symphonies. The book is an enormous rebus that leads the reader astray at first, but whose pattern becomes apparent little by little as he makes his way.

Joyce employs here Giordano Bruno's ideas, creating a system of symbols bringing together mutually complementing antagonisms: man and woman, old age and youth, life and death, love and hate. Through their attractions and affinities, their conflicts and their repulsions, they supply the antinomial energies that animate the universe. Joyce uncovers these constants everywhere in history: in the individual, in the family, in the state, in the atom, in the universe. Everywhere he comes across the same dynamic.

The book re-creates the human and cosmological tension of birth, marriage, death, and resurrection. From a philosophical point of view, Joyce's allegory is grounded in the cyclical doctrine of Vico who, in his *Scienza nuova,* professes his belief in the eternal progression-regression of humanity. Vico proposes that humanity will pass through four phases, the first of which, corresponding to prehistory, constitutes the theocratic or religious age. That is the birth of the primitive humanity. The second age is heroic, the age of marriage and of love, and represents the aristocratic age. The third age is the humanistic and democratic age, which, in the end, leads to chaos, or "re-barbarization," and thus merges with the first. Although it is evident that Joyce has not strictly followed this schema—his themes telescope frequently—overall we can discern the "morphology of human destiny" underlying the entire work.

According to Campbell and Robinson, the final phase—ours—represents the nadir of man's fall. It ends with a thunderclap that terrifies but also, at the same time, reawakens man to the demands of the supernatural. The cycle thus reopens with a return to a primitive theocracy, for, according to Vico, in the beginning there was thunder and the thunder roused man's religious instinct. In *Finnegans Wake* the thunderclap plays an essential role as the prelude to Finnegan's fall. It is announced by a multilingual "sonorism":

Babababadalgharaghtakamminarronnkonnbronntonnerronntuonnthunn-
trovarrhounawnskawntoohoohoordenenthurnuk!

All of the world myths are synthesized in the magnum opus of this alchemist of the word. Besides the myth of Finn MacCool, which constitutes the main motif, we find the myth of Edda, the Egyptian myth of the dead, the myth of the city builders, the myth of the golden salmon,* the myth of Yggdrasil, the myth of the purgatory, the Hindu myth of the cosmic dreamer, the myth of the devils, the angels, the original fall, the Paschal resurrection, and many others.

The tale begins in the middle of a phrase:

> riverrun, past Eve and Adam's, from swerve of shore to bend of bay, brings us by a commodius vicus of ricurcultaion back to Howth Castle and Environs. . . .

and comes to an end on page 628 with the following phrase which flows into the first:

> a way a long a last a loved a long the . . .

The author ushers in the action by playing a guide who tells us the story of Finnegan's fall. This will also be a story of Lucifer's fall, of the fall of Adam and Eve, the decline of the sun which will rise anew, the fall of Rome, Humpty Dumpty's fall, the fall of Newton's apple, and the Wall Street *Krach*. At the same time, it concerns the everyday fall from grace of every human being. Each of these falls liberates the energy that makes the universe spin, just as water spins the wheel, and thus sets in motion the cycle of universal history: a spatial-temporal chain where one Dublin night is projected onto the night of ages as onto a stage background.

Campbell and Robinson claim that Joyce hints at the premises and the secret of his narrative at the very beginning of the first book, as he recounts the fall, wake, and resurrection:

> the great fall of the offwall entailed at such short notice the pfchute of Finnegan.

Joyce draws here upon an Irish-American song that tells how an old builder, Finnegan, drinks too much whiskey while working on the construction

---

* According to Clémence Ramnoux, who has recently published two remarkable essays on Celtic myths in the journal *Psyché* (June–October 1947), the golden salmon is identified with Finn himself. Although she is by no means familiar with the works of Joyce, Ramnoux draws conclusions in her study of the cycle of Finn that shed light on his works. Speaking of the order of time, she writes: "So we find juxtaposed and coexisting three species of being and three temporal orders: 1. the immortal gods of the underworld; 2. the heroes endowed with marvelous longevity, yet mortal, and 3. the ordinary men."

of a wall to erect a tall tower, gets drunk, and falls down the ladder. His friends collect the seemingly dead Finnegan and, having laid him in his coffin, gather round the corpse for a true Irish wake, which is marked more by gaiety than by mourning. Someone pronounces the word "whiskey," [whereupon] the dead man comes back to life and joins the dance. The song captures the moment:

> Och, he revives! See how he raises!
> And Timothy, jumping from the bed,
> Cried out, while he lathered round like blazes,
> Soul of the divil! Did ye think me dead?

And it ends with the refrain: "Lots of fun at Finnegans Wake. . . ."

Yet, outside of this general story line, what is *Finnegans Wake* about? In their summary of the novel, the commentators explain that it is composed of four books: Book I is the book of the parents; Book II is the book of the sons; Book III is the book of the people; and Book IV is the *recorso.* This classification seems somewhat arbitrary, because we must bear in mind that all of these themes intertwine and recur incessantly in *Finnegans Wake,* and all of the characters dissolve into one another in each of the four parts. Nevertheless, the authors successfully unveil the mystery of the characters in a quasi-didactic précis, which shows us Finnegan's fall and his palingenesis, and his metamorphosis into HCE (Here Comes Everybody), who then repeats the theme of the fall and the resurrection on another plane, and who further becomes the protagonist of the novel. The authors introduce us to HCE's wife, Anna Livia Plurabelle, their two sons Shem and Shaun, and their daughter Isabelle.

Avoiding a cursory interpretation, Campbell and Robinson give a thorough account of the novel's complex plot and interpret the whole in detail. We are invited to share their difficulty of reducing the extensive synthetic to an accessible analysis. Campbell and Robinson point out that Joyce is a master card player who does not often reveal his hand. Sometimes Joyce might describe the Neolithic night or surprise us with his own comments by mocking those whom he allows to speak or by reciting eruditely in gobbledygook. Conversations constantly change with a deliberately omitted syllable, a transformed name, a mutilated, invented, or hybrid word. Even the more or less realistic conversations are launched in the blink of an eye onto a totally different level. Thus all the action of the *Wake* takes place either in the clairvoyant mind of an alert observer, who appears to be a guide, a scholar, or a madman, or it occurs in an oneiromantic evocation. The ordinary novelistic chronology has been eliminated and we journey indiscriminately into the macrocosmos, or microcosmos, of the night.

The first book unravels the story of Finnegan and his successor HCE and sketches all the other characters who will come to play a role: Anna Livia Plurabelle, Shem and Shaun, and Iseult. In the manner of banter in Irish slang, Joyce follows point by point the Finnegan song. There are a dozen mourners gathered around the bier, and we witness a grandiose presentation of Dublin's prehistoric and topographic landscape. As the dead Finnegan blends into the landscape, we notice the first movements of the archetypes of existence: Mutt and Jute, coming from distant epochs, enter the stage, and we realize that Finnegan is in fact a great giant of prehistory. His head lies at Ben Howth, his clay feet come out near the Magazine Wall at Chapelizod where he fell off the ladder, and all his colossal body fuses with Dublin's geography.

We enter the little Wellington museum in Phoenix Park, where we hear a humorous account of the battle of Waterloo and of all the world battles. Suddenly someone utters the Gaelic word for whiskey, "Usqueadbaugham!" and Finnegan awakes and joins the dance. But the mourners try to calm him down by telling him that an important traveler, arriving from distant countries, has just disembarked at Dublin Bay. That's HCE, who sets foot on land with his wife, his two sons, and a daughter, and who is about to settle in Chapelizod, a small district of Dublin, where he opens a tavern on the shores of the river Liffey. Finnegan disappears once more.

HCE is Finnegan's double and descendant, and his fate will follow the latter's. If Finnegan represents a giant, a god-hero, the man of obelisks and cromlechs, the man-Titan of the Finn cycle, or *homo divinans,* HCE, the newcomer, symbolizes the patriarch of history, *homo sapiens,* the city builder. In the second chapter of the first book, Joyce traces the childhood of this man-king and explains his name. Gossips tell us of a sin HCE once committed in Phoenix Park, and a great scandal breaks out. It is Adam's original sin. HCE is apparently guilty of affronting the decency of two young girls. Although three soldiers witnessed the act, they can no longer clearly remember any details of the story that quickly spreads across the town.

HCE (Here Comes Everybody, or Humphrey Chimpden Earwicker, or Haveth Childers Everywhere) is a likeable creature. He is a stutterer and a hunchback, a victim of jeering fate. He is also a jovial migrator who has scattered families around the world, a city builder who has left behind whole civilizations in his wanderings across Asia Minor, the lands of Goths, Franks, the Nordic people, and through the British Isles. This back-story has its place in the novel. HCE is, in short, a man-universe and an inn-keeper. He is the hero of Culture, the king, the pioneer, the marauder, the vagabond, the voluptuary, the saint; he is a man who is beyond birth and death, a pauper and a man of great fortune. He represents all heroic types and constantly changes names throughout the book. He is called Crom-well, Finn MacCool, Noah, Napoleon, Nelson, Saint Patrick, Krishna, Jesus, Perse O'Reilly, Buddha, Papa Browning, Osirin, Tristan, Thor, and so on. The human races live under his inspiration, because it is through the reappearance of the hero following the disappearance of the Titan Finnegan that humanity gains strength and hope.

When HCE is arrested, we find ourselves in a criminal court where the jury is made up of a dozen drunk citizens. These twelve are also the twelve clients at HCE's tavern, in addition to being Finnegan's twelve friends, twelve Zodiac signs, and the twelve apostles. There are also four senile judges who remember ancient legends. Here, they symbolize the four winds, the four evangelists, and the four chroniclers of Irish history. The four judges reappear throughout the novel. HCE is accused by a police-man, at which point he clumsily defends himself—stuttering, speaking in puns, jokes, and spoonerisms. HCE's sin is a parody of the original sin which, according to St. Augustine, was committed in order to make redemption through Christ possible. "O foenix culprit!" Joyce exclaims and adds mockingly: "ex nickylow malo comes mickelmassed bonum." HCE pines from guilt, as do all of Adam's descendants. He feels shame, even though he is content with his sin. The theme of guilt recurs constantly in the book in such cases as the relationship between the young girl and the old man (Marc and Iseult, Swift and Vanessa, etc.), and even in HCE's incestuous passion for his daughter Isabelle, who is identified with Iseult.

Joyce gives us to understand that all these events took place long ago and that their participants no longer inhabit the earth. A number of dubious or outlandish characters try to explain HCE's guilt, as he languishes in his prison cell. HCE's fall constitutes his apparent death, and an underwater grave meanwhile has been dug for him at the bottom of Lake Neagh, which he is forced to enter. Wars break out everywhere, and a rumor spreads that HCE has escaped. A certain housemaid, the widow Kate, intervenes and makes an allusion to a deeply mysterious letter that is supposed to reveal the whole truth about the missing aged HCE.

That letter was HCE's "mamafesta" and was written by his wife, Anna Livia Plurabelle, who tries to apostrophize her husband. The document opens with a prayer to ALP as to the World Mother, holder of all the virtues of Maya, of the Virgin Mary, the Great Mother, and the waters of the river Liffey combined, as well as of the qualities of the little chick, Belinda, who, while scraping the ground, found the letter. The letter is recovered by Shem, but it is his brother Shaun who claims the credit of its discovery. A professor analyzes the letter in a pedantic manner and finds pre-Christian, post-barbaric, and Celtic influences. The account principally focuses on the conflict between the two brothers.

We then follow the extremely complex development of two opposing principles. HCE and ALP represent the male-female antinomy that lies at the basis of all life. Shem and Shaun, who also constantly change names (to Jerry and Kevin, Mutt and Jute, etc.), represent an exclusively masculine antinomy which is at the basis of all historical events. The character traits that are strangely united in their father are isolated and separated in the sons. Joyce gives us a portrait of Shem in the seventh chapter of the first book and a portrait of Shaun in the first two chapters of the second book.

Shem, or Jerry, is an introvert. He is a writer, a calligrapher, and an explorer. Respectable persons spontaneously discard the books he writes because they threatened to dissolve the protective boundaries between good and evil. He has access to secret sources and possesses arcane powers. No one wishes to listen to him and he is denounced by the top public officials. He is an asocial man, a disinherited bohemian, an outlaw. But he is also a seer and a poet. This could also be an autobiographical portrait of the author himself.

Shaun, on the other hand, is an extrovert par excellence. He is a shepherd of the people, a public orator, he is prudent and sanctimonious, the people's favorite, the one who succeeded in life; he is the planet's policeman, the conqueror of the rebels. He does not concern himself with spiritual or esthetic matters; the life of flesh and the senses is enough for him. He hates Shem, his brother. Under the name of "Shaun the postman," he delivers humanity the grand message that was discovered by Shem, while taking for himself the reward reserved for bearers of good news.

Joyce gives us the portrait of Shem and Shaun in four hypothetical transformations and, in the end, we learn that the little mother Anna Livia Plurabelle (giddgaddy, grannyma, gossipaceous Anna Livia) is going to bless both of them. The first book thus ends with one of the most charming passages of the saga, which contains the theme of the mother. Two of her representatives, under the form of two washerwomen, chat about HCE and ALP, about their children and their neighbors, each on either bank of the river Liffey. It is evening. One of the washerwomen is old; the other is young, like the young temptresses of Phoenix Park. Finally, both washerwomen, one identified with a tree trunk, the other with a rock, retransform themselves as the night is falling into their primitive elements.

> Can't hear with bawk of bats, all thim liffeying waters of. Ho. Talk save us! My foos won't moos. I feel as old as yonder elm. A tale told of Shaun or Shem? All Livia's daughtersons. Dark hawks hear us. Night! My ho head halls. I feel as heavy as yonder stone. Tell me of John or Shaun? Who were Shem and Shaun the living sons and daughters of? Night now! Tell me, tell me, tell me, elm! Night night! Telmetale of stem or stone. Besides the rivering waters of. Hitherandtithering waters of. Night!*

ALP turns out to be the symbol of the "matriarch," of the river, of the Heraclitean flux, of Vico's eternal return.

The first book comes here to a close. It belongs to the depths where history turns into a legend. This legend has the aura of a myth that introduces us to the mysteries of what the authors of the *Skeleton Key* call the "Form of Forms."

The second book, which is divided into four chapters, belongs to the present. Its figures display a plasticity and a solidity that differentiate them from the strange metamorphic fluidities of the first book.

As the book opens, we witness a children's game played on the road that runs by the tavern. The game portrays the recurrence of the ages: children tread Vico's Road (there exists an actual "Vico Road" in the Dublin suburb of Chapelizod), and scuffle in a game called "angels and devils." This is a little dramatic skit performed in the Phoenix Theatre, and the participants include Glugg (Shem), Chuff (Shaun), and Izod (Isabelle), while Hump (HCE) and Ann (ALP) watch them from the house. The game begins with Glugg, who three times risks exploits destined to failure. First, it is a charade, then the composition of a love letter, and finally an act meant to put his spirit in touch with the "house of breathings." Each of his failures gives

---

* *Finnegans Wake* (New York: Viking, 1945), 215–16.

the occasion for a triumphal dance on the part of the little girls (Isabelle's twenty-eight pretty girlfriends), and Shem gets angry. At first he repeats his three vows of silence, exile, and cunning from the *Portrait of an Artist.* Then he repents. Eventually he confesses, recounting scrupulously the sins of his father and his mother and, in the end, lets himself be carried away by lascivious thoughts. His rival brother then throws himself at him and they fight until the father's voice calls them back to the house. This chapter, whose progression is marked with frantic youth and gaiety, contains numerous references to Joyce's own life and to his revolt against Dublin, and to the entire folklore background of his childhood.

In the second chapter, the children have retired to their rooms, where they are doing their homework. We are confronted with one of the most inscrutable chapters of the book. Joyce intensifies the moment through an image that encompasses all schoolchildren of the world and magnifies their little tasks in representations of grand tasks of all professors throughout history. We recognize many references to the trivium and quadrivium, as well as to the esoteric doctrines of the Kabbala. In the margins of this description, Joyce adds little notes: those on the left (Shem) express ridiculous and farcical opinions, while those on the right (Shaun) are more solemn.

The chapter opens with a description of the students' perplexity and of the problems they face. First, there is an allegorical review of the processes of creation. Twenty-six pages are used to describe the descent of the spirit in time and space. The creative will incites the father to engender the universe. The world becomes possible and acquires form. Man appears with his primitive passions and taboos and is then placed in HCE's tavern. The whole human comedy is played out in the children's room. The boys work while their sister looks at the letters. The good child Kev (Shem) has difficulties solving his geometry problems. The bad boy Dolph (Shaun) simultaneously helps him and scoffs at him. Kev slaps him but they then reconcile. It is time to go to bed.

The third chapter's opening is constituted by an introduction of the people who are present in the tavern, followed by a summary of their respective themes. The chatter does not cease, for everyone is drunk. The radio emits nasal sounds, and HCE leans on his elbow at the bar. Everyone listens to the radio broadcasts, which are all based on the old story of HCE's sin. There is a general brouhaha. Nine stories intersect: (1) a story of a scuffle; (2) a story of a Norwegian captain who is investigating the case of a tailor in the town; (3) a radio play containing a dialogue of two brothers, Butt and Taff; (4) Butt tells another story about (5) an Irish soldier who killed a Russian general during the battle of Sevastopol; (6) stock market bulletins; (7) televised news; (8) a story of atomic experiments; and (9) a radio report about a hero's dismemberment. In the end, Finnegan himself tells a story made up of all these parts.

Once the tavern is closed, HCE the innkeeper begins to empty all the glasses and ends up collapsing stone drunk on the floor. In his inebriation, he has a vision in which he sees King Marc betrayed by Tristan, who flees with Iseult. Flying round the honeymoon ship is a circle of four seagulls, representing the four old men.

In the course of the night, the drunk rises. This is the beginning of the third book, and HCE has now changed into his sons. He climbs the staircase and sleeps next to his wife ALP. His dream of the future starts to unfold, a dream in which the conflicts between Shem and Shaun become exacerbated. Shaun the pragmatist departs, later to be found on the top of a hill at the heart of Ireland. The four old men arrive with their donkey and open an investigation, but Shaun disappears. It becomes evident that Shaun is the colossal representative of all the HCEs. The investigation continues, and we hear the cries and protests from Ireland and from India, the garbled reports of witnesses. The episode ends with the scene of Finnegan's fall.

Now the four old men are sitting around the conjugal bed. The day breaks. The oneiric imagery takes the form of the furniture in HCE and ALP's room. Everyone sleeps. Suddenly a cry is heard; it is one of the children (Jerry or Shem) who has just had a nightmare. The mother goes to console him and then comes back to her bed. The shadows on the window mimic the copulation of HCE and ALP. The shadows disappear, the spouses go back to sleep.

In the fourth book, the *recorso*, seraphic voices announce the break of day. The two sleepers see the light. The world awaits the great hero of the dawn. The form of the innocent Saint Kevin rises, recalling the idyllic moment of the Christian dawn in fifth-century Ireland. The ambiguities of the night will soon be resolved. The arrival of Saint Patrick marks yesterday's triumph over the mythological dream and its conquest of druidism. Everything proceeds toward illumination. The morning newspaper arrives, and the letter ("mamafesta") that Anna Livia Plurabelle receives contains all the news of the past night.

In the course of her morning sleep, the wife felt her husband turn away from her. They have both been abused by time. Their hopes now rest with their children. HCE has become Humpty Dumpty's shattered carcass, and ALP identifies herself with the river at the point where it hurls itself into the sea. Her nostalgia, which drives her toward the liberation of constraining shores and toward a reunion with her father the Ocean, concludes with a magnificent monologue. As her eyes open, Anna Livia Plurabelle, Anna Liffey, the beautiful river Liffey, returns to the grand Triton, to the Father. The dream dissolves and the cycle is ready to start again.

In order to depict this world of nocturnal mists, Joyce employs a language all his own, a language often entirely invented. It is the language of night. Even though the Irish-American-English language is incredibly rich, there was no language able to express the processes of the unconscious life. There was no means of representing directly the turbulent existence of dreams, of half-dreams, of the hypnogogic life, of waking dreams, and so on. The vocabulary was lacking.

Fortunately, Joyce was not only a remarkable mathematician, but also a talented linguistic. At the Jesuit College in Dublin, he had learned Latin and Greek. Due to his admiration for Ibsen, he studied Norwegian. He spoke Italian, French, and German fluently; he acquired a knowledge of Russian and Sanskrit. Curiously, though, he was never interested in Spanish and was totally indifferent to Gaelic.

In *Finnegans Wake,* Joyce continues to utilize a process that he had already started to employ in *Ulysses:* he deliberately deforms words and creates amazing neologisms. He plays with onomatopoeia. He uses a "sonorist" vocabulary, but one which always has a precise and mythical signification. All his words form multiple associations. He enjoys the pun, which, under his pen, turns into poetry and phantasm. He borrows sounds from all the world languages and transforms them into new ones. He unearths obsolete English-Irish words and uses them in new ways, giving them a different meaning.

James Joyce has kneaded the human tongues so completely that his followers will be but epigones. He rendered the creator's task difficult, and his successors will suffer the consequences. He transcribed the infantile, prehistoric, psychological, and traditional languages; he took up slang, the language of dreams, daydreams, intoxication, liturgy and rites, ecstasy, corruption, debauchery, and love and hate. He realizes the words of Blake: "the voice of excess leads to the palace of wisdom."

In his vast philological treasury, Joyce places particular emphasis on his revolutionary concept of etymology. He invents his own semantics. He intermingles modern languages, dead languages, ancient and secret languages, which he channels into a linguistic crucible. He goes so far as to use the Inuit grammar. But he never forgets the purely psychological element of language, and all those who have heard him read the chapter of the washerwomen notice the phonetic quality of his writings.* Joyce was up to date on the theories of Rev. Jousse and Sir Richard Paget, both of whom studied sign language. He picked up fragments of conversations, pieces of words overheard in the street or in cafés, and he incorporated them into his text. How many times would his friends run across their own words spoken in a conversation and appropriated verbatim, or deformed, by the work. Joyce had an acute sense of the ambiguity of language, and the theme of the Tower of Babel often recurs in *Finnegans Wake.*

To offer a classic example of Joyce's manifold mythological and philological symbolism, let us cite a phrase found at the very beginning of the book:

> . . . a waalworth of a skyerscape of most eyeful hoyth entowerly, erigenating from next to nothing and celescalating the himals and all, hierarchitectiptoloftical, with a burning bush abob off its baubletop and with larrens o'toolers clittering up and tumbles a'buckets clottering down.

We have here a mythological description of the fall, a revivification of many myths: the ladder joining heaven and earth, a powerful mythic image; Jacob's ladder in the Bible; the kabbalistic ladder or the tree of emanations; Yggdrasil; the Tower of Babel. Allusions abound. He telescopes the words "hierarchy," "architect," "tipsy," and "toplofty" so that they climb up and down like a skyscraper. *Eyeful hoyth* is "most awful height." The word "tower" is in the pun *entowerly. Erigenating* is made of *ériger,* "to erect," and "origin." *Himals* evokes the German word for "sky," and the Himalayas. *Baubletop* brings to mind Babel. *Larrens o'toolers* and *tombles a'buckets* are Lawrence O'Toole and Thomas Becket, the bishops of Dublin and Canterbury in the time of Henry II. O'Toole represents the conflict between Shem and Shaun, because he is a man of profession, and Becket was assassinated. *Clittering up* and *clottering down:* here the word *clitter* suggests the German *klettern,* which means "to climb," and *clotter* comes close to the English "clatter," which indicates noisy movements.

* Recorded in 1931.

To quote Campbell and Robinson:

Finnegans Wake is above all an essay in permanence. From its perspective, the hopeful or fearful may learn to behold with a vast sympathy the prodigious upsurging and dissolution of forms, the continual transvaluation of values, the inevitable ambiguities, which are the stuff of life and history. Through the notes that finally become tuneable to our ears, we hear James Joyce uttering his resilient, all-enjoying, all-animating "Yes,"* the Yes of things to come, a Yes from beyond every zone of disillusionment, such as few have had the heart to pronounce.

Finnegans Wake is at the same time the requiem for a civilization and the announcement of a new era. James Joyce, with poetic prophecy, announces the atomic age in the repetition of the Viconian motif of thunder. The terrible roar of the bomb of Hiroshima was foreheard by Joyce, who nevertheless did not despair of man.

* According to Joyce, his family was of French descent, and was called "Joyeux" [Joyous]—an idea that was dear to him.

Part Seven : **Literature, Culture, and Politics**

Introduction

The word "ruin" is an apt term to describe Germany's total devastation as a result of the Second World War. A ruin, however, is also a potent symbol, which, for the Romantics, held out the promise of renewal and redemption. Jolas's essay on the state of postwar German literature as "German Letters in Ruins" thus would seem to have a dual meaning perhaps applicable to most of his end-of-the-war and post-World War II reflections concerning the state of Europe. In fact, for a view of regeneration his thoughts turn wider than ever before: the Americas have become a new haven for thousands of refugees from the old, war-ravaged continent, reinforcing Jolas's utopian idea of a "Super-Occidental," or "Atlantic language" in tune with Walt Whitman's singing of a great democracy. Mexico and Central and South America too are in fermentation, producing a vast literary culture, with a plentitude of new names in cultural criticism, poetry, and the novel of "magic realism" (a term that Jolas had already applied to the "paramyths" of the interwar European avant-garde). The revival here owes much to Europe, of course, but increasingly more to the Americas' indigenous peoples, cultures, and languages, since it blends an "*Indianista* consciousness" into a new interethnic *unidad Americana* as "the antithesis of Hitler's grotesquely stupid racism."

Jolas's essays thus continue to follow a widening pattern of a "revolution of the word," which he increasingly understands to have political impact, yet its formulations are so abstract (super-, meta-, pan-) that it remains, after all, an aesthetic education of man, however radicalized. The author had himself experienced the concrete brutality of Nazism in Berlin,

Saarbrücken, Forbach, and Paris (see *Man from Babel,* chap. 8). However, his continued valorization of the aesthetic experience remains a conscious, quite traditional choice previously made versus the Communist politics of Surrealism. By contrast, others, like *transition*'s "advisory editor" Carl Einstein, participating with gun in hand but also as a journalist in the Spanish Civil War, had decided that the perverse myths of Nazism could not be countered effectively with "white" myths. For Jolas, however, borrowing and somewhat straining a term from his eclectic encounter with the gnosticism of the anti-Fascist Parisian Collège de sociologie in the late 1930s, myth remains the only path for reconnecting with what is existentially at stake: "the sacred."

Indeed, in this transitional phase from war to peace, the essayist perceives the sentiment of a broad global revival: a "Goodbye to Yesterday." A movement toward a "metaphysical renascence" is also at critical stake in his 1940–41 reviews of contemporary publications on Anglo-American poetry from T. S. Eliot to W. H. Auden, and editions of the poetry of Edna St. Vincent Millay to Stephen Vincent Bénet. After the war, the author asks whether Germany will understand its cultural devastation under the Third Reich as so much debris or, like elsewhere, as the possibility of a new beginning. However, his return to a culture he once left as a young man, from Forbach for New York before the outbreak of the First World War, on the surface leads to little more than the lament that "a compulsive synthesis [in German letters] is still lacking, and will be lacking, in my opinion, until the German writers recognize a priori their country's full responsibility for the totalitarian horrors." Jolas's scepticism regarding Germany's ability to come to terms with its past was informed by his own conviction about what was needed to restore the German spirit. Germany's intellectual elite needed to acknowledge its guilt and responsibility in overcoming a "revolting pathological self-pity," become involved in the democratization of cultural life, and, last but not least, there needed to be a thorough denazification of the German language. Jolas himself was to act on these insights in unison with some of the best minds in postwar Germany.

—K.H.K.

Super-Occident (February 1929)

The year 1929 has begun with a general disorder all along the line. Confusion reigns in the various camps on this and the other side of the Atlantic, negative and positive modalities are chaotically superimposed on each other, everywhere we look there is a bankruptcy of the spirit. Collective materialism seems triumphant, the notion of man in relation to the totality of the real is thoroughly vague, literary exhibitionism and senile estheticism lingering in ideals of the past, are the order of the day.

The gratuitous act of the creator having become apparently abhorrent to him, Mr. T. S. Eliot constrains his reformatory forces into the straitjacket of political and religious dogma. Although I retain a profound admiration for the great poet that he was, and although I try to have tolerance for another man's viewpoint, I cannot help feeling that Mr. Eliot has committed intellectual treason. His conversion may be sincere (though his royalism is suspicious)—and I cannot sneer at mystic or transcendental hunger—but, for a creative mind, complete absorption in a party or religious institution is paralysis. In France we have seen Surrealism fighting desperately for the purity of the spirit. In Germany the Bauhaus group takes up the cudgels for the conscious and utilitarian mass man, while the "New Objectivity" has ended in a ridiculous philistinism. The proletarian ideology makes Russian mass-life and expression the paramount ideal, and every functional element is rationalistic. In America we observe a groping tendency toward a new life-sense, but also the triumph of superficiality, the abdication of the better spirits in the face of an overwhelming leveling process, the lone struggle of a revolutionary minority for survival.

In the present crisis we will have to go back once more to the problem of the spirit in relation to the external world. What attitude is the
individual to take, as he contemplates the increasing sociological central-
ization around him, while noting at the same time a decadence of internal values? He is dimly aware that some radical change will have to take
place in himself, if he wishes to retain his stability in the onward march
of a century that is deterministic and anti-individual. He has observed the
fixation of Marxism, the progress of collectivities, the eternal disillusion
of the solitary minds avid for freedom. He has before him a capitalistic,
money-drunken civilization bent on reducing man to the rank of an "economic animal"—with feudal tyranny continuing, under the guise of pater-
nalism, the oppression of the worker—and a nascent communistic culture
which is aping the former's economic vision, while attempting to retain a
revolutionary mobility for the working out of a new civilization. Between
these two he sees a more or less transitory democracy desperately struggling
to hold on to a frail kind of reality, a desiccated humanitarianism, and Fascism envisaging a Nietzschean utopia.

Seeking the central, the all-human point in the play of those contra-
puntal elements—spirit and nature, mechanical life and instinctive life—
seems still the aim of every philosophic speculation today. The essential
problem is man. We are waiting for a new type of man—not a collective
being, but a universal being, a harmonious being, synthesizing in himself
the impulsions of the spirit and the social sense of the twentieth century.
The industrial civilization has made the clash between the rational and irrational a grave one. But the technological age and its dynamic forces contain elements that make possible a union of both categories. Mutual adaptation, according to Max Scheler, is the process by which the variegated
elements will bring about the *All-Mensch,* the universal man, the complete man. The modern man has at his disposal new instruments which
he may use as a lever for the accelerating of his vision. He has no desire to
compete with the machine; he wants to create a plastic feeling of life. His
senses might become more acute, his reflexes might change, but the eternal
human springs will forever remain immutable. In him the individual and
the universal are being merged—the conscious and the subconscious. He
has an urge for totality of being and becoming.

But before this development is possible, a continuous subversive action
will have to take place. Sympathy for any creative action that tends to
destroy the present system should be encouraged. It is up to the intellectual proletariat to engage itself in the struggle for the destruction of a social

entity which is based on hypocrisy, injustice, and a-humanity. For the present, rule holds its power by virtue of the economic intimidation of labor and the supremacy of fraudulent ideologies for the masses. Combating the sociological and esthetic defenders of this anachronistic regime must be the fundamental aim.

But the deification which European-American idealism brings to mechanics as a mystic thing per se does not lead us anywhere. Here we have, I believe, a time phenomenon that is rapidly developing into a craze, a hysteria, a fashion for the new philistine, the "nepman" of the machine. I have followed with considerable interest the ideations of those who have suddenly, Columbus-like, discovered the mechanical continent. They are dazzled by the delusion of American prosperity, speed, mass action. The magical spell of American dynamics and violence cannot be denied. But underneath this there is a metaphysical sordidness which repels. While concentration of wealth is getting more and more absolute, self-satisfaction, megalomania, cynicism run riot. Mad with a mercantile-utilitarian vision, the power of the bankers has centralized everything so that all variations from their arbitrarily established norm are considered pathological cases. A wave of intolerance will sweep the country under the guise of democratic liberalism. The ruthless suppression of all protesting voices will be the result. Bad taste engendered by sentimentalism will be rampant. But underneath all this show, there is still the volcano of the barbarians.

The arts of tomorrow must find their expression in the double reality of the natural and the supernatural. The universal man must find a mythos which is adequate to his changed outlook. Art must find an equilibrium between the eternal or immutable and the conscious. It must express the new age.

Pure individualism, as a counteraction in the social crisis, is no longer possible. Anarchism was one phase of our development, but we know now that it belongs to another age. The genius, the rebel, the iconoclast, however, must continue his revolt. He is forever the autonomist of the spirit, the defender of the regional. He alone can bring the "I" into relation with the cosmos. He alone realizes that, while the masses march along the highroads with their step of steel, the old human hatreds persist under the hypocrisy of brotherly love. He alone can oppose the danger of overestimating the mechanical. He will defend the right to revolt, the right to think in eternal terms, to help bring about the upheaval that may scatter the threatened coagulation of mediocre values around him.

Much has been done in painting. The "motif" has been replaced by the camera, and perspective has been eliminated in favor of pure composition. The evolution from Impressionism to Cubism, Neo-Plasticism, Suprematism, Surrealism, and so on is an evolution toward geometric purity and the crystal harmony of planes and color through a supra-earthly imagination. With the development of technology, the possibilities of enlarging the magical have become automatically emphasized. The new use of the camera, with its light and dark contrasts, has made it possible to create expressions of the enigmatic and marvelous beyond all our expectations.

Music, too, is liberating itself from historicism. The search for new instruments, a minimizing of the use of the old melodic instruments, such as the voice and the violin, a search for new percussions and new intervals that will require a reeducation of the human ear, and for a new scale, the development of rhythms that are both violent and unfamiliar, and a complete departure from the conception of music as a drug, a balm, a soothing-syrup, or as a literary-programmatic composition, an attempt to give it its place as one of the vital forces of modern life corresponding to the forces of our time—this is the direction music is now taking.

In architecture, certain men (Le Corbusier, Bouroff, Gropius, Mallet-Stevens, etc.) have also envisaged a purer form of building. America and Russia work out huge creations in concrete. Constructivism, demonstrating the epoch of the machine to its most logical conclusion, by the use of concrete and steel, and their application to new problems for the construction of mills, offices, and so on, emphasizes the changed viewpoint.

While these arts are going ahead, literature is still rooted in the ideas of the past. The reality of the *universal word* is still being neglected. Never has a revolution been more imperative. We need the twentieth-century word. We need the word of movement, the word expressive of the great forces around us. Huge, unheard-of combinations must be attempted in line with the general tendency of the age. We need the technological word, the word of sleep, the word of the half-sleep, the word of chemistry, biology, the automatic word of the dream,. and so on. With this must go the attempt to weaken the rigidity of the old syntactic arrangements. The new vocabulary and the new syntax must help destroy the ideology of a rotting civilization.

Literature must give us the composite picture of the eternal human currents in relation to the twentieth century. We are creatures and creators of our epoch. Seeing before us the unfolding of a new sense of life, we no longer feel despair. Immense possibilities are contained in life. The things of the absolute are within our grasp. Do we feel that most of the writers who today, in America, fill the magazines and newspapers with their esthetic drivel, their imbecile apologies for their financial-literary cartels, their frail lyricism, are visualizing the new spirit? They describe the little psychological situations and portray the contours of middle-class scenes. They express with "common" words the experiences of the fat and mediocre. They are the servants of the bankers, the materialistic exploiters of thought. They think of indigenous literature in terms of patriotic, megalomaniacal ballyhoo. They reflect the cynical sophistication of the shallow-pated leisure class which this era is developing, and cater to the bad taste of the snobs. They have substituted for a loving interest in their soil a pretentious interest in Mr. Mencken's Americana. They are always respectable. With the exception of a pitiful minority, they try to fill the lives of the newly rich with pseudo-sensations. The essence of life has become stale to them.

There is a tendency among certain groups in Europe to oppose poetry entirely as a possible creative expression. To them prose alone is important—especially the feuilleton, the bald, journalistically direct narrative. The poetic vision, however, remains as an organic force, whether it is expressed in prose or poetry. The American poet has a suprematic world to bear out of his chaos. He is called upon to defend the pure spirit. Under the whip of the engineer's creation, under the impulse of the bill-poster, he can find autonomous laws for his universe. In his composition, being and appearance must merge. It is up to him to recapture for us a new *Wunderglauben,* an orphic vision and faith!

We love in America that which it was and that which it might become. North, Central, and South America, like Russia, contain in themselves the germs of an immense creative force. The Anglo-Saxon's supremacy is being wrested from him by the future intercontinental man who may well become the universal man. I should like to imagine a super-America which might be the idealistic intensification and sublimation of the Occident. But a long struggle must face us before a super-Occident can be realized. We must continue to oppose the present plutocratic materialism, fight for a new orientation of life based on the need for a universal humanity and on the idea of the American mythos in relation to the dynamic century, defend at all costs man's inalienable right to dream and rebel and create for himself the possibilities of the organic cosmos. We must strive for the duality of the infinite and the material, the primitive and the mechanical, the hallucinatory and the concrete. The art of the future must be conceived as a universal art, with regional autonomy. We want the most complete decentralization in life and expression, while at the same time working for the new humanity, which will, as always, be biologically monistic, but evolutionary in manifestations, totalistic and autochthonous.

Goodbye to Yesterday (October 1940)

The Poet abhors regimentation. He is a born anarch. His is the visionary élan, and he seeks forever absolute values. Can he be an activist? I am sorry to have to say *no* to Archibald MacLeish, whose recently published essay "The Irresponsibles" challenges all those who believe in the autonomy of poetry. His pamphlet is a new and, we might say, an American version, of Julien Benda's *Treason of the Clerks,* published in 1928. Mr. MacLeish adds little to that interpretation. To be sure, as a human being the poet reacts to the barbarism of his surroundings with all the force of the liberty-loving individual. But as a creator, he simply records a kind of paroxystic emotion before the social convulsions he witnesses. He certainly sympathizes with the cry for freedom and the universal hatred against Nazi despotism. Yet Mr. MacLeish would be more convincing if he were less the political partisan (which he undoubtedly is) than merely the Humanist creator. There is a great *political* poem by Heinrich Heine which, as far as I am aware, none of the political poets of today have ever duplicated in violence and lyric force. But he lives as a poet of love. I cannot say that Edna St. Vincent Millay's poem "There Are No Islands Any More" approximates in the slightest degree to poetry. We may dismiss it as the expression of a poet whose conviction and sincerity are obvious, but whose creative spirit has burned out. Nor is Stephen Vincent Benét's far superior poem of protest, "Nightmare at Noon," more than a versified editorial which leaves you cold. These ubiquitous tracts about the poet's role in the present, quite unsatisfactory, civilization, and especially Mr. MacLeish's public speeches, begin to annoy me. It is a complete misunderstanding of the essence of poetry.

Fortunately there are other tendencies. I am interested in seeing some American poets engaged in an attempt to write lyric rhythms in which the conquest of the law of gravitation is a basic direction. Muriel Rukeyser, Selden Rodman, Kay Boyle seek a solution in the modern myth of aeronautics, in the myth of Icarus. Others, like Raymond E. F. Larsson, Elder Olson, Richard Eberhart, the present writer, seek it in the metaphysical transmutation of values. They feel, with Franz Werfel, "that the revolutionary movements in literature of the last decades are nothing but passionate attempts to safeguard the nihilistic state of the time-spirit from the metaphysical peril." Flight is the theme. Not ivory tower escape. But existential flying. Flight into space and time. Flight toward astronomic marvels. Flight into the night and dream. Flight into the cosmos. Flight to a transcendental reality. Flight to God.

Poetry is truly becoming cosmic. A voice long neglected in American poetry—at least since the New England Transcendentalists—is being heard again. It is the voice of mystic aspiration, of the nostalgia for ascension. It is an attempt to conquer the fear of existing which the present mechanistic civilization of totalitarianism has accentuated for some years. It is an attempt to declare the primacy of the logos. Jean-Pierre Jouve, De Miloscz, T. S. Eliot, Rainer Maria Rilke foreshadowed it. So did James Joyce. So did Pablo Picasso and André Masson. They were not afraid to face the great paralysis before the catastrophe. They were not unwilling to represent violence and death. They suffered with humanity in its social and religious *convulsions*. Certain American poets are willing to draw the consequences from this ideological dissociation. They are engaged on a pilgrimage to the holy grail. They want to emancipate man from his organic anguish by insisting that he look at the stars again.

This is a *verticalist* tendency. The outlines are still somewhat nebulous, but we can already see certain contours emerging from the mist of words and sounds. There is a new aspiration toward a communal feeling, a Romantic reconstruction, a revolt against individualism. Poetry seeks a return to myth and ritual. It seeks to capture a sense of ecstasy and stupor before the cosmic forces. It seeks to reinstate the sacred, and it combats the utilitarian and mechanistic tyranny of the machine by sublimating the technological, by giving it spiritual dimensions. It is in revolt against the pseudo-religious myths of the dictators. The ritualistic renaissance which could be observed here and there on the European continent for the past few decades is beginning to take place in America also. In Europe men with delicate antennae broke new ground. They pushed back the frontiers of consciousness and language, and I regret to say that ignorant littérateurs, with three-dimensional minds, still sneer at the innovators. A group of young men in Paris, dissatisfied with the Surrealist cul de sac, *Marxist* Naturalism, and the frenetic preoccupation with the political theme, banded themselves together and, in great obscurity, constructed a laboratory for ritualistic symbolism, basing themselves on the sociological philosophy of Durkheim. Traditional religion, especially the Catholic Church, revived the interest in liturgy and ceremony with extraordinary results. Even before the war, this rebirth in cloistral and metaphysical activity could be noted. All of them tried to combat exaggerated individualism, to search for a new collective spirit, to reestablish the sacred symbols and sigils in the shifting quotidian reality. Mythologies were reconstructed. Icarus, Dionysos, Ulysses, and so on. The poets knew that men are only uplifted by a mystique that can be entertained by feasts and rites. For doctrines always remain dead, if they cannot affect the sensibilities. They recognized the impotence of intellectual concepts and knew that nationalistic rituals lead to explosions and death. They felt that a remedy was needed for the autointoxication of the I. They wanted to get away from the impressionistic caprices and the anarchy of the senses. They wanted to be fugitives to the *absolute*.

Liturgy and ritual were the antidote and the remedy. A sacramental sense of life took hold of poetry again. It wanted to return to the unity of a supernatural order and become integrated in the planetary system. A four-dimensional consciousness was developing. In the hour of mechanistic philosophy, of blood and steel, poetry sought a nexus with the super-rational forces. The epoch began to break with the positivism that had enchained the individual and strove for the collective—not collective nationalism, but collective spiritualism. Utilitarian criteria were overthrown. The object of poetry was to praise and sing, was to play and dance, like David before the arch. All of man, total man, corporeal and spiritual, was involved in this monistic aspiration. The liturgical was conceived as a social and living link in the urban existences.

Language itself needed a metaphysical dimension. "Language is Delphi," said Novalis, the Romantic poet. The language of poetry had to become sacred again. There was no room any longer for the journalistic Naturalism that had dominated creative expression during the impressionistic and naturalistic epoch. This linguistic Naturalism had brought into rhythmic expression the dynamic contemporaneousness, the common speech vaunted by that infantile movement called *Imagism,* and had debased the mystic element of the word. Its mediumistic force was abolished. The time-spirit demanded a language of three dimensions, the everyday ambient, the universe without magic. Activism persecuted the sacred sigil. But language had to become logos again. It had to have a pentecostal, hymnic feeling and liturgical consecration. It had to recapture the cosmic and transcendental once more.

Raymond E. F. Larsson is one of the poets whose awareness of this state of things can be noted in all his work. His new book *Weep and Prepare: Selected Poems, 1926–1939,* is a spiritual migration. Already in his earliest poems like "The Inward Turning Eye," we observe the turning away from the sensual objects.

> Heavy the lid
> of sky
> the heavy-lidded eye
> of sky turns inward—
> inward
> the inner eye
> inward on the vast
> grey vapors
> of a decomposing past

Henceforth his pilgrimage becomes more and more mystic and profoundly Catholic. Against the fetid spirit of the urban collectivities he places his vision of the Augustinian *civitas Dei.* In "O Cities, Cities" we have a strange nostalgia for a medieval Gothicism, a wandering in the dark night of the soul toward the celestial dream."

> O cities, cities—
> full-lipped
> full-throated singing
> singing cities all embogued
> of light like an increasing choral
> column
> and column

```
                    cornice
      and arcade
                    columns ascending all around
      like bursts of silver
      trumpet sound
```

More and more liturgical become the stanzas. Prayers and hymns and odes and psalms are the forms he chooses for the substance of his mystic nomadism. He ends with a magnificent recitative for choir with speaking voices, "Good Friday Music," which summarizes his entire attitude. Raymond E. F. Larsson is an American Catholic mystic whose work begins a new cycle in poetry.

Elder Olson, also a metaphysical poet, seeks a slightly different direction. His *The Cock of Heaven* is an apocalyptic creation of an authentic modern myth. It is a poem composed of lyrics, plays, and prose texts, and attempts to present a legend of a grandiose vision. The world goes toward its destruction and the *Cock of Heaven* tells his cosmic story. We witness the creation of the earth, the fall of man, the pilgrimage of man into the countries of the seven deadly sins, the wanderings of the magi in search for a messiah, and the final catastrophe. Mr. Olson writes vigorously in many styles, sometimes taking over directly texts from other poets, but when he writes himself, his work is rich in imagery and lyric power. His erudition is profound. His language is bold and many-faceted. In the "Night Journey" we read:

```
I went in woldway dark as sleep
Bearing no lantern save the mind's.
I mournfulness had for cloak and hood.

Thence morningward through the sad
    veils
Rode I, nor knew what mount I rode,
But came on castled ruin at last,

And beat on the great graven bell.
That weft-world lifted then as lifting
Mist-fold: mead, stream, draped barge
    drifting
```

Saw, and Three cypress-stoled,
That shewed One bound and burning-
   haired,
Whose only substance was sky-gold

The new issue of *Fantasy,* a literary quarterly ably edited by Stanley Dehler Mayer in Pittsburgh, Pa., has a rich fare in creative and critical work. Although eclectic in taste, *Fantasy* conveys a stirring picture of the esthetic battleground in America, opening its pages to vigorous analyses of the poetic spirit. Harvey Breit challenges the critics of Kenneth Patchen's poetry in a brilliant essay. Parker Tyler studies "Literature and the Image" with a scintillating profundity. There are excellent poems by Joy Davidman, Harvey Breit, Nicolas Moore, William Pillin, Harry Roskolenko, Oscar Williams, and many others. *Fantasy* is one of the most important literary galleries of the advance-guard in America.

The poetry number of the *Saturday Review of Literature* (August 10, 1940) contains illuminating articles by William Rose Benét, Selden Rodman, Louis Untermeyer, C. P. Lee, Mark Van Doren, with some of which I can hardly agree, and poems by Horace Gegory, Raymond Holden, Robinson Jeffers, Max Lerner, and others, in which the sense of our stupefaction before the present catastrophe is movingly expressed. I was particularly struck by C. P. Lee's essay "Adulation and the Artist," with excerpts from the late Vachel Lindsay's letters to a young girl which emphasize his bewilderment before his success.

View, edited by Charles Henri Ford and published by James A. Decker, uses the newspaper form, and reminds me of that remarkable predecessor, *Journal des poètes,* which Charles Flouquet edited in Brussels before the deluge.

The Irresponsibles. By Archibald MacLeish. New York: Duell, Sloan and Pearce. 34 pages. $1.00.

There Are No Islands Any More. By Edna St. Vincent Millay. New York: Harper and Brothers. 10 pages. $.50.

Nightmare at Noon. By Stephen Vincent Benét. New York: Farrar and Rinehart. 8 pages. $.50.

Weep and Prepare. By Raymond E. F. Larsson. New York: Coward-McCann. 168 pages. $2.50.

The Cock of Heaven. By Elder Olson. New York: Macmillan. 105 pages. $2.00.

Toward a Metaphysical Renascence?
(October 1940–March 1941)

The Spiritual Aspects of the New Poetry, by Amos N. Wilder. Harper & Brothers.

Poetry between the two wars passed through an epoch of cynical nihilism and abject materialism, and the preoccupation with the purely demonic resulted in a "Satanism" that precluded all possibilities for creative ascension. The language of poetry became journalistic. It was filled with the aura of cheapness and superficiality which usually mark transitional eras. The incantatory or simply liturgical quality went out of poetry altogether, and could be found, in fragmentary passages, only in occasional poems by T. S. Eliot, whose religious evolution has definitely stamped his creative effort since *The Waste Land.*

A bewildered disquiet has marked all the poetry written during the past two decades in England and America. Mr. Amos N. Wilder studies this phenomenon at length in a well-documented book in which he applies the creative Christian principle as an ethical gauge. He examines the experimental and revolutionary phases of modern poetry in relation to the disarray of "a world without roots." In analyzing the work of such poets as Conrad Aiken, Hart Crane, W. H. Auden, Robinson Jeffers, Robert Frost, Archibald MacLeish, D. H. Lawrence, W. B. Yeats, T. S. Eliot, and others, he tries to bring to emergence the confusion of the modern writers before the metaphysical anguish and the dissolution of modern society. The solution of each of these writers is explained: Jeffers's "deliverance from our human state"; D. H. Lawrence's animal primitivism; T. S. Eliot's Christian Protestant direction; Kenneth Patchen's social romanticism. Numerous apposite examples emphasize the inner struggle mirrored in their work. He interprets the general tendency toward an attitude of negation which differs vitally from the attitude of traditionalist poets. We follow his interesting analysis of Aiken's psychological researches in the latter's dissection of identity and individuation. He finds that Aiken is morbidly attracted by the disintegrated consciousness of modern man.

The malady of the soul from which Mr. Wilder believes these poets to be suffering is a real pathological fact today. Agnosticism, the law of causality, scientism, dialectical materialism, pessimistic nihilism, philosophic vitalism—all these forces have militated against a religious revival. "This main malady or sense of alienation and lostness of contemporary man," he says, "expresses itself for one thing as a vertigo, or what we have called a sense of the abyss." Meditating death is part of this mood. The general dissociation of urban man makes Mr. Wilder feel that "we are playthings of some blind vortex." He quotes the exiled Russian philosopher Berdyaev to the effect that man has lost the human image or identity as a result of the havoc wrought by Humanism since the Renaissance. Surrealist irrationalism leads us to perdition, asserts Mr. Wilder. Like most observers, he makes Romanticism responsible for these facts, without being aware that the Romantic movement, historically speaking, had two currents to which Görres once gave the name of "descending and ascending mysticism."

Mr. Wilder believes that he has found a new pantheism, a new ethos, a new Christian orientation in many of the poets whose work he examined. T. S. Eliot undoubtedly has a metaphysical tendency. But I, for one, fail to discover this trend in any of the other poets. For they write as Humanists, as vitalists, as social revolutionaries. To measure the gulf dividing them from such writers, for instance, as Gerard M. Hopkins or Patrice de la Tour du Pin or Rainer Maria Rilke, we need only analyze the contents of the work of modern poets. There is no search for a new dimension in their verses. We see no super-rational expansion of consciousness. The "night" they evoke has no relation to that of St. John of the Cross and his mystic operations, but to the mechanistic night of the senses, of vitalism, of determinism. The emphasis is on primal chaos and despair.

Mr. Wilder fails to recognize that the malady of the human personality is followed by the malady of language. We notice in these poets the corruption of language. A spiritual poetry can only grow in an atmosphere favorable to the development of liturgical symbolism and liturgical language. A mere continuation of the Calvinist, Anglo-Saxon tradition is therefore not enough. The "diversity of racial strains in American life" ought to make possible a vast synthesis of all mystic tendencies, with an emphasis on the sacred logos in poetry.

Mr. Wilder's book comes at the right time. It is challenging and stimulating. It is a straw in the wind. It is a prospection in that *verticality* of thinking which the apocalypse of our times seems to be resuscitating.

Super-Occident and the Atlantic Language
(June 1941)

Professor M. L. Hansen published a remarkable study last year which he called the *Atlantic Migration*. In it he analyzed the great migratory movements from Europe to America, particularly the period that began one hundred years ago, with the population shift which ended in the transmigration to the American hemisphere of almost forty million persons. This movement is still going on. The religious, political, and social dissidents are once more streaming across the Atlantic to find a refuge here from the barbarism and robotism of Hitler's dark age.

I was once part of this westward journey before World War I, and a feeling of fraternity joins me to the Neo-Americans of World War II. We are all in the interracial crucible of modern America. We are all elements of the Eur-American melting pot which is beginning to glow white-hot, and which will ultimately create a new democratic universe.

We are all part of the great American Dream. We poured from the British Isles, and from the variegated regions of the European continent to these shores, bringing with us our archetypal memories and images, our languages and dialects, with the idea of welding them with the living phenomenon of America.

As creators of the word, we are naturally interested in the evolution of the American language. What will be the future of this language, the Elizabethan richness of which is today a phenomenon that excites the philologist, but should excite the writer even more? I have a feeling that it will eventually absorb all the other tongues now being spoken on the American continents, that it will weld them into a Super-American expression. It will probably be a continuous expansion of the Anglo-Saxon tongue: the realization of Rilke's grandiose vision of "a technique comprising all the advantages of particular languages in one."

The Super-Occidental, or the Atlantic Language—is this not Walt Whitman's vision of a great democracy?

Arts and Letters in Latin America (July 1941)

War in Europe has given impetus
to the "Indianista" renaissance

While efforts to combat Nazi-Fascist infiltration continue below the Rio Grande with increasing vigor, a creative ferment is sweeping through the southern continent. Literature and the arts are flowering in every Ibero-American republic, in spite of the malaise caused by the war. The publishing trade, especially in Mexico, Chile, Peru, and Argentina, is passing through a boom period, and the plastic manifestations are vigorous in the various social strata of the principal national units. Recent reports from Argentina, for instance, state that 1,582 new titles were brought out in 1940, as against 1,090 in 1939 and 842 in 1938. Of this number, 453 were accounted for by the social sciences; 289 by general literature; 266 were devoted to the applied sciences; 223 to history and geography; and university publications numbered about 250.

Literary life in Ibero-America is dominated by a Neo-Romantic revival in poetry. The essay, which always flourished in the southern part of the hemisphere, is making vast strides, while the novel and other manifestations of the narrative are searching for new forms in the framework of a magic realism. There has appeared, as yet, no colossus such as Yeats, or Proust, or Joyce. Esthetically, too, the general style still derives from European pioneers. But the substance of the work is American and indigenous. The writers are busy exploring the infinite variety and color of the people, the life and culture of their own continent. They seek to penetrate the ritual element of folklore, especially the grandiose beauty of primitive myths and customs. The *Indianista* renaissance, which began about twenty years ago, is growing, and this racial consciousness is a major preoccupation. The quest for a synthesis, the desire to weld together the multiple divergences across the many frontiers of climate and temperament, race and language, results in daring speculations that are influencing the work of the best creators in every land. In all these countries, from Mexico to Argentina, they are finding a common denominator in a radical aspiration toward a new democratic populism.

It must not be forgotten that there exist great temperamental and spiritual differences throughout the Ibero-American world. A Mexican's attitude toward life differs radically from that of the Argentine, and a Peruvian's outlook has little in common with that of the Brazilian. The climatic conditions, which are often violently changing, dominate, to a great degree, the inner state of mind. Here human geography is a factor of the first importance. Nevertheless, there is a melting pot at work among the many races in these countries. Pre-conquest Indians, Hispanic Americans, Negroes, Japanese, Chinese, Irish, Continental Europeans have mingled in these lands and are still mingling, and modern anthropologists predict the ultimate emergence of a new race. The mixture of races, Indian-Negro, Mestizo-Negro, Indian-Chinese, Portuguese-Negro, and others, is an ethnological fact that has already deeply influenced the psychic characteristics of the growing new race. Necessarily, too, this has brought with it a welding of languages. The Spanish and Portuguese languages are being constantly enriched with words and syntactical innovations from native pre-Columbian Indian languages.

Two main currents influence the formation of the Ibero-American races: the Spanish cultural tradition and the Indian heritage. The latter, originally suppressed, has emerged under the influence of the pro-Indian and mestizo intellectuals, such as José Carlos Mariateguí and Luis Valcarcel in Peru, Moisés Sáenz in Mexico. This movement, which became a powerful cultural force, *Indianismo,* places emphasis on the retention and continuation of Indian culture and handicraft, on the supremacy of pre-conquest customs and rituals, on the creative sources inherent in the new world itself. It seeks a link with the autochthonous forces. Both these tendencies have been at war for some decades, a war which was brought to emergence especially by the Mexican revolution against Diaz. In the past decade, however, the tendency to look for a common denominator seems to be gaining the upper hand. A natural blending would appear to be taking place.

Nothing reveals this more than a trip through the tropical, temperate, and glacial regions of the continent. Some years ago—in 1931, to be exact—I visited the South American countries and later Central America, from the Pacific side, in a leisurely British freighter. In Guatemala, where I stopped for two months, I felt that a new world was opening up to me. It was vastly different from Panama or Colombia, and later, when I reached Mexico, the difference seemed even more pronounced. I met a number of writers and artists during this trip and was impressed by their close contact with the people. I found a sincere sympathy for the Indio's struggles, for his spiritual and physical pain. The writers everywhere were seeking to learn to know their environment, in order to depict the new man and his ethos. There was a spirit of creative vitalism abroad.

This interracial world of Ibero-America is still the principal preoccupation of the writers. Already, in 1931, I noticed a phenomenon that has not yet spent itself, but, on the contrary, is beginning to assume vast proportions. This is *la época de la plaqueta,* of the little poetic booklet. Today books and pamphlets are rolling off the presses in great streams. A new lyrical golden age is at hand. Next in point of interest is the philosophical essay—especially having to do with existential philosophy—which is followed by the narrative. The novel pursues the social vision and silhouettes human geography in a new realism.

In Mexico I met Bernardo Ortiz de Montellanos. He was, at that time, editor of the advance-guard review *Contemporáneos,* which has since been suspended. De Montellanos is a leading Mexican poet, together with Xavier Villarutia, Manuel Maples Arce, Jaime Torres Bodet, Carlos Pellicer, Manuel M. Ponce, José Muñoz Cota. All of these men are in the Neo-Romantic tradition. De Montellanos recently published his new book *Cinco horas sin corazón* (*Five Hours Without a Heart*), in which the Romantic motif of subconscious explorations is applied with gusto. He has written little, but each volume has marked a date: *Sueños* (*Dreams*), *Himno a hypnos* (*Hymn to Sleep*), and *Muerte de cielo azul* (*Death of the Blue Sky*). His new poems, which he also calls *entresueños* (half-dreams), are daring flights into the unconscious. Among the novelists in Mexico are to be found such men as Mariano Azuelo (*Los de abajo; The Underdogs*), Mauricio Magdalena, and Bernardino Mena Brito (*Paludismo*). In the work of all these writers is to be found a preoccupation with the earth and man's labors.

Sculpture and painting continue to thrive in Mexico. It is no longer the great awakening of the Revolutionary Union of Technical Workers, Painters, and Sculptors. In fact, some of the pioneers of this movement have left the country. Diego Rivera is in California; Jean Charlot is in New York; the Communist painter David Alfaro Siqueiros, who was in jail accused of having organized the first attempt to assassinate Trotsky, left for Chile after his release and is now en route to Soviet Russia. But Mérida and Orozco are still active. Murals are still being painted, as they were when the Madero revolution released the creative forces of the *Indianista* consciousness. Among the talented new painters, the name of Orozco Romero must be mentioned.

The interest in folklore, which was initiated by an American woman, Frances Toor, is profoundly influencing artistic and literary creation in Mexico. Her magazine, *Mexican Folkways,* has been a cultural rallying point for many years. It has made available folk songs, narratives of ancient Indian and Hispanic folk customs, as well as many little-known ritualistic texts gathered throughout the country. This review, with which such men as Diego Rivera and Jean Charlot have been identified, has been officially recognized as being of national importance.

The experimental theater in Mexico has made great strides in the last few decades. Since the revolution, the interest in the people's struggle and fate became the preoccupation of the playwrights and actors, and the people's response was vigorous. The theater Orientación had an especially brilliant career. It became a school for actors and directors. There are many other groups scattered throughout the nation, and the esthetic and sociological discussions have been extremely stimulating to the students of contemporary drama.

Numerous reviews pullulate in Mexico and add to the dynamics of the cultural treasure. Among them may be mentioned *Revista Ibero-Americana,* published by the universities of Seattle, Wash., and Mexico City, with contributors like Carlos Prada, Juan Ramón Jiménez, Cesar Barja; *Tierra nueva,* which publishes Mexican and foreign writers like Antonio Caso, Manuel Cabrera, Alfonso Reyes, and Ali Chumacero; and others of equal interest.

In Guatemala and other Central American countries, where the popular art is essentially one of handicrafts, there is an intellectual fermentation as well. Guatemala City is the home of Miguel Angel Asturias, whose *Leyendas de Guatemala* is a literary monument. These are stories of his picturesque homeland, fantastic tales set against a Mayan background, for Asturias has Mayan blood in his veins. Indeed, he seemed to me to resemble an ancestral Mayan deity when I met him some years back. In San José (Costa Rica), J. Garcia Monge edits a review of the advance-guard, *Repertorio americano* (*Semanario de cultura hispánica*), which publishes work by Central American and Caribbean writers. This is an especially well-edited magazine containing poetic work by Mejía Robledo of Costa

Rica and Alexandro Manrico Campio of Peru; chronicles by Emilia Rieto, Juan Marín, Alicia Castro Argüello, Mario Santa Cruz, Fernando Luján, Eduardo Ines González. *Repertorio americano* is a stimulating magazine that deals with esoteric and philosophical subjects as well as with literature. The well-known Spanish poet Rafael Alberti, last heard from in May from Costa Rica, recently made a tour of Latin America and is preparing a book on his experiences. Alberti fled Spain after the Franco government put a price on his head.

The old-world *Hispanismo* of Chile has safeguarded the purity of its culture. The melancholy strain that runs through the national temperament is due to conditions of climate as well as to the volcanic nature of the land. These influences are reflected in the work of the writers, which is marked by a fierce Humanism, *el grito de la fraternidad* (the call for fraternity). Pablo Neruda is doubtless the greatest of contemporary Chilean poets. His work, which has been translated into many languages, possesses a Whitmanesque feeling for human solidarity and achieves a lyrical contact with the violent nature of the country. Vincente Huidobro, another leading poet, is bilingual. I knew Huidobro in Paris in the 1920s, when he was writing modernistic poems in French that constituted his participation in the insurgent literary manifestations of Dada and Surrealism. Huidobro returned to Santiago in 1930 and began to write in Spanish again. A convinced anti-Fascist, like Neruda, he has been prominent in the ranks of the poetic opposition. Among the better-known novelists of Chile, the names of Ruben Azocar and Maria Luisa Bombal may be mentioned.

Peru lost its leading writer and essayist, Carlos Mariateguí, several years ago. He edited *Amanta,* a revolutionary magazine which divided its interest between *Indianista* folklore and the activities of the new poets and artists. His essays, in which an American type of Marxism predominated, are among the most stimulating expressions of his humanitarian genius. Among Peru's best novelists is Ciro Alegria, who wrote *La Serpiente de oro* (*The Golden Snake*). Among the poets may be mentioned Xavier Abril and Abraham Arias Larreta.

Argentina is celebrating today a literary and artistic renaissance that promises a new golden age. It is fortunate in the possession of a centralizing agency constituted by the review *Sur,* which is edited by the brilliant Victoria Ocampo. Waldo Frank, whose work has frequently appeared in translation below the border, and who has a marked influence on the new writers of these countries, regards this review as the best anywhere. *Sur* tries to present the most significant work of all South America; it was also a bridge to the Europe that is now immersed in the blackout. Its list of contributors ranges from Jorge Luis Borges, Leopoldo Marechal, Francisco Luiz Bernárdez, Silvina Ocampo, Salvador de Madariaga, Carlos Alberti Erro, to such European spirits as Paul Valéry, Jean Paulhan, Franz Werfel, André Breton, and others. Borges, Bernárdez, Marechal are among the better native poets who are published in *Sur*. A number of French refugee writers such as Georges Bernanos and Roger Caillois contribute their share to the intensely alive atmosphere of Buenos Aires.

The novelists who have emerged in recent years show an increasing interest and love for the people and their landscape. Roberto Artl, Eduardo Mallea, Jorge Luis Borges, Morel Adolfo Cesares present in their novels a daring panorama of Argentine life. A moving novel, *Gente sin suelo* (*People Without Soil*), by Clemente Cimorra should not be neglected. Cimorra is a Spanish refugee writer who attempts to present a grandiose fresco of the Spanish tragedy.

There are women poets of interest in Argentina. Maria Alicia Domínguez, Silvina Ocampo, Norah Borges, Clementina Azlor, and, especially, the village schoolteacher Ida Réboli have conquered a prominent place in lyric poetry.

José R. Destéfano, who just published *Cánticos de la muerte* in Buenos Aires, gives apocalyptic images in grandiose verses that seem to have gone through the school of Surrealism. Rimbaud and Eluard are the sources of his delirious lyrics.

The Argentine essayists have long been recognized as important explorers of the spirit. Chief among these is Carlos Alberti Erro.

The interest in North American literature is profound and intelligent. Ernest Hemingway's *Farewell to Arms,* recently republished in Buenos Aires, was the occasion of a remarkable critical reception. Argentine critics analyzed it with perspicacious insight and agreed that the North American novel occupies a first place in the world today.

There are numberless reviews scattered throughout the various republics. *Claridad, American Tribune for Free Thought,* edited by Antonio Zamora, appears in Buenos Aires, and devotes its pages to esthetic essays on Picasso, James Joyce, Martí, as well as to sociological subjects dealing with the Latin American world. Other reviews are *Nosotros,* under the direction of Alfredo A. Bianchi and Roberto F. Giusti, published in Buenos Aires; *Revista Bimestre Cubana,* directed by Fernando Ortiz; *Atenea,* published in

Concepción, Chile; *Revista Nacional de cultura,* under José Nucete-Sardi, in Caracas, Venezuela; and many others, particularly university magazines of great cultural value.

There are a great many other novelists and poets scattered throughout the South American continent. Each, in his own way, contributes to the aspiration toward spiritual unity which is one of the most cherished desires of the writing clan in those countries. In Ecuador, Jorge Icaza has emerged with a powerful novel, *Huasipungo,* which even had a good sale. In Venezuela there is Uslar Pietri, who wrote *Las Lanzas coloradas (Red Spears).* Perez Cabral's novel *Jengibre,* recently published in Caracas, presents the dour life of the Negro workers and reveals a powerful epic talent.

Uruguay's most prominent poet is Gaston Figueira, who has just published his *Geografía Poética de America,* an attempt to present synthetically the human struggle of the races on the South American continent. This is permeated with the vision of *unidad americana.* Blanca Luz Brum, whose very human poems with socialist leanings are so moving, also lives in Uruguay. The poetry of the Bolivian visionary Avila Jiménez, especially his *Cronos,* attempts to weld *Indianista* and Hispanic motifs into an organic whole. M. A. Puga recently published *3 poemas civiles,* in which the rebel cry against political tyranny and oppression resounds in strong accents. This social consciousness also is found in *Kollasuyu,* poems by Emilio Vázquez. The twenty-fifth anniversary of the death of the Nicaraguan poet Rubén Darío elicited numberless essays in the reviews of the Spanish-American countries. Revaluations of his position in the literary history of Latin America appeared. Some of them—like that of Luis Alberto Sánchez in his essay "Balance and Liquidation of 1900"—refused to join in the homage to the poet and criticized the poet's work from the standpoint of the modernist orientation.

Victor Llona, a native Peruvian, who lived for several decades in Paris, writing in French, has recently returned to Lima. He has written a number of interesting articles in Spanish on the work of the late James Joyce, who was his friend in the French capital.

But unfortunately we know relatively little of Bolivian poetry. The recently published *Poetas Jóvenes de Bolivia* under the direction of the Ministry of Foreign Affairs by Guillermo Viscarra F. simply adds to the confusion. It is badly edited and does not add anything to our knowledge of Bolivian poetry.

In the vast interracial crucible of Brazil, where Afro-Creole, Indian, Portuguese, Italian, French, German, and other races live side by side, the literary and artistic life goes on in close association with the ethnic complex. Novelists and poets like Jorge Faleiros, Padua de Almeida, and essayists like Eurialo Canabroa, Guirrido Torres, and Mario Vieira de Melo are making important contributions to the creative heritage. Tasso de Silveira edits from Rio de Janeiro his review *Cadernos da hora presente* (*Records of the Present Hour*), which gathers the more essential forces of cultural Brazilian life together. The composer Heitor Villa Lobos continues his musical innovations in the operatic and choral mediums. His work is also well known in the United States. Although there is an official indifference to the folklore sources of the country, the primitive mentality is, nevertheless, influencing creative activity. I have been told that the official world of Brazil looks askance at Miss Elsie Houston's presentations of *Macumba,* or African and mestizo folk music, which it is said to consider as being too limited in its interpretation of the national spirit. It cannot be denied, however, that her contribution is a highly significant one.

The Afro-Creole element in Latin American life is everywhere in evidence. The West Indian tropics possess a distinct character of their own in which the African elements mingle with the Hispanic ones. In Puerto Rico, Luis Palés Matos writes *Tuntún de pasa y grifería, poemas afroantillanos,* in which the Negro rhythm is mingled with Spanish words and vice versa. He tries to invent new composite words to express the primitive soul. The same thing applies to Cuba, where *jitanjáforas* are playing a great role in lyric poetry. Drumbeats are translated into poetry. These phrases are untranslatable, since they really have no logical meaning. They are merely rhythmic sounds to express ritual movement, a combination of pre-Columbian Indian with aboriginal African incantations. The bongo, a feature of Afro-Cuban orchestras, can be heard in the meters of such poets as Guillén, Ballagas, Giran, and others. The famous Mexican poet Alfonso Reyes gave his tendency the onomatopoetic name of *jitanjáfora.* Augusto Malaret and Luis Florens Torrens also use this form occasionally.

Cuba is extremely rich in its literary life. Its greatest poet is probably Mariano Brull, but there are others; Renée Potts, Amparo Rodríguez Vidal, and Isabel Alvarez. Its novelists, who deal principally with the underworld, are Novas Calvo and Enrique Sierpo. It has a plethora of remarkable essayists such as Juan Marinello, Jorge Mañach, Felix Lizaso, Jorge Ichaso, and

Alejo Carpentier. Cuba has also extended its hospitality to many anti-Fascist Spanish writers. These men publish a review of their own, *Nuestra España,* and the poet Manuel Altolaguirre is its director.

The death during the Spanish Civil War of Pablo de la Torriente-Brau, author of *Aventuras del soldado desconocido cuban* (*Adventures of the Unknown Cuban Soldier*), deprived Cuban letters of a brilliant promise in creative literature. His humor and irony and sometimes his acid violence against injustice lend a special note to his style.

The American film has completely captured the entire hemisphere. The inroads of the American language—already noted in the Hispanic versions of *futbol* and *beisbol*—are familiarizing millions of our southern neighbors with the vocabulary of our rich American speech. The *estrellas* (stars) of Hollywood are as well known in Buenos Aires, Lima, Rio de Janeiro, and in the smallest town of the provinces as in our own United States. Certain Hollywood deformations of South American national characteristics have caused resentment, but attempts are now being made by our movie producers to correct this. The very existence of the films tends to build a bridge with the southern world. In Mexico, Argentina, and Brazil, native screen producers have recently made films that use the language, and their success, in many cases, has been marked.

The great Mexican educator José Vasconcelos once declared: "Latin America is the home of the cosmic race." There is no doubt but that a huge fermentation of cultural-creative values is taking place in our neighboring continent. We may be confident that this world of racial and democratic equality—the antithesis of Hitler's grotesquely stupid "racism"—will add brilliant new chapters to the arts of our hemisphere.

German Letters in Ruins: A Report from Frankfurt (July 4, 1948)

The visitor in the American zone of Germany who looks for significant creative work is liable to receive a shock. He will find that most of the post-war work now being written and published is like the rubble he sees every-where in the big cities and towns, like the eviscerated houses that yawn spectrally into the summer-sheen. He will find literary manifestations frag-mentary, confused, nihilistic. He will wander through the desolation of a mental wasteland, where only occasionally he stumbles over an exotic plant amid the heaped-up masonry. Three years after Germany's surrender, intel-lectual life strikes the outsider as being under the sigil of irrationality, and he looks in vain for constructive ideas in this vacuum.

While attending the recent celebration of the German revolution of 1848 in this city, I had an opportunity of meeting German writers at their congress and of listening to their speeches. With a few notable exceptions their utterances were pompous, hollow, and full of resentment against the occupational powers. I heard not a single admission of Germany's guilt. In the verbose and often puerile discourses there was no intercontinental per-spective, only a narrow Teutonic self-sufficiency and insistence on a resur-gent nationalism. One man alone, Fritz von Unruh, the playwright who recently returned from eight years of exile in the United States, spoke words from a democratic consciousness and shook his listeners with a masterful exposé of Hitler's crimes against the spirit. Von Unruh, one of the great writers of the Expressionist movement that flourished about twenty-five years ago, remained an exponent of the international Humanism which marked the Expressionist era.

This was the second writers' congress held in the American zone since the capitulation, the first one having taken place in Berlin about six months ago, when authors from both the western and eastern zones confronted each other. At the Frankfurt conclave not a single scribe from the Soviet zone was allowed by SMA to be present, and their absence accentuated the latent antithesis in creative life today, to wit: the meaning of *Dichtung* as a spiritual or intellectual experience and its meaning as an activistic or political function. Certain of the writers taking their cue from France tried timidly to face the problem as the combat between "la poésie pure" and "la poésie engagé," but the discussion was tepid and amateurish.

Using nebulous philosophical terms, the sixty-five-year-old poet Rudolf Alexander Schröder spoke about "time" in poetry and tried to demolish Surrealism, while Elisabeth Langgässer, one of the rising young prose writers, wallowed in high-flown verbiage in postulating a "new consciousness of reality." Theodor Plivier, author of *Stalingrad*, who recently fled from the Soviet zone into the western zone, spoke of the new writer's will to liberty and the hope for a rebirth of the "soul of the old Continent."

American observers were particularly struck with the fact that none of the speakers seemed to be aware of the confusion that lies so heavily on language in Europe today. Nazi and Communist banalities clung to the style of the lecturers, some of whom still used Nazi clichés and parroted the Bolshevist vocabulary. The books being published today still show many traces of this, despite the fact that Dr. Dolf Sternberger, editor of *Die Wandlung*, initiated a semantic purge of the Nazi lexicon in his "Vocabulary of the Monster" almost three years ago. American press control officers encouraged the systematic denazification of the German language from the earliest days of the American occupation.

We know that during the war there was little literature of resistance inside Germany against Hitler and that there was no intellectual underground that expressed itself in creative work against the Nazi crimes. Is it therefore to be wondered at that the theme of the age-old struggle for freedom is hardly noticeable in contemporary German letters? In talking to German writers, one finds an almost revolting pathological self-pity. They repeat ad nauseam threnodies about their economic plight and sputter lyrical inanities about the *Dachböden* (attics) where they are compelled to live. This can also be discovered in reading their novels, short stories, essays, or the "feuilleton" pages of the newspapers. Over six thousand books have been published since the end of the war by the 374 publishing houses licensed by the Information Control Division of the United States Military Government. To a large extent, these books represent translations from French and American, while hardly a single new German book can be considered a major contribution to the spiritual evolution of the country or of Europe.

The *Neue Zeitung,* the overt paper of the American Military Government, recently launched a symposium to explore the state of mind of the young writers. Walter Kolbenhoff, the author of *Of Our Flesh and Blood,* a novel imitative of Ernest Hemingway, said: "Give us time!" He arrogantly rejected the "polished articles and stories of the older men, because they are sparkling pearls and the achievements of experienced littérateurs." "The new men," he asserted, "have no time for exercises in literary style. They speak the language of the age and will express what has not yet been expressed about the tortured, bewildered people to which we belong. . . . Our generation stands before zero." Carl H. Ebbinghaus felt that there was "much ado about nothing" and proceeded to defend the "polished writers" against the onslaughts of the half-baked iconoclasts. Another young man wondered why his contemporaries were so certain they were writers, "for to be a writer is not a profession or calling like that of a stonemason. . . . It is simply a destiny." These vacant affirmations are characteristic of the post-Nazi generation's reasoning.

The older generation that left the Germanic countries in 1933—Thomas Mann, Franz Werfel, Alfred Döblin, Hermann Broch, Fritz von Unruh, Leonhard Frank, and others—are little read today, because their works are hard to obtain. But certain writers who claim to belong to the "inner emigration," like Kasimir Edschmid, Walter von Molo, and others (although they continued to publish during the Hitler regime), are reemerging. The recent death of Ricarda Huch at the age of seventy-eight left a gap in German letters. She was in some ways a great writer (poet, novelist, and historian) who left a bulky production behind. Her work on German Romanticism, brilliant interpretations of that controversial movement, is one of the best.

The documentary literature on Himmler's concentration camps is still growing. Besides Eugen Kogon's *The SS State* and Ernst Wiechert's *The Forest of the Dead,* a number of new testimonies to Nazi depravity have recently appeared. Among them are *2,000 at Dachau,* by K. A. Gross; *Night and Fog,* by Arnold Weiss-Ruethel; *Journey Through the Last Act,* by Isa Vermehren, which depict the laboratories of evil in starkly graphic prose. Here we glimpse the transition from individual cruelty to an organized sadism unique in the history of mankind. These personal records show Hitler's hatred of the human personality in the terror acts of the SS beasts who coined the cynical phrase "Action Springtime Wind" as a code word for their mass executions.

What do the young novelists think about this? Very little, if my perusal of the new writing and my conversations with them mirror their minds. One cannot escape the impression that the process of democratization has not yet taken root in their spirits. Even the conversion of that archmilitarist, Ernst Jünger, in his insolent screed *Peace: A Word to Europe's Youth,* does not convince us that he has forsworn his Caesarean directions. Some of the young writers have now adopted an apolitical attitude, but we know that many of them were formerly Nazis, militarists, and pan-Germans in spirit. Those who today are Communists or fellow travelers are so only because they are still haunted by the idea of a dictatorship—it matters little whether it be brown or red. Much of their jargon is still totalitarian.

As for the new novelists, no first-class talent has emerged so far. A group of young storytellers recently banded themselves together under the banner of "magischer Realismus," or, as some called it, "blutiger Realismus," at a meeting in the Odenwald. About thirty of them read their work. They have published little for the most part.

A vague Neo-Romanticism is also in the air among the prose writers. It is a synthesis of Expressionism and Surrealism, and emphasizes the metamorphosis of the narrative into fables and magic tales of terror. Its representatives are Elisabeth Langgässer, Hermann Kasack, and Gustav René Hocke. A recent anthology, *End and Beginning,* presents the work of six young men and women, among whom Werner Illing, Susanne Kerkhoff, and August Scholtis show promise in creating a fantastic reality out of the experiences of their battered world. Wolfdietrich Schnurre uses the nightmare fantasy as his favorite motif for depicting man's inner disarray. Doubtless the most gifted of the new "visionaries" is Kasack, whose powerful evocations of the night-side of existence deserve to be known outside the frontiers of Germany. *Die Stadt jenseits des Stromes* (*The City Beyond the River*) is his last novel.

The "little magazine" which presents such a rich proliferation of experimental writing in the United States is practically unknown in Germany. A number of serious reviews—most of them having an uncommonly large circulation—appear irregularly, presenting literary, philosophical, and sociological themes in great abundance.

The oldest postwar magazine in the American zone is *Die Wandlung*, for which I suggested the name and selected the editorial staff in the summer of 1945. It has a circulation of forty thousand and is edited by Dr. Dolf Sternberger, with an editorial board consisting of the Heidelberg existentialist philosopher Karl Jaspers, the Heidelberg sociologist Alfred Weber, and the Marburg philologist Werner Krauss. Since the review appears in Heidelberg, it mirrors to some extent the ambience of the university spirit. Jaspers has just left Heidelberg to follow a call from the Swiss University of Basle, where he plans to complete his philosophical life work.

Magic Realism or Neo-Romanticism: it is hard to predict what will come out of the present apocalyptic chaos in which we Americans live in Germany as observers. A compulsive synthesis is still lacking, and will be lacking, in my opinion, until the German writers recognize a priori their country's full responsibility for the totalitarian horrors. Perhaps the creative forces now dammed will then flow forth into the Western world and mingle with the pan-democratic tendencies of a new age.

The Migrator and His Language (1948)

Since my earliest childhood, I have always been a nomad, an emigrant, a traveler. Born in the United States, I came to Europe at the age of two, only to return to New York as an adolescent. From then on, a trilingual reporter, I lived a life of constant migration between the two continents. I have just cast my anchor in Paris after five years of work for the Allied troops in the States and in Europe, work that has tied me intimately to the events whose apocalyptic reverberations can be felt even now. It is quite likely that in less turbulent times I would be now prudently thinking of settling down some-where. And yet, more than ever I find myself attracted by distant things, by geographical displacements, by travels.

Is my case unique? I don't think so, since today we all suffer from anguish. It is getting darker and darker around us, and the worm of primordial apprehensiveness crawls across the halls of our sleeping and waking hours. Every element of religion and philosophy, of poetry and language seems to disintegrate. Schizophrenic lesions torture the psychic skin of our society. The somatic being seems suspended in midair, fearing the heights and the abysses, prey to a Magdalenian trembling. The anonymous masses gaze with the eyes of despair, and their speech is no more than the clapping of tongues.

In that collective hunger for a new Humanism, we dream of ships and airplanes which would take us further than magic carpets which merely allow us to fling off our daily burden; we dream with a pervasive desire to attain some sense of life's dynamism. We dream with the hope to intensify and illuminate our lives. We would like to meditate over man's destiny:

456

on love and death, on fraternity and war, on progress and the atomic age. We would like to meditate on our language as a means of communication between men and on the tragedy of fleeting words.

My thoughts carry me toward the country of my birth. I am nostalgic. The sound of old Indian names comes back as an echo in my ears; I can hear the Anglo-American speech, the French-Canadian accents, and the Mexican mixed with the Aztec tongues. And the megalopolis of New York rises like a fiction, like a vertical image bathed in the light of an explosive springtime. The dream of a new world, this emancipatory dream still haunts me since my schoolboy years in Europe, before I emigrated: Thule, the Island of Happiness, Utopia. At that time, thousands shared my dream, and I would venture to say that they share it to this day. Each man experiences a moment in his life when he would like to discover an America, a new America, an America of his own, a mysterious and unknown America, an *America fantomatica*, a *mystical America.*

I recall my last departure from New York, during the troubled war days at the beginning of 1944. I had been working at a government agency for war intelligence, and I was preparing to join the Allied armies in Europe. I had just left behind the binary tapping of teleprinters, the staccato hammering of typewriters, the breathtaking conversations of my coworkers. I was spurred by a nomadic fervor even as I was strolling along Broadway, toward the Columbus Circle where the delicate stele of the explorer grew tall in the air, outlined against the metallic sky. A bitter wind swept through the dilapidated streets where I used to like walking a quarter of a century earlier, a solitary and anxious immigrant, my head spinning with thousands of French and English words, with journalistic jargon, with army slang words that I had just finished typing up in the office, with words of encouragement for the occupied countries. Europe slept, somber and sick, deep in my unconscious.

A few days later, on the road, I felt that the travels would never come to an end. Our French cargo, displaying the flag of the Lorraine Cross, left a Canadian port one foggy evening; we traveled without convoy across the oceanic deserts infested with submarines. In London, bombs were about to growl over the city as we, the journalists, retorted with words of steel meant to prepare our friends from the Continent for the battle of France. In the month of June, we disembarked on the Cotentin Peninsula to live in the middle of the Breton Maquis. Then, the liberation of Paris, and we were helping our French colleagues from Reims, from Nancy, and other cities to restart their democratic press. Then, the battle of Ardennes. Our task was then, in Aix-la-Chapelle, to hammer democratic principles into hard-headed Nazis. We were just in Germany, one sunny day, when the enemy signed the unconditional capitulation. We stayed on for a while. Now, back in France, I am seized by an Atlantic nostalgia that only a ship or a clipper heading west could appease.

Westward! To New York, to Quebec, to New Orleans, to Veracruz, to Buenos Aires. Departing toward the world of emigrants, the world of the synthesis of races, the world of transformed vocables of the new Americans. I think of seven and a half million inhabitants who "enjoy the privileges of democracy," as the speaker on the New York City radio proclaims. I think of sixty-five nationalities represented in the Manhattan melting pot, of all these languages, of all these dialects spoken in that city alone. Within the bounds of a single city we can traverse all national borders. I ponder over this heterogeneous night of Europe and I feel that I, an almost symbolical migrator, belong in that "melting pot." As a part of that multiracial and multilingual cosmos, I feel I belong to the future. For New York is but an immense urban mirror of a much vaster melting pot that is the United States; the United States being themselves but a reflection of an even larger whole that extends to Canada and Latin America.

Yes, we would all like to go West, the visionary West of liberty. Today, however, our creative imagination unfurls its sails toward other shores: toward a spiritual liberation.

Crossing "the demon-infested ocean," Christopher Columbus sought a new way to China. Instead, he finds an island inhabited by caciques. Pizarro, Cortez, and Balboa follow. In their turn, the conquistadors attract thousands of other adventurers hungry for gold and silver. Then Cartier, Champlain, Father Marquette, La Salle, and Bienville discover Canada, the Great Lakes, the Mississippi basin, and finally the Delta and the Gulf of Mexico. Captain Smith embarks on a voyage to Virginia, and the Pilgrims go ashore by the Plymouth Rock in New England. New York is founded by the Dutch, under the original name of New Amsterdam. In the foot-steps of these pioneers, feudal and turbulent Europe will send thousands and thousands of immigrants who will settle down on the new continent before penetrating inland. The first hundred years unleash a wave of migra-tion that would continue until the beginning of the First World War. Over seventy million men and women reach the shores of the United States and Canada, especially farmers and workers from eastern and southeast-ern Europe, from central Europe and Scandinavia. They cultivate Mid-western soils, build railroads and factories, construct giant cities, veritable nests of international communities. The last wave of migrations dates from the rise of Fascism and Nazism, when Jews and leftist political refugees escaped persecutions and the menace of concentration camps of the new "Caesars."

Today, the aim of migrations has changed. It is no longer the one described by Henry Thoreau in his beautiful essay "Walking":

> When I go out of the house for a walk, uncertain as yet whither I will bend my steps. . . . I turn round and round irresolute sometimes for a quarter of an hour, until I decide, for the thousandth time, that I will walk into the southwest or west. Eastward I will go only by force; but westward I go free. . . . I must walk toward Oregon, and not toward Europe.

This passage contains in a nutshell the isolationist philosophy of the bygone century. The world wars opened a new chapter in the history of migrations. For the first time in centuries the journey leads equally in the opposite direction: toward the East, from the new to the old world. It is a mythical return to the mother. This time, entire armies pour out onto the old beaches of Europe and Africa. On the European continent itself, the inter-migration of displaced people, in a ferocious flow and ebb caused by Hitler's tyranny, was able to upset within a few years all demographic charts. The Occidental tensions begin to dissolve, at least partially, into a geographical and spiritual union. We are no longer all heading for Oregon.

The scientific progress, the triumph of the machine in the service of *homo faber,* the rise of aeronautics and of the atomic age have changed our prospects. The world is planetary. We travel toward Europe just as well as toward America, Asia, the Aleutian Islands, as well as to Africa and Australia. The airplane (the Flying Fortress, Superfortress, Spitfire) has shown that Europe borders America, that China is located at our doorstep, that Brazil is close to Africa and to the United States, just as Canada is close to Siberia and to Greenland. We have acquired a pluralist consciousness of the universe.

Despite all these facts, the modern man is gripped by an inexpressible anguish that forebodes future catastrophes and upheavals. Yet, standing upright amidst the ruins, man who awaits his fall, also awaits his resurrection. He dreams of a chiliastic voyage across the surges of time. Dispossessed and a nomad, man tries to elude his fear, to vanquish the sense of isolation, to escape the solitude created by the borders. Are we witnessing the birth of a new type of human being: a universal man, man of interracial confraternity, a visionary? This man aspires to a metaphysical liberty. Don't the Americas, in love with aviatic adventures, give us a natural example of such a metamorphosis? An anthropological transmutation is already at work on this vast continent. In this laboratory of the New West, the modern man, whose unconscious contains the memory of innumerable myths of pre-logical Europe, seeks a sacred alchemy, a meta-cosmic religion, a new Holy Grail. He reaches out for the high as well as for the low, to the East as well as to the West, toward the interior as well as toward the exterior; his pilgrimage is horizontal as well as vertical.

The myth of migration imprints an obsessive image upon our minds. It is a primitive myth of our times. Amidst chaos, it is but the configuration of archaic nostalgia aiming at the destruction of human chains; it is an impulse that seeks to overcome physical obstacles, such as the law of gravity, and to reach the zenith, as man's third eye is being opened. It is a myth of mystic travelers searching an esoteric reality which would abolish the sense of nothingness and the anguish of crowds. Each of us wishes to undertake this intense voyage toward light, toward freedom, toward the fullness of life. Each of us wishes to participate in that mythical migration toward a communal liturgy, toward a new cosmological dimension, toward a vertical Humanism. We wish to climb the stairs dotted with stars in a blinding ecstasy.

Gripped by fear, man of the atomic age strolls among the crises and ruins of his time and trails his language with him. His language suffers from the same diseases as the man. "The malady of language" to which, since 1927, I have frequently drawn the attention of *transition* readers, can be felt in all domains of human activity. We are no longer just a handful of avant-garde writers to share the feelings expressed by the young Lord Chandos (in the admirable essay by Hugo von Hofmannsthal) who wrote in his "Letter to Lord Bacon":

> I can no longer write, because the language in which I might be able not only to write but to think is neither Latin nor English, neither Italian nor Spanish, but a language none of whose words is known to me, a language in which inanimate things speak to me and wherein I may one day have to justify myself before an unknown judge.

Since the war, young people are becoming more aware that this pathology of words is now a reality. Words have lost their meaning. There is a semantic decadence which necessitates new definitions and neologisms. The word has become an instrument of negation.

To observe the statesmen groping for a peace agreement capable of withstanding the threat of the nuclear era, it becomes evident, in the light of nomadic currents, that a metamorphosis of means of communication is inevitable. More than ever, the new civilization needs a universal language. But the malady of languages in use cannot be cured by the fire of ecumenical consciousness acquired in the process of migration and the growing interdependence among nations. We are doubtless moving, slow as it may be, toward a fusion of languages. The migrating man, in quest of new words, no doubt incorporates words drawn from all modern languages in order to attain a monolithic structure of a world language. Why English, whose birth itself constitutes such a striking and efficient example of amalgamation, and which is already used by approximately six hundred million people, couldn't serve as the basis for that future language, for that expanding language?

I leave up to philologists all the speculations on the manner in which this desirable union could be accomplished. Nevertheless, I am convinced that if this world language—let's call it, for the moment, "Atlantica"—is not known to my grandchildren, it will be to theirs. It will have very little or nothing to do with the artificial inventions that we have known so far: the Neutral Idiom, Ido, Esperanto, Novial. It will certainly be an antithesis of "Basic English," notable mostly for its stiffness and its creative paucity.

The poet will once more assume the role of an explorer. Navigating between grammatical islands of the linguistic New West, he will cross many storms, in danger of a shipwreck. The corruption and the decadence of all languages are setting an ambush. But he will reach a hospitable port, loaded with gifts of invention: new vocabularies, new sounds, and new syntaxes gathered along the way. The creative imagination is more than ever on the point of new discoveries, of yet unthought-of realities, of unconceivable conquests. We follow the great cultivators of virgin lands: we travel toward a mythomorphosis of the logos.

Part Eight : **Across Frontiers**

Introduction

In 1944, only days after the Allied landing in Normandy, Eugene Jolas set foot on Utah Beach as an American press officer. Via Cherbourg, Paris, Nancy, and Luxembourg, traversing the smouldering remains of French towns and villages, and always just one step behind the fighting troops, he entered the city of Aachen, where he and his team set up the first Allied newspaper in occupied Germany. He did similar work in Heidelberg before he came to Bad Nauheim, where the American Military Government appointed him as editor in chief of a news agency called Deutsche Allgemeine Nachrichten-Agentur (DANA; now the Deutsche Presse-Agentur).

At first sight, Jolas's work had little in common with his literary interests, since he had to confine himself to teaching young Germans basic journalistic principles—meaning the American way of strictly reporting the facts—for a new democratic press. However, the Office of Military Government in the American zone soon asked Jolas to set up an intellectual journal, for which he chose the title *Die Wandlung* (*Metamorphosis*), echoing the Expressionist credo of change for the better. He found a kindred spirit in fellow editor Dolf Sternberger, and they were supported by editorial advisors such as Karl Jaspers and Alfred Weber. Jolas established contact between Sternberger and writers like T. S. Eliot, some of whose poems were published in *Die Wandlung*. Subsequently, Jolas set out upon on an advanced quest for the sobriety of words. He realized that the National Socialists had deeply perverted the German language, and he therefore felt faced with the challenge of a denazification of the German language. He compiled a list of compromised words and banned terms for the journalists at DANA and undertook a critical analysis of Nazi language with Dolf Sternberger, who published a series called "Aus dem Wörterbuch des Unmenschen" ("From the Dictionary of the Monster") in *Die Wandlung*.

Jolas's work as a press officer was completed when he returned to Paris to live with his family and work on the revival of *transition*, but he came back to Munich and Frankfurt only a year later, working as a journalist for the American-controlled *Neue Zeitung*. Moreover, twenty-five years after the "Rambles Through Literary Paris," Jolas reported from Europe again, once more compiling a column, "Across Frontiers," for the European edition of the *New York Herald Tribune*. These contributions were dedicated to the latest European developments, specifically in the French and German literary scene. In his column, the utopian project of transatlantic bridging is necessarily eclipsed by a topical interest in steps toward advancing cooperation and understanding between continental Europe's crucial nations, France and Germany. He does, however, retain his sympathies for the "spiritual," which cause him, for example, long before it would come into vogue, to review the emergence of African literary contributions to the European and global contexts; this literature is no longer seen as coming out of a "dark" continent, but as vital for the expansion of the European discourse. Within these wide parameters, Jolas was particularly interested in the postwar reception of compromised German intellectuals like Ernst Jünger, the most complex representative of the "conservative revolution" of the interwar era, a militarist with a unique literary imagination, who remains suspect in his newly adopted role of a European Paulus. Similar reservations are directed at Martin Heidegger, who had supported National Socialism at some point. Yet Jolas is not quite enthusiastic for Jean-Paul Sartre's version of existentialism as an alternative, as he abhors any type of programmatic "ism," however evolved. Thus his interest lies with Jasper's historically more circumspect philosophical position. In spite of certain signs of change and growth with postwar literary circles like the Gruppe 47, Jolas remains predictably nostalgic for the dynamics of the historical European avant-garde.

—D.D.

Some Notes on Existentialism, Martin Heidegger, and Poetry Sales (November 1, 1949)

In this atomic autumn of 1949 the traveler in search of Europe's culture finds the great capitals congeries of activity. Everywhere the poets, artists, and novelists are busy creating their vision, and ideas are once more exchanged across national borders. Yet it is not a particularly striking year as regards inventions, and a comparison between the two postwar periods—that of the twenties and that of the forties—easily gives advantage to the former. To the intellectual tourist the artistic mood seems to be more quiescent, and the bulk of active ideas would appear to derive principally from the cerebral flashes of an earlier period.

Having just returned to Paris from Frankfurt and Munich (where nothing really new—save perhaps a post-Expressionist mood—is flourishing in the arts), this particular traveler is struck by the Alexandrian splendor of the Seine capital. The autumnal *rentrée* in letters, the plastic arts, and the theater appears to be brilliant and fertile, although breathtaking new schools or "isms"—such as Surrealism, existentialism, Lettrism, and so on—have ceased to emerge in that bewildering sequence of public demonstrations and controversial manifestoes that made certain previous epochs so exhilarating. The poets of the older school, such as Pierre Reverdy, Jules Supervielle, Blaise Cendrars, Henri Michaux, continue to produce with rich maturity, while such younger men as Henri Pichette, Romain

Weingarten, André du Bouchet—to mention only a few—are also ready-ing new books and *plaquettes*. Publishers are inclined to whine about the difficulty of launching new writers, but a number of the big houses—Gallimard, Julliard, Michel, Plon, and others—are nevertheless preparing to present their *poulains* in the race for glory and the literary prizes that will be awarded the end of the year. There is feverish speculation about the new members soon to be elected to the seats left vacant by the deaths of Lucien Descaves and Edmond Jaloux in the Académie Goncourt and the Académie française. Colette was recently elected president of the former *académie,* thus becoming the first woman president of that august insti-tution. Existentialism is still a dominating force, particularly on the Left Bank, and Gallimard has just published Jean-Paul Sartre's latest opus—the third volume of his tetralogy, *Les Chemins de la liberté*—under the title *La Mort dans l'âme.* This time Sartre has plunged deep into the war and given a vivid account of the Nazi occupation of Paris. Existentialist fiction flour-ishes, but where is the poet of the movement? One wonders sometimes whether that school is not essentially anti-poetic. . . .

And speaking of existentialism, it may be of interest to note that one of the founders of that turbulent doctrine, the German philosopher Martin Heidegger, has just celebrated his sixtieth birthday at his Black Forest her-mitage in the French zone of occupied Germany, where he has been living in complete isolation since the Nazi capitulation. According to friends, he has been preparing a major work intended to present the *summum* of his metaphysical explorations. Heidegger recently published two books—said to be fragments of his definitive opus—one a small pamphlet called *Über den Humanismus,* and the other bearing the recondite title of *Holzwege.* The humanistic brochure is a study of modern man's "homelessness." Writ-ten in his customary abstruse style, it is filled with the tortured neologisms that are the despair of his translators. Rejecting both individualism and col-lectivism, he seeks "the truth of being," declaring that "man is not the lord, but the shepherd of that which is." The other work concerns principally his ideas about poetic form in art, with such chapter headings as "Origin of the Work of Art" and "Why Poets?"

Heidegger's disciples believe that his organic notion of philosophical nihil-ism continues to stem from his now famous pamphlet *What Is Metaphysics?* (circa 1932), in which he posited "existential anguish" as the point of depar-ture for his speculations on the genesis of being. He has had less influence in postwar Germany than his famous disciple Jean-Paul Sartre has had in France, and even less than his antipodes, the Heidelberg philosopher Dr. Karl Jaspers, whose existentialism tends more toward a Kierkegaardian, Christian solution. Before the war Heidegger taught at the University of Freiburg, where, in 1937, he delivered an address eulogizing Nazism and embracing the infamous regime. Jaspers, on the other hand, took a vigorously anti-Nazi stand from the very beginning and was forbidden either to lecture or to publish anything during the period of Hitler's despotism. After the war he brought out a pamphlet in which he asserted Germany's guilt before history. In 1947 he left Germany for Basel, where today he teaches at the university while completing his life work. Jaspers was recently one of the principal speakers at the Rencontres Européennes which took place in Geneva early in September.

Before leaving the subject of existentialism, it is curious to recall that discussions about the philosophy played a considerable role during the recent International Congress for Humanistic Studies in Rome. Pope Pius XII, who received the delegates at his residence in Castel Gandolfo, made a devastating attack on both the conceptions and language of Heidegger. He addressed the visiting scientists in the French language, but in speaking of Heidegger he revealed his familiarity with these Teutonic notions. "Human nature," concluded the pope, "can do much when it turns to the Christian faith. . . . For faith is able to save man from the entanglements of technocracy and materialism. . . . Man's destiny does not lie in what Heidegger calls *Geworfenheit*."

The August–September issue of Jean-Paul Sartre's *Temps Modernes* is devoted to an analysis of Western Germany. These documents comprise articles by twenty-three German writers dealing with the war, the occupation, and the Year Zero. Eugen Kogon, author of *The SS State,* who spent [six] years at Buchenwald, analyzes the German people's attitude to the concentration camp, and finds a stubborn attempt to forget the iniquities of the Nazi period. Arnold Bauer relates the ideas and emotions of the "generation of the lost men." There are three articles on German "resistance" against Hitler. Literary creations by Wolfgang Schnurre and Wolfgang Borchert are presented in translation. The general impression of these interesting and revealing documents is that despair and hopelessness dominate the new Germany. It should be emphasized, however, that the material was prepared before the currency reform in June 1948, and therefore does not really give a psychological portrait adequate to today's changed reality.

Young existentialists, Surrealists, epiphanists gathered for a unique occasion before the church of Saint-Séverin in Paris two weeks ago. For Paris now has a poets' fair, after the *foire aux puces,* the *foire aux pains d'epices,* the *foire aux croûtes.* A number of young French poets left their attics and their ivory towers and went into the streets to sell their verbal "wares" to a public that consisted of the typical *Parigot* and a few amateurs. In the picturesque little street of the Prêtres Saint-Séverin, they initiated for the first time a market for the sale of books of verse, *plaquettes,* reviews, and manifestoes. For several days one could see the devotees of Pegasus acting as "barkers" for their creative efforts and appealing to the curious and astonished passersby to buy their productions. Their books were offered from little mobile bookshelves covered with their printed effusions and even with manuscripts.

Among the younger poets who stood before the Saint-Séverin church for many weary hours were Maurice Fombeure, Claudine Chonez, Paul Chaulot, Hervé Bazin, Philippe Dumaine, Jean Rousselot, Jean Lazare, and other refugees from Saint-Germain-des-Prés. The older poets, Francis Carco, André Breton, Jacques Prévert, Jean Cocteau did not appear. It cannot be said, however, that the *poètes des quatre saisons* had a great success, and the sales were practically nonexistent. Nevertheless, they were not discouraged and planned a new fair, this time to be held on the Right Bank— at the Palais Royal—some time after Christmas.

Reemergence of Heidegger (November 1949)

The existentialist philosopher Martin Heidegger is gradually emerging from the isolation in which he has lived in his native Germany for many years. He has just given his first lecture in Baden-Baden, in the French zone of occupied Germany, on the general theme of "Aspects of that which is," and his apodictic statements have aroused widespread discussion. The essay he read marked a continuation of his morbid system and thought and emphasized his nihilism, which leaves no hope to the modern man.

The English poet and editor Stefan Schimanski described some time ago in *The Listener* a visit he had made to Heidegger in his retreat:

> Like a monk in his cell, he lives in the cobweb of his own house of truth, timid by nature, harassed by circumstances, a peasant by birth and tradition. This is not a metaphorical description. On both occasions when I met him, I had to drive for an hour toward the small town of Todtnau, high up in the Black Forest mountains, then to climb still further until the road became a path and all human habitation scattered and invisible. There, on top of a mountain, with nothing but space and wilderness all around, in a minute skiing hut, five hours' walk from Freiburg, I spoke to Heidegger. He had not been to town for six months, when I saw him the second time. His living conditions were primitive; even his books were few; and his only relationship to the world was a stack of writing paper.

Schimanski tries to give an analysis of Heidegger's philosophy in the following words:

Heidegger's so-called nihilism is not far removed from Dostoevsky's interpretation of suffering, which to the Russian not only awakens conscious thought but also has the power to redeem evil. Heidegger agreed when I submitted this comparison to him. He does not deny that man has lost his dignity and that God is absent from the world. But absence, as he stated with emphasis, does not mean nonexistence. It means not being present. Whether or not God will reappear, whether or not man shall regain his dignity—that is none of Heidegger's concern. But he is very much concerned with the possibility of a God and the possibility of man's dignity. To Heidegger both reside in being as such.

"We have," he says in effect,

lost our relationship to being-in-totality. Instead we are rooted in an existence which is a void. Although being surrounds man and is nearest to him, we have moved furthest from it. Yet in this nearness alone—if anywhere—is the decision being taken whether or not God shall deny himself to man and darkness remain; or whether the days of the saints shall dawn. . . . This loss of relationship to the nearest—caused by our lack of ability to think of it—is the real rootlessness of modern man; his homelessness has become the world's destiny; and his own destiny has become his estrangement both from the world and from his fellow men.

In his lecture a few weeks ago, Heidegger stated that he regarded modern technics as man's destiny, as something historic, as "something real within the real." "Man," he said, "is unable to overcome the technological existence, for it cannot be stopped, and is part of his life." He says that "the essence of mechanic is the essence of being in the technological world age." Thus being becomes a danger. To be sure, we are not conscious of it; for during more than two thousand years it looked as if being had been without danger, although the world is obviously full of danger and pitfalls. The real pitfall, he asserts, is the apparent lack of it. Now we are no longer mortal. The man of the mass age does not die, he simply is liquidated and replaced by new ones—just like the mechanical framework.

Heidegger now goes back to his basic idea of universal dread and existential anguish. He says that being frightened by the daemonic quality of technics makes us afraid before the consideration of that which is. He . . .

Heidegger in the Atomic Age (November 1949)

Martin Heidegger, the German existentialist philosopher, lectured recently for the first time in Baden-Baden, in the French zone of occupied Germany. He gave two lectures on the general theme of "Aspects of that which is" in his first public appearance since the capitulation. According to those who attended his apodictic interpretations, his lectures marked a new phase in his evolution motivated by World War II.

I learn from various sources that he philosophized along new lines with respect to technics and its relation to nature, man, god, world, and being. He apparently went beyond Nietzsche and Kierkegaard. He regards now technics as man's destiny, as something historic, as "something real within the real." Man is unable to conquer technics, for it cannot be stopped. He himself is *einbezogen* in it. Man today has become an object that can be liquidated. Man in the age of the masses is replaceable, he says.

Modern technics began with the substantial trait of *bestellen* or manufacture. Contemporary natural science, up to and including nuclear physics, is only the application of this trait of ontological technics. The substance of nature which Kant thought out is the basis. Heidegger says that nature is the "basis of the *Bestand*" of energy and matter. *Das Wesen, man,* he regards also as the constantly exchangeable equal. Its constancy is replaceability.

His basic teaching is in the sentence: "The essence of the framework (*Gestell*) (technics) is the essence of being—in the world age of technics." Thus being becomes a danger. To be sure we are not conscious of it; for it too hides itself. Since two thousand years it looks as if being were dangerless, assured, although the world is obviously full of dangers and distresses.

The apparent lack of distress of being, he says, is the real distress. We all are no longer mortal. The man of the mass age does not die, he falls out (*fällt aus*), is liquidated, is replaced by new ones—like the *Gestell*. Is it possible that technics in the end is more than a man in the hands of man? The being frightened before the daemonic of technics is basically the fear before the consideration of that which is.

He quotes Hölderlin's words, "Where danger is there is also that which rescues." But rescue presupposes an *Einblick* in that which is. Technics must be thought not only in the sense of technical fragmentation. The constellation of being talks to us. Through the *Gestelle* itself (radio and film) we are not aware of the constellation. Refusal of the world negligence of the thing is the highest mystery within the rule of the *Gestell*. Whether God lives or is dead, that comes from the constellation of being. As long as we don't learn while thinking that which is we will never know what will be. Only in the *Einblick* man places himself into the "expanding" world, into the God vicinity of the thing, which is the mirroring quadrangle of sky, earth, of mortal and immortal.

The lectures were followed by discussions. Benno Riefenberg wondered whether in man itself there lies the possibility for a decision. (The concept of liberty had not been mentioned up till then.) Heidegger replied he would not like to go so far, that man should decide himself, what being should be. Then man would be master of being, in other words, free. In this way we would have reached Sartre. That was not possible. It would be important to become "mistakable" again, after we had been "unmistakable" for a long time. He only wanted to open the eyes to that which is. He thought it important to give a suggestion, an insight, . . . not a faith in authority.

Irrealism, Immoralism, Naturalism, Concretism (November 8, 1949)

Blaise Cendrars, who once called himself an "irrealist," is a poet for whom the dynamics of modern life have always constituted a creative stimulus, and in his book of poems entitled *Kodak* (1914) he gives an almost startling account of his position with regard to photographic reality. However, his biographer, the late Louis Parrot, in a recently published volume entitled *Blaise Cendrars* (in the collection *Poètes d'aujourd'hui*), reveals a hitherto unknown Cendrars, a poet haunted by the esoteric and the luminous. This little book consists of poems and prose poems, as well as photographs and manuscript reproductions.

Cendrars, who is a lyrical globetrotter, the migratory poet par excellence, and who turns up at the most unexpected moments in Rio de Janeiro or New York, from where he usually departs with a minimum of fuss, possesses also, apparently, the inner eye, a transcendental awareness, a metaphysical vision. In his last book, he relates how he discovered in the south of France, during his activities in the Maquis, the biography of an Italian monk who had the gift of levitation. In this little volume, in which he equates flight with creation, Cendrars pays homage to the medieval visionary and presents detailed documents by contemporaries who witnessed the flight and sudden loss of gravitational force.

One of the sensations of intellectual Paris is the impatiently awaited publication, in a literary weekly, of the correspondence between André Gide and Paul Claudel. Two hundred letters were exchanged between them, the first dated 1899 and the last 1926, when it became evident to both that they had nothing more to say to each other. The underlying problem of our time—that of religious belief—seems to have been the real subject of this remarkable correspondence, and it was only when the author of *L'Annonce faite à Marie* realized the futility of his attempt to convert to the Catholic faith the author of *L'Immoraliste* that all contact ceased. Both men have now celebrated their eightieth birthdays, a negligible fact, however, when one considers the extent of their *rayonnement*. For Claudel continues to be one of the most frequently played of living French dramatists, and Gide one of the most widely read prose writers anywhere. Gide's present activities include a series of twenty interviews now being heard over the French national radio. It was recently announced that the Vatican theater will open its Holy Year program with Claudel's *Annonce*.

Before leaving this generation of octogenarian giants, the news that Henri Matisse, the greatest color-magician of the century, has been working some time on the decoration of a convent near Vence, perhaps surprised certain of his admirers. Those who have seen his sketches say that the artist has outlined the theological-mystic elements of the life of Jesus not only with his usual luminous color but also with a reverence for the theme that will astonish the spectator. Matisse has been quoted as saying that he wanted to make his chapel a place where one might like to live, rather than a place of gloom.

The American influence on new German writing is considerable, and it is especially Ernest Hemingway whose concise, lyrical form of the modern narrative sets the pattern for the majority of the younger writers in Germany today. This influence was quite manifest during the recent meeting of the Group 47, in the little town of Utting, on the Bavarian Ammersee, where some fifty writers representing both the pre- and postwar periods gathered for a week's exchange of ideas and critical conversation. Swiss and French representatives participated in the discussions, especially Enrique Beck, of Zurich, who spoke on "Poetry as Order and Adventure." Certain speakers noted that the economic difficulties of the writer in France are not entirely dissimilar to those in Western Germany, and many present admitted that they were obliged to supplement their earnings by working for "pulp" magazines. Walter Kolbenhoff, whose writings show strong traces of the Hemingway influence, and whose first novel, *Of Our Flesh and Blood,* has appeared in English translation in the United States, read excerpts from his latest novel, a vagabond story situated between the two wars. A new literary form for Germany, derived from the American short story, could be seen in Franz Josef Schneider's two stories, "Tomorrow Fear Will End" and "The Almond Ripens in Broscher's Garden." Another writer with neo-American influence was Heinz Ulrich, author of "A Nice Story." The form now developing would appear to be a nicely balanced mixture of reportage and lyrical narrative, and certain Western observers were reminded not only of Hemingway but also of Faulkner and Kay Boyle. Günther Eich, a poet of real stature, read from his latest work. He admitted that he makes his living by writing gewgaws for the films. Before separating, the group decided to invite writers from a number of foreign countries to be present at their 1950 conference.

A Strindberg revival would appear to be taking place in Europe today. The actor-producer Fritz Kortner, who returned to the Continent some time ago after thirteen years in the United States, is now playing to packed houses in *The Father,* at the Schauspielhaus in Munich. He gives a remarkable performance, all the more tragic for its overtones of humor and grotesqueness. The naturalism of the play has, however, obfuscated certain theater lovers who have declared that they prefer a lighter form of entertainment to the gloomy nihilism of the Swede. In Zurich the same author's *Dance of Death,* with Rudolf Forster in the main role, is eliciting the bravos of both critics and public; and in Paris, at the Gaité-Montparnasse, Roger Blin is playing the Student in his own sensitively staged production of *The Spook Sonata.*

Jean-Paul Sartre's success of two seasons ago, *Mort sans sépulture,* had its opening performance in the West German federal capital of Bonn recently. During the scene depicting the infliction of torture on the resistants by members of the Milice, a number of spectators left the hall, protesting loudly.

On his first visit to Western Germany, T. S. Eliot is being given an enthusiastic reception by German students and intellectuals. The Anglo-American poet and Nobel Prize winner arrived Oct. 28 in Hamburg and immediately began a tour which will take him to Braunschweig, Göttingen, Münster, Berlin, Hermannsburg, Frankfurt, Stuttgart, and Munich. He delivered his first lecture in Hamburg on "The Aims of the Poetic Drama." On this occasion he outlined how he himself had used a "broken mirror" in the writing of his *Murder in the Cathedral* which, he said, attempted to make the spectator witness a drama of the fourteenth century while listening to the language of the seventeenth. He insisted that the modern play may also be written in verse.

The interest in Eliot's work and personality is great. Before setting out on his journey he gave interviews to German newspapers in London, and he has continued to maintain cordial relations with the press in Germany. In an interview with the British-licensed newspaper *Die Welt,* he discussed the possibility of founding an international newspaper or review. "The main difficulty of such a scheme," he said,

> would, of course, be the problem of language. Either each contributor would have to be presented in his original tongue—the contributors from small countries as well as those writing in the better-known languages—or the publication could not really be international. In this case, however, only a few people in every land would benefit from it. One might also limit linguistic presentation to the two or three most important European languages, excluding the smaller countries, and publish one or several simultaneous translations of each original contribution. This last solution, however, would be technically complicated and above all expensive. . . . What I have long had in mind is a group of reviews, one in each capital, which might have much in common on the intellectual plane. The task of each one would be to bring its readers into contact with the best foreign writing. Thus there would not be one review, but half a dozen in as many languages.

Mr. Eliot added that the danger of intellectual and moral lack of color was also inherent in the notion of an international review. "A review expressing as many viewpoints as possible would surely have none of its own. In my opinion, in order to have character, a magazine would need to be conducted by a group of people who are not only representative of different nations, but who share the same intellectual outlook." In Hamburg, replying to an interviewer who addressed him "as a passionate proponent of the Western spirit," and who sought to learn his ideas as to how this spirit might become a "common possession," Eliot said:

> Both the past and the future are based on it. This does not exclude the possibility of the growth of another new element for common possession. I also think it erroneous to link this unity together with economic

and political aspects. It has always been my opinion that Christianity should erect no cultural barriers. No cultural influences should be excluded, shall we say, because they are of non-European origin or out of consideration for political frontiers. Culture is not a machine. It stems from the whole of life. And that is always fluid.

Switzerland stands today, as before, at the artistic crossroads of Europe. In Zurich, Geneva, Lausanne, Winterthur, and even in other small cities, may be seen examples of both modernistic and classical painting. At the Kunsthaus in Zurich, an exhibition of three "concretists," Antoine Pevsner, Georges Vantongerloo, and Max Bill, presents experiments in space and time that are attracting interested crowds. These geometrical conceits are based on a purely spatial experience and go well beyond mere abstract art. At Winterthur a twentieth-century exhibition of canvases loaned from private collections, comprising the works of Redon, Maillol, Rousseau, Utrillo, Matisse, Picasso, Marquet, Bonnard, Giacometti, Lautrec, and Rodin, is now in progress, and in Lucerne an exhibition of "Three Centuries of French Painting," in which Henri Matisse and Marc Chagall triumphed, has just closed, after a showing of several months. Schaffhausen is presenting an exhibition of Rembrandt and works by such of Rembrandt's contemporaries as Vermeer, Fabritius, Franz Hals, and others. In Basel, a show of French Impressionists includes Corot, Manet, Cézanne, Degas, Pissarro, Monet, Sisley.

Arnold J. Toynbee, the British philosopher-historian, has just arrived in Germany from London to lecture before the Joachim Jungius Society on "The Uniformity and Uniqueness of History." In a brilliant image-laden talk he told his audience of the result of his empirical speculations.

He said that he saw hope for mankind in the apocalypse of World War II, and declared that his comparative history of the world allows of continuous evolution into a better existence. His optimistic picture of Western civilization elicited tremendous applause. Toynbee pointed out that "the national epoch is coming to a close" and that a true universal epoch is about to begin. He regards history as a kind of phenomenal form of the celestial kingdom, thus leading it into theology.

Origin and Aim of History
(November 15, 1949)

A new interpretation of world history comes from Basel, where the former Heidelberg professor Karl Jaspers—one of the leading modern exponents of the existentialist philosophy—has just published a thesis entitled *Origin and Aim of History,* which promises to create something of a stir in intellectual circles.

In contradistinction to the pessimistic exponents of the decline of Western civilization (one thinks immediately of Spengler and his followers), Jaspers believes that history is still in its infancy, and he situates its beginnings some time about 500 years B.C. He points out that at this period Confucius and Lao-tse were teaching in China, Zoroaster in Iran, and Buddha in India. In Palestine the prophets were forewarning the people, and it was then that Greece gave birth to Homer and the philosophers.

Jaspers draws attention to the enigmatic phenomenon of these simultaneous events in China, India, and southern Europe, as well as to the fact that the Occident continues to live by the basic categories of thought they engendered. He offers no explanation as to how this flowering should have occurred among civilizations that were so widely scattered over the face of the ancient continents and had little or no contact with one another, but points out that no other humanistic unity has ever existed or exists today.

Speculating about the future, Jaspers declares that history is the process of man's struggle toward a consciousness of his own being and that it is through his attempt to understand the essence of existence that he is gradually transformed. The philosopher notes, however, that man does not appear to change biologically and that he can conceivably lose his traditions and revert to mass murder and cannibalism.

In the second part of the book, Jaspers examines the role of modern technology and the functions of the masses as well as the progress of socialist organization, world unity, and faith. He concludes that it is still within man's power to metamorphose himself into "a unique, irreplaceable being," capable of conquering nature.

History is transition, he says, and the freedom of the soul with respect to God is never lost. He urges that this desirable transformation be undertaken through a reconstitution of the religious life, along biblical lines. It is the belief of Jaspers that we must re-create ourselves and "make a new attempt at realization of what is within the grasp of man." The book is optimistic in its outlook, a fact that will undoubtedly astound many who are the prey of a darker vision.

Following in the footsteps of the late Georges Bernanos, author of *France Versus the Robots* and the standard-bearer of a virulent anti-machine philosophy, André Siegfried, of the Académie française, recently expressed a similar if more moderately couched opinion.

Siegfried, it will be recalled, is the author of *America Comes of Age,* that important post-World War I analysis of the United States which, perhaps more than any other book by a foreign writer, made twentieth-century America aware of both the stature and problems of their machine-age civilization. In an article entitled "La Machine au pilori," Siegfried pointed with satisfaction to the current toward a New Humanism to be found in the University of Chicago review, *Measure, a Critical Journal.*

He commented:

This Humanism will be called reactionary by all those who . . . condemn culture in the name of technology. . . . It is, however, in the real Western tradition. If the United States is to lead the world, the contribution of technical superiority is not enough. The United States has moreover something else to give. I am not among those who believe that America expresses herself through the machine and the dollar. I believe that she expresses herself quite as much through the still-vital eighteenth-century Jeffersonian tradition, and this is an essentially humanistic tradition.

Those who followed the series of talks given in Paris a year ago by the veteran Hungarian philosopher and esthetician George Lukács will undoubtedly be surprised to learn that this apparently very orthodox defender of a "wholesome as opposed to an unwholesome art" has recently been the object of a virulent attack, published in the official *Tarsadalmi Szemle,* in connection with the appearance of his latest work, *Literature and Democracy.*

The author of the indictment, Laszlo Rudas, accuses the former party spokesman of "cosmopolitanism" at a time when, on the contrary, "a complete and definitive break with Occidental culture, in whatever form, is essential." According to François Fegto, who relates the incident in the October number of *Paru,* Lukács has been retired from his post as professor of esthetics at the University of Budapest.

More recent accounts state that, as twice before in his rather spectacular career, Lukács has now made his mea culpa, and that his reinstatement may be expected.

The return of emigrants who fled Hitlerian Germany continues. Among the latest to go back is Elisabeth Bergner, famous actress and film star. Miss Bergner arrived home via Zurich, where she stopped long enough to give a German-language recital consisting of readings from the Bible, Angelus Silesius, and so on.

In Munich, which was the scene of her 1933 debut, her program included recitations from the works of Arthur Schnitzler, and excerpts from Shaw's *Saint Joan.* Although the large and critical audience would have preferred her in a conventional dramatic vehicle, the reaction to her recitations was cordial, if lacking in enthusiasm.

Miss Bergner told a reporter that she hoped to regain her place in the German theater and that this recital tour was little more than a visiting card. She plans to visit Germany, Holland, Scandinavia, Austria, and Palestine.

After spending the war years in the United States, Salvador Dali, the Catalonian Surrealist, is back in Barcelona, where he is busy working on the decoration for a new play, *Don Juan's Return,* which will be produced at the Maria-Guerera Theater.

Another Surrealist painter, Max Ernst, has arrived in France from Arizona, where he has been living since 1944. Ernst belonged to André Breton's group at the time of its inception in the twenties. He has brought back from the United States a collection of canvases which will be seen in exhibitions throughout Europe this winter. He is at present on the Riviera.

The death of J. W. Dunne, the British engineer and psychologist, reminds me of the great interest James Joyce manifested for all unconscious phenomena. During several weeks in 1934, I read out loud to him Dunne's work on "prophetic" dreams, entitled *An Experiment with Time,* which had just appeared. At that time Joyce himself often related his dreams to me—dreams which on several occasions seemed to have foreshadowed events in his life. Dunne's later book, *The Serial Universe,* which assumes many egos in the human consciousness participating in a metamorphosis of time, was read attentively by Joyce while he was working on *Finnegans Wake.*

Edouard Dujardin, author of *Les Lauriers sont coupés,* died recently in Paris. He was one of the better-known poets of the Symbolist period, but since World War I his work had been followed only by a few connoisseurs. When James Joyce published *Ulysses* in 1922, he reminded his friend and admirer Valéry Larbaud that the technique of the interior monologue had been used some twenty years earlier in Dujardin's *Les Lauriers,* and when the French translation of Joyce's supernovel appeared, he inscribed a copy to Dujardin as follows: "A Edouard Dujardin, le larron impénitent, J. J."

Dujardin was an old *Parigot,* possessed a considerable wit and, when necessary, aggressive energy, which showed itself one evening in the early thirties, when the French translation of Joyce's "Anna Livia Plurabelle" was being read in Adrienne Monnier's bookshop to a distinguished audience of French, British, and Irish writers. Among them was Dujardin, who listened to the neologist carnival with concentrated attention.

Suddenly, while Mlle. Monnier was reading the subtle French version of Joyce's hermetic prose, there stumbled into the back room of the shop a young American poet from the Middle West, one of the pillars of the expatriate group that was turbulently visible and audible in every bistro in Montparnasse at the time. The young man was in an advanced state of ebullient alcoholism, and he obstreperously interrupted the recital until he found a seat beside M. Dujardin. Soon he began making faces at the audience, mumbling dark words at the venerable French poet, and showing complete irreverence toward the proceedings in the front room. Finally, he decided to divert M. Dujardin's attention by humming "Auprès de ma blonde."

At this point the old gentleman rose calmly and gave the Midwesterner such a smack that it reverberated throughout the two rooms. Strange to say, this did the trick. The garrulous intruder suddenly became quiet and listened reverently till the end of the reading.

From Rome come reports that Giovanni Papini, the sixty-eight-year-old poet and philosopher, is about to reenter the literary arena after a long silence. Papini will shortly publish two books, one a lengthy study of Michelangelo and the other a 2,000-page volume entitled *World Judgment*, which he began during the war. The poet, who is almost blind, started to write this latter book while living in the refuge of a monastery during the height of the battle in his native Tuscany.

Curiosity about this forthcoming literary event is considerable in Italy, and it is expected that the Catholic concert will present a modern apocalyptic work of sensational nature. Papini's name was mentioned recently in connection with the Nobel Prize.

A German Nationalist (December 6, 1949)

A new novel by Ernst Jünger, *Heliopolis,* has been announced for early appearance in the French zone of Germany.

This nationalist, militarist writer who, after 1918, eulogized war in a book entitled *Storm of Steel,* and during the second war brought out that remarkable novel *On the Marble Cliffs,* is probably the most gifted writer in Germany today.

The first volume of Jünger's diary, *Gardens and Roads,* which detailed his experiences during the 1940 invasion of France, was published during the war. An expression of nationalist pride and arrogance, it was for a time a bestseller although, for as yet unknown reasons, it was eventually banned by the Nazis.

Under the title *Irradiations,* he recently issued the second volume of this diary, covering the years 1941 to 1944, during which a change of heart would appear to have taken place. Here the author accentuates an alleged antipathy toward the Nazi regime and even refers with astonishing frankness to the "lemuroid" nature of German cruelty. The arch-nationalist has become metamorphosed into a dreamer and even a mystic, a lover of international peace and the domestic virtues. In 1943, having perceived the inevitable end of the Hitler regime, Jünger was a penitent man, one who felt morally impelled to write an "appeal for peace to the youth of Europe." (This would have perhaps been more convincing if he had first addressed himself to the youth of Germany.)

Despite these concessions, however, the general impression is that of a continental German who has no genuine feeling for Western democracy, one who lives and thinks in an atmosphere of traditional Teutonic nebulousness, and the reader closes the book unconvinced that the author's conversion to anti-militarist thinking is a sincere one.

Jünger's influence on the postwar generation in Germany is today very great. He is being widely discussed, exegetical books on his doctrines are becoming increasingly numerous, and it has become impossible to ignore him.

In a recent essay published by *Der Monat*—edited by Melvin Lasky and probably the best international magazine in Western Germany—Peter de Mendelssohn has sought to evaluate the work of Jünger. De Mendelssohn himself is a bilingual writer who left Germany for England before Hitler came to power and not long after began to publish novels in the English language. During the war he returned to Germany with the British army.

Under the title *Counter-Irradiations,* he examines Jünger's diary with almost clinical precision. He finds in the 400-page account of wartime Paris, as seen through the eyes of a German writer, a multitude of serious contradictions. According to de Mendelssohn, Jünger believes in the possibility of a modern revival of the age of "knighthood." The critic finds, however, that Jünger's definitions still retain the militaristic aura of his earlier works, and he points out that nowhere, throughout the book, is there an allusion to the simple historic fact that it was Hitler and his Nazis that began the war against the democracies. For de Mendelssohn, Jünger's religious conversion is merely a return to a too-recent militaristic past in which Jünger's god was identical with military power.

De Mendelssohn's thesis has both psychological and literary force and, in the face of Jünger's growing influence, it constitutes a necessary *mise au point.* It is to be hoped that it will be the point of departure for a more complete study of the German, an up-to-date version of Jacques Rivière's classic *L'Allemand,* which the late editor of the *NRF* wrote as a prisoner during the First World War.

In a recent interview granted to a Paris correspondent, the existentialist philosopher Martin Heidegger stated that he had never read a line of Franz Kafka's or Jean-Paul Sartre's works. Heidegger gave as his favorite book by a contemporary French writer Antoine de St. Exupéry's *Le Petit Prince,* a heavily annotated copy of which he keeps in a convenient spot on his bookshelves. "Here we find the beginning of a philosophy of technology," he said.

Replying to a politically oriented question, Heidegger declared: "Politics cannot be isolated from philosophy, since both have metaphysical implications. As for ethics, there exist as many shades of ethical conduct as there do individuals, so that any attempt to find a unique solution is impossible, even absurd. Man must keep in a state of spiritual disquiet, in order that he may find his solutions through his own disquiet and anguish." The sixty-year-old philosopher told the interviewer that his recently completed work *Holzwege* is now being translated into French.

The controversy initiated by the Italian painter Giorgio de Chirico, who has announced the death of modern art, continues. De Chirico once belonged to the Surrealist advance-guard, but he now regards all manifestations of Cubist, Expressionist, Surrealist, or abstract art as mere "street-fair painting," and he has asserted that the public in Europe and America is "tired of these ugly pictures." He has, in fact, only contempt for the international art world, even hurling his objurgations at such precursors as Cézanne and Vollard.

"Modern art must die," says de Chirico, "for it has permitted persons without conviction and without scruple to deceive their neighbors and exploit dishonestly human vanity and stupidity."

Although these ideas are much the same as expressed by de Chirico some twenty years ago in his book *Hebdomeros,* this more recent declaration has elicited renewed opposition among advocates of the modern idioms, and only a small group in Rome, the so-called Instinctivists, has accepted his pronunciamento.

Meanwhile, also from Rome, comes the news that the dapper Salvador Dali, early Surrealist and former impenitent diabolist, has not only made his voyage to Canossa, but has succeeded in converting even the Vatican to the notion that a statue of the Virgin with a show-window torso possesses heightened "spiritual" possibilities.

The bewildered public, which after many years of rather rough handling in these matters must by now be somewhat inured to new suggestions, will probably react with a shrug to both these events and conclude simply that "when the Devil is old, the Devil a saint would be."

In that mysterious old building opposite the church of Saint-Germain-des-Prés which houses under one roof and one concierge the Deux Magots, La Hune, and the Club Saint-Germain, and which bears over its main portal the slightly archaic inscription: "Société pour l'Encouragement de l'Industrie Nationale," Jean Wahl's "Collège philosophique" inaugu-rated last week its fourth season with a talk by Wladimir Weidlé on "Le trompe-l'oeil de l'esthétique."

At the suggestion of certain of his more academically minded colleagues, Jean Wahl, who is himself probably one of the most attentively followed lecturers at the Sorbonne, has agreed to change the title of these extracur-ricular discussions to "Colloques philosophiques," the name by which they will be known henceforth.

The December program announces nine meetings to take place before Christmas, the discussions to be led by Professor E. Minkowski, Boris de Schloezer, Clémence Ramnoux, Lionel Abel, J. Beaufret, Lévy-Strauss, and others. After the first of the year, Merleau-Ponty, Jankélévitch, Gurvitch, Lacan, Médieu, de Broglie—to mention only a few—will be heard.

Jean Wahl recently made a tour of the Dutch universities, where he spoke on the subject of existentialism.

The Absent Avant-Garde (February 7, 1950)

The situation of literature and the arts in the world today presents a curious anomaly: for the first time in many years there would appear to exist no avant-garde, no cohesive group possessed of an intellectual esthetic conviction that is sufficiently arresting and dynamic to form the basis of a real "movement," in the etymological sense of this word.

Not that there aren't to be seen here and there individuals whose lonely, exasperated gesturings only succeed in attracting attention to their anomaly and more especially to their own persons. The ex-Rumanian "Lettrist," Isidor Isou, who, in the Paris of 1947, tried vociferously to take over certain inventions of another postwar generation, is one of these. (Isou will bear watching, however, for he is young and active and he is also a proselytizer.) Another is the former New Yorker and Parisian Henry Miller, now settled out California way and who, although nearing the three-score milestone, is still mailing out manifestoes of his anarchic credo with a conviction that their contents would hardly seem to warrant. "Life is a phenomenon," announces the Sage of Big Sur, "that has neither rule nor morality." Continuing, we learn that he "spits on seriousness and the beards of dignified old men" (what to do about the seriousness and beards of undignified young men is not indicated); that culture is a delusion and a snare and that you can't cultivate your intelligence, anyway. In conclusion, we are urged for inspiration to turn to "our hearts, our sex, and our heads." (To be filed, in my modest opinion, under B, for balderdash, or P, for platitudes.)

The Last "Ism"

Unfortunately, the last great "ism"—existentialism—which is in reality much older than it seems to the general public, has shown no esthetic dimension. On the contrary, it is not entirely impossible that it may to a certain extent have precipitated the present state of affairs. For existentialism has remained primarily a philosophical or ontological aspiration, at once a new and an old ethos with many possible interpretations: atheistic or Christian, materialistic or spiritual; and Jean-Paul Sartre, despite his dynamism, is anything but a literary inventor.

As for Surrealism—now nearly thirty years old—it has become a sort of generic term for the merely macabre and deformed that is indiscriminately applied to fashions and paintings, to literature and theatrical settings, without awareness of its unifying concept. Breton's vision, however, was once a great purifying movement which swept across continents, and it has, in fact, fructified two entire generations. (Like Romanticism, from which it stems, there is no reason, either, why it should not fructify future generations, its ferment having remained intact.) Dadaism, on the other hand, which preceded Surrealism, is dead—quite dead—despite the attempts made by three of its founders, Tristan Tzara, Hans Arp, and Richard Huelsenbeck, to resuscitate its once witty, nihilistic cadaver.

In other words, the merry time of experimentations would seem to be over for the moment and the "isms," which were once living organisms possessing an electric potency that delineated our confused subjective tendencies and created formulae capable of becoming veritable spearheads, have given way to a period of groping, solitary research for a new "reality" that may well last for years.

Dead Branches

Significant of this trend is the gesture of Herbert Read, one of England's most famous modernists, who has apparently turned his back on what is generally termed "modern" art.

In a recent essay, he made a frontal attack on the plastic expressions of the last decades and urged as well new methods for teaching art to the generations being formed. It is Read's opinion that the general public is not the least interested in modern art, and he goes so far as to question even the future existence of painting. State-inspired museums, he feels, can do little toward the development either of public taste or that of the artist himself.

In France, an analogous attack, this time aimed at contemporary letters, has been made with far less amenity by Julien Gracq, a younger novelist and playwright in the Surrealist tradition (his best-known work is *Le Château d'Argol*) who, in an article entitled "La Littérature à l'estomac," in the January number of *Empédocle,* states that the reading public has been systematically deceived by the critics through their eulogy of mediocre bestsellers and exploitations of personalities. He also attacks what he considers the hypocrisy of certain littérateurs, and pokes scathing fun at the so-called great writers of 1950, more specifically at existentialism, which is his bête noire. "We have reached a point," says Gracq, "when in literature—and this time there's no joking allowed—it is Caliban who has the floor. Metaphysics has landed in literature with a thud of heavy boots that invariably commands respect," . . . and he adds: "A friend of mine, the editor of a literary review, has expressed to me his dismay before the rising tide of unreadable Jasperian, Husserlian, Kierkegaardian manuscripts that pile up each day on his desk."

To some the picture may seem a bleak one. Personally, I welcome these gestures of aggressivity. Our troubled apocalyptic time may not be conducive to artistic innovation. Sawing off the dead branches, however, is an essential feature of preparation for a new flowering.

Recorded Biography

Just as the cinema is being used more and more frequently to preserve for posterity an authentic image of the men and women who mark our time, so the new biographical form that consists of recorded interviews with persons who knew the subject, will probably give access to incidents and impressions that, in many cases, would never have been written down. The BBC has already in its archives such an "eyewitness" account of the late William Butler Yeats, which it presented to the public over a year ago. Now it has announced a similar recording (Third Program, Feb. 13, 17) to be devoted to the personality and works of James Joyce, who died in Zurich in 1941.

Since Joyce, like his own *Ulysses,* was a great traveler, the author of the program, the Irish poet W. R. Rodgers, has been obliged to make numerous visits to the various cities in which Joyce lived. In addition to these trips, however, not the least of his difficulties has been the reluctance of many who had known Joyce to record their reminiscences. Joyce himself was extremely reticent; the reaction was comprehensible. Although in most cases Rodgers was able to conquer this hesitation, unfortunately, several persons whose testimony would have been of great interest did not record. Many others did, however, both in Ireland and on the Continent, and the result—later to be consigned to the BBC archives—should be of inestimable value to future biographers.

Lord Russell

The English philosopher Lord Russell visited Paris last week, where he spoke on three occasions: before the Société française de philosophie, on "Liberty of the Individual and the State"; before the Centre d'études de politique étrangère, on "Problems Confronting Political Democracy Today"; and at a meeting of the Colloques philosophiques, on "The Position of the Philosopher in Times of Crisis."

On this last subject, Lord Russell expressed the opinion that although history contains illustrious examples of different types of conduct, ranging from participation through action to complete detachment, detachment today is impossible. It is the philosopher's duty, he declared, to teach men to think clearly, to maintain freedom of discussion, and to practice at all times an "extreme" form of veracity.

A curious detail of his visit was that on all three of these occasions Lord Russell, whose distrust of Communism is no secret, was accompanied by an unobtrusive, though adequate, police protection.

German Letters Today (February 21, 1950)

The postwar generation of German writers has not yet found the road back to the European integration which, before Nazism, constituted the literary ideal of twentieth-century letters, and although a lot is being published, one has the impression that there is no lasting voice to be heard. Rainer Maria Rilke and Stefan George have many followers. Here and there too, one even hears echoes of Expressionism. As with most "neo" movements, however, the present-day exponents lack the vigor and profundity of the founders. The picture is too often little else than that of an amalgam of old-fashioned Naturalism with a modern existentialism that is both cynical and pessimistic.

The majority of the poets whose work has come to my attention in the last year seem still to be living under the aegis of a strictly central European consciousness and, although this was probably to be expected, one is nevertheless constantly disappointed not to feel in their creations the authentic Occidental signature which, for a brief period, marked the era of Weimar.

Vocabulary Purge Overdue

To begin with, an indispensable purge of vocabulary is long overdue, for in the plethora of trite verse that is to be found in the magazines, there are still evidences of the baleful influence of Nazi banality. To be sure, Dolf Sternberger, editor of the now defunct *Wandlung* did, with his *Vocabulary of the Monster*, initiate an important semantic *epuration*. But the evil clichés of the Goebbels machine are still rooted in the minds of many writers, and such Hitlerian terms as "Gedankengut," "Betreuung," and so on still pullulate. (Just here it should be stated that the death of *Wandlung* was universally regretted. It was the first serious review to be licensed by the American Military Government, in 1945, and it gave many new poets, who do not enjoy the outlet of the "little magazines" so prevalent elsewhere, a much-needed forum.)

But in addition to the problem of needed eliminations, none among the numerous poets I have read during these last months seems to possess the savage will toward verbal adventure that characterized certain predecessors who fairly reveled in the invention of new words and grammatical arrangements, and who in fact gave to lyricism the language required to express the psychology of depth. There is no Georg Heym, no August Stramm or Rudolf Borchardt to be found among the German poets writing today.

On the contrary, the most remarkable tendencies are a return to Classicism, Neo-Romanticism, and a sort of apocalyptism. The outstanding names are those of Günther Eich and Elisabeth Langgässer, both of whom show genuine creative faculties and technical mastery. Others are Egon Holthusen, who is profoundly influenced by T. S. Eliot, and Wilhelm Lehmann, a nature-poet possessing Dionysian imagination.

Western Influence

The fact that he represents a much-needed contact with the outside world may explain the liberating force of the recently published verses by Maurice Gumpert, who has just been in Germany after having lived as an émigré in America during the Hitler regime. His poems, *Gedichte aus der Fremde,* in which the atmosphere of America's great spaces and the genuine friendliness of its people find powerful expression, are also lacerating autobiographical confessions, cries of uprooted loneliness. "Never can we fugitives find peace," he writes,

Until our fists have torn out the weeds
Until our liberated hands
Have touched wounded German earth again.

Storytellers and Reviews

More fortunate than the poets as regards publishing, the storytellers find ready outlet in such well-established houses as that of Suhrkamp, in Frankfurt, which recently brought out excellent translations of Hemingway's *For Whom the Bell Tolls* and Saroyan's *The Human Comedy.* There is also the old firm of Rowohlt, which is bringing out a monthly magazine with the English title of *Story,* entirely devoted to translations of international writers. *Story's* current issue contains work by Eudora Welty, James Thurber, Curzio Malaparte, Carl Zuckmayer, and even—Knut Hamsun.

Interesting to observe is the postwar influence of the review *Hochland,* founded by the late Karl Muth some forty years ago. This Catholic magazine was suppressed by the Nazis in 1936 and revived by the American authorities in 1945. It has succeeded in maintaining its high intellectual quality and, as before, its pages are divided between creative writing and speculation along neo-Thomist lines. Recent issues published poems by Claudel, Fargue, Guardini, Bunin, and Péguy.

The *Frankfurter Hefte,* edited by Eugen Kogon and Walter Dirks, is an aggressive polemical magazine publishing a continuous examination of the democratic philosophy by Kogon and his young disciples. Kogon spent [six] years in the Buchenwald camp and is the author of *The SS State,* one of the earliest and most remarkable of the works that have appeared throughout Europe on the subject of the world of the concentration camp.

Another, more esthetically orientated magazine, *Prisma* (formerly called *Vision*), publishes poems and prose of the Expressionist era as well as reprints from the classics.

Abstractionism in Denmark

Raymond Cogniat, editor of the French weekly *Arts,* writing his impressions of a recent visit to New York, expressed his astonishment that abstract art, which "in certain other circles is now considered to have been a passing mode already ended," should still be so much in favor in the United States.

According to a letter from Copenhagen signed Frank Rubin (*Art News and Review,* London), the same situation would appear to exist in Denmark, where, writes this correspondent, a widely commented exhibition of abstract art was held recently under the auspices of an organization of younger artists, grouped together under the title "Linjen" and mainly interested in abstract art. Beside the work of "Linjen" members, the exhibition included examples of that of such pioneer abstractionists as Kandinsky, Arp, and Le Corbusier, as well as a number of non-Danish contemporaries: Domela, Hartung, Massen, and others.

Rubin reveals that, until this exhibition, the works of Arp, Kandinsky, and Klee were practically unknown in Denmark and, in fact, Klee is not even represented in the current exhibition. In addition, all three have been ignored by those responsible for the collections owned by the Danish government. The result of this long quarantine against an experiment that began elsewhere in the twenties is that these works, looked at in 1950 by new eyes, seem "new, puzzling, and obscure," and they have caused considerable "stir and discussion." They have also, apparently, given rise to a new generation of abstractionists, more "barren, more frighteningly intellectual" than their predecessors and who are seeking "parallels with modern atomic theories" at a time when, in other capitals, most of the younger artists are groping toward a new realism.

Any attempt to draw conclusions or to explain these manifestations of an identical esthetic time lag in as widely distant parts of the world as Denmark and the United States would be vain, for the causes must be multiple and of a quite different order in the two countries. It might be pertinent to recall again, however, that nowhere does there exist so direct, so immediate a contact between the artist and his public as is to be found in France today. The light of Paris is not the only explanation of the fact that it remains, par excellence, the ideal painter's city.

Negro Culture (March 14, 1950)

The work of Negro writers, whether they live in Africa, Europe, or the American hemisphere, seems generally to follow the main current of contemporary creative expression, and this despite the recentness of its inclusion in world literature. Their contributions are nevertheless frequently marked by a luxuriance of image and emotional antennae which may well indicate that here is a distinctive literary vein as potentially rich and "different" as their musical vein has shown itself to be. In any case, whether they write in English, French, or one of the many Caribbean derivations of Spanish (not to mention the numerous African languages), they represent an increasingly articulate viewpoint that will need more and more to be taken into consideration.

It is because of these facts that *Présence africaine,* a review entirely devoted to Negro creation, has quickly made a unique place for itself among contemporary Paris publications. Edited by the African poet Alioune Diop, its contributors are usually of Negro origin, but it also boasts the friendly patronage and occasional collaboration of André Gide, Albert Camus, Michel Leiris, Emmanuel Mounier, Paul Rivet, Jean-Paul Sartre, and Richard Wright. The seven issues that have appeared thus far compose a representative anthology of poems, stories, and chronicles dealing with the Negro world and comprising not only the world of writers from the French African colonies, but also poems and prose by American Negro writers, in the original English, as well as studies of native Negro poetry and folklore in Brazil and the Antilles. (Somewhat similar in aim to the volume *The*

Poetry of the Negro, edited in America in 1948 by Langston Hughes and Arna Bontemps.)

It is the African continent, however, that constitutes the underlying theme: Africa, no longer the "dark" continent of Conrad's *Heart of Darkness,* or even the moral quagmire of Graham Greene's more recent *Heart of the Matter,* but a great reservoir of spiritual and cultural dynamism, a universe whose magical vision of the Magdalenian *homo divinans* presents striking analogies with certain twentieth-century modes of European thinking.

Bantu Philosophy

Thus the major part of the current issue is devoted to an *enquête* on the subject of "Bantu Philosophy," as presented in a work by the Dutch Franciscan priest Father Placide Tempels. Among the replies are those of the Sorbonne philosophers Gaston Bachelard and Jean Wahl; the Catholic existentialist philosopher and playwright Gabriel Marcel; the novelist Albert Camus; and others.

The existence of this deeply intuitive philosophy, which Father Tempels had the opportunity of studying during long years of missionary work, gives the lie to the generally accepted notion that the Bantu is a man of "primitive" or "unevolved" mentality. (The latter term apparently being the one usually applied to the native who has had no contact whatsoever with European civilization.)

The Bantu's cosmos is not a chaotic tangle of disordered, conflicting forces. On the contrary, he thinks in essentially hierarchical terms, and his world is one in which each living man, because he represents force, can influence directly or indirectly other reasoning beings.

European Comment

Jean Wahl points out that one of the most recent stages of Occidental philosophy, that represented by the teachings of Henri Bergson, was not far removed from a number of these ideas or from the ontology of "vital" force. He also sees in it a relationship to the ideas of D. H. Lawrence and certain modern thinkers, who believe that contact must be reestablished with the hidden, active forces of the world below.

For Gabriel Marcel, objective study of such a philosophy is hopelessly complicated not only as a result of the teachings of Descartes "that have for so long dominated European thinking," but also because of racial prejudice and language barriers. He suggests, however, that there would be much to gain by approaching it with humility and, particularly, by ridding ourselves before we approach it of what he terms a certain "prétension scientiste" which, he believes, underlies many of our most regrettable errors of thought.

Father Tempels's point of view is based on long experience. He is very doubtful as to the quality of the civilization Europeans have given the Africans in exchange for their own, and he would like to see the traditional "vital" elements of their philosophy retained as the basis of whatever further teaching they are to receive. He considers that by cutting them off entirely from their past they have suffered an amputation that condemns them to wander disoriented between two teachings, unable to give genuine meaning to their lives.

"One of the best things Europeans have given the Negroes," he writes, "is the lesson and example of their activity. However, industrialization and . . . permanent overproduction do not necessarily give the measure of a civilization, but on the contrary, may bring about its destruction, if sufficient attention is not focused on the human personality. Civilization is a value which resides in man himself, and not in the exterior things that surround him."

Father Tempels concludes: "It is a crime against education to impose on members of the human race a civilization without philosophy, wisdom, or spiritual aspirations. But it is even more serious to rob peoples of a patrimony that constitutes their only possession capable of serving as a point of departure toward a superior civilization."

An International Poet

News has reached me that my friend of many years, Yvan Goll, died recently, after a long and painful illness, at the American Hospital in Paris. He was fifty-nine years old.

I first met Goll in Paris in the early twenties, soon after he and his poet-wife, Claire, arrived from Zurich, where they had spent the war years in a milieu of Expressionist poets and painters that included Else Lasker-Schüler and Leonhard Frank. It was then that he published one of his first books of poems, a *Requiem für die Gefallenen in Europa,* in German. This was soon to be followed by a little volume entitled *Elégies internationales,* in the French language, which was to become his exclusive medium for the next two decades.

After Munich, Goll emigrated to New York, where he soon published an English-language volume entitled *Fruits from Saturn.* While there, he edited an excellent bilingual Franco-American review, *Hemispheres,* which appeared until he returned to Europe, in 1947. Back in Paris, he brought out two more French volumes: *Le Mythe de la roche percée* and *Elégie d'Iphétonga,* the latter with illustrations by Picasso.

Shortly before his death, Goll broke his thirty-year silence to work on a poem in the German language entitled "Das Traumkraut." It is to be feared that this, his return to his *Muttersprache,* remained unfinished.

Here was a poet of international dimensions; a visionary of the logos, the European frontier-man par excellence—he hailed from Metz—whose entire life was devoted to the search for a frontierless universe. His going will leave a void in international letters, for he was truly the international poet, both in spirit and language.

State of the Novel

Listeners to the BBC Third (Literary) Program of the last two Wednesday evenings were left somewhat in the dark as to the actual condition of the contemporary English novel. After having been told by one speaker on March 1 that it had never recovered from the shock of Joyce's *Ulysses* and might be considered definitely dead, others, among whom were Rose Macauley, John Lehmann, and L. P. Hartley, on March 8, told a world in mourning that although science, anthropology, psychology, and "all the other ologies" had tried to take it over, the novel had nevertheless survived somehow and was going strong with Henry Greene, Ivy Compton-Burnett, and Elizabeth Bowen way out in the lead.

Mrs. Macauley wants poetry and still more poetry for background. Mr. Hartley finds a tendency to move from things said to things seen and wonders if the cinema has not had a slightly "cinesta" influence. One of the men (voice unidentifiable) is delighted to see the return to a Sterneian type of satire, and he cited George Orwell. Mr. Lehman feels that we are in a period of transition (ah, that word again!), that the young people are finding their way. All, whatever their slight differences of opinion, are emphatically agreed that the novel is neither dead nor dying.

This is good news and makes excellent listening. I wish I felt as sure about it as they do.

Marginalia

Raymond Queneau, author of *Chiendent, Gueule de Pierre, L'Instant fatal,* and so on, has just returned to Paris after his first visit to the United States. . . . James Joyce's only play, *Exiles,* was produced recently by the BBC in the Third Program. The fugal treatment of this intensely interior drama by the adapter John Kier Cross was declared a complete success by the critics. . . . Henry Miller, author of the *Tropic of Cancer* and other banned books, will leave his Big Sur tusculum next summer to see Montparnasse again after an absence of a decade. . . . The last issue of the French review *Arts et lettres* published a tribute to Jules Verne, pioneer of atomic literature and "the greatest literary genius of the centuries." . . . The German poet Elisabeth Langgässer, author of *The Labyrinth, The Inextinguishable Seal,* and so on, gave a recent lecture in Paris on contemporary German writing. . . . Foujita, the Japanese painter who had quite a vogue in prewar Paris, is back in Montparnasse after an absence of ten years. He arrived via Manhattan, where he spent a year.

Franco-German Cultural Exchanges
(March 21, 1950)

Attempts to bring about a general European consciousness in the political sphere are finding their corollary today in more localized efforts toward Franco-German understanding in cultural matters. This is particularly true of the French zone in Western Germany, where there is to be seen a genuine striving for an amalgam of the apparently antipodal viewpoints of the two countries, and where contacts between representatives of both neighbors are becoming more frequent and more cordial. In the university towns of Tübingen, Mainz, and Freiburg, as well as in private conversations, a real "bridge" may be said to be under construction, and it is not without significance that the term *Brückengedanke* should have become almost a cliché in reports of these activities.

Crossing the Rhine at Mainz, one is immediately struck by the prevailing atmosphere of internationalism which this quest for intellectual accord engenders, an atmosphere that becomes more evident as one travels further in the zone. Nowhere is the suggestion of Franco-German political union—until very recently regarded as utopian—being discussed with more fervor, nowhere is the proposal more rapidly transposed to the cultural plane. Even the language barrier would appear no longer to constitute a serious obstacle. Knowledge of French is spreading, and translations from one language to the other are increasingly numerous.

Salutary discussions between French and German writers have taken

place in Mainz and Baden-Baden, as well as in the harmoniously beautiful country contiguous to Lake Constance, where the international wind
seems to blow with particular force. Bookstores throughout the zone are
well supplied with both German and French books and magazines, and
frequent lectures in both languages on cultural subjects contribute to a
continuous interchange of ideas. The intensive spadework undertaken by
the Paris Information Services immediately after the capitulation is beginning to bear fruit.

The Golden Gate

It is interesting to note that a German émigré, Alfred Döblin, is playing
a major role in this cultural exchange. Before 1933, Döblin was one of the
better-known writers of the Expressionist group in Berlin. Today he directs
Das Goldene Tor, a review of literature and the arts which has appeared in
Mainz-Gonsenheim for four years.

The last two issues of this well-edited review offer a rich fare of French
and German examples of the literature of this and other epochs that constitute a characteristic cross-cut of western European writing. Side by side
with stories by Oscar Maria Graf and Hans von Savigny are German poems
by the late Yvan Goll, and Döblin himself gives a deeply human analysis
of contemporary poetry. He also presents German translations of a number of the French Symbolist poets, ranging from Baudelaire and Villiers de
l'Isle-Adam to Mallarmé, whom he juxtaposes to their German counterpart, Stefan George.

Döblin, who has a number of novels to his credit, is perhaps best known
outside Germany as the author of the highly original *Berlin Alexanderplatz*
(ca. 1930), the scene of which is laid in that part of the former German
capital where he once worked as a doctor. Shortly before the Nazi regime
he emigrated to France, and from there to the United States. On his return
to Europe in 1945 he joined the French Information Services and has since
lived in the French zone of Germany. His latest novel, *The New Forest Primeval,* set against the background of the South American landscape, was
brought out recently in Baden-Baden.

Other Reviews

Another excellent review appearing in Baden-Baden and Stuttgart is
Merkur, edited by Joachim Moras and Hans Paeschke, and described as

"a German review for European thought." This monthly magazine seeks to lead away from merely parochial interests toward a supra-national concept that takes in not only modern literature but philosophical and what Peter Viereck has called "meta-political" evaluations as well. A recent issue published fragments from a posthumous novel, *The Venetian,* by Gerhart Hauptmann, along with an elucidating essay on "America's European Policy," by Robert Ingrim.

Any account of intellectual life in the French zone would be incomplete that neglected to mention Benno Reiffenberg's *Die Gegenwart,* also edited in Baden-Baden. This magazine, which is somewhat similar in presentation to the English *New Statesman and Nation,* deals for the most part with current topics, and its comments on international events are closely followed. Its literary pages are especially well documented, and one senses in them a genuine desire to interpret both French and European modes of thinking. One would like, however, to see greater vigilance exercised with regard to the recent political past of certain of its contributors.

Finally, the Catholic monthlies, *Documents* in French, and a German-language edition, *Dokumente* (Offenburg, Baden), give an extremely informative account of many phases of the Franco-German problem, as well as doing all in their power to create better understanding between the two peoples.

Further "Brückengedanken"

If I have given first mention to activities within the French zone, where, in all probability, the most efficacious nucleus of understanding will first take form, it is with no intention to minimize what is being achieved elsewhere; on the contrary.

Since 1945, many important Paris reviews have devoted entire numbers to examination of the problems involved (the German issues of *Esprit* and *Temps modernes* were of a very high quality); a number of thoughtful books have appeared on the subjects, such as Robert Minder's *Allemands et allemagnes,* Henri Berr's *Allemagne, le contre et le pour,* Alexandre Arnoux's *Contacts Allemands;* and a French committee of some twenty-five writers, formed for the purpose of "furthering exchanges with new Germany," includes Jean-Paul Sartre, Maurice Merleau-Ponty, Emmanuel Mounier, Remy Roure, David Rousset, Vercors, and Claude Bourdet. This group publishes a regular bulletin, organizes lectures in both countries, and so on.

In the academic world, there are fifty German students working in French universities on scholarships offered by the French Ministry of Education, and a certain number of other young Germans is scattered throughout France on scholarships offered by the Cultural Relations branch of the Ministry of Foreign Affairs. I hear, too, that in the border town of Saarbrücken, both the university and the newly founded Conservatory of Music are flourishing in an atmosphere of increasing Franco-German cooperation that includes both students and faculty.

Last, but by no means least, the fact that plays by Sartre and Giraudoux—to mention only these two—are playing to capacity houses in Western Germany, the genuine enthusiasm that greeted the 1949 tour of the Sorbonne theatrical group "Les Theophiliens," the warm reception accorded Marianne Oswald's recitals of French poetry by Berlin students and workers—all these are straws in the wind which, taken together, make heartening reading.

And certainly no citizen of good will in either country can be unaware of the high odds that are at stake.

Marginalia

Robert Flaherty, the famous director of *Louisiana Story, Man of Aran,* and other great documents of the cinema, is at present in Berlin, where he is studying the problem of the cultural film. . . . The American writer Meyer Levin has founded an English-language house in Paris, under the name "Authors' Press." . . . Franz Pfemfert, who emigrated from Nazi Germany before 1933, recently celebrated his seventieth birthday in Mexico City. Pfemfert edited the important Expressionist review *Aktion* in Berlin in the twenties. . . . Mark Reinsberg announces from Amsterdam that he is launching a publishing house under his name. The first book scheduled for publication is Margaret Anderson's sequel to *My Thirty Years' War.* . . . The former Austrian novelist Hermann Broch, author of *Die Schlafwandler* and *Der Tod des Vergil,* will visit Europe this summer for the first time since his flight from Austria in 1936. . . . Elliot Stein, the twenty-year-old American editor of a new Franco-American poetry review, *Janus,* which has just appeared in Paris, has an interesting essay in the current issue of the Dutch review, *Podium,* in which he attempts to situate the post-World

War II American writers in Paris. . . . Fernand Léger will leave shortly for Switzerland, where he will lecture in the principal cities on painting and architecture, under the auspices of the recently formed Lausanne group "Carreau." . . . It has been officially stated that 1,088 works by foreign authors were published in France in French translations during 1949. The word "chauvinistic" is no longer applicable.

German Literary Trends (May 23, 1950)

It is still difficult to report in anything but general terms on recent developments in contemporary German literature. A great deal is being written in the three western zones, and a certain amount of jockeying for position may be observed among the writers who have come to the fore since the capitulation. From conversations with both publishers and authors I gather, too, that reader interest in the new writing has been growing apace during the last year. But although I have read books and reviews galore, a clear picture is still lacking.

There is, however, óne evident and important development: the violent antagonism which existed until recently between the emigrant writers and those who stayed behind during the infamóus regime would appear to be subsiding. In this connection, I recall Thomas Mann's famous letter to the novelist von Molo, in which the former expressed his moral repugnance toward Hitler's dictatorship and declared that he could not read the men who had continued to write in Nazi Germany because he felt they had profited from its conquests. Feigning to ignore the existence of the camps in which over seven million innocent victims of race hatred had perished, von Molo, in his reply, claimed that these writers had lived in what he euphemistically termed an "inner emigration," and had had no knowledge of the sadism which the regime had fostered. Few were taken in by this sophism, however, and it soon disappeared a bit shamefacedly from the vocabulary.

A Publishing Bridge

Today the famous publishing house of S. Fischer is taking the lead in an attempt to reconcile these groups. Mrs. E. Beermann-Fischer, daughter of the late S. Fischer, and her husband, Gottfried Beermann-Fischer, are well equipped for this task, for they were themselves fugitives from Hitler's tyranny as early as 1933, and their long odyssey took them from Berlin to Vienna, to Amsterdam, to Stockholm, and finally to New York. They have recently returned to Western Germany for a temporary stay (they now have American citizenship), and have undertaken to reestablish the publishing firm in Frankfurt, linking it up with already existing branches in Amsterdam and New York.

"We hope to make of the house of Fischer a meeting-place for these two forces," Beermann-Fischer told me recently, when I interviewed him in his Frankfurt office. He declared that he is particularly desirous to build a bridge between German-language writers inside and outside Germany, thus constituting a link with the past. He proposes to publish both early and recent works of Thomas Mann, as well as the work of Johannes von Jensen, posthumous work of Gerhart Hauptmann, Henrik Ibsen, Hugo von Hofmannsthal, and others whom this firm made famous during the last half-century. Most of the stock of the old S. Fischer firm, having been stored in Leipzig and Frankfurt during the war, was destroyed, so that republication of their earlier titles is also an early objective.

A Talented Nucleus

Beermann-Fischer has now added a number of younger authors to his lists: some who left Germany before 1933, as well as certain others who stayed behind, but managed to stay politically untainted. He says that here is quite a nucleus of talented German-language writers in the "diaspora" whose creations should flow quite naturally into the stream of the new literature, and he spoke with particular enthusiasm of Joachim Maas, whose recent *The Magic Year,* a volume of childhood reminiscences, he regards as an important contribution. Another novelist living in the United States is Friedrich Torberg, whose *Interrupted Flight* appeared recently. The names of Leonhard Frank, in Paris, and Hermann Kesten, in New York, are also mentioned.

Other Activities

To have relaunched the famous review *Neue Rundschau,* founded in 1890 (although Beermann-Fischer began with Peter Suhrkamp as coeditor, he now directs it alone), is also no mean achievement. In its international outlook and catholicity of taste, this eminent review recalls the *Nouvelle Revue française,* of before 1940, or T. S. Eliot's prewar *Criterion.* The most recent issue contains work by Eliot, excerpts from Thomas Mann's unpublished new novel, *The Elect,* posthumous documents by Hugo von Hofmannsthal, Virginia Woolf, and W. B. Yeats, as well as such new German writers as Fritz Usinger, Franz Josef Schneider, and others. The review is edited and published in Amsterdam and has three branch editorial offices: one in Frankfurt (Friedrich Podszus), one in New York (Joachim Maas), and one in Amsterdam (Rudolf Hirsch).

Then there is the plan for a special series to be called *Sonderhefte,* which will present excerpts from new novels, collections of short stories, and sociological and philosophical essays by the new younger writers now being corraled from all over Germany. Among those on the list are Alfred Andersch, Nicolas Sombart, Hans-Jürgen Söhring, Jürgen von Hollaender, Rudolf Kramer-Badoni. (Kramer-Badoni's novel *In the Turmoil* constitutes, with Hans Werner Richter's *Those Who Were Beaten,* one of the first important German expressions of the war epoch.)

Alfred Andersch will make a six months' tour through the occupied zones of Western Germany with a view to writing an account of his findings that will include reporting as well as political and sociological analyses. The main object will be to give a clear picture of the country's human problems, as well as to permit the reader to judge for himself whether Germany represents "a threat or a promise" for the Western world now in the making.

I asked young Andersch what, in his opinion, might be considered the new tendencies in German writing. "Above all, neo-Realistic," was his reply. "The younger men are violently anti-esthetic, almost existentialist in spirit. They want to 'report' their experiences in a form they call *Aussage* (statement), and they reject all pseudo-Romantic *fatras.*"

"Group 47"

The Fischers are enthusiastic about certain discoveries made at the annual meeting of "Group 47," which took place last week at Inzighofen, near Sigmaringen, in the French zone. Here a hundred or so German writers gathered in a former monastery to read aloud their poems and narratives, which were later discussed with great frankness and critical acumen.

Many new writers received their first hearing in the beautiful sylvan landscape of the Black Forest. Arnold Bauer read from his novel; Günter Eich his new poems; Walter Kolbenhoff a radio play that reminded some of the *Beggars' Opera;* Wolfdietrich Schnurre a fabulous animal story; Hans-Jürgen Söhring a powerful chapter from a "Zeitroman"; and Adrian Morrien, a Dutchman, his extraordinary *The Disorderly Man.*

A poetry prize of one thousand marks was awarded to Günter Eich for his collected poetical works. (I was happy to hear this, as I had translated him in *transition* as early as 1927.) His writing has a half-magical, half-realistic force that expresses the disquiet of modern man.

Another prize of six thousand marks, founded by the Munich publisher Kurt Desch to crown the best novel of a young writer (it is to be called the "René Schickele Prize," after the bilingual Alsatian writer who died just after the war), will be awarded by a jury composed of Thomas Mann, Annette Kolb, Alfred Neumann, Hermann Kesten, and Ernst Petzold. Ten publishers, including American, French, British, and Swiss houses, will take an option on the new novel. The René Schickele Prize, according to the founders, is intended to mark the new unity of German literature, and its objective is "to bridge the gulf between the German writers who emigrated and those who remained behind."

Hermann Kesten, who is today an American citizen, summed up the situation in a recent address: "The concept of 'emigration' no longer exists. There is only our common language."

The American sculptor Alexander Calder, accompanied by Mrs. Calder and their two daughters, has arrived in Paris to prepare an important exhibition of his works which will be shown at the Galerie Maeght at the end of June. . . . A telegram signed by sixteen French writers, among whom were Simone de Beauvoir, Claude Bourdet, Michel Leiris, Merleau-Ponty, Jacques Prévert, Raymond Queneau, Jean-Paul Sartre, Jean Schlumberger, Vercors, and Jean Wahl, has been sent to President Ismet Inonu of Turkey urging the liberation of the ailing poet Nazim Hikmet, imprisoned since 1937 on a political charge. . . . Sylvia Beach, publisher of James Joyce's *Ulysses,* was awarded the 1950 Denyse Clairouin prize for her translation of Henri Michaux's *A Barbarian in Asia.* . . . The Académie française last week voted unanimously against a proposal to introduce the teaching of local dialects in French primary schools.

Biography of Eugene Jolas

1894	John George Eugene born in Union Hill (Union City), New Jersey, to parents Eugene Pierre Jolas, French, and Christine (née Ambach), German, on October 26.
1897	The Jolas family moves back to Forbach in Lorraine, then in Germany. Bilingual language acquisition (German-French).
1901–09	Eugene attends grammar school, High School College in Forbach; Catholic seminary, Montigny, near Metz, Lorraine.
1909	Decides to return alone to America. He attends DeWitt Clinton Evening High School, New York, while working several delivery jobs; learning English.
1912–16	Begins writing for the German-language *Volksblatt und Freiheitsfreund* in Pittsburgh and then the *Pittsburgh Sun* as a local and automobile reporter.
1917	Joins U.S. Army Medical Corps and is stationed in Camp Lee, Virginia; editorial assistant to the camp newspaper, *The Bayonet;* launches in 1918–19 at Fort Sheridan, Illinois, a newspaper for wounded war veterans, *The Recall.*
1919	Honorably discharged from the army. Returns to New York and works as a proofreader for the newspaper *Women's Wear.*
1920–23	In pursuit of a career in journalism: police and political reporter for the *Waterbury Republican,* court reporter for the *Savannah Morning News,* caption and feature writer for the *New York Daily News.*
1923	Returns to his family in Forbach, now in France. Contacts with bilingual Strasbourg literary circles; visits Paris.
1924–25	Joins the *Chicago Tribune*'s Paris edition, writing as city reporter; replaces Ford Madox Ford as literary editor; and is a columnist via his weekly "Rambles Through Literary Paris."
1924	First book of poetry, *Ink* (New York: Rhythmus).

1925	Meets Maria McDonald in Paris. She was born in Louisville, Kentucky, on January 12, 1893; died in Paris in 1987.
1926	Returns to New York City and marries Maria at St. Patrick's Cathedral, January 12. For six months after his marriage, lives in New Orleans and works as feature writer for the *New Orleans Item Tribune*. Second volume of poetry, *Cinema,* introduction by Sherwood Anderson (New York: Adelphi). First daughter, Betsy, born. Betsy Jolas is now one of France's leading avant-garde composers, winner of prestigious national and international awards; since 1983 member of the American Academy of Arts and Letters.
1927	Returns with his family to Paris, then moves to Colombey-les-Deux-Eglises, Haute-Marne. Founds and begins work on the review *transition* with coeditor Elliot Paul. Thanks to the mediation of Sylvia Beach in whose bookshop, Shakespeare & Co., James Joyce lectured, the seriatim publication of Joyce's *Work in Progress* commences with its "Opening Pages" in the first issue. *Transition* would be published over a period of eleven successive years.
1928	Publishes *Le Nègre qui chante* (Paris: Editions des cahiers libres) and *Anthologie de la nouvelle poésie américaine* (Paris: Kra). Translates, together with his wife Maria, Franz Kafka's *Das Urteil* as *The Sentence* in *transition,* no. 11. Acquaintance with Carl Einstein, German avant-garde art critic and writer, settled at Paris since that year, who arranges Jolas's visits to Berlin Expressionist artists (Benn, Döblin, Grosz, Sternheim, and others) and functions as "advisory editor" to *transition.* Jolas develops a great deal of social and creative activity among European artists and American expatriate writers.
1929	Publishes *Secession in Astropolis* (Paris: Black Sun) and *Transition Stories* (New York: Walter V. McKee). Second daughter, Marie-Christine, born: a noted ethnologist and translator of modern poetry, wife of poet André du Bouchet, then longtime companion of René Char, she died in 1999.
1931	Translates Alfred Döblin's *Berlin Alexanderplatz* into English (New York: Viking). Visits Mexico.

1932	Publishes *Hypnolog des Scheitelauges* (Paris: Editions Vertigral), *Epi-vocables of 3* (Paris: Editions Vertigral), and *The Language of Night* (The Hague: Servire).
1933	Publishes *Mots-Déluge: Hypnologues* (Paris: Editions des cahiers gris).
1935	Takes a sabbatical to work in New York City for the Havas News Agency, translating news from America for transmission to France, Canada, and South America.
1936–38	With his wife Maria, translates Kafka's *Metamorphosis* for *transition,* nos. 25, 26, 27.
1937	Returns to Paris and resumes work on *transition.*
1938	Publishes *I Have Seen Monsters and Angels* (Paris: Transition).
1939	Officially suspends production of *transition* and moves back to New York to work as a freelance writer. His family joins him in New York in 1940, fleeing German occupation. Begins to work on his autobiography, posthumously published by Andreas Kramer and Rainer Rumold under the title *Man from Babel* in 1998.
1939–40	Lives in Iowa for a year with his brother Jacques, pianist and music instructor at Cornell College.
1940	Publishes *Planets and Angels* (Mount Vernon, Iowa: English Club of Cornell College). Publishes *Words from the Deluge* (New York: Gotham Bookmart).
1940–44	Resides in New York.
1941	Publishes an anthology, *Vertical: A Yearbook for Romantic-Mystic-Ascensions* (New York: Gotham Bookmart).
1942	Works for the Office of War Information in New York as a writer, translating war news into French for the Allied forces in North Africa, and for the French underground.
1944	Transfers to London in March to continue translating war news for radio transmission to the French underground. Relocates in June to

France to help reestablish journalistic communications in recently liberated towns.

1945   Enters Germany in January to set up "denazified" newspapers in captured German towns. Establishes *Aachener Nachrichten* and *Die Heidelberger Mitteilungen* successfully, leading to his appointment as editor in chief of the Deutsche Allgemeine Nachrichten-Agentur (DANA, later changed to DENA, today's Deutsche Presse-Agentur). Teaches American newspaper methods at Aachen and Bad Nauheim from January 1945 to February 1947. Works with Dolf Sternberger, Karl Jaspers, and others on a new literary review, *Die Wandlung.*

1946   Receives the U.S. Medal of Freedom for his services as chief of a field press team and press control officer from 1944 to 1945.

1947   Resigns his post with DENA and the Allied School of Journalism, rejoins his family who have now moved to Paris. Works for a revival of *transition* with Georges Duthuit as editor. Works extensively on his autobiography, *Man from Babel.*

1948   Returns to his journalism career as news editor for the *Neue Zeitung* in Munich. Writes and compiles a textbook, *Der moderne Reporter,* published in 1949, as part of his duties in the occupation government's Information Services Division. His definitive "elucidation" of Joyce's *Finnegans Wake* appears in *Critique: Revue générale des publications françaises et étrangères.*

1949–50   Contributes a weekly column, "Across Frontiers," to the *New York Herald Tribune*'s Paris edition.

1950   In April resigns his post with the Information Services Division, returns to Paris, and continues freelance writing.

1951   His essays on Novalis and Ernst Jünger appear in *Critique.*

1952   Eugene Jolas dies in Paris on May 26.

Notes

Part One: Rambles Through Literary Paris

Number 17 (June 8, 1924)

embarras du choix: Fr. to be spoilt for choice; impossibility to choose.

Jacques Rivière (1886–1925): French critic and novelist, Rivière cofounded the *Nouvelle Revue française* (1910) and remained its director from 1919 until his death.

Henry Cowell (1897–1965): American composer. Cowell experimented with tone clusters, string pianos, and the indeterminacy of elastic form.

la réclame: Fr. advertising.

Valéry Larbaud (1881–1957): Novelist, poet, critic, and translator from Spanish and English, Larbaud was the cosmopolitan coeditor of *Commerce.* Closely associated with the *Nouvelle Revue française,* he helped introduce Whitman, Butler, and Joyce to French audiences.

tout à fait en bois: Fr. entirely wooden; stiff.

Maurice Barrès (1862–1923): French conservative novelist, publicist, and politician whose books are characterized by a mystical nationalism. His popular, patriotic novels set in Lorraine express his political preoccupations.

Raymond Poincaré (1860–1934): French politician who served as finance and foreign minister and senator; 1913–1920, president; member of the Académie française.

Paul Bourget (1852–1935): French Catholic poet, novelist, and essayist, Bourget used spiritual pathos in his didactic works as a means to revive social thought.

psychographe du coeur: Fr. psychograph of the heart.

Henri Solveen (1891–1956): Strasbourg-born artist and writer, an intimate friend of Eugene Jolas; in 1924 Solveen founded an Alsace-Lorraine artists' and writers' group, l'Arc, whose work he edited the same year. He was also the editor of *Les Nouveaux Cahiers Alsaciens / Neue Elsässer Hefte* (1921–23) and *Elsässisch-Lothringischer Kunst- und Heimatkalender* (1926–33).

carrefour du monde: Fr. world's crossroads.

Number 18 (June 15, 1924)

plain-chant: Fr. plainsong; singing in the Catholic tradition.

Jean Cocteau (1889–1963): Novelist, playwright, screenwriter, and painter, Cocteau was a versatile artist associated with most currents of modernism, from the

Russian ballet and Les Six to the Surrealists. He identified himself as a poet above all. His work on the stage and screen was often inspired by classical mythology.

Ernst Toller (1893–1939): Expressionist playwright. Exiled in New York by the rise of Nazism, Toller put an end to his own life (autobiography: *Eine Jugend in Deutschland,* 1933).

Norman Bel-Geddes (1893–1958): American stage designer, architect, and producer, Bel-Geddes founded the Theatre Guild (1920), which helped promote European avant-garde theater in America.

André Maurois (1886–1967): French historian, novelist, and essayist.

Franz Werfel (1890–1945): Lyric poet, dramatist and novelist, Werfel was associated with Expressionism in poetic works like *Wir sind* (1913); his novels evinced a pacifist and humanitarian sentiment.

secrétaire de rédaction: Fr. assistant editor.

Number 19 (June 22, 1924)

Waldo Frank (1889–1967): American novelist and journalist; Frank's work advocated social and political reform.

Harold Vinal (1891–1965): American poet and editor; Vinal directed the journal *Voices.*

André Spire (1868–1966): French poet and militant Zionist; Spire promoted the idea of a new Jewish literature.

Charles Vildrac (1882–1971): French poet and playwright who cofounded the Groupe de l'Abbaye with Georges Duhamel.

George Antheil (1900–1959): American avant-garde composer associated with Ezra Pound in the 1920s; Antheil toured Europe as a concert pianist before earning renown for his compositions *Jazz Symphony* and *Ballet mécanique* (1927) scored for airplane propellers, automobile horns, electric bells, and player pianos.

Russian composer [. . .] Spanish counterpart: Allusions to Stravinsky and Picasso, respectively.

Savonarola (1452–1498): Influential Italian preacher; Savonarola led an austere theological democracy in Florence under Charles VIII.

Number 20 (June 29, 1924)

Guillaume Apollinaire (1880–1918): French poet who participated actively in all the artistic movements flourishing in France during his short lifetime. From Art Nouveau and Symbolism to Cubism, Apollinaire helped define the aesthetic agenda of twentieth-century art.

Henri Martineau (1882–1952): French doctor and literary critic.

Jon Dos Passos (1896–1970): American novelist of Portuguese origins; Dos Passos is famous for his monumental *U.S.A.* trilogy (1937), as well as *Manhattan Transfer* (1925), where his use of montage introduced a cinematic scope to the realistic novel.

Gilbert Seldes (1893–1970): Critic, writer and contributing editor of the *Dial;* Seldes is often hailed as one of the first American intellectuals to lend legitimacy to popular culture.

Pierre Reverdy (1889–1960): "Cubist" poet and precursor to Surrealism in his review *Nord-Sud* (1917). Soon after, the French poet secluded himself in a monastery to write metaphysical and mystic verse.

Spoon River Anthology: Edgar Lee Masters (1869–1950) published his most famous collection of free verse in 1915.

Paul Géraldy (1885–1983): French poet and playwright, Géraldy cofounded Cénacle 20 with Chaplin and Gershwin in 1920.

livre de chevet: Fr. bedside reading.

Rémy de Gourmont (1858–1915): French novelist, poet, playwright, and philosopher; de Gourmont cofounded the review *Mercure de France.* His influential criticism of Symbolism helped define and disseminate the movement's aesthetic doctrines.

Blaise Cendrars (1887–1961): French writer and poet, Cendrars initiated the poetics of *Simultanéisme,* which would prove decisive for Apollinaire and the Surrealists. Cendrars mythologized his experiences abroad in his autobiographical works.

Number 22 (July 13, 1924)

Max Jacob (1876–1944): French Jewish poet; Jacob converted to Catholicism after having a vision of Christ. A forerunner of Surrealism, his poetry is spiritual and humoristic by turns while remaining unrelentingly self-reflexive.

Margaret Anderson (1886–1973): After having worked for the *Dial* in Chicago, Anderson started her own *Little Review,* a literary magazine, devoted to "Life for Art's Sake," that published many key figures of Anglo-American modernism.

Scofield Thayer (1889–1982): Editor of the *Dial,* Thayer had a vast network of friends in artistic circles in Europe and America.

Cowper Powys (1872–1963): Welsh poet and novelist.

Louis Untermeyer (1885–1977): American author and editor noted for his anthologies of modern American and British poetry; see Jolas's letters to Untermeyer on March 8, 1918, February 4, 1919, and June 30, 1921 (University of Delaware Library, Newark).

Renée Dunan (?–1936): A provocative French writer and critic, Dunan published erotic works under multiple pseudonyms and was associated with anarchist circles.

Raymond Radiguet (1903–1923): Precocious French poet and novelist, Radiguet was introduced to literary circles by Cocteau and Salmon. His promising career was cut short by typhoid.

Fritz von Unruh (1885–1970): German poet and playwright who started his career with plays and poems about military heroism, only to turn toward pacifist and universal themes after his experiences in the war.

René Schickele (1883–1940): Franco-German author, editor, and journalist, Schickele began his career as part of the modernist group Jüngstes Elsaß, which attempted to renew Alsatian literature independently of nationalist movements.

B. J. Kospoth (1883–1940): Wrote about Jolas in "The Poems of a Reporter," *Chicago Tribune Sunday Magazine* (European edition), no. 40 (November 16, 1924): pp. 3 and 6.

Mme. Rachilde (1860–1953): Born Marguerite Eymery, married Vallette, Rachilde held literary salons for the review *Le Mercure de France* and was a prolific novelist; anti-German racist.

Number 28 (August 24, 1924)

Douglas Fairbanks (1883–1939): American actor who was dubbed the "King of Hollywood" in the 1920s.

Cénacle: A literary circle formed around the various early leaders of French Romanticism such as Lamartine, Vigny, de Musset, and Hugo.

Marcel Schwob (1867–1905): Journalist, essayist, and writer, Schwob's work is a testament to his eclectic interests including the study of slang, translation, pastiche, and poetry.

Catulle Mendès (1848–1909): French poet and novelist, Mendès founded *La Revue fantaisiste* (1891) and edited the anthology *Le Parnasse contemporain* (1866–76), which lent its name to the group of pre-Symbolist formalist poets.

Unanimism: French literary movement that took up the place left by Symbolism. Jules Romains wrote its manifesto (*Les Sentiments unanimes et la poésie*) in 1905 in the magazine *Le Penseur*. With fellow poets Charles Vildrac and George Chennevière, Romains aimed to establish a new lyric poetry celebrating the "collective soul," as materialized by the city, and acceding to divinity through solidarity.

le tact [. . .] trop loin: Fr. tact in audacity is knowing how far one can go too far.

Number 30 (September 7, 1924)

recueil de vers: Fr. a collection of poetry.

Homme de Péché [. . .] de Patience: Fr. sinful man, angry man, patient man.

le voyageur [. . .] de l'Europe: Fr. the traveler whose journeys link the members of Europe, like ample blood flow.

imprimé aux dépens de l'auteur: Fr. printed at the expense of the author.

Ivan [or Yvan] Goll (1891–1950): Bilingual Franco-German poet, novelist, playwright, and translator, Goll went from his native Alsace to Berlin, where he took part in the Expressionist movement. In Paris he founded the review *Surréalisme* in 1924, thus breaking with Breton's group. Exiled in the United States, he edited the review *Hémisphères* and the eponymous publishing house.

Claire Goll (1891–1977): Bilingual Franco-German poet, novelist, and translator; married to Yvan Goll.

Benjamin Crémieux (1888–1944): French writer and critic, Crémieux translated Pirandello and introduced Italo Svevo to French audiences. He died in deportation to Buchenwald.

Paul Morand (1888–1976): French writer and diplomat, Morand's poetry and novels describe the chaos of modern life.

Number 36 (October 19, 1924)

Darius Milhaud (1892–1974): French composer known for his development of polytonality, associated with Les Six; Milhaud worked regularly with poets such as Cendrars, Cocteau, and Claudel.

Goll's anthology: *Les cinq continents: Anthologie mondiale de poésie contemporaine* (1922).

Heimatkunst: Ger. Regionalism; a Germanophone literary movement that sought to re-create the life and atmosphere of the provinces.

Homer Croy (1883–1965): American novelist, journalist, and humorist.

Number 40 (November 16, 1924)

tendenzlos: Ger. unbiased.

Carl Sternheim (1878–1942): German dramatist and satirist of middle-class life; Sternheim has been associated with Expressionism, although he always claimed to be a Realist.

Henri Massis (1886–1970): Politically active French writer, Massis was involved with the Action Française and codirected the *Revue universelle* from 1920 to 1944.

Number 2686 (November 23, 1924)

Charles du Bos (1882–1939): Oxford-educated French essayist and literary critic; Du Bos lectured widely in Europe and America.

The Gumps: A Harold Gray comic strip published in the *New York Daily News*.

Number 2714 (December 21, 1924)

drame comique: Fr. comic drama.
Poèmes d'amour: Claire and Yvan Goll; illustrated by Marc Chagall (1925).
assurance contre le suicide: Fr. suicide insurance.

Number 2735 (January 11, 1925)

François Mauriac (1885–1970): Nobel Prize-winning French novelist, critic, and playwright; Mauriac wrote about the conflict between lust and spirituality, between renunciation and revolt.
roman d'analyse: Fr. novel of analysis.
sans-gêne: Fr. inconsiderate.

Number 2763 (February 8, 1925)

mondialisme: Fr. internationalism (lit. "world-ism").
André Maurois: Jolas conflates the titles of Maurois' novel *Les silences du Colonel Bramble* (1918) with *Les discours du Docteur O'Grady* (1922).
Victor Llona (1886–1953): Peruvian writer; Llona was a prolific translator of Russian and American literature into French. He also contributed to the *Nouvelle Revue française.*
Coeur de ténèbres: French title of Joseph Conrad's *Heart of Darkness* (1902).

Number 2805 (March 22, 1925)

Qui est là? [. . .] entrer l'infini: Fr. Who's there? Very well, let infinity in.
Francis Jammes (1868–1938): French poet and novelist with pastoral themes; his work has been referred to as Naturism.
Nathalie Clifford Barney (1876–1972): American writer and heiress who held a literary salon at her Latin Quarter home in the rue Jacob. A lesbian icon, she was the inspiration for heroines in the work of Djuna Barnes, Colette, and Rémy de Gourmont.
la dame, une femme expurgée: Fr. the lady, an expurgated woman.

Mrs. Pinchwife: Character in a play by William Wycherley, *The Country Wife* (1675).

Number 2875 (May 31, 1925)

Super-Realism: With this term Jolas oscillates between a desire to distinguish Breton's brand of Parisian Surrealism from Goll's more congenial, Romantic Alsatian version and the desire to confound them by applying the various terms used by the latter to the former.

Adolphe: Hero of the eponymous Romantic novel (1816) by Benjamin Constant (1767–1830) about his tumultuous affair with Mme de Staël.

Pierre Drieu La Rochelle (1893–1945): Right-wing French writer who described the decadence of postwar society. Drieu La Rochelle declared himself the epitome of the young European (*Le Jeune Européen,* 1927) before adhering to Fascism. He replaced Jean Paulhan as the director of the *Nouvelle Revue française* during the German occupation, committing suicide in 1945.

Number 2889 (June 14, 1925)

The Silver Vessel: i.e., the French journal *Le Navire d'argent.*
brevet élémentaire de Parisianité: Fr. basic diploma of Parisianness.

Number 2910 (July 5, 1925)

bagarre: Fr. fight.
dictée automatique: Fr. automatic dictation.
le faux bon sens: Fr. false common sense.
vaste saloperie: Fr. absolute crap.

Part Two: Revolution of the Word: *Transition* Manifestoes and History

Proclamation

Source: "Proclamation," *transition: An International Quarterly for Creative Experiment,* no. 16–17 (June 1929): 13.

Harry Crosby (1898–1929): Writer and publisher who contributed to *transition* in 1928–29 both intellectually and financially, and became associate editor in 1929. His Black Sun Press published Jolas's *Secession in Astropolis* in fall 1929.

Caresse Crosby (1891–1970): Born in a prominent New England family, Mary Phelps Jacobs dubbed herself Caresse Crosby to better market her invention, the backless brassiere. After having sold her patent to the undergarment industry, she went on to marry Harry Crosby, became an editorial assistant for *transition,* and helped run the Black Sun Press.

Stuart Gilbert (1883–1969): British writer and translator from French, Gilbert is best known for his 1930 study *James Joyce's Ulysses.* He co-translated Artaud and Béguin for *transition* with Jolas and took part in the first French translation of *Ulysses.*

Matthew Josephson (1899–1978): American writer and translator of French and German avant-garde writers for little magazines such as *Broom* and *Secession.* Josephson contributed to *transition* as a poet and a critic.

Elliot Paul (1891–1958): American journalist, musicologist, film critic, and writer who contributed to the Paris edition of the *New York Herald Tribune,* the *Chicago Tribune,* and was a coeditor of *transition.* As the Paris correspondent for the *Tribune* from 1925 to 1929, Paul took over Jolas's literary column, retitling it "From a Littérateur's Notebook."

Robert Sage (1899–?): Associate editor of *transition,* Sage also came to the group from the Paris edition of the *Chicago Tribune.* Drawn to Surrealism, he continued in his post until 1929, when he was transferred to the London office of the *New York Herald Tribune.*

Kay Boyle (1903–1993): American novelist, poet, and short story writer. She worked with Richard Brault on the experimental literary magazine *Broom,* with Archibald Craig on *Living Poetry,* contributed to *transition* from the very first issue, and later worked as a European correspondent for the *New Yorker.*

Whit Burnett (1899–?): American journalist, founder of *Story* magazine in 1931, contributed dreamlike stories written in a surreal, neologistic style. His wife, Martha Foley, cofounder of *Story,* also had a short story of hers appear in *transition,* no. 18 (November 1929).

Hart Crane (1899–1932): American poet made famous by *The Bridge* (1930) and *The Broken Tower* (1932). While an admirer of Eliot's poetry, Crane sought to go beyond what he found to be its spiritual sterility toward a "mystical synthesis of America," a stance which resounded with Jolas's own Neo-Romantic idiom. Numerous poems by Crane appeared in *transition,* including *The Bridge,* illustrated by Joseph Stella, in *transition,* no. 16–17 (1929).

Abraham Lincoln Gillespie (1895–1950): Philadelphia schoolteacher who became an expatriate writer in Paris.

Leigh Hoffman, Douglas Rigsby, Harold J. Salemson: Journalists with varying degrees of literary aspiration.

Theo Rutra: Jolas first used this pseudonym—meaning "God-root"—in *tran-*

sition, no. 8 (November 1927). Later, he used it to sign a prose poem dedicated to André Masson in *transition,* no. 15 (February 1929).

Laurence Vail (1857–1934): American novelist, poet, and painter married to Peggy Guggenheim and later to Kay Boyle; he contributed three stories to *transition.*

The Novel Is Dead—Long Live the Novel

Source: "The Novel Is Dead—Long Live the Novel," *transition: An International Quarterly for Creative Experiment,* no. 18 (November 1929): 239.

Preface to the New *Transition*

Source: "Preface to the New *Transition,*" *Transition: An International Workshop for Orphic Creation,* no. 21 (March 1932): 6.

a mantic laboratory: A place for the art or practice of divination and prophecy.

What Is the Revolution of Language?

Source: "What Is the Revolution of Language?" *Transition: An International Quarterly for Orphic Creation,* no. 22 (February 1933): 125–26.

Léon-Paul Fargue (1876–1947): French poet; Fargue was a student of Mallarmé who distanced himself from both the Surrealists as well as contemporary revolutionary movements. Author of intimate verse about Parisian life, he founded the journal *Commerce* in 1923 with Valéry Larbaud and Paul Valéry.

Lucien Lévy-Bruhl (1857–1939): French sociologist; a critic of abstract notions of morality, he worked from a perspective of sociological relativism to define a science of morals ("une science des moeurs"). After having studied the moral, religious, and mental lives of primitive tribes (*La Mentalité primitive,* 1922), he came to the conclusion that mystic thought was present in all human minds, albeit at variously perceptible levels.

Adolf J. Storfer (1888–1944): Journalist, linguist, director of the Internationaler Psychoanalytischer Verlag and a correspondent of Freud; Storfer worked on the possibilities of psychoanalytic etymology.

Frontierless Decade

Source: "Frontierless Decade," *Transition: Tenth Anniversary,* no. 27 (April–May 1938): 7–9.

Transition: An Occidental Workshop, 1927–1938

Source: "*Transition:* An Occidental Workshop, 1927–1938," in *transition work-shop,* ed. Eugene Jolas (New York: Vanguard, 1949), 13–18.

James Johnson Sweeney (1900–1986): curator of the Museum of Modern Art, 1935–46; and director of the Guggenheim Museum, New York, 1952–60.

Part Three: The Language of Night

The Revolution of Language in Elizabethan Theater

Source: "La révolution du langage chez les Elisabéthains," *Les Cahiers du sud* (Marseille) 20, no. 154 (June–July 1933): 73–76, trans. L.S. and C.R.

Dr. Samuel Johnson (1709–1784): Published his *Dictionary of the English Language* (1755) in two volumes. The first lexicographical work on the English language, Johnson's dictionary carries greater authority for its definitions and its quotation of English authors from the Elizabethan period to his own time, rather than for its idiosyncratic etymologies.

Neoplatonism: The last school of Greek philosophy, Neoplatonism (3rd century A.D.–6th century A.D.) develops certain ideas of Plato and Platonism, in combination with elements from Aristotle, the Stoics, and Gnosticism. It posits a single source from which all existence emanates and with which an individual soul can be mystically united. Its most famous proponents were Plotinus (A.D. 205–250) and Porphyry (A.D. 234–c. 305).

malgré: Fr. despite. "I love thee so, that, maugre all thy pride,/Nor wit nor reason can my passion hide" (Shakespeare, *Twelfth Night,* 3.1).

George Gordon: See *Shakespeare's English,* S.P.E. Tract No. 29, vol. 2 (1925–28).

Richard Puttenham (1520–1590): English writer ascribed authorship, with his brother George Puttenham, of *The Arte of English Poesie* (1589), a major Elizabethan treatise on versification.

Thomas Nash (1567–1601): Pamphleteer, poet, dramatist, and author of *The Unfortunate Traveller, or The Life of Jacke Wilton* (1594), the first picaresque novel in English.

Ben Jonson (1572–1637): English dramatist, lyric poet, and critic renowned for his comedies.

revised by Craig: Between 1899 and 1931, Craig coedited the Arden Shakespeare edition with H. R. Case. His 1914 Oxford edition of the *Complete Works of William Shakespeare* ranks among the most authoritative published in the last century.

alchemy of the word: A reference to Arthur Rimbaud (1858–1891), who was widely hailed by the Surrealists as a precursor of the permanent revolution of the mind. Turning away from Hugo and other early Parnassian influences, Rimbaud attempted to forge a new poetic idiom by defying the norms of diction and prosody, in a venture that he often compared to alchemy and hallucination. The precise allusion here is to the cycle of poems called "Alchimie du verbe" (1873), a subsection of the longer autobiographical poem *Une saison en enfer.*

One happied a woman: There appears to be no occurrence in Elizabethan literature of that phrase. However, "happy" was used as a verb in other instances: "That use is not forbidden usury,/Which happies those that pay the willing loan" (Shakespeare, Sonnet 6).

askance (used as a verb): "O, how are they wrapp'd in with infamies/That from their own misdeeds askance their eyes!" (Shakespeare, *The Rape of Lucrece*).

since of my crime: "O, hear me then, injurious, shifting Time!/Be guilty of my death, since of my crime" (Shakespeare, *The Rape of Lucrece*).

malice (used as a verb): "Your forc'd stings/Would hide themselves within his malic'd sides" (Jonson, *The Poetaster*).

The King's English Is Dying: Long Live the Great American Language

Source: "The King's English Is Dying: Long Live the Great American Language," *transition: An International Quarterly for Creative Experiment,* no. 19–20 (June 1930): 141–46.

V. F. Calverton (1900–1940): Born George Goetz, Calverton was a leftist intellectual who welcomed important literary figures such as F. Scott Fitzgerald, Langston Hughes, Alain Locke, Max Eastman, and Norman Thomas to his home in Baltimore. In 1923 he founded the *Modern Quarterly,* an independent Marxist journal for social critique which he would edit until his death. He wrote an influential literary history, *The Liberation of American Literature* (1932).

Marcel Jousse (1886–1961): Jesuit priest and French professor of anthropology, Jousse specialized in the study of oral style, rhythm, and gesture. He is generally accredited as a forerunner of ethno-linguistics.

On ne parle pas comme on écrit: Fr. We don't speak the way we write.

aurochs: an extinct species of wild ox which formerly inhabited Europe.

Jean Paulhan (1884–1968): Director of the *Nouvelle Revue française,* Paulhan was a French writer and art critic. He started his career as a gold digger in Madagascar, wrote a volume on Malagasy poetry, and went on to become a professor of Eastern languages.

F. W. J. Schelling (1775–1854): A German idealist philosopher, Schelling was one of the major successors of Kant, along with Fichte and Hegel. He developed his own philosophy of nature, as well as a philosophy of spirit around a conception of absolute identity recognizable through intellectual intuition rather than speculation.

Esperanto, Volapük, and [. . .] Novial: Constructed by Ludwik L. Zamenhof, a Russian physician, Esperanto is the best-known attempt at creating a universal language. Volapük was created in 1879–80 by Johann Martin Schleyer, a Catholic priest in Baden, Germany. While Esperanto works on a base of Romance languages, Volapük relies on English and German, with some French. Novial, an artificial language constructed in 1928 by the Danish philologist Otto Jespersen, intended for use as an international auxiliary language, is also based on Germanic word roots.

Sherwood Anderson (1876–1941): Mainly a novelist and a short story writer, he was interested in the use of colloquial speech in prose and poetry. A close personal friend of the Jolases from New Orleans, Anderson wrote a glowing introduction to Jolas's collection of poems, *Cinema* (1926).

The Language of Night

Source: *The Language of Night* (The Hague: Servire, 1932).

Max Scheler (1874–1928): A German ethical and social philosopher, Scheler attempted to develop Husserlian phenomenology in keeping with his Catholic faith. After formulating an intensive critique of Kantian ethics (*Der Formalismus in der Ethik und die materiale Wertethik,* 1913–16), Scheler took on a meta-anthropological study of the place of man in the universe (*Die Stellung des Menschen im Kosmos,* 1928). Jolas was attracted to Scheler due to his own affinity for what he called "White Romanticism" in the works of Novalis, Jean Paul, and others Romantics, as well as following his discussions with Carl Einstein.

Ruskin's gentleman's tradition: Jolas sets up the influential Victorian art critic, writer, and social reformer John Ruskin (1819–1900) as a model of clearly expressed erudition left untouched by the dominant crisis of language.

Luis de Góngora y Argote (1561–1627): Author of *Fábula de Polifemo y Galatea* (c. 1613) and *Soledades* (c. 1613); Góngora y Argote was an influential Spanish poet known for his convoluted, Baroque style known as Gongorism (*Gongorismo*). His introduction of Latinisms into Spanish and his use of complex syntax, allusions, and imagery won him as many epigones as enemies.

Comte de Lautréamont (1846–1870): Little is known about Isidore Ducasse's brief life except that he came to Paris to study at the Ecole polytechnique. Taking his pseudonym from a novel by Eugène Sue, Lautréamont is famous for his *Chants de Maldoror* (1868–69). He was taken up by Breton and the Surrealists as one of the rare precursors of their poetic revolution.

Stefan George (1868–1933): A lyric poet, George was chiefly responsible for the revival of fin de siècle German poetry. His verse is symbolic, classical, and erudite, with an emphasis on form. Having visited the Symbolists and Mallarmé in Paris and the Pre-Raphaelites in London, George returned to Germany to found his own movement known as the George-Kreis. He cofounded the art journal *Blätter für die Kunst* (1892–1919) with Hugo von Hofmannsthal.

Filippo Tommaso Marinetti (1876–1944): French-Italian writer, novelist, poet, and dramatist, Marinetti founded Futurism by publishing the *Manifeste du Futurisme* in *Le Figaro* (February 20, 1909). He exalted modernity in a proto-fascistic cult of speed, machines, and machismo. His works display a similar intensity exploding syntax, punctuation, and typography. See also Marinetti's *Manifeste technique de la littérature futuriste* of 1912.

August Stramm (1874–1915): German Expressionist poet and playwright; while serving as an army captain, Stramm was killed in World War I. Stramm's "Wortkunst" poems appeared in Herwarth Walden's art review *Der Sturm.*

Herwarth Walden (1878–1941): Founder of the Berlin periodical and gallery *Der Sturm,* Walden was instrumental in the Expressionist circle from 1910 onward. He introduced the Futurists, the Cubists, and other major contemporary European art to Germany and provided a forum for the poetry of Else-Laske Schüler, August Stramm, and George Heym and the stories of Gottfried Benn and Kurt Tucholsky in his review. The activities linked with the review later spread out to salons, art institutes, and experimental theaters (*Sturmabende, Sturmschule,* and *Sturmbühne*).

Liliencrons and Dehmels: Detlev von Liliencron (1844–1909) was a playwright and poet known for his naturalistic verse; Richard Dehmel (1863–1920), a poet influenced by Nietzsche, wrote on naturalistic social themes, but also on the mystical power of sex and love.

Gottfried Benn (1886–1955): German Expressionist poet and essayist; Benn's early poems were influenced by his work as a doctor (*Morgue,* 1912). He regained influence, in spite of a short-lived involvement with Nazism in 1933–34, in post-World War II Germany. Jolas published translations of his stories in *transition* as well as his scientific work on the unconscious ("The Structure of Personality," *Transition,* no. 21, 1932).

Kurt Schwitters (1887–1948): German artist and poet, Schwitters was a fringe member of the Dada group. Having been denied full membership in the Berlin circle by Richard Huelsenbeck due to his overtly aesthetic stance and his "bourgeois face," Schwitters went on to form "Merz" in Hanover, based on a similar principle of montage; an architectural version of these experiments was the series of dwellings or *Merzbau* that Schwitters built. A selection of his visual work and poems can be found in *transition.*

Carl Einstein (1885–1940): Art historian and essayist, Einstein wrote groundbreaking studies on African art and Cubism, while in his early novel *Bebuquin* (1906–12), he experimented with a form of literary "Cubism." During his time in Paris, Einstein cofounded the influential review *Documents* with Georges Bataille and others in 1929, served as an artistic advisor to the filmmaker Jean Renoir, and contributed to *transition.* Politically committed throughout his life, Einstein would go on to fight in the Spanish Civil War alongside Durutti. A German Jew, he committed suicide in 1940 close to Pau, while trying to escape from the Nazis.

Hugo Ball (1886–1927): Writer, dramatist, and actor, Ball, after a short military adventure, turned pacifist and left Germany for Switzerland during World War I. He founded the Dada movement with Tristan Tzara and others in Zurich (see his autobiography, *Die Flucht aus der Zeit*, 1927; *The Flight from Time*). His "Laut-poesie" (sound poetry) inspired Jolas.

Hans (Jean) Arp (1887–1966): an Alsatian; Arp with Ball, Tzara, and others created Dada in Zurich. His abstract drawings, automatic poems, paintings, and sculptures all sought to fuse art and accident, while flouting formal conventions. Later he was involved with Surrealism.

Tristan Tzara (1896–1963): Romanian-born Francophone poet; "Tzara" was the pseudonym of Samuel Rosenstock. Tzara wrote some of the movement's manifes-toes; see, for example, *Sept manifestes Dada* (1924). In the 1930s he worked to rec-oncile Surrealism with Marxism.

Richard Huelsenbeck (1892–1974): Huelsenbeck was a cofounder of the Dada movement in Zurich and Berlin. He later traveled abroad as a correspondent for German publishing houses, worked as a ship's doctor, and finally immigrated to the United States, where he lived under the name of Charles Hulbeck and prac-ticed Jungian psychoanalysis.

Alfred Jarry (1873–1907): Jarry is widely associated with his recurrent mario-nette character King Ubu, a farcical tyrant with a penchant for scatological mal-apropisms (*Ubu Roi*, 1896). Apart from his Ubu writings, Jarry's work has often been considered complex and difficult. His reflections on theater would inspire the Theatre of the Absurd, and especially Antonin Artaud. Jarry also wrote an intro-ductory manual to a mock science called "pataphysics."

Benjamin Péret (1899–1959): French Surrealist who took part in the first exper-iments to record dream speech under hypnosis. Although Péret was staunchly against moral and political influence on literature, he went on to fight in the Span-ish Civil War alongside the Anarchists.

Roger Vitrac (1899–1952): French poet and playwright; Vitrac joined Artaud when he founded the Théâtre Alfred Jarry, attacking bourgeois values and illustrat-ing the destructive powers of language.

Robert Desnos (1900–1945): French poet; Desnos had a real flair for verbal automatism and participated in Breton's hypnotic sleep experiments. Although closely linked with Surrealism, he gave his poetry a more lyric, humorous accent in the development of Nerval's Romanticism (*La liberté ou l'amour*, 1927; *Corps et biens*, 1930). Desnos was later a resistant in World War II and died in Theresien-stadt, a concentration camp in former Czechoslovakia.

Henri Michaux (1899–1984): Belgian-born, poet and painter; Michaux's works deal with the inner experience of dreams, fantasies, and drug-induced hallucina-tions. He contributed to various avant-garde journals in the 1920s and published travelogues based on his experiences in the merchant marine.

Gerard Manley Hopkins (1844–1889): English poet and Jesuit priest; his works were published posthumously in 1918, influencing a great number of poets from

Eliot and Auden to Stephen Spender and Joyce. Inspired by Duns Scotus, the medieval Franciscan thinker, Hopkins sought to depict the "inscapes," or the individual essence of natural life. His experiments with rhyme, "sprung rhythm," alliteration, and repetition lend a strong musical quality to his verse.

Giambattista Vico (1688–1744): Italian philosopher; Vico is considered a forerunner of historiography and the history of philosophy. He developed a cyclical conception of history. A critic of Cartesian rationalism, Vico relied on philology to study the formation, development, and decline of nations, which all passed through three phases in his theory: the age of gods, the age of heroes, and the age of men, followed by the *recorso,* or the return of the first phase. His principal work is translated as the *New Science* (1725). As Jolas points out in "The Revolution of Language and James Joyce" (*transition*, no. 11, 1928), Vico played a critical role for Joyce's vision of history and narrative in *Finnegans Wake.*

C. K. Ogden (1889–1957): Founder of the *Cambridge Magazine* (1912); Ogden was a British linguistic who developed "Basic English," a pared-down, standardized version of English intended for international communication (*Basic English,* 1930). He coauthored *The Meaning of Meaning* (1923), a study on semantic ambiguity, with the critic I. A. Richards.

new-sounders: Jolas transliterates a term from Karl Kraus's German term "Neutöner." Kraus uses it as a critical epithet for the Expressionists, whereas Jolas puts a positive spin on it.

Biedermeier: Refers to the dominant style in furniture, architecture, and later as a modus vivendi of the middle class in Austria and Germany between 1815 and 1848; Jolas uses it in its derogatory meaning of being conventional or bourgeois.

Sachlichkeit: The term "Neue Sachlichkeit" or "New Objectivity" is generally attributed to the museum director Gustav Hartlaub (1884–1963), who used it in 1923 while preparing an exhibition of paintings in Mannheim by the "Verists"— Expressionist painters such as Max Beckmann, Otto Dix, and George Grosz.

Eleusinian mysteries: The secret religious rites of Demeter, the earth goddess, as celebrated on Eleusis in Attica.

Novalis (1772–1801): pseudonym of Friedrich Freiherr von Hardenberg; Novalis was an early German Romantic poet, novelist, and theorist who greatly influenced later generations of Romanticism. His *Hymnen an den Nacht* (1800) are an elegiac series of poems that celebrate night, death, and the promise of a mystical reunion with his absent beloved in the afterlife. He went on to write philosophical romances which idealized the quest of a poet in the Middle Ages (*Heinrich von Ofterdingen,* 1800), whose visions of longing crystallized in the image of the "blue flower." Jolas placed Novalis at the center of his personal genealogy of a "White Romanticism," in which he saw a precursor to avant-garde movements of his time.

Pierre Janet (1859–1947): French psychologist and professor at Collège de France and the Sorbonne; Janet worked with Charcot to develop the notion of the unconscious in his doctoral work on automatic acts (1889). He went on to become the director of the Salpêtrière hospital and remained an advocate for the conjunction of research psychology and clinical treatment both in the United States and France.

Léon Daudet (1868–1942): French journalist and writer; Daudet was a virulent columnist in Charles Maurras' right-wing journal *Action française* (1919–24; 1929–42).

Master Eckhart (ca. 1260–1327): Dominican theologian and philosopher; Eckhart is considered to be Germany's greatest mystic. In his sermons he set out the course of the union of the soul and God. His thought offers a unique blend of Greek, Neoplatonic, Arabic, and Scholastic elements, along with personal mystic experiences. By naming them, he introduced many abstract neologisms into German.

Wilhelm Schlegel (1767–1845): Along with his brother Friedrich, Wilhelm Schlegel founded the review *Athenäum*. As a critic, Schlegel was a follower of Herder and Lessing in his defense of Romanticism against Classicism. In his conferences on *Literature and Art* (1801–4) he would develop his major ideas on language, poetry, myths, and the unconscious creations of the imagination.

Wanted: A New Symbolical Language!

Source: "Wanted: A New Symbolical Language!" *Transition: An International Workshop for Orphic Creation*, no. 21 (March 1932): 284.

Wanted: A New Communicative Language!

Source: "Wanted: A New Communicative Language!" *Transition: An International Workshop for Orphic Creation*, no. 21 (March 1932): 285.

Confession About Grammar

Source: "Confession About Grammar," *Transition: An International Workshop for Orphic Creation*, no. 22 (February 1933): 124.

Introduction to *The Negro Who Sings*

Source: Introduction to *Le Nègre qui chante* [*The Negro Who Sings*], ed. and trans. Eugene Jolas (Paris: Editions des cahiers libres, 1928), 9–28, trans. A.D. and C.R.

Erik Satie (1866–1925): French composer who was an exponent of several important trends in twentieth-century composition, including bitonality, polytonality, jazz, and non-triadic harmony.

Parade: In 1917 Satie collaborated with Jean Cocteau and the Cubist painter Picasso on the ballet *Parade*. The composition consisted of three pieces representing three different viewpoints of a single musical concept, an approach similar to the one used by the Cubist painters.

Roland Hayes (1887–1977): African American musician and composer; Hayes was the first black male to win acclaim in America and Europe as a concert artist.

Paul Robeson (1898–1976): African American athlete, singer, actor, and advocate for the civil rights movement.

Fisk Singers: The Fisk Jubilee Singers, in the chaotic decade following the Civil War, were a group of young ex-slaves in Nashville, Tennessee, who set out on a mission to save their financially troubled school by giving concerts. Traveling first through cities in the North, then on to venues across Europe, the Jubilee Singers introduced audiences to the power of spirituals, the religious anthems of slavery.

Irving Berlin (1888–1989): American musician; he was one of America's most prolific writers of patriotic songs from World War I through World War II.

Josephine Baker (1906–1975): Iconic African American dancer, she became a French citizen after marriage and performed extensively in Paris. Her 1925 act with an all-black troupe, *La Revue nègre,* proved to be a turning point in her career. She gained a reputation for working the Paris Music Hall audiences into a frenzy with her uninhibited movements.

Albert Henry Krehbiel (1873–1945): American critic and Impressionist painter.

George Antheil (1900–1959): American composer known for his ultramodern compositions in the 1920s.

Aaron Copland (1900–1990): American composer, whose works blend national musical influences—such as Mexican folk and Shaker music—with modern compositional techniques.

Race and Language

Source: "Race and Language," *Transition: A Quarterly Review,* no. 24 (June 1936): 111–12.

Inquiry into the Spirit and Language of Night

Source: "Inquiry into the Spirit and Language of Night," *Transition: Tenth Anniversary,* no. 27 (April–May 1938): 233 and 243–45.

Preface to *Words from the Deluge*

Source: Preface to *Words from the Deluge* (New York: Gotham Bookmart, undated [1940]), unpaginated.

H. L. Mencken (1880–1956): Dubbed the Sage of Baltimore; Mencken was a satirical journalist, columnist, and essayist who wrote for the *Baltimore Morning Herald* and the *Baltimore Sun.* He cofounded the literary magazine *Smart Set* (1914–23) and was a contributing editor to *American Mercury.* A leading authority on American English, Mencken published his study *The American Language* in 1919.

Logos

Source: "Logos," *transition: An International Quarterly for Creative Experiment,* no. 16–17 (June 1929): 25–30.

From Jabberwocky to "Lettrism"

Source: "From Jabberwocky to 'Lettrism,'" *Transition: Forty-eight,* ed. Georges Duthuit, no. 1 (January 1948): 104–20.

Isidore Isou (1928–?): Romanian-born poet; Isou came to Paris after World War II with the express intention of renovating the arts with his pan-esthetic movement called Lettrism. A form of "hyper-graphic" visual poetry, or phonetic Cubism, Lettrism aimed at the production of sound using the human body as an instrument. It was later linked with Guy Debord's Situationism and other utopian anarchist movements, thus playing a part in the events of May 1968.

Hugo von Hofmannsthal (1874–1929): Austrian poet, dramatist, and essayist; both in his poems and his plays, Hofmannsthal composed metaphysical lyric reflections on the nature of life and the transient world. After a personal crisis, which he staged in a fictive letter to Francis Bacon ("Ein Brief," the so-called Lord Chandos Letter, 1902), he gave up purely lyrical forms.

Paul Scheerbart (1863–1915): German poet, grotesque and humorist novelist, and "glass architect." Scheerbart was obsessed with the esthetic and architectonic qualities of glass as a material.

Rudolf Blümner (1874–1945): German actor, poet, and essayist linked with *Der Sturm,* Blümner appeared in such Expressionist classics as Fritz Lang's film *M* (1931), and wrote the study *Der Geist des Kubismus und die Kunst* (1921).

Philippe Soupault (1897–1990): French poet and novelist, Soupault cofounded the review *Littérature* with Breton and Aragon in 1919 and cowrote *Les Champs magnétiques* with Breton (1920). Soupault was interested in bridging the transatlantic divide as much as Jolas, and he often contributed to little magazines such as *Tambour, transition,* and *La Revue Européenne,* finding the *Nouvelle Revue française* too traditional for his taste. In this vein, he worked closely with Jolas while editing an *Anthologie de la nouvelle poésie américaine* (1927) and the collection of spirituals entitled *Le Nègre qui chante* (1927).

Raymond Roussel (1887–1933): French poet and writer; Roussel's influence stretches from Surrealism to structuralism and the *nouveau roman.* Roussel had a nervous breakdown when his early poetic works met with no success. He went on to publish the imaginary travelogues *Impressions d'Afrique* (1910) and *Nouvelles impressions d'Afrique* (1932). His posthumous volume of meta-commentary, *Comment j'ai écrit certains de mes livres* (1935), gave rise to intensive studies of his complex creative procedure—by Foucault, Kristeva, and Leiris—ruled by a set of complex language games.

Fernando Ortiz (1881–1969): Essayist, anthropologist, and philologist who pioneered in the study of neo-African cultures in the Americas, particularly in Cuba.

Iliazd (1894–1975): Russian writer and printer; Ilia Zdanevich took part in the Futurist and Dada movements both in Russia and France. Author of *Lidantiu faram* (1923), a dramatic poem written in "Zaoum," he went on to work as a typographer with Max Ernst, Pablo Picasso, and Joan Miro on illustrated books.

Part Four: From Romanticism to the Avant-Garde

Romanticism and the Dream

Source: "Romanticism and the Dream," *Transition: A Quarterly Review,* no. 24 (June 1936): 109–11.

Johann Georg Hamann (1730–88): German philosopher of language and aesthetics, who—quite similar to Johann Gottfried Herder—involved himself in a meta-critical reflection of Kant's *Critique of Pure Reason.* However, his Christian-based discourse and highly allusive and hermetic literary style proved to be in the way of a proper understanding of the latter's epistemology.

Ludwig Tieck (1773–1835): early German Romantic author.

William Lovell: Ludwig Tieck's epistolary novel *Die Geschichte des Herrn William Lovell* (1795–96) describes the self-destruction of a young man.

Romanticism Is Not Dead

Source: "Romanticism Is Not Dead," in *Vertical: A Yearbook for Romantic-Mystic Ascensions,* ed. Eugene Jolas (New York: Gotham Bookmart, 1941), 157–61.

Gérard de Nerval (Gérard Labrunie, 1808–55): French Romantic poet (*Aurélia, ou Le rêve et la vie*), translator of Goethe's *Faust.*

Gustav Theodor Fechner (1801–1887): German physicist and philosopher who helped found psychophysics, the study of the relations between sensations and physical stimuli. His work in psychology addressed the mind-body problem, claiming that the two entities were different aspects of the same phenomenon (*Elemente der Psychophysik*, 1860).

Pan-Romanticism in the Atomic Age

Source: "Pan-Romanticism in the Atomic Age," in *transition workshop,* ed. Eugene Jolas (New York: Vanguard, 1949), 393–95.

Achim von Arnim (1781–1831): German poet, folklorist, and novelist; von Arnim was part of the Heidelberg Romantic circle with Görres, Creuzer, and Brentano (*Des Knaben Wunderhorn*, 1806–08).

Schwärmerei: Ger. exaltation, reverie; used pejoratively by enlightened critics of occultism and Romanticism.

Maurice Maeterlinck (1862–1949): Belgian Symbolist poet, playwright, and essayist. Maeterlinck's atmospheric plays influenced Hofmannsthal, Yeats, Synge, and Beckett. He won the Nobel Prize in 1911.

Romanticism and Metapolitics

Source: "Romanticism and Metapolitics," Gen Mss 108, box 5, folder 125 (after 1949), Eugene and Maria Jolas Papers, General Collection of Rare Books, Beinecke Rare Book and Manuscript Library, Yale University, New Haven, Conn.

Johann Gottfried Herder (1744–1803): German critic and philosopher of language and history; Herder was a leading figure in the Sturm und Drang movement, a mentor of young Goethe, and a forerunner of the philosophy of culture and history in his defense of national folk traditions against "classical" ideals (*Ideen zur Philosophie der Geschichte der Menschheit*, 1784–91).

Götterdämmerung: Ger. twilight of the gods.

Lebensraum: Ger. "living space," in nationalist and Nazi terminology.

Stars and Angels: Homage to G. Th. Fechner, Romantic Savant and Visionary

Source: "Stars and Angels: Homage to G. Th. Fechner, Romantic Savant and Visionary," in *Vertical: A Yearbook for Romantic-Mystic Ascensions,* ed. Eugene Jolas (New York: Gotham Bookmart, 1941), 173–75.

Prolegomenon, or White Romanticism and the Mythos of Ascension

Source: "Prolegomenon, or White Romanticism and the Mythos of Ascension," Gen Mss 108, box 28, folder 386 (undated), Eugene and Maria Jolas Papers, General Collection of Rare Books, Beinecke Rare Book and Manuscript Library, Yale University, New Haven, Conn.

das Wunderbare: Ger. the marvelous; fantastic.

Wunderbare Mondennacht, / Steig' empor mit alter Pracht: Ger. Wonderful moonlight / Rise with the old magnificence.

Nacht and *Sehnsucht:* Ger. night and nostalgia.

Mary Colum (1883–1957): Irish critic and short story writer (*Our Friend James Joyce,* 1959; *Life and the Dream,* 1966).

plaquette: Fr. leaflet.

Albert Béguin (1901–1957): Prolific Swiss literary critic and essayist; Béguin edited the *Cahiers du Rhône* and *Esprit.* A translator of German Romantics into French, his doctoral thesis examined their influence on modern French poetry (*Le rêve chez les romantiques allemands et dans la poésie française moderne,* 1937).

Surrealism and Romanticism

Source: "Surrealism and Romanticism," Gen Mss 108, box 5, folder 128 (undated), Eugene and Maria Jolas Papers, General Collection of Rare Books, Beinecke Rare Book and Manuscript Library, Yale University, New Haven, Conn.

Surrealism: Ave atque Vale

Source: "Surrealism: Ave atque Vale," *Fantasy* (Pittsburgh), no. 1 (1941): 23–30.

cadavre exquis: Fr. "exquisite corpse," a Surrealist game of folded paper that consists in having a sentence or a drawing composed by several people, each ignorant of the preceding collaboration.

Marcel Noll (1890–?): Director of the Surrealist Gallery from 1926; Noll's writings appeared in *La Revolution surréaliste,* and Jolas published two of his poems in *transition.*

coulée de mots: Fr. flow of words.

poèmes en commun: Fr. poems in common.

Max Morise (1903–1973): Cartoonist, poet, and writer who contributed to *La Révolution surréaliste.*

Michel Leiris (1901–1990): French writer and anthropologist; Leiris is remembered for his monumental, multivolume autobiography *La Règle du jeu* (1948–76). His early Surrealist poetry, showing his fascination with puns and wordplay, appeared in *La Révolution surréaliste* (*Simulacre*, 1926).

calembours: Fr. pun, play on words.

Il faut changer le monde: Fr. One must change the world.

Nous sommes en quête du merveilleux: Fr. We seek the marvelous.

Monk Lewis: Matthew Lewis's (1775–1818) Gothic novel *The Monk* (1796) earned such notoriety that he was known as "Monk" Lewis thereafter.

Saint-Pol-Roux (1861–1940): Born Paul Pierre Roux; French Symbolist poet given to baroque lyricism. Saint-Pol-Roux's use of the image as a force of liberation made him a precursor celebrated by the Surrealists.

poncif: Fr. commonplace; cliché.

Part Five: Crisis of Man and Language: Verticalist/Vertigralist Manifestoes

On the Quest

Source: "On the Quest," *transition,* no. 9 (December 1927): 191–96.

William Carlos Williams (1863–1963): Williams was influenced by Imagism, Cubism, and Dadaism and yet was one of the singularly American modernist poets, both in his diction and his themes.

De Soto (1496–1542); Spanish explorer and conquistador.

Daniel Boone (1734–1820): American pioneer.

Notes on Reality

Source: "Notes on Reality," *transition: An International Quarterly for Creative Experiment,* no. 18 (November 1929): 15–20.

Wilhelm Stekel (1868–1940): Austrian psychiatrist; Stekel was a student of Freud, but distanced himself in 1912. He wrote widely on sexual problems and questioned the notion of the unconscious; his critique would later be used by Sartre.

Preface to *Transition* Stories

Source: "Preface," in *Transition Stories: Twenty-three Stories from "Transition,"* ed. Eugene Jolas and Robert Sage (New York: Walter V. McKee, 1929), ix–xii.

Literature and the New Man

Source: "Literature and the New Man," *transition: An International Quarterly for Creative Experiment,* no. 19–20 (June 1930): 13–19.

daemon: Gk. divinity; the genius attached to each individual, identified as his or her destiny.

Johann Jakob Bachofen (1815–1887): Swiss jurist and anthropologist who studied Roman law, kinship, and funeral symbolism (*Das Mutterrecht,* 1861).

Allan Tate (1899–1979): American poet, critic, and novelist. Tate was a forerunner of the New Criticism.

Irving Babbitt (1865–1933): American critic and Harvard professor of French and comparative literature; Babbitt was the leader of the conservative New Humanist movement.

Lemonnier and Thérive: Camille Lemonnier (1844–1913), Belgian writer; André Thérive (1891–1967), French novelist and critic.

Robinson Jeffers (1887–1962): American philosophical poet with a pantheistic vision; Jeffers declared that his poetry dealt with "Inhumanism."

Night-Mind and Day-Mind

Source: "Night-Mind and Day-Mind," *Transition: An International Workshop for Orphic Creation,* no. 21 (March 1932): 222–23.

Poetry Is Vertical

Source: "Poetry Is Vertical," *Transition: An International Workshop for Orphic Creation,* no. 21 (March 1932): 148–49.

On a été trop horizontal/j'ai envie d'être vertical: Fr. We have been too horizontal/I want to be vertical.

The Primal Personality

Source: "The Primal Personality," *Transition: An International Workshop for Orphic Creation,* no. 22 (February 1933): 78–83.

Ludwig Klages (1872–1956): German psychologist and philosopher, a leader of the vitalist movement; Klages made important contributions to characterology and graphology (*Prinzipien der Charakterologie,* 1910; *Geist und Leben,* 1935).

Hans Leisegang (1890–1951): German mythologist and philosopher.

ens a se: Lat. being from itself.

Parmi les différences qui [. . .] habitudes d'esprit: "Among the differences that separate the mentality of inferior societies from ours," says M. Lévy-Bruhl, "there is one that catches the attention of a large number of those who have observed them in the most favorable conditions, that is, before they could have been modified by an extended contact with White people. They have noticed that there is a marked aversion amongst the primitives for reasoning, for what the logicians call discursive operations of thought; they have remarked at the same time that this aversion does not rise from a radical incapacity, or a natural impotence of their understanding, but that it was explicable rather by the ensemble of their mental habits."

Edgar Dacqué (1878–1945): German paleontologist, author of *Urwelt, Sage und Menschheit* (1925), in which he sought to reconcile science, myth, and religion.

oor-world: Jolas's neologism, oor- from German ur- (Urwelt), primeval world.

Wesensschau: Ger. intuition of essence, or eidetic seeing; a term often associated with Husserlian phenomenology.

Twilight of the Horizontal Age

Source: "Twilight of the Horizontal Age," *Transition: An International Workshop for Orphic Creation,* no. 22 (February 1933): 6.

Vertigralist Transmutation

Source: "Vertigralist Transmutation," *Transition: An Intercontinental Workshop for Vertigralist Transmutation,* no. 23 (July 1935): 107, trans. E.K. and C.R.

Georges Pelorson (1909–?): George Belmont, French translator and poet. Pelorson worked closely with Beckett, Henry Miller, and Raymond Queneau.

Paramyths

Source: "Paramyths," *Transition: An Intercontinental Workshop for Vertigralist Transmutation,* no. 23 (July 1935): 7.

Workshop

Source: "Workshop," *Transition: An Intercontinental Workshop for Vertigralist Transmutation,* no. 23 (July 1935): 97–106.

restitutio in pristinum: Lat. restoration to the original (condition).

Ofterdingen's blue flower: Vision of longing in Novalis's *Heinrich von Ofterdingen* (1800).

formule magique: Fr. magic spell.

O certe necessarium Adam peccatum: Lat. "O truly necessary sin of Adam," phrase ascribed to St. Ambrose of Milan.

n'en déplaise aux collectivistes: Fr. even if it bothers collectivists.

Vertigral

Source: "Vertigral," *Transition: A Quarterly Review,* no. 24 (June 1936): 114.

Vertigralist Pamphlet

Source: *Vertigralist Pamphlet* (Paris: Transition, 1938).

Nous descendons [. . .] la respiration: Fr. We are going down spirally, for fifteen years, into a vortex of infamy and our descent is speeding up to breathlessness.

weltangst: Ger. world anxiety.

urangst: Ger. primal anxiety.

la grande peur de l'an mil: Fr. the great fear of the year thousand.

le mal: Fr. evil.

Georges Bernanos (1888–1948): Conservative French Catholic writer and journalist (*Sous le soleil de Satan,* 1926; *Le Journal d'un curé de campagne,* 1936).

tremendum: Lat. usually *mysterium tremendum,* that is, the overwhelming mystery, or the mystery that repels.

The Quest and the Myth

Source: "The Quest and the Myth," in *Vertical: A Yearbook for Romantic-Mystic Ascensions,* ed. Eugene Jolas (New York: Gotham Bookmart, 1941), 98–100.

Poetry of Ascent

Source: "Poetry of Ascent," in *Vertical: A Yearbook for Romantic-Mystic Ascensions,* ed. Eugene Jolas (New York: Gotham Bookmart, 1941), 17–18.

Threefold Ascent: Verticalist Manifesto

Source: "Threefold Ascent: Verticalist Manifesto," in *Vertical: A Yearbook for Romantic-Mystic Ascensions,* ed. Eugene Jolas (New York: Gotham Bookmart, 1941), 11–14.

Part Six: Literary Encounters

Novalis

Homage to Novalis

Source: "Homage to Novalis," *transition: An International Quarterly for Creative Experiment,* no. 18 (November 1929): 72–73.

Herrnhuter: Ger. literally "God's watchmen"; a German missionary sect founded in America in 1723 by Nikolaus Ludwig Graf von Zinzendorf, and more commonly referred to as Moravians.

Novalis, the Mystic Visionary

Source: "Novalis, the Mystic Visionary," Gen Mss 108, box 21, folder 394 (undated), Eugene and Maria Jolas Papers, General Collection of Rare Books, Beinecke Rare Book and Manuscript Library, Yale University, New Haven, Conn., partly used for "Novalis, or the White Romanticism."

Oscar Vladislas de Miłosz (1877–1939): French poet and Lithuanian diplomat; Miłosz settled in Paris after World War I, where he wrote poetry, dramas, philosophical essays, and adapted Lithuanian folk tales. He exercised considerable literary influence over his nephew, Czesław Miłosz.

Joseph Görres (1776–1848): German writer, critic, and theologian; leading member of the Heidelberg Romantic group; together with Clemens Brentano and Ludwig Achim von Arnim, he edited the famous *Zeitung für Einsied-ler* (subsequently renamed *Trost-Einsamkeit*). In 1814 he founded *Der Rheinische Merkur.*

Böhmist mysticism: Mysticism based on the doctrines of Jakob Böhme (1575–1624), philosopher and mystic who greatly influenced German idealism and Romanticism.

felix culpa: Lat. "happy fault"; in Christian theology, it refers to the felicity of Original Sin, which permits redemption through Christ.

Aufklärung: Ger. Enlightenment.

Tiberius Hemsterhuys (1685–1766): Dutch scholar and classical lexicographer.

Vedic writings: Sacred writings of the Vedic religion, compiled over ten centuries from the 15th to the 5th century B.C. The Vedas, written in old Sanskrit, compose the Sruti or the divinely revealed part of Hinduism.

Novalis, or the White Romanticism

Source: "Novalis ou le romantisme blanc" ["Novalis, or the White Romanticism"], *Critique: Revue générale des publications françaises et étrangères* 7, no. 44 (January 15, 1951): 3–15, trans. E.K. and C.R.

Devotional Songs: Geistliche Lieder, compare Jolas's own translation from German into English (p. 312); the poem is numbered there as ninth, here tenth; in a modern German edition, *Beck's Kommentierte Klassiker,* eleventh, v. 25 ss: "Ein Engel zieht dich wieder. . . ."

Goethe

The Case of Goethe: Was He a Heroic Figure or Merely a Philistine?

Source: "The Case of Goethe: Was He a Heroic Figure or Merely a Philistine?" *Transition: An International Workshop for Orphic Creation,* no. 21 (March 1932): 206.

Binsenwahrheiten: Ger. tautology, home truths.

standpatter: Someone who "stands pat," being an opponent or resistant to change.

Gide

André Gide, Mystic and Dionysian

Source: "André Gide, Mystic and Dyonisien [*sic*]," *Chicago Tribune Sunday Magazine* (European edition), no. 22 (July 13, 1924): 3 and 10.

récits: Fr. "narrative" or "account;" a brief novel with a simple narrative structure.

soties: Short satirical plays popular in France in the fifteenth and early sixteenth centuries, in which a company of fools would mix chatter with farcical acrobatics.

Les Extrêmes se touchent: Fr. the ends meet.

José-Maria de Hérédia (1842–1905): Cuban-born French poet remembered for his sonnets (*Les Trophées,* 1893).

Les Nourritures terrestres: Fr. *The Fruits of the Earth.*

La Porte étroite: Fr. *Strait Is the Gate.*

La Symphonie Pastorale: Fr. *The Pastoral Symphony.*

Les Caves du Vatican: Fr. *The Cellars of the Vatican.*

Les Faux Monnayeurs: Fr. *The Counterfeiters.*

Franz Kafka's Stories and Ascending Romanticism

Source: "Franz Kafka's Stories and Ascending Romanticism," in *Vertical: A Year-book for Romantic-Mystic Ascensions,* ed. Eugene Jolas (New York: Gotham Book-mart, 1941), 169–72.

Heinrich von Kleist (1777–1811): German dramatist and writer. Kleist was profoundly impressed by Kant and Rousseau, whose works destroyed his belief in the value of knowledge, and fed his naturally audacious and irrational imagination. Although he was encouraged by Goethe and Schiller early on, his career ended in failure and suicide. His tumultuous life and works made him an avatar for Realist, Expressionist, and Existentialist poets.

Georg Trakl, Poetry

Source: "Georg Trakl, *Die Dichtungen*" ["Georg Trakl, *Poetry*"], *Critique: Revue générale des publications françaises et étrangères* 7, no. 49 (June 15, 1951): 552–55, trans. E.K. and C.R.

Georg Trakl (1887–1914): Austrian Expressionist poet; influenced by Hölder-lin and French Symbolism, Trakl began his career under the patronage of Ludwig Wittgenstein.

Menchenheitsdämmerung: Ger. dawn of humanity.

Weltunglück geistert: Ger. the misfortune of the world lurks.

Gottfried Benn

Source: "Gottfried Benn," *transition,* no. 5 (August 1927): 146–49.

Arno Holz (1863–1939): German critic and poet; Holz was one of the founders of the Naturalist school.

Ernst Jünger and the Twilight of Nihilism

Source: "Ernst Jünger et le crépuscule du nihilisme" ["Ernst Jünger and the Twilight of Nihilism"], *Critique: Revue générale des publications françaises et étrangères* 8, no. 54 (November 1951): 937–45, trans. E.K. and C.R.

In Stahlgewittern: Ger. *The Storm of Steel.*

Der Kampf als inneres Erlebnis: Gr. *Combat as Inner Experience.*

Der Arbeiter: Ger. *The Worker.*

Blätter und Steine: Ger. *Leaves and Stones.*

Lob der Vokale: Ger. *The Eulogy of Vowels.*

Auf den Marmoklippen: Ger. *On the Marble Cliffs.*

Gärten und Strassen: Ger. *Gardens and Roads.*

Strahlungen: Ger. *Irradiations.*

Gabriel Marcel (1889–1973): French playwright and Christian existentialist philosopher.

Das Fürchterliche: Ger. the horrible.

Naturphilosophie: Ger. "philosophy of nature," associated in German idealism with the work of Hegel and Schelling, who opposed it to logic and the phenomenology of the spirit.

André Breton's Surrealism in 1950

Source: "André Breton's Surrealism in 1950," Gen Mss 108, box 4, folder 83, Eugene and Maria Jolas Papers, General Collection of Rare Books, Beinecke Rare Book and Manuscript Library, Yale University, New Haven, Conn. Heading: Report from Europe, dated Paris, June 1950.

bilan: Fr. appraisal, assessment.

Malcolm de Chazal (1902–1981): Mauritian writer, painter, and aphorist.

Mélos: Founded in 1950, this short-lived group consisted of the musicians Robert Caby, Marcel Despard, and Anne-Terrier Lafaille, who declared themselves against "music for technique's sake" and for "music for the people." The contemporary composers they admired were Chabrier, Satie, Koechlin, Poulenc, and Sauguet.

The Revolution of Language and James Joyce

Source: "The Revolution of Language and James Joyce," *transition,* no. 11 (February 1928): 109–16.

Jules Michelet (1798–1874): French historian; Michelet was the author of the six-volume *History of France* (1833–44) and the seven-volume *History of the French Revolution* (1847–53). He was the French translator of Vico who, along with Victor Cousin and Herder, greatly influenced his philosophy of history.

Erich Auerbach (1892–1957): Literary critic and professor of Romance languages at Yale, Auerbach was one of the principal exponents of the German philological tradition. His work, informed by Vico's historicism, addresses a panoramic range of literature while aiming to describe the changing patterns of Western literary history (*Mimesis*, 1946).

Benedetto Croce (1866–1952): Italian literary critic, historian, philosopher, and politican; Croce was a polymath figure who founded the review *Critica* (1903) and served as a senator and a minister. His writings on history, aethetics, and literature were heavily influenced by Vico and Hegel.

Marginalia to James Joyce's *Work in Progress*

Source: "Marginalia to James Joyce's *Work in Progress*," *Transition: An International Workshop for Orphic Creation*, no. 22 (February 1933): 101–5.

das Ewig' Weibliche: Ger. "the eternal Feminine"; the verse 12110 from Goethe's *Faust II* reads "Das Ewig-Weibliche/Zieht uns hinan" (The eternal Feminine draws us onward).

Theodicee ex consensu gentium: Lat. literally "theodicy out of the agreement of the community"; a proof of the existence of God based on the common consensus that there is a God.

Sir Richard Paget (1869–1955): Cambridge linguist who expounded a "gesture theory of human speech" in Babel.

Robert Bruce and the spider: Legend about an exiled Scottish king, Robert I (1274–1329), who, while hiding out in a cave, is said to have been inspired to continue his struggles—"try and try again"—upon observing a spider quietly toiling away at its web.

Homage to the Mythmaker

Source: "Homage to the Mythmaker," *Transition: Tenth Anniversary*, no. 27 (April–May 1938): 169–75.

Giordano Bruno (1548–1600): Italian philosopher, astronomer, and occultist; Bruno was a critic of the Aristotelian system whose theories about the infinity of the universe anticipate modern science. A pantheist, he affirmed the eternity and unity of substance, thus seeming to foreshadow Spinoza. After an arduous trial, Bruno was burned by the Inquisition for heresy.

Henri Bergson (1859–1941): French philosopher and professor at the Collège de France. Bergson pioneered his own process philosophy of consciousness and time, focusing on intuition and lived experience, while criticizing the methods of contemporary science, materialism, and neo-Kantianism.

My Friend James Joyce

Source: "My Friend James Joyce," *Partisan Review* 8, no. 2 (March–April 1941): 82–93; reprinted in *James Joyce: Two Decades of Criticism,* ed. Seon Givens (New York: Vanguard, 1963), 3–18.

Sylvia Beach (1887–1962): American expatriate and publisher; Beach was the owner of the legendary Parisian bookshop Shakespeare & Co., at 12 rue de l'Odéon, which was frequented by Pound, Stein, Hemingway, and Fitzgerald, as well as French figures curious about English and American literature. She played the rather thankless role of being Joyce's publisher for *Ulysses* (1922).

Adrienne Monnier (1894–1976): French publisher and writer, Monnier ran the Left Bank bookshop La Maison des amis des livres, at 7 rue de l'Odéon. A mecca for interwar Parisian intellectuals, her bookshop functioned as a lending library and a literary salon and was visited by Valéry, Paulhan, Larbaud, and others. Monnier was the first to publish a French translation of *Ulysses* (1929) and created the review *Le Navire d'argent.*

Edmund Wilson (1895–1972): American literary critic and novelist, Wilson wrote groundbreaking studies on American and European modernism.

Laurence Sterne (1713–1768): Irish born-English author of the *Life and Opinions of Tristram Shandy* (1760–67), an intricately conceived, digressive novel presented as an autobiography; Sterne was described by Diderot as the English Rabelais. He serves as a counterpoint to Swift in *Finnegans Wake.*

Frank Budgen (1881–1971): Joyce's close friend and confidant from his Zurich days; Budgen wrote the anecdotal *James Joyce and the Making of Ulysses* (1932) and *Myselves When Young* (1970).

Karl Radek (1885–1939): Soviet politician and journalist; Radek was a member of the Central Committee of the Communist Party and the Komintern.

J. W. Dunne (1874–1949): British aeronautical engineer, author of *An Experiment with Time* (1927), a meditation on the relation between precognitive dreams and time, in which the author presents his theory of "infinite regress" and the four-dimensional universe. His ideas sparked a brief yet considerable scientific and literary interest, drawing the attention of J. B. Priestly, J. R. R. Tolkien, and Joyce.

Nobel Prize [. . .] Finnish writer: Frans Eemil Sillanpää (1888–1964), Finnish novelist, author of *The Maid Silja,* was awarded the Nobel Prize for "his deep understanding of his country's peasantry and the exquisite art with which he has portrayed their way of life and their relationship with nature."

Elucidation of James Joyce's Monomyth: Explication of *Finnegans Wake*

Source: "Elucidation du monomythe de James Joyce: L'explication de *Finnegans Wake*" ["Elucidation of James Joyce's Monomyth: Explication of *Finnegans Wake*"],

Critique: Revue générale des publications françaises et étrangères 4, no. 26 (July 1948): 579–95, trans. Z.P. and C.R.

Campbell and Robinson: authors of *A Skeleton Key to "Finnegans Wake"* (New York: Harcourt, Brace, 1944).

Allier: Central French region situated between the Loire valley and the mountains of Auvergne.

Paul Léon (1893–1942): A close personal friend and aide of Joyce, Léon was an émigré who tutored him in Russian. He had studied literature and law. Léon saved Joyce's manuscripts from being confiscated as collateral for unpaid rent during World War II.

Part Seven: Literature, Culture, and Politics

Super-Occident

Source: "Super-Occident," *transition: An International Quarterly for Creative Experiment,* no. 15 (February 1929): 11–16.

Goodbye to Yesterday

Source: "Goodbye to Yesterday," *The Living Age: The World in Review* (Boston) 359, no. 4489 (October 1940): 192–96.

Archibald MacLeish (1892–1982): American poet, professor, and statesman. MacLeish's early poetry shows the influence of Pound and Eliot, whereas his mature works deal with his long-standing concern for the fate of liberal democracy.

Julien Benda (1867–1956): French novelist and philosopher; Benda criticized Romanticism and Bergsonian intuition throughout his career. His major work, *La Trahison des clercs* (1927), denounced the lack of moral commitment to justice among intellectuals.

political poem by Heinrich Heine: Although much of Heine's (1797–1856) poetry is underlain with political commentary, Jolas is probably referring to *Deutschland: Ein Wintermärchen* (1844), a satirical attack on reactionary circles in Germany.

Stephen Vincent Benét (1898–1943): American poet, novelist, and short story writer, author of *John Brown's Body* (1928), a long poem on the American Civil War.

Muriel Rukeyser (1913–1980): American poet.

Selden Rodman (1909–2002): American poet and critic.

Raymond E. F. Larsson (1901–?): American Catholic poet.

Elder Olson (1909–1992): American poet, playwright, and critic.

Richard Eberhart (1904–2005): American poet and teacher.

A group [. . .] in Paris: Jolas's description fits the activities of the secretive Acéphale and its counterpart, the Collège de sociologie (1937–39) founded by Georges Bataille and Roger Caillois, both concerned with "sacred sociology." Their group drew the attention of contemporaries including Alexandre Kojève, Pierre Klossowski, Michel Leiris, and Jean Wahl.

Stanley Dehler Mayer (1913–?): Mayer founded *Fantasy* magazine in Pittsburgh in 1931 for the publication of "good free verse." While its original scope was limited to local poetry, the magazine featured national and international poets, as well as an essay by Jolas on Surrealism, before the end of its run in 1943.

Vachel Lindsay (1879–1931): American poet; Lindsay consecrated himself to spreading the "gospel of beauty" in hopes of regenerating American spiritual life.

Toward a Metaphysical Renascence?

Source: "Toward a Metaphysical Renascence?" *Poetry: A Magazine of Verse* (Chicago), vol. 57 (October 1940–March 1941): 49–52.

Amos N. Wilder (1895–1993): American poet, literary critic, and professor of divinity at Harvard.

Conrad Aiken (1889–1973): Poet, critic, and short-story writer whose work was heavily influenced by T. S. Eliot and psychoanalytic theory.

Kenneth Patchen (1911–1972): Experimental poet, painter, novelist, and graphic designer.

Super-Occident and the Atlantic Language

Source: "Super-Occident and the Atlantic Language," *Decision: A Review of Free Culture,* ed. Klaus Mann, vol. 1, no. 6 (June 1941): 51–52.

M. L. Hansen (1892–1938): History professor at the University of Illinois; Hansen's *The Atlantic Migration 1806–1938* (1940) won a Pulitzer Prize in 1941.

Arts and Letters in Latin America

Source: "Arts and Letters in Latin America," *The Living Age: The World in Review* (Boston) 360, no. 4498 (July 1941): 421–28.

José Carlos Mariategui (1895–1930): Peruvian political leader and Marxist thinker.

Luis Valcárcel (1891–1986): Peruvian historian and anthropologist.

Moisés Sáenz (1888–1941): A leading *Indigenista* intellectual, Sáenz was an advocate of the rights of Indians and the founder of the secondary school system in Mexico.

revolution [. . .] Diaz: The Mexican Revolution (1910–20) was a violent uprising that led to the overthrow of the thirty-year dictatorship of Porfiro Diaz (1830–1915) and the foundation of a constitutional republic.

Miguel Angel Asturias (1899–1974): Guatemalan poet, novelist, and diplomat; Asturias won the Nobel Prize in 1967. While studying anthropology at the Sorbonne, Asturias became a Surrealist and went on to combine Mayan myth with themes of social protest in his work.

Pablo Neruda (1904–1973): Chilean poet and diplomat, Neruda was awarded the Nobel Prize in 1971. His vast body of work, ranging from intimate love poetry to political protest poems and Whitmanesque epic poems, earned him a strong international following.

Vincente Huidobro (1893–1948): Chilean poet; Huidobro played a critical role in introducing European avant-garde aesthetics to Chile. During his time in Paris, he worked with Apollinaire and Reverdy on the literary journal *Nord-Sud* and founded the short-lived *Creacionismo* movement.

Victoria Ocampo (1890–1979): Argentinian essayist and editor; Ocampo founded the groundbreaking literary review *Sur* (1931–70), which offered Spanish translations of European authors. Ocampo's essays challenged the dominantly masculine literary establishment, and she was the first woman inducted into the Argentinian Academy of Letters (1977).

Gastón Figueira (1905–?): Uruguayan poet.

Heitor Villa Lobos (1887–1959): Brazilian composer whose work combined elements of indigenous Afro-Brazilian rhythms with classical music.

Elsie Houston (1902–1943): Brazilian singer, musicologist; Houston was married to the Surrealist poet Benjamin Péret.

Luis Palés Matos (1898–1959): Puerto Rican lyric poet known for introducing the diction and music of Afro-American culture into Spanish poetry.

German Letters in Ruins: A Report from Frankfurt

Source: "German Letters in Ruins: A Report from Frankfurt," *New York Times Book Review,* no. 27 (July 4, 1948): 7 and 13.

SMA: Soviet Military Administration, also known as the SMAD (Sowjetische Militäradministration in Deutschland), directly ruled the eastern areas of Germany from 1945 until the establishment of East Germany in 1949.

la poésie pure and *la poésie engagé:* Fr. "pure poetry" and "politically committed poetry."

Rudolf Alexander Schröder (1878–1962): German writer, critic, poet, architect, and painter.

Dolf Sternberger (1907–1989): Sternberger was the cultural editor of the *Frankfurter Zeitung*, which he kept free of Nazi propaganda by concentrating on purely abstract and literary themes. He was also the author of a critique of Heideggeran phenomenology, *Death Understood* (1936). Jolas included Sternberger in his editorial committee when he was given the task of launching the first postwar German "intellectual" review, *Die Wandlung*.

magischer Realismus or *blutiger Realismus:* Ger. "magical Realism" or "bloody Realism."

The Migrator and His Language

Source: "L' homme migrateur et son langage." In *Peuples et Evolution*, 266–73. Paris: Editions de Clermont, 1948 (Chemins du Monde vol. 6), trans. E.K. and C.R.

Part Eight: Across Frontiers

Some Notes on Existentialism, Martin Heidegger, and Poetry Sales

Source: "Some Notes on Existentialism, Martin Heidegger, and Poetry Sales," *New York Herald Tribune* (European edition), no. 20767 (November 1, 1949): 5.

poulain: Fr. foal, colt; figuratively, a promising young person, a protégé.

Sindonie-Gabrielle Colette (1873–1954): French writer, whose realistic, humorous novels chronicle the poverty of a provincial childhood in Burgundy, as well as the leisurely lives of wealthy Parisians.

Les Chemins de la liberté [. . .] *La Mort dans l'âme:* Fr. translated as *Roads to Freedom* (1945–49); *Troubled Sleep* (1951).

Martin Heidegger, *Über den Humanismus* [. . .] *Holzwege:* Ger. translated as *Letter on Humanism* (1977); *Off the Beaten Track* (2002).

Geworfenheit: Ger. "thrown-ness;" a term used by Heidegger in *Sein und Zeit* (1927), where it suggests the facticity of being "delivered over" or "thrown into the world."

Les Temps Modernes: Fr. *Modern Times;* a monthly review of politics, philosophy, and art founded in 1945 by Jean-Paul Sartre.

Eugen Kogon (1903–1987): Austrian activist, sociologist, and political scientist; Kogon was imprisoned in Buchenwald from 1939 to 1945, not "twelve years" as Jolas writes in the original, also p. 495. In addition to being one of the main authors of the Buchenwald report and a witness at the Dachau commission, Kogon wrote *The Theory and Practice of Hell* (*Der SS-Staat,* 1947), which detailed the system of concentration camps.

Wolfdietrich Schnurre (1920–1989): German writer, journalist, and critic, cofounder of Gruppe 47.

Wolfgang Borchert (1921–1947): postwar playwright and short story writer (*Draußen vor der Tür,* 1947).

foire aux [. . .] croûtes: Fr. flea market, gingerbread market, crust market.

Parigot: Fr. Parisian.

poètes des quatre saisons: Fr. poets of the four seasons.

Reemergence of Heidegger

Source: "Reemergence of Heidegger," Gen Mss 108, box 4, folder 83 (November 1949), Eugene and Maria Jolas Papers, General Collection of Rare Books, Beinecke Rare Book and Manuscript Library, Yale University, New Haven, Conn.

Heidegger in the Atomic Age

Source: "Heidegger in the Atomic Age," Gen Mss 108, box 4, folder 83 (November 1949), Eugene and Maria Jolas Papers, General Collection of Rare Books, Beinecke Rare Book and Manuscript Library, Yale University, New Haven, Conn.

Irrealism, Immoralism, Naturalism, Concretism

Source: "Irrealism, Immoralism, Naturalism, Concretism," *New York Herald Tribune* (European edition), no. 20773 (November 8, 1949): 5.

L'Annonce faite à Marie: Fr. *Tidings Brought to Mary* (1912).

rayonnement: Fr. influence, radiance.

Group 47: A literary association founded by Alfred Andersch, Walter Kolbenhoff, and Wolfdietrich Schnurre, Gruppe 47 was meant to promote democratic culture and postwar German literature. Amongst its illustrious members were Heinrich Böll, Paul Celan, Hans Magnus Enzensberger, and Günter Grass.

Enrique Beck (1904–1947): German writer and translator.

Walter Kolbenhoff (1908–1993): A militant anti-Nazi writer and journalist, Kolbenhoff was exiled to Denmark in 1933. In 1946 he returned to Germany to work on the journal *Der Ruf,* and he started Gruppe 47 the following year.

Mort sans sépulture: Fr. *Death Without Burial,* or *Men Without Shadows,* was produced in English in 1947 at the Lyric Theatre in the West End.

Arnold J. Toynbee (1889–1975): English historian and professor; Toynbee was the author of the twelve-volume *A Study of History* (1934–61), which contained his lifelong research in world history according to civilizations rather than nation-states.

Origin and Aim of History

Source: "Origin and Aim of History," *New York Herald Tribune* (European edition), no. 20779 (November 15, 1949): 5.

Karl Jaspers (1883–1969): German philosopher, whose early work brought the insights of phenomenology to psychiatry; his major philosophical work, albeit existential in nature, was bound by his Christian faith in the necessity of new ethical foundations. His later writings dealt with long-standing political concerns with Nazism, as well as the future of humanity in the atomic age.

André Siegfried (1875–1959): French economist, sociologist, and professor at the Collège de France.

"La Machine au pilori": Fr. "The Machine in the Pillory."

Georg Lukács (1885–1971): Hungarian philosopher and literary critic; Lukács was deeply influenced by Hegel and Marx in both his aesthetic and political thought (*Theory of the Novel,* 1916; *History and Class Consciousness,* 1923).

Edouard Dujardin (1861–1949): French writer, poet, and editor of the *Revue independante;* Dujardin is remembered for his pioneering use of the stream of consciousness in his novel *Les Lauriers sont coupées* (1887).

le larron impenitent: Fr. the impenitent thief.

Giovanni Papini (1881–1956): Italian writer and journalist.

A German Nationalist

Source: "A German Nationalist," *New York Herald Tribune* (European edition), no. 20796 (December 6, 1949): 5.

Melvin Lasky (1920–2004): American editor; Lasky would play a key role in the cultural Cold War with his anti-Communist magazine *Encounter* (1958–90), which attracted such authors as Bertrand Russell, Arthur Koestler, and Vladimir Nabokov. It was revealed later that Lasky's project was funded by the CIA.

Peter de Mendelssohn (1908–1982): German journalist and editor; de Mendelssohn had a double career as a writer in Britain. After the war, he returned to report on the Nuremberg commission and helped to set up newspapers such as the

Berliner Tagesspiegel and *Die Welt.* He would go on to write a biography of Thomas Mann and edit his correspondence.

mise au point: Fr. clarification, update.

Giorgio de Chirico (1888–1978): Italian painter; de Chirico renounced his proto-Surrealist *pittura metafisica* in the 1930s to become a classicist in the style of Titian instead.

Jean Wahl (1888–1974): French philosopher who was a historian of existential currents in philosophy from Hegel and Kierkegaard to Heidegger; Wahl wrote his own negative ontology in *Traité de métaphysique* (1953).

The Absent Avant-Garde

Source: "The Absent Avant-Garde," *New York Herald Tribune* (European edition), no. 20850 (February 7, 1950): 5.

Herbert Read (1893–1968): British poet and critic, Read was one of the principal supporters of modern art in Britain from the 1930s onward (*The Philosophy of Modern Art,* 1952).

Julien Gracq (1910–?): French writer, critic, and professor of history and geography; Gracq's work shows the influence of German Romanticism, Surrealism, and Ernst Jünger.

German Letters Today

Source: "German Letters Today," *New York Herald Tribune* (European edition), no. 20862 (February 21, 1950): 5.

Gedankengut: Ger. "ideas," "views," having in postwar German less an ideological than a conservative meaning.

Betreuung: Ger. "care," "support"; in the context of the "Final Solution," the term was a euphemism for "taking care of" in the sense of extermination.

Negro Culture

Source: "Negro Culture," *New York Herald Tribune* (European edition), no. 20880 (March 14, 1950): 5.

Alioune Diop (1910–1980): Senegalese editor; Diop founded the review *Présence africaine* in 1947 and the homonymous publishing house two years later. In addition to his editorial work, he would be a key promoter of African culture via the first Congrès des écrivains et artistes noirs in 1956 and the creation of the Society of African Culture.

homo divinans: Lat. divining man.

enquête: Fr. investigation, survey.

Father Placide Tempels (1906–?): Belgian priest and author; Tempels wrote *Bantu Philosophy* (1946), which described the thought systems of the Luga people of the Congo and opened the debate about the possibility of an African philosophy.

Requiem für die Gefallenen in Europa: Ger. *Requiem for the Fallen in Europe.*

Le Mythe de la roche percée and *Elégie d'Iphétonga:* Fr. *The Myth of the Pierced Rock* and *Iphétonga's Elegy.*

"*Das Traumkraut*": Ger. "The Dream Herb."

Muttersprache: Ger. mother tongue.

Henry Greene (1905–1973): British industrialist and novelist.

Ivy Compton-Burnett (1884–1969): British writer.

Elizabeth Bowen (1899–1973): Anglo-Irish novelist.

Franco-German Cultural Exchanges

Source: "Franco-German Cultural Exchanges," *New York Herald Tribune* (European edition), no. 20886 (March 21, 1950): 5

Brückengedanke: Ger. bridging thought.

Alfred Döblin (1878–1957): German medical doctor and Expressionist writer; Döblin is best remembered for his montage novel *Berlin Alexanderplatz* (1929), which Jolas translated into English in 1929–30 (printed 1931).

Das Goldene Tor: Ger. *The Golden Gate.*

chauvinistic: Gallicism; in French, *chauvin* describes someone who is insular and nationalistic.

German Literary Trends

Source: "German Literary Trends," *New York Herald Tribune* (European edition), no. 20939 (May 23, 1950): 5.

Samuel Fischer (1859–1934): German editor who founded the prestigious S. Fischer Verlag (publishing house) in 1886 in Berlin; now in Frankfurt am Main.

Neue Rundschau: Ger. *The New Review.*

Sonderhefte: Ger. special editions.

Alfred Andersch (1914–1980): German writer and journalist; Andersch founded the journal *Der Ruf* in 1945 in a prisoner-of-war camp in America. Upon returning to Germany, he worked for the *Neue Zeitung* and actively promoted the writers of Gruppe 47.

fatras: Fr. jumble, hodgepodge.

Zeitroman: Ger. literally "novel of its time"; figuratively, "engaged novel." The genre was especially popular in German literature during the Weimar republic with writers such as Willi Bredel, Irmgard Keun, Erich Kästner, and Ernst von Salomon.

Günter Eich (1907–1972): German poet, translator, and writer; Eich was a member of Gruppe 47.

Selected Bibliography

In line with the overall concept of this volume, the bibliography's "Primary Sources" section contains only Jolas's nonfictional or nonpoetic works. They are arranged in chronological sequence under "books," "essays," and "articles" (mostly in newspapers), as well as "translations"—amounting to a survey of his prose. This gives us a clear insight: it is only in the late 1920s that Jolas turns from journalist—a metier which he never gave up altogether—to writer, and finally to "respected" author. His genuinely literary and poetic works are hence relegated to the "Biography of Eugene Jolas" of our edition. Of course, the boundaries of genres are quite fluid; moreover, we must not forget that neither Jolas's poetic oeuvre nor his nonfictional writings are conclusively accessible. His early journalistic writings, assuming they were relevant, are altogether unknown so far. Moreover, Jolas's activities in postwar Germany are little documented. Thus his handbook *Der moderne Reporter,* with which he trained German journalists, cannot be found. Likewise, his sizable unpublished literary estate in Yale University's Beinecke Library for Rare Books and Manuscripts (see the 1993 catalogue by Timothy Young listed under "Secondary Sources" below) has hardly been evaluated in its entirety. This is true also for his vast correspondence. In the "Primary Sources" section of the bibliography we have listed the dated items that were included in our volume and separately the non-dated texts from the unpublished holdings. Thus we are talking of a bibliography which makes no claims to completeness. Our register is based specifically on the preliminary work of Andreas Kramer and Céline Mansanti; it was compiled and edited by Tanja Trumm. The texts published in the present edition are marked with an asterisk.

The "Secondary Sources" section of the bibliography is divided into two subsections, "Critical Reception (to 1955)" and "Research (from 1956)" Under "Critical Reception (to 1955)" are listed in alphabetic order the reviews of Jolas's publications. The critical reception of his literary production, and also of his *transition* project, commenced around 1929. In about 1956, a few years after his death, the reception turns into academic research, which is listed under the subsection "Research (from 1956)." Interest in Jolas has increased, in both America and internationally, as related to topical issues such as "intercultural communication," "English as a global language," "the Americanization of our world," and so on. Given the centrality of James Joyce for *transition,* actually relatively little has been contributed by Joyce research, and relatively more by Carl Einstein research. The reviews named relate in one way or another to Jolas's poetic work or to the journal *transition;* yet they are cited here as long as they pertain to issues this volume focuses on, such as "language," "anthropology," and so forth. Jolas himself had collected numerous reviews of his work, or he had chosen to have them collected by the Romeike Press Clipping Bureau or by Argus de la Presse ("Voit Tout"). These numerous clippings, important or not, are found in the Beinecke archive. Here, too, we could only be selective.

Since not all of the numerous and often quite remote sources could be viewed and evaluated on-site, some of the references may be open to amendment. In the posthumous papers at the Beinecke Library there are numerous documents, clippings from local newspapers, and so on, without any sources being given. Sometimes one cannot even establish which work is being reviewed. Thus one can say here with some confidence that in spite of some lacunae, we have at least laid a solid basis from which future research can depart, research which should before all pay special attention to Jolas's entire poetic work and its reception.

PRIMARY SOURCES

1923

Articles

"The Peasant." *The Liberator* 5, no. 4 (April 1923): 17.

1924

Articles

"Through Paris Bookland." *Chicago Tribune Sunday Magazine* (European edition), no. 15 (May 25, 1924): 2.
"Through Paris Bookland." *Chicago Tribune Sunday Magazine* (European edition), no. 16 (June 1, 1924): 2.
"Rambles Through Literary Paris." *Chicago Tribune Sunday Magazine* (European edition), no. 17 (June 8, 1924): 2 and 13.*
"Rambles Through Literary Paris." *Chicago Tribune Sunday Magazine* (European edition), no. 18 (June 15, 1924): 4.*

"Rambles Through Literary Paris." *Chicago Tribune Sunday Magazine* (European edition), no. 19 (June 22, 1924): 4.*

"Rambles Through Literary Paris." *Chicago Tribune Sunday Magazine* (European edition), no. 20 (June 29, 1924): 2.*

"Rambles Through Literary Paris." *Chicago Tribune Sunday Magazine* (European edition), no. 21 (July 6, 1924): 2.

"Rambles Through Literary Paris." *Chicago Tribune Sunday Magazine* (European edition), no. 22 (July 13, 1924): 2 and 9.*

"André Gide, Mystic and Dyonisien." *Chicago Tribune Sunday Magazine* (European edition), no. 22 (July 13, 1924): 3 and 10.*

"Rambles Through Literary Paris." *Chicago Tribune Sunday Magazine* (European edition), no. 23 (July 20, 1924): 2.

"Rambles Through Literary Paris." *Chicago Tribune Sunday Magazine* (European edition), no. 24 (July 27, 1924): 2 and 8.

"Rambles Through Literary Paris." *Chicago Tribune Sunday Magazine* (European edition), no. 25 (August 3, 1924): 2 and 9.

"Rambles Through Literary Paris." *Chicago Tribune Sunday Magazine* (European edition), no. 26 (August 10, 1924): 2.

"Rambles Through Literary Paris." *Chicago Tribune Sunday Magazine* (European edition), no. 27 (August 17, 1924): 2.

"Rambles Through Literary Paris." *Chicago Tribune Sunday Magazine* (European edition), no. 28 (August 24, 1924): 2.*

"Rambles Through Literary Paris." *Chicago Tribune Sunday Magazine* (European edition), no. 29 (August 31, 1924): 2.

"Rambles Through Literary Paris." *Chicago Tribune Sunday Magazine* (European edition), no. 30 (September 7, 1924): 2.*

"Rambles Through Literary Paris." *Chicago Tribune Sunday Magazine* (European edition), no. 31 (September 14, 1924): 2.

"Rambles Through Literary Paris." *Chicago Tribune Sunday Magazine* (European edition), no. 32 (September 21, 1924): 2.

"Rambles Through Literary Paris." *Chicago Tribune Sunday Magazine* (European edition), no. 33 (September 28, 1924): 2.

"Rambles Through Literary Paris." *Chicago Tribune Sunday Magazine* (European edition), no. 34 (October 5, 1924): 2.

"Rambles Through Literary Paris." *Chicago Tribune Sunday Magazine* (European edition), no. 35 (October 12, 1924): 2.

"Rambles Through Literary Paris." *Chicago Tribune Sunday Magazine* (European edition), no. 36 (October 19, 1924): 2.*

"Rambles Through Literary Paris." *Chicago Tribune Sunday Magazine* (European edition), no. 37 (October 26, 1924): 2.

"Rambles Through Literary Paris." *Chicago Tribune Sunday Magazine* (European edition), no. 38 (November 2, 1924): 2.

"Rambles Through Literary Paris." *Chicago Tribune Sunday Magazine* (European edition), no. 39 (November 9, 1924): 2.

"Rambles Through Literary Paris." *Chicago Tribune Sunday Magazine* (European edition), no. 40 (November 16, 1924): 2.*

"Rambles Through Literary Paris." *Chicago Tribune Sunday Magazine* (European edition), no. 2686 (November 23, 1924): 5.*

"Rambles Through Literary Paris." *Chicago Tribune Sunday Magazine* (European edition), no. 2693 (November 30, 1924): 5.

"Rambles Through Literary Paris." *Chicago Tribune Sunday Magazine* (European edition), no. 2700 (December 7, 1924): 5.

"Rambles Through Literary Paris." *Chicago Tribune Sunday Magazine* (European edition), no. 2707 (December 14, 1924): 5.

"Rambles Through Literary Paris." *Chicago Tribune Sunday Magazine* (European edition), no. 2714 (December 21, 1924): 5.*

"Rambles Through Literary Paris." *Chicago Tribune Sunday Magazine* (European edition), no. 2721 (December 28, 1924): 5.

1925

Articles

"Rambles Through Literary Paris." *Chicago Tribune Sunday Magazine* (European edition), no. 2728 (January 4, 1925): 5.

"Rambles Through Literary Paris." *Chicago Tribune Sunday Magazine* (European edition), no. 2735 (January 11, 1925): 5.*

"Rambles Through Literary Paris: Pierre Loving and the *Transatlantic Review.*" *Chicago Tribune Sunday Magazine* (European edition), no. 2742 (January 18, 1925): 5.

"Rambles Through Literary Paris." *Chicago Tribune Sunday Magazine* (European edition), no. 2749 (January 25, 1925): 5.

"Rambles Through Literary Paris: Words, Words, Words!" *Chicago Tribune Sunday Magazine* (European edition), no. 2763 (February 8, 1925): 5.*

"Rambles Through Literary Paris." *Chicago Tribune Sunday Magazine* (European edition), no. 2770 (February 15, 1925): 5.

"Rambles Through Literary Paris." *Chicago Tribune Sunday Magazine* (European edition), no. 2777 (February 22, 1925): 5.

"Rambles Through Literary Paris." *Chicago Tribune Sunday Magazine* (European edition), no. 2784 (March 1, 1925): 5.

"Rambles Through Literary Paris: The Middle West and Mr. Ford Madox Ford, etc." *Chicago Tribune Sunday Magazine* (European edition), no. 2791 (March 8, 1925): 5.

"Rambles Through Literary Paris." *Chicago Tribune Sunday Magazine* (European edition), no. 2798 (March 15, 1925): 5.

"Stravinsky Predicts Musical Future for America; Jazz Thrilled Him." *Chicago Tribune Sunday Magazine* (European edition), no. 2804 (March 21, 1925): 5.

"Rambles Through Literary Paris: A Literary Portrait of the Amazone." *Chicago Tribune Sunday Magazine* (European edition), no. 2805 (March 22, 1925): 5.*

"Rambles Through Literary Paris." *Chicago Tribune Sunday Magazine* (European edition), no. 2812 (March 29, 1925): 5.

"Rambles Through Literary Paris." *Chicago Tribune Sunday Magazine* (European edition), no. 2840 (April 26, 1925): 5.

"Rambles Through Literary Paris." *Chicago Tribune Sunday Magazine* (European edition), no. 2847 (May 3, 1925): 5.

"The Skyscraper Age and Harold Stearns." *Chicago Tribune Sunday Magazine* (European edition), no. 2847 (May 3, 1925): 5.

"Rambles Through Literary Paris." *Chicago Tribune Sunday Magazine* (European edition), no. 2854 (May 10, 1925): 5.

"Rambles Through Literary Paris." *Chicago Tribune Sunday Magazine* (European edition), no. 2861 (May 17, 1925): 5.

"Rambles Through Literary Paris." *Chicago Tribune Sunday Magazine* (European edition), no. 2868 (May 24, 1925): 5.

"Rambles Through Literary Paris." *Chicago Tribune Sunday Magazine* (European edition), no. 2875 (May 31, 1925): 5.*

"Rambles Through Literary Paris." *Chicago Tribune Sunday Magazine* (European edition), no. 2882 (June 7, 1925): 5.

"Literary Rambles." *Chicago Tribune Sunday Magazine* (European edition), no. 2889 (June 14, 1925): 4.*

"Literary Rambles." *Chicago Tribune Sunday Magazine* (European edition), no. 2896 (June 21, 1925): 5.

"Rambles Through Literary Paris." *Chicago Tribune Sunday Magazine* (European edition), no. 2903 (June 28, 1925): 5.

"Literary Rambles." *Chicago Tribune Sunday Magazine* (European edition), no. 2910 (July 5, 1925): 5.*

"Rambles Through Literary Paris." *Chicago Tribune Sunday Magazine* (European edition), no. 3044 (November 15, 1925): 4.

"Rambles Through Literary Paris." *Chicago Tribune Sunday Magazine* (European edition), no. 3051 (November 22, 1925): 5.

"Rambles Through Literary Paris." *Chicago Tribune Sunday Magazine* (European edition), no. 3058 (November 29, 1925): 5.

"Literary Rambles." *Chicago Tribune Sunday Magazine* (European edition), no. 3072 (December 13, 1925): 5.

1926

Articles

"Ernest Walsh, Poet and Editor, Dies in Monte Carlo at Age of Thirty-one." *Chicago Tribune Sunday Magazine* (European edition), no. 3389 (October 26, 1926): 1.

"A Chronicle of Reviews." *Chicago Tribune Sunday Magazine* (European edition), no. 3436 (December 12, 1926): 5.

"A Chronicle of Reviews." *Chicago Tribune Sunday Magazine* (European edition), no. 3450 (December 26, 1926): 5.

1927

Essays

["Response to Enquête on Foreign Literatures"]. *Les Cahiers du sud* 13, no. 89 (April 1927): 276–77.

(With Elliot Paul). "Introduction." *transition,* no. 1 (April 1927): 135–38.

(With Elliot Paul). "K.O.R.A.A." *transition,* no. 3 (June 1927): 173–77.

(With Elliot Paul). "Suggestions for a New Magic." *transition,* no. 3 (June 1927): 178–79.

"Gottfried Benn." *transition,* no. 5 (August 1927), 146–49.*

"Revolt Against the Philistine [on Carl Sternheim]." *transition,* no. 6 (September 1927): 176–79.

"Enter the Imagination [on Jacques Maritain and Lautréamont]." *transition,* no. 7 (October 1927): 157–60.

(With Elliot Paul). "The Pursuit of Happiness." *transition,* no. 8 (November 1927): 179–80.

(With Elliot Paul and Robert Sage). "First Aid to the Enemy." *transition,* no. 9 (December 1927): 167–76.

"On the Quest." *transition,* no. 9 (December 1927): 191–96.*

Translations

Carl Sternheim. "Busekow." *transition,* no. 1 (April 1927): 36–56.

André Breton. "Introduction to the Discourse on the Dearth of Reality." *transition,* no.5 (August 1927): 129–45.

Kurt Schwitters. "Revolution: Causes and Outbreak of the Great and Glorious Revolution in Revon." *transition,* no. 8 (November 1927): 60–76.

André Gide. "Food of the Earth." *transition*, no. 8 (November 1927): 117–19.
André Gide. "Roundelay." *transition*, no. 8 (November 1927): 120–22.

1928

Books

Le Nègre qui chante: Chansons traduites et introduites par Eugène Jolas. Paris: Editions des cahiers libres, 1928.
Anthologie de la nouvelle poésie américaine. Paris: Kra, 1928.

Essays

Introduction to *Le Nègre qui chante*, 9–28. Paris: Editions des cahiers libres, 1928.*
"Flight into Geography: A Scenario." *transition: An International Quarterly for Creative Experiment*, no. 10 (January 1928): 75–85.
"The Revolution of Language and James Joyce." *transition: An International Quarterly for Creative Experiment*, no. 11 (February 1928): 109–16; reprinted in *Our Exagmination Round His Factification for Incamination of Work in Progress* (Paris: Shakespeare and Company, 1929), 77–92.*
(With Elliot Paul). "A Review." *transition: An International Quarterly for Creative Experiment*, no. 12 (March 1928): 139–47.
"Daily Graphic." *transition: An International Quarterly for Creative Experiment*, no. 13 (Summer 1928): 174–75.
"Inquiry Among European Writers into the Spirit of America." *transition: An International Quarterly for Creative Experiment*, no. 13 (Summer 1928): 248.
"Glossary." *transition: An International Quarterly for Creative Experiment*, no. 13 (Summer 1928): 271–73.
"Transatlantic Letter." *transition: An International Quarterly for Creative Experiment*, no. 13 (Summer 1928): 274–77.
"Notes." *transition: An International Quarterly for Creative Experiment*, no. 14 (Fall 1928): 180–85.
"Glossary." *transition: An International Quarterly for Creative Experiment*, no. 14 (Fall 1928): 275–79.

Articles

"Auf der Suche." *Neue Schweizer Rundschau* 21 (1928): 244–48.

1929

Books

Transition Stories: Twenty-three Stories from "Transition." Selected and edited by Eugene Jolas and Robert Sage. New York: Walter V. McKee, 1929.

Essays

"Preface." In *Transition Stories: Twenty-three Stories from "Transition,"* selected and edited by Eugene Jolas and Robert Sage, ix–xii. New York: Walter V. McKee, 1929.*

"Super-Occident." *transition: An International Quarterly for Creative Experiment,* no. 15 (February 1929): 11–16.*

"Slanguage." *transition: An International Quarterly for Creative Experiment,* no. 15 (February 1929): 32–33.

"The New Vocabulary." *transition: An International Quarterly for Creative Experiment,* no. 15 (February 1929): 171–74.

"Notes." *transition: An International Quarterly for Creative Experiment,* no. 15 (February 1929): 187–88.

"Necessity for New Words." *Modern Quarterly* (Fall 1929): 273–75.

"Document." *Blues* 1, no. 4 (May 1929): 80–82.

(With others). "Revolution of the Word." *transition: An International Quarterly for Creative Experiment,* no. 16–17 (June 1929): 1.

(With others). "Proclamation." *transition: An International Quarterly for Creative Experiment,* no. 16–17 (June 1929): 13.*

"Logos." *transition: An International Quarterly for Creative Experiment,* no. 16–17 (June 1929): 25–30.*

"The Innocuous Enemy." *transition: An International Quarterly for Creative Experiment,* no. 16–17 (June 1929): 207–12.

"Notes." *transition: An International Quarterly for Creative Experiment,* no. 16–17 (June 1929): 219–22.

"Glossary." *transition: An International Quarterly for Creative Experiment,* no. 16–17 (June 1929): 326–28.

"Notes on Reality." *transition: An International Quarterly for Creative Experiment,* no. 18 (November 1929): 15–20.*

"Homage to Novalis." *transition: An International Quarterly for Creative Experiment,* no. 18 (November 1929): 72–73.*

"The Industrial Mythos." *transition: An International Quarterly for Creative Experiment,* no. 18 (November 1929): 123.

"Statement." *transition: An International Quarterly for Creative Experiment,* no. 18 (November 1929): 175.

"The Novel Is Dead—Long Live the Novel." *transition: An International Quarterly for Creative Experiment*, no. 18 (November 1929): 239.*

Translations

Ernst Robert Curtius. "Technique and Thematic Development of James Joyce." *transition: An International Quarterly for Creative Experiment*, no. 16–17 (June 1938): 310–25.

1930

Essays

"'Que font les mots . . .'" *Documents: Archéologie, beaux-arts, ethnographie, variétés*, no. 3 (1930): 175.
"Literature and the New Man." *transition: An International Quarterly for Creative Experiment*, no. 19–20 (June 1930): 13–19.*
"The Dream." *transition: An International Quarterly for Creative Experiment*, no. 19–20 (June 1930): 46–47.
"Towards New Forms?" *transition: An International Quarterly for Creative Experiment*, no. 19–20 (June 1930): 104.
"The King's English Is Dying: Long Live the Great American Language." *transition: An International Quarterly for Creative Experiment*, no. 19–20 (June 1930): 141–46.*
"Letter to Mr. Walter Winchell." *transition: An International Quarterly for Creative Experiment*, no. 19–20 (June 1930): 166.
"Harry Crosby and Transition." *transition: An International Quarterly for Creative Experiment*, no. 19–20 (June 1930): 228–29.
"Announcement." *transition: An International Quarterly for Creative Experiment*, no. 19–20 (June 1930): 369.
"The Machine and 'Mystic America' [on Edward J. O'Brien and Waldo Frank]." *transition: An International Quarterly for Creative Experiment*, no. 19–20 (June 1930): 379–83.

Translations

C. G. Jung. "Psychology and Poetry." *transition: An International Quarterly for Creative Experiment*, no. 19–20 (June 1930): 46–47.
Carola Giedion-Welcker. "Work in Progress: A Linguistic Experiment by James Joyce." *transition: An International Quarterly for Creative Experiment*, no. 19–20 (June 1930): 174–83.

1931

Books

Transition: An Epilogue. New York: Knopf, 1931.

Essays

"Faula-and-Flona." In *READIES for Bob Brown's Machine,* edited by Bob Brown,
    136–37. Cagnes-sur-Mer: Robing Eye, 1931.
"Elysian Invention: An Acoustic Scenario." *Front* 1, no. 2 (February 1931): 121–23.
"*Transition:* An Epilogue." *American Mercury,* no. 23 (June 1931): 185–92.
"Frontier." *The Morada* (Albuquerque) 2, no. 5 (Winter 1931): 7.

1932

Books

The Language of Night. The Hague: Servire, 1932.

Essays

"Preface to the New *Transition.*" *Transition: An International Workshop for Orphic
    Creation,* no. 21 (March 1932): 6.*
"Crisis of Man." *Transition: An International Workshop for Orphic Creation,* no. 21
    (March 1932): 106.
"Poetry Is Vertical." *Transition: An International Workshop for Orphic Creation,* no.
    21 (March 1932): 148–49.
"The Case of Goethe: Was He a Heroic Figure or Merely a Philistine?" *Transition:
    An International Workshop for Orphic Creation,* no. 21 (March 1932): 206.*
"Night-Mind and Day-Mind." *Transition: An International Workshop for Orphic
    Creation,* no 21 (March 1932): 222–23.*
"Mantic News." *Transition: An International Workshop for Orphic Creation,* no. 21
    (March 1932): 240–44.
"Wanted: A New Symbolical Language!" *Transition: An International Workshop for
    Orphic Creation,* no. 21 (March 1932): 284.*
"Wanted: A New Communicative Language!" *Transition: An International Work-
    shop for Orphic Creation,* no. 21 (March 1932): 285.*
["Note on *Transition's* Revolution-of-the-Word Dictionary"]. *Transition: An Inter-
    national Workshop for Orphic Creation,* no. 21 (March 1932): 323.

"For a Revision of Grammar!" *Transition: An International Workshop for Orphic Creation*, no. 21 (March 1932): 325.

"Appel orphique." *Stimmen aus Lothringen* 2, no. 4 (April 1932): 97–98.

Translations

Gottfried Benn. "The Structure of the Personality (Outline of a Geology of the 'I')." *Transition: An International Workshop for Orphic Creation*, no. 21 (March 1932): 195–205.

Carl Einstein. "Obituary: 1832–1932 [on Goethe]." *Transition: An International Workshop for Orphic Creation*, no. 21 (March 1932): 206–14.

Ludwig Klages. "The Essence of Metaphysics." *Transition: An International Workshop for Orphic Creation*, no. 21 (March 1932): 224–25.

Justinus Kerner. "The Inner Language." *Transition: An International Workshop for Orphic Creation*, no. 21 (March 1932): 299–301.

1933

Essays

"Twilight of the Horizontal Age." *Transition: An International Quarterly for Orphic Creation*, no. 22 (February 1933): 6.*

"The Primal Personality." *Transition: An International Quarterly for Orphic Creation*, no. 22 (February 1933): 78–83.*

"Marginalia to James Joyce's *Work in Progress*." *Transition: An International Quarterly for Orphic Creation*, no. 22 (February 1933): 101–5.*

"From a Letter." *Transition: An International Quarterly for Orphic Creation*, no. 22 (February 1933): 113.

"Transition's Revolution-of-the-Word Dictionary." *Transition: An International Quarterly for Orphic Creation*, no. 22 (February 1933): 122–23.

"Confession About Grammar." *Transition: An International Quarterly for Orphic Creation*, no. 22 (February 1933): 124.*

"What Is the Revolution of Language?" *Transition: An International Quarterly for Orphic Creation*, no. 22 (February 1933): 125–26.*

"The Interior Dialogue." *Transition: An International Quarterly for Orphic Creation*, no. 22 (February 1933): 126.

"Anathema Maranatha." *Transition: An International Quarterly for Orphic Creation*, no. 22 (February 1933): 128.

["Note to '*Transition* Bibliography'"]. *Transition: An International Quarterly for Orphic Creation*, no. 22 (February 1933): [146].

"Laboratory of the Mystic Logos." *Transition: An International Quarterly for Orphic Creation*, no. 22 (February 1933): 177.

"La révolution du langage chez les Elizabéthains." *Les Cahiers du sud* 20, no. 154 (June–July 1933): 73–76.*

Translations

Friedrich Marcus Huebner. "The Road Through the Word." *Transition: An International Quarterly for Orphic Creation*, no. 22 (February 1933): 110–13.

Max Pulver. "Handwriting and the Symbolic Words." *Transition: An International Quarterly for Orphic Creation*, no. 22 (February 1933): 114–21.

1934

Articles

"Verbirrupta for James Joyce." *Contempo* 3, no. 13 (February 15, 1934): 3.

1935

Books

Testimony Against Gertrude Stein. The Hague: Servire, 1935.

Essays

"Paramyths." *Transition: An Intercontinental Workshop for Vertigralist Transmutation*, no. 23 (July 1935): 7.

"Little Mantic Almageste." *Transition: An Intercontinental Workshop for Vertigralist Transmutation*, no. 23 (July 1935): 44–51.

"Workshop." *Transition: An Intercontinental Workshop for Vertigralist Transmutation*, no. 23 (July 1935): 97–106.

"Vertigralist Transmutation." *Transition: An Intercontinental Workshop for Vertigralist Transmutation*, no. 23 (July 1935): 107.*

"Inquiry About the Malady of Language." *Transition: An Intercontinental Workshop for Vertigralist Transmutation*, no. 23 (July 1935): 144.

"Malady of Language." *Transition: An Intercontinental Workshop for Vertigralist Transmutation*, no. 23 (July 1935): 175.

Translations

Lothar Mundan. "Vertrigral Poetry: The Third Eye." *Transition: An Intercontinental Workshop for Vertigralist Transmutation,* no. 23 (July 1935): 60–61.

Franz von Baader. "From: Extasis as Metastasis." *Transition: An Intercontinental Workshop for Vertigralist Transmutation,* no. 23 (July 1935): 85–86.

Hugo Ball. "Gnostic Magic." *Transition: An Intercontinental Workshop for Vertigralist Transmutation,* no. 23 (July 1935): 86–87.

Franz Werfel. "From a Discourse on the Religious Experience." *Transition: An Intercontinental Workshop for Vertigralist Transmutation,* no. 23 (July 1935): 87–88.

Carola Giedion-Welcker. "New Roads in Modern Sculpture." *Transition: An Intercontinental Workshop for Vertigralist Transmutation,* no. 23 (July 1935): 198–201.

1936

Essays

"Glossary." *Transition: A Quarterly Review,* no. 24 (June 1936): 109.

"Romanticism and the Dream." *Transition: A Quarterly Review,* no. 24 (June 1936): 109–11.*

"Race and Language." *Transition: A Quarterly Review,* no. 24 (June 1936): 111–12.*

"Dreamers of the World Unite." *Transition: A Quarterly Review,* no. 24 (June 1936): 113.

"Notes for a Lexicon of Night." *Transition: A Quarterly Review,* no. 24 (June 1936): 113.

"Vertigral." *Transition: A Quarterly Review,* no. 24 (June 1936): 114.*

[Editor's Note to Paul Nelson, "Study of Surgical Pavillion for the Suez Canal"]. *Transition: A Quarterly Review,* no. 24 (June 1936): 134.

Translations

"Description by a Schizophrenic Patient" [from Hans Prinzhorn, *Bildnerei der Geisteskranken: Ein Beitrag zur Psychologie und Psychopathologie der Gestaltung,* Berlin: Springer, 1922]. *Transition: A Quarterly Review,* no. 24 (June 1936): 93–94.

Siegfried Giedion. "Construction and Aesthetics." *Transition: A Quarterly Review,* no. 24 (June 1936): 181–84 and 197–201.

1937

Translations

Andre Lhote. "The Unconscious in Art." *Transition: A Quarterly Review,* no. 26 (June 1937): 82, 87–90, 93–96.
L. Moholy-Nagy. "An Academy for the Study of Light." *Transition: A Quarterly Review,* no. 26 (June 1937): 113–17.
Leo Frobenius. "Birth of a Fable." *Transition: A Quarterly Review,* no. 26 (June 1937): 191–92.

1938

Books

Vertigralist Pamphlet. Paris: Transition, 1938.*
Vertical. Paris: Editions Sagesse, Librairie Tschann, 1938 (Les Feuillets de "Sagesse," Collection Anthologique, no. 64).

Essays

"Vertigral, ou la volonté cosmique; Babel." *Volontés,* no. 3 (February 20, 1938): 19–21.
"Frontierless Decade." *Transition: Tenth Anniversary,* no. 27 (April–May 1938): 7–9.*
"Homage to the Mythmaker [on James Joyce]." *Transition: Tenth Anniversary,* no. 27 (April–May 1938): 169–75.*
"Inquiry into the Spirit and Language of Night." *Transition: Tenth Anniversary,* no. 27 (April–May 1938): 233 and 243–45.*
"Glossary." *Transition: Tenth Anniversary,* no. 27 (April–May 1938): 377–82.
"Ten Years *transition.*" *Plastique,* no. 3 (Spring 1938): 23–26.
"Le Langage de la nuit." *Volontés,* no. 12 (December 1938): 19–27.

Translations

Carola Giedion-Welcker. "Prehistoric Stones." *Transition: Tenth Anniversary,* no. 27 (April–May 1938): 335–43.

1939

Essays

["Inquiry About Dream and Language"]. *Sur*, no. 51 (1939): 89–97.
"Crise du Langage." *Volontés*, no. 19 (July 1939): 8–11.

1940

Essays

Preface to *Words from the Deluge*. New York: Gotham Bookmart, undated [1940], unpaginated.*
"James Joyce." In *We Moderns: Gotham Book Mart 1920–1940*, 38–39 and 83–89. New York: Gotham Bookmart 1940.
"Euramerican Chant." *Fantasy: A Literary Quarterly with an Emphasis on Poetry* (Pittsburgh) 6, no. 4 (1940): 5–6.
"French Poetry and the Revival of Mysticism." *Poetry* (Chicago) 56, no. 5 (August 1940): 264–71.
"Goodbye to Yesterday." *The Living Age: The Word in Review* (Boston) 359, no. 4489 (October 1940): 192–96.*
"Patmos." *American Prefaces* 6, no. 1 (Fall 1940): 36–38.
"Remembering an Ascension in Strasbourg." *American Prefaces* 6, no. 1 (Fall 1940): 103–4.

1941

Books

Vertical: A Yearbook for Romantic-Mystic Ascensions. Edited by Eugene Jolas. New York: Gotham Bookmart, 1941.

Essays

"Foreword." In *Vertical: A Yearbook for Romantic-Mystic Ascensions,* edited by Eugene Jolas, 1. New York: Gotham Bookmart, 1941.
"Threefold Ascent: Verticalist Manifesto." In *Vertical: A Yearbook for Romantic-Mystic Ascensions,* edited by Eugene Jolas, 11–14. New York: Gotham Bookmart, 1941.*
"Poetry of the Ascent." In *Vertical: A Yearbook for Romantic-Mystic Ascensions,* edited by Eugene Jolas, 17–18. New York: Gotham Bookmart, 1941.*

"The Vertical Language." In *Vertical: A Yearbook for Romantic-Mystic Ascensions,* ed. Eugene Jolas (New York: Gotham Bookmart, 1941), 94–95.

"Suggestions for a Verticalist Vocabulary." In *Vertical: A Yearbook for Romantic-Mystic Ascensions,* ed. Eugene Jolas (New York: Gotham Bookmart, 1941), 95–96.

"The Quest and the Myth." In *Vertical: A Yearbook for Romantic-Mystic Ascensions,* edited by Eugene Jolas, 94–100. New York: Gotham Bookmart, 1941.*

"Romanticism Is Not Dead." In *Vertical: A Yearbook for Romantic-Mystic Ascensions,* edited by Eugene Jolas, 157–61. New York: Gotham Bookmart, 1941.*

"Stars and Angels: Homage to G. Th. Fechner, Romantic Savant and Visionary." In *Vertical: A Yearbook for Romantic-Mystic Ascensions,* edited by Eugene Jolas, 173–75. New York: Gotham Bookmart, 1941.*

"Poetry and Mysticism." In *Vertical: A Yearbook for Romantic-Mystic Ascensions,* edited by Eugene Jolas, 189–90. New York: Gotham Bookmart, 1941.

"Franz Kafka's Stories and Ascending Romanticism." In *Vertical: A Yearbook for Romantic-Mystic Ascensions,* edited by Eugene Jolas, 169–72. New York: Gotham Bookmart, 1941.*

"My Friend James Joyce." *Partisan Review* 8, no. 2 (March–April 1941): 82–93.*

"Surrealism: Ave atque Vale." *Fantasy: A Literary Quarterly with an Emphasis on Poetry* (Pittsburgh) 7, no. 1 (1941): 23–30.*

"Towards a Metaphysical Renascence?" *Poetry: A Magazine of Verse* (Chicago) 57, no.1 (October 1940–March 1941): 49–52.*

"Super-Occident and the Atlantic Language." *Decision: A Review of Free Culture,* edited by Klaus Mann, vol. 1, no. 6 (June 1941): 51–52.*

"Art and Letters in Latin America: Nightmares, Up-to-Date." *Living Age: The World in Review* (Boston) 360, no. 4498 (July 1941): 421–28.*

1943

Translations

Gustav Theodor Fechner. *Live After Death.* New York: Pantheon, 1943.

1944

Articles

Anonymous. "Le débarquement en Normandie vu d'Amérique." *Journal de Genève,* no. 142 (June 16, 1944), 1 (Jolas's authorship uncertain).

1946

Essays

"My Friend James Joyce." In *The Partisan Reader: Ten Years of Partisan Review, 1934–1944: An Anthology,* 457–68. New York, 1946.

1948

Essays

"My Friend James Joyce." In *James Joyce: Two Decades of Criticism,* edited by Seon Givens, 3–18. New York: Vanguard, 1948.

"From Jabberwocky to 'Lettrism.'" *Transition: Forty-eight,* ed. Georges Duthuit, no. 1 (January 1948): 104–20.*

"German Letters in the Ruins: A Report from Frankfurt." *New York Times Book Review,* no. 27 (July 4, 1948): 7–13.*

"Elucidation du monomythe de James Joyce: L'explication de *Finnegans Wake.*" *Critique: Revue générale des publications françaises et étrangères* 4, no. 26 (July 1948): 579–95.*

"L' Homme migrateur et son langage." In *Peuples et Evolution,* 266–73. Paris: Editions de Clermont, 1948 (Chemins du Monde, vol. 6).*

1949

Books

transition workshop. Edited by Eugene Jolas. New York: Vanguard, 1949.

Essays

"*Transition:* An Occidental Workshop, 1927–1938." In *transition workshop,* edited by Eugene Jolas, 13–18. New York: Vanguard, 1949.*

"Pan-Romanticism in the Atomic Age." In *transition workshop,* edited by Eugene Jolas, 393–95. New York: Vanguard, 1949.*

"Reemergence of Heidegger." Gen Mss 108, box 4, folder 83 (November 1949), Eugene and Maria Jolas Papers, General Collection of Rare Books, Beinecke Rare Book and Manuscript Library, Yale University, New Haven, Conn.*

"Heidegger in the Atomic Age." Gen Mss 108, box 4, folder 83 (November 1949), Eugene and Maria Jolas Papers, General Collection of Rare Books, Beinecke Rare Book and Manuscript Library, Yale University, New Haven, Conn.*

Articles

"Across Frontiers." *New York Herald Tribune* (European edition), no. 20761 (October 25, 1949): 5.
"Across Frontiers: Some Notes on Existentialism, Martin Heidegger, and Poetry Sales." *New York Herald Tribune* (European edition), no. 20767 (November 1, 1949): 5.*
"Across Frontiers: Irrealism, Immoralism, Naturalism, Concretism." *New York Herald Tribune* (European edition), no. 20773 (November 8, 1949): 5.*
"Across Frontiers: Origin and Aim of History." *New York Herald Tribune* (European edition), no. 20779 (November 15, 1949): 5.*
"Across Frontiers: Under Tyranny." *New York Herald Tribune* (European edition), no. 20785 (November 22, 1949): 5.
"Across Frontiers: Gordon Craig's Influence." *New York Herald Tribune* (European edition), no. 20790 (November 29, 1949): 5.
"Across Frontiers: A German Nationalist." *New York Herald Tribune* (European edition), no. 20796 (December 6, 1949): 5.*
"Across Frontiers: Left-Bank Scuffle." *New York Herald Tribune* (European edition), no. 20802 (December 13, 1949): 5.
"Across Frontiers: Americans Abroad." *New York Herald Tribune* (European edition), no. 20808 (December 20, 1949): 5.
"Across Frontiers: Poetic Renaissance in Belgium." *New York Herald Tribune* (European edition), no. 20814 (December 27, 1949): 5.

1950

Essays

"André Breton's Surrealism in 1950." Gen Mss 108, box 4, folder 83 (Heading: Report from Europe, dated Paris, June 1950), Eugene and Maria Jolas Papers, General Collection of Rare Books, Beinecke Rare Book and Manuscript Library, Yale University, New Haven, Conn.*

Articles

"Across Frontiers: Dominant Ten." *New York Herald Tribune* (European edition), no. 20820 (January 3, 1950): 5.

"Across Frontiers: Plethora of Goethe." *New York Herald Tribune* (European edition), no. 20826 (January 10, 1950): 5.

"Across Frontiers: Cosmic Man." *New York Herald Tribune* (European edition), no. 20832 (January 17, 1950): 5.

"Across Frontiers: Friends and Partisans." *New York Herald Tribune* (European edition), no. 20838 (January 24, 1950): 5.

"Across Frontiers: Art in Switzerland." *New York Herald Tribune* (European edition), no. 20844 (January 31, 1950): 5.

"Across Frontiers: The Absent Avant-Garde." *New York Herald Tribune* (European edition), no. 20850 (February 7, 1950): 5.

"Across Frontiers: Totalitarian Criticism." *New York Herald Tribune* (European edition), no. 20856 (February 14, 1950): 5.

"Across Frontiers: German Letters Today." *New York Herald Tribune* (European edition), no. 20862 (February 21, 1950): 5.

"Across Frontiers: Trend Toward Religion." *New York Herald Tribune* (European edition), no. 20868 (February 28), 1950: 5.

"Across Frontiers: The Old, Well-Trodden Paths." *New York Herald Tribune* (European edition), no. 20874 (March 7, 1950): 5.

"Across Frontiers: Negro Culture." *New York Herald Tribune* (European edition), no. 20880 (March 14, 1950): 5.

"Across Frontiers: Franco-German Cultural Exchanges." *New York Herald Tribune* (European edition), no. 20886 (March 21, 1950): 5.

"Across Frontiers: Keyserling's School of Wisdom." *New York Herald Tribune* (European edition), no. 20892 (March 28, 1950): 5.

"Across Frontiers: Death of a Crusader." *New York Herald Tribune* (European edition), no. 20898 (April 4, 1950): 5.

"Across Frontiers: Mushrooming Magazines." *New York Herald Tribune* (European edition), no. 20904 (April 11, 1950): 5.

"Across Frontiers: Semantic Warfare." *New York Herald Tribune* (European edition), no. 20910 (April 18, 1950): 2.

"Across Frontiers: Henri Matisse's Chapel." *New York Herald Tribune* (European edition), no. 20916 (April 25, 1950): 2.

"Across Frontiers: Literary Censorship." *New York Herald Tribune* (European edition), no. 20921 (May 2, 1950): 2.

"Across Frontiers: Post-War Austrian Letters." *New York Herald Tribune* (European edition), no. 20927 (May 9, 1950): 5.

"Across Frontiers: Cultural Synchronization in Prague." *New York Herald Tribune* (European edition), no. 20933 (May 16, 1950): 5.

"Across Frontiers: German Literary Trends." *New York Herald Tribune* (European edition), no. 20939 (May 23, 1950): 5.

"Across Frontiers: Congress for Intellectual Liberty." *New York Herald Tribune* (European edition), no. 20945 (May 30, 1950): 5.

"Ferien in Frankreich: Ein Blick in französisches Landleben." *Frankfurter Rundschau* 6, no. 200 (August 30, 1950): 2.

"Meine Begegnung mit James Joyce." *Die Neue Zeitung* 6, no. 84–85 (April 8, 1950): 12.

"James Joyce auf der Reise nach Amerika: Das Schicksal seines literarischen Nachlasses." *Frankfurter Rundschau* 6, no. 203 (September 2, 1950): 4.

"Wiedersehen mit der Pariser Boheme." *Die Neue Zeitung,* 1950, archived in Beinecke Rare Book and Manuscript Library (folder 350), but can't be found in the newspaper.

1951

Essays

"Novalis ou le Romantisme blanc." *Critique: Revue générale des publications françaises et étrangères* 7, no. 44 (January 15, 1951): 3–15.*

"Georg Trakl: Die Dichtungen." *Critique: Revue générale des publications françaises et étrangères* 7, no. 49 (June 15, 1951): 552–55.*

"Ernst Jünger et la crépuscule du nihilisme" ["Ernst Jünger and the Twilight of Nihilism"]. *Critique: Revue générale des publications françaises et étrangères* 8, no. 54 (November 1951): 937–54.*

Articles

"Latin Quarter Is Still Center of Cultural Life." *New York Herald Tribune* (European edition; Paris Bimillenary special edition), June 12, 1951, 1, 14, and 18.

1963

Essays

"My Friend James Joyce." In *James Joyce: Two Decades of Criticism,* edited by Seon Givens, 3–18. New York: Vanguard, 1963.

1990

Essays

"James Joyce." In Eugène Jolas, *Sur Joyce,* presented and translated by Marc Dachy, 33–127. Paris: Plon, 1990.

"Proclamation: La Révolution du mot." In Eugène Jolas, *Sur Joyce,* presented and translated by Marc Dachy, 131–33. Paris: Plon, 1990.

"La Poésie est verticale." In Eugène Jolas, *Sur Joyce,* presented and translated by Marc Dachy, 134–35. Paris: Plon, 1990.

1998

Books

Man from Babel, edited, annotated, and introduced by Andreas Kramer and Rainer Rumold. New Haven and London: Yale University Press, 1998.

Selected Undated Writings

"The Migrator and His Language." Gen Mss 108, box 4, folder 100, Eugene and Maria Jolas Papers, General Collection of Rare Books, Beinecke Rare Book and Manuscript Library, Yale University, New Haven, Conn.*

"Surrealism and Romanticism." Gen Mss 108, box 4, folder 128, Eugene and Maria Jolas Papers, General Collection of Rare Books, Beinecke Rare Book and Manuscript Library, Yale University, New Haven, Conn.*

"Romanticism and Metapolitics." Gen Mss 108, box 5, folder 125 (after 1949), Eugene and Maria Jolas Papers, General Collection of Rare Books, Beinecke Rare Book and Manuscript Library, Yale University, New Haven, Conn.*

"Novalis, the Mystic Visionary." Gen Mss 108, box 21, folder 394, Eugene and Maria Jolas Papers, General Collection of Rare Books, Beinecke Rare Book and Manuscript Library, Yale University, New Haven, Conn.*

"Prolegomenon, or White Romanticism and the Mythos of Ascension." Gen Mss 108, box 28, folder 386, Eugene and Maria Jolas Papers, General Collection of Rare Books, Beinecke Rare Book and Manuscript Library, Yale University, New Haven, Conn.*

SECONDARY SOURCES

Critical Reception (to 1955)

Allen, Charles. "American Little Magazines: *transition.*" *American Prefaces* 4, no. 8 (May 1939): 115–18 and 125–28.

Anonymous. "Eugene Jolas gestorben." *Die Neue Zeitung* (Berlin edition), no. 124 (May 31, 1952).

———. "Gedenkblatt für den lothringer Dichter Eugène Jolas: Die Welt zur Heimat—Die Heimat seine Welt." *Chez Soi en Lorraine,* June 20, 1953.

———. "Periodicals: English [review]." *Criterion* (London) 18, no. 71 (January 1939): 395–97.

——— [M., D.]. "Repostes [review]." *Partisan Review* 5, no. 3 (September 1938): 74–75.

———. "Review [of *Transition Stories*]." *Tambour* (Paris), no. 2 (April 1929): 57.

———. "Review [of *Transition Stories*]." *The Dial,* vol. 86 (1929): 525.

———. "Review [of *The Language of Night*]." *Les Nouvelles Littéraires* 12, no. 507 (July 2, 1932): 6.

———. "Review." *London Mercury,* vol. 32 (1935): 510.

———. "Review [of *transition*]." *John O'London's Weekly,* no. 1001 (June 24, 1938): 472.

———. "Review." *New York Times Book Review,* March 15, 1942, p. 9.

———. "Revue des revues." *La Nouvelle Revue française* 40, no. 235 (April 1, 1933): 702.

———. "*Transition* and Its Contemporaries: Some Opinions." *transition,* no. 18 (November 1929): 288–91.

———. "*Transition:* In a New Dress It Renews Its Experimental Lease." *Newsweek* 8, no. 2 (July 11, 1936): 40.

———. "Zululand." *Time* 28, no. 2 (July 13, 1936): 56–57.

Barker, George. "Review." *The Nation,* vol. 154 (February 7, 1942): 170.

Boyle, Kay. "A New Mythology." *Chicago Tribune* (European edition), no. 4254 (March 10, 1929): 5.

Brion, Marcel. "Review." *Les Cahiers du sud* (Marseille) 17, no. 4 (April 1930): 234–35.

Bryher, Winifred. "Review." *Life and Letters,* vol. 33 (May 1942): 132–36.

Calverton, V. F., et al. "The Revolution of the Word (A Symposium)." *Modern Quarterly* 5, no. 3 (Fall 1929): 273–91.

Eastman, Max. "The Cult of Unintelligibility." *Harper's Magazine* 158 (April 1929): 632–39.

Fitts, Douglas. "Review [of *Transition Stories*]." *Hound & Horn* 2, no. 4 (July–September 1929): 436–37.

Forgotson, E. S. "Review." *Poetry* 61, no. 1 (October 1942): 396–99.

F[ourman, Jacques]. "Review [of *transition* 21]." *Stimmen aus Lothringen* 2, no. 4 (April 1932): 111–12.

Giedion-Welcker, Carola. "James Joyce und die Sprache." *Die Weltwoche* (Zurich) 6, no. 225 (March 4, 1938).

Gilbert, Stuart. "Why a Revolution of the Word?" *Modern Quarterly* 5, no. 3 (Fall 1929): 284–85.

Godwin, Murray. "Mantic Almageste." *New Republic* 84, no. 1084 (September 11, 1935): 137.

Gold, Michael. "Three Schools of U.S. Writing." *New Masses* 4, no. 4 (September 1928): 13–14.

Grossmann, D. Jan. "Un poète international." *Critique* 8, no. 62 (July 1952): 592–604.

Highet, Gilbert. "The Revolution of the Word." *New Oxford Outlook* 1, no. 3 (February 1931): 288–304.

Hoffman, Frederick J., et al. *The Little Magazine: A History and a Bibliography.* Princeton, N.J.: Princeton University Press, 1946.

Hoops, Reinald. "*transition.*" *Englische Studien,* vol. 65 (1930–31): 474–75.

Huebner, Friedrich Markus. "Das andere Amerika." *Elsässisches Literaturblatt* (Strasbourg) 4, no. 7 (July 1, 1933): 2.

Hughes, Riley. "Review." *Renascence* 2, no. 2 (Spring 1950): 172–73.

Hutt, G. A. "Jolas' Julep." *Left Review,* no. 12 (September 1935): 528.

Jewell, Edward Alder. "In the Realm of Art: Along Paths That Summer Fields. Whichness of the What. Concerning the Revived *Transition* and Various Thorny Problems of the Day." *New York Times* 85, no. 28 (July 12, 1936): X7.

Kospoth, B. J. "The Poems of a Reporter." *Chicago Tribune Sunday Magazine* (European edition), no. 40 (November 16, 1924): 3 and 6.

———. "Passing of *transition.*" *Chicago Sunday Tribune* (European edition), no. 4695 (May 25, 1930): 9.

Leavis, F. R. "Review [of *The Language of Night*]." *Scrutiny* 2, no. 2 (1933): 193.

Loving, Pierre. "Experiment and Expression." *Pagany* 1, no. 4 (October–December 1930): 98–103.

Muir, Edwin. *Transition: Essays on Contemporary Literature.* New York: Viking, 1926.

North, Jessica Nelson. "Convention and Revolt." *Poetry* 34, no. 4 (July 1929): 212–16.

O'London, John. "Literary Jazz." *John O'London's Weekly,* no. 856 (September 7, 1935): 783.

Paul, Elliot H. "From a Littérateur's Notebook [review of *Cinema*]." *Chicago Tribune* (European edition), no. 3464 (January 9, 1927): 5.

Polsky, Ned. "Review." *Chicago Review,* vol. 4 (1950): 43.

Pound, Ezra. "Small Magazines." *English Journal* 19, no. 9 (November 1930): 689–704.

Putnam, Samuel. *Paris Was Our Mistress: Memories of a Lost & Found Generation.* New York: Viking 1947.

———. "The Revolution of the Word: A Symposium." *New Review* 1, no. 2 (May–July 1931): 144–45.

Rea, Gardener. "Dessin." *Life Magazine* 93, no. 2422 (April 5, 1929): 18.

Sage, Robert. "Magazines in General and One in Particular." *Chicago Tribune* (European edition), no. 3535 (March 20, 1927): 5.

Small, Alex. "Latin Quarter Notes." *Chicago Tribune* (European edition), no. 3487 (February 1, 1927): 4.

Smith, Bernard. "Books." *New Masses* 4, no. 11 (April 1929): 16.

Solveen, Henri. "Meine Freundschaft mit Eugen Jolas." *Die Tat* (Zürich) 17, no. 257 (September 20, 1952): 11.

Spector, Herman. "Liberalism and the Literary Esoterics." *New Masses* 4, no. 8 (January 1929): 18–19.

Sweeny, James Johnson. "Review [of *Vertical*]." *Cincinnati Enquirer,* no. 274 (January 8, 1933): n.p.

Tracy, T. F., and Abraham Lincoln Gillespie. "Clarity in Literature." *New Review* 1, no. 2 (May–July 1931): 98–100.

Vogel, Joseph. "Literary Graveyards." *New Masses* 5, no. 5 (October 1929): 30.

Research (from 1956)

Anderson, Elliot, and Mary Kinzie. *The Little Magazine in America.* Yonkers: Pushcart, 1978.

Attridge, Derek. "The *Wake*'s Confounded Language." In *Coping with Joyce: Essays from the Copenhagen Symposium,* edited by Morris Beja and Shari Benstock, 262–68. Columbus: Ohio State University Press, 1989.

Bennett, David. "Periodical Fragments and Organic Culture: Modernism, the Avant-Garde, and the Little Magazine." *Contemporary Literature* 30, no. 4 (Winter 1989): 480–502.

Benstock, Shari, and Bernard Benstock. "The Role of Little Magazines in the Mergence of Modernism." *Library Chronicle of the University of Texas at Austin* 20, no. 4 (1991): 69–87.

Biro, Adam, and René Passeron, eds. *Dictionnaire général du surréalisme et de ses environs.* Paris: Presses Universitaires de France, 1982.

Bishop, Edward. "RE: Covering Modernism: Format and Function in Little Magazines." In *Modernist Writers and the Marketplace,* edited by Ian R. Willison, Warwick Gould, and Warren Chernaik, 287–319. London and New York: Macmillan and St. Martin's, 1996.

Chielens, Edward E. *American Literary Magazines.* Westport, Conn., and London: Greenwood, 1992.

——. *The Literary Journal in America, 1900–1950: A Guide to Information Sources.* Detroit: Gale, 1977.

Cummings, Maurice. "*transition:* Eugene Jolas's Quest to Overcome Alienation." Ph.D. diss., Catholic University of America, Washington D.C., 1977.

Dachy, Marc. "Jolas-Joyce: Une amitié dans la tour de Babel." In Eugène Jolas, *Sur Joyce,* presented and translated by Marc Dachy, 9–31. Paris: Plon, 1990.

Dasher, Thomas E. "Eugene Jolas." In *American Writers in Paris, 1920–1939: Dictionary of Literary Biography,* 4:218–31. Detroit: Gale Research, 1980.

Deissler, Dirk. *Die entnazifizierte Sprache: Sprachpolitik und Sprachregelung in der Besatzungszeit.* Frankfurt am Main and Oxford: Peter Lang, 2004.

Dollenmayer, David B. "'*Wessen* Amerikanisch?'—Zu Eugene Jolas' Übersetzung von Döblins *Berlin Alexanderplatz.*" In *Internationale Alfred-Döblin-Kolloquien Münster 1989–Marbach a. N. 1991,* edited by Werner Stauffacher, 192–205. Bern: Peter Lang, 1993.

Fargnoli, Nicholas, and Michael Patrick Gillespie. *James Joyce A to Z: The Essential Reference to the Life and Work.* New York: Facts on File, 1995.

Finney, Michael. "Eugene Jolas, *transition* and the Revolution of the Word." *Tri-Quarterly,* no. 38 (Winter 1977): 39–53.

Fitch, Noel Riley, ed. *In Transition: A Paris Anthology: Writing and Art from "Transition" Magazine 1927–1930.* New York: Doubleday, 1990.

Fletcher, John. "The Anglo-American Avant-Garde: Continuities and Discontinuities with Special Reference to the Magazine *transition.*" In *Proceedings of the Eighth Congress of the International Comparative Literature Association,* 911–23. Stuttgart: Bieber, 1980.

Folio, Marta Alyssa. "Eugene Jolas and *Transition:* Bridging European and American Modernism." Ph.D. diss., Vanderbilt University, Nashville, Tenn., 2001.

———. "'Wüsten aus Stahl und Stein': The Urban Poetry of Eugene Jolas." Master's thesis, University of Delaware, 1996.

Ford, Hugh, ed. *The Left Bank Revisited: Selections from the Paris "Tribune" 1917–1934,* with an introduction by Matthew Josephson. University Park: Pennsylvania State University Press, 1972.

Forster, Leonard. *The Poet's Tongues: Multilingualism in Literature: The de Carle Lectures at the University of Otago, 1968.* Cambridge University Press and University of Otago Press, 1970.

Giedion-Welcker, Carola, ed. *Anthologie der Abseitigen/ Poètes à l'écart.* Zurich: Arche, 1965.

Heideking, Jürgen. "Melting Pot." In *USA-Lexikon: Schlüsselbegriffe zu Politik, Wirtschaft, Gesellschaft, Kultur, Geschichte und zu den deutsch-amerikanischen Beziehungen,* edited by Rüdiger B. Wersich, 461–62. Berlin: Schmidt, 1995.

Kiefer, Klaus H. "Dialoge—Carl Einstein und Eugene Jolas im Paris der frühen 30er Jahre." In *Carl Einstein et Benjamin Fondane. Avant-gardes et émigration dans le Paris des années 1920–30,* edited by Liliane Meffre and Olivier Salazar-Ferrer, 153–72. Bruxelles: P.I.E. Peter Lang 2008 (Comparatisme et Société, vol. 6).

———. *Diskurswandel im Werk Carl Einsteins: Ein Beitrag zur Theorie und Geschichte der europäischen Avantgarde.* Tübingen: Niemeyer, 1994. (Communicatio: Studien zur europäischen Literatur- und Kulturgeschichte, vol. 7.)

———. "Einstein in Amerika: Lebensbeziehungen und Theorietransfer." In *Carl-Einstein-Kolloquium 1994,* edited by Klaus H. Kiefer, 173–84. Frankfurt am Main: Peter Lang, 1996. (Bayreuther Beiträge zur Literaturwissenschaft, vol. 16.)

———. "Eugene Jolas' multilinguale Poetik." In *Multilinguale Literatur im 20. Jahrhundert,* edited by Manfred Schmeling and Monika Schmitz-Emans, 121–35. Würzburg: Königshausen & Neumann, 2002. (Saarbrücker Beiträge zur Vergleichenden Literatur- und Kulturwissenschaft, vol. 18.)

———. "Krieg der Wörter? Eugene Jolas' Babel-Dichtung ['Babel: 1940']." In *"Das Gedichtete behauptet sein Recht": Festschrift für Walter Gebhard zum 65. Geburtstag,* edited by Klaus H. Kiefer, Armin Schäfer, and Hans-Walter Schmidt-Hannisa, 147–63. Frankfurt am Main: Peter Lang, 2001.

———. "Modernismus, Primitivismus, Romantik—Terminologische Probleme bei Carl Einstein und Eugene Jolas um 1930." *Jahrbuch zur Kultur und Literatur der Weimarer Republik,* vol. 12 (2008): 117–37.

———. "Multilinguale Jugend und multilinguale Poetik: Zu Eugene Jolas' Leben und Werk." In *Osaka Gakuin University: International Colloquium 1994: Youth,* 125–53. Osaka: Osaka Gakuin University Press, 1995.

———. "Multilingualismus und Multikulturalismus als Herausforderung des Deutschunterrichts und der (interkulturellen) Germanistik." In *Kanon und Text in interkulturellen Perspektiven: "Andere Texte anders lesen,"* edited by Michaela Auer and Ulrich Müller, 215–38. Stuttgart: Heinz, 2001. (Publikationen der Gesellschaft für Interkulturelle Germanistik, vol. 7.)

———. "*Wortkunst* in Paris: Eugene Jolas und der deutsche Expressionismus." In *Frankreich und der deutsche Expressionismus/France and German Expressionism,* edited by Frank Krause, 141–59. Göttingen: Vandenhoeck & Ruprecht, 2008.

Kostelanetz, Richard. "*transition.*" In *A Dictionary of the Avant-Gardes,* 619–20. New York: Schirmer Books, 2000.

Koster, Beatrix De, and David Applefield. "Les Revues américaines à Paris, des années 20 à nos jours." *La Revue des revues,* no. 2 (November 1986): 22–26.

Kramer, Andreas. "August Stramm, Eugene Jolas und die 'Revolution of the Word': Eine Fußnote zur internationalen Stramm-Rezeption." In *August Stramm: Beiträge zu Leben, Werk und Wirkung,* edited by Lothar Jordan, 85–89. Bielefeld: Aisthesis, 1995.

Kramer, Andreas, and Richard Sheppard. "Raoul Hausmann's Correspondence with Eugene Jolas." *German Life and Letters,* n.s., 48, no. 1 (1995): 39–55.

Mansanti, Céline. "Bibliographie." In *Revues modernistes anglo-américaines: Lieux d'échanges, lieux d'exil,* edited by Benoît Tadié, 287–304. Paris: Ent'revues, 2006.

———. "De *The Criterion* à *transition:* L'évolution des revues littéraires et la désintégration de l'esprit d'avant-garde." In *Revues modernistes anglo-américaines: Lieux d'échanges, lieux d'exil,* edited by Benoît Tadié, 59–72. Paris: Ent'revues, 2006.

———. "'The Novel Is Dead: Long Live the Novel': Réponses de la revue américaine d'exil *transition* (1927–1938) à la crise française du roman." *Roman 20–50,* no. 43 (June 2007): 141–53.

———. "Présence du surréalisme français dans la revue américaine *transition* (Paris, 1927–1938): Eugène Jolas entre André Breton et Ivan Goll." *Mélusine,* no. 26 (February 2006): 277–304.

———. *"transition* de Eugene Jolas, une revue victime de son avant-gardisme?" In *Les oubliés des avant-gardes,* edited by Barbara Meazzi and Jean-Pol Madou, 339–50. Chambéry: Presses Universitaires de Savoie, 2006.

Marek, Jayne E. *Women Editing Modernism: "Little" Magazines and Literary History.* Lexington: University Press of Kentucky, 1995.

McGee, Patrick. "Joyce's Pedagogy: *Ulysses* and *Finnegans Wake* as Theory." In *Coping with Joyce: Essays from the Copenhagen Symposium,* edited by Morris Beja and Shari Benstock, 206–19. Columbus: Ohio State University Press, 1989.

McMillan, Dougald. *"Transition": The History of a Literary Era, 1927–1938.* London: Calder and Boyars, 1967; reprint New York: George Braziller, 1976.

Meffre, Liliane. *Carl Einstein 1885–1940: Itinéraires d'une pensée moderne.* Paris: Presses de l'Université de Paris-Sorbonne, 2002.

Monk, Craig. "Eugene Jolas and the Translation Policies of *transition.*" *Mosaic* 32, no. 4 (December 1999): 17–34.

———. "Modernism in Transition: The Expatriate American Magazine in Europe Between the World Wars." *Miscelánea: A Journal of English and American Studies,* vol. 20 (1999): 55–72.

———. "Photography in Eugene Jolas's *transition* Magazine." *History of Photography* 20, no. 4 (Winter 1996): 362–65.

———. "Sound Over Sight: James Joyce and Gertrude Stein in *Transition.*" In *Re Joyce: Text, Culture, Politics,* edited by John Brannigan, Geoff Ward, and Julian Wolfreys, 17–32. New York: St. Martin's, 1998.

Morrisson, Mark S. *The Public Face of Modernism: Little Magazines, Audiences, and Reception, 1905–1920.* Madison: University of Wisconsin Press, 2001.

Mott, Frank Luther. *A History of American Magazines: Sketches of 21 Magazines, 1905–1930.* Cambridge, Mass.: Harvard University Press, 1968.

Mousli, Béatrice, and Guy Bennett. *Poésie des deux mondes: Un dialogue franco-américain à travers les revues 1850–2004.* Paris: Ent'revues, 2004.

Perloff, Marjorie. "'Logocinéma of the Frontiersman': Eugene Jolas's Multilingual Poetics and Its Legacies." *Kunapipi:* Wollongon, 1999, pp. 145–16.

Poli, Bernard. *Ford Madox Ford and the Transatlantic Review.* Syracuse, N.Y.: Syracuse University Press, 1967.

Rabaté, Jean-Michel. "Joyce and Jolas: Late Modernism and Early Babelism." *Journal of Modern Literature* 22, no. 2 (1998–99): 245–52; reprinted in *Joyce and the Joyceans,* edited by Morton P. Levitt (Syracuse, N.Y.: Syracuse University Press, 2002), 51–58.

Rainey, Lawrence. *Institutions of Modernism: Literary Elites and Public Culture.* New Haven: Yale University Press, 1998.

Ritchie, James M. "Translations of the German Expressionists in Eugene Jolas's Journal *transition.*" *Oxford German Studies,* vol. 8 (1973): 149–58.

Rothenberg, Jerome. *Revolution of the Word: A New Gathering of American Avant Garde Poetry 1914–1945.* New York: Seabury, 1974.

Rumold, Rainer. "Archeo-logies of Modernity in *transition* and *Documents* 1929/30." *Comparative Literature Studies* 37, no. 1 (2000): 45–67.

Scheppard, Richard, and Andreas Kramer. "Raoul Hausmann's Correspondence with Eugene Jolas." *German Life and Letters,* no. 48 (1995), pp. 39–54.

Schmitz-Emans, Monika. *Die Sprache der modernen Dichtung.* Munich: Fink, 1997.

Silet, Charles L. P. *Transition: An Author Index.* Troy, N.Y.: Whitston, 1980.

Sullivan, Alvin, ed. *British Literary Magazines.* Westport, Conn.: Greenwood, 1983.

Wickes, Georges. *Americans in Paris.* Garden City, N.Y.: Doubleday, 1969.

Young, Timothy G. "Yale University: Beinecke Rare Book and Manuscript Library: General Collection of Rare Books and Manuscripts: Eugene and Maria Jolas Papers, Gen Mss 108 (1993)."

Index

Abel, Lionel, 488
Abin, César, 397
Abril de Vivero, Xavier, 446
Aiken, Conrad Potter, 437–38
Alberti, Rafael, 446
Alegria (Bazán), Ciro, 446
Alexandre, Maxime, 232
Alibert, François-Paul, 86
Altolaguirre, Manuel, 450
Alvarez, Isabel, 449
Ambelain, Robert, 193
Andersch, Alfred, 509
Andersen, Hans Christian, 222
Anderson, Margaret, 80, 505
Anderson, Sherwood, 49, 52, 76, 139, 260
Andrews, Wayne, 123
Anet, Claude (Jean Schopfer), 45
Anquetil-Duperron, A. H., 313, 323
Antheil, George, 23, 61, 71, 171
Apollinaire, Guillaume, 26, 56, 71, 97, 103, 148, 153, 196
Aquinas. See Thomas Aquinas, Saint
Aragon, Louis, 81, 85, 89, 95–96, 103, 232, 235
Arce, Manuel Maples, 444
Ariosto, Ludovico, 64
Aristotle, 205, 250
Arland, Marcel, 57
Arndt, Ernst Moritz, 216, 316
Arnim, Ludwig Joachim Achim von, 205, 211, 213, 215–16, 226–27, 235, 315–16
Arnoux, Alexandre, 504
Aron, Robert, 82–83
Arp, Hans (Jean), 124, 126, 147, 189, 212–13, 232, 258, 267, 379, 490, 495–96

Artaud, Antonin, 90, 213, 232
Artl, Roberto, 447
Asturias, Miguel Angel, 445
Auden, Wystan Hugh, 437
Auerbach, Erich, 381
Augustine, Saint (Augustinus, Aurelius), 310, 350, 390, 413
Auslander, Joseph, 22
Azlor, Clementina, 447
Azocar, Ruben, 446
Azuela, Mariano, 444

Baader, Franz von, 156, 205–6, 210, 272, 314, 319–20
Babbitt, Irving, 260–61
Bach, Johann Sebastian, 63
Bachelard, Gaston, 225, 318, 498
Bachofen, Johann Jakob, 260, 269–70, 286
Bacon, Francis, 188, 460
Baillon, André, 18–19
Baker, Josephine, 165
Balagas, Patricio, 449
Balboa, Vasco Núñez de, 458
Balde, Jean, 15
Ball, Hugo, 146–47, 184, 189, 212–13, 232, 273
Balzac, Honoré de, 17, 43, 64
Barbey d'Aurévilly, Jules, 25
Barbusse, Henri, 24
Barja, Cesar, 445
Barney, Natalie Clifford, 92
Baron, Jacques, 90, 232, 235
Barrès, Maurice, 10–11, 14, 51, 78, 335, 339
Barrès, Philippe, 10
Basave, René, 30
Basso, Hamilton, 123

Bataille, Georges, 318
Baudelaire, Charles, 37, 63, 144, 185,
    196, 209, 224, 318, 339, 503
Bauer, Arnold, 469, 510
Bazin, Hervé, 470
Beach, Sylvia, 8–9, 36, 40–41, 47, 66,
    101, 122, 125, 394–95, 406, 510
Beauduin, Nicolas, 27
Beaufret, Jean, 488
Beauvoir, Simone de, 510
Becher, Johannes Robert, 39
Beck, Enrique, 476
Becket, Thomas, 419
Beckett, Samuel, 124, 150, 267, 397,
    402, 406
Bédier, Joseph, 17
Bédouin, Jean-Louis, 372
Beer-Hoffmann, Richard, 59
Beermann-Fischer, E., 508–9
Beermann-Fischer, Gottfried, 508
Beethoven, Ludwig van, 374
Beguin, Albert, 217, 224, 227, 316, 318
Bel-Geddes, Norman, 16
Benda, Julien, 15, 86, 431
Benét, Stephen Vincent, 431, 436
Benn, Gottfried, 146, 263, 349, 351,
    355–57
Benoist-Méchin, Jacques, 38, 47
Benoît, Pierre, 27
Béraud, Henri, 7, 24
Berdyaev, Nikolai Alexandrovich, 438
Berence, Fred, 17
Berge, André, 96
Bergner, Elisabeth, 482
Bergson, Henri, 30, 44, 225, 269, 318,
    390, 498
Berkeley, George, 234
Berlin, Irving, 165
Bernanos, Georges, 290, 447, 481
Bernárdez, Francisco Luiz, 447
Bernhardt, Sarah, 42

Berr, Henri, 504
Bertaud, Jules, 86
Bertrand, Louis, 87
Besset, Maurice, 313–14, 319–20,
    322–23
Betz, Maurice, 11, 44, 91
Bianchi, Alfredo A., 447
Bianquis, Geneviève, 316
Bibesco, Martha (Princess Bibesco), 15
Bienville, Jean-Baptiste Le Moyne de,
    458
Bill, Max, 479
Billy, André, 8
Bismarck, Otto von, 361
Blackwood, Algernon, 219
Blake, William, 111–12, 225, 281, 292,
    307, 340, 418
Blin, Roger, 477
Bloch, Jean-Richard, 45
Bloom, Marion, 389
Bloy, Léon, 289, 363
Blümner, Rudolf, 189
Boch, Jean-Richard, 92
Bodet, Jaime Torres, 444
Böhme, Jakob, 280, 292, 314, 319, 320,
    323
Bohr, Niels, 225, 318
Bombal, Maria Luisa, 446
Bonnard, Pierre, 479
Bontemps, Arna, 498
Boone, Daniel, 246
Bopp, Léon, 38
Borchardt, Rudolf, 494
Borchert, Wolfgang, 469
Bordeaux, Henry, 15
Borel, Petrus, 280
Borges, Jorge Luis, 447
Borges, Norah, 447
Bosch, Hieronymus, 390
Bosquet, Alain, 373
Bouchet, André du, 468

Boulenger, Jacques, 10, 17
Boulenger, Marcel, 15
Bourdet, Claude, 504, 510
Bourget, Paul, 10–11, 14
Bouroff (architect), 428
Bouteron, Marcel, 15
Bowen, Elizabeth, 500
Boyd, Ernest, 42, 79–80, 93
Boyle, Kay, 112, 121, 124, 151, 432, 477
Brâncuşi, Constantin, 126, 397–98
Braque, Georges, 126
Brauchbar, Edouard, 400
Breit, Harvey, 436
Bremond, Henri, 15
Brentano, Clemens, 205, 210
Breton, André, 33, 49, 56–57, 81,
    89–90, 102–5, 148, 192–94, 209,
    211, 213, 224, 227–29, 231–37, 318,
    371–74, 378, 396, 447, 457, 470,
    482, 490
Bridges, Robert Seymour, 24
Brion, Marcel, 406
Brisset, Jean-Paul, 193
Brito, Bernardino Mena, 444
Broch, Hermann, 453, 505
Brod, Max, 344
Broglie, Louis-Victor de, 488
Brooke, Rupert, 24
Brooks, Van Wyck, 260
Brousse, J. R. de, 18
Brugière, Francis, 126
Brull, Mariano, 195, 449
Brum, Blanca Luz, 448
Bruno, Giordano, 389, 409
Brunschvicg, Léon, 45
Buchert, Raymond, 11, 60, 92
Buddha, 400, 413, 480
Budgen, Frank, 400, 406
Budry, Jean, 94, 147, 190
Bunin, Ivan Alekseyevich, 495
Burnett, Whit, 112, 151

Butcher, Fanny, 53
Butler, Samuel, 67

Cabral, Perez, 448
Cabrera, Manuel, 445
Cahn, Sulvain, 92
Caillois, Roger, 447
Calder, Alexander, 126, 510
Caldwell, Erskine, 123
Callaghan, Morley, 124
Calverton, V. F., 134–38
Calvin, John, 132
Calvo, Novas, 449
Campbell, Joseph, 405–6, 408–11,
    420
Campio, Alexandro Maurico, 446
Camus, Albert, 497–98
Camus, Marcel, 316, 325, 497
Canabroa, Eurialo, 449
Cannan, Gilbert, 66
Carco, Francis, 15, 24, 27, 93, 470
Carlyle, Thomas, 324
Carpentier, Alejo, 449
Carroll, Lewis (Charles Lutwidge
    Dodgson), 149, 184, 282, 329
Carrouges, Michel, 315–16, 372
Cartier, Jacques, 458
Carus, Carl Gustav, 209, 269–70
Caso, Antonio, 445
Cassou, Jean, 43, 81, 83, 374
Castro Argüello, Alicia, 446
Cendrars, Blaise, 31, 318, 467, 475
Cesares, Morel Adolfo, 447
Cézanne, Paul, 63, 479, 487
Chagall, Marc, 75, 94, 479
Chalupt, René, 69
Chaminade, Marcel, 69
Champlain, Samuel de, 458
Chaplin, Charlie, 73
Chapman, John A., 53
Charlot, Jean, 444–45

Chateaubriand, François-Auguste-
  René de, 51
Chaulot, Paul, 470
Chazal, Malcolm de, 227, 373
Chérau, Gaston, 97
Chirico, Giorgio di, 126, 232–33, 236,
  371, 487
Chonez, Claudine, 470
Chumacero, Ali, 445
Churchill, Winston, 299
Cimorra, Clemente, 447
Clairouin, Denyse, 510
Claudel, Paul, 33, 46–47, 63, 102, 236,
  476, 495
Climacus, Joannes, 292
Coates, Robert, 121, 139, 150
Cocteau, Jean, 15, 45, 93, 97, 103, 148,
  339, 470
Cogniat, Raymond, 43, 495
Cohen, Gustave, 12
Coiplet, Robert, 30
Coleridge, Samuel Taylor, 209–10,
  280, 401
Colette, Sindonie-Gabrielle, 468
Colon, Marguerite ("Jenny"), 321
Colum, Mary, 224
Colum, Padraic, 403
Columbus, Christopher 458
Compton-Burnett, Ivy, 500
Comte, Auguste, 144, 269
Confucius, 480
Conrad, Joseph, 48, 86, 340, 498
Copland, Aaron, 171
Corot, Jean-Baptiste-Camille, 479
Cortés (de Monroy y Pizarro),
  Hernán, 458
Cota, José Muñoz, 444
Cowell, Henry, 7–8
Crane, Hart, 112, 122–23, 151, 437
Crastre, Victor, 372
Crémieux, Benjamin, 51, 63, 69, 83
Crevel, René, 57, 86, 97, 213

Croce, Benedetto, 381
Crosby, Caresse (Mary Phelps Jacobs),
  112, 151
Crosby, Harry, 112, 114, 123, 151
Cross, John Kier, 501
Croy, Homer, 53–54
Cummings, Edward Estlin, 8, 69,
  151–52

Dacqué, Edgar, 271
Dali, Salvador, 229, 237, 482, 487
Dano, Rubén, 448
Dante Alighieri, 16, 295
Darío, Rubén, 448
Darwin, Charles, 156
Daudet, Léon, 156, 207
Davidman, Joy, 436
Deberly, Henri, 21
Debussy, Claude, 63, 185, 334, 374
Decker, James A., 436
Deffoux, Léon, 24
Degas, Edgar, 479
Dehmel, Richard Fedor Leopold, 146
De La Salle (René Robert Cavelier),
  458
De la Tour du Pin, Patrice, 438
Delaunay, Elie, 57, 71
Delteil, Joseph, 57, 82, 90, 96, 104, 231
Derème, Tristan, 15, 27, 147
Dermée, Paul, 49, 56
Descartes, René, 89, 100, 381, 498
Descaves, Lucien, 468
Desch, Kurt, 510
Desnos, Robert, 89, 105, 121, 124, 146,
  148, 193, 213, 230–31, 235–36
Desoille, Robert, 225, 318
De Soto, Hernando, 246
Destéfano, José R., 447
Desthieux, F. J., 8
Dionysius Areopagita, 280
Diop, Alioune, 497
Dirks, Walter, 495

Döblin, Alfred, 453, 503
Domela, César, 495
Domínguez, Maria Alicia, 447
Dongen, Kees van (Cornelis Theo-
    dorus Maria van Dongen), 97
Doren, Mark van, 436
Dorgelès, Roland, 24
Dos Passos, John, 27, 139, 262
Dostoevsky (Dostoevskij), Fyodor
    Mikhaylovich, 17, 58, 64, 78, 309,
    317, 339, 361, 363, 472
Doysie, Abel, 24
Drapkin, Tsilye (Celia Dropkin), 25
Dreiser, Theodore, 52–53
Du Bos, Charles, 21, 69
Duchamp, Marcel, 126, 148, 193
Dufay, Pierre, 24
Duff, Charles, 150
Du Gard, Maurice Martin, 56–57, 89,
    334
Duhamel, Georges, 24
Dujardin, Edouard, 483
Dumaine, Philippe, 470
Dumont, Arsène, 340
Dunan, Renée, 9, 37
Dunne, J. W., 176, 402, 483
Durkheim, Emile, 44, 433
Durtain, Luc, 46, 48
Duse, Eléanore, 84
Duvernois, Henri, 15

Ebbinghaus, Carl H., 453
Eberhart, Richard, 432
Eboué, Félix, 194
Eckhart, Master. See Master Eckhart
    (Eckhart von Hochheim)
Edschmid, Kasimir, 453
Eich, Günter, 477, 494, 510
Eigeldinger, Marc, 372
Einstein, Carl, 123–24, 146, 212, 225,
    267, 330, 352
Eizenstat (poet), 25

Elbée, Jean d', 14
Eldridge, Paul, 92
Eliot, Thomas Sterns, 21, 101, 151, 184,
    425, 432, 437–38, 477–78, 494, 509
Ellington, Duke, 374
Ellis, Havelock, 28, 340
Eluard, Paul, 90, 102, 148, 213, 229,
    230, 232, 235–36, 447
Emerson, Ralph Waldo, 283
Engels, Friedrich, 234
Eon, Francis, 27
Epstein, George, 11
Ernst, Max, 126, 232, 371, 482
Erro, Carlos Alberti, 447
Ewers, Hanns Heinz, 37

Fabre, Guillermo Viscarra, 448
Fabre, Lucien, 15, 27
Fabritius, Carel, 479
Fagus (Georges Eugène Faillet), 23
Fairbanks, Douglas, 43
Faleiros, Jorge, 449
Fargue, Léon-Paul, 42, 46–48, 69, 88,
    116, 119, 124, 148–49, 191, 235, 258,
    266, 378, 495
Faulkner, William, 364, 477
Faÿ, Bernard, 32, 69–70, 83, 144
Fayard, Jean, 8, 16
Fechner, Gustav Theodor, 205, 209,
    219–20, 225, 251, 269, 292
Fegto, François, 482
Fehr, Bernard, 400
Fernandez, Ramon, 21, 28
Fichte, Johann Gottlieb, 215–17, 314,
    316, 319–20
Ficker, Ludwig von, 349
Fierens, Paul, 38
Figueira, Gastón, 448
Fischer, Samuel, 508
Fiske, Dwight, 22
Flaherty, Robert, 505
Flaubert, Gustave, 334

Fleg, Edmond, 45
Flers, Robert de, 15
Flouquet, Charles, 436
Foley, Martha, 112, 151
Fombeure, Maurice, 470
Ford, Charles Henri, 436
Ford, Ford Madox, 395
Forster, Rudolf, 477
Foujita, Leonard Tsuguharu, 501
Fourcade, J. O., 148
France, Anatole, 85
Franck, Henri, 45, 63
Frank, Leonhard, 453, 499, 508
Frank, Waldo, 21, 52, 260, 446
Frantz, C. A., 92
Frazer, James, 143
Freitag-Loringhoven, Elsa van, 150
Freud, Sigmund, 17, 23, 27–28, 56–57,
    78, 116, 136–37, 148, 156, 176, 209,
    211–13, 224, 233–35, 237, 249, 252,
    257–59, 265, 269, 271, 371
Frost, Robert Lee, 29, 76, 437

Gabo, Naum (Naum Neemia Pevs-
    ner), 126
Gachot, M., 21
Galantière, Lewis, 93
Gauguin, Paul, 63, 198
Gautier, Théophile, 339
Gegory, Horace, 436
George, Stefan, 145, 188, 493, 503
Géraldy, Paul, 30
Giacometti, Alberto, 126, 479
Gide, André, 7, 21, 37, 46, 48, 55,
    61–63, 78, 97, 121, 333–40, 475–76,
    497
Giedion, Sigfried, 126, 400
Giedion-Welcker, Carola, 188
Gilbert, Stuart, 112, 114, 123, 134, 140,
    151, 158, 396, 402, 406–7
Gillespie, Abraham Lincoln, 112,
    150–51

Ginsberg, Louis, 92
Giran (poet), 449
Giraudoux, Jean, 69, 505
Giusti, Roberto F., 447
Glatstein, Jacob, 25
Godwin, Murray, 139, 150
Goebbels, Joseph, 362, 493
Goethe, Johann Wolfgang von, 223,
    280, 286, 311, 321, 329–30, 356, 367,
    399
Gogh, Vincent van, 60
Goldoni, Carlo Osvalo, 100
Goll, Claire, 49–50, 72–73, 75, 92, 94,
    499
Goll, Felix, 74
Goll, Ida, 74
Goll, Ivan/Yvan, 11, 32, 48–50, 52,
    55–56, 71–75, 92, 94, 349–50, 499–
    500, 503
Gomez de la Serna, Ramon, 43–44, 69
Góngora y Argote, Luis de, 143
González, Eduardo Ines, 446
Gordon, George, 132, 143
Gorman, Herbert, 36, 134, 402
Görres, Joseph, 60, 215, 309, 318, 438
Goudal, Jean, 90
Gourmont, Jean de, 31
Gourmont, Rémy de, 31
Gracq, Julien, 372, 491
Graf, Oscar Maria, 503
Grasset, B., 84
Greene, Graham, 364, 498
Greene, Henry, 500
Gregory, Horace, 436
Grimm, Jacob, 222
Grimm, Wilhelm, 222
Gris, Juan (José Victoriano
    González-Pérez), 126
Gropius, Walter, 428
Gross, K. A., 454
Grosz, George, 126
Grünewald, Matthias, 390

Guardini, Romano, 495
Guegen, Pierre, 30
Guerne, Armel, 316, 319, 323
Guillén, Nicolás Cristóbal, 449
Gump, Andy, 70
Gump, Chester, 70
Gump, Min, 70
Gumpert, Maurice, 494
Gutermann (member of Esprit), 234
Gurvitch, Georges, 488

Halpern, Moyshe-Leyb, 25
Hals, Franz, 479
Hamann, Johann Georg, 205, 208, 249
Hammond, Percy, 53
Hamsun, Knut, 495
Hansen, M. L., 440
Harry, Myriam, 87
Hartley, L. P., 500
Hartung, Hans, 495
Haulleville, Eric de, 258
Hauptmann, Gerhart, 394, 504, 508
Hayes, Roland, 165
Heap, Jane, 34–35
Hébertot, Jacques, 18
Hegel, Georg Wilhelm Friedrich, 104,
    215, 217, 234, 249
Heidegger, Martin, 176, 269, 270–71,
    290, 363–64, 387, 467–69, 471–74,
    486–87
Heine, Heinrich, 55, 60, 223, 431
Hélion, Jean, 126
Hemingway, Ernest, 59–60, 68, 124,
    139, 211, 364, 447, 453, 476–77, 495
Hemsterhuys (Hesterhuis), Tiberius,
    320–21
Henriot, Emile, 15
Heraclitus of Ephesus, 155, 205, 250
Herder, Johann Gottfried, 205, 207–8,
    215, 249, 313, 316, 324
Hérédia, José-Maria de, 335
Hermant, Abel, 10

Hérold, A. Ferdinand, 31
Herrick, Robert, 89
Herrmann, Henri, 92
Heym, Georg, 349–51, 494
Hikmet, Nazim, 510
Himmler, Heinrich, 453
Hippocrates, 250
Hirsch, Rudolf, 509
Hitler, Adolf, 217, 299, 316, 352, 362,
    367, 440, 450–54, 459, 469, 485–
    86, 507–8
Hiver, Marcel, 24
Hobbes, Thomas, 364
Hocke, Gustav René, 454
Hoddis, Jakob van, 349–51
Hoffmann, Ernst Theodor Amadeus,
    205, 223, 226
Hoffman, Leigh, 112, 151
Hofmannsthal, Hugo von, 188, 209,
    352, 460, 508–9
Holden, Raymond, 436
Hölderlin, Friedrich, 92, 212, 215, 234,
    280, 315–16, 363, 474
Hollaender, Jürgen von, 509
Holthusen, Egon, 494
Holz, Arno, 357
Homer, 53, 480
Honegger, Arthur, 16
Hopkins, Gerard Manley, 149, 438
Houston, Elsie, 449
Huch, Ricarda, 453
Huelsenbeck, Richard, 147, 189, 212,
    490
Hughes, Langston, 498
Hugnet, Georges, 232
Hugo, Victor, 12, 144, 224, 309, 317
Huidobro, Vincent, 192, 446
Huot, Martha Champion, 195
Huysmans, Joris-Karl, 14, 25, 37

Ibsen, Henrik, 394, 418, 508
Icaza, Jorge, 448

Ichaso, Jorge, 449
Iliazd (Ilia Zdanevich), 192, 196
Illing, Werner, 454
Imbs, Braving, 122
Ingres, Jean Auguste Dominique, 63
Ingrim, Robert, 504
Inonu, Ismet, 510
Isou, Isidore, 185, 196–99, 489
Istrati, Panait, 13, 85

Jacob, Max, 33, 51, 71
Jaloux, Edmond, 15, 27–28, 30, 69, 468
James, Henry, 28
James, William, 219
Jammes, Francis, 12, 33, 90, 339
Janet, Pierre, 156, 250
Jankélévitch, Vladimir, 488
Jarry, Alfred, 148, 231
Jaspers, Karl, 455, 469, 480–81
Jeffers, Robinson, 436–38
Jensen, Johannes von, 508
Jesperson, Otto, 137
Jiménez, Avila, 448
Jiménez, Juan Ramón, 445
John of the Cross, Saint (Juan de Yepes Alvarez), 157, 176, 280–81, 292, 309, 317, 438
Johns, Orrick, 49, 52, 75
Johnson, Samuel, 123, 131
Jolas, Eugene, 112, 114, 228, 267, 403
    See also Rutra, Theo
Jolas, Jacques, 229
Jones, William, 313, 323–24
Jonson, Ben, 132
Josephson, Matthew, 123
Jouhandeau, Marcel, 121
Jousse, Marcel, 135, 181, 381, 392, 401, 419
Jouve, Jean-Pierre, 432
Joyce, George (Georgio), 396–97, 407
Joyce, Helen, 396–97

Joyce, James, 8–9, 30, 33–36, 40–41, 46–47, 67, 69, 80, 116, 118–19, 121–24, 133, 149–50, 158, 185–87, 211, 219, 224, 258, 263, 282, 325, 365, 377–83, 385–94, 396–98, 400–403, 405–14, 416, 418–20, 432, 442, 447–48, 483, 491, 500–501, 510
Jung, Carl Gustav, 28, 116, 137, 156, 176, 224, 250, 257, 259, 269, 271
Jünger, Ernst, 361–68, 454, 485–86
Jünger, Friedrich Georg, 367
Jungius, Joachim, 479
Just, August Coelestin, 310, 320

Kafka, Franz, 124, 212, 290, 343–45, 364, 486
Kahn, G., 196
Kaiser, Georg, 38
Kandinsky, Wassily, 126, 495–96
Kant, Immanuel, 45, 319–20, 330, 473
Kasack, Hermann, 454
Katz, Nathan, 92
Kazin, Alfred, 403
Keller, Gottfried, 59
Kempis, Thomas à, 77
Kerkhoff, Susanne, 454
Kerner, Justinus, 156, 205
Kessel, J., 24, 83
Kesten, Hermann, 508, 510
Keurtz (poet), 25
Keyserling, Eduard von, 58, 270
Kierkegaard, Søren, 176, 212, 225, 269, 271, 290, 344, 363, 473
Kipling, Rudyard, 24, 401
Kissin (poet), 25
Klages, Ludwig, 269–70
Klee, Paul, 126, 496
Klein, Carl August, 145
Kleist, Heinrich von, 215–16, 315–16, 344
Klemm, Wilhelm, 349
Knapp, Ethel Marjorie, 92

Knickerbocker, Harmen Jansen, 99
Knopf, Alfred A., 333
Kogon, Eugen, 453, 469, 495
Kolb, Annette, 510
Kolbenhoff, Walter, 453, 476, 510
Kortner, Fritz, 477
Kospoth, B. J., 39
Kra, Suzanne, 50
Kramer-Badoni, Rudolf, 509
Krauss, Werner, 455
Krehbiel, Henry Edward, 169
Kühn, Sophie von, 309–10, 313, 319–
  21, 323–24, 419

Lacan, Jacques, 488
Lalou, René, 25
Langgässer, Elisabeth, 452, 454, 494,
  501
Lanux, Pierre de, 69
Lao-tse (Laozi), 480
Larbaud, Valéry, 8–9, 30, 33, 41–43,
  46–48, 51, 65–69, 79–80, 88–89,
  99–101, 394–95, 483
La Rochelle, Pierre Drieu, 96
Larreta, Abraham Arias, 446
Larsson, Raymond Ellsworth F., 122,
  432, 434–36
Lasker-Schüler, Else, 121, 499
Lasky, Melvin, 486
Lassaigne, Jacques, 374
Laurens, Paul Albert, 335
Lautréamont, de (Isidore-Lucien
  Ducasse), 144, 209, 213, 224, 234,
  258, 286
Lavaud, Guy, 27
Lawrence, David H., 437–38, 498
Lazare, Bernard, 45
Lazare, Jean, 470
Le Corbusier (Charles-Édouard
  Jeanneret-Gris), 126, 428, 495
Lee, C. P., 436
Lefèvre, Frédéric, 8

Léger, Fernand, 24, 71, 126, 506
Le Grix, François, 14, 97
Lehmann, John, 500
Lehmann, Wilhelm, 494
Leibowitz, Rene, 374
Leiris, Michel, 146, 148, 231, 235–36,
  378, 497, 510
Leisegang, Hans, 269
Lemonnier, Camille, 261
Léon, Lucy, 397
Léon, Paul, 397, 402, 406
Lerner, Max, 436
Levin, Harry, 403, 408
Levin, Meyer, 505
Lévi-Strauss, Claude, 488
Levy, Simon, 21
Lévy-Bruhl, Lucien, 116, 156, 176, 257,
  259, 269, 271, 387, 488
Lewis, Sinclair, 52, 262
Lewis, Wyndham, 236, 286
Lewisohn, Ludwig, 121
Leyeles, A., 42
Lichtenberg, Georg Christopher, 208,
  224
Lichtenberger, André, 223
Lichtenberger, Henri, 321
Lièvre, Pierre, 27
Liliencron, Detlev von, 146
Lindbergh, Charles, 291
Lindsay, Vachel, 52, 75–76, 436
Lizaso, Felix, 449
Llona, Victor, 69, 84, 406, 448
Lobos, Heitor Villa, 449
Lord Russell (Bertrand Arthur Wil-
  liam Russell), 492
Lourdin, Rose, 68
Louys, Pierre, 334–35
Loving, Pierre, 92, 134
Lowell, Amy, 49, 52, 75–76
Lowenfels, Walter, 150
Luján, Fernando, 446
Lukács, Georg, 482

Maas, Joachim, 508–9
Macauley, Rose, 500
MacGreevy, Thomas, 124, 267, 397, 406
Machiavelli, Niccolò, 386
MacLeish, Archibald, 122, 431, 436–37
MacOrlan, Pierre, 25
Madariaga, Salvador de, 447
Maeterlinck, Maurice, 29, 209, 212, 223, 234, 335
Magdalena, Mauricio, 444
Magnus, Albertus, 154, 250
Maier (writer), 313, 324
Maillol, Aristide, 479
Malaparte, Curzio (Kurt Erich Suckert), 495
Malaret, Augusto, 449
Mallarmé, Stéphane, 44, 144, 181, 185, 212, 224, 280, 282, 334, 503
Mallea, Eduardo, 447
Mallet-Stevens, Robert, 428
Malraux, André, 364
Mañach, Jorge, 449
Manet, Edouard, 479
Mann, Erika, 374
Mann, Klaus, 374
Mann, Thomas, 374, 453, 507–10
Mannon, O., 92
Man Ray (Emmanuel Radnitzky), 90, 126
Mantle, Burus, 53
Marais, Xavier de, 17
Marcel, Gabriel, 364, 498
Marcus, B., 61
Marechal, Leopoldo, 447
Margolin, Anna, 25
Mariateguí, José Carlos, 443, 446
Marín, Juan, 446
Marinello, Juan, 449
Marinetti, Filippo Tommaso, 146, 188, 282, 379

Maritain, Jacques, 86, 97
Marlowe, Christopher, 132, 184
Marquet, Albert, 479
Marquette, Jacques, 458
Marsan, Eugène, 15
Martí, Marcel, 447
Martineau, Henri, 26–27
Marx, Karl, 234
Masefield, John, 24
Massen, Osa 495
Massis, Henri, 61, 86, 97
Masson, André, 126, 213, 232–33, 371, 432
Massot, Pierre de, 28
Master Eckhart (Eckhart von Hochheim), 157, 280, 292
Masters, Edgar Lee, 49, 52, 75–76
Matisse, Henri, 97, 476, 479
Matos, Luis Palés, 449
Matthews, Brander, 48
Maupassant, Guy de, 93
Maurer, Th., 92
Mauriac, Claude, 372
Mauriac, François, 15, 77–79, 81, 85, 290
Maurois, André, 17, 45, 83
Maurras, Charles, 15
Maury, A., 251
Mayer, Stanley Dehler, 436
Mayr, W., 50–51
McAlmon, Robert, 406
Médieu (discussion leader), 488
Melo, Mario Vieira de, 449
Melville, Herman, 363
Mencken, H. L., 119, 139, 178, 429
Mendelssohn, Peter de, 486
Mendès, Catulle, 44
Mercier, Gustave L. S., 225, 318
Merleau-Ponty, Maurice, 488, 504, 510
Michaux, Henri, 148, 258, 467, 510
Michel, Michel-Georges, 8, 24, 29

Michelangelo (di Lodovico Buonarroti Simoni), 484
Michelet, Jules, 381
Migot, George, 7–8
Milhaud, Darius, 52
Millay, Edna St. Vincent, 431, 436
Miller, Henry, 365, 489, 501
Miłosz, Oscar Vladislas de, 309, 317, 432
Minder, Robert, 504
Minkowski, E., 488
Miró, Joan, 126
Moeller, Philip, 35
Moholy-Nagy, László, 126
Molière (Jean-Baptiste Poquelin), 17, 44
Molo, Walter von, 453, 455, 507
Mondrian, Piet (Pieter Cornelis), 126
Monet, Claude, 479
Monge, J. Garcia, 445
Monk Matthew Lewis, 234
Monnerot, Jules, 194
Monnier, Adrienne, 41–42, 46–48, 66, 69, 85, 101, 395, 483
Monnier, Emmanuel, 497, 504
Monnier, Marie, 47
Montaigne, Michel de, 132, 340
Montellanos, Bernardo Ortiz de, 444
Montford (author), 27
Montherlant, Henry de, 77
Moore, Nicolas, 80, 126, 436
Moorhead, Ethel, 152
Morand, Paul, 38, 51, 55, 60, 69, 78, 98
Moras, Joachim, 503
Morel, Auguste, 42
Morhange (member of Esprit), 234
Morien, Adrian, 510
Morise, Max, 230–31
Mounier, Emmanuel, 497, 504
Mozart, Wolfgang Amadeus, 374
Müller, Otto, 349
Munson, Gorham, 21

Mussorgsky (Moussorgski), Modeste Petrovitch, 63, 374
Muth, Karl, 495

Nash, Thomas, 132
Nelson, Paul, 126
Neruda, Pablo, 446
Nervaise, Raoul de, 67
Nerval, Gérard de (Gérard Labrunie), 209, 211, 224, 280–81, 321
Neumann, Alfred, 510
Newbolt, Henry, 24
Newton, Isaac, 410
Nicholson, Ben, 126
Nietzsche, Friedrich, 65, 154, 157, 209, 269–70, 289, 352, 361, 363, 366, 389, 473
Nin, Anaïs, 124
Noailles, Anna de, 30
Nohain, Franc, 15
Nolhac, Pierre de, 15
Noll, Marcel, 229–30, 236
Novalis (Friedrich von Hardenberg), 156, 176, 205, 208–10, 212–13, 217, 222–27, 234, 249, 260, 269, 280–81, 289, 291, 307–26, 373–74, 433
Nucete-Sardi, José, 448

Ocampo, Silvina, 447
Ocampo, Victoria, 446
Ogden, C. K., 150
Olson, Elder, 432, 435–36
O'Lynn, Lyon, 379
O'Neil, Dave, 60
O'Neill, Eugene, 16, 21, 52, 251
Oppenheim, James, 52
O'Reilly, Perse, 390
Ortiz, Fernando, 195–96, 447
Orwell, George, 500
Ossendowski, Ferdinand, 15
Oswald, Marianne, 505

Otfried (Otfrid of Weissenburg), 91
O'Toole, Laurentius, 386, 419
Otten, Karl, 350
Ouspensky, P. D., 289

Pachman, Vladimir de, 197
Padua de Almeida, 449
Paeschke, Hans, 503
Paget, Richard, 386, 392, 401, 419
Painlevé, Jean, 57
Papini, Giovanni, 484
Paraclete, 300
Parrot, Louis, 475
Pascal, Blaise, 12, 14, 290, 299, 340
Pascal-Bonetti, 12
Patchen, Kenneth, 436, 438
Paul, Elliot, 112, 121, 123, 151, 230, 236,
    256, 394–96, 406
Paul, Emile, 13
Paul, Jean, 205–6, 208, 212–13, 223,
    226–27, 237, 280, 289, 311, 321
Paulhan, Jean, 21, 136, 149, 158, 284, 447
Péguy, Charles, 181, 495
Pellicer, Carlos, 444
Pelorson, Georges, 267, 276
Pereschke, Hans, 503
Péret, Benjamin, 146, 148, 193, 213,
    230, 236
Perse, St. John, 42, 124, 235
Petzold, Ernst, 510
Pevsner, Antoine, 479
Pfemfert, Franz, 505
Piaubert, Jean, 374
Picabia, Francis, 126
Picasso, Pablo, 97, 104, 126, 229, 233,
    371, 432, 447, 479, 500
Pichette, Henri, 467
Pietri, Uslar, 448
Pillin, William, 436
Pinthus, Kurt, 349
Pius XII (Eugenio Maria Giuseppe
    Giovanni Pacelli), 469

Pissarro, Camille, 479
Pizzaro, Francisco, 458
Plivier, Theodor, 452
Plotinus, 157
Plutarch, 205
Podszus, Friedrich, 509
Poe, Edgar Allan, 13, 52, 255, 282, 318,
    363
Poincaré, Raymond, 10
Politzer, Georges, 234
Ponce, Manuel M., 444
Porché, François, 27
Porter, Gene Stratton, 54, 124
Porter, Katherine Anne, 124
Potts, Renée, 449
Poulenc, Francis, 15
Pound, Ezra, 23, 36, 49, 52, 60, 151–52,
    396
Powell (photographer), 126
Powys, John Cowper, 35
Prada, Carlos, 445
Prairie, Gopher, 45
Praviel, A., 18
Prévert, Jacques, 470, 510
Prevost, Jean, 21, 101
Proust, Marcel, 21, 23, 61, 64, 339, 364,
    442
Puga, M. A., 448
Pulver, Max, 272
Puttenham, Richard, 132

Queneau, Raymond, 501, 510
Quinn, John, 34–35

Rabelais, François, 132, 143, 329
Rachilde (Marguerite Eymery), 39,
    102, 235
Racine, Jean, 100, 184, 340
Radek, Karl, 401
Radiguet, Raymond, 37
Rameau, Jean-Philippe, 63
Ramnoux, Clémence, 410, 488

Rascoe, Burton, 84
Raus, Alphonse, 55
Read, Herbert, 490
Réboli, Ida, 447
Redon, Odilon, 479
Regnier, Henry de, 30
Reiffenberg, Benno, 504
Reinolt, Claus, 92
Reinsberg, Mark, 505
Rembrandt (Rembrandt Har-
    menszoon van Rijn), 479
Renan, Ernest, 10
Renard, Jules, 25
Renard, Maurice, 25
Reverdy, Pierre, 17, 29, 33, 57, 60, 467
Reyes, Alfonso, 195, 445, 449
Rhine, Joseph Banks, 292
Ribemont-Dessaignes, Georges, 192,
    232
Richter, Jean Paul, 223, 237
Richter, Werner, 509
Riding, Laura, 150
Riefenberg, Benno, 474
Rieto, Emilia, 446
Rigby, Douglas, 112, 151
Rilke, Rainer Maria, 89, 209, 227, 352,
    373, 432, 438, 441, 493
Rimbaud, Arthur, 89, 111, 116, 144, 193,
    209, 213, 224–25, 234, 236, 258, 280,
    282, 318, 363–64, 447
Ringelnatz, Joachim, 60
Riou, Gaston, 30
Rivera, Diego, 444–45
Rivet, Paul, 497
Rivière, Jacques, 7, 20–21, 28, 61,
    62–63, 65, 86, 209, 333, 339, 486
Robeson, Paul, 165
Robinson, Henry Morton, 405–6,
    408–11, 420
Robledo, Mejía, 445
Roché, Louis, 15
Rodgers, W. R., 491–92

Rodin, Auguste, 479
Rodman, Selden, 432, 436
Rolland, Romain, 11
Romains, Jules, 46, 48, 69
Romero, Orozco, 445
Ronsard, Pierre de, 11–12, 14, 37, 143
Rosenberg, Alfred, 217, 316
Roskolenko, Harry, 436
Roth, Joseph, 262
Rouault, André Thomas, 126
Roud, Gustave, 316
Roure, Remy, 504
Rousseau, Henri Julien Félix (Le
    Douanier), 97
Rousseau, Jean-Jacques, 208, 216, 223,
    316, 350, 479
Roussel, Raymond, 193
Rousselot, Jean, 470
Rousset, David, 504
Rouweyre, André, 25
Rubin, Frank, 495–96
Rubiner, Ludwig, 350
Rudas, Laszlo, 482
Rukeyser, Muriel, 432
Rutra, Theo (Eugene Jolas), 112, 114,
    150–51, 267
Ruysbroeck, Jan van, 157, 280, 292
Rysselberghe, Théo van, 21

Sacher-Masoch, Alexander, 50
Sacher-Masoch, Wanda, 50
Sade, Donatien-Alphonse-François
    de, 237
Sáenz, Moisés, 443
Sage, Robert, 112, 114, 123, 134, 151, 256,
    396, 406
Saint-Exupéry, Antoine de, 364, 486
Saint-Pol-Roux (Paul Pierre Roux),
    102, 209, 235, 309, 317, 438
Salemson, Harold J., 112, 151
Salmon, André, 25, 32
Sánchez, Luis Alberto, 448

Sandburg, Carl, 21, 29, 49, 50, 52, 75, 76
Santa Cruz, Mario, 446
Sapir, Edward, 92
Sardou, Victorien, 10
Saroyan, William, 495
Sartre, Jean-Paul, 468–69, 474, 477, 486, 490, 497, 504–5, 510
Satie, Erik, 15, 165, 374
Sauvage, Marcel, 30
Savigny, Hans von, 503
Savonarola, 25
Savoy, Prew, 30
Schaffner, Georges, 92
Scheerbart, Paul, 188
Scheler, Max, 140, 269, 426
Schelling, Friedrich Wilhelm Joseph, 137, 158, 205–6, 208, 215, 269, 311, 313–14, 319–21, 323–24, 392
Schickele, René, 11, 38–39, 91, 229, 349–50, 510
Schiller, Friedrich, 223
Schimanski, Stefan, 471
Schlegel, Karl Wilhelm Friedrich, 158, 205–6, 208, 215, 311, 313, 321, 323–24, 392
Schloezer, Boris de, 21, 488
Schlumberger, Jean, 510
Schmalhausen, S. D., 134
Schneider, Edouard, 84
Schneider, Franz Josef, 477, 509
Schnitzler, Arthur, 59, 482
Schnurre, Wolfdietrich, 454, 510
Scholtis, August, 454
Schopenhauer, Arthur, 249, 251, 313, 323
Schröder, Rudolf Alexander, 452
Schubert, G. H., 205, 209
Schwab, Raymond, 313, 324
Schwerke, Irving, 7
Schwitters, Kurt, 124, 146, 189, 191, 197, 352

Schwob, Marcel, 25, 44, 335
Scribe, Augustin Eugène, 394
Scudéry, Madeleine de, 100
Sebas, Jean, 11, 92
Segal, Erich, 25
Segalen, Victor, 25
Seghers, Pierre, 372
Seldes, Georges, 28
Seldes, Gilbert, 28
Shakespeare, William, 15, 41, 66, 69, 101, 131–33, 143, 340
Shaw, George Bernard, 11, 16, 482
Sheeler, Charles, 126
Shelley, Mary, 225, 318
Shipman, Evan, 122
Siegfried, André, 481
Sierpo, Enrique, 449
Silesius, Angelus, 281, 482
Silveira, Tasso de, 449
Sinclair, Upton, 262
Siqueiros, David Alfaro, 444
Sisley, Alfred, 479
Smith, John, 458
Söderberg, Hjalmar, 121
Söhring, Hans-Jürgen, 509–10
Sollier, J. M., 101
Solveen, Henri, 11, 91–92, 229
Sombart, Nicolas, 509
Sorel, George, 44
Soupault, Philippe, 57, 83, 90, 95–96, 121, 148, 192, 213, 231, 233, 235–36, 407
Spengler, Oswald, 58, 480
Spire, André, 22–23, 44–45
Stadler, Ernst, 349
Stalin, Joseph, 217
Starr-Untermeyer, Jean (Jean Starr), 36
Stein, Elliot, 505
Stein, Gertrude, 116, 121, 124, 125, 150, 152, 232, 258, 378
Steiner, Rudolf, 58
Stekel, Wilhelm, 251

Stendhal (Marie-Henri Beyle), 27
Sternberger, Dolf, 452, 455, 493
Sterne, Laurence, 399
Sternheim, Carl, 60, 121, 329
Stevenson, D. E., 22
Stierlin, Henri, 316, 323, 349–50
Storfer, Adolf J., 116
Stramm, August, 146, 189, 349, 352,
    379, 494
Strauss, Richard, 59
Stravinsky, Igor Fyodorovich, 49, 71
Strindberg, August, 477
Suhrkamp, Peter, 509
Supervielle, Jules, 101, 467
Swedenborg, Emanuel, 292
Sweeney, James Johnson, 123–24, 267
Swift, Jonathan, 400
Symond, Ronald, 267
Synge, John Millington, 80

Tagore, Rabindranath, 339–40
Tal-Coat, Pierre, 374
Tanaquil, Paul, 22
Tanguy, Yves, 126, 233, 371
Tate, Allan, 260
Taeuber-Arp, Sophie, 232
Tauler, Johannes, 292
Tempels, Placide, 498, 499
Tennyson, Alfred, 389
Tharaud, Jérôme, 87
Tharaud, Jean, 87
Thayer, Abbott Handerson, 126
Thayer, Scofield, 35
Thérive, André, 10, 17, 261
Thibaudet, Albert, 12, 15, 30, 86
Thomas, Dylan, 212
Thomas Aquinas, Saint, 61, 154–55,
    250
Thomas, Guillaume, 93
Thompson, Francis, 281
Thomson, Virgil, 125
Thoreau, Henry, 459

Thurber, James, 495
Tieck, Luwig, 205–6, 208, 222–23,
    280, 313, 323–24, 326
Tisserand, Ernest, 23
Tocqueville, Alexis de, 363
Toller, Ernst, 16, 59
Toor, Frances, 445
Torberg, Friedrich, 508
Torren, Luis Florens, 449
Torres, Guirrido, 449
Torriente-Brau, Pablo de la, 450
Toulet, Paul-Jean, 27
Toulouse-Lautrec, Henri de, 479
Toynbee, Arnold J., 479
Trakl, Georg, 121, 212, 349–52
Trotsky, Leon, 237, 445
Troxler, Ignaz Paul Vital, 209–10
Troy, William, 403
Tyler, Parker, 436
Tzara, Tristan, 28–29, 32, 147, 189–90,
    212, 232, 490

Ulrich, Heinz, 477
Untermeyer, Louis, 36, 55, 58–59, 69,
    75, 436
Unruh, Fritz von, 38, 451, 453
Usinger, Fritz, 367, 509
Utrillo, Maurice, 479

Vail, Laurence, 112, 151
Vaillat, Léandre, 87
Valcárcel, Luis, 443
Valentino, Rudolph, 18
Valéry, Paul, 8–9, 15, 30, 33, 37, 41–43,
    46–48, 51, 65–69, 79, 88–89, 99,
    101, 104, 184, 244, 339, 394, 447, 483
Vanderem, Fernand, 45
Vantongerloo, Georges, 479
Vasconcelos, José, 450
Vaudoyer, Jean-Louis, 15, 21, 27
Vázquez, Emilio, 448
Vercors (Jean Marcel Bruller), 504, 510

Verlaine, Paul, 196
Vermeer, Johannes, 479
Verne, Jules, 318, 501
Vico, Giambattista, 149, 187, 381, 387, 389, 400, 409, 415
Vidal, Amparo Rodríguez, 449
Vidal, Armand, 18
Viélé-Griffin, Francis, 29
Viereck, Peter, 504
Vigneaud, Jean, 87
Vildrac, Charles, 23, 48
Villarutia, Xavier, 444
Villiers de l'Isle-Adam, A. de, 25, 224, 503
Vinal, Harold, 22
Vioux, Marcelle, 8
Vitrac, Roger, 146, 148, 231, 235
Voisins, Gilbert de, 25
Vollard, Ambroise, 487
Voltaire (François-Marie Arouet), 189–90, 212, 216, 316

Wagner, Richard, 63, 389
Wahl, Jean, 217, 319, 488, 498, 510
Walden, Herwarth, 146, 189, 330, 352
Walleser, J. G., 13
Walsh, Ernest, 152
Weaver, Harriet, 395
Weber, Alfred, 455
Wedekind, Frank, 209
Weidlé, Wladimir, 488

Weingarten, Romain, 468
Weiss-Ruethel, Arnold, 454
Wells, Herbert George, 318, 395
Welty, Eudora, 495
Werfel, Franz, 17, 39, 212, 349–50, 432, 447, 453
Werth, Léon, 45
Whitman, Walt, 13, 52, 441
Wiechert, Ernst, 453
Wilde, Oscar, 32, 60, 334, 339
Wilder, Amos N., 437–39
Williams, Oscar, 436
Williams, William Carlos, 60, 124, 246, 406
Wilson, Edmund, 224, 396, 403, 408
Wolff, Charles, 92
Wolff, Kurt, 350
Wolf, Robert R., 22
Woolf, Virginia, 509
Wrangel, Peotr Nikolayevich, 39
Wright, Richard, 497
Wylie, Eleanor, 16
Wyss, Dieter, 373

Yeats, William Butler, 24, 42, 80, 401, 437, 442, 491, 509

Zamora, Antonio, 447
Zavie, Emile, 24
Zola, Emile, 24, 27, 253
Zuckmayer, Carl, 495

Eugene Jolas was born in Union City, New Jersey, in 1894 but was raised by his Franco-German parents in the borderland of Lorraine. In 1927 he and his wife, Maria McDonald, along with the author Elliot Paul, were founders of the influential Parisian literary magazine *transition*. In Paris, Jolas met James Joyce and played a major part in encouraging and defending Joyce's *Work-in-Progress*, later to become *Finnegans Wake*, a work Jolas viewed as the perfect embodiment of his manifesto "Revolution of the Word."

Klaus H. Kiefer is a professor of German at the University of Munich and a Fellow at the Center for the Humanities at Northwestern University. He has published widely on European literature from the eighteenth, nineteenth, and twentieth centuries.

Rainer Rumold is a professor of German and comparative literature at Northwestern University. He has published numerous books, editions, and articles on European modernism, the avant-garde, and Expressionism.